# Vichy Law and the Holocaust in France

"A well-researched document of cruel times and insensitive oppressors. The author's words will long reverberate in the reader's memory and arouse essential questions about the human condition."

*Elie Wiesel*

"Immensely informative...Weisberg sees the 'racial' laws promulgated by Vichy against the Jews as basically 'religious' laws. His bold thesis, which will no doubt stir controversy, but is argued cogently and with sadness, is that Catholic spirituality, which had stereotyped Jewish faith as legalistic, helped lawyers to tolerate the anti-Jewish legislation, despite the real possibility of challenging it in the name of egalitarian republicanism and guaranties in the French constitution itself."

*Geoffrey Hartman*
Sterling Professor
of Comparative Literature
Yale University

"Richard Weisberg's prodigious research and provocative analysis reveals that Vichy laws on the status of Jews outstripped Nazi texts in their legalistic zeal, and that personalities of considerable prestige favored the exclusionary laws, not only marginal bigots brought to power by an aberrational regime. Weisberg reveals the resentment felt by some eminent and even 'liberal' French lawyers about the 'exaggerated place' held by Jews in the Third Republic. This book amply supports the claim that 'Vichy, seen in this way, is less an aberration than a cyclical French phenomenon.' "

*Jane Ginsburg*
Morton L. Janklow Professor
of Literary and Artistic Property Law
Columbia University

"*Vichy Law and the Holocaust in France* tells an appalling and still-contemporary story of the xenophobia of lawyers and of genocide and law. Weisberg has labored meticulously through archival and contemporary sources to document the lowest hour of the French legal profession. This is not only a monumental work of record but also an essay in interpretation of the failure of law."

*Peter Goodrich*
Birkbeck College
University of London

# Vichy Law and the Holocaust in France

Richard H. Weisberg



by

NEW YORK UNIVERSITY PRESS
Washington Square, New York

First published in the U.S.A. in 1996 by
NEW YORK UNIVERSITY PRESS
Washington Square
New York, N.Y. 10003

Second printing 1998

---

**Library of Congress Cataloging-in-Publication Data**

Weisberg, Richard H., 1944–
Vichy Law and the Holocaust in France / Richard Weisberg.
p. cm.
Includes index
ISBN 0-8147-9302-9 (hardcover)
ISBN 0-8147-9336-3 (softcover)
1. Jews–Legal status, laws, etc.–France–History–20th century.
2. Lawyers–France–History–20th century. 3. World War, 1939–1945–Deportations from France. 4. France–History–German occupation, 1940–1945–Collaborationists. 5. Holocaust, Jewish (1939–1945)–France. I. Title.
KJV4207.J49W45 1996
346.4401′3–dc20
[344.40613]

95-25844
CIP

COVER
Jews 1942 © BHVP/Keystone/SYGMA

EDITING AND COMPOSITION
Alifa Saadya

Printed and bound in Canada by University of Toronto Press Incorporated.

To Monroe Price
whose vision realized this book

To Cheryl Weisberg
whose love inspired its author

# Contents

# List of Archival Sources

ALL *Alliance israélite universelle,* Paris

AN *Archives National*

Paris:
*Commissariat Général aux Questions Juives (CGQJ) et Service de Restitution des Biens Spoliés,* $AJ^{38}$: "Inventaire", and files 7, 14, 58, 61, 67, 69, 70, 80, 99, 100, 106, 115, 116, 118, 120, 127, 148, 331, 592–601, 801, 1020, 1075, 1076–80

*Régime de Vichy (1940–1944),* $BB^{30}$: files 1708–1718

*Seconde Guerre Mondiale, Comité d'histoire de la Deuxième Guerre Mondiale (1951–1980),* 72 AJ: Joseph Barthélemy, ministre de la Justice, 1940–1943: 411, 412, 413

Fontainebleau:
*Archives Personnelles et Familiales,* Papiers Maurice Garçon, 304 AP

*Bar Association of the City of Paris:* Memorandum, "On the Attitude of Attorneys Inscribed at the Court of Appeals of Paris Concerning the Authorities of the French State from 1940–1944," Bar Association archivist, *Palais de Justice*

CDJC *Centre de Documentation juive contemporaine,* Paris

YV *Yad Vashem,* Jerusalem: file 0/9; IV-VI (Documents of the CDJC); 98-d; Leo Israelowicz file; Klarsfeld notebook; Kurt Schendel file

# Foreword

Nearly twenty years ago, while researching *Vichy France and the Jews,* Robert Paxton and I were struck by the degree to which the murders of Jews from France during 1942–44 were facilitated by two years of aggressive persecution of the Jewish minority, initiated and implemented by the collaborationist régime at Vichy. That persecution stigmatized the Jews in French society, stripped them of their property and livelihood, turned them into fugitives, and, we argued, facilitated the Nazis' deportation of some 75,000 of them to death camps in the east. Many factors contributed to the isolation and victimization of the Jews. But among them, we noted, was a veritable cascade of French laws regulating their situation specifically—no fewer than 143 laws and *actes réglementaires* generated by the Vichy government. Remarkable as these laws were, so also was the rigor with which they were enforced by the French courts. Even when taking account of local variation, their severity in dealing with Jews seemed outstanding. We noted, for example, that over 650 Jews were convicted for having violated anti-Jewish laws between June 1941 and the middle of 1944, with the overwhelming majority of these being in the period extending through the massive deportations of 1942. Taking the lead from the Conseil d'État, at the very pinnacle of the French legal system, lower courts doggedly worked away at enforcing the anti-Jewish laws—almost until the very end—in what may seem to us a stunning habituation to a sordid routine. In addition, an army of legal practitioners looked up the laws, furnished opinion, filled out forms, and otherwise had untroubled recourse to the legal machinery of Vichy's antisemitic enterprise.

We also thought it noteworthy that the anti-Jewish laws slipped into the canon of legal disputation. Working energetically within the system, learned jurists published their opinions on technical and interpretive issues concerning the instruments of persecution. Academics did their part, lending the name of distinguished institutions to their writings on anti-Jewish laws. Careers were enhanced by learned publications on these themes. In reading this material, one should not forget that when it was being written and when some of it was read Jews were being cast into destitution, torn loose from their families, thrown into camps and in some cased deported to their deaths. *Elle est pourtant la loi. Obéissance lui est due* (The law is the law. It must be obeyed), one high official recalled having told head of state Philippe Pétain about the *Statut des Juifs*—a claim that may be taken as emblematic of the entire process.

Having reported the importance of the legal framework—prompted in part, I should add, by the urging of our friend Roger Errera of the Conseil d'État—Paxton and I went no further. Particularly in retrospect, I can see, we left vital questions unexplored. And that is why I take particular pleasure in introducing this excellent volume. For Richard Weisberg's *Vichy Law and the Holocaust in France* not only examines these questions, it provides answers informed by the author's extraordinary research and wide learning. Floersheimer Professor of Constitutional Law at the Benjamin N. Cardozo School of Law of Yeshiva University, Weisberg brings to the task his formidable legal expertise, and also a literary sensibility attentive to the subtle interrelationship between Vichy's legal discourse and what he calls its "interpretive community."

Weisberg's starting point is that law was critical to the fate of Jews in France: "life on—and death from—French soil remained for victim and oppressor alike matters of law, negotiated by ordinary people using the tools of their prosaic craft." These 'ordinary people', the legal professionals, are the focus of this book. Examining the work of lawyers and judges, policy makers and administrators, prosecutors and defenders, reporters and academics, the author shows how legalized persecution—what was know at Vichy as *antisémitisme d'état*—actually worked. The overwhelming impression is that it functioned with remarkably little friction. In both the Occupied and the Unoccupied Zones, anti-Jewish laws were energetically enforced—sometimes even more zealously so than the politically-minded Germans preferred. Notably, this legal community operated autonomously, outside the framework of government control and free of coercion or government regulation. Which is to say: the legal practitioners had choices. Yet in contrast with their colleagues in Belgium or in Italy, they displayed their "pervasive willingness to accept and work with the language of racial exclusion," a near-universal accomodation to the universe of Vichy's antisemitic legislation. Which is to say: they knowingly did what they did. Notwithstanding occasional departures from the general rule, including some instances in which lawyers, courts, or tribunals assisted individual Jews, the system maintained an exclusionary discourse that was pervasive in the legal profession—a "discourse that all too often screens lawyers from the corrupt atmosphere lurking above the surface of their words," Weisberg tells us.

What accounts for pervasiveness of this particular 'exclusionary discourse' in the wartime French legal system? Why did Vichy lawyers contemplate no other option? Venturing an interpretation that has important ramifications for an understanding of French culture, Weisberg identifies an approach toward Jews which he terms "dessicated Cartesianism"—"a uniquely French desire to see the elaborate interpretation of the religious laws through to every logical conclusion." Deriving ultimately, he suggests, from a particular French Catholic reading of the place of law in Jewish history, this view contemplated Jews as being unalterably different from Frenchmen. So widespread was this perception, the author argues, that even Léon Blum, the former conseilleur d'état who seems to us to be French to his fingertips, could be so widely seen as an incorrigible Talmudist—alien, strange, and vaguely repulsive; someone, said one of his accusers, who "didn't even think French."

Opening a new theme for research and debate, Weisberg finishes his book with an explanation to the riddle of French exclusionary legal rhetoric that posits a particular French Catholic hermeneutic on the subject of Jews and the law. This solution will have to be tested and refined in the years to come, but however interpreters decide, they will undoubtedly refer to this important book as a major landmark, and one whose importance extends far beyond the French context. For *Vichy Law and the Holocaust in France* shows not only how cruel persecution was once cloaked in a legalistic process, but how easily this can happen, how the instruments of a seemingly liberal legal system can be adapted to this end, and how readily quite ordinary practitioners can be drawn into the process. This ought to give pause to those—like most of us—who do not regularly question just what it is we do with the rules of the game we inherit. Having learned much from this book, I commend it to readers as first-rate legal history, as a distinguished contribution to the understanding of the Holocaust in France, and also as a cautionary tale.

*Michael R. Marrus*

# Preface

This work sets forth data about the role of law and lawyers during the Holocaust in France, a period between 1940 and 1944 in which some 75,000 Jews were sent from French soil to death camps 'in the East'. The vast majority of these deportations occurred under cover of French law, for as early as September and October of 1940, an independent French government, with its seat of operations in Vichy, had promulgated a widespread series of laws, regulations, and decrees about the Jews. These proved sufficiently thorough in their application and effect that the Germans largely imported them for use in the occupied zone of France as well.

This is a work of empirical research, involving the identifying and amassing of over 2,500 primary documents relating to Vichy law, conversations with countless French witnesses from the period, and formal interviews with twenty-five or so lawyers or legal functionaries whose careers spanned the Vichy years. The data spans all areas of legal activity, and all participants in the legal arena. Documents made available to the researcher over the twelve-year period of this project (1982–94) illuminate the work of magistrates, administrative agencies and courts, government lawyers and ministries (particularly the Ministry of Justice), private legal practitioners and their professional associations, legal academicians and their books and journals.

Legal activity during the full four years of Vichy was pervasive. Courts functioned much as they had always functioned, although bound by an unusual oath to Vichy's leader, Marshal Pétain; administrative actors fought for jurisdictional space and increasing power under the Marshal's authoritarian brand of leadership; private legal practitioners—avocats, avoués, notaires—with greater autonomy from their government, took up the new materials of racial, religious and ethnic ostracism and worked with them in volume and without substantial protest. Legal academicians wrote doctoral theses and had them published on the subject of the anti-Jewish laws, made their reputations as young law professors by discussing 'neutrally' the stuff of exclusion, tried to explain how French constitutional norms could co-exist with laws designed to persecute people *ex post facto* and because of immutable traits or private beliefs.

The data reveals that all this French activity occurred largely without German *Diktat.* The French did it mostly on their own, with a zestful logical thoroughness that often seems to defy easy explanations such as endemic antisemitism. Too many people were involved, on all sides of the political and social spectrum, to ascribe the totality of the legal record under Vichy to virulent forms of anti-Jewish feeling. And the data reveals more than a few doctrinal areas that developed over the four year period to *protect* certain categories of Jews. The system was working on its own—certainly aware of the presence of the Germans—but within its own characteristic self-conception.

While many legal actors may well have assisted individual Jews (or, more likely, people suspected of being Jews but who could argue a legal loophole and escape that beleaguered status), their pervasive acceptance of the laws made possible the exclusion of a thousand Jews for every one that was saved. Judicial doctrine or individual advocacy often worked to *expand* the scope of the laws beyond what either their literal sense, or even the German precedents, demanded. More than once, the Nazis formally asked the French to limit the pace of definitional or evidentiary decisions that had the effect of encompassing categories of individuals that German law itself had never considered Jewish. All of this occurred because of the 'rich' debate that involved French legal actors in increasingly thick volumes of prose related to the 'Jewish question'.

Under French law, billions of francs of Jewish property were pillaged. The process was rational, bureaucratic, and 'lawful'. Many Jews consulted with lawyers and found ways to protect their property. The courts and agencies heard many hundreds of cases dealing with the new figure of the 'administrateur provisoire', the Aryan 'trustee' who was charged with dealing with any property not so protected. The politics of inevitable German defeat did not substantially deflate the rhetoric of religious definition, economic aryanization, denationalization, arrest, and deportation.

This study seeks eventual norms of understanding about French legal activity under Vichy. Adopting a kind of hourglass structure, the work expands from the first chapter, which identifies Léon Blum as the paradigmatic victim of Vichy law during the political trial at Riom, to an intensely substantive second chapter on the religious laws themselves and then a third chapter on the manner in which Vichy law treated Jewish lawyers. Chapter 4 again bends inward as Justice Minister Joseph Barthélemy's blend of Catholic constitutionalism comes to center stage (having been a key secondary player at Riom); then the work expands outward again in a fifth chapter devoted to the personal power struggles between the magistrates and the administrative agencies and courts, and a sixth dealing with the manner in which Vichy exceeded Nazi precedents. Chapter 7 deals in detail with property law, including landlord-tenant (where suffering Jews almost always won judicial support in their search for rent reductions) as well as aryanizations, corporate housecleaning, estate planning, spousal gifts, intergenerational transfers, and community property (in all of which domains Jews did not fare as well). Chapter 8 broadens the hourglass further, with dozens of descriptions of private lawyers, and all manner of situations for which the considerable talent of individual French practitioners was brought to bear on one side or the other of the exclusionary laws. Chapter 9 speaks of legal reform projects, particularly those in the fateful months of late 1943, when the Germans awaited Vichy laws to abide their need for more Jewish bodies. Chapter 10 bends inward, as the study attempts to understand the special hermeneutics of French law, an anti-Talmudism that combined one aspect of traditional xenophobia with the sense that the Jew's choice of a peculiar and 'non-French' approach to law somehow made reasonable and even necessary special laws dealing with the Jew. Catholic hermeneutics and theology, centering on Vichy ambassador Léon Bérard's consoling letter to Pétain about Vatican acceptance of French exclusionary legislation, play an interweaving role, as secular law counts on the dominant religion to rationalize ostracism.

It is because of the latter analysis that the study mostly eschews use of the word 'racial' to describe the laws. Vichy law surely contained racial components, ranging from the enormously contested definition of grandparental heritage to the exalted language of constitutionalism itself; but in the main, the laws against the Jews in France were the product of an ingrained way of seeing and understanding the Talmudic outsider. This was a person who not only had "too little French soil in his sandals" (to quote a legal treatise of 1943) but whose religion—far more than moral laxity or depravity, the slogans of less typical antisemites—set him legitimately apart from the universe of protected Frenchmen, who still enjoyed the great constitutional gifts of equality and due process, never fully repealed by Vichy. To this extent, the adjectives 'religious', 'exclusionary', or even 'ethnic' better modify the nouns 'legislation' or 'laws' in the Vichy context.

Individuals also play a great role in this study. Woven into various substantive chapters are pervasive legal actors such as Justice Minister Barthélemy, Paris Bar Association head Jacques Charpentier, Constitutional Law Professor Jacques Maury, practicing lawyer Joseph Haennig, Riom defense counsel and active private practitioner Maurice Garçon, as well as men trained in law such as Pierre Laval, Raphäel Alibert (the first Minister of Justice), Philippe Serre—who courageously joined a mere handful of other parliamentarians to vote against granting full powers to Pétain, and whom I interviewed about Vichy in 1988—and the victimized lawyers who range from the masterful and distinguished Pierre Masse to the communist Hajje (shot as a hostage) to the poignant Jacques Franck, so demoralized to see what his own country was doing to law that he threw himself from a window.

Hundreds of other individuals play their role here. Vichy is not an abstraction. It was a fully functioning, largely 'Franco-French' phenomenon. It is everything that needs examining, fifty years after the Liberation, about France; and it is much that is ennobling and inspiring as well. No reader should claim for himself or herself a path of action unencumbered by the complex choices these largely unexceptionable men and women made in the face of laws passed by their own government. Yet none should assume either that the mere promulgation of the laws dictated any particular outcome.

People created whatever Vichy's record eventually became. They used the tools of legal reasoning. They managed to avoid protest on high levels of legal generalization that were surely available to them, particularly at the beginning, before the discourse had settled on lower levels of analysis, such as the four-year long debate about the status of mixed-heritage individuals. In Italy, a Fascist régime and ally of Hitler, similar laws went largely unenforced. In France, legal actors instead brought their considerable rhetorical, logical, and even creative abilities to bear. The Germans, never really able to expend manpower in great quantities to enforce their own version of racism on Vichy's Jews, quickly and pragmatically saw that it would be enough to 'let the French do it'. How and why the French 'did it' we are now about to discover.

People also have made this project possible. My thanks go to archivist Jacobson at the Centre de documentation juive contemporaine, who assisted me in 1982 in Paris when little else was available. How rich and how generous is that archival center! To Cynthia Haft, archivist of the French collection at Yad Vashem in Jerusalem, go my friendship and my gratitude. To archivist Mme. Bonazzi of the twentieth-century collection of the Archives Nationales in Paris, my enduring thanks for guiding me through the collections relevant to my topic and for unfailing support for a project that had only recently become even thinkable much less implementable without such aid. The relatives of Vichy legal actors were most generous with their time, their thoughts, their documents. I am thinking especially of Jean Barthélemy, a Parisian lawyer and grandson of the Justice Minister. He must have known that I disagreed with many of his assessments of his distinguished grandfather's Vichy years, yet he unstintingly opened his thoughts and his generous spirit to me. I am thinking of Maurice Garçon's son, a lawyer in Beaunes, who greeted me warmly and assisted me to gain access to his father's extensive collection at Fontainebleau. My thanks go to Serge Klarsfeld—a figure of unparalleled moral stature in shedding light upon Vichy for working with me to gain access (as no earlier researcher had) to a part of the files of the Bar Association of the City of Paris. To the archivist there, M. Azanam, go my thanks for understanding a three-year long attempt to open the door just a bit to the multifaceted collection that exists at the Palais de Justice. To Laurence Craig, an American lawyer in Paris, I offer thanks for selflessly assisting with that same, finally fruitful, process.

I cannot express sufficiently my gratitude to Eric Freedman, my friend, confidant and co-worker, whose importance to this project ranged from assisting me on his day off, to sort out the 11,000 individual files of Maurice Garçon at Fontainebleau, to discussing the entire range of issues provoked by this study over a twelve-year period. To Eric's spouse, Claire Estryn, a superb French jurist, go further thanks for assisting me with numerous technical issues of French administrative law. I must also mention French scholars Annette Wieviorka, André Kaspi, Dominique Gros, and Pierre Birnbaum, who shared their thoughts with me and opened many doors. My fine friend and colleague, Claude Klein, lent me inspiration, advice, and the further friendship of Liliane Abendsour; both encouraged my efforts at every turn. Geoffrey Hartman, with whom I have been fruitfully discussing for thirty years what has become this book's developing thesis, offered his consistent support and constructive criticism. My brother, Prof. David Weisberg, has also inspired and taught me along many of this project's pathways. Finally, an inexpressible debt of thanks goes to my wife, Cheryl, and my children, who not only supported me with their humor and their love but also accompanied me both to Paris' proud sites and to the mournful monuments and documentary centers that reveal every bit as much about the French and, indeed, about ourselves. My family assisted me to live with this darkside without losing my affection for the French and for their wonderful country.

I would like to thank my Cardozo Law School colleagues, who patiently sat through several versions of my thesis and offered their comments along the way, and particularly among them I wish to acknowledge Telford Taylor and Eva Hanks.

Several institutions have underwritten this work. The American Council of Learned Societies, under the leadership of Stanley Katz, saw something at an early stage that they were willing to assist. The Vidal Sassoon International Center for the Study of Antisemitism in Jerusalem was vitally important to the continuation of this work. I was further privileged to have the extraordinary editorial assistance of Alifa Saadya, whose commitment to making this the best book it could be went far beyond the call of duty. And Yeshiva University, my law school's home institutional base in New York City, has been unstintingly generous to this project.

For her supervision of the secretarial assistance I received at Cardozo, I warmly thank Anne Kamlet. To Joel Grantz, my friend and indispensable assistant in computing my data, and in figuring out the best technical strategies for producing this book, I convey great gratitude.

And to the French. Oh, the French! Those ultimate creditors of my upbringing, my wellbeing, my love of what is stunning in art and in nature! I hope that they will be able to see what follows as a form of still admiring exchange for all they have given to me.

# Introduction: On the Continuing Myth of Vichy

I began the research for this study in 1982. At that time, the seminal work of Marrus and Paxton, *Vichy France and the Jews,* had not yet achieved wide readership in France. Few documentary centers were open to those seeking enlightenment about Vichy. At that time, there still prevailed a dominant myth about the French people during World War II and several related corollaries about the régime itself. The myth, intoned to me by almost everyone whom I interviewed: "We were all in the Resistance." The corollaries, as to the question of the persecution of Jews: Vichy had to do what the Germans ordered *(Diktat);* stateless Jews were the unfortunate victims of a Vichy policy designed to protect native French Jews, the former becoming a shield *(bouclier)* for the latter.

At the completion of this volume—with the notable contemporaneous exception of Jacques Chirac—the French continue to mythologize about Vichy, although considerably more realism has been forced upon them. Some now say, for example, that "If 25% of Jews on French soil perished because of the Vichy government, 75% of Jews were saved because of the efforts of the French people." Regrettably, and with reverence for the individuals who courageously saved Jewish lives, my research (and surely also that of other scholars within the past five years) contradicts this assessment.

The availability in the archives of three kinds of documentation particularly tends to the conclusion that Vichy was a *pervasive phenomenon,* involving tens of thousands of public and private French participants. The first—chronologically—are the documents dealing with the "aryanization" of property (chapters 6 and 7). The second archival source is the record of the *private bar* (chapter 8). Difficult to crack, and still largely unexplored, these sources reveal that the phenomenon of religious persecution was known, tolerated, and implemented by hundreds of important legal figures, and perhaps thousands of ordinary practitioners of the law-related professions (avocat, avoué, notaire, etc.). And the third kind of documentation relates to academic writing during the period (chapters 2 and 10).

Vichy was the work not of a small group of fringe zealots or Quislings; it involved the French system as a whole—one might also say French culture as a whole. Essentially unchanged from its prewar form—as the son of prominent lawyer Maurice Garçon put it to me several years ago—the post-vanquishment legal system digested the new religious and racial material and made it its own. In the process, legal actors displayed ingrained cultural and religious (as well as legalistic) proclivities that permitted them to assimilate with relative ease a bizarre system of legalistic exclusion. Protestations of ignorance as to the laws against the Jews cannot any longer be credited. Thousands of French legal and bureaucratic actors participated—whatever their inner doubts—in a predominantly French system that proceeded as follows:

1. Definition of Jew;
2. Rationalization of the laws of exclusion;
3. Exclusion of the Jew from various careers and activities;
4. "Aryanization" of property;
5. Arrest and encampment;
6. The first transportation steps toward deportation.

Maurice Garçon, a distinguished lawyer, a fine man and surely no anti-semite, wrote on one of his wartime dossiers that his client was a *"juif déporté en Silésie."* There were numerous such files. People knew of the deportations, and they also knew that the French system more than the Germans led even to that ultimate disaster. Garçon himself had written several legal memoranda (as early as mid-1941) analyzing the French-authored laws of Jewish definition, analyzing them with the acuity and logic of the exceptional practitioner. He knew—at least by one year after—that arrest and deportation were connected to those laws. He tried to assist Jewish clients. He regretted the "madness" that had taken hold. But he participated. While nothing explicitly indicates that he or his colleagues knew of the *fate* of deported Jews, there is a tone of sadness and ultimate tragedy to Garçon's files where missing Jews were concerned.

Selective forgetfulness has no place in the post-Holocaust world. The case of France is of capital importance: 75% of the population cannot be exonerated at the stroke of a pen. As Philippe Serre told me, "There would have been no racial policy in France if the French had refused." But *why* did the French offer up 75,000 Jews to the Final Solution? Antisemitism is surely part of the answer. French academicians and manual writers, in rationalizing the new religious laws, rehashed ancient arguments of a twofold nature. Jews, even those who had lived in France for centuries, were organically incapable of being truly French: Jews were "Talmudists"; their allegiance to the literalism and moment-to-moment dictates of the Talmud automatically distanced them from the French approach to law and made them the legitimate object of laws recognizing their (voluntary) alienation from France and its culture.

Of course, there was virulent antisemitism connected to Vichy. The first Justice Minister, Raphäel Alibert, leapt into statutory print with the infamous statutes of 3 and 4 October 1940 (chapter 2), in which he surely was articulating—albeit with technical legalistic skill—his own prejudice. But few legal actors contributing to the tragedy were really antisemites of this persuasion. Far more typical was the second Justice Minister, Joseph Barthélemy (chapter 4), a man of liberal and humane vision and a highly respectable professor of constitutional law who had written against Hitler and against racial persecution. Called to Vichy, he managed not only to accommodate but to sign, and more actively to participate in the drafting of the second religious statute, of the detailed statute on the aryanization of Jewish property, of the institution of the "special section" courts, of a draft constitution explicitly employing the word "race" as a factor of exclusion in the new France, and of countless individual decisions relating to the new laws.

So antisemitism, although perhaps called more to the surface by Vichy, cannot in and of itself explain the passion with which the legal community authored, accepted and implemented the laws. I believe that an answer to the "why" requires an understanding of the peculiar Cartesian logic that led French lawyers to carry the open questions (as they defined them) of Jewish definition to their drily logical extremes. Impervious to German influence, they fought among themselves to seize jurisdiction over the Jewish question (chapter 5), and then followed through on the identified ambiguities (is a mixed-heritage individual Jewish or not?; who has the burden of proof? what kind of proof is admissible on the question?, etc.) with a rigorous, internal professional logic that would be admirable if it were not so tragic in its precise context. The Germans rarely interfered; when they did, it was as often to chastise the French for going too far than to suggest that they were being too liberal on the Jewish question (chapter 6).

My sense is that the French profession behaved pervasively to make the Jewish statutes live, for one reason that is native to legal professionalism in other countries as well, particularly perhaps in the United States, the United Kingdom, Canada and Australia. That reason has to do with *an ingrained approach to the reading of legal texts*. The French, at one and the same time read their constitutional text flexibly so as to accommodate the noble values of the 1790s *and still exclude* from those protections a selected group of "others." They also read their statutory texts narrowly to identify only a single low-level generalization issue as consistently important and to rule out immediately other legal issues that might have led to a very different set of outcomes for the population persecuted by the statutes.

This two-headed coin is emblematic of risks always tangible in liberal constitutional régimes. The story of embedded values may at any time be distorted to exclude people and groups from the otherwise still egalitarian tale; and the work of statute reading may always fall prey to an ingrained professional sense that almost delights in limiting legal discourse to the narrowest range of issues possible under the statute. Maurice Duverger, whose wartime treatise on the new laws has led to much controversy even in very recent years, protests that his treatise advised lawyers to expand their understanding of the Jewish statutes so that they could be understood sharply *to limit* those who could be persecuted under them. Whether or not one can find this approach in Duverger's actual wartime language (chapter 10), it is surely the case that the statutes of 3 October 1940 and 2 June 1941, could have provoked the legal community to focus on much higher levels of generalization that would have tended to protect substantially greater numbers of Jews.

That they did not do so does not, again, largely result from antisemitism as it is usually understood. Rather, it reveals the narrowness that always risks appearing when lawyers do their technical work. Unless legal education changes—in part because it has learned from these events—liberal constitutional cultures must turn to the other side of the coin, and they must constantly insist on *less flexible* readings of the legal system's egalitarian stories. To do this, however, one must change the tradition (which I associate in chapter 10 with a subtle form of Catholic hermeneutics, specific to Vichy but also more serviceable elsewhere) of distorting foundational texts to suit the demands of the given moment. This may require a more fundamental shift yet in the reading strategies of authoritative lawyers and their larger communities. Perhaps, as to foundational beliefs, a bit of Talmudic literalness will be worth two millennia of hermeneutic flexibility.

For the myth of Vichy will fall—and its lessons be understood by other cultures that are not so different from that of France—only if people are willing to look reality in the face. Neither Catholic spiritualism in reading texts and applying them to situations nor, for that matter, post-modern strategies of deconstructive subtlety and even beauty, can finally help us to fathom the fact and the lesson of Vichy law.

## Chapter 1

# Léon Blum, The "Stranger" at Riom: Legalized Ostracism and Vichy's Political Trial

*Il est bien l'étranger, le nomade asiatique, le négateur, le destructeur de toute race qui n'est pas la sienne.*
He is surely the outsider, the asiatic nomad, the negator, the annihilator of every race that is not his own.

Description of Léon Blum on 28 March 1942 in *L'Alerte*

I have chosen to begin this study with Léon Blum, one of twentieth century France's most fascinating figures. A leading light in literary circles around the time of Proust and Valéry, Blum was also an accomplished lawyer and eventually one of the Third Republic's foremost leaders. After World War II, Blum returned from imprisonment in Germany, again to become a key policymaker. He died a venerated man—indeed a uniquely admired politician and writer, whose lifelong Socialist ideals were upheld in such a way that few who differed with him on principle could manage to resent his politics.

In just a single period during this exemplary life did France itself (as opposed to his most extreme political opponents) come to detest and ostracize Leon Blum. Having abided him, sometimes grudgingly, having recognized his moral force in affairs ranging from the persecution of Dreyfus (which he passionately opposed) to the establishment of the forty-hour workweek (which he earnestly managed to bring about), and from the occupation of the Ruhr (opposed by Blum) to the firm alliance with beleaguered Poland (hailed by Blum in the tense atmosphere of prewar Paris), Vichy turned on him with legalistic ferocity in 1940 and attempted to silence him forever. The means to this end was a criminal indictment virtually tailor-made for Blum and several other leaders of the Third Republic. The charge was responsibility for the French defeat and betrayal of the duties of his office as Premier and Vice Premier during the prewar period.

The complainant, the authority that spoke for France as it moved to excise from the French polity Blum and everything he stood for, was the government of Vichy France. From its arrest of Blum in September 1940, to its formal indictment of him some thirteen months later, through its political trial of him in the town of Riom that began on 19 February 1942, until its transfer of Blum in March 1943 from the French prison at Bourassol to the concentration camp Buchenwald, Vichy's treatment of Blum spans the years of its greatest power and—as I here argue—typifies the régime's adoption of legalized racism on French soil.

In the year of that Riom trial, 1942, a novella appeared from the pen of a young French writer, himself a member of the Resistance. In the story, French law defines and banishes from its midst a man whose values it cannot tolerate. That classic tale, *L'Étranger* (The Stranger), does not explicitly mention the political and legal horrors of Vichy. Only much later, this same storyteller—Albert Camus—would explicitly associate the malaise that was Vichy with the eloquent professionalism of a lawyer.[1] If, in *The Stranger,* the heterodox Meursault is convicted of *being different,* in Camus' last story, *La Chute* (The Fall, 1956), the tables are turned and we are asked to sit in judgment of the successful lawyer Jean-Baptiste Clamence, he who in the depths of Vichy's evil rationalizes himself into non-resistance. Like hundreds of French magistrates, lawyers, bureaucrats, and law professors during Vichy, Clamence uses his gifts of reason and eloquence to tolerate what he was trained as a lawyer to oppose.

Blum—the flesh and blood stranger—is the quintessential victim of Vichy law. And Clamence—the fictional lawyer—represents many lawyers during Vichy who participated articulately in the régime's racial

---

[1] For the literary genealogy of the present study, see Richard Weisberg, *Poethics: And Other Strategies of Law and Literature* (New York: Columbia, 1992), 127–87.

policies, participated because they lacked the professional and moral capacity to say no.[2]

Riom epitomizes the struggle for the French soul that went on in Vichy and that, in a sense, has been going on ever since. It also stands as a comparative constitutional model from which lawyers generally need to draw wisdom. For Riom came to pass under a government that thought of itself as controlled by constitutional principles very similar to those in systems like the English and American. Due process talk permeates the investigation and trial, but process, in a fairer sense, was due neither Léon Blum nor the Jews on French soil whose fate he sometimes seems to embody. Nor did he or his co-religionists count any more under the guaranties (still nominally present because still so theoretically dear to these descendants of 1789) of "equal protection."

The paradox of Riom as a challenge to the French rhetorical allegiance to their constitutional heritage is furthered when we cast light upon the proponent of the government's proceedings against Blum, Joseph Barthélemy. Universally admired and even revered as a leading prewar scholar of French administrative and constitutional law, Barthélemy was Vichy's justice minister, and as such played the key role of antagonist to Blum's embattled defense. No mere martinet and surely no zealot, Barthélemy was considered a voice of reason and even liberality.[3] He could not be confused with the occasional virulent bigot attracted to the government. But he did enjoy power, and he was fiercely loyal to the aging but charismatic Pétain. Contemporaneous with the Riom proceedings, he had

---

[2] For more on the comparison of literary and actual legal rhetoric in France and on the continent generally, see Weisberg, "Comparative Law in Comparative Literature: The Figure of the Examining Magistrate in Dostoevski and Camus," 29 *Rutgers L Rev* 237 (1976), reprinted, expanded, and integrated into the Vichy research in *The Failure of the Word: The Protagonist as Lawyer in Modern Fiction* (New Haven: Yale, 1984).

[3] See, e.g., Arnaud Teyssier, "Joseph Barthélemy, Garde des Sceaux, 1941–43" (unpubl. master's thesis, Paris X, 1980), 4: "The entire *oeuvre* of this lawyer proclaimed his indefatigable attachment to the intangible dogmas of the liberal tradition. For all his students at the Faculty of Law and at Sciences politiques, he was the liberal leader *par excellence,* who taught in his courses the most spirited admiration for parliamentary régimes. A deputy for nine years (1919–28), Barthélemy retained that reputation among his parliamentary colleagues." For more on Barthélemy's liberalism, see below, note 19, and chapter 4 of this study.

signed the comprehensive religious statute of 2 June 1941, broader in its terms and in its application than the Nazi models.[4]

Joseph Barthélemy micromanaged the proceedings against Blum and the other prewar leaders. He jots down the words "The Jew Blum" in his notebook as he listens to the defense, observing that "No Jew would be allowed to speak up against Hitler the way Blum does here against Pétain."[5] Later, upset that the defense has managed to score legal and even public relations victories (despite his carefully wrought censorship program) against the prosecutors, Barthélemy suspends the trial without releasing the defendants. He goes on to underwrite the infamous "Special section" courts that summarily try Communists, resistance fighters, and Jewish hostages;[6] Barthélemy dies of tongue cancer awaiting his own trial after the Liberation. And some fifty years later, with the publication of his extensive memoirs, he posthumously provokes the debate about French legal values in the face of crisis and moral debasement.[7]

As Barthélemy and the defense lawyers sparred, the notion of French constitutional law itself became a player at Riom. Contemporaneous with the trial, an elaborate committee established by Vichy under Barthélemy's leadership was actually drafting a new constitution that would cite all the traditional safeguards of equal protection and due process while it also considered Barthélemy's suggestion that "race" be introduced to deprive unwanted outsiders of those very rights.[8] Meanwhile, a tiny minority of courageous French lawyers, including the Riom defense team, loudly invoked the still-existing rights established in 1789, rights that had been reiterated in texts of the 1880s that remained nominally in force to protect their clients until Vichy promulgated its own chartering document.

Constitutional arguments abounded at Riom, in the presence not only of government ministers but even of occasional German authorities, most

---

[4] See Dominique Rémy, *Les lois de Vichy* (Paris: Romillat, 1992), 116. For a wartime analysis noting already the greater breadth of Vichy religious definition, which it calls "quite natural" given the French need to control Jewish influence, see Henri Baudry and Joannès Ambre, *La Condition publique et privée du juif en France* (Lyon: Desvigne, 1942), 25.

[5] Joseph Barthélemy file held by his grandson, Jean Barthélemy.

[6] Rémy, *Les lois,* 140.

[7] Joseph Barthélemy, *Ministre de la Justice: Vichy, 1941–1943* (Paris: Pygmalion, 1989).

[8] Ibid., 20.

of them down from occupied Paris and visiting the "free zone" controlled by Vichy. The fact that Blum himself, as well as his lawyers and those retained by the others, could raise a specific legalistic attack on the *ex post facto* laws under which they had been indicted, on the breach of separation of powers that had permitted Pétain to declare their guilt before the trial began, on the impediments to the production of evidence necessary to the defense but found in the Occupied Zone, and on violations of the basic rights of man confirmed by 150 years of French constitutional law—this fact indicates that no Vichy lawyer was *forced* to collaborate in the new system. For, if the imprisoned and indicted Blum and his fellow defendants could protest with such eloquence, surely their compatriots, influential Vichy lawyers, whom we will have occasion here to analyze by the dozens, had all their rhetorical options available to them. Defense counsel at Riom, who challenged on behalf of their clients the very *bona fides* of Pétain's government, were treated with respect throughout the proceedings. (Barthélemy, zealously desiring Blum's conviction, nonetheless lunched collegially over beef and wine with the defendant's lawyers, whose skill and idealism had been turning the courthouse into a forum for ancient French ideals. Not one defense lawyer, including the Jewish litigator, Sam Spanien, was ever sanctioned or even professionally penalized for his Riom constitutional claims.)

Yet no Vichy lawyer or group ever directly protested against the régime's religious laws and extensive persecution of Jews on French soil.[9] This is yet another of Riom's paradoxes: it reveals that lawyers could without significant risk protest fiercely against oppressive Vichy laws; it casts into a tragic light the profession's pervasive willingness to accept and work with the language of racial exclusion.

So, Riom exposes much about Vichy law more generally. It is a tale of a proud legal system, self-consciously autonomous from the Germans, developing over four years its own peculiar blend of rationalized racism in a constitutional context. It is the story of lawyers, most of them trained to believe in equality and due process, precipitously—in a flash, as it were—using their skills to argue and apply antisemitic laws that exceeded in their scope of definition what the Germans demanded or indeed promulgated in the Third Reich. It is the story of selected and rare moments of courage within the legal profession. And, above all, it is the story of

---

[9] See chapter 2.

Vichy's pervasive "Barthélémisme," the ability of decent people to use their professional skills narrowly and perversely, to avoid myopically the central issues of their legal workday, and to employ low levels of generalization to produce high levels of grotesque and aberrational French legal rhetoric.

## A. Morality and Law: the Justification for Riom

### 1. Constitutional Reform as an Exclusionary Process

Much has been written about the political and historical dimensions of Riom, and these are not the pages to rehearse those excellent earlier findings.[10] We are interested in Vichy law as a whole, and in Riom as a microcosm of that larger organism. We are interested in the fact that Blum, a Jew, was the quintessential (but not the only) target of Vichy persecution; that his Jewishness was an important part of the state's resentment of him; that an elaborate scheme was concocted by the régime to dramatize his expulsion; and that, at least in part, Vichy sought through Riom to re-Christianize a people and a government that it felt had come under the "wrong" influences during the Third Republic.

The self-styled "revolution" that Vichy was creating had as a significant aim the elimination of certain specific nefarious influences that it felt had debased France and brought about its spiritual degradation and military defeat. Reacting against the French Revolution's motto, "Liberté, égalité, fraternité!," Vichy adopted the desultory triad, "Travail, famille, patrie."[11] Truer still perhaps to the spirit of the régime might have been a negative variation on these tripartite themes through a call for the elimination of everything that was wrong with prewar France: its *leaders,* its *morals,* and its *racial minorities.* From the beginning—long before any German Diktat—Vichy promulgated a series of anti-Jewish laws, signalling that its program was resentful, reactive, and negative. Whatever the strengths or weaknesses of its claim of distinctness from Nazi models,

---

[10] See. e.g., Henri Michel, *Le Procès de Riom* (Paris: Albin Michel, 1979); Christian Howie, tr., *Leon Blum Before His Judges* (London: Routledge, 1943); Louise Elliott Dalby, *Léon Blum: Evolution of a Socialist* (London: Yoseloff, 1963); Joel Colton, *Leon Blum: Humanist in Politics* (New York: Knopf, 1966).

[11] For "liberty, equality, fraternity" was substituted "work, family, fatherland."

this violent resentment of perceived enemies links Vichy's policies to the worst aspects of Hitler's Germany.

While not always speaking explicitly about Jews, the entire framework of Vichy law embodied this principle of exclusion. Thus Marshal Pétain, the aging World War I hero to whom the defeated French granted full powers to head their new government in Vichy, reflecting on the process of constitutional revision that Vichy set for itself, insists upon the need to condemn in order to re-define:

> The institutions that have brought us moral dissipation, economic ruin, and military defeat, can only be irremediably condemned. France, with a sure instinct, attributes to them the misery of the Nation. It does not wish to see them again. It will not see them again.[12]

What place, given the project of ostracism, would human rights have in the new constitutional scheme? Pétain goes on:

> The State, however, emphasizes its respect for the human personality, first achievement of Christian civilization.[13]

The interpolation of Christianity into constitutional law as a signpost to Vichy's notion of individual liberties becomes a central theme. Henry Puget, the official reporter for the new constitutional reform committee, would say:

> There is a complete break between the constitutional reform project and the political system that has dominated France for many years. Still, if we reject the official ideologies of the Third Republic, we also completely distance ourselves from Fascist and Hitlerite theories. The project both accepts the recent tendencies of our people and restores and prolongs our old national traditions, aligning itself with an idea of civilization that comes from Christianity.[14]

And Barthélemy would insist that the new constitution include:

> The grouping of rights that constitute the notion of the human personality.... The family, source of preservation and development of the race. The State exists as the politico-juridical expression of the Nation.... The State con-

---

[12] AN 72 AJ 412, Dossier no. 2. Copies or notes regarding archival sources are in the author's possession; translations by the author.

[13] Ibid.

[14] Ibid.

> siders itself subordinate to the superior rules of morality and of law.... In this way, the State differentiates itself from totalitarian States.[15]

But how *was* a constitution that would speak of "the family as the source of preservation and development of the race" going to "differentiate itself from the totalitarian states" of Europe? (Barthélemy opines that Vichy's continuing allegiance to free ownership of property clearly marks it off from Soviet Russia, failing—as he often did in discussing the proposed constitution—to take account of new French laws stripping Jews of their property.)[16] Would the simple and frequent invocation of "Christianity," "Christian values" or "Christian morality" suffice to separate Vichy from Nazi Germany? Barthélemy's own draft constitution would go on to include the following explicitly racial Article IV:

> The French community requires from its members an absolute allegiance. It does not accept into its breast as a constitutive element a race that conducts itself as a distinct community that resists assimilation.[17]

In the thinking of Pétain and his legalistic servants, there arises a consistent interweaving of the restoration of "French" or "Christian" civilization with the elimination of certain tendencies, and these tendencies are political, moral, and racial all at the same time. Rights that were to be safeguarded—like ownership of property, freedom from arbitrary detention, or from prosecution for *ex post facto* crimes—were vouchsafed only to the protected, morally sound, majority. Article 28 of the Barthélemy draft constitution guarantied to "All Frenchmen the right to move about and to establish a residence or a domicile in any lawful place," and the next article assured that "No one can be arrested or detained unless under law and by the prescribed formalities." But Articles 28 and 29, drafted well after the Vichy Jewish laws had authorized the stripping of Jewish property, the relegation of Jewish movement to certain areas, and the establishment of arbitrary arrest and detention for merely being a Jew, were apparently not applicable to all Frenchmen. As

---

[15] Ibid.

[16] By law of 22 July 1941, see Rémy, *Les lois,* 148; Vichy authorized the "aryanization" of Jewish property and businesses to eliminate "Jewish influence" in both zones.

[17] Michèle Cointet-Labrousse, *Vichy et le fascisme* (Paris: Editions complèxe, 1987), 177.

Article 29 put it in conclusion: "But whoever is summoned or seized by force of law must obey instantly."[18]

Barthélemy—who as late as 1938 adopted public positions of anti-fascism and egalitarianism[19]—this liberal academician and life-long fervent Catholic, speaks this way of an essential feature of Pétain's legislative scheme:

> The government of the National Revolution sees it as indispensable to rid the French community as quickly as possible of certain elements who have insinuated themselves in high leadership positions in the State, in industry, and in the Bank.[20]

Just as integration into the New France was legally limited to predefined groups and denied to others, so a membership card into the Vichy Revolution would not be granted to the politically incorrect. To be excised from the polity were Barthélemy's deliberately described "elements who *insinuated themselves*" in leadership positions under the Third Republic.

## 2. Léon Blum as Perfect Target

Vichy was able to demonize Léon Blum, because he embodied in one visible entity the three traits it most detested. He was a socialist prewar leader; he urged France to adopt the lax values that had led to defeat and demoralization; and he was a Jew. As historian Michèle Cointet-Labrousse puts it:

> There is the problem of Vichy's antisemitism, which comes to the fore in laws excluding Jews from numerous activities. Its source is largely French. To the old Christian urging of distrust towards the "Christ-killers," there

---

[18] AN 72 AJ 412, Dossier no. 2.

[19] On this point, see also Marrus and Paxton, *Vichy France and the Jews* (New York: Basic Books, 1981). They add that Barthélemy "defended Jews and Italian antifascist refugees that year," ibid., 56. So, too, in J. Lubetzki, *La condition des Juifs en France sous l'Occupation allemande* (Paris: CDJC, 1947), 9. Lubetzki praises the prewar Barthélemy but adds that "Once Minister of Justice in an authoritarian government...he denaturalizes countless irreproachable citizens for the sole reason of being Jewish or adversaries of the régime." Henri Michel's praise for Barthélemy seems to extend into his performance as Justice Minister; see Michel, *Le Procès*, 71, but was based on earlier information sources not including (it appears) the archival material that researchers more recently have had at their disposal.

[20] AN 72 AJ 412, Dossier no. 2.

> were many other negative assessments added since the 19th Century.... For certain proponents of the National Revolution, the *front populaire* of Léon Blum—blamed for the weakness of armaments caused by the 40-hour week and paid vacations—had been supported and profited from by the Jews. The minister from the Ardeche, X. Vallat had been sorry [in 1936] to see his "old gallo-Roman country...governed by a Jew." He [Vallat] would be granted on 29 March 1941 the leadership of [Vichy's] Bureau on Jewish Questions. This rightist Catholic preached a statist antisemitism and was convinced that the Jews could no longer be assimilated.... He thought they were driven to dominate and wanted to "neutralize" them. He defined his targets: politicians (especially revolutionaries), businessmen, the merchant class, professional people, the press, radio and theater: even the workers and the ordinary Jewish employee would be pursued since they formed the support on which their more prosperous coreligionists relied.[21]

The longtime antisemite, Xavier Vallat, whose parliamentary attack on Blum in 1936 had been silenced by the Chamber's newly elected president, Herriot,[22] now had no vocal enemies; he was to find his own way to power under Vichy. From his base of operations at the central Vichy administrative agency on racial questions—the "Commissariat général aux questions juives," or CGQJ—Vallat watched the still-polite world of French law deal with his detested Blum.

Indeed, in Riom, where everything was done by law and where statist antisemitism remained largely covert—to be discovered later in Barthélemy's courtside doodling[23]—the "strangeness" to France that Vallat associated with Blum in 1936 was rearticulated. Blum was on trial not just for poor prewar armament preparations; a prosecution witness, General Langlois, formulated the deeper structure of the case against Blum: "It's too bad for France that the leaders did not believe in war.... There were some who didn't even think French."[24] Blum asked aloud

---

[21] Cointet-Labrousse, *Vichy et le fascisme,* 197–99.

[22] Colton, *Leon Blum: Humanist,* 144; Dalby, *Leon Blum, Evolution,* 91.

[23] See text at note 5.

[24] AN 72 AJ 411, Dossier no. 15, Roger Genebrier's notes for the session of 1 April 1942. Genebrier, a *prefet,* after citing the phrase "il y avait quelques uns qui ne pensaient pas Français," and Blum's indignant rejoinder, adds "General Langlois responded patiently, 'I do not deal in personalities...,' and with magnificent courage he concluded 'anyway, I believe that the atmosphere was poisoned by the League of Nations.' "

if the witness were referring to him, to which Langlois responded that he did not "deal in personalities." Blum said:

> There are many ways to deal in personalities. I would think that if the witness was referring to me, if he was thinking of me in using such a weighty and insulting expression, that he would express his thought in a categorical manner.[25]

Langlois' resuscitation of Vallat's thought occurred in open court on 1 April 1942. Like the tip of the iceberg, it evoked more than it showed. Vichy's frigid treatment of Blum and his people was becoming foundationalized, far below the surface of the trial.

## B. Setting the Stage for a Morality Play

### 1. Blum *contra* the Supreme Leader

Near Vichy, at the Chateau of Chazeron, a prison had been set up to accommodate a series of illustrious political prisoners, all of whom had been arrested without charge by a Vichy law of 3 September 1940, legitimizing administrative detention.[26] Léon Blum took his place there on 15 September, thus gaining the dubious distinction of being among the first Jews to be arrested under Vichy statutory law. There would eventually be tens of thousands of such cases, none (perhaps unfortunately) as well publicized. Blum was joined the following 25 April by fellow socialists such as Auriol, Dormoy, Grumbach, and Moch—three-quarters of the influx were Jews.[27]

---

[25] Ibid.

[26] This law was itself modeled after a decree of 18 November 1939; it permitted "the taking from their residences of people deemed dangerous to the national defense or to national security," and such people under appropriate circumstances could be held "at a place designated by the Minister of Defense or of the Interior." This administrative detention was subject to no other law. It was carefully chosen by Vichy from among several ways of imprisoning political undesirables without due process of law. See AN $BB^{30}$ 1710. Typical of Vichy's devious legalism was its rejection of arrest under the more traditional provision of the code d'instruction criminelle, for under Article 15, evidence to substantiate arrest was required within twenty-four hours, and there was fear that a court would dismiss charges given the lack of tangible proof of any wrongdoing.

[27] Michel, *Le Procès,* 36.

His case was special though, as was that brought against his illustrious co-defendant, Édouard Daladier. These prominent Third Republic leaders were to endure a process that lasted from their imprisonment in fall 1940 through their indictments a year later and their trial in February 1942. Both fates would involve continuing imprisonment, both in France and in Germany. They never ceased battling the charges against them. But Blum's case was the more personalized, the more *allegorized,* and finally, the more representative of the Vichy years.

Blum at Chazeron was kept in a kind of Kafka-esque limbo as to the nature of the charges against him until, on 18 October 1940, these were revealed. Although he would contest eloquently every substantive accusation, his lawyer-like attention was drawn first to the question of the jurisdiction of the court charged with his case. Under the terms of the fifth of the new "actes constitutionnels," passed on 30 July 1940,[28] Vichy had created a new court, and it was this "Cour suprême" that indicted Blum and others for "Treason against his duties in actions that led from a state of peace to a state of war." Specifically, the régime saw dereliction in duty when Blum, as prime minister, nationalized the war industry, introduced the forty-hour week, and failed to suppress strikes. The charge laid the beginning of French demoralization and unpreparedness at Blum's feet.[29]

Blum, a distinguished lawyer both in France's highest administrative court (the Conseil d'État) and at the private bar, was not long to answer the methods used to arrest him. In what stands as the first major peroration on the illegality of the régime itself, and on its various "constitutional acts," Blum replied in early November 1940:

> Since I have been confronted with the first procedural move against me, I want to make a preliminary statement. The acts that have been held against me are of a political nature. Under the Constitution of 1875, the body having jurisdiction over crimes committed by ministers in the exercise of their functions was the Senate, assembled as a High Court of Justice. An act of the Head of State has eliminated the High Court and created a Cour suprême. This act was itself undertaken pursuant to a delegation of power granted by the National Assembly in a resolution of 10 July [1940]. I must

[28] Rémy, *Les lois,* 60.

[29] See, e.g., AN BB[30] 1710, describing the 62-page file on Blum outlining and detailing the government's case against him.

declare, therefore, that I do not recognize the validity of that law, which I believe was infected by a substantial absence of consent.[30]

Blum's theory was that not only the new court, but also the régime that had created it, had no constitutional validity. From this point until the suspension of the trial, he and others at the defense table maintained that the "constitutional acts" under the legislation of 10 July 1940 that created Vichy were *all* invalid. These latter included the National Assembly's grant of full powers to Pétain,[31] the legitimacy of which was a *sine qua non* for the appointment of the special Riom jurisdiction.

The argument was momentous, and in some ways it still rages in France: did any law or new governmental body promulgated by the Vichy government indeed have legitimacy?[32] The defense team at Riom declared that the Cour suprême, a creature of the new régime's constitutional plan, had no jurisdiction; political prisoners should be tried by the Senate, not a puppet court.

Easily the most explosive—because the broadest—of Blum's foundational arguments against the validity of the prosecution, this constitutional attack provoked almost immediate internal debate at Vichy. Barthélemy agonized over the strategy, which called into question Vichy's leader, who was otherwise achieving near-mythic dimensions as France's savior

---

[30] Ibid.

[31] Rémy, *Les lois,* 31.

[32] AN 72 AJ 411, Dossier no. 15. How could the court have jurisdiction, asked the defendants, if the constitutional order establishing it first needed to be ratified—on the terms of Parliament's grant to Pétain of full powers—"by the people"? The court rejected this jugular attack on its own existence by agreeing with the prosecutor that all French laws take immediate effect (even if requiring some additional legal element in the future), including the new constitutional decrees. See also, e.g., Michèle Cointet-Labrousse, "Le conseil national de Vichy: Vie politique et réforme de l'état en régime autoritaire. 1940–1944," (unpubl. Ph.D. diss., Paris X, 1984), 113: "The Pétainists must resolve a problem.... The constitutional acts [of the new régime] do not correspond to the delegation of power granted to Pétain. They cannot be thought of as a 'constitution.' " Vichy aide-de-camp Moulin de Labarthète describes the uneasiness with Vichy legitimacy felt even by Pétain at times in idem., *Le temps des Illusions* (Geneva: Bourquin, 1946), 110–20. For an excellent recent summary of Vichy's historical and present-day legal legitimacy, see Dominique Rousseau, "Vichy, a t-il éxisté?," in *Le Monde des débats,* November 1992, 22. The reader should also bear in mind that many laws passed by Vichy are still operative today, none of course racial in nature.

in a time of defeat and desperation.[33] Over the course of the entire Riom process, this man of law never resolved the constitutional attack in his own mind; as late as 14 February 1942, the constitutional lawyer in him still pondered Blum's foundational attack on the court's legitimacy:

> The National Assembly may not really have abdicated. It only gave its mandate to the Marshal to make a constitution, for it, with it, and under its control, after which he would retire.[34]

Publicly, however, Vichy at Riom gave not an inch on the question of its own validity, and the matter never gained enough momentum outside the defense team to make a difference. As a matter of constitutional law, the government prevailed in its view that the National Assembly's July 10 grant of full powers was an authentic "going-out-of-business" transfer to the new government, and that each successive constitutional act—including the establishment of the Cour suprême—had complete legitimacy as a matter of positive law. The National Assembly recognized, on this view, the need for authoritarian leadership in the hands of the hero of Verdun, the charismatic if ancient World War I hero who would reform the state and bring it only gradually (if at all) back to republican legislative procedures. On 10 July, the argument proceeds, the Assembly fully intended to let Pétain do anything he wanted for as long as he felt necessary to do it.

Having survived constitutional attack from the outside, however, the Cour suprême ironically faced its greatest challenge from the head of state himself. Pétain was frustrated by the pace of his new court's proceedings. He wanted quicker disposition of these political pariahs. A year after the arrest of the defendants, and still many months before the preliminary inquiry into their case was completed, Pétain made a declaration of the Riom defendants' guilt.[35] At the same time, he shocked even his closest advisors by attempting to substitute for the Cour suprême the jurisdiction of a hand-picked "Conseil de justice politique." This council of political justice—more an executive advisory board than a court—

---

[33] As Barthélemy's grandson, the Parisian lawyer Jean Barthélemy told me, for the first few years of the régime, "There were 40,000,000 Pétainistes in France"; personal interview with author, Paris, December 1988.

[34] AN 72 AJ 411, Dossier no. 8.

[35] See, e.g., Barthélemy, *Ministre,* 238–42, "La Justice du Maréchal"; see also AN 72 AJ 411, Dossier no. 7.

would remedy the delays of the Cour suprême and hasten the verdict and punishment against Vichy's foremost enemies.

As was to be true virtually each time Vichy brought its authority to bear against individuals and peoples, Pétain's second intervention against the Riom defendants had the appearance of legality, indeed of constitutional legitimacy. Just as Constitutional Act 5 permitted the establishment of the Cour suprême and other special Vichy courts, Constitutional Act 7 permitted Pétain—*personally*—to investigate and punish all government functionaries or ministers who "betrayed their duties."[36] No matter that the council was completely unchecked by the ordinary procedures of French criminal investigations, impermeable even to the influence of the Marshal's faithful Barthélemy.[37]

If authoritarian government had been mandated by the French people in their representatives' final act, Pétain forced the further argument that he alone could administer justice as well as promulgate legislation. A memorandum rationalizing the council, and Vichy's other "exceptional courts"—there were to be nine altogether—invokes the memory of Saint Louis (a provocative but hardly unique conjuration)[38] to justify what otherwise seemed like a gross breach of separation of powers:

---

[36] Article 3 of the Constitutional Act of 27 January 1941, Rémy, *Les lois,* 108.

[37] Barthélemy, *Ministre,* 238. Pétain's loyal justice minister was troubled by his leader's *diktat* prior to a trial. Barthélemy jotted on his letterhead: "Peine provisoire prononcée par le Maréchal—et si les accusés sont ensuite acquittés?" (Sentencing pronounced by the Marshal—and if the defendants are eventually acquitted?), AN 72 AJ 411, Dossier no. 1. Yet Barthélemy himself may have originated the idea of such a "council," luncheon menu, Barthélemy file of Jean Barthélemy on which is written: "The Committee on Political Justice—a project I prepared for the Marshall."

[38] St. Louis (Louis IX, a thirteenth-century king of France) turns out to be a favorite source of Vichy legal thinking, and his antisemitism in this regard not unpleasant to some legal (or at least legalistic) theorists of the régime. Contemporaneously with the Riom change of jurisdiction, for example, the eminent writer Henri de Montherlant, in *La Reine morte,* was applauding the announcement of the new courts that would summarily try and execute Vichy undesirables; in a column for the newspaper *Aujourd' hui* of 25 August 1941, Montherlant quotes Saint Louis: "None can govern his country until he learns as well to say 'no' as to say 'yes.' " Montherlant continues, "Let us work to say 'no' to all who are mediocre, to all who are beneath us." Employing medieval French royalist precedents to define Vichy law, Charles Maurras had vociferously endorsed the merging of executive and judicial power for some time. See discussion in Barthélemy, *Ministre,* 239.

> A chief-of-state jurisdiction? This seems to many a surprising innovation.... And yet in all cultures the power and the duty of rendering justice have long been among the most prized prerogatives of the leader. When societies have begun to move from private vengeance to penal justice, the leader has been the first judge.... Who has not heard of Saint Louis, presiding under an oak tree in Vincennes...? It is a return to this old judicial tradition, interrupted for a century and a half, that is consecrated by [the new courts].[39]

Although only the defendants and their counsel had protested against the Cour suprême and the legitimacy of the régime as a whole, Pétain's insistence on the council proved too much for others as well. Having tacitly accepted by that summer and fall of 1941 many other fundamental violations of French legal tradition,[40] some of France's most distinguished private lawyers now decided to speak up. Jacques Charpentier, *bâtonnier* (chair) of the Bar Association of the City of Paris, may have been willing to engage in a self-described "honeymoon" with Vichy (accepting without batting an eyelash its anti-Jewish statutes, which quickly involved some of his colleagues in the pillaging of "aryanized" property[41]); he may eventually have tolerated the sight of the Star of David on the robes of surviving Jewish litigators in the Palais de Justice; he may have grudgingly given Vichy authorities the names of court personnel who might fall prey to the racial *numerus clausus*. These parts of his story, like his postwar rationalization of the quotas levelled against his Jewish colleagues at the bar, are the stuff of a different Vichy chapter.[42]

At Riom, however, Charpentier would not quietly accede to the blatant denial of due process embodied in Act 7 and its consequent executive council of justice. On 28 August 1941, in his official capacity as head of France's largest grouping of private lawyers, Charpentier wrote directly to Pétain, as follows:

---

[39] AN 72 AJ 413, Dossier no. 10.

[40] See especially Vichy's religious statutes, Statut des juifs of 3 October 1940 and 2 June 1941, Rémy, *Les lois,* 87, 116; the breach of separation of powers inherent in the fifth constitutional act, discussed above, n. 32; laws permitting the incarceration in "special camps" of stateless Jews, such as the Vichy law of 4 October 1940, long before the Germans had turned their attention to the subject at all, Rémy, ibid., 91.

[41] See Jacques Charpentier's own postwar book, *Au service de la Liberté* (Paris: Fayard, 1949), where he admits that some of his colleagues had been appointed "Aryan trustees" over Jewish property.

[42] See chapters 3 and 8.

> M. le Maréchal: In a recent speech, you announced your intention to judge on your own those "responsible for our disasters," by using Constitutional Act #7. Soon after that text was published, you did me the honor of receiving me, and you assured me that you did not intend to apply such a procedure against those indicted before the court in Riom.... Now it seems from the newspapers that their trial will occur before you, and it is also difficult to guess whether the Cour suprême is to be dissolved or if new investigations will follow the old.
>
> Whatever may be the case, I believe it to be my duty as Bâtonnier respectfully to call your attention to the extraordinary nature of such a measure, which I believe to be without precedent in the history of our country. All great political figures that come to mind...were judged by courts—the Duc d'Enghien himself was tried before a court martial.
>
> In each case, the accused retained the right to defend himself, and almost always to call witnesses and to have a lawyer present. Never has the head of state taken on the grave responsibility to remove them from their judges, to sit as sole adjudicator, and to pronounce sentence unbound by the most elementary guaranties of justice....
>
> The Bar Association is both by nature and secular tradition the logical defender of accused people. I would betray the confidence of those who have chosen me their leader if I remained silent before a measure that must be judged by History, but that surely at present constitutes a violation of the defendants' rights.[43]

Jacques Charpentier, like Joseph Barthélemy, was another basically decent lawyer who found a way to work with Vichy, but who picked his spots to protest vigorously when he felt that his own, or his constituency's, vital interests had been compromised. Neither man would find his way clear to attack at the heart the wide-ranging Vichy legalistic sickness that was antisemitism. But, thanks largely to their efforts, the Council of Political Justice did not crush the Cour suprême.

## 2. Barthélemy's Prideful Intervention

Charpentier in Paris was not alone in his anxiety over the proposed shift from the court to the council. Joseph Barthélemy claims to have heard the news for the first time, during the intermission of a performance of

---

[43] AN 72 AJ 411, Dossier no. 3. See also Charpentier's account of his protest in *Au service*, 148, where he speaks of the "problem" of having too many Jews at the prewar Paris bar.

*Boris Godunov* at the Grand Casino in Vichy.[44] Pétain was making a speech over the radio, amplified for all in attendance to hear. Although respected by the Marshal, and close to him on almost all legal decisions, Barthélemy appeared shocked by the announcement. He decided to work immediately to have the Cour suprême restored to full jurisdictional power over the Riom defendants. Part of his reaction smacked of political pique:

> That the Minister of Justice be left out of the preparations for a political address, perhaps. But that such a direct intervention in the most important judicial business of the country take place without the Minister of Justice even being informed, that was intolerable.[45]

Part of Barthélemy's response was surely based on the illogicality of having one body pronounce a sentence while another was still in the process of amassing and assessing evidence.[46] But it seems fair at this distance to speculate that Barthélemy's aversion to the council was far less imbued with constitutional idealism than, say, Charpentier's. His opposition, which marks the only disagreement he pursued (however respectfully) with Vichy's charismatic old man, grew out of a wish to preserve the forms of law while still wreaking vengeance upon the régime's political and moral foes. Without any doubt, too, he sought to preserve his own preeminent spot as manager of the Riom proceedings. He had personally chosen most of the Cour suprême and the prosecutors connected to it[47]; he could have little influence, however, on this new council.

Barthélemy took upon himself the task of explaining his master's reasoning to the offended Cour suprême and to the people of France.[48] Although the council went on formally to condemn Blum, Daladier, and their co-defendant Gamelin, to immediate imprisonment in the maximum security prison at Portalet (far less comfortable than the one at Bourassol), the mediation of leading lawyers brought jurisdiction over

---

[44] Barthélemy, *Ministre,* 239. Barthélemy was to suffer other stresses that August; see chapter 9, note 97, for a discussion of his role in the infamous special section courts.

[45] Ibid.

[46] For a description of Blum's response to this "Catch-22," see Colton, *Leon Blum: Humanist,* 399–400.

[47] See Barthélemy, *Ministre,* 218–20.

[48] Ibid., 240.

their fates back to the Cour suprême for a trial on the merits. At the behest of his trusted minister, Pétain's intermeddling ceased, but his presence as a kind of mythic savior whose sacred nature the defendants insisted on attacking, still dominated the Riom courthouse.

## C. The Preliminary Investigation: Blum as Talmudic Interloper

The jugular attack by the defendants against the régime itself had failed for lack of broadscale support outside Riom, but because the Council of Political Justice did offend many influential lawyers, that body at least had been suppressed. Now continued the long period preceding the trial, the traditional French "preliminary investigation." In this process, little familiar and less comparable to Anglo-American criminal law,[49] a detailed psychological portrait is drawn of the suspect. Novelists like Camus revel in depicting preliminary investigations, and Blum's—taking place as Camus wrote *The Stranger*—would have been grist for his aesthetic mill.

During the seventeen months before Blum came to trial, the theme of his "strangeness" to the values of Vichy was composed as the preliminary investigation's dominant *Leitmotif.* This allegorical element was quietly at work during the very months in which the jurisdictional battle was being fought more openly. For, although the Marshal's pretrial pronouncement of guilt and insistence on his own tribunal drew attention and disapprobation from most Vichy lawyers, the Cour suprême and its agents proceeded without interruption or publicity in a manner those same lawyers would only applaud as typical of French criminal law.

The preliminary investigation into the guilt of Blum and the other Riom defendants—during which some 650 witnesses would be heard[50]—was designed both to uncover the facts and to cloak Blum in the colors of Vichy's direst enemies. This pretrial phase spanned the calendar year 1941, peaking perhaps in June, the very month in which the definitive Vichy religious statute was signed by Barthélemy and offered to a France that was awash in regulatory antisemitism.

---

[49] See Weisberg, *Failure of the Word,* chapter 3.

[50] Michel, *Le Procès,* 85. The figure takes us through the end of August 1941, by which time the bulk of the preliminary inquiry had taken place.

The indictment levied against Léon Blum contained, of course, no explicit reference to his Jewishness. As we have seen, however, the issue arose during the trial, and it was much in the mind of Barthélemy and many onlookers. The régime held against Blum the combination of idealistic republican virtues he embodied *and* the Jewishness they associated with the political and moral excesses of his prewar Socialist governments. No individual case better exemplifies Vichy's program: the confounding of political, spiritual, and religious elements in a reactive response at least to the politics of the 1930s and arguably to the idealism of the previous 150 years.[51]

And, in another sense, no prosecution so compellingly complements, by its mixture of law and storytelling, of procedural forms and mythic allusions, the story being written by Camus as he contemporaneously lived through the Vichy experience. As in Camus' *L'Étranger,* the French state conducts an investigation that has as much to do with the *character* of the defendant as with the crime he allegedly committed. And in Riom as well as in the Algeria of the novella, a preliminary investigation sets the tone (often more subtly than does the prosecution at the public trial itself); the allegory of good and evil emerges early, and the defendant finds himself answering charges that are as much metaphysical as they are based on historical "fact." In a manner quite distinct from Anglo-American criminal procedures, the French pretrial inquiry provides the ideal *narrative structure* for this admixture of law and myth.[52] Just as Camus depicts the *juge d'instruction* (examining magistrate, or preliminary inquisitor) finding Meursault's *moral weakness* and making it

[51] As Pierre Birnbaum recently demonstrates with majestic scope, Vichy thus constitutes a particularly ironic denouement to the fate of generations of loyal "Juifs d'état"–Jews in the service of the French state. Blum was chief but not unique among them. Julien Reinach—a distinguished member of the Conseil d'État—found himself arrested and sent to Drancy under the new religious laws that eventually the Conseil itself would both affirm and seek to expand. Julien and his brother Leon were deported; only the former survived to return to the homeland that had so debased his family's service to it. Many other functionaries of the Republican past found themselves riven by the awareness that all their assumptions about being "un Français d'origine israélite" (a Frenchman of Jewish origins) had been reversed and reduced to the ethno-racial epithet "juif." See Birnbaum, *Les fous de la République* (Paris: Fayard, 1992), 15–16 and passim.

[52] See Weisberg, *Failure of the Word,* Parts 2 and 3.

central to his legal case, so the Riom *juge* seeks to associate Léon Blum with the "sickness" of Republican weakness and spiritual debasement.

Camus in 1942 gives us a process frighteningly close to the contemporary reality: French law capitalizes on the surrounding political and cultural atmosphere to allegorize its case against the Riom defendants. Léon Blum, like Meursault, is punished for being "other." But where the fictional character is painted as an amoralist, the real defendant is stamped with a *foreign morality*. Its name is "Jewishness" and its trademark is the Talmud.

During the unfolding of the preliminary investigation, much was happening in both French zones that colored the strategy of Blum's pretrial inquisitors. Xavier Vallat, the exogenous prewar parliamentarian whose racism was then silenced,[53] now typified the mythic background from which prosecutors and other Vichy lawyers could find sustenance even as their egalitarian blood cells continued to fight for recognition in the corrupted organism. In 1937, Darquier de Pellepoix, eventually to be Vallat's successor at the CGQJ, had included the following series of "quotations" in his publication, *L'Antijuif:*

> "It's a commandment for every Jew to try to wipe out everything that concerns the Christian church and those that serve it." Talmud
> "To bolster their trusts, their guilds, the Jews have decided to ruin trade. Small businessmen are inept, they constitute a social anachronism and it would be good if they disappeared." Léon Blum
> "Non-Jews have been created to serve Jews, night and day." Talmud
> "Only Jews are people; other nations are a species of animal." Talmud.[54]

Vichy legal theorists, too—with more art, perhaps—interwove religious antisemitism and social policy. In treatises on the new religious laws by such authorities as the lawyers Henri Baudry and Joannès Ambre, legalized sanctions against Jews are discussed in the context of citing neutrally Vallat's 1936 libel against Blum on the floor of the National Assembly.[55] Legal scholar André Broc contemporaneously condones the laws against Jews as correctly symbolizing the *essential religious differences*

---

[53] See note 21.

[54] Cited in Jean Laloum, *La France antisémite de Darquier de Pellepoix* (Paris: Syros, 1979), 18.

[55] Baudry and Ambre, *La Condition publique et privée,* 14, citing Vallat as per note 21, above.

between Christian and Jew, epitomized by the latter's alleged devotion to the Talmud:

> Judaism has no real mystical aspect, which might somehow correspond directly to religious needs.... On the contrary, Judaism consists since the Exile essentially of a system, supported by the Talmud, designed to maintain the patriotic goal of the social cohesiveness of the Jews, dispersed in the midst of the Gentiles. This system, although intellectualized, has so marked the Jewish people that it seems objectively today to be their moral law, at least as regards the essential rules, the details having been nitpicked to death by them. One might ask if this system, by its corporeal restraints, particularly as regards sexual matters, has not itself contributed to the enforcement of racial categories....[56]

If the citations to the Talmud—and to other Jewish texts and "rules" are almost always erroneous or totally fabricated,[57] the Talmud nonetheless symbolizes the ineffable "otherness" that legitimizes—nay necessitates—the imposition of the status of "other" through law.

Furthermore, as we shall explore in greater depth in this study's final chapter, a loose "interpretation" of the Talmud itself was justified, since flexibility in the reading of texts is itself a mark of the elevated Christian law, compared, in this view, to the literalness of the Jewish religion. For the Jews, every act is dictated by the letter of the law, whereas French law has risen to an elevated level of spiritualistic generalization.[58]

Vichy law's twisted use of the Talmud rationalized the need for a special law to regulate a group that had defined itself as legally special and legitimatized persecution of that group through loose, amorphous, and often incoherent readings of history, religion, and sacred texts. In *L'Etranger,* Camus brilliantly captures this "spiritualization" of the criminal law; Meursault is tried for failing to show the proper sentiments at his mother's funeral or for starting an affair on that same day. Analogously, Blum is tried for "poisoning" French morale, and for the twin

---

[56] André Broc, *La Qualification juive: une notion juridique nouvelle* (Paris: Presses universitaires de France, 1943), 14.

[57] Ibid., 19, where Broc confidently asserts that Jewish fathers circumcise their sons.

[58] Ironically, the spirit-letter dichotomy would be used *against the French* by none other than the Nazis, who felt that Vichy was always insufficiently sensitive to the spirit of the laws and too attached to literal textual meanings; see chapter 10, notes 31–36. The Germans, however, quickly came to depend on French literalistic legalism and learned how to use it for their own ends; see chapter 6, notes 1–9.

infecting agencies, Socialism and Judaism. Although hardly an observant Jew, and although more celebrated for his knowledge of French letters than for his Talmudic wisdom, Blum would continue to be associated with a foreign strain of thinking.[59] The preliminary examination into the Riom charges against him, along with the occasional revelatory moment at the public trial, indicate that the "making strange" of Léon Blum was at the heart of the matter.

While answering a question put to him at the trial by presiding judge Caous, Blum alluded to his preliminary inquisitor's strategy:

> In making notes for my personal use, there is what I call "the poison" argument. The Prosecution seems convinced—and wishes to convince public opinion—that my policy injected into French social life, and especially into the working classes, a venom, a poison, a toxic element, so toxic in fact that its harmful effects went on indefinitely and perhaps still lasts even to-day. I think that is the crux of the charge against me. I think it is the essence of what underlies the various counts, the various heads, of the indictment, and the questions of every kind put to me during the [preliminary] Examination. I do not say that it was anywhere explicitly expressed, but I do not think I am wrong in affirming that one feels the idea latent and always present. I have poisoned the country by what is called my weakness and complaisance, my weakness and complaisance in face of subversive plots, and primarily, I imagine, towards the Communist Party.[60]

Like Camus' examining magistrate, who makes of Meursault a moral monster, Blum's apparently also consciously fashioned a narrative that extracted from the letter of the charge a far more powerful allegorical "spirit." Blum proceeds:

> I am, then, trying to find out what is the tangible, concrete, content of this indictment, of which nobody could say that it is not present in all the charges brought against me. And when I endeavour to discover, to examine, what is the meaning of these charges of weakness and complaisance by which the soul of this nation is alleged to have been corrupted, I return

---

[59] "Although Blum always retained a respect for the faith of his fathers, he took the path of many other assimilated French Jews. At an early age, he considered himself 'emancipated,' heir to the rationalism and the anticlericalism of the Enlightenment. Blum's indifference to the Jewish faith in which he was reared did not mean that he rejected 'being Jewish.' He always remained a Jew in the face of antisemitism, which he despised in all its forms," Colton, *Leon Blum: Humanist,* 5.

[60] Howie, *Leon Blum Before His Judges,* 148.

always in the last analysis to this everlasting occupation of the factories about which I have said so much.[61]

Blum the lawyer—Blum the Talmudist?—is seeking to find in the charges against him *something specific*. Perhaps it was his government's relationship with the Communists; perhaps it was his unwillingness to bring violent state action to bear on the strikers who occupied the factories during 1936. Or, perhaps too poignant for the always idealistic "Juif d'État" to surmise out loud,[62] perhaps it is the Jewish value system, the quest for justice on this earth, that once had seemed harmonious with France but that to the new régime was anathema.

Ironically, Blum's very insistence on finding the "substance" of the seemingly amorphous charges against him reenforced the prosecution's allegorical treatment of his personality. Who but a Jew, who but a Talmudist, would insist on literal details at a time of such moral urgency for the French?[63]

Like Meursault's pretrial inquisitor, too, Blum's eventually adopted a kind of unsolicited, easygoing familiarity with the defendant. To Blum's essential assertion that his policies were born of compromise, discussion, and political necessity (as well as of idealism and the mandate Blum felt he had received from the people), the rejoinder was this:

> During one of the visits he paid me at [Blum's first prison, the Chateau of] Chazeron, the Examining Magistrate said to me with flattering, certainly, but also intimidating suavity, "Why, when a man like you is in the government, everyone knows he is the real Head!"[64]

Who can forget the scene when, during an equally lengthy preliminary investigation into moral guilt, Meursault's inquisitor taps him on the shoulder in a most friendly way and labels him "M. Antichrist," thus establishing humorously what turns into the deadly serious justification for a capital sentence. So Blum's inquisitor posits him as the supreme

---

[61] Ibid., 154.

[62] See Birnbaum, *Les fous*, passim, for the difficulties those faithful Jewish servants always experienced in even thinking—much less expressing—the thought that their "madness" for France would ever be repaid with statist antisemitism.

[63] Justice Minister Barthélemy reveals his own assessment of Blum's "morals" in his discussion of the Riom trial: "The values of the Blum family were biblical, sometimes strict, always patriarchal," Barthélemy, *Ministre*, 226.

[64] Howie, *Leon Blum Before His Judges*, 28.

leader—the unquestioned source—of what the prosecution now submits was a poisoned politics and a venomous morality that must be ruthlessly eliminated from the French bloodstream.

A set of non-legal assumptions informed the Riom strategy from the outset. Blum was the uncontested leader of a Third Republic that was poisoning the French people through both its policies and its inner moral essence. Vichy wanted to remove the venom of Jewish morality and to restore France to its Christian place in a new Europe. At the end of the day, however, Blum's sheer perspicacity, his brilliant control of the facts, his awareness of the literary techniques that inform French criminal procedure,[65] his superb and courageous defense team, and his good fortune both in his strong co-defendants (particularly Daladier) and his weak judges, would compromise the strategy of his persecutors.

## D. The Trial Itself: A Failure of "Liberal/Catholic" Pétainisme

Joseph Barthélemy, perhaps as much as any other individual, sought to translate the Marshal's antipathy to these Riom prisoners into an official verdict. A lawyer to his roots, he surely deserves some of the credit for the eventual openness with which the Cour suprême engaged the defendants' arguments; but of considerably greater moment is the fact that he tolerated along the way so many detours from established French principles. The *ex post facto* nature of both the charges and the jurisdictional innovations, the censorship and spying on the defendants' communications that were largely his own creation,[66] the closed nature of some of the proceedings[67]—these and other breaches of due process that would have shocked the law professor of 1937 or 1938 were endorsed by the reincarnated Minister of Justice of 1941 and 1942.

---

[65] Blum's first career, of course, was as a celebrated and highly sensitive literary critic and journal editor. See, e.g., Dalby, *Leon Blum: Evolution,* ch. 3: "Literary Criticism."

[66] AN 72, AJ 411, Dossiers nos. 8, 16, 20. See also Barthélemy, *Ministre,* 231.

[67] AN 72 AJ 411, Dossier no. 6. Barthélemy's decision to make the trial public came quite late, perhaps as late as 22 February 1942. He decided that a *huis clos* (closed trial) would only invite the curious to seek their own accounts and might compromise the control he would otherwise have over the press.

At the same time, the rationalized bitterness that tugged at so many otherwise accomplished Frenchmen—the resentment of the Outsider—was given voice: "Atmosphere of the courtroom. A Jew who insults the Marshal."[68]

Barthélemy's memoirs reveal his inner doubts about the *substantive* nature, too, of the Riom charges, particularly those against Blum, "who was not in the government at the time hostilities commenced."[69] Yet again, he found a way to ignore the pleas of his best inner self by employing halfway measures that did nothing to change the grim reality of Vichy's departure from French legal norms. In this case, he substituted forms for substance and was content to organize a trial at which the *trappings of tolerance* replaced real fairness. His characterization of the defense's view of the trial borders on self-deception:

> Although the defendants are always called "Monsieur"...the judges sometimes must interrupt their speeches.... The defendants and their counsel have expressed their confidence in the independence of the judges and have confirmed that this is a judicial—and not a political—process.[70]

Barthélemy sought less, throughout the trial, traditional French due process than the gloss of gallic chivalry. (Approached by Blum's counsel Spanien, he granted the defendant's request to receive his companion, Mme. Reichenbach, while in prison.[71]) The basic, inner man seemed to rejoice at the prospect of this trial, which would be a showplace for the Marshal's values. Barthélemy's notes even include a detailed architectural and ceremonial plan for the courthouse, from the curtains on the windows to the robes of the judges.[72]

Eventually, however, Blum's appeal to republican virtues won considerable public support, as dispatches emerged from Riom despite Barthélemy's quite illiberal attempts to censor the proceedings and to dictate the form of their public dissemination. Although the major constitutional arguments Blum raised—often articulated in court by the lawyer Le

---

[68] AN 72 AJ 411, Dossier no. 1.

[69] Barthélemy, *Ministre,* 217.

[70] AN 72 AJ 411, Dossier no. 15.

[71] Ibid., 229. See also AN $BB^{30}$ 1710.

[72] Barthélemy, *Ministre,* 221; AN 72 AJ 411, Dossier no. 15.

Troquer—did not succeed,[73] Pétain's technical defeat liberated Blum to take on the merits of the case, and he did so with gusto. The substantive arguments have been transcribed and discussed in other places as a matter of French political history,[74] but their sheer legalistic force so contrasts with Vichy's "spiritualized" persecution that they deserve summary here. Blum, eager to go to the merits of the case against him, once his jurisdictional and constitutional arguments had lost, was clearly masterful: his government had reduced tensions among striking workers, not created or increased them;[75] the forty-hour week, which helped to end the strikes, had no real effect on military production;[76] the nationalization of some industries was to prevent profiteering at a time of general economic difficulty;[77] his policies were those mandated by the people, through the overwhelming victory they had given him.[78] Blum's remarks exuded the republican *credo,* which incontrovertibly justified even policies that may have gone on to fail; his passion for the Republic still found receptive ears at Riom and beyond.

As Blum juxtaposed the substantive legal issues to an unimpeachable belief in French Republican traditions, Barthélemy raged inwardly. Indeed, it would be only a mild exaggeration to find in Barthélemy's approach to Blum at the late stages of Riom no small measure of *"ressentiment,"* of severely reactive negativity against this man whom Pétain saw as the archetypal enemy. (We shall return to this theme in chapter 4.) The

---

[73] See note 29 above. But, even in defeat, Le Troquer exhibited his enormous courage, extending the constitutional argument to an attack on the rottenness of the Vichy regime: "Capitalism is denounced as sordid, and the head of state has proclaimed its deficiencies often; but meanwhile liberty, liberties generally, are suppressed. It is dangerous to express an opinion, to formulate a criticism that might run against the dominant tastes of those in charge. Men and women by the thousands, by tens of thousands, are in concentration camps [sont en prison dans des camps de concentration], too often because of their origin, of their religion.... Civic and professional penalties are inflicted for the same reason.... France is not this, it will not be this." AN 72 AJ 411, Dossier no. 15.

[74] See, e.g. Howie, *Leon Blum Before His Judges,* with a forward by one of Blum's defense counsel, Felix Gouin. See also, Dalby, *Leon Blum, Evolution,* 330–39.

[75] Howie, *Leon Blum Before His Judges,* 35, 56.

[76] Ibid., 39, 73f, 126f.

[77] Ibid., 100–106.

[78] Ibid., 52.

contemporaneous jottings evoke a vulgar antisemitism.[79] But the latter description somehow seems less fair to the inner Barthélemy than the notion that he found himself increasingly powerless to bring this particular Jew to heel. Barthélémisme shows itself here as the perennial Christian frustration before the resisting and virtuous Jew.

Perhaps as the trial wore on, Barthélemy started to think about the early days with Blum, and this would only have aggravated his resentment. Their relationship began when Blum was with the Conseil d'État in the years prior to 1919, when both men entered the National Assembly together. Barthélemy describes their relations as cordial until 1924, when Blum's party vanquished Barthélemy's; from that point, in the Justice Minister's words, Blum "stopped acknowledging my presence when we crossed paths in the halls."[80]

Barthélemy's understandable spite before these memories from the 1920s might have been exacerbated by the "dignity" and "biblical paternalism" with which he always associated Blum and his family.[81] Together, the characterizations evoke a more polite, traditional antisemitic language than we saw in the jottings, one that defines the Jew by his arrogance, his otherness, and his tribal loyalty.[82]

For Barthélemy, the last straw was the explicit conjuration of Pétain's name by the defendants, together with the implication that the Marshal himself—on the logic of the indictments—also deserved to be in the dock. Blum and his lawyers made much of the use of the phrase "ultérieurement à 1936" [after 1936] in the charges against the defendants, a phrase that limited the court's investigations to the post-1936 period. But it was obvious to all that this tactic was designed to prevent a full inquiry into Marshal Pétain's own place, during the early to mid-1930s, when he played an active role in France's prewar policies.[83]

---

[79] See text at note 5.

[80] Barthélemy, *Ministre,* 226.

[81] Ibid., 226–27.

[82] Barthélemy, when criticized mildly for permitting Blum the prison visits of his friend, Mme. Reichenbach, observed "Why not, they're of the same tribe [Ils sont de la même tribu]," Barthélemy, *Ministre,* 232.

[83] See, e.g., Colette Audrey, *Léon Blum ou la Politique du Juste* (Paris: Julliard, 1955), 170.

No one could prevent Blum, even on the terms of the indictment, however, from answering a question relating to a *1937* meeting of the Permanent Committee for National Defense as follows:

> [Citing the minutes of the meeting:] "Upon a remark by Marshal Pétain, M. Léon Blum asked the following question: 'What will happen if Germany and Italy do not agree to take part in the work of the [Disarmament] Commission?' He replied by indicating that, in that case, our interests lie in pushing on with the work as much as possible.... The meeting ended with unanimous agreement."[84]

For Barthélemy, this implication of his sacred leader's complicity in pacifism and unpreparedness for war must have been "the most unkindest cut of all." Despite self-described "cordial and frequent meetings with the lawyers (Le Troquer, Spanien..., Ribet) [including even] my accepting a luncheon invitation from Ribet,"[85] Barthélemy found himself hearing his revered leader's name cleverly inserted almost daily into the defense argument. Would no one play the game any more by the "correct" rules? Would this man, the nemesis to Vichy, be permitted to sully the hero who had come to save the soul of a defeated nation?

Moments such as these led Barthélemy to note, in a less than even hand:

> Le Maréchal ne doit pas être discuté.
> On commence à discuter son pouvoir et sa légitimité
> On se propose [illegible] de discuter sa personne
> (The Marshal must not be challenged./They're beginning to challenge his power and his legitimacy./ They ponder [ ] challenging even his person.)[86]

To avoid such threats to Pétain's person, he began to see the need to suspend the trial altogether:

> The government may be called upon to make grave resolutions. I am ready to take this upon myself since my sole concern in this whole business is that the Marshal must not be challenged.[87]

---

[84] Howie, *Leon Blum Before his Judges,* 9, 120–21.

[85] AN 72 AJ 411, Dossier no. 21.

[86] Ibid., Dossier no. 8.

[87] Ibid.

Barthélemy's "sole concern" lay not in safeguarding the rights of the defendants but in protecting the aura of the Marshal. Fittingly, it was he who would eventually end the trial prior to a verdict, for "the spiritual values and eternal certainties upon which the Marshal intends to base the renewal of the country have been flouted." His leader's charismatic goodness was to be safeguarded from the morally poisonous strategies of Blum.

The national interest in protecting the régime—and no German Diktat—led Barthélemy to recommend to Pétain that the trial be suspended, with the Cour suprême retaining its jurisdiction and with the defendants remaining in prison. On 11 April 1942, Barthélemy and Pétain signed an order to those effects, and on 14 April, their decision was announced to the public.[88] For Barthélemy, it always came down to the allegory, to the level of personalities:

> Daladier and Blum have nothing to lose and everything to gain. The government has nothing to gain and everything to lose.... No good can come of it; much harm may ensue....[89]

In the public dispatch, through the press agency Havas, Barthélemy used more formal language to explain the suspension of the trial, but it was no less moralistic:

> We only had a limited trial, limited to the unpreparedness for the War. From a limited trial only a limited truth can emerge. And a limited truth is not really the truth. It will be necessary to start over.... The spiritual values and the eternal certitudes on which the Marshal intends to base the renewal of the country have been flouted [bafouées].[90]

It had been an allegory without an uplifting ending, this Riom trial. Its investigations were to continue,[91] but its major contribution to the cause of Vichy morality was in its *Leitmotif* rather than its denouement. And the theme was that of estrangement and ostracism, of removal of the poison, of expurgation of the soul.

---

[88] Ibid., Dossiers nos. 15, 16.

[89] Ibid., Dossier no. 16.

[90] Ibid., Dossier no. 19.

[91] Ibid., for example, a 191-page report was issued to the court as late as 16 December 1942 on the state of aeronautic preparedness during the prewar period.

## E. Blum in Hell

Blum, arrested and tried as the very symbol of what Vichy law intended to expunge from its midst, had survived and even prevailed. Riom thus not only clarified in its choice of Blum an entire constitutional approach, it also permitted French lawyers and others to perceive that there was an opening for resistance, resistance through law as well as violence. Yet, as we now shall see, how rarely the courage of Blum, his fellow defendants and their lawyers was emulated by the French legal establishment.

Although the Cour suprême never rendered a verdict, Blum and his co-defendants were still "guilty" according to the judgment of Pétain's other "court," the Council of Political Justice. Temporarily elated by the suspension of the public trial, Blum had to celebrate his seventieth birthday, a month later, still behind bars. Before turning seventy-one, he would be handed over by the French to the Germans. From April 1943 until April 1945, his prison would be in the valley of the shadow of Death—at Buchenwald.

# Chapter 2

# The Basic Scheme of Ostracism

## A. The Vichy Statute of 3 October 1940

### 1. Nazi Indifference; Vichy Innovation

Before it had time to consider much else, the new régime turned to questions of nationality and race. In its first 20 days of legislative power, the bulk of its statutory work was directed to denaturalization policy, including bars to government employment for those deemed no longer to be French.[1] Within another few weeks, on 3 October 1940, Vichy had promulgated its own religious statute.[2] And the following day, 4 Octo-

---

[1] Dominique Rémy, *Les Lois de Vichy* (Paris: Romillat, 1992), 48–59. Denaturalization laws worked against Jews throughout the Vichy years, although Jews were not specially earmarked for loss of citizenship by these early laws. See chapter 9.

[2] It was authored by Vichy's first justice minister, the antisemite Raphaël Alibert. See ibid., 87. See also R. Sarraute and P. Tager, *Les Juifs sous l'Occupation: Recueil des textes officiels français et allemands* (Paris: CDJC, 1982), 19. Race was explicitly introduced to Vichy legislation at this time; see, e.g., AN AJ[38], Inventaire, 1[er] cahier: "On 3 October, the Vichy government promulgated the Jewish law and introduced into it the notion of race." In a companion law of 4 October 1940, the regime set up its own concentration camps for stateless people, preponderantly Jewish, and this attracted the Germans' attention. See, e.g., note from *Hauptsturmführer*Dannecker to *Sturmbannführer* Zeitschel, dated Paris, 28 February 1941: "I notice that these concentration camps for stateless Jews have already been set up in the unoccupied zone, under the terms of the *Vichy law of 3.10.40.*" [emphasis added], YV V-63.

ber, it legalized the internment of stateless Jews in "special camps." None of these actions was forced upon Vichy by the Germans; on the contrary, as we shall see pervasively, the conquerors noted the rapidity and scope of French legislation with bemusement, opportunistic glee, and even occasional annoyance.[3] Claude Singer observes in his recent study:

> In the archives that we so far have, there is not a single document indicating any pressure brought upon the government of Vichy by the German authorities to obtain the promulgation of a law regarding the Jews, and still less the elimination of Jews from public office. This legislation is thus a French idea, even if the departments that elaborated it were greatly influenced by models then in existence in countries like Italy, Rumania, Germany.[4]

The religious statutes of October 3 and 4 seem to have been developed without much discussion after a full cabinet meeting on 30 September.[5] Raphaël Alibert, Vichy's first Justice Minister, authored and signed them.[6] Of Alibert's brief tenure as Vichy's first Justice Minister, the

---

On the purely French origins of these and subsequent religious laws, only the second justice minister, Joseph Barthélemy, seems to disagree, an oddity coming from the man who himself signed the second major religious law eight months later: "This legislation is not a French initiative: it is entirely of German origin," Joseph Barthélemy, *Ministre de la Justice: Mémoires* (Paris: Pygmalion, 1989), 311.

[3] Eventually there would be at least twenty-eight laws and nineteen decrees published by Vichy that dealt with Jews. There were countless less lofty "actes réglementaires."

[4] Claude Singer, *Vichy, l'Université et les Juifs* (Paris: Les Belles Lettres, 1992), 76.

[5] See, e.g., ibid., 78. Henri Moulin de Labarthète, Pétain's chief-of-staff, reported after the war that "a lot of the basic laws, the laws on the Jews and the freemasons, for example, were signed at the end of a meeting of the cabinet, in the midst of the noise of the chairs and the smoke of cigarettes, and the Marshal, impressed by the attitude of his ministers, affixed his signature often without reading them." Labarthète, *Le Temps des Illusions* (Geneva: Bourquin, 1946), 119.

[6] See, e.g., Michèle Cointet-Labrousse, *Vichy et le fascisme* (Paris: Editions complèxe, 1987), 199; Michael Marrus and Robert Paxton, *Vichy France and the Jews* (New York: Basic Books, 1981), 5. Marrus and Paxton add: "Any simple notion of German *Diktat* can be dismissed summarily. When Raphaël Alibert...came to trial in March 1947, the attorney-general found, to his astonishment, that the accused's dossier contained no evidence of contact with Germans, official or not, and was obliged to drop, from among the charges, the accusation of *intelligence avec l'ennemi.*" Yet Alibert's "name is inseparable from the beginnings of the government...the laws removing citizenship status, on divorce, on the Jews," Moulin de Labarthète, *Le Temps des Illusions,* 134.

régime's courageous opponent Philippe Serre would remark to me: "Alibert was a remarkable jurist who acted very badly.... He was one of the group of rascals [fripons] [at Vichy]."[7]

Alibert's antisemitism was well-known and was surely one of several important reasons for the haste and the expansive thoroughness demonstrated by the régime in dealing with the racial question.[8] Serre perceived that the absence of opposition to Alibert made Vichy, and not Germany, the prime mover on racism in wartime France.[9]

What were the terms of these two early religious statutes? The law of 3 October established the French definition of "Jew," which was to set the tone for all subsequent religious legislation, judicial and bureaucratic implementation, and academic and professional analysis:

> Article I. For the purposes of the present law, a Jew is one who has three grandparents of the Jewish race; or who has two grandparents of that race, if his or her spouse is Jewish.
>
> Article II. The availability and exercise of the following public functions and duties are denied to Jews:
>
> 1. Head of State, member of the government, the Conseil d'État, the national council of the Legion of Honor, the Cour de Cassation..., the courts of appeal, courts of first jurisdiction, justices of the peace, etc.
>
> [Remainder of Article II and other articles omitted]

The definitional section of the 3 October 1940 statute applied at first only to individuals who were in the Vichy zone of governance. Those in the Occupied Zone were at that time covered by the language of the following German ordinance of 27 September 1940:

---

[7] Philippe Serre, personal interview with author, Paris, 21 December 1988. Accord, Cointet-Labrousse, *Vichy et le fascisme,* 36.

[8] See, e.g., the contemporaneous account of Jacques Charpentier, wartime chair (bâtonnier) of the Paris Bar Association: "M. Alibert was antisemitic [but]...to do justice to M. Alibert, one must note that in the midst of all those chimeras he was deeply devoted to the state...." Jacques Charpentier, *Au Service de la liberté* (Paris: Fayard, 1949), 124–27.

[9] Philippe Serre, personal interview with author, Paris, 21 December 1988.

A Jew is one who belongs or used to belong to the Jewish religion or who has more than two Jewish grandparents. Any grandparent who belongs or has belonged to the Jewish religion counts as being Jewish.[10]

While the 3 October statute is less important to this overall study than is the revised Vichy statute of 2 June 1941, it sets the trend in French religious legislation throughout the war years of being *more comprehensive* than the equivalent German ordinance.[11] Unlikely though it may at first seem, the Vichy authorities exceeded the Nazis in two ways:

1. Vichy explicitly includes a notion of *race* in the statutory formula; the word is absent from the first German ordinance. This difference is perhaps more of theoretical than practical significance. It indicates Vichy's early interest, independent of German pressure, in race, an interest that will be present as a dominant thread in a variety of completely autonomous Vichy legal developments from then on.[12]

2. Vichy innovates—somewhat paradoxically, given the rhetorical invocation of *race*—by including a person of mixed heritage in the definition of Jew if he or she has married a Jew. Vichy's consistent drive to include more people under the definition of Jew than anyone was demanding of them is signalled here. Mixed marriages (German: *Mischehe*) and mixed-heritage individuals (German: *Mischlinge*) become implicated, and a person who never thought of herself as Jewish now becomes subject to the law if married to a Jew.

---

[10] Sarraute and Tager, *Recueil des textes,* 18.

[11] Accord, e.g., Jean Laloum, *La France antisémite de Darquier de Pellepoix* (Paris: Syros, 1979), 5: "the law is harsher and more coercive than the Nazi occupier was demanding"; Joseph Billig, *Le Commissariat général aux questions juives* (Paris: CDJC, 1955), vol. 1, 42–43. Robert Aron, *Histoire de Vichy* (Paris: Fayard, 1954), 227, observes that the French statutory scheme was "more severe than that of several of the Reich's satellite countries."

[12] Compare Barthélemy's introduction of the notion of race into the proposed new constitutional scheme; see chapters 1 and 4. There seems to be some evidence that Barthélemy had discussed racial prerequisites with Pierre Laval, and that they had reached agreement on considering race in making governmental and bureaucratic appointments, even prior to the vote of 10 July 1940 that created the Vichy regime; see Joel Colton, *Leon Blum, Humanist,* 380.

The Vichy statute's mention of race quickly caught the attention of French legal commentators.[13] What, particularly in the absence both of a German model and a French racist legal tradition, could the word mean? Two lawyers opined as follows in a 1942 treatise on the subject of "The Public and Private Status of the Jew in France"[14]:

> We must ascertain what the statute meant[15] by "race juive." The law was silent on this point. We believe, with Professor E. H. Perreau ("Le nouveau statut des Juifs en France," *La Semaine juridique,* 1941, étude 216, #36), that, in the absence of legal criteria, we must fall back on the norms of civil status. We know the traditional analysis of that notion: *nomen, tractatus, fama.*
>
> *Nomen:* the fact of having a name or first name generally thought of as Jewish; *tractatus:* the fact of having always been treated as racially Jewish by everyone with whom one has had business relations; *fama:* the fact of having been publicly known as such.[16]

The authors go on to criticize the use of racial concepts, although their objections are more historical and pragmatic than legal or ethical. They cite Prof. Perreau's observation that, in the rare cases of antecedent French legislation against Jews, it was religion and nothing else that distinguished Jews from others.[17] The theme of "Talmudism" is invoked, as it was by many French legal commentators, to rationalize special statutes for a people whose religious practice, after all, had already set them apart as believers in a legal system that contradicted French

---

[13] The Germans appropriated the term in their *third* ordinance of 26 April 1941; see Sarraute and Tager, *Receuil des textes,* 41.

[14] Henri Baudry and Joannès Ambre, *La Condition publique et privée du juif en France* (Lyon: Desvigne, 1942).

[15] The past tense is used because, by the year of publication of their treatise, the authors knew that the second Vichy statute (of 2 June 1941) was fully operative, replacing the 3 October law; the later statute retained its predecessor's mention of "race," and hence the authors' analysis here continued to be quite relevant.

[16] Ibid., 35.

[17] Danièle Lochak, "La Doctrine sous Vichy ou les Mésaventures du positivisme," in Serge Klarsfeld, ed., *Le Statut des Juifs de Vichy* (Paris: F.F.D.J.F., 1990), 135–37 discusses Prof. Perreau at considerable length; she does not, however, cite Baudry and Ambre.

traditions.[18] If the 3 October statute was to be regretted, according to such analyses, it was for its misdirected emphasis on race instead of the centrality of Jewish Talmudism.[19] The law of 2 June 1941 would redeem these academic and political lawyers' belief in the central *religious* justification for the new thinking on Jews (already present in the proceedings against Léon Blum): the Jew as "other," as bizarre, as Talmudist and hence as the legitimate object of an ostracizing law.

Aside from this theoretical internal debate, we have no record of any direct attack on the régime for its unsolicited introduction of *race* into the statutory language,[20] but there is one curious document attesting to some *internal* stress about the law's second innovation. Its provenance was Xavier Vallat's Commissariat général aux questions juives (CGQJ).[21] This agency was charged with the bulk of the administrative work relating to the new Jewish legislation; it of course needed to come to an internal understanding of such major statutes as this. Yet, as late into the existence of the law as 11 April 1941, Vallat's own Legislative Director, Giroud—a man "directly attached to Vichy, where he spends half his time"[22]—still seemed to be grappling with the unfairness of his own régime's innovation. His "distress" underlines the part of the law that would make a person Jewish by mere fact of marrying a Jew:

---

[18] See chapters 1 and 10 for the Talmudic theme in French law.

[19] Baudry and Ambre, *La Condition publique et privée du juif,* take pains to note that the 3 October 1940 French statute *limits* the definition of Jew by featuring the individual's heritage rather than his actual religious practice (a loophole that Vichy would remove in its 2 June revisions), but do not analyze the statute's addition of marriage to a Jew, an element far more likely to increase the numbers of individuals coming under the law's penalties.

[20] We will discuss shortly the courage of Prof. Jacques Maury in attacking—during 1940 itself—the denaturalization statutes and in alluding to the breach of French traditions in pitting one "kind" of Frenchman against another; but Maury himself did not, to my knowledge, specifically take on the racial features of the religious statutes.

[21] The CGQJ was innovated by Vichy in a law of 29 March 1941; see Sarraute and Tager, *Recueil des textes,* 39.

[22] Memorandum, 8 August 1941, cited in Billig, *Le Commissariat général,* vol. 1, 108.

> The [statutory] section including among Jews a person who, were it not for marriage, would be considered an Aryan, is highly objectionable, for it shocks good sense, violates equity, and is juridically unprecedented.[23]

Whether or not a man of Giroud's stature actually wrote the memo (it is unsigned, but his name is handwritten above the typed document, as though by a higher official in the CGQJ), it is noteworthy that he was in the middle of this argument six months into the life of Vichy's first definitional statute.[24] Time and again we will see such examples of internal debate, impervious to German influence, on crucial questions of Vichy racial policy. The Giroud memo analyzing the 3 October statute constitutes merely the first of many proofs that—as to French law during the Occupation—the French considered themselves an autonomous system subject to, but not bound to follow, surrounding political influences.

Again, the first internal dispute was as to the "fairness" of the Vichy innovation rendering Jewish a mixed-heritage individual who marries a Jew; the *racial* features of the régime's statute are not only accepted but indeed—with a peculiar logic that becomes all too characteristic of French legal commentary and practice during Vichy—fully integrated:

> On the racial level, it is difficult to concede that an individual already of a determined race might—by the sole fact of marriage—cease belonging to that race and instead acquire that of his or her spouse.[25]

---

[23] CDJC CXIV-9a, henceforth Giroud memo. The memo writer uses the strong word "unprecedented" and is correct in that the Vichy law on mixed-heritage Jews went beyond the German ordinance of 27 September 1940. In fact, the Nuremberg laws themselves did include provision for an individual with only two Jewish grandparents who was also married to a Jew. See Billig, *Le Commissariat général,* vol. 2, 155. As commentators such as Billig put it, "Contradicting in France the Nuremberg laws," the German ordinance included neither race nor mixed-heritage categories. (Billig seems to me to exaggerate when he proceeds to assert that the German ordinance's emphasis on religion might penalize "un demi-Juif" nonetheless, because it included a mixed-heritage person who *at any time* was a practicing Jew. These cases were rare, or difficult to prove, compared to the hundreds of sustainable cases under the Vichy statute.)

[24] A comparable internal Vichy debate related to the thorny issue of *burden of proof* under the religious statutes; see below, note 112.

[25] Giroud memo. On the proposition that racism of a particular French variety—but racism nonetheless—was at work throughout the Vichy period, see Marrus and Paxton's excellent analysis of Xavier Vallat, *Vichy France and the Jews,* 90–92.

Thus the protest arises in terms of a constrained logic in which *race plays an affirmative and unchallenged role:*

> If the statute's reasoning prevailed, the same individual could be considered, in succession, as being an Aryan during his bachelorhood, then of the Jewish race once married to a Jewess, then again an Aryan once the marriage is dissolved either through divorce or the death of the spouse.[26]

The audience for this memo (probably Vallat himself) took pains to write an underlined *"no"* in the margin of the final phrase above. Did the CGQJ at the highest levels thus indicate that, despite the plain meaning of the statute, an individual with only two Jewish grandparents but having married a Jew would irrevocably retain that persecuted status, even upon termination of the transfiguring relationship? In any event, the same hand had already indicated boldly at the top of the document, "This memorandum does not modify the point of view of the Commissioner-General." In fact, the following "equitable" argument against the mixed heritage inclusion is explicitly rebutted in the reader's hand:

> "[The disputed sections] will lead to different treatments under law of two brothers with identical father and mother, as long as one marries an Aryan and the other a non-Aryan."
>
> "Yes" [responds the reader in the margin] "but there was an intent on the part of one of the two to return to his origins."

The memo writer (again, probably Giroud) closes by stressing two other arguments. First, the new category punishes couples who "could not have weighed the costs at the time of their marriage."[27] Second, it surpasses the model of the German ordinance of 27 September 1940.[28]

---

[26] Giroud memo, 2. Eventually Vallat himself became convinced that Alibert's innovation making *race* central was unworkable; see Billig, *Le Commissariat général,* vol. 2, 159f. This led to the revised definition in the 2 June 1941 statute. However, as Vallat later recalled, that revision retained the word "race" nonetheless; he bemoaned his mistake in not substituting the phrase "peuple juif."

[27] Giroud memo, 3.

[28] Ibid., 4. As Léon Poliakov put it after the war, "Contrary to popular belief, the Nazi laws were not on all points of larger scope or more implacable than those passed by satellite or allied countries. In particular, certain categories of 'Mischlinge,' or of marginal ethnic groups, could more easily adapt to antisemitic measures in Germany than even in France...," Léon Poliakov, "Lois de Nurembourg et lois de Vichy" (available in the library

One might think that the first argument, grounded in the inequities of punishing actions that were fully lawful when first done, would find little hope of prevailing, because the régime by then had firmly established the legitimacy of a great number of *ex post facto* laws. But the very presence of the argument as part of an internal debate indicates that the discourse was still in flux, still malleable on this important point. The reader of the memo in fact avoids the *ex post facto* argument and answers instead on the merits: "Yes [they could have weighed the costs]—on the moral level." The unfavorable comparison to the Nazi ordinance goes unanswered, as does a prayer for reform of the statute, suggesting new language that would penalize only the mixed heritage individual who married a Jew (or another such individual) *after* the date of promulgation of the law. "This will have the double advantage," concludes the writer, "of not gravely compromising the status or the future of Aryans who have married Jews without reckoning with the costs to them of the race of the future spouse; and of restraining the number of unions between Aryan and Jew, as was clearly the wish of the legislator."[29]

No authoritative mind was changed by the memorandum of 11 April 1940. The 3 October statute remained in full force and effect, and (as we shall see) courts and agencies remained quite busy determining the status of individuals with only two Jewish grandparents. When less than two months later, the second and definitive Vichy statute was promulgated, it would retain both innovations (mention of race and inclusion of mixed heritage individuals); its only relevant "clarifications"—which in effect poured salt in the wound of the rejected memo writer—lay in its assuming race from the religious practice of the individual's grandparents and in its replacing for "if his or her spouse is Jewish" the new language "if his or her spouse is also the descendent of two grandparents of the Jewish race."[30]

---

of the Alliance Israélite Universelle, Paris), #8 U Br 1832, 182.

[29] Giroud memo. As we shall see pervasively, the fiction "legislator" is consistently used by analysts during Vichy, even though all legislative powers had been given to the executive branch.

[30] Sarraute and Tager, *Recueil des textes,* 49. This revision makes crystal clear that two mixed-heritage individuals marrying each other would—as much as one mixed-heritage individual marrying a full Jew—both be considered Jewish. However, this was already the uniform interpretation of the 3 October law cited here, as the 11 April memo makes

The internal CGQJ memorandum of 11 April 1941 is of great interest because the dialogue between the memo writer and his audience reveals a textured and nuanced openness to discussion. Its moral outrage, which, in retrospect, is myopic, is couched in a careful use of language that would flatter the racist perspective of its audience. (Would the memorandum have achieved some results if its writer had *directly* attacked the very notion of a French-authored religious law? This distinction—between what I will call the "polite" and the "jugular" modes of protest—will inform many areas of the present study.)

Eager to legislate, prideful of tracking its own course on questions of race, Vichy declined all opportunities to soften the effect of its statutes.[31] The die was cast. To track how far Vichy had managed to project its homegrown approach to racism, we need do little more than contrast two German documents of the period. The first, an Ordinance of 10 May 1940, declares:

> Orders and rules promulgated by the German military command override all indigenous laws. Nonetheless, indigenous laws remain in effect as long as they do not oppose the goals of the Occupation.[32]

The second, which relates specifically to the vital question of Jewish definition discussed thus far, is dated 1 July 1942 and contemplates both Vichy religious statutes. In the opinion of its author, SS *Hauptsturmführer* Theodor Dannecker, a lawyer by training and "the first true professional of antisemitism in France,"[33] "the French definition being broader, it will now serve as a basis in all doubtful cases."[34]

---

clear. (In fact, the 2 June language might have provided a literal defense to one marrying a *full* Jew, namely that he or she was not included under the new statute. No one seems to have made this argument. For an elaboration of this paradox, see chapter 6, notes 125–26.)

[31] On the contrary; as Marrus and Paxton, *Vichy France and the Jews,* 115, report, one of Vallat's central aims was to have the Germans actually *rescind* all their religious ordinances in favor of the French approach.

[32] AN $AJ^{38}$, Box 594, 4.

[33] Lucien Steinberg, *Les Allemands en France* (Paris: Albin Michel, 1980), 212.

[34] Dannecker memorandum, 1 July 1942, CDJC XXVI-36.

## 2. To Protest or Not to Protest: Reception of the 3 October Statute by Lawyers Outside the Government

Much is made by respected historians of the changing political climate, internally to Vichy or as regards Franco-German relations; the theory seems to be that decisions as to legal developments largely depended on those factors.[35] My sense is quite different: beginning with (or at least right after) the important basic text of 3 October 1940, French *legal* developments proceeded on a continuum that had surprisingly little to do with *political* influences, either internal[36] or German-inspired.[37] Vichy had no reason to feel that they had anything but full autonomy over their developing religious laws.[38]

A key early indication of this autonomy is the degree of *extrinsic* criticism the régime received and even tolerated about its new racial approach.[39] This question of how much controversy was generated by the religious laws is of primary importance and has attracted most of the still small group of scholars who have treated Vichy legislation.[40] The present writer has already made the claim that the legal establishment's response to statutory racism not only *permitted* the worst to occur but

---

[35] See, e.g., Marrus and Paxton, *Vichy France and the Jews,* 115, for their account of the fall of Xavier Vallat, which they place under the two-toned sign of Vallat's not having satisfied his Vichy colleagues by procuring "the withdrawal of the German anti-Jewish ordinances"; and of the Germans' considering him "lukewarm" on such matters as the aryanization of Jewish property, ibid., 117f.

[36] Vallat's inability, for example, to procure complete rescission of German religious laws was of little practical consequence to Vichy. After all, as is proven by the 26 April 1941 German ordinance's specific tracking of the 3 October 1940 Vichy religious definition, the Germans *quickly adhered to Vichy's legal norms anyway!* If the cat was following the tail on racial policy throughout these four years, then the cat was the German Occupier and the tail was the Vichy "legislator."

[37] Indeed, even as to aryanization, there was broad early agreement that French law controlled instead of German; see generally, chapter 7.

[38] See, e.g., below at note 85.

[39] For a discussion of protests within the regime itself, see notes 22–30.

[40] See, e.g., Danièle Lochak, "La Doctrine sous Vichy"; François Dominique-Gros, "Le 'Statut des juifs' et les manuels en usage dans les facultés de droit (1940–1944)," in Philippe Braud, ed., *La Violence politique dans les Démocraties européenes occidentales* (Paris: L'Harmattan, 1993), 139–92.

was largely responsible for the extent of Jewish suffering in both zones![41] The "interpretive community," I argued, not only validated the work of Alibert (and his successors); it took up that work, made it its own, and on every level created an indigenous system of rationalized persecution. Its pervasive interest in religious definition cannot be explained by antisemitism alone; too many unprejudiced and even "liberal" players were involved for too long. Instead, we see a legal system exemplifying what Niklas Luhmann has called "autopoeisis," recently described by Luhmann as systemic "self-causation," as an "autonomous" and "operationally closed" enterprise.[42] In Vichy law, the self-referential system nurtured what I have called a "dessicated Cartesianism," a uniquely French desire to see the elaborate interpretation of the religious laws through to every logical conclusion, whoever might be winning the war or nominally influential at any given time.

Because of the thoroughness of its approach, Vichy law and lawyers rendered unnecessary the investment in racial matters of significant German intellectual and manpower resources. As happened in Italy and Denmark, for example, organized resistance or simple refusal to implement religious laws might have brought about very different outcomes, particularly if legal resistance had broken through at the very origins of Vichy's religious laws and become dominant.

These claims have been controversial,[43] for they do not merely chal-

---

[41] See Weisberg, "Legal Rhetoric Under Stress: the Example of Vichy," *Cardozo Law Review* 12 (1991): 1371.

[42] Niklaus Luhmann, "Operational Closure and Structural Coupling: The Differentiation of the Legal System," 13 *Cardozo Law Review* 13 (1992), 1420; see chapter 10, note 22.

[43] Dominique-Gros, "Le 'Statut des juifs,' " has usefully studied legal manuals of the period, which he finds to have produced *mixed results* characterized more by silence or cautious reserve than by passionate support for the new laws. Further, he claims that doctrinal commentary generally should not be confused with the "normative activity of the CGQJ," ibid., 1. But I myself allowed that there were "mixed results" and include that very range of responsiveness within the risks of discursive acceptance by intelligent communities of what they previously would have considered unspeakably horrible. (Without some protest—and Dominique-Gros's chart indicates that legitimation far outweighed protest among the manual writers—those abhorring the religious laws but willing to live with them would have felt worse about their tolerance. We always feel better knowing that there is some protest going on somewhere.) As to whether academic writing should be put in the same category as administrative or judicial writing, I believe strongly that it

lenge the denial of widespread French collaboration that has been so much a part of the myth of universal resistance. Some of the work of the present volume is designed to reenforce my arguments. It must be emphasized here, in the context of discussing reactions to the régime's first religious statute, that *any response would have been tolerated at the beginning* and that *the nature of the opening response by the immediately affected community was crucial and regrettably indifferent.* To justify these remarks, it is decidedly *not* necessary to show that there was a uniformly positive reception to Alibert's 3 October statute among French lawyers, judges, and law professors.[44] On the contrary, it suffices to show that there *were* some protests, which neither disempowered the protestors nor worked any known hardship to their careers. For this would indicate that the Vichy legal community in fact had all options at its disposal—including sharp, passionate protest against the central racism of the new statute. Once it is shown that the French legal community was free to protest but that, by comparison to some other legal cultures under Nazi influence, the French badly underperformed in terms of a preliminary show of repulsion towards legalized racism, we must then reckon with a community fully involved in the business of *making* religious law. No longer will the twinned rationalizations of Vichy "un-Frenchness"[45] and German political pressure on legal matters rule our understanding of this phenomenon. Instead Vichy law will be seen as a fully integrated, subtly developed, and virtually all-encompassing creation of, by, and for the French themselves. Beleaguered the institution of French law surely was during World War II, although also profitable and lively. But to say that pressure, even intense pressure, made the 3 October law and its racist progeny a non-French matter is like saying that the pressures of poor diet and insufficient education explain Hitler's

should and will further defend this argument in my section on the academicians in chapter 10, e.g., notes 2–3.

[44] See note 43.

[45] The tradition from de Gaulle ("We are the real French") to Mitterrand ("the French nation and French republicanism had nothing to do with what happened at Vichy") is unanimous on this perspective. Jacque Chirac's July 1995 statement finally broke from this unfortunate preservation of the Vichy myth. See, e.g., "Chirac Affirms France's Guilt in Fate of Jews," *New York Times,* 16 July 1995, A1.

genocidal ideas. It would be to ignore more cogent, if perhaps more upsetting, explanations.

I began this study with the figure of Léon Blum, whose Jewish "otherness" made him a paradigm for everything the new régime detested. Yet when Vichy put Blum and his codefendants before the bar of justice at Riom, a handful of courageous lawyers publicly challenged the very norms under which the new government was basing its prosecutions. Well over a year after Alibert's religious statute was promulgated, these lawyers felt they could attack centrally not that law itself but features of Vichy legality that the 3 October law also had revealed: *ex post facto* penal liability, breach of separation of powers, breakdown of republican principles. No one ever punished or (as far as the records show), even chastised these lawyers.

By the same token, however, there was revealed at Riom a subtle distinction between what lawyers would not tolerate and what they had been willing to abide. The head of the Paris Bar Association, Jacques Charpentier, played a role in the team of defense counsel at Riom and firmly chastened Pétain about the importance of client/attorney relations and of non-intervention by the executive in matters of guilt and innocence. But the same Charpentier admitted that there had been a yearning among mainstream French lawyers for the kind of legislation that Vichy provided early against foreign, and specifically immigrant, Jewish influences at the bar.[46]

Graphically different had been the response of the beleaguered bar in Belgium to religious legislation, where (unlike in France) little was preserved of legal autonomy after the country was vanquished. Upon promulgation of the first German religious ordinance (similar to the one issued in the Occupied Zone of France on 27 September 1940), three of that small nation's most distinguished lawyers issued a strong letter of protest directly to the Military Field Commander for Belgium and the North of France:[47]

---

[46] See especially, chapters 3 and 8.

[47] Under the cease-fire agreement, the French ceded a part of their northern frontiers to outright German military rule.

> The ordinances of 28 October 1940, touching on the STATUT DES JUIFS[48] in Belgium, have profoundly moved the legal world [ont profondément ému le monde judiciaire].
>
> The undersigned scrupulously avoid discussing the principles that underlie the Institutions of the Reich.
>
> But the ordinances as applied to Belgium are in opposition to the principles of our constitutional law and of our laws.
>
> Belgium continues to exist as a country. A foreign occupation, under the terms of the Hague Convention of 18 October 1907, does in fact substitute the authority of the occupier for that of the established legal power, but only insofar as this relates to maintaining public order.
>
> It does not seem that—in the administration of Justice—the presence of Jews [Israelites] has in any way troubled the public order....
>
> The ordinance, in excluding Jews from the magistrature, is in opposition to Articles 6, 8, 14 of the Constitution and with Article 100 thereof, under which terms any judge who is appointed for life can only be removed by adjudication. As for lawyers, they can only be removed from the bar by disciplinary action....[49]

Like their colleagues in Belgium, French lawyers were *capable of strong protest*. But when it came to the religious laws, *there was no organized response in France—there was no outcry.* Whether Jacques Charpentier's view of the superabundance of foreigners at the bar explains this silence or not, it stands as one of the signally shameful sins of omission among lawyers during the period of Vichy.

Again, would protest have changed things? The magnificent gesture of its three legal leaders did not, after all, prevent the ultimate deportation of some 25,000 Jews from Belgium. This figure constitutes over one-half of the registered Jewish population there, whereas deportations from French soil have been estimated at only one-fourth of its Jewish population.[50] But this *ex post* reasoning should be questioned: it is entirely unclear that the Vichy situation of virtual autonomy can be compared to Belgium's or indeed any other defeated country's. Furthermore, 20,000

---

[48] Capitalization in original.

[49] YV IV-203.

[50] Contrast, e.g., Lucy Dawidowicz, *The War Against the Jews* (New York: Holt Rinehart, 1975), 403, with others' figures on France, e.g., note 109, for Xavier Vallat's postwar figures.

Belgian Jews never registered and were saved, and 25,000 others had (unfortunately for them) fled to France itself. Playing the percentage game proves to be tricky, for here it would lead to similar outcomes in the two countries, but with France having enjoyed considerably greater freedom in determining its own racial policy and fate.

So we can only guess as to what an organized reaction of antipathy to the French-made 3 October statute might have accomplished. Nor is it likely that the Germans would have severely limited French legal autonomy if there had been lively protests against the Vichy form of racism.

In fact, the French were always free—and considered themselves such—to protest, to innovate, to implement, to refuse to collaborate. Like the Belgian lawyers, French authorities deemed themselves unbound by German occupation law (except as to matters of public order); but Vichy's aim in making that assertion was considerably different from the admirably pro-Semitic flavor of the Belgian jurists' position. In a centrally important inter-ministerial document written several months after the 3 October statute and addressing directly the authority of Vichy to legislate on racial matters when such actions might conflict with those of the Germans, the French government declared itself free to rule in all situations not directly touching the maintenance of public order. The exact context is the aryanization of Jewish property in the Occupied Zone, and the date is 14 January 1941:

> A German ordinance of 20 May, 1940 calls for the naming of administrative trustees [*administrateurs provisoires;* hereafter "a.p."] for companies now lacking formal structure either because the managers are absent or because of *force majeure.*
>
> This ordinance, as its preamble indicates, responds to the desire to maintain economic life in the Occupied Zone. In this regard, the ordinance touches on a subject that has not been ceded to the Germans under the Armistice Convention and which, according to human rights [!] would only become a matter for the occupier if the legal authorities were not capable of handling it themselves. In all the territories where the French administration has been established, it is to them and not to the German occupier that the task of regulating economic life descends; therefore, in those territories, the ordinance must no longer apply because it goes beyond the power of the occupier.[51]

[51] Foreign Ministry and Interior Ministry, internal memorandum, 14 January 1941, AN AJ[38], Box 594, 4.

This surprising memo goes on to analyze the Hague Convention, making the claim that the Germans' right even to protect German property in France by placing it under seal is sharply limited by the Convention since article 43 "makes it incumbent upon the occupier to respect French law unless there is an absolute need."[52] The memo writer is now positioned to comment directly on the basic conflict between the German 1940 ordinances relating to Jews and the French laws relating to the same subject:

> The second ordinance relating to measures taken against the Jews on 18 October 1940 exceeds the limits of the occupier's power. The measures it requires are not necessitated by any security need of the occupying army; they trample on an area left exclusively to the French authorities; they conflict with French laws that the occupier should wish to respect except in extraordinary situations. The appointment of administrative commissars, by the ordinance of 18 October, constitutes therefore an abuse of power on the part of the occupying authority.
>
> Thus, French administrators must refuse to recognize the validity of any a.p. named under the terms of this ordinance.[53]

This strong position, maintained by the Vichy government with some consistency throughout the Occupation, was therefore of early origin and authoritative belief.[54] Nor was it theoretical; a mere fortnight after the internal memo was circulated, a functionary at the Finance Ministry explicitly cited it to the head of the French Railway System, Monsieur Fournier, and copied its full text for him.[55] Influential players in the corporate structure of French finance and transportation were to understand that the French were the masters of their own fate—and of Jewish property.

The French thus took the Belgian position—but with a difference. Whereas the Brussels legal establishment asserted its remaining rights over law in order to *upset* the new racism, the French cited the Hague Conventions and the "rights of men" in order to vouchsafe the supremacy of *their indigenous form of racism*. Eventually Vichy would complement its 3 October religious law with the 22 July 1941 law specifically dealing

---

[52] Ibid., 6.

[53] Ibid., 7.

[54] See, e.g., note 85.

[55] Letter, 28 January 1941, AN $AJ^{38}$, Box 594.

with aryanization. Whether (as Joseph Billig suggests[56]) the French statute placated the Germans, or whether (as I tend to believe, in view of the latter memorandum) the French were furthering a rigorous plan to maintain their own legal supremacy even in the Occupied Zone, the key difference between Vichy and Belgium was that—in Billig's words: "On matters of principle, the Vichy Government was not in contradiction to the Nazi occupiers."[57]

There was little inclination to question the need for or the appropriateness under French legal traditions of ostracizing Jews on the basis of race. Only in occasional forums, and usually somewhat quietly did some French lawyers in and around October 1940 or shortly thereafter *go for the jugular*. (As Dominique-Gros very recently reports, the number of outright protests did not increase substantially as the war wound to a close and Allied victory appeared inevitable.[58]) But the rule was for the 3 October statute to be digested, like the 2 June 1941 law that succeeded it, and assimilated into the French system without much effort.[59]

Perhaps the only notable protest on the high level of generalization we saw in the Belgian response was that of Prof. Jacques Maury of the Toulouse Law School. Maury, in the authoritative *Journal officiel* for the period just after promulgation of the Vichy denaturalization and religious laws of 1940, states that making exceptions of individuals on the basis of immutable traits

> has been substituted for or (better) juxtaposed with that of a required progressive change. The French people find themselves placed in three categories of non-identical stature. There is an increasing abandonment of our

---

[56] Billig, *Le Commissariat général,* vol. 3, 138f.

[57] Ibid., 139.

[58] Of thirty-nine legal manuals studied, Prof. Dominique-Gros cites only two that fall into his category of expressing "clear hostility" to the religious laws. Another handful contains "commentaire assorti de réserves." Dominique-Gros, "Le 'Statut des juifs,' " 8.

[59] French internal documents made no pretense about the origins of the religious laws under which most Jews (in both zones!) were persecuted: these laws were of Vichy derivation. Typically, the tragic case of a Paris Court of Appeals judge, Laemle, involves a set of Vichy documents tracing his fate, all citing the law of 3 October 1940 (and no German ordinance), under the terms of which "on 17 December 1940," he was "mis à la retraite" (fired), CDJC VI-140; on Laemle's eventual arrest and deportation see chapter 3.

long-held rule safeguarding equality in their rights as well as in their responsibilities to all French people.[60]

Although Maury did not specifically attack the 3 October law, his lengthy statement—elaborated over several articles—in one of the profession's most prominent publications surely stood as a challenge to the already tangible legislative policies dividing citizen from citizen (and citizen from "non-citizen") on the basis of race. But the progression in Prof. Maury's own discourse over the next few years indicates that internal professional pressures led even a right-minded analyst such as himself to adapt to an apologetic way of speaking about religious definition.[61] The progression in legal discourse towards an interpretive "mainstream" that abided and utilized the religious laws can be preliminarily revealed by watching Maury's subtle rhetorical shift as the Vichy years wore on.[62] First, however, let us turn to the other major statute on the Jews promulgated by Vichy early in its existence, long before any tangible German pressure had been exerted upon the autonomous régime to move in these directions.

---

[60] *Journal officiel,* 18 October 1940; Doc. 169. The full text is: "The legislator of 1940 goes much further [than did some prewar precedents establishing unequal legal treatment according to existing characteristics]: he opposes on principle one Frenchman from another; on the specific characteristic thus emphasized, the great majority of nationals are safeguarded rights that all the others, unless excepted, definitely and even retroactively lose. The notion of a quality indigenous to the person, of an essential quality, has been substituted for or (better) juxtaposed with that of a required progressive change."

[61] Thus Prof. Dominique-Gros does not disprove my early position that the French "interpretive community" brought on the debacle when he says merely that there are different "modulations" to be found in the legal manual writers. Dominique-Gros, "Le 'Statut des juifs,' " 1. The essential is to *trace* the progression of discourse from an original protest to a more (or less) conciliatory position, etc. This is how professional discourse develops in the kind of free-flowing environment characterizing French law during 1940–44. Maury was quite outspoken at first. No one cared to join him in his protest. To see how his discourse softened over time, see text after note 122.

[62] For the causes of this rhetorical phenomenon, see chapter 10.

## B. The Vichy Statute of 4 October 1940

A day after it fixed its racism into definitional law, Vichy jumped the gun on the Germans by establishing "camps spéciaux"—special camps—into which stateless Jews could be herded by mere prefectoral fiat.[63] The text, in pertinent part, reads as follows:

> Law of 4 October 1940 on foreign nationals of the Jewish race. I. Foreign nationals of the Jewish race may, from the promulgation date of the present law, be interned in special camps by a decision of the prefect of the department of their residence. II. A commission charged with the organization and administration of these camps shall be constituted within the Ministry of the Interior.... III. Foreign nationals of the Jewish race may at any time be assigned a forced residence by the prefect of the department in which they reside.[64]

In the "free" zone, stateless Jews were now outlaws, by virtue solely of their religious status. The full story of these camps—their horrors and their occasional glimpses of humanitarian aid—falls outside this study.[65] But the fact that the French came up, on their own, with the idea of concentration camps for Jews cannot be underemphasized. (Although Jews were not explicitly mentioned there was precedent for "centers" for stateless individuals towards the end of the Third Republic,[66] and even the extreme measure of deportation, never codified into Vichy law, had its legal origins in an old French statute of 28 April 1832.[67]) The first convoys from French soil to Auschwitz, which began on 27 March 1942,

---

[63] "Loi sur les ressortissants étrangers de race juive," signed 4 October 1940. For the text of the statute, see Sarraute and Tager, *Recueil des textes,* 22; Rémy, *Les lois,* 91.

[64] Rémy, ibid. The law was published in the *Journal officiel* of 18 October 1940.

[65] See Marrus and Paxton, *Vichy France and the Jews,* 165–66; Gilbert LeSage, personal interviews with author, Paris, December 1988. LeSage, a Quaker, was assigned a post by Vichy relating to this statute. His individual story was one of attempting to do some good within a system that dehumanized and terrorized its victims.

[66] See Marrus and Paxton, *Vichy France and the Jews,* 57.

[67] An internal Vichy memorandum of 27 January 1941 refers to this old law. See AN $BB^{30}$, 1715.

consisted largely of Jews who had been arrested under the terms of this 4 October Vichy statute.[68]

Naturally, the Nazis took great interest in the 4 October law, although we have no indication of their discussing it formally until several months after its promulgation. Their own first steps into racism on French soil had been fairly cautious: the ordinance of 27 September 1940 defining Jewishness[69]; and an ordinance published the same day as the Vichy statute (18 October 1940) but dealing with the new juristic notion of the "Jewish enterprise" in the Occupied Zone. The Nazis, as of early 1941, were not yet ready to broach the idea of concentration camps.

But they seemed curious and generally delighted to see what Vichy was creating. The most important observations were made by SS *Sturmbann-führer* Helmut Knochen in a memorandum of 28 January 1941 to the Military High Command in Paris. He writes as follows:

> "Establishment of Concentration Camps [*Konzentrationslagern*] for Stateless Jews" ...
>
> About half the Jewish population in France consists of foreign nationals. The antisemitic developments of the past months show that French ill-will towards Jews is directed primarily toward foreigners. The French régime has reckoned with this by promulgating a law of 10 [read: "4"] October 1940 on foreigners of the Jewish race, making it possible to gather foreign Jews in specified concentration camps.... There are at the moment no further incisive anti-Jewish measures planned, and the French régime is not particularly concerned about the rest of its Jewish population given the concern of its 4 October 1940 statute to build concentration camps. [As to the remaining Jews, including those in the Occupied Zone,]...I suggest that a meeting of all interested parties be convened as soon as possible at which a piecemeal solution of this problem can be set in motion towards the final solution [*Bereinigung*] of the Jewish question.[70]

Knochen's remarks indicate how seriously the Nazis took French legal initiatives, even on the most compelling questions of racial annihilation. Throughout the war, the Germans carefully crafted their own project to conjoin with French legality. But here, as in some other situations, the

---

68 Klarsfeld, *Vichy/Auschwitz,* (Paris: Fayard, 1983), 199, note.

69 Sarraute and Tager, *Recueil des textes,* 18–19.

70 Yad Vashem V-64.

French actually took the lead as to the project itself. Before Wannsee, and before conferences later that winter had been convened by the Germans on the subject of mass arrests and deportations, the French acted.[71]

By the end of January 1941 the German reliance on French law for the internment of Jews *in the Occupied Zone* became quite explicit:

> The juridical basis for the internment of Jews is supplied by a French law of 4 October 1940. This is why it [any order for internment of Jews in the Occupied Zone] must also be executed by the French Government if only to prevent in large measure by this procedure any foreign policy difficulties. The task of the Military Administration and any other German section must be to insure the complete application of French law and to collaborate for the solution of technical difficulties that will follow.[72]

French law was the linchpin for the extremes of German policy and performance in the Occupied Zone. Whether the French went along with the Nazis to keep Jews from being transferred in great numbers to the "free" zone,[73] or because they felt constrained for other reasons to do so, it was their own October statutes that became the prime mover in the "cleansing" of Jews from all of French soil.

## C. The Law of 2 June 1941: Extension and Expansion

### 1. Innovations as to *Mischlinge* and *Mischehe*

The definitive sequel to the Vichy law of 3 October 1940,[74] this "2 June statute," as I shall call it, was designed to eliminate Jewish property ownership and to restrict or even eliminate Jewish participation in many professions and trades. Eventually it, too, would be supplemented by almost two hundred laws, decrees, and rulings authored by French lawyers

---

[71] Marrus and Paxton, *Vichy France and the Jews,* 81, gives February 1941 as the time when the Germans focussed on the Final Solution; but Knochen (who is characterized, ibid., 209, as believing that French antisemitism could best be exploited through economic measures) in fact was forced to think about final solutions even earlier, and his prod was Vichy legislation.

[72] Billig, *Le Commissariat général,* vol. 3, 313, citing CDJC LXXV.

[73] Ibid., 314.

[74] See note 2, above.

and officials.[75] But it remained in full force and effect until the end of the war, generating intense debate on all levels of the legal and administrative hierarchy. The 2 June statute begins, as had its predecessor, with a definition of the word "Jew":[76]

> 1. A Jew is: He or she, of whatever faith, who is an issue of at least three grandparents of the Jewish race, or of simply two if his/her spouse is an issue herself/himself of two grandparents of the Jewish race.
> A grandparent having belonged to the Jewish religion is considered to be of the Jewish race;
> 2. He or she who belongs to the Jewish religion, or who belonged to it on June 25, 1940, and who is the issue of two grandparents of the Jewish race.
> Non-affiliation with the Jewish religion is established by proof of belonging to one of the other faiths recognized by the State before the law of 9 December 1905.
> The disavowal or annulment of recognition of a child considered to be Jewish is without effect as regards the preceding sections.
> [There follow the prohibitions for such people on property ownership and many means of employment; sanctions—including imprisonment—are then declared for failing to register or for engaging in proscribed activities; administrative internment is extended and covers anyone suspected of being a Jew. Finally, a number of "dérogations" or exceptions to coverage under the statute are noted.]

As the contemporary legal commentators Baudry and Ambre noted, the 2 June statute filled "the blank in the statute of 3 October" that had failed to define "Jewish race."[77] Now the "race" of the individual could be gleaned by looking at the *religious practice* of his or her grandparents. The French religious statute now posed the "irrebuttable" presumption that he who practiced the Jewish religion was thus a member of the Jewish race. Continuing, Baudry and Ambre's treatise opined:

> It is indisputable that the two notions of race and religion are theoretically foreign one to another.... [But] in many countries religion is the surest sign of race, and the most distinguished lawyers posit that religion can be taken

[75] Sarraute and Tager, *Receuil des textes,* 185–92, giving a full list of these laws.

[76] Ibid., 49–53.

[77] Baudry and Ambre, *La condition,* 36.

account of in the establishment of a religious law. (See Plianol, Ripert, and Boulanger, *Basic Treatise on Civil Law,* 1942, volume I, no. 420.)[78]

Speaking to the press just after promulgation of the statute, Xavier Vallat (the head of the CGQJ) had emphasized the link—one that we saw subtly articulated in the case against Léon Blum—between a Jew's religious practice and the qualities that justified a religious statute such as this one:

> Thus the antisemitic legislation has been based on the religious factor, the criterion for the definition of Jew, who, as Bernard Lazare once described him "is a confessional type, who is what he is because of the law and the Talmud that made him."[79]

Vallat emphasized, speaking from Vichy, that the law "will equalize—to both zones—the removal of Jews from all influence."[80] Calling attention also to the companion statute of the same date requiring a census of Jews[81], Vallat promised that the "free zone where most Jews have fled from many European countries will no longer provide such refuge."[82]

The new definition of Jew girded the state against those mixed-heritage individuals who might claim non-Jewish status. While the 3 October law made such people Jewish only if they were married to a Jew, and while the German ordinance for the Occupied Zone had included them only if they were practicing Jews, the 2 June statute combined these racial and religious factors by including all such people who in fact "belong to the Jewish religion" or had so belonged as of 25 June 1940. The latter cutoff date cynically barred post-Occupation conversions and even made the baptisms of newborns suspect after that date. Furthermore, early analysts of the statute like Baudry and Ambre felt that it placed on the mixed-heritage individual the *burden* of proving non-Jewishness and limited evidence of another "affiliation" to official adherence to a religion recognized by the state under the law before 9 December 1905 (effectively

---

[78] Ibid.

[79] Interview, *Le Temps,* 14 June 1941, ALL # 8 U Br 526.

[80] Ibid.

[81] Sarraute and Tager, *Recueil des textes,* 53.

[82] ALL # 8 U Br 526.

speaking, Protestantism or Catholicism).[83] And the statute's definitions crudely disallowed any action taken by a Jewish parent to distance himself or herself from a child in order to protect the latter from Jewish definition.

The 2 June statute went even further, by extending the coverage as to *Mischehe* first declared in the 3 October statute it was replacing. There, as we will recall, a person with two non-Jewish and two Jewish grandparents, if married to a full Jew, became Jewish under the law. The new statute explicitly rendered Jewish *both* mixed-heritage marital partners, so that two people who never thought of themselves as being Jewish suddenly would become so by the mere fact of having married each other.

## 2. Franco-German Understandings as to Whose Law Controls from Definition to Arrest and Deportation

What was the interrelation of the new Vichy statute with the German ordinance in effect in the Occupied Zone? Analysts noted that the French law was "more rigorous" in defining as Jewish mixed-heritage individuals who had married *another* mixed-heritage individual (the German laws stopped short of this) or who could not prove that he belonged to another recognized religion. Just as innovative and dramatic in its effect, the new Vichy statute placed at risk individuals married to *Aryans,* a category often granted favored status by the German. Whereas the Nazis, until 1944, insisted that many such people—even if fully Jewish themselves—should not be deported from France, the French definition disregarded the Aryan status of the spouse as long as the individual had at least three—and in many cases, even two—Jewish grandparents.

Furthermore, Vichy legal theorists argued with substantial success that their own new statute should instantly become applicable in the Occupied Zone:

> This presumption of the French law is obviously applicable in the occupied zone because it merely completes (without contradicting) the less explicit German text.[84]

---

[83] Baudry and Ambre, *La Condition,* 36.

[84] Ibid., 37. Baudry and Ambre go on to note that the German ordinance was more stringent in defining as Jewish "in doubtful cases" those who had at any time practiced Judaism, ostensibly covering even those whose grandparental heritage could not be shown, but such cases were quite rare.

Categories of people who would not otherwise be made subject to the German ordinances in the Occupied Zone were now to be included because Vichy's definitions "filled in the blanks" left open by the German ordinances. Whatever Franco-German tensions there may have been as to this approach, the matter was apparently resolved some time before December 1941, when Vichy could confidently write to the German High Command:

> In many situations and more frequently still in recent days, the German authorities and my government have been in agreement on the principle of the substitution of French regulation against the Jews for German regulation thereof.[85]

Subsequent sections of this study will treat in greater detail the irony of Vichy's outdistancing the Nazis in religious definition and implementation. Remarkable already, however, is that on a key issue of German concern—the "Final Solution of the Jewish Question in France"[86]—the French were deemed more than capable of establishing the legalities themselves.[87] Nazi concern that its ordinances be strictly followed in the Occupied Zone quickly yielded to a sense that Vichy's laws, policies, and administrative agencies would produce just what the overall Nazi war machine needed, and with considerable benefits in manpower, public relations, and bureaucratic efficiency. (Thus in a cable of 2 July 1943, Berlin felt comfortable *denying* Helmut Knochen's request for 250 additional SS to help with the French-initiated round-ups of denaturalized Jews in Paris; four Germans and four alone would be sent to help out. To the decision makers in Berlin, by mid-1943 the French had displayed a more than sufficient zeal in racial matters to limit sharply the need for Nazi manpower.)[88]

If the theme of "Let the French do it!" resonated harmoniously within the broader German *Leitmotif* of "efficient" genocide, it paradoxically

---

[85] Memorandum to German High Command, Paris, 9 December 1941. CDJC CVIII-5. See also Dannecker's memorandum confirming this general principle a few months later, above, note 34.

[86] Cable, Müller, RSHA Section IV-B, Berlin to Helmut Knochen, Paris, 2 July 1943, CDJC XXVII-23.

[87] See also Billig, *Le Commissariat général,* vol. 3, 138, 164, 205, 224, 253.

[88] See note 86, above, and chapter 9.

created some dissonances as well. There came a point at which the orchestra conductors themselves became upset with the innovative zeal of their subordinate musicians. We will have many occasions—again, particularly in chapter 6—to note the bizarre recurrence of German pleas to the French to slow down and restrict religious legislation and policy to the sometimes more restrained *tempi* of the Nazi ordinances.[89]

Indeed, even as to the relatively short-lived Vichy statute of 3 October 1940, there were a few absorbing examples of German annoyance at how far the French had gone. Article 2, Paragraph 1 (cited above) included bridge and street workers ("Corps des ponts et chaussées") from among those trades barred to Jews. So, on 31 March 1941, the personnel director of the German Commerce Ministry in Paris found himself pleading with the Vichy authorities in East Africa to help him find a loophole in the statute that would permit Jews to continue in their much-needed work in the Tunis area. Might these workers at least fall under one of the statute's exceptions? Or might they not be employed on a temporary basis, always under the stipulation that they not take leadership positions?[90]

German disaffection with French legalistic excesses was not always phrased so prayerfully or done for merely pragmatic reasons. Their approach to mixed marriages and individuals of mixed heritage, subjects on which the Germans had historically displayed "a bizarre obsession,"[91] is instructive. Documents relating to the arrest and even deportation of purported Jews in these two categories indicate a continuing uncertainty among Germans as to their inclusion among Jews that would be persecuted; recall that the first German ordinance specifically *limited* Jewish definition to those who had at least three Jewish grandparents or who otherwise confessed to being practicing Jews. But Vichy consistently

---

[89] Again, with the possible—although still quite complex—exception of the French approach to *aryanization*. See chapter 6 for this conflict, and chapter 7 for a full analysis of property law.

[90] CDJC (unnumbered German-language document).

[91] The phrase is Marrus and Paxton's, *Vichy France and the Jews*, 291. As Lucien Steinberg puts it about the gravest questions of life and death, "for rather obscure reasons, the Germans set up a kind of 'hierarchy of departures' at the transit centers. This is how, for quite some time, Jewish members of mixed marriages were spared," Lucien Steinberg, *Les Allemands en France* (Paris: Albin Michel, 1980), 217; see also above, note 28.

tended "to outstrip even the Nazis"[92]; the 3 October statute on its terms included mixed-heritage individuals as long as they were also married to Jews. The 2 June statute went on to include many *Mischlinge* who were *not* married to Jews.[93] The Germans throughout 1942 and 1943 consistently sought to restrain French arrests and deportations of individuals whose "Jewishness" was either in doubt or negated by German standards. Thus a secret SS memorandum of 2 February 1942 (probably authored by Walter Nährich[94] for Dr. Werner Best, head of Civil Administration for the German High Command in Paris) underscores in the gravest context German concerns about the scope of Jewish definition under French law:

> Subject: Deportation of Jews, specifically, Jews married to Aryans.
> I am of the opinion that Jews married to Aryans should be—as they are in the Reich—exempted from deportation. In keeping to this principle, a certain number of Jews should be liberated from the detention camp in Compiègne or transferred to the camp in Drancy....[95]

Unlike the French, whose statutory approach to mixed-heritage individuals explicitly included mixed-marriage cases under all the sanctions of the religious laws, the Germans equivocated on *Mischehe* and *Mischlinge*. Around the time of the first convoys to Auschwitz, Eichmann personally insisted that "Jews in mixed marriages are not presently deportable."[96] While the French were not ready to contemplate the exclusion of full-Jews from any statutory penalty—and surely not just because they might

---

[92] Marrus and Paxton, *Vichy France and the Jews,* 291, here discussing the half-Jews *(Mischlinge)* only, and at a later period of Vichy policy.

[93] Marrus and Paxton oversimplify this point in their treatment—which they of course did not claim to be thorough in 1981—of Vichy religious law. See, e.g., *Vichy France and the Jews,* 291: "(Vallat's statute had exempted those with two Jewish grandparents who were not married to a Jew)." In fact, Alibert's statute, of 3 October 1940, on its terms so restricted Jewish definition; but the 2 June 1941, statute, promulgated after much study by Vallat's CGQJ, included many other ways of finding Jewishness in mixed-heritage individuals, unleashing a significant component of the caselaw and the policy arguments analyzed here and in other chapters, particularly chapter 5.

[94] A senior SS official in Paris, who was killed there shortly before the end of the Occupation; see Lucien Steinberg, *Les Allemands en France,* 328.

[95] Yad Vashem # IV-183 (from the French translation).

[96] Serge Klarsfeld, *Vichy/Auschwitz,* 199.

be married to Aryans!—the Germans seemed prepared to consider last minute pleas such as that of Mrs. Armand Taub to the German Military Command at 16 rue Kléber. An Aryan, Mrs. Taub in mid-1942 perhaps realized that a direct appeal to the Germans to block her Jewish husband's impending deportation from Drancy stood a better chance of success than going to her compatriots; but Mrs. Taub, despite German intervention on her behalf,[97] was too late. Taub was already on his way "to the East."

On the level of official policy, still later in 1942 and now months after the Wannsee conference itself, the Germans were still trying to reign in French overzealousness on questions of definition that specifically related to arrest and deportation. In a memorandum of 11 July 1942, the German high command issued its directives to the French police for the impending, infamous roundups of Jews of 16–17 July 1942 (the "Vel d'Hiv" roundups); the memo explicitly states, "As to mixed marriages only the stateless spouse will be arrested."[98] For the following summer's roundups, the German instructions on this point were similar: a memorandum to the Paris police prefects relating to the impending action of 16 July 1943 reveals the German High Command's relative solicitude for mixed-marriage *(Mischehe)* individuals. The latter are explicitly exempted from arrest, along with their children, in Section 5 (b) of the memo, although its following section withdraws the exception for 17 categories of stateless Jews.[99]

Only very late in the Occupation did the Nazis apparently move more firmly, but not universally, in the direction of what I would here call the Vichy statutes' "overinclusiveness" as to religious definition. In March 1944, despite their obscene hunger to fill the ovens back east to which they were retreating, the Nazis equivocated on whether "Mixed-heritage

[97] Memorandum, German High Command to Paris SD, 14 May 1942; Taub had already been deported, probably among the first transports from French soil, and the German police official notes on the face of the memo that saving him "can no longer enter into the question," CDJC XXVb–27.

[98] CDJC XXVI-44. The next section of this memo specifically directs the French to *release* all arrested children after first taking them to the Vélodrome d'Hiver. The infamous French demand (originated by the lawyer, Laval) to have the children deported, too, will be discussed in due course.

[99] CDJC XXVI-76.

as well as mixed-marriage Jews should be arrested?" in France;[100] one month later *Hauptsturmführer* Harnig informs regional prefectures in Dijon that "all other Jews without exception" are to be arrested later in the month, having first advised them that "surveillance in special residences and lodgings is lifted on Jews married before 1 July 1940 to Aryans."[101]

The twinned innovation penned by Alibert and elaborated later by Vallat—those "convinced antisemites"[102]—but signed in its gruesome final form into law by the Catholic prewar liberal Joseph Barthélemy, thus permanently extended all the risks of "Jewishness" to hundreds of individuals who were not affected by the first German ordinance.

## 3. Application of Vichy's Definitions within the French Legal Structure

Little more than a month after the promulgation of the new statute, which was supposed to fill many lacunae in the 3 October text, a Parisian named Adrien Jacques wrote to the CGQJ confidently expecting that his case would be removed from any suspicion of "Jewishness." He and his spouse were *first cousins;* they had two Jewish grandparents in common and a total of four separate non-Jewish grandparents. Baptized at birth, they were married in a Roman Catholic church in 1905. "It is inconceivable," writes Jacques, "that the marriage sacrament is going to annul the baptismal sacrament and stick us into the Jewish community, although we

---

[100] See a series of questions posed by the Union Générale des Israélites Français (UGIF) to the SD, 20 March 1944: "Are mixed-heritage Jews comparable to mixed-marriage Jews? [marginal answer: "yes"]; What about mixed-heritage individuals who were baptized *before* 25 June 1940 and possess a certificate of non-adherence to the Jewish race? [no marginal answer]; there are also in Drancy some wives of prisoners of war and other special cases—are these to be transferred if there is no Aryan in the family? [marginal answer: "yes"]; Should I treat these people like mixed-marriage Jews? [marginal answer: "yes"]", Yad Vashem, Kurt Schendel file (Schendel was SD liaison with the UGIF).

[101] French translation of Harnig memorandum, Dijon, 14 April 1944, YV IVB (unnumbered).

[102] The phrase is Marrus and Paxton's, *Vichy France and the Jews,* 368. For a fine analysis of Vallat's brand of Maurrasian antisemitism, see also Laloum, *La France antisémite,* 5f.

have always on the contrary been part of the Catholic community."[103] But was it inconceivable under Vichy law? Not at all, opined the CGQJ about a month later:

> The Commissaire général [Vallat] has noted, in fact, that two half-Jews who both became Aryans by baptism at their birth, could—by application of Article I paragraph 2 of the law of 2 June 1941—without illogicality become Jewish again by the fact of their religious marriage subsequently to a spouse who is also Aryan.[104]

So weird was this approach that M. François of the prefectural division of CGQJ notes

> The law will be modified—to state that a person having two Jewish grandparents and who is baptized is not Jewish if he marries someone who also has two Jewish grandparents and is herself baptized.[105]

As we shall see in chapters 5 and 6, such a change never occurred; the surpassing of the Nazi models continued, and many cases had to be litigated in French courts.

But by far the most contentious part of the new statute was to become the question of burden of proof in the case of the mixed-heritage individual. The 2 June statute is not explicit on the point, although its language "is established by proof of belonging to one of the other faiths...," etc., might imply that the individual has the burden. The procedural issue, vital (as lawyers know) to the outcome of any piece of litigation, divided courts, commentators, and administrators for four long years.

Upon this burden-of-proof question hung many a career, a fortune, a life. It was here that the law coerced litigation and legal rhetoric. Anyone with three or more Jewish grandparents was irrebuttably Jewish, as a matter of "race"; anyone with one or no Jewish grandparents was an "Aryan" under this still primarily race-based approach, even if Jewish under Jewish law (by having a Jewish maternal grandmother) and even if (secretly) a Jew. Unless married to another Jew (or half-Jew), however,

---

[103] Letter to CGQJ, 11 July 1941, CDJC CXIV-39. For first cousin analysis, see also chapter 5, note 85; chapter 6, note 130; chapter 8, note 207.

[104] Ibid., memo, CGQJ to the police prefecture, 9 August 1941.

[105] Ibid.

the person with exactly two Jewish grandparents was an ambiguous case. Would this person need to prove non-Jewishness or would Vichy have to prove the contrary?

This is the kind of question that lawyers love to attack. American as well as French lawyers might find here the tempting kind of statutory void that volumes of verbiage will soon fill. How can an interpretive community that thrives on such problems resist? What choices do members of that community have? Before returning to that last question, which is for my claim a vital one, let me continue empirically by revealing what French lawyers actually did. First, they drew up charts to clarify the various perambulations.[106] Then they began to debate the ambiguous statutory point; within a matter of weeks, they were, as an observer put it (making it sound more like a young wine than a legal matter of the gravest consequence), divided on "cette matière fort délicate et nouvelle" (this new and delicate matter).[107]

Government lawyers, judges, and private attorneys all had much to say about the "delicate" debate. Anticipating the problem in an early memorandum, a justice department lawyer wrote to the Minister of the Interior of

> a yet more delicate case, although admittedly unusual and manageable, that of an individual, presumably of Jewish origins, but the issue of grandparents who practiced no religion or who were married civilly. How can we find the key to this problem? Arduous genealogical research might have to be on an international scale.[108]

For Xavier Vallat of the CGQJ, there was no doubt that the 2 June statute placed this occasionally overwhelming burden on the individual; writing just after the war of this problem, he says:

> But *how could we know* if the grandparents were of the Jewish religion, since Jewish communities in France did not have records like those of the parish churches? It was only possible to determine this by forcing their descendants to furnish the contrary proof, that is evidence establishing that

---

[106] CDJC XVIIa-38 (166 and 167).

[107] "Qu'est-ce qu'un juif?," in the "Bulletin quotidien d'études et d'informations économiques," Paris, No. 380, 19 August 1942, CDJC CDXXIX-1.

[108] AN BB[30], 1714.

> their grandparents had belonged to other recognized religions then in France: Catholic, Protestant, Orthodox or Islam.
>
> And what about atheists, some will ask us? The answer is simple. We were dealing with people born in the first half of the 19th century and, in that period, atheism practically did not exist.[109]

As early as 10 October 1941, Vallat's CGQJ and its "service de législation et contentieux" were alerting all regional directors to the agency's firm position (theoretical—since there was no explicit language in the statute—but firm nonetheless) that the individual and not the CGQJ bore the burden of proof.[110] The following month, CGQJ was busy slapping the wrists of such magistrates as the Procureur in Toulouse who dared to reverse the burden. Declaring itself the best judge of the 2 June statute, "because of the minute study of the texts...our position is unattackable. It consists of this affirmation: that the burden of proof, in all contests relating to the quality of Jewishness, must be carried by the individual and not by our Commission."[111]

Not everyone connected with the Vichy government revelled in placing this almost insurmountable burden on the individual rather than the state. But it may be significant that the strongest statement from Vichy against such an interpretation came from a writer, not a lawyer. It was René Gillouin, an essayist and writer who briefly served in Pétain's cabinet, who complained directly to the Marshal on this point:

> It is regrettable, according to [Gillouin], that from now on the putative Jew will have to prove her/his innocence [*sic*], and not for the State to prove her/his guilt. This judicial innovation is disquieting for everyone. The

---

[109] Xavier Vallat, *La Vie de France Sous l'Occupation* (Hoover Institute, Stanford University, 1947), vol. 2, 659–60. Xavier Vallat wrote this essay, which he called, "Affaires juives," from prison. The essay goes on to assert, among other things, that the Vichy religious laws helped to save "95% of French Jews" (p. 672), while admitting that, of the 330,000 Jews he counted on French soil before the war, only 180,000 remained in 1946.

[110] CGQJ memorandum, 10 October 1941, AN AJ[38]. On the question of burden of proof throughout Vichy courts and agencies, see chapter 5, subsections A–C.

[111] CDJC XVIIa-45 (2501).

> dispersion of property by dissolution of the community will sap the family. French law is more severe than German law.[112]

If the government debated the point, soon deciding that the individual would have to prove his non-Jewishness ("innocence" as even the sympathetic Gillouin's position was just characterized), a second domain of legalistic rhetoric—the courts—even more extensively and controversially entered the fray. In the case of *Michel Benaim,* for example, a court in Rabat stated that:

> an individual, issued from two Jewish grandparents and two non-Jewish grandparents, who is both baptized according to the Catholic faith and circumcised according to the rites of the Hebraic law, but who has never really belonged to the Catholic religion [must], by reference to Article One, Section Two [of the 2 June statute], be declared Jewish as not having proved his non-adherence to the Jewish religion by an actual membership in one of the other religions recognized by the French state before the law of December 9, 1905.[113]

Elsewhere, the Tribunal correctionnel of Brive decided that two small children had not sufficiently shown their "innocence." Aged two and three, Jack and Claude *Lang* had two Jewish and two non-Jewish grandparents; they were both baptized, and neither was circumcised. But the court decided that truly to "belong" to another religion required "une volonté réfléchie et nettement exprimée que ne sauraient posséder des enfants de 2 et 3 ans" (a considered and clearly expressed will that no child of the age of Jack and Claude Lang can possess). Their father was thus convicted of not having declared the children to be Jewish and accordingly fined 1200 francs.[114]

---

[112] Michèle Cointet-Labrousse, "Le Conseil national de Vichy, Vie politique et réforme de l'état en régime autoritaire. 1940–1944" (unpubl. Ph.D. diss., Paris X, 1984), 960.

[113] CDJC CXV-20.

[114] *Charles-Robert Lang* case, *Tribunal correctionnel de Brive,* 30 April 1942, reversed on appeal. See also chapter 6, note 17. Reported in *Semaine juridique* of 12 July 1942 and in J. Lubetzki, *La Condition des Juifs en France sous l'Occupation allemande* (Paris: CDJC, 1945). In an expert opinion rendered on a similar matter in 1944, to which we shall shortly return, law professor Jacques Maury indicates that this case was ultimately reversed by the Court of Appeals of Limoges; see CDJC XVIIa-44 (240). Accord on the reversal, Lubetzki, *La Condition,* 36. The Lang children, of course, included a future government minister.

The decisions of these various civil or "ordinary" courts bothered the CGQJ less on the merits perhaps than because the CGQJ thought that *it alone had the jurisdiction* to make decisions about Jewish matters. After all, it declared proudly, only the agency could provide to those denying their Jewish status some tangible proof that they were "Aryans." This prized document was the "certificate of non-affiliation with the Jewish race."

The "Certificat de non-appartenance à la race juive" referred to here was the passport to relief from the life-threatening strictures of the religious laws. For hundreds of cases similar to the ones we have noted, the "inside," "delicate" debate on the meaning of the 2 June statute decided whether the individual would receive such a certificate.[115] Such certificates would have a magical effect, allowing the bearer or, less frequently, her spouse to avoid special curfews and travel restrictions imposed on Jews, to fend off Aryan administrators all too eager to take over businesses and real property, to engage in various professions and trades otherwise prohibited to Jews, to avoid, finally, deportation—sometimes at the last minute as lawyers rushed to the internment camp at Drancy with the certificate, thus plucking their clients from the line heading for the bus, heading for the train "to the East."

---

In contrast to the principal case was the view of such legal analysts as Dr. Mosse of Perpignan that, at least as regards proof of Jewish ancestry, the personal feelings of the *ancestor* are irrelevant. Hence: "From the point of view of the Law of 2 June 1941, it is irrelevant to argue the lack of religion or the impurity of race of the Jewish ancestors. The law inquires neither into the religious beliefs nor the greater or lesser racial purity of the ancestors...," CDJC XVIIa-38 (165).

Dr. Mosse's view renders irrelevant the personal beliefs of the grandparents, as long as they were nominally Jewish; the principal case renders highly relevant the personal beliefs of infants being baptized. The only way to harmonize the opinions is to see that both made life more difficult for individuals trying to show their non-Jewishness.

See also, and interestingly, the more "liberal" approach to baptized babies taken by the CGQJ [!] which, in an advisory opinion, declared that war babies born of mixed parentage, although not in fact belonging to a recognized faith "before June 25, 1940," would be viewed (if baptized immediately) as non-Jewish. Why? "Obviously it could not have been baptized before June 25, 1940, because it was not yet born," CGQJ to regional director, Toulouse, 18 August 1942, CDJC XVIIa-38 (158).

[115] For a cinematic re-creation of the life and death legalisms required to get the Vichy certificate, see Joseph Losey's *Mr. Klein* (1976).

The CGQJ treasured its monopoly on this jurisdiction, but the civil courts kept finding ways to compete. Throughout 1943, opinions such as the following appear, from the Tribunal civil de la Seine in Paris, in the *Touati* case:

> it appears from the [2 June] statute that definition as a Jew is a function of the number and the race of the individual's grandparents.
>
> Whereas Charles Touati...was born on 22 December 1898 in Algiers of Israel and Eugenie Temime, themselves born of unknown fathers and mothers who never acknowledged them;
>
> That there are neither maternal nor paternal grandparents on which his race can be determined;
>
> That thus the law of 2 June 1941 is not applicable to him.
>
> Therefore, it is held that Charles Touati is not Jewish under the meaning of the law of 2 June 1941.[116]

As the war was ending, and even the hitherto supportive Conseil d'État could see the handwriting on the wall, it, too, began opposing the CGQJ. The latter bitterly attacked its administrative ally when, on 9 February 1944, the Commissariat formally complained about a Conseil decision declaring as an Aryan a woman with two Jewish grandparents who had "spontaneously declared herself to be Jewish."[117]

Voluntary declarations were rare, so all kinds of other evidence were solicited. In a document of unknown, but bureaucratic origin, called by a contemporary observer, "une perle de la jurisprudence vichyssoise," the lawyer for a certain M. Élina was advised as follows:

> My dear colleague: In order finally to dispose of this case, which has been pending since 4 February, 1943, I would be in your debt if you could have sent to me by a member of the Medical Association a declaration as to whether or not your client benefits from his entire preputial integrity. [que votre client jouit de toute son intégrité préputiale][118]

---

[116] Session of 12 February 1943, lere Chambre. For Vichy's special solicitation for even Jewish out-of-wedlock children, see chapter 4, notes 144, 147; chapter 5, note 81, and chapter 9, subsection C.

[117] The *Françoise Raphael* case, CDJC XVII-36 (154a). For a fuller analysis of this case, as well as developments in the various jurisdictions competing for control of racial doctrine, see chapter 5, note 92.

[118] CDJC XXIII-19.

Sadly, the use of circumcision evidence was pervasive, particularly where the state was deemed to have the burden of proof. Civil prosecutors used such data in their rigorous efforts to detect Jews even toward the end of the war. As late as 17 May 1944, the 2 June statute narrowly avoided depriving someone hitherto untouched—unlike tens of thousands of other Jews on French soil who had already been deported—of his liberty. Before the Tribunal civil de première instance of Ceret, *Marcel Joseph Weiller* was accused of failing to register himself as a Jew, even though the prosecutor could not prove that he had at least three Jewish grandparents. Weiller's "crime"? The court put it this way:

> being born of at least two grandparents of that race, he would be Jewish if found to belong himself to the Jewish religion. Weiller's belonging to the Jewish race is apparent from the discovery, in his house, of the Tablets of the Law, and of Hebrew prayers; from the fact that he was circumcised at birth, and, contrary to his allegations, never baptized, the certificate of baptism delivered by the vicar Berges of Toulouse being just an accommodation to him.[119]

Weiller's production of a baptismal certificate, always less convincing to French courts than to German,[120] to the extent that the German High Command in Paris once had to urge the French administrative courts to accept such evidence irrebuttably (advice rejected at the time by the French),[121] availed him little. The court thought it not quite a forgery, but almost so, and they had the evidence of the Jewish sacred objects in Weiller's home, and of a Dr. Cortade that Weiller was indeed circumcised. On the other hand, a maid testified that she had seen Weiller perform certain Catholic rites. Because the state (in this tribunal) had the burden, and because the evidence was equally balanced, Weiller escaped retribution and deportation. On such thin reeds, wispier than the words themselves of which they are made, were fates decided, over and over again, in Vichy France.

Throughout this period of increasing litigation and complexity, academic and doctrinal discourse paralleled and—in my view rationalized—

[119] CDJC XVIIa 45 (254).

[120] See, e.g., chapter 6, text at notes 33–41.

[121] Memorandum, Röthke to CGQJ advising them to accept as definitive affirmative testimony provided by Catholic priests about the baptism of suspected Jews, CDJC CXV-83.

the courts' treatment of the Jewish population in France. A singularly important example of the manner in which intellectualized and analytical rhetoric contributed to the terror gets us back to Jacques Maury. When, just three months before D-Day. Prof. Maury was asked to opine about the Jewishness of three young issue of a mixed marriage in Toulouse, he had come far from his stance of jugular protest to the first fruits of Vichy legislation. Too much had happened in those almost four years since the régime launched its program. There was no longer any doubt of the religious laws' "Frenchness," no longer any talk of the unacceptability of distinguishing one person from another on the basis of immutable characteristics. The discourse had softened; lawtalk had accomodated. And the issues had sorted themselves out on a far lower level of generalization. French law, without much prodding from the Germans (except in the form of Nazi slaps on overzealous Vichy wrists), had gradually come into existence by just this process of rhetorical give and take, of professional discourse, of learning what is right and wrong not through "basic ethics" or even "established French constitutional principles," but instead by watching and listening to what other lawyers were saying and doing.[122] For the Maury of March 1944, there persisted none of his original—one might say "foundational"—objections:

> "Consultation on the Aryan-ness of the Levy children." The undersigned professor, Jacques Maury, professor of comparative law on the faculty of the University of Toulouse, offering on that faculty the course in private international law, director of the institute of comparative law at the University, provide the following opinion on the racial quality [le caractère racial] of the Levy children.
>
> The following facts have been given to us: three children have been born of the marriage, celebrated on 23 November 1936 [*sic?*] in Toulouse between M. LEVY, an Argentinian national of the Jewish race, and Mlle MAGNE Simone,

---

[122] See Stanley Fish, e.g. *Is There A Text in this Class? The Authority of Interpretive Communities* (Cambridge: Harvard, 1980), chapters 15 and 16. For Fish, a professional discourse is never subject to overriding "rules" because only the way people talk and behave in a given community can establish what the "rules" of the group are at any given time. See also, on Vichy itself, Danièle Lochak, "La Doctrine sous Vichy," who speaks of the "banalisation" of the religious laws partly in terms of the academic lawyers' "measured, neutral, and detached tone...," ibid., 125. Lochak, to the best of my knowledge, does not cite Prof. Maury's writings; most other writing that she does utilize will be discussed later in this book; see chapter 10, note 14.

Aryan and French by nationality, remaining French despite this marriage; the three are Gilbert, born 24 October 1934...Serge, born 15 November, 1935...and Michelle, born 28 January, 1940.... These children were baptized; Gilbert on 15 August 1935, Serge on 15 May 1941, and Michelle on 18 June 1940. Their birth and baptismal certificates have been presented.

On this state of the facts, we have been asked to opine on the race of the LEVY children.[123]

Prof. Maury then cites the prevalent statute of 2 June 1941, which tracked the 3 October law's ambiguous treatment of people with two Jewish and two non-Jewish grandparents (the case here) but added that such people would be considered Jewish if "belonging to the Jewish race or having belonged to it on 25 June 1940." Are the Levy children to be considered Jewish?

The negative answer is clearly applicable to Gilbert, and to Michelle, both baptized before that date according to the Catholic rite.... Although some courts of first jurisdiction at the outset of the application of the law of 2 June, 1941 held that what was needed was a "real" commitment to Catholicism or Protestantism and that such a commitment could not be found in a child of tender years [see above, note 114[124]]...the law has moved, apparently with good sense, to the opposite conclusion [cite omitted]. Today the point is settled that baptism suffices to prove the non-affiliation with the Jewish religion ["la non-appartenance à la religion juive"], the decision of the Conseil d'État of 7 January, 1944 ... [preserving the job of a mixed-heritage functionary who produced a baptismal certificate from the reformed church.] Against such proof, no contrary presumption can prevail....

The issue is different, both factually and legally, when it comes to Serge, baptized on 15 May 1941.

The law once held that only belonging to one of the religions recognized by the state before the law of 9 December, 1905 can prove the non-affiliation to the Jewish religion, which would lead to declaring as Jewish all those with

---

[123] Maury opinion, March 1944, CDJC XVIIa-44 (240) (henceforth Maury opinion).

[124] The CGQJ consistently took the line that a mere baptism without attendant "conviction" of belief would not suffice to disprove Jewish status. See Armilhon (director of CGQJ legal department) to Limoges regional bureau of CGQJ, 19 August 1942, AN AJ[38], *Robert Meyer* case, instructing them to appeal a Périgueux lower court decision affirming the Catholicism of two non-circumcised but baptized minor children: "these facts do not seem to show the element of conviction needed to remove the legal presumption [of Jewishness]."

> two grandparents of the Jewish race who could not demonstrate that they were Catholics or Protestants before 25 June, 1940. But this approach has been justly criticized by almost all the analysts, and has also been rejected by both ordinary and administrative courts. Although the Cour de Cassation has not to our knowledge ruled on the point, many courts including Appeals Courts have ruled that non-affiliation with the Jewish religion can be proved by all other means [besides baptism alone]. [Cites omitted.] This is incidentally the solution reached by German courts, whether on the basis of the occupation ordinances of 1940, 1941 or 1942 or the [indigenous German] law of 15 September 1935. [The citation to the articles by French attorney Joseph Haennig are omitted here, but Haennig's approach will be taken up imminently.][125]

Maury now turns to the difficult issue of Serge's adherence or non-adherence to Judaism. He first adopts a controversial stance:

> Now in fact Serge LEVY has never belonged to the Jewish religion, and all the indications presented to us consititute, in this regard, sufficient factual presumptions. It would be inexplicable, by the way, to find one child out of three, or one son out of two raised in the Jewish religion while the other son, or the two other children, would be raised as Catholics. Such an arrangement would be completely untypical of the approach of spouses of differing religions.[126]

Perhaps because Maury's logic in 1944 contrasted with that of official Vichy (which, as we have seen, held that different family members *should* be treated differently by the religious laws),[127] the professor extends his argument on the absurdity of finding Serge Jewish but his siblings Aryan by stressing the indifference of father Levy to his Judaism compared to the familial concern about Catholic ritual:

> It has been shown that M. LEVY, completely detached from the Jewish religion, did not participate at all in it.... [Serge's] baptism in 1941 might be suspect if it stood alone. It is in a way authenticated by the baptisms of his brother and sister, which show by their very existence that the family religion was Catholicism, although by the tardiness [of the baptisms] that perhaps the rites of that religion were not strictly adhered to. The actual practice of the Catholic religion by the two [other] children, their keeping

---

125 Maury opinion.

126 Ibid.

127 See text at notes 27–30.

to the catechism, confirms as well the reality of their religious life, which their parents surely chose for them. There was certainly no adherence by Serge to Catholicism before 25 June 1940. *From the facts, as they have been reported, we can deduce that Serge LEVY did not belong to the Jewish religion, and therefore he is not Jewish under the law of 2 June 1941.* (Emphasis added.)[128]

Maury concludes by harmonizing his findings with German law and concluding that "In the Occupied Zone, unless there is a new ordinance that has not yet come to our knowledge, the LEVY children would not be Jewish. There is not the slightest reason to consider them such in the southern zone, since according to existing French law they are Aryans."[129]

Jugular protest, although rare, did attend the promulgation of the 3 October 1940 religious statute. Foundational attacks on Vichy legislation were published and abided, and they would continue (in very small doses) throughout the four years of the régime. The political trials at Riom, as we have seen, inspired some prominent lawyers to pick up on Maury's 1940 theme of the "unfrenchness" of the régime's laws, although the Riom protest unfortunately did not specifically address the religious laws *per se*. But Maury's own rhetorical shift, over the years, to a neutral tone accepting the racial premise as a given (where he once saw it as grotesque and aberrational) is typical of French professional discourse during the period. It is not so much that some protested, continued to protest and then gave up or were somehow silenced; rather the religious laws became a viable reality because the discourse of direct protest *never caught on*. Instead, moving in the gradual way that professional rhetoric will, French lawyers and courts found racism tolerable. They easily learned to accommodate those few colleagues whose nausea in the face of what they were seeing placed them increasingly at the margins of polite legal discourse.

Appellate lawyer Joseph Haennig, a member of the Parisian Bar, was not a man at the professional margins. Like Maury, his position permitted him to write with authority, and also like Maury, he was turning his attention to the hermeneutics of the religious statute. Haennig, too, seems motivated by a kind of right-minded effort to do some "good" by seizing

---

[128] Maury opinion.

[129] Ibid.

a low-level debate about the French approach to religious definition; at the same time, and like the law professor, this practitioner's decision to discuss the laws this way could do little—at the time—to avoid an appearance of accepting their legitimacy and their continuing authority.

Haennig had tracked legal developments during the contentious years of 1942 and 1943, during which (as we saw above) the crucial questions of burden and evidentiary appropriateness as to proof of "Jewishness" were played out in French courts. Late in 1943, he published a prominent article, suggesting with the more liberal magistrates and thinkers that the broadest inquiry be allowed into the Jewishness of the individual. The state should present evidence, and so should the individual. Not only the individual's belonging to a recognized religion should satisfy the courts, Haennig argued, but also any other proof he might mount. This, Haennig advised, using the gentle rhetoric he felt comfortable with at the time, was the approach of the Nazi courts in Germany itself, whose "largeness and objectivity of spirit" he hoped the French would emulate.[130] He also explicitly cited to a committee of the Conseil d'État that had also demonstrated some liberality on racial litigation.[131]

Haennig's analysis, published in the authoritative reporter of French law, attempts to "work from within" the racial system and to induce some benignity in it by limiting its consequences in certain situations. We will see a good measure of this kind of ameliorative discourse as this study proceeds; it is quite typical of a kind of "liberal" French spirit, projected by lawyers who clearly were not villains but in fact were unexceptionable members of a profession whose strictures they surely felt they were fulfilling in these discussions. Haennig's plea reads as follows:

> "What Means of Proof Can the Jew of Mixed Blood Offer to Establish His Nonaffiliation with the Jewish Race?"
>
> The Commission on the Jewish Laws has been established by the head of State to give its view on the interpretation of Article I of the Law of 2 June 1941 concerning the subject of nonaffiliation with the Jewish race.
>
> The Commission believes that the statute writers allowed more proof than merely that of belonging to another religion recognized by the State prior to the law of 9 December 1905. It has noted that "in each case, the adjudicator

---

[130] For my earlier discussion of Haennig, see Weisberg, *The Failure of the Word: The Protagonist as Lawyer in Modern Fiction* (New Haven: Yale, 1984), 1–3, 181.

[131] See chapter 5 at notes 52–53.

may ascertain that the claimant either has never belonged or has ceased to belong in fact, to the Jewish community" (*Gazette du Palais* 1943, 1st sem., Doctrine, p. 14)....

We believe that neither good sense nor the law could lead to the view that the statute writers required of an individual having only two Jewish grandparents proof of his belonging to the Catholic or Protestant denominations in order to avoid being included on the lists of Jews....

Since the courts must now decide each case on its own merits, we would do well to cite as an example German law, and thus to see how it overcomes any difficulty relating to proof of nonaffiliation with the Jewish race. This exercise reveals a largeness and objectivity of spirit....

A recent case of particular note dealt with the female descendant of two Jewish grandparents, baptized as a Protestant, who, under the Article stipulating the definition of a citizen of the Reich, only would become Jewish if she adhered to the Jewish religion, the same solution incidentally as is reached under the law of 2 June 1941.

This woman of mixed Protestant and Jewish heritage had, for a period of six months, at the express request of her Jewish father and against the wishes of her Protestant mother, attended classes at religious school to learn about the Jewish faith. Once each year until her father's death in 1931, she accompanied him to synagogue on the New Year.

On the other hand, she never contributed to the synagogue, while still retaining her name on the list kept there.

Under these circumstances and facts, the Supreme Court of Leipzig was called on to consider her case. It first noted that, as soon as she learned of the presence of her name on the Jewish lists, she requested its removal, in the spring of 1938.

The Court affirmed the lower court judge's view that she had only attended New Year's services in order to preserve family peace. The view that there was no sufficient tie to the Jewish community in this case was thus deemed correct.

[However, the defendant had called herself a Jew in order to obtain employment from a Jewish agency.] Theoretically, the Court of Leipzig refused to consider the motives leading an individual to certain specific acts apparently linking him to the Jewish community. However, where these links are apparently merely for pretense, the court instructed lower courts not to take them into account if it has been established, as in the instant case, that the defendant was merely using the Jewish religion as a means to acquire an advantage by that way.

This analysis of the German law furnishes an interesting contribution to the study of a subject still little understood by the French courts. The analysis

indicates a possible route, without risk of distorting the statute writers' intention, and in conformity with the principles which underlie the religious statutes and cases.
Joseph Haennig,
Member of the Appellate Bar
Paris[132]

Haennig's 1943 essay takes a seemingly more benign doctrinal position than the one espoused by Baudry and Ambre just after the 2 June statute was promulgated.[133] A mixed-heritage individual was to be allowed full evidentiary recourse in disproving his Jewishness. Yet the very "liberality" of the discourse raises the most dreadful questions of how law is made and enforced. Placed in the context of Vichy rhetoric on Jewish definitional questions, it stands as a paradigm for the French legal profession's willingness to abandon allegiance to its textual traditions and to "think the unthinkable, write the unwritable." As I discussed in *The Failure of the Word,*[134] Haennig's statement typifies the immersion in discourse that all too often screens lawyers from the corrupt atmosphere lurking above the surface of their words.

At the turning point of Vichy power, with the Axis armies largely in retreat and the Normandy landing about a year off, Haennig and most of his colleagues were just warming to the jurisprudence of Jewish identity. Professor Maury engaged even later in racial nitpicking, a mere three months before D-Day. Gone were thoughts of the still-existing Constitutional guaranties of equal protection, safeguarding of property, and avoidance of *ex post facto* laws.

The "jugular attack" on the very premises of the religious laws—which we have seen mounted both at Riom and by the early Jacques Maury, without penalty to those who had so protested—was transmuted by 1943 and 1944 into a learned discourse that felt comfortable urging Nazi

---

[132] This analysis originally appeared as an article by Haennig in the edition of the *Gazette du Palais* (the traditional reporter of French statues and cases) covering the first semester of 1943, 31.

[133] See text at notes 82–83.

[134] See the response of Judge Richard Posner, *Law and Literature: A Misunderstood Relation* (Cambridge: Harvard University Press, 1988), 171–75. Posner has more recently moved closer to my position—and used my evidence for it; see Posner, "Review of Ingo Müller, *Hitler's Justice,*" *New Republic,* 17 June 1991, 36.

models upon French lawyers. Considering himself only bound by the internal discourse of the "Jewish question," and not by any external norm, Haennig deftly juggled issues that shortly before he would have considered inadmissibly grotesque.

Haennig's apparent lack of viciousness thus makes his case compelling for us today. Lawyers like Haennig, more than those few who relished the infliction of suffering upon the Jews, made that suffering possible. Once the Nazi state and its courts could be cited *by a mainstream lawyer* as precedent for "a largeness and objectivity of spirit," French law became unanchored—dashing towards its own doom with no one at the helm but the most recently published rhetorician.

For any lawyer in 1943 who might still have wavered on the professional propriety of debating religious laws in "free" as well as Occupied France, Haennig's seeming benevolence must surely have been persuasive. If such a man, trying to narrow the already overly broad French definition of Jew, could discourse freely on such a subject, surely racism was now within the fabric of French law. No statutory language alone could produce that result; rather, the *low level of generalization* that lawyers managed to use in discussing the statute brought about its pervasiveness and ultimate acceptability. For every threatened person able to make the arguments Haennig sought to validate, there might be another—or five or ten—who could not and hence who would be considered irrebuttably "Jewish." As long as the discursive parameters remained narrow and avoided attacking the very principle of racism head on, people were going to suffer at the hands of the legal system. And, indeed, the French bar (always, as we shall see in chapter 8, remarkably autonomous from governmental control) had by then taken the statute to its bosom, nurtured it, discovered its defects and its strengths, and—like the parents of a still youthful upstart—discussed its future with a combination of wariness and optimism.[135]

---

[135] Marrus and Paxton, *Vichy France and the Jews,* 143, have noted Joseph Haennig's description of German law as dealing more "objectively and broadmindedly" than the French cases. They opine that "this suggestion was not, to our knowledge, taken seriously by any French jurisdiction." They misunderstand, in that passage, that Haennig was trying to convince French courts that had *already* exceeded German jurisprudence on the burden of proof/evidentiary standard issue discussed in this section. Indeed, Haennig's superficially bizarre rhetoric continued to be necessary throughout the war to French lawyers urging more benign interpretations on their courts and colleagues.

# Chapter 3

# The Special Treatment of Jewish Legal Professionals

## A. Summer and Fall 1941: Laws of Exclusion, Special Arrests

One of the ways in which the statute of 2 June 1941 "completed" that of 3 October 1940 was in its special treatment of "the liberal professions." Whereas the earlier statute's Article IV permitted Jews access to such fields as law,[1] the ultimate religious law provided as follows:

> Article IV. Jews cannot exercise a liberal profession...except according to the limits and conditions that will be set by decrees of the Conseil d'État.[2]

So to the old scheme, which had definitively barred Jews from being magistrates or court-related functionaries, the 2 June law conjured sharp restrictions on practitioners who fell under the Vichy religious definitions. The early summer of 1941 must have been an anxious period for many lawyers, indeed for many clients who had come to rely on professional advice or on courtroom advocacy from people whose livelihoods were now at risk.

Law students, as well as all others seeking higher education, needed to wait only a fortnight longer to learn of the three percent *numerus clausus*

---

[1] R. Sarraute and P. Tager, *Les Juifs sous l'Occupation: Recueil des textes officiels français et allemands* (Paris: CDJC, 1982), 20.
[2] Ibid., 50.

decreed by Vichy on all university student populations.[3] With exceptions envisioned for long-established French families ("vieille souche"—typically families tracing their roots in France back at least five generations), Jewish students would have to line up and plead for admission before a statutorily-mandated faculty committee (named by the Dean).

> Article I. The number of Jewish students permitted to inscribe each year to study on a faculty, school, or institute of higher education cannot exceed 3% of non-Jewish students inscribed for that same year during the prior academic year. (Law of 21 June 1941)

The other shoe was to drop on 16 July, with the promulgation of the following decree:

> Article I. The number of persons defined in Article I of the law of 2 June, 1941, admissible to be a lawyer ["avocat"], may not exceed, in the jurisdiction of each Court of Appeals, 2% of the total of non-Jewish lawyers inscribed at the Bar of each jurisdiction.
>
> In any case, the number of Jewish lawyers inscribed at the Bar may not exceed the number that was there inscribed before 25 June 1940.

The decree proceeded to carve out the usual exceptions (war veterans or those wounded in wars), adding the following laborious procedure in recognition of distinguished careers at the Bar:

> Those lawyers may also be maintained who, on the request of the given Bar association [conseil de l'ordre], after consent given by the Court of Appeal acting collectively, and on the proposal of the commissioner general on Jewish questions,[4] [are] authorized by the Minister of Justice in recognition of the eminent quality of their professional service.

---

[3] Ibid., 56. For a superb account of the internal French pressures resulting in the educational *numerus clausus,* see Claude Singer, *Vichy, l'Université et les Juifs* (Paris: Les Belles Lettres, 1992), chapter 2.

[4] The CGQJ had recently been formally created by the decree of 19 June 1941. Sarraute and Tager, *Recueil des textes,* 55, and it was thus that the present decree on lawyers—which originated with the CGQJ as an administrative arm of the Conseil d'État—was promulgated.

Article II required registration at the Bar by lawyers defined as Jewish, excepting only those who were still prisoners of war,[5] although the latter needed to register within two months of their being freed. Removal ("radiation") from the Bar would result from voluntary retirement or, once the numbers were amassed and calculated, from forced expungement. Fired Jewish lawyers were to be given two months notice. The elaborate process was to involve, in terms of enumerating all practitioners, the Bar associations, the courts of appeal and the public prosecutor's office, as well as the administrative officials named above.

Vichy's alacrity in dealing with the liberal professions—the doctors were to be similarly regulated a month later[6]—once again is not properly understood as bowing to German pressure. Although, as we shall shortly see, French lawyers *did* attract an unusual amount of attention from the occupiers during this period, restrictions on "foreign influences" in law and medicine had been contemplated by France during the 1930s and the "invasion of the semites" specifically bemoaned.[7]

Rather, and perhaps especially regarding lawyers, Vichy was responding to professional pressure to limit Jewish practice, and the régime had every reason to believe that its measures would be politically popular. Adequate proof of this is found in a *postwar* statement by Jacques Charpentier, the head of the Paris Bar during most of the war, and a man generally thought to have resisted both the Nazis and Vichy on many points of principle having to do with private lawyers. (Charpentier was Paul Reynaud's defense counsel at Riom, where he courageously chastised Pétain for interfering with the trial by prematurely issuing an edict of guilt.) But when it came to Jewish colleagues, or more specifically to those many Jewish lawyers who did not have distinguished careers or old-line families, Charpentier had this to say:

---

[5] A fair number of Jewish lawyers had been captured, along with tens of thousands of others fighting the Germans under the French flag during the "drôle de guerre" that ended with the fall of France and the creation of Vichy.

[6] Decree of 11 August 1941, Sarraute and Tager, *Recueil des textes,* 69.

[7] Claude Singer, "Les médecins juifs en France," seminar lecture, Sorbonne, 13 December 1992. In 1934, for example, Darquier de Pellepoix (the eventual second commissioner of the CGQJ during Vichy) was calling for legislation to loosen "the Jewish grip on the liberal and artistic professions." Michèle Cointet-Labrousse, *Vichy et le fascisme* (Paris: Editions complexe, 1987), 207. See also Marrus and Paxton, *Vichy France and the Jews* (New York: Basic Books, 1981), 160.

> At the Paris Bar, there had always been a Jewish problem. A number of refugees had a conception of justice very different from our own.[8]

Charpentier's association surely did not endorse overt racism, but his own words indicate that the ostracism of "strange" lawyers was not wholly antipathetic:

> Since 1940,[9] a law excluded the sons of such refugees from the profession of law. For several prior years, this type of measure was strongly desired by the Paris Bar.... Before the war, we were invaded by those recently naturalized, almost all of eastern origin, whose language was ridiculed by the Press, thus covering us with shame. They brought to the conduct of their practice the customs of their bazaars. In this respect, the Vichy policies comported with our own professional interests, but I only envisioned their application after the fact.[10]

Charpentier and his Bar Association, unlike the legal leadership in Belgium who strongly protested in a far less autonomous atmosphere the ostracism of their Jewish colleagues, abided the various statutes that persecuted many of their number.[11]

The Paris Bar's complex response to these laws of ostracism will be treated in chapter 8, but the basic approach is familiar to us. Like Joseph Haennig and Jacques Maury, Charpentier knew how to protest against other actions taken by Vichy against lawyers, and he felt empowered to do so articulately; like them, too, he found a way to formulate questions as to race on so low a level of generalization that it never amounted to a jugular attack upon the new laws. For Charpentier, the surprising thing was not the restrictive legislation; it was the application *ex post facto* of the new laws. Had he managed to be upset or at least surprised by the restrictions themselves, France's history relating to the legal profession might have been quite different.

---

[8] Jacques Charpentier, *Au Service de la Liberté* (Paris: Fayard, 1949), 151.

[9] Charpentier is referring here not so much to the law of 3 October 1940 as to the denaturalization initiatives such as the Vichy law of 10–11 September 1940 (*Journal officiel* No. 3315: "No one may remain on the list of lawyers at the Bar who does not have French nationality as descending from a French father.") See chapter 8, section A.

[10] Charpentier, *Au Service,* 127. His assessment of recently-admitted non-French Jewish lawyers was analogous; see chapter 8, section B.

[11] Bar Association of Brussels to German High Command, 19 November 1940, YV IV-203.

What did bother Charpentier was the *arrest* of several colleagues at the Paris Bar whose eminence in the field and whose respectable collegiality were unquestioned. Many of these were French—not foreign—and so the incidents challenged any complacent assumption that only the "riffraff" would be excised. And it is surely one of the stranger episodes of that summer of 1941 that found the Germans unusually interested in this single profession and its prominent Jewish exemplars. A full year prior to the mass roundups and the "Vel d'Hiv," scores of lawyers were randomly arrested, most at their domiciles, and sent to such local camps as Drancy or Compiègne.

The arrests of 20 and 21 August 1941 thrust many of these victimized lawyers into a vortex of emotional turmoil from which—even if they managed to regain their freedom—many would not recover. Meanwhile, various French negotiators attempted to appeal to the Germans for the release of selected lawyers. It was not until after the war that the Bar expressed its official affection and grief for *all* those who had been arrested:

> On 21 August, 1941, when the rumor floated that 40 of our colleagues had been arrested, although nothing except the fury of persecution itself commended them to the invader, we sensed by the rebellion of our consciences and the anxiety of our hearts, how spurious had been the illusions that had cushioned some of us.
>
> What danger did these peaceful men [and women] pose for an occupier certain of its victory? He [the occupier] had already carved them out of the civilized world, exempted them from all employment and stripped them of their goods [*sic*]. This condition, almost lower than that of ancient slaves, did not manage to satisfy his cruelty and his appetites....
>
> The abrupt awakening, the violent eruption of a hypocritical and brutal police, the frayed good-byes, the departure without any luggage for a terrifying unknown, the only certainty being of terrible treatment: this is what the survivors have told us of this ignominious roundup.[12]

Although somewhat inaccurate as to legal chronologies affecting Jews generally (many of those arrested had not been affected by the *numerus*

---

[12] "Discours prononcé par M. Marcel Poignard, Bâtonnier de l'ordre des avocats, à la mémoire des avocats à la cour de Paris morts pour la France (1939–45), 11 July 1946" (Paris: Imprimerie du Palais, 1946), 22–23 (henceforth Poignard's eulogies; available at the archives of the Palais de Justice).

*clausus* and few had been stripped of property) and as to the source of these woes (still ascribed almost exclusively to the Germans), the postwar eulogies were moving and tell us that the legal community did feel the repercussions of these arrests. In large measure, it was the sheer prominence of many on the following list that unsettled their colleagues:

> Théodore Bernard, Edmond Bloch, Pierre Masse, Marcel Bloch,[13] Jacques Franck, Léon Bzourowski, Jean Lévy-Hollander, Léon Netter, Marcel Uhry, Jacques Rosenthal, Théodor Valensi, Gaston Weill, Maurice Weill-Raynal, Claude Rosenthal, Henri Reitlinger, Henri Blaustein, Benjamin Veinstein, Edmond-Charles Kahn, Fischgrund, Pierre Lehmann, Jean Ignace, Marcus, J-P Mayer, André Cahen, Robert Bilis, René Kahn, Moise Taboul, Jean Weill, Paul Léon, Albert Ulmo, Maurice Azoulay, Elie Kowner, Gaston Crémieux, Gaston Strauss, Lucien Weill, François Montel, Boitel, Fain, Charles Maurice Garson, Marcel Skop, and (Cour de Cassation:) Lyon-Caen and Mayer.[14]

Others on the eulogist's list include Jean Oestreicher, Léon-Maurice Nordmann, René Bloch and his wife Odette Cahen-Bloch, Nelly Gaston-Bloch, Jean-François Bokanowski, Raymond Cahen, Kadmi Cohen, Claude Gompel, Lucien Haas, Maurice Hesse, René Idsowski, Léon Jacob, J-P Kahn, Marc Lauer, Odette Mayer, Louis Schmoll, Jean Schonfeld, Benoit Stein, Alfred Valensi and Yvonne Strauss.

Why lawyers? Although there had been random roundups and arrests in Paris from about the middle of May,[15] the late summer focus on lawyers almost uniquely finds the Germans singling out one field for special punition. Not only that, but for the first time in the still fledgling game of arrest and deportation, the August roundups of lawyers saw French nationals imprisoned, among them individuals of great prominence. Three themes in the German understanding of law and lawyers, both more generally and as regards the specific French situation, may help explain these arrests:

---

[13] The Germans later released "der jüdische Rechstsanwalt Marcel Bloch" as being "blind since birth." CDJC V-48.

[14] Culled from AN $AJ^{38}$, no. 7, this list is in rough conformity with others, such as Poignard's eulogy, or the "Liste des avocats détenues par les autorités allemands," CDJC CVIII-10.

[15] Georges Wellers, André Kaspi and Serge Klarsfeld, eds., *La France et la Question juive, 1940/44* (Paris: Sylvie Messinger, 1981), 62.

1. Germanic distrust of lawyers;
2. Association of some French lawyers with "subversive" causes;
3. Use of arrested French Jewish professionals as bargaining tools with opinion makers in the field of law.

The Third Reich started its own campaign against Jewish lawyers very early in the régime. A "Law regarding admission to the Bar" was passed on 7 April 1933,[16] permitting rapid and immediate dismissals of Jewish lawyers (with exceptions for pre-1914 admissions or for active service or family-related deaths in World War I). The Nazis, who tended to proceed—much like the French—within the seeming traditions and even forms of law, never felt (as did the French) comfortable with the letter of the law itself as a valid mainstay of folk values; this led them to question the more positivistic French approach to the religious laws, even when such laws surpassed in their scope the reach of their own statutory models. No wonder that they moved so rapidly in their own country to undermine any Jewish influence over a profession that they already distrusted.[17] To the extent Jewish lawyers may have survived professionally until as late as the outbreak of hostilities, they were often formally banned from participating in key corporate or litigious circumstances.[18]

The Nazis' special focus on law carried over to the conquered territories, but perhaps nowhere more so than in France, upon whose legal system they came so much to rely. Earlier in 1941, they had granted permission for the use of German-speaking French lawyers in cases before military courts, and a Parisian lawyer named Stoeber had in fact represented French defendants in Nantes. As we have already seen and shall discuss more fully in chapter 6, the Germans exhibited a kind of love-hate relationship with the French legal system generally, but their approach to Jewish influence on law was of course another matter. Throughout the war, they maintained with the CGQJ (only recently created when the Paris arrests took place) a special file called *Jüdische*

---

[16] CDJC XV-44, English translation from postwar trials.

[17] For superb surveys of German legal behavior under the Third Reich, see Ingo Müller, *Hitler's Justice* (Cambridge MA: Harvard, 1991); and David Richards, "Terror and the Law," *Human Rights Quarterly* 5 (1983): 171–85; see chapter 10.

[18] See, e.g., postwar description of ministerial meeting of 15 March 1938, in which it was determined that "Paragraph 157: Jewish lawyers will not be used to defend I. G. [Farben] interests," CDJC CLIX-38.

*Rechtsanwälte.*[19] And, although the denaturalization and *numerus clausus* initiatives came exclusively from Vichy, it was a German drive to reduce that influence that apparently led to the late summer and subsequent arrests of lawyers during 1941.

The French authorities seem to have understood the August arrests as answering Nazi fears of subversive behavior by at least some Jewish lawyers. The minutes of the weekly interministerial meeting, held on 26 August, of the various French agencies in Paris, described the situation as follows:

> Jews—Arrests. The representative from the Ministry of Interior noted that the German authorities have undertaken vast operations against Jews whom they consider to be particularly responsible for communist agitation. The roundups that have taken place have for the first time included French Jews. They have been directed not only at Jews who might themselves participate in communist agitation but also at controlling elements (rich or intellectual Jews).
>
> The arrest of a significant number of lawyers is particularly noteworthy, including lawyers inscribed at the Cour de Cassation, at the Court of Appeals and before the Conseil d'État.
>
> The General Delegation has protested against the arrests of the most notable of these individuals. The German authorities have responded that orders from above are involved and that the decision had been made to decapitate the leadership of the Jewish masses [décapiter l'encadrement de la masse juive].[20]

A myth that we saw prevalent at Riom—the perverse influence of Jewish leaders and the poisoning through subversion of their followers and hence of all of French culture—glimmers through this memorandum. In this sense, the arrest of prominent Jews would follow quite naturally from the dismissals and the quotas that had been part of Vichy policy from the beginning.[21] Of course, the French delegation would not articulate any such connection of German arrests to their own policies, but the proceedings at Riom (well into its preliminary investigation of leaders such as Blum at the time) also constituted a "decapitation" attempt.

Arrests of lawyers to satisfy German fears of subversive activities were to continue over the next few months, although there was no evidence

---

[19] See, e.g., memorandum, SS to the CGQJ, 9 September 1942, CDJC XXIII-7.

[20] CDJC CII-8a.

[21] Wellers et al., *La France,* 61–65.

that the Germans intended to round up "all the Jewish lawyers residing in Paris," as a later interior ministry document exaggeratedly put it.[22] On 11 December, sixteen prominent lawyers were arrested, most while taking their lunch near their offices.[23] These joined a handful of lawyers who had already fallen as part of the German plan to take prominent leaders as hostages against "terrorist" attacks on German personnel. Three from the earlier group, the lawyers Georges Pitard, Michel Rolnikas, and Antoine Hajje, were to be eulogized after the war as martyrs of 19 September 1941:

> What was their crime? That of having professed a political belief to which they ardently adhered? Or that, even more grave, of remaining faithful to their professional mission of defending their comrades? The hypocrisy of their executioners claimed that they were punishing adherence to a detested (because redoubtable) party. We must restore to the drama its true sense.
>
> Yes! All three were involved in social and political idealism for which they preserved their enthusiasms and their strength; and they were considered dangerous because they were known to be incapable of renunciation or weakness.
>
> But above all they were lawyers. Their speech was free and they pleaded undisguisedly.... They stepped to the bar, especially in the criminal courtrooms, where those they defended were unpopular. They spoke with fervor: they denounced intolerance, and they exclaimed their passion for justice.... Taken as hostages, just before being shot at the fortress of Ivry during a feeble dawn of day, they addressed to their professional leader [à leur Bâtonnier] moving farewells that resonate still for us as we read them, with appeals to the freedom of defending others that these executioners could never stifle.[24]

It is surely true that the organized French Bar was moved by the arrests, and certainly the shootings, of their left-leaning members. Thus Jacques Charpentier, head of the Paris Bar Association, would receive with compassion and admiration, such pre-execution letters as that of the communist Hajje, who offered himself "for the profession that I have loved."[25] The individual fates of early resistance leaders from the left

---

[22] Memorandum, 18 September 1941, CDJC CII-8b.

[23] Wellers et al., *La France,* 64.

[24] Poignard's eulogy, 11 July 1946.

[25] Charpentier, *Au Service,* 157.

such as Léon-Maurice Nordmann also caught Charpentier's attention and sympathy.[26] Nordmann, arrested in January 1941 for distributing tracts and for attempting to join de Gaulle in London, was first sentenced to six months detention but eventually executed in late February 1942.[27] But the Bar's attitude to radical activities largely paralleled their ambiguous reaction to the "Jewish question" writ large. Hence, Charpentier, who spoke after the war of the "bazaar"-like atmosphere created by most foreign Jewish members of the Bar, said this about the communist alternative to fascism:

> I had every reason to fear that under their control the place Vendôme would become a subsidiary of Moscow [la place Vendôme ne devînt une succursale de Moscou].[28]

The 1941 arrests surely were connected in the German (and French) mind to the advocacy—or the mere defense—of left-wing subversion. No profession offered as tempting a target to those who wished to cut off this kind of "Jewish" influence—which we have placed here under the general symbol of Léon Blum as outsider—more broadly. Yet the most prominent of the arrested lawyers were hardly terrorists or even necessarily left-wing idealists in the sense just expressed. The Paris press delighted instead in emphasizing the wealth of "ces juifs millionnaires," now imprisoned with their less fortunate co-religionists in Drancy.[29] Photos of Weill, Valensi, Azoulay, Ulmo, Crémieux, Edmond Bloch, and perhaps especially Pierre Masse, filled the public eye in September 1941, along with descriptions of the life in prison these men were leading (painted to seem far less atrocious than it was).[30] They were all part of the original roundup of the month before, and their fates varied widely from that of the lawyers who were arrested as hostages and usually murdered within a short period on French soil.

It was around these prominent individuals that the German desire to affect public opinion eventually focussed. For, although Jacques Char-

---

[26] Ibid., 175.

[27] See postwar eulogy for Nordmann by Lucienne Scheid at the Bibliothèque des avocats, Palais de Justice, 183.

[28] Charpentier, *Au Service*, 225.

[29] *Paris Soir*, 12 September 1941, 1, headline. For full text see Richard Weisberg, *Poethics* (New York: Columbia University, 1992), Appendix 14.9.

[30] *Le petit Parisien*, 12 September 1941.

pentier's words about foreign Jewish lawyers color adversely the Bar's postwar claim that "Nowhere, even in France, was the indignation [at these arrests] more keen than at our Bar, supreme rampart of liberty,"[31] and although no formal protest ever was mounted by the Bar against their Jewish colleagues' treatment,[32] private delegations of lawyers *did* appeal to the Germans on behalf of some of those arrested. One quick result of this contact was the release of the blind lawyer, Marcel Bloch, whose prison spot was immediately filled by an engineer with exactly the same name.[33] But other negotiations were more complicated.

The sensitivity of the arrests concerned the Germans on the highest levels. In October, von Bose wrote to "Jewish Question" specialist Carl-Theodor Zeitschel, and the latter then also reported to Dannecker, that the release of certain Jewish lawyers would have the ironic effect of appeasing important segments of antisemitic French opinion at the Bar. Such prominent lawyers as Aulois, Vallier, and Mettetal, led by Cathala, were asking for the release of six of the arrested Jews: Jacques Franck, Edmond Bloch, Weill-Raynal, Montel, Ulmo, and Edmond Kahn.[34] The Germans felt that releasing these six would mollify many whose sympathies already extended to Vichy policies, but who were aggrieved to see such colleagues arrested. Zeitschel gave his theoretical blessing to their freedom (in some cases, temporary), noting that the French brought a punctiliousness to law that such a gesture would flatter. Ulmo, Franck, and Kahn were released.

---

[31] "Discours de M. Poignard," 29. For the Bar's true story, see chapter 8.

[32] Charpentier claims to have protested privately the arrest of the forty through French channels, through a note to Jacques Bardot, whom Vichy had placed in charge of its constitutional reform project. There is no documented record of the actual protest letter and apparently no aftermath affecting the lawyers' fates; see Charpentier, *Au Service,* 154.

[33] Memorandum, Paris Gestapo to Zeitschel, 5 January 1942, CDJC (YV) V-48, 3.

[34] See memorandum of von Bose (himself a lawyer), Legal Counsel to the German Ambassador in Paris, 5 October 1941. In that memo, von Bose reports to the Gestapo that he had been visited by these lawyers (Pierre Cathala was to be finance minister and Félix Aulois was named to Pétain's Council of Political Justice) who had asked that some of the more prominent of the forty arrested lawyers be released from Drancy, "in the interests of antisemitism." The French lawyers' reasoning appears to have been that, with so many mediocre, "undesirable" Jewish lawyers still free, the average French lawyer might be disgusted to see these prominent ones imprisoned, and the arrests might "inspire pity in a segment of their antisemitic colleagues," CDJC, VI-138.

On the other hand, the memos seem to indicate that a deal was cut that would permit further arrests of "less desirable" lawyers, and indeed that happened, as we noted. Furthermore, as of November, although Ulmo, Franck and Kahn had been released, Edmond Bloch remained in detention, and others (like René Bloch and his wife, alleged to be known Communist lawyers) were still at large. Others, such as the socialist Gaston Strauss, never emerged from Drancy. His fate was described after the war by an admiring colleague:

> Everything was falling apart around him, his country captured by barbarians.... He took consolation in his profession and in waiting for revenge. No more than most of us did he think he was running a risk as a Jew, because he was French. He wore his yellow star with pride because it was a star and because it distinguished him from the race of the conquerors who had imposed it.[35]
>
> On 19 August, 1941, his daughter, who had unhesitatingly crossed the demarcation line and who brought him his final joys, begged him to leave with her. The next day he was arrested and interned at Drancy. One of his cellmates paints a disturbing picture of him, which describes his stupor and his bitterness. It is as though he had just perceived that life was worse than he had judged it to be, and he was discovering with sad surprise a reality that far surpassed his expectations.
>
> A bit later, he was sent towards Germany. No one will ever know where or when he would be massacred, along with an entire trainful of outlaws, crammed together like beasts being sent to the slaughterhouse....
>
> So Gaston Strauss, my friend, executed like a guilty convict, an entire life devoted to Justice was incapable of keeping you from the tragic end that fate should have preserved to wrongdoers. But in succumbing, you have merited the citation on the tables of our Association, "Died for France through Deportation."[36]

---

[35] Since the German order requiring Jews to wear the Star of David in the Occupied Zone was not effective until 15 March 1942, this detail may be an anachronism on the part of the speaker. Remaining Jewish lawyers at the Palais de Justice did have to wear the star on their robes while pleading, but this seems to have been after the arrest and deportation of Strauss.

[36] "Discours de M. le Bâtonnier Marcel Héraud pour Gaston Strauss (1946)," available at the Palais de Justice, Bibliothèque des avocats, 423–24.

And what of Ulmo, Franck, and Kahn? The first two—released as a result of the negotiations[37]—did not survive the war. Albert Ulmo, distinguished lawyer and war veteran, was to be arrested again and deported. Jacques Franck, whose health had been very poor since early in the year, and who was inconsolable despite his release and worried for the welfare of his family, jumped out his office window at the Palais.[38] Edmond-Charles Kahn was re-arrested and deported.[39] The husband and wife attorneys, René Bloch and Odette Cahen-Bloch, whose provisional release was so resented because of their alleged communist leanings, were both re-arrested and deported.[40]

Perhaps the most distinguished of those arrested in August was Pierre Masse, the descendant of a soldier decorated by Napoléon I whose vieille souche Lorraine family had already lost seven members during the brief war against Nazi Germany. Somewhat like Léon Blum, he was noted for his broad culture:

> Always superior to the tasks he set for himself, he traversed and was familiar with all humane fields. Literature and the arts found in him an *amateur* and an enlightened defender, at the same time as legal problems of exceptional complexity drew him into arduous investigations.
>
> A certain judgment, an unbelievable quickness in seizing difficulties and discovering the salient point, a profound knowledge of legal science, and a keen psychological sense allowed him to be ready to plead—without lateness or apparent fatigue—more important matters than anyone had ever taken on before.[41]

As summer turned to fall and winter approached, Pierre Masse was to meet his fate as a deportee with courage, writing to Charpentier on 14 December 1941 that "I will die for my country, my faith, and my pro-

---

[37] The negotiations included such tactics as bringing forth Jacques Franck's World War I records and presenting to the Germans documents describing his heroism and his receipt of the Croix de guerre with palme, Roussilon to de Brinon, 6 October 1941, YV VI-14.

[38] See postwar eulogy of Jacques Franck by Maurice Alléhaut, available at Bibliothèque des avocats, Palais de justice, 229–34. Alléhaut notes that "The lawyers' room (Cell 4), was the only one in those dark early days of Drancy in which spirit reigned.... Only the lawyers regained themselves and, from their souls, showed a strong face," ibid., 221.

[39] Serge Klarsfeld, *Vichy/Auschwitz* (Paris: Fayard, 1983), 26, note 1.

[40] See Poignard's eulogies, 11 July 1946, tables of those lawyers who died in deportation, and 23–24.

[41] Poignard's eulogies, 25.

fessional community [mon Ordre]."[42] But even as regards the arrest and deportation of a man like Pierre Masse, Charpentier and his Bar Association could not find a way to raise a formal voice of protest. (There were many antisemites at the Bar, Charpentier later would confess, and many who were already earning fees as administrators of Jewish property.)[43] Still, Charpentier personally remained in close touch with his revered colleague, and the complicated story of the Bar chief's personal response to Drancy, and his ensuing rupture with Vichy on many issues, awaits a detailed account in chapter 8.[44]

Meanwhile, Pierre Masse was interviewed by Dannecker, but unlike several of his colleagues for whom negotiations were secretly attempted by French lawyers, Masse did not gain his release. Yet he maintained his optimism throughout the Drancy horror; as Charpentier was to put it:

> Like many of his co-religionists, he had a messianic faith that sustained him.... I never saw Pierre Masse again. They took him in one of their trains—from Compiègne—their cargo condemned to death.[45]

Thus before the large-scale roundups of July 1942, which involved for the most part stateless Jews and their children, Jewish lawyers of French and foreign nationality became a single focus for Nazi oppression. Pierre Masse epitomizes the vulnerability of all Jews at the time, whatever their citizenship status or position in society. Their arrest by French police, their experiences at Drancy, the equivocal nature of the reaction of their peers, and the doleful end to which most of these lawyers came, stand as a remarkable and fitting early paradigm for law and the legal profession under Vichy.

## B. Subsequent Arrests of Legal Professionals

On 27 March 1942, the first convoy left French soil (*ex* Compiègne) for Auschwitz.[46] Among their number were several of the arrested lawyers

---

42 Charpentier, *Au Service,* 157.

43 Ibid., 151–2; see also 97.

44 Ibid., 154.

45 Ibid. Masse is also the subject of chapter 7, notes 115–18.

46 Klarsfeld, *Vichy/Auschwitz,* 59.

from the prior year.[47] Making the same tragic trip were many individual lawyers, some of whose representative stories will be told chronologically in the bulk of this sub-section. Just before Convoy 1 left the Paris environs, a decorated lawyer named Laemle and a provincial notary[48] named Bloch were transferred along with 176 other Jews from the camp at Royallieu to Drancy to await deportation. Police Commissioner Bielle of the Compiègne camp noted that "100 French gendarmes" had assisted with the transfer.[49] The use of French police for arrest[50] and transport within France of Jews was by then commonplace if not universal. At age 65, Laemle could boast of a distinguished career at the Algerian Bar and admittance to the Court of Appeals in Paris; he had received the Legion of Honor. Most favorably for his chances of release, Laemle was married to an Aryan.[51] All of these facts were pointed out in a written memorandum from the Minister of Justice's office in Vichy to the French ambassador in Paris. Laemle himself did not hesitate to protest loudly, while he waited on line for transfer to Compiègne: "This is what it has come to. And yet one remains French nonetheless." Brielle reports that, upon this pronouncement, someone in the crowd of onlookers offered the aging lawyer two bars of chocolate. It was the only succor that Laemle was to receive.

---

[47] Serge Klarsfeld, *Memorial to the Jews Deported from France, 1942–44* (New York: Beate Klarsfeld Foundation, 1983), 1, notes that Convoy 1 included "in part...foreign Jews arrested in Paris in the round-ups of...August 20, 1941 [and]...French Jews arrested in their homes on December 12, 1941." (Recall that a second group of lawyers was arrested around that date in Paris.)

[48] Throughout this book, I will be recounting histories not only of lawyers (avocats, avoués) but also of the unique European figure—part lawyer but mostly designated functionary for wills and real estate conveyances—the notary (notaire).

[49] Note of 20 March 1942, YV VI 140.

[50] Accord, Charpentier, *Au Service,* 230. Most if not all of the forty prominent lawyers arrested in their homes in August were taken by Parisian police, in full uniform, using such formulae as "You are the Jew, Jacques Franck? Follow me," as found in the eulogy by Maurice Alléhaut.

[51] Laemle's case is noted in interministerial documents around the middle of 1942 where, for example, his name is mentioned among ex-magistrates currently "interned at Drancy," AN BB[30], 1714. For the diminishing importance to the French of Laemle's mixed marital status, see discussion, chapter 2, of the basic French religious statutes, under which the German interest in the race of one's spouse became largely irrelevant for Vichy purposes.

As to the notary Bloch, there, too, and not uncommonly, the Minister of Justice gathered a small file. The procureur général of the Besançon Court of Appeals informed the ministry that, on 10 March, "during his absence" (a common euphemism for arrest), Bloch had been replaced in his functions by a certain Jean Rossel. The tribunal civil of Montbelliard had so decreed.[52] As in hundreds of other cases relating to Jewish careers in the French legal system, dismissal, arrest, and deportation followed hard one upon the other (arrest sometimes preceding dismissal). From these beginnings until the very end of the occupation—as late as November 1944, Jewish servants of the court system suffered arrest, special treatment by the infamous Milice, deportation, and death. All three Vichy Ministers of Justice (Alibert, Barthélemy, and Gabolde) took note of the effect of such attrition on Vichy law. Perhaps because of this, we have many individual stories of arrested magistrates like Laemle.

On 19 September 1942, career government attorney Adrien Sée and his wife—"tous deux de race juive"—were arrested. Sée, a former public prosecutor in the town of Orléans who had begun his service to the law in 1904, was not to go quietly into the long dark night of deportation. Indeed, a year earlier, he had formally requested a "dérogation" (or exception) under Article 8 of the law of 2 June 1941. At the time, he would have had to fill out a standard form justifying his exemption from the rigors of the religious law. His claim for professional reinstatement followed his official dismissal from the Orléans court system, announced for all to see in the *Journal officiel*.[53] Now he was fighting for his life, and on essentially the same legalistic grounds. Propounding the case for the release of Sée and his wife, a certain Guernier wrote as follows to the Vichy justice ministry:

> I ask you to turn your gracious attention as quickly as possible to the request made to the Justice Minister by honorary first president[54] Adrien Sée, in which he seeks to benefit from the exceptions of Article 8 of the law of 2 June, 1941, including those for Jews whose families have been established in France for at least five generations and who have rendered to France exceptional service. These seem to hold true for Adrien Sée, whose

---

[52] YV VI 140.

[53] AN $BB^{30}$, 1712.

[54] This was the title given to Sée in the *Journal Officiel* when he was dismissed as public prosecutor.

> French ascendancy goes back five generations and at least since 1705, including generals, high officials and scholars whose merits have been recognized by every régime....
>
> The sense of high equity that has inspired the text of Article 8 is fully satisfied in the case of first president Sée.[55]

Sée's case for exceptional status, like the vast majority of such requests by legal professionals, did not succeed.[56] Prior to his arrest, the patience of the bureaucracy had seemed to wear thin, as the new public prosecutor at Orléans remarked in writing to the justice ministry that Sée "did not bother to respond" to a request made of him by his former employer.[57]

Arrest and deportation, like dismissal from one's post in the legal profession, was often a matter of case-by-case scrutiny. Thus Pierre Isaac, arrested on 13 March 1943,[58] like Sée, had his own file in the ministry of justice. Born in 1906, Isaac had built a short but apparently successful career as an assistant judge and legal draftsman (magistrat/substitut de 2[e] classe), "appreciated by his superiors and enjoying the universal sympathy of his colleagues." As early as July 1942 (nine months before his arrest), the ministry of justice was noting:

> Remarkably gifted and intellectually brilliant, this magistrate also possesses true juridical knowledge, the fruit of judicial experience acquired at trial level cases.... Attentive to all legal questions and unwilling to be stumped by even the hardest, he participates actively in the study and preparation of legislative texts. His work is done with care; his style is clear and concise.[59]

The cause of his arrest, which took place in Vichy, was due "essentially to his belonging to the Jewish race and to his affiliation with a Catholic group suspected of anti-German maneuvers." The records indi-

---

55 AN BB[30] 1712.

56 Of well over a hundred applications for dérogation mentioned in AN BB[30] 1716, only seven succeeded in bringing some relief to the applicant under Article 8 of the 2 June statute. The Paris Bar association recommended maintaining fourteen of its number on the lists for exceptional professional merit; none was eventually permitted. Memo, archivist, Bar Association of the City of Paris to author, Serge Klarsfeld, and another researcher, 6 January 1992, 3. See also chapter 8.

57 AN BB[30] 1716.

58 AN BB[30], 1712.

59 AN BB[30], 1715.

cate that Joseph Barthélemy—the Justice Minister himself—became aware of the arrest immediately, and indeed Isaac was released and thought the matter finished.

Unfortunately, he was re-arrested the very next day, and for about a year no one heard of him again. There is evidence that Barthélemy intervened, but to no avail. As late as February 1944, the Vichy justice ministry took note that "neither his family nor his administrative employer has been able to find out anything about his fate." However, on 17 November 1944, on "a list of magistrates deported to Germany," Pierre Isaac's name appears one final time.[60]

Another such case was Pierre Isidore Lévy, a law clerk at the Conseil d'État; a Parisian, Lévy was en route through Vichy when he was arrested on 7 July 1943:

> He seems to have been considered a Jew, the certificate of non-Jewishness he received earlier having just been removed by the CGQJ.[61]

Lévy apparently argued without success that his wife (née Latreuille) was an Aryan and would prove—if contacted—that he was indeed not Jewish.

Although we have just noted that the highest levels of Vichy government established files and sometimes actively intervened for some Jewish legal functionaries, the vast majority of clear-cut Jewish magistrates and court assistants had been fired or placed on early retirement by that same government. Now, these individuals were being arrested in great numbers, both in Vichy and in the northern zones. Adrien Sée had been one of these. So were former magistrates Coen and Blum (the latter arrested as "a Jewish hostage after unknown individuals had been seen distributing Communist tracts").[62]

For most Jewish lawyers, judges, functionaries, and legal assistants, the fight for life and death that failed in 1943 and 1944 began as a struggle for *professional* survival in 1940 and 1941. How many "anciens magistrats" like Coen and Blum, or their lower-level assistants such as clerks, or even court-appointed translators[63] had been living as outcasts, fired

---

[60] AN $BB^{30}$, 1712.

[61] AN $BB^{30}$, 1712.

[62] AN $BB^{30}$, 1712.

[63] As early as 6 February 1941, the justice ministry signed an order honoring the request of the Occupation authorities "to stop court translations by Jewish expert-translators"; some fifteen people were immediately affected by the directive. AN $BB^{30}$, 1712.

by Vichy from their jobs due to Vichy's earliest legislation; how many practicing lawyers dismissed and removed from the lists at their bar association because of Vichy naturalization laws or the *numerus clausus* implemented by the law of 17 July 1941! We turn now to the official policies toward Jews desperately trying to continue their careers in the midst of the nightmare.

## C. Vichy Policy towards Jews Providing Legal Services

The *numerus clausus* for lawyers permitted some small percentage of Jewish lawyers to continue to practice in each Bar Association's territory. A tiny number of Jewish law students was matriculated as well. But, unless able to satisfy the rigorous requirements for an "exception" to Article 2 of the law of 2 June 1941, *no* Jew was permitted to serve as a government functionary "de la cour de cassation, la cour des comptes...des cours d'appel, des tribuneaux de première instance, des justices de paix, des tribuneaux répressifs d'Algérie, de tous jurys...etc."[64]

From the uppermost echelons of France's two highest courts—the Cour de Cassation and the Conseil d'État—to the lowliest justice of the peace, and to all their assistants, the blanket Vichy policy against Jewish personnel retained its full force and scope. Even in the darkest days of dangerously reduced judicial personnel—for Vichy was a litigious society in a time of low morale and low salaries for its judges[65]—Vichy at the highest levels refused to accept any Jewish talent available to help in its midst. An interesting and typical example of this obsessional and self-defeating racism arose in mid-July 1942, when various courts asked if dismissed or retired Jewish lawyers could be used even temporarily to assist with pending trials. Joseph Barthélemy, whose justice ministry we

---

[64] Law of 2 June 1941, Sarraute and Tager, *Recueil des textes,* 49f. See below, note 66.

[65] A Vichy memorandum of 17 February 1943 is typical in its request for more judges as it points out that litigation has increased dramatically—in part because of "the complexity of recent legislation"—so that in the criminal court in Montpellier, for example, 966 cases were adjudicated in 1938 compared to 2,980 in 1942; in Limoges 696 rising to 2,502; in Bordeaux, 2,557 rising to 4,601; and in Quimper, 389 rising to 990. AN $BB^{30}$, 1715.

saw operating to intervene in certain cases of arrest, joined with the Conseil d'État to answer their request in the negative:

> The question has been posed to my cabinet agency whether Jewish avocats or avoués...can be called to supplement judges under conditions prescribed in [various laws dating back to the Revolution and to Napoléon I]. The Conseil d'État, at its meeting of 30 December, 1941, adopted an approach to this question.... Strict adherence to its approach should be maintained.
>
> Conseil d'État.... The Justice Minister having authorized the Section on legislation, justice and foreign affairs of the Conseil d'État to deal with the question...In view of the decree of 30 March, 1808; of those of 16 July, 1941 regulating the profession of lawyer (no 2956) and the functions of public or ministerial office (no. 2957); of the law of 2 June, 1941 dealing with the status of Jews...; Considering that...*avocats* or *avoués* cannot be designated to serve on courts if they are affected by a legal incapacity so to serve such as that now relating to Jews...[Such service is prohibited.][66]

The extreme irony of finding Jewish legal talent rebuffed absolutely when Vichy litigation was increasing by a factor sometimes of 4:1 over prewar figures is exacerbated when we realize that part of the litigiousness of the period *was a direct result of new laws on Jewish status!*[67] Yet, from the earliest weeks in 1941, Justice Ministry documents begin to track judicial "resignations, deaths, and retirements" as follows:

> For the Tribunal de la Seine. Judge Durkheim, Jew;
> Councillor, Nancy. Meiss, Jew;
> Councillor, Algiers. Journau, Jew;
> Councillor, Rabat. Jean, retired;
> Assistant, Toulon. Sudaka, Jew;
> Judge, Belfort. Franck, Jew....[68]

At around the same time, the simple marking "Law of 3 October 1940" was used to explain the "retirement" of such Alsatian Jewish magistrates as Brunschwig, Lang, Lehmann, G. Lévy, Loeb, Mayer, and Samuel.[69]

---

[66] CDJC CCXVI-18

[67] See, on this decision, J. Lubetzki, *La Condition des juifs en France sous l'Occupation allemande* (Paris: CDJC, 1945), 52. For further decisions by Barthélemy about Jewish magistrates and lawyers, see chapter 4, note 158; on the crisis in the Vichy magistracy, see chapter 5, notes 59–60.

[68] Vichy memo, 28 January 1941, AN $BB^{30}$ 1712.

[69] Ibid.

Still in the heavily German-influenced eastern regions, a local memo at Mulhouse notes that a certain regional judge named Neher is "a well regarded magistrate," but a handwritten addendum in red pencil observes "Israelite à signaler à Vichy...mère Shomos [Jew, tell Vichy, mother Shomos]."[70]

The ministry of justice under the prewar liberal Joseph Barthélemy was unremitting in its denial of functionary positions to Jews, except in the very rare cases of "exceptions." As late as 2 April 1943, this cabinet agency needed to remind even the CGQJ that Jewish functionaries such as magistrates were to be terminated altogether; unlike private practitioners, government lawyers and judges were not redeemable by any *numerus clausus*. They were simply out:

> You have asked me by memo of 17 March if there were still Jews among the magistrates, and in the affirmative to send you two lists, the first containing those who are maintained according to the *numerus clausus* of the law of 2 June 1941, the second containing those satisfying one of the four conditions of Article 3 of that law.
>
> I feel I must remind you that Article 2 of the law of 2 June 1941 specifies that the access to and exercise of magisterial functions is prohibited to Jews, without reference to proportionality, and that the special exceptions [dérogations] of Article 3 of that law do not apply on their terms [to magistrates]. I therefore cannot send you either of the two lists.[71]

Fascinating in this exchange is the friction between Justice and the chief administrative agency on Jewish questions. Typically, as we shall see in the next chapter, that tension worked with the CGQJ bemoaning what it saw as too liberal a ministerial position on Jews, often expressed through the latter's support for civil court—as opposed to administrative— jurisdiction over basic Jewish matters; but here, CGQJ opens a window to quotas for Jewish magistrates and functionaries that Justice slams shut.

In effect, there were two very difficult and tortuous routes that a Jew needed to follow if he or she wished to pursue a legal career despite the religious laws. If a functionary, the sole possibility was to fall under one of the exceptions provided by Article 8 (not usually Article 3, as we have just seen) of the law of 2 June 1941. If a private legal professional, the recourse was either to Article 3 or Article 8 exceptions under the latter

---

[70] Ibid.

[71] CDJC CVIII-16a. See also chapter 4, note 156.

law, or to the *numerus clausus,* as established by the law of 16 July 1941 and spelled out from time to time by directive of the CGQJ, or to the recommendation of the local bar association under the terms of the 16 July law itself.

For the general exception outlined in Article 8 of the basic religious statute of 2 June 1941, an individual otherwise prevented from employment because Jewish must "have rendered to the French state exceptional service" or "have a family established in France for at least five generations that has rendered to the French state exceptional service." The statute sets out the procedure for such an exception, and individuals seeking one typically had to fill out something like the following questionnaire, responding, as to the first twelve questions, both for the paternal and maternal lines:

> DECLARATION towards application of the law of 2 June 1941 regarding the status of Jews:
> 1. Is your or was your grandfather a member of the Jewish religion?
> 2. If no, did he belong to another religion prior to 25 June 1940?
> 3. Indicate which religion (attach probative documents).
> 4-6. Is your or was your grandmother [same as first three questions]
> 7-12. [Same questions regarding grandparents of applicant's spouse]
> 13. Do you belong to the Jewish religion?
> 14. Did you belong to another religion prior to 25 June 1940?
> 15. Indicate which religion.
> 16. Can you take advantage of articles 3, 7 and 8 of the law of 2 June 1941 by claiming one of the following conditions:
> a. holding a *carte du combattant* [World War I];
> b. having been cited for *Croix de guerre;*
> c. holding the *Légion d'honneur* or the *Médaille militaire;*
> d. being a ward of the State; or
> e. having rendered exceptional service to the French State;
> f. having a family established in France for five generations and having rendered exceptional service to the French State.[72]

In practice applications for Article 8 treatment usually originated in Vichy. (Recall the files that had been set up in the justice ministry for certain magistrates who were eventually arrested; many poignant letters with detailed family histories were sent directly to Pétain.) If the ministry

---

[72] Numerous such declarations can be found in AN $BB^{30}$, 1716.

receiving the request found it spurious, the matter would end there. If there was potential merit of any kind, the ministry in question would forward the file to the CGQJ, even if its own judgment was that the request should be denied. (Under the law of 29 March 1941, as amended by that of 19 May 1941, the CGQJ was made the primary arbiter of Jewish questions.) If the CGQJ found merit, that agency then would forward the file to the vice president of the Conseil d'État—France's high administrative court and the immediate hierarchical superior to the CGQJ. Depending on the chief proponent of the request, if it was to be granted, either the ministry or the CGQJ would then prepare the official announcement (by formal "decree," the same formula used to announce most dismissals) of the exception.[73]

As to other fields barred to Jews, other openings for exception existed, specifically under earlier provisions of the 2 June statute.[74] But, as noted previously, judges and law-related government functionaries had to show individual exceptional service to France and demonstrate five generations of vieille souche French roots.

There remained some question as to the *scope* of the law's coverage: would even low level court employees be fired? An early example (still under the law of 3 October 1940) is representative of the difficulties throughout the war experienced by those like M. Ruben Auguste Posso, who had to leap the double hurdle imposed. Posso, a stenographer *(greffier)* with twenty years' seniority in the town of Bayonne, was summarily dismissed in April 1941 by a letter from the Justice Minister. He and his supervisor, M. Abadie, immediately wrote to the CGQJ; Abadie stressed his employee's service record, and Posso emphasized his family roots.

---

[73] Interior ministry memorandum, September 1941, CDJC CXIV-59a. The Conseil d'État's procedure for considering exceptions was elaborate in itself, assuming all other parts of the process had been satisfied to reach its jurisdiction. The vice president of the Conseil d'État would have to be petitioned; if satisfied that there was a colorable case for an exception, he would take the matter to the high counsel [haute assemblée] of the full body. If the latter granted the request, the exception would finally be ready for formal declaration, through a decree signed by Marshal Pétain and usually also by the justice minister, AN $BB^{30}$, 1714.

[74] See, e.g., CGQJ memorandum, November 1941, calling for an interministerial meeting to bring the kind of clarity to these fields that had been brought to the procedures for magistrate exceptions, CDJC XXIII-62.

First, part of Abadie's letter:

> Is it necessary that he be punished for the sins of others, when his own past of probity and selflessness speaks loud? I do not believe that this can be the spirit of the law. I ask that M. Xavier Vallat [first head of the CGQJ] examine personally this case.
>
> The members of the Tribunal of Bayonne are distressed at the departure of M. Posso, and if I am intervening on his behalf it is because I know him personally. It is thus my duty to describe his case to you and it would only be just to allow him to continue the functions he has always performed with such tact and conscientiousness.
>
> Also—is M. Posso truly a public functionary? He had to post a surety to perform his service as stenographer and he only receives a monthly disbursement of 300 francs; he has no right to a pension.
>
> I add that M. Posso is responsible for two children who are not in the best of health, his mother and his sister-in-law.[75]

Posso's handwritten letter of 16 April says in part:

> M. le commissaire général for Jewish questions. I thought that distinctions were going to be made for Jews of "vieille souche." This is why I am submitting to your wise attention my own case.... I am the head of a household involving the support of six people who live exclusively from my courtroom work....
>
> French, and descended from French, my family has been established either in Bayonne or Bordeaux for almost three centuries....[76]

Nine days later, the CGQJ answered Posso by letter: there would be no exception for him.[77]

Whenever breaches in its severe policy appeared, Vichy could count on court officials to bring them to its attention. Thus, in another case involving stenographers, Prosecutor General Joppe of the Court of Appeals in Tunis complained in 1943 to his superiors that a fired employee of the Justice of the Peace there had resurfaced in another registry and was back in contact with fellow workers and with the public at large:

> It is not a question of making the laws more rigorous but of asking frankly whether those laws are being applied uniformly.

---

75 CDJC CXV-10.

76 Ibid.

77 Ibid.

> One might ask oneself how the man in the street can understand an administration that fires a Jew only to take him back a few days later into another service of the same administration, preserving his salary and benefits that had just been stripped away...? Maybe this is a simple blunder, but after all there are blunders that just shouldn't happen.[78]

In fact, there was no good reason to bring stenographers, for example, under the absolute proscription of the statute barring Jews from government or magisterial service. As in so many other areas of Vichy law, the process of barring these human beings from their lifelong work derived from arbitrary and overly logical individual decisions. Thus as to greffiers, a predecessor to the Conseil d'État's eventual committee on Jewish

---

[78] CDJC LIV-6. French North Africa produced interesting variations on the *numerus clausus* theme. First, the *process* of extending it to Vichy's overseas territories involved careful legal planning, and originated at least as early as 29 May 1941, when the CGQJ formally requested that François Darlan's ministry take up the quota question for North Africa; see CDJC CX-47. In Algeria, the repressive law was established on 5 November of that year, and the dispute in the text for this note is not unique. A similar but undated and unsigned document from Algeria notes the phenomenon of Jewish lawyers retaining their influence and in fact continuing their practice through such guises as "turning the management of their practice over to Jewish colleagues maintained at the bar. They appear to be only assistants, but in fact they continue to greet their clients, prepare and even finish their cases, and sometimes even plead the matters as simple agents of their clients," CDJC CCXXXVII-80. The *numerus clausus* was established for Tunisia at 5% on 30 March 1942; see CDJC CVIII-9, and one was in place in Morocco around the same time. Some of these North African Vichy sites were liberated by late 1942. In a post-liberation assessment of February 1943, Moroccan authorities reported that 32 of 37 private lawyers had been thrown out under their *numerus clausus,* established by the law of 18 August 1941. They went on to blame the quotas exclusively on the French authorities in Vichy ("la France nazifiée"), noting that the Sultan and the Grand Vizier were only tools of that régime. Citing a tradition of equality dating to a law of 5 February 1864, the report states that "Sultan Sidi Mohamed formally and often assured notable Jews...that he considered them to be Moroccans fully equal to Moslems...." However, even after the Americans entered Morocco, specifically in November 1942, there were antisemitic outbreaks; Frenchmen were heard to shout "The Americans have come to avenge the Jews!" and "The American president is a Jew!" CDJC LXXXIV-12. Lubetzki, *La Condition des Juifs,* 51, recounts the North African case of a Jewish lawyer in Oran whose father could have claimed for him "ward of the nation" status, thus privileging him in the *numerus clausus* but failed to do so. When the lawyer turned to the Court of Appeals of Algiers, that body declined his request, saying that one who had reached his majority could no longer make a valid claim for that status, and the lawyer was removed from the lists of the bar association.

matters decided early and strangely that they did fall under the strictures of the racial restrictions. On 21 March 1941, the Conseil d'État opined that "The stenographer, by the nature itself of his functions, is so tied to the work of doing justice [!] that even though he is not a magistrate in the rigorous sense of the word, he is nonetheless one of the necessary auxiliaries to the tribunal."[79]

Somewhat more liberal was the Ministry of Justice's position on the *numerus clausus* and the various exemptions under the law of 16 July 1941[80] having to do with the private practice of law. Although the bulk of our discussion of quotas upon private practitioners will await chapter 8 of this study, some governmental aspects of the attack on Jewish lawyers are relevant at this point. For example, a law of 31 October 1941, not referring to any religious status,[81] permitted lawyers from the occupied zone who could justify their inability to regain their home base to inscribe at the bar of their new residence. In a typical struggle with the CGQJ, Barthélemy's office on 27 January 1942 proposed that certain lawyers who had not been inscribed at their local bar associations the prior July when the anti-Jewish law was passed—because, for example, earlier legislation had already removed them from such inscription[82]—might now re-enroll and become potential candidates for continuing practice under the *numerus clausus* for a new locality. Despite the October statute, the CGQJ prevailed in its somewhat draconian view that these already removed lawyers now had the status simply as applicants to the new bar; that they could not benefit from the exemptions envisioned by the 16 July statute (e.g., war veterans); and that they were not to be thought of as competitive in assessing the *numerus clausus*.[83]

The agency persevered with this policy but ran into trouble when testing it before certain courts. Thus, when four Marseilles Jews were removed from the bar association's list there, five Parisian lawyers temporarily in the southern zone attempted to resume practice by taking their place. The CGQJ indulged in statutory interpretation—this time

[79] AN $BB^{30}$, 1716.

[80] Sarraute and Tager, *Recueil des textes,* 58; see above, text at note 4.

[81] AN $BB^{30}$, containing *Journal Officiel,* 14 November 1941.

[82] See, e.g., the Vichy statute of 10 September 1940, eliminating from the practice any lawyer not born of a French father, discussed above at note 9.

[83] CGQJ to the Justice Minister, 18 February 1942; CDJC XXIII-3.

comparing the 31 October text with that of the 16 July law; an internal memo of 12 August 1942, bemoans the view of the Court of Appeals of Aix-en-Provence, which permitted the Parisian lawyers to join (temporarily) the Marseilles bar:

> This decision goes against the spirit and the letter of the law.... A bar can support a limited number of Jews, 2%. Above that, the Jewish element becomes threatening and can only be assimilated with great difficulty. If, on the other hand, one claims that the 2% has been fixed arbitrarily to show tolerance [!], it is hard to understand greater tolerance for lawyers coming from another city about whom people know neither their ancestors nor their habits, when the bar welcoming them has been obliged to let go from its association colleagues whom it has known for years.
>
> The letter of the law is equally violated [by the Aix court decision].... Article 2 of the law of 31 October 1941 stipulates that "The preceding sections do not apply to lawyers covered by the provisions of the decree of 16 July, 1941, No. 2956." Which again indicates clearly that lawyers from the occupied zone may ask for temporary inscription at the bar of their residence, but that Jewish lawyers may not benefit from these provisions.[84]

Vichy also tried to shut off other avenues to practice that Jewish lawyers strove to follow. To avoid lawyers "forum shopping" and moving to bar jurisdictions that had fewer Jewish lawyers and hence greater opportunities under the *numerus clausus,* it was decreed that the number of Jews inscribed at a given bar could in no case increase over the number already in place as of 25 June 1940.[85] Thus, even if there were fewer than 2 percent of Jewish lawyers compared to the population of Aryan lawyers in a given jurisdiction, lawyers seeking a slot could not capitalize on the situation if their candidacy would raise the absolute number of Jewish lawyers to more than had been there as of that specified date.[86]

Disputes about the *numerus clausus* between the CGQJ and the ordinary courts were legion, and Aix-en-Provence was not the only troublemaker from the agency's point of view. Beginning a debate that would involve many central Vichy players, the Court of Appeals of Limoges,

---

[84] CDJC CVIII-11/12.

[85] See Lubetzki, *La Condition,* 50.

[86] The date chosen was the same as for the religious statute of 2 June 1941 as the cut-off moment after which proof of belonging to another religion became irrelevant.

for example, had even more rapidly violated the spirit and letter of the quota laws by a decision of 14 November 1941. There, the court had affirmed the dismissal of a Maître Israel but had retained his colleague, Maître Schwob, who had apparently asked for temporary inscription, having fled his Mulhouse point of origin. The Regional Director of the Service of Economic Aryanization of Limoges (located at 8, rue des Coopérateurs in that town) hastily informed the CGQJ of the decision. CGQJ agreed with its service's view that "since there were no Jews inscribed in the jurisdiction of the court before 25 June 1940, the *numerus clausus* prescribed absolutely by Article I, paragraph two of the law of 16 July, 1941 must apply and M. Schwob cannot be maintained."[87]

What remedy did CGQJ have when it saw violations of quota laws—or the many other laws it oversaw as administrators of Jewish fates? The result in the Limoges situation was typical: it urged its informant to go to the district prosecutor and to ask that the matter be reopened in court. In other words, the CGQJ did *not* have ultimate authority to fix interpretations of laws regulating Jewish lawyers.

Dutifully, the district prosecutor took the Schwob matter under advisement. What could his office accomplish? After all, "The Court of Appeals, meeting *en banc,* rendered its November decision favorably to Maître Schwob, and gave him temporary inscription at the Limoges bar, finding that he was the holder of the *carte de combattant* of the '14-'18 war." The district prosecutor continues:

> The inscription of Maître Schwob has resulted, therefore, from a decision of the courts that has become *res judicata* ["la chose jugée"] and that does not seem to me to be currently attackable.

The prosecutor saw only the option of returning to the bar association the following year to urge that body to remove Schwob from the lists.[88]

Frustrated but self-righteous, the CGQJ decided in May to bring the matter directly to the attention of Joseph Barthélemy. "I must tell you," moaned the administrator, "that I cannot accept the legality of such a decision.... The decision of the Court of Appeals of Limoges is itself illegal. M. the district prosecutor believes that this decision has the status

---

[87] CDJC CX-176.

[88] CDJC XXIII-5.

of *res judicata*. But this view seems unacceptable to me, since this matter is not a dispute and hence cannot result in *res judicata*."[89]

Typically, the matter was becoming more and more legalistic, and the arguments used were increasingly based on traditions of French law long predating the racial scheme. Was the Limoges court's decision absolutely binding on the case as *res judicata* [the matter has been determined] or was the decision merely advisory, since it did not involve a case or controversy but rather merely a determination of the appropriateness of the bar association's decision relating to Schwob? French analysis of matters of career, of property, of life and of death remained rigorously legalistic and indicated the ability of the system to thrive *internally* and to devour the new subject of race as though it were not at all a foreign organism.[90]

Joseph Barthélemy took up the Schwob matter and replied to the CGQJ on 8 July 1942. In this prewar liberal's most liberal formal pronouncement on the religious laws, the Justice Minister fully supported the court's decision in permitting Schwob's inscription at Limoges. First of all, Barthélemy read the conflicting statutes as giving refugee Jewish lawyers the same rights at their temporary bar association as they would have had at their point of origin.[91] Hence, if Schwob—as the holder of the *carte de combattant*—would have been eligible under the Mulhouse *numerus clausus* to continue to practice, he deserved his status at Limoges, even if there were otherwise no room for Jews at that particular bar. "The decree of 16 July, 1941 cannot have the effect of modifying on this point the prescription of a law anterior to itself."[92]

> Any other interpretation of these two texts would have the effect of applying the *numerus clausus* twice to the refugee Jewish lawyers... placing them in a far worse position than that of their colleagues of the same faith who did not have to flee.[93]

---

[89] CDJC XXIII-5a.

[90] See Richard Weisberg, "Autopoiesis and Positivism," *Cardozo Law Review* 13 (1992) 1721, challenging (in light of Vichy) Niklas Luhmann's acceptance of the self-contained system.

[91] Further complicating the Schwob situation is the fact that his claim for asylum at Limoges was predicated on a 29 July 1941 law relating to refugees from such areas as Alsace and Lorraine, which had their own special histories under German control. But in effect the issues raised are the same as in the earlier cases of displaced lawyers.

[92] CDJC XXIII-5c.

[93] Ibid.

Barthélemy closes by reassuring the infuriated agency that no Jewish lawyer would escape the constraints of the 16 July law by virtue merely of having fled to a new jurisdiction, and that only two lawyers from Alsace and Lorraine—Schwob and Dreyfus-May[94]—had so far sought such solace.

The district prosecutor and the CGQJ persevered in the former's strategy of seeking bar association rethinking on the Schwob matter. However, on 20 April 1942, the association *reconfirmed* Schwob's affiliation. When the prosecutor appealed this decision to the same Limoges court, his plea was rejected. On 10 December 1942, Maître Schwob was again supported by a French court and permitted to continue his practice.[95]

Generally speaking, the government could take as personal an approach to private lawyer dismissals as it did to the release of Jewish magistrates and court officials. Sometimes this highly personalized administrative agenda led to altercations with the civil courts who were ostensibly in charge of establishing the lists of those who could or could not continue to practice. Thus in 1942, the CGQJ heeded the request of a Jewish lawyer in Marseilles (Maître Paul-Clément Bernheim) that the Court of Appeals had wrongly used *seniority,* as opposed to personal histories of Jewish lawyers, as the way to decide continuing practice. Although, in its letter to the district prosecutor in Aix-en-Provence, the agency rejected Bernheim's calculations—as he insisted that 303 non-Jewish lawyers should lead to six instead of five retained Jewish colleagues[96]—it allowed that his status as a war veteran with an established French family should have been accounted for by the Court of Appeals. The agency concluded that "the legislator wanted the court to heed the personal history of each applicant." Seniority alone was, in its view, too mechanical an approach to the law.[97]

---

[94] Dreyfus-May had been under CGQJ investigation at least since the prior September; see CDJC CXCV-155.

[95] CDJC XXIII-5c, 5d.

[96] See chapter 8, note 40, for the computational wizardry of the CGQJ in determining how many private lawyers could remain in practice at any given bar.

[97] CDJC CXI-28.

The application of the *numerus clausus* not only to avocats but also avoués,[98] notaries,[99] auctioneers,[100] legal counsel,[101] and translators,[102] thus involved the Vichy government in internecine quarrels involving legal reasoning and case-by-case resolution substantially autonomous of German interest or influence. Even the phenomenon of German arrests of lawyers, as we saw early in this chapter, involved Vichy participation and the conscious decision of legal players to protest or not to protest the debilitating treatment of their Jewish colleagues. But the Vichy-originated quotas and their elaboration across the legal profession raises with specificity the question of how odious internal policies *become the law as practiced* within a self-defining system under stress. Joseph Barthélemy, a key component of the enigma, and a "liberal" at the origins of antisemitic policy, will now occupy us for awhile in all his contradictory legality.

---

[98] See, e.g., the cases of Maître Lucien Frank and Jean Dreyfus, both retained in Paris by the "Chambre des avoués" as the only two Jewish solicitors remaining in April 1943, CDJC CVIII-15

[99] Avoués and notaries were covered, along with bailiffs (huissiers) and auctioneers (commissaire-priseurs) by a companion decree to that of the law of 16 July 1941. See CDJC CVIII-2. The "Chambre des notaires" of the various jurisdictions was polled quite often by the CGQJ as to numbers, lists of names, and the other technicalities we have seen applied to avocats. See, e.g., demand of 17 March 1943 to the Paris chambre for the list of notaries under the 2 percent *numerus clausus,* to which the response was that of 150 notaries only one was Jewish, CDJC CVIII-16; see above, note 48.

[100] The president of the Chambre des commissaires-priseurs reported to the CGQJ in March 1943 that of 82 Parisian auctioneers only one was Jewish and that the *numerus clausus* thus was followed, CDJC CVIII-15a.

[101] For conseils juridiques, see the list of four Jews remaining as of April 1943 in the Paris region (Chicurel, Feigelman, Robert Israel, and Felix Jacobi), CDJC CVIII-14. An early decree held that "No Jew can serve as a court-appointed expert...," Law of 11 December 1940, cited in AN BB[30] 1713.

[102] Although subject to the *numerus clausus,* translators in the Unoccupied Zone, along with some other court-appointed experts, were treated by a special circular from the justice minister's office of 28 October 1941, permitting the hiring of Jewish experts if "the most qualified" to assist in a given matter. Xavier Vallat cites this circular in permitting the retention of a Jewish translator, Stucki, for litigation before the court of appeals of Toulouse, CDJC XVIIa-40 (193). However, prior to the October circular, the first justice minister, Alibert, had taken a much harder line on translators, honoring what he called the German request "to see no more expert translations by Jews in court," AN BB[30] 1709. See above, note 63.

# Chapter 4

# Barthélemy: A Catholic Prewar Liberal Is Called to Vichy

> Justice Minister Joseph Barthélemy declared to the newspaper "Le petit Parisien" on April 13, 1941, that the new law he had drafted closed many loopholes that permissively encouraged divorce. The former law, he said, came about after "a violent campaign by Naquet. This Jew from the Rhône Valley sought his revenge against the Restoration Catholics." The paper described the new divorce laws as a "return to the former approach."
>
> Paris, AN, $BB^{30}$, 1711.

For those in the French legal establishment prior to the debacle of World War II, few names rang so clearly with distinction and honor as that of Joseph Barthélemy, and few individuals would have endowed by his presence alone a certain respectability to any government he would choose to join.[1] A law professor whose eminence in constitutional and admini-

[1] See, e.g., Michèle Cointet-Labrousse, "Le Conseil national de Vichy: Vie politique et réforme de l'état en régime autoritaire. 1940–1944," (unpubl. Ph.D. diss., Paris X, 1984): "Joseph Barthélemy's reputation is solidly established.... Author of the magisterial *Essai sur le Travail parlementaire et le système des commissions* (1934)...(p. 156). [H]is legal knowledge, his reform ideas, his circle of political friends, justified his being called [to Vichy]. He possessed a number of other qualities of mind that made him the ideal replacement for R. Alibert" (p. 162).

strative law was of the highest order, Barthélemy had also served in the National Assembly and been a government advisor on many essential Third Republic matters. His relationship with socialists such as Léon Blum, although marked during the turbulent 1930s by strong political differences,[2] was collegial. Nothing at all during the prewar years would in any way have signalled to the French world of law that such a man was less than first rate; indeed, he was a "liberal,"[3] broad in his culture, renowned for his wit, esteemed for his writings and for his range of acquaintances.

On 26 January 1941, this man of moderation joined the government at Vichy as its second Minister of Justice, as the "Garde des sceaux," the keeper of the seals of French law. He replaced Raphaël Alibert, the author of the heinous Vichy statutes of 3 and 4 October 1940. Despite misgivings that he articulated privately and sometimes publicly, Joseph Barthélemy remained at his post for two years and two months. He signed the definitive religious statute of 2 June 1941; he introduced the notion of "race" into the constitutional reform project of the time; he orchestrated the Riom trial against his former colleague, Blum, and the other Third Republic leaders; stranger still, in the eyes of many, he signed into law the infamous "special section" courts[4] that brought swift and violent ends to the lives of Frenchmen denied any right of appeal.

Yet throughout his tenure at Justice, Barthélemy preserved a sense of analytical distance from his own actions. He jousted with the eternal conundrum faced by normal people living in the midst of evil: do they stand on the sidelines or try to work from within—retreat to an academic passivity or wade in and make the horrible reality slightly "better"? If we have seen this awful predicament implicitly thrust on such figures as Jacques Charpentier, Joseph Haennig, or Prof. Jacques Maury, in the case of the Justice Minister it became explicit. For Barthélemy kept contemporary notes of his term in office, and in reading them and the other documents he and his family have decided to make public, we seize in its pur-

---

[2] See Joseph Barthélemy, *Ministre de la Justice: Vichy 1941–1943* (Paris: Pygmalion, 1989), 226.

[3] See, e.g., Arnaud Teyssier, "Joseph Barthélemy, Garde des Sceaux, 1941–43," (unpubl. master's thesis, Paris X, 1980), 4, cited at chapter 1, note 3.

[4] The film-maker Costa-Gavras portrayed a thinly-veiled Barthélemy as an odious figure in his film, *Special Section* (1975).

est form the questions of law and morality that permeate the present study.

Claude Singer has recently described Barthélemy this way:

> Author of *La valeur de la liberté,* he protested prior to the war against the antisemitism of the dictatorships, then denounced the decree of 12 November, 1938 that threatened the removal of French citizen status from naturalized people, those deemed "unworthy of the name of French citizen."[5] A fervent Catholic, and National Block deputy from Gers between 1919 and 1924, he then opposed the Front populaire. A pacifist and supporter of Munich, he publicly supported Pétain in an article he published on August 20, 1940 in *Le Temps.*
>
> In the Vichy régime, neither his functions nor his acts were in line with his prior record. It was he who in effect elaborated the second *statut des juifs,* prepared the law on functionaries of 14 September 1941, and was working on the unfinished constitutional project that referred to "Christian civilization." He co-signed all the extraordinary laws promulgated during his presence at the Justice Ministry (the *ex post facto* special sections, measures against communists, Jews, and freemasons).
>
> Barthélemy, unlike Alibert, was no ideologue and no militant antisemite. Above all, he was a man of order, of duty, and he was an administrator.... This Catholic intellectual who never masked his moral scruples, was in no sense an "extremist."[6]

For Barthélemy's grandson, the editor (with the historian Arnaud Teyssier) of the Justice Minister's wartime notes,[7] the depiction of the man would be quite different. In several interviews with this author, and in the exacting notes to his grandfather's writings, Jean Barthélemy attempts to redeem the prewar Catholic humanist from the Vichy cabinet minister. Himself a lawyer, the grandson has scrupulously researched the Vichy years as they relate to Joseph Barthélemy. His account helps us to fathom the phenomenon of "the good man persuaded to do wrong" that so characterizes the French legal profession during those years.

---

[5] On this point, see chapter 1, notes 3 and 19.

[6] Claude Singer, *Vichy, l'Université et les Juifs* (Paris: Les Belles Lettres, 1992), 89–90.

[7] Joseph Barthélemy, *Ministre de la Justice: Mémoires* (Paris: Pygmalion, 1989).

"My grandfather's mother was a Catholic and his father was a radical."[8] These two influences colored Barthélemy's whole life and partly explain the paradoxical combination of his prewar liberalism and his attraction to Vichy through its charismatic and authoritarian leader, Philippe Pétain.[9] For the present study, the grandson's bipolar description holds immense significance.

The aim of this chapter is not so much to reiterate the factual side of Barthélemy's behavior as Vichy's second minster of justice—although there is need to correct some impressions left by his posthumously published recollections[10]—as it is to elaborate what I consider to be the response of a *representative* legal intellectual to the religious laws in particular. The way in which, as I shall argue, Barthélemy's *Catholicism outweighed his liberal impulses* offers a richly detailed retrospective on an entire cast of thought.

The chapter's argument runs roughly as follows: Barthélemy took with him to Vichy a set of beliefs and practices that had brought him distinction and that he was unlikely to change during his tenure as Minister of Justice. He neither "worked to do some good from within" nor did he change his stripes altogether to become a clear villain. Instead, like hundreds of lesser legal lights, his willingness—whatever his motive—to work with Vichy *became the "within"* that was Vichy. Had he and others like him refused to accept a racist premise within Vichy, that strain might well have become desiccated or even dead. On the other hand, Barthélemy's actions are not indicative of a marked alteration from the prewar law professor. Something innate to him survived and came out in Vichy where it was benign previously. That element, in my view, is a form of French Catholic racism of a rather polite variety. It employs a notion of race subtly different from the Nazis' but equally as destructive to its victims. While not totally distinct from ideas of blood and hierarchy, the French variety situates race in terms of the "irremediable otherness" of a certain group. With their own supposed sense of law and morality, and

---

[8] Jean Barthélemy, personal interviews with author, Paris, 1988. All quotations and paraphrases are from these interviews.

[9] Barthélemy's descriptions of Pétain can only be characterized as panegyrical. See *Ministre,* chapter 3. I will refer to these from time to time in the text, as they indicate an authoritarian impulse within the most liberal French spirit.

[10] See especially below, text at notes 141–61.

their relative lack of attachment to French soil, these "others" become ripe for ostracism and legalistic violence. Yet all this can occur within a framework otherwise moderate or even liberal in appearance, where republican and even revolutionary values are preserved (Barthélemy's constitutional scheme). Harking to imagery of biblical origin, the irremediable other is recalled as always being separate and even threatening—Christ-killers in the less polite language of the extreme right. In more considerate terms, these are the alien organisms that need from time to time to be cleansed from the healthy organism that is the true French nation. And all this can and *should* be done by law, because it is these others' differing *notion* of law that particularly sets them apart.

The structure of our Barthélemy page permits an interweaving of factual data and intellectual theory, hoping here in particular to add to what Marrus and Paxton call the "archaeology of consciousness" of Vichy.[11] Always central is Barthélemy's personal commitment to the elaboration of the 2 June statute and other religious laws, during Vichy's heyday and especially in 1942, a period during which he claims he deliberately absented himself from the racial arena.[12]

## A. From Alibert to Barthélemy

The transition from Vichy's first ministry of justice to its second—there was to be only one more, that of Gabolde—must have seemed to most respectable French lawyers and intellectuals like a breath of fresh air. Raphaël Alibert was, after all, a known right-wing extremist, a follower of Charles Maurras,[13] and a man whose influence over Marshal Pétain

---

[11] Michael Marrus and Robert Paxton, *Vichy France and the Jews* (New York: Basic Books, 1981), 353.

[12] Barthélemy, *Ministre,* 314.

[13] See, e.g., Pierre Birnbaum, *Les fous de la République* (Paris: Fayard, 1992), 467; Christian Lépagnot, *Histoire de Vichy,* 5 vols. (Geneva: Idégraf, 1978–81), vol. 3, 72: "Charles Maurras who often spoke through Alibert to Pétain." For a recent analysis of Maurras' theories and their integration into Vichy circles, see Pierre Birnbaum, *Anti-Semitism in France,* trans. Miriam Kochan (Oxford: Basil Blackwell, 1992), particularly 242–47.

rivalled that of any other government leader.[14] Incontestably the author of the Vichy statutes of 3 and 4 October 1940, Alibert had surely employed "his science of manoeuvering the Marshal"[15] to bring about not only the quick signing of those laws but also the arrest of such Jewish prewar leaders as Blum and Mandel. Barthélemy's very name would have brought hope even to the persecuted class that his predecessor had already so badly injured; indeed, a testimonial from just such a victim indicates this fragile but vital contemporaneous faith. Boris Mirkine-Guetzevitch, a Jew naturalized in 1933 and hence already at risk of losing his job under early Vichy legislation, and also a professional colleague of Barthélemy's on the journal *La revue d'Histoire constitutionnelle* and at the Institute for political and constitutional history (he was soon to join the faculty of the New School for Social Research in New York City), telegrammed the newly appointed minister as follows: "29 January, 1941. France resides its justice in its most eminent lawyer."[16]

In a letter of the same day from Marseilles, where Mirkine-Guetzevitch had taken temporary refuge from the persecution he felt all around him in Paris, he writes: "At this moment you—garde des sceaux—this is the greatest guaranty of justice, of law."[17]

If even the already insulted and injured might find a ray of light in the appointment of such a man, it goes without saying that Barthélemy's ascension delighted a whole host of still active law professors, diplomats, journalists, practitioners, and former students (one of whom wrote, "Young people have not lost their liberal ideal; they know it will be reborn").[18] The strength of belief in the new Justice Minister's potential attests not only to his reputation but also to the belief in the régime's capacity—even many months into its existence—to be flexible and to chart its own legal course. Many in the legal world expected changes from the Alibert policies.

To one like Philippe Serre, Alibert had typified the "petit groupe des fripons"—the little band of rascals—that Pétain brought into his first

---

[14] See, e.g., the depiction of Alibert as Pétain's constant dining companion, Lépagnot, *Histoire de Vichy,* vol. 3, 93. Accord Barthélemy, *Ministre,* 44.

[15] Lépagnot, *Histoire de Vichy,* vol. 1, 36.

[16] AN 72 AJ 413, Dossier no. 9; see also the reference in Barthélemy, *Ministre,* 415.

[17] AN 72 AJ 413, Dossier no. 9.

[18] This as part of a listing of well-wishers' names in Barthélemy, *Ministre,* 414–15.

government.[19] Serre and many others among the parliamentary minority were too busy avoiding the régime's retribution to wire congratulations to Barthélemy, even if they had wanted to do so, but surely the law professor would have seemed like a step up from the "espèce de violent"—the "violent type"—that was Alibert.[20]

Not that Alibert's considerable legal abilities had been ignored or even minimized; some professional leaders might not have been unhappy to see him continue. Jacques Charpentier knew that Alibert was antisemitic[21]—but is able to observe:

> He wasn't such a bad guy. [Cet homme, qui n'était pas un mauvais diable].... His prodigious memory, his perspicacity, his superiority in the knowledge of texts [made of him a good cabinet minister].... To do justice to M. Alibert, we must recall that in the midst of all those illusions [au milieu de tous ces chimères], he was profoundly devoted to the State and that this monarchist was French.[22]

Charpentier, whose attitude about Barthélemy was quite equivocal, emphasized Alibert's fierce anti-German sentiments.[23]

Alibert's independence from German control, coupled with his "science of maneuvering the Marshal,"[24] indicate together the force of his ministry and the proudly perceived "Frenchness" of the religious laws of 3 and 4 October 1940. But, to return to the main point, all those who were both alert to and also distressed by the 1940 legislation—and the volatile author of those laws—would have warmed to the thought of a Barthélemy guarding the "Seals" of justice. Indeed, by January 1941, even some who might have appreciated Alibert's view of the Jews (including the Germans) also were pleased to see him go.

---

19 Philippe Serre, personal interview with author, Paris, 1988.

20 Barthélemy's phrase, transcript of his interrogation by the post-Liberation authorities in the early months of 1945; see Barthélemy, *Ministre,* 569.

21 Jacques Charpentier, *Au service de la liberté* (Paris: Fayard, 1949), 127. H. du Moulin de Labarthète, *Le Temps des Illusions* (Geneva: Bourquin, 1946), 38, recalls that Alibert "peignait à la fresque," excessively legislating his own antisemitism without any constraining influence.

22 Charpentier, *Au service,* 124.

23 Accord Cointet-Labrousse, "Le Conseil national," 135.

24 Lépagnot, *Histoire de Vichy,* vol. 1, 36.

Alibert's "violent" streak was, by many accounts, of a particularly frightening strain, for it derived from an active and rancorous intellect. To Barthélemy,[25] and to other such contemporary writers as Maurice Martin du Gard, his personality was marked by "rancune," inspired by "a long and aggressive passivity..., as though he found himself avenged of a gap [vengé d'une vacance] of which he had exaggerated the injustice!"[26] Cointet-Labrousse, more recently, probably hits the mark, too, in using the word *"ressentiment"* to describe Alibert's "bitterness,"[27] observing that he was at one and the same time a loser at universal suffrage, an agitated *eminence grise,* and an ideologue:

> A fervent adherent of Charles Maurras, he is incontestably one of the instigators of Vichy's antisemitic legislation. Of a shadowy character and unstable and violent temperament, always bitter, he was never able to reap the benefits of universal suffrage.... He believes only in the power of *élites* and in the virtue of high bureaucrats and experts upon whom he would like to impose parliamentary commissions.[28]

Turning his striking abilities to resentful vengeance, Alibert—as we have seen in chapters 1 and 2—instituted proceedings against his Third Republic foes and authored comprehensive statutes against the Jews. These laws he then proceeded to interpret aggressively for all government workers who would have to implement them. Not letting the words of the 3 October 1940 law speak for themselves, the

> Justice Minister, in a communication to the Minister of the Interior of November 1940, affirmed that proof [of Jewishness] could be sustained by any evidence bearing on the issue. The legislator [*sic*[29]] in declining to elaborate and enumerate such evidence thus gave to none of them a special weight and excluded none of them. Under these conditions, the task of the administration [in proving Jewishness] was relatively easy: it was enough to invoke any evidence: religion, family name, first name, place of burial,

---

[25] Barthélemy, *Ministre,* 44.

[26] Maurice Martin du Gard, *La chronique de Vichy, 1940–44* (Paris: Flammarion, 1948), 36–37.

[27] Michèle Cointet-Labrousse, *Vichy et le facisme* (Paris: Editions complexe, 1987), 132.

[28] Ibid., 36.

[29] See chapter 2, note 29.

> and the burden of proof was thus displaced to the individual who had to rebut the proofs....[30]

Eventually Alibert went too far and directed his rancorous energies to the task of having Pierre Laval removed from the government, which event (only partly orchestrated by Alibert)[31] in fact took place on 13 December 1940. So Alibert soon became one of those whose heads the Germans demanded as atonement for the (temporary) loss of their favorite Vichy presence[32]—Laval was to return to the government as its effective head of state in spring 1942. On 27 January 1941, Alibert's resentful and excitable nature detached itself from Vichy, although Barthélemy paints a colorful picture of his predecessor "hanging on" and shouting resentfully at the Vichy rooftops.[33]

But did *ressentiment* itself, as a prevalent emotion, leave the justice ministry along with Alibert? Most of his juristic *substance* survived his departure: the religious laws, the denaturalization and internment laws, the Riom proceedings, the constitutional reform project Pétain vested in his ministry.[34] Surely, however, the elevation to the *Sceaux* of a man like Joseph Barthélemy at least put an end to the spiritual venom and exaggerated intellectualized revenge that, under Alibert, had characterized Vichy Justice.

After all, no one associated Barthélemy with any of the venomous impulses of his predecessor. This was an upstanding individual, whose behavior in the turbulent 1930s was unexceptionable. He had not sought after Vichy (although he certainly was not averse to attaining powerful positions); his appointment may in fact have marked a liberal concession,

---

[30] Memo on Interior Ministry letterhead, 10 December 1941, CDJC, CXIV-78. The past tense is used because the 2 June 1941 law was by then in effect, but the memo writer observes that the "Administration" (i.e., the state) has an even easier time of proving Jewishness under the new statutory approach. See chapter 2.

[31] For an excellent account of the way in which Laval was politically wounded by his refusal to publicize Alibert's passionate protest against the German expulsion of thousands of Lorrains into the French zone, see Jean-Paul Cointet, *Pierre Laval* (Paris: Fayard, 1993), 313-17.

[32] Cointet-Labrousse, *Vichy et le fascisme,* 57; see also Jean-Paul Cointet, *Pierre Laval,* 334.

[33] Barthélemy, *Ministre,* 44–45.

[34] P. Baudouin, *Neuf mois au gouvernement* (Paris: Editions de la Table ronde, 1948), 282.

particularly as regards the constitutional reform project and its cousin, the new Conseil national, to Pierre Etienne Flandin, who was probably responsible for having Barthélemy invited to Vichy.[35] Flandin had been fighting for a "liberalization of the régime",[36] and although he would lose that war (and his government position), he did manage to install a man in the justice ministry who might stand for greater allegiance to republican traditions.

But it is fair to ask what qualities of spirit—in addition to the liberality and humanism of intellect—the new minister of justice in fact demonstrated while in the post. Would innovations occur to eliminate, or at least minimize the effect of, the Alibert racial program, born in part of a Maurrasian antisemitism reactively lashing out at France's perennial scapegoat? Would an end be put to the Riom political trials or at least a different coloration be placed on the persecution of such Third Republic Jews as Blum and Mandel? Would the new constitution conserve Flandin's vision of considerable ties to the republican past or would it move towards Pétain's (or Darlan's) more authoritarian concept?[37] Would denaturalization of increasing numbers of French residents occur, thus making them ripe for the humiliation and incarceration established by Barthélemy's predecessor?

With the benefit of 20-20 hindsight, analysts can find what they need to explain Barthélemy's record in office. To post-Liberation interrogators, ironically, the explanation lay partly in a perceived linkage between Alibert and his successor that made the latter both knowledgeable of and

---

[35] See Barthélemy, *Ministre,* 23, and 607. Moulin de Labarthète, staff leader to Pétain, actually made the invitational phone call, ibid., 126; and Labarthète, *Le Temps des Illusions,* 135.

[36] The phrase is Cointet-Labrousse's, "Le Conseil national," 119. Cointet-Labrousse, in her later book, defines "neo-liberals" and situates them (including Barthélemy) within Vichy politics; see Cointet-Labrousse, *Vichy et le fascisme,* 156ff. Flandin has his place in that description, although he is seen as "a fluctuating parliamentarian," ibid., 158. Many of these "liberals" were made welcome in Vichy because they had been pacifists and publicly urged cooperation with Nazi Germany from an early date. This was certainly true of Flandin; see, e.g., Lépagnot, *Histoire de Vichy,* vol. 1, 129.

[37] See discussion in Cointet-Labrousse, "Le Conseil national," 121–24. While Flandin wanted real concessions to republican opinion and a renewed parliamentary presence, Darlan saw the Conseil as a political tool to keep as many factions happy as possible, and Pétain wanted it to serve the ends of the "national revolution" by substituting a designated group of "élites" for the parliamentarians he detested.

responsible for Alibert's radical rightist proclivities. But Barthélemy responded to this implication:

> M. Alibert and I once belonged to the same *milieu,* but our relations were virtually non-existent. He has always been a violent type.[38]

To his grandson, Barthélemy proceeded along the tragic lines of the decent individual compelled to adopt a "politique de sauvetage."[39] As many other lawyers whose actions collectively provoke this study's conclusions, Barthélemy in this light was an incrementalist, doing small amounts of good in an unalterably bad context. To Barthélemy himself, Vichy was "mon Calvaire."[40]

To the present writer, the fullest explanation would be an amalgam of these three. There *is* a linkage between the two dissimilar Justice Ministers, but it is not the political one implied right after the war. A central element of this linkage, as Michèle Cointet-Labrousse first observed, was (with Pierre Caziot among Vichy ministers) "solid contact with the Church".[41] And it is true that Barthélemy accomplished some good in areas (such as assistance of individual Jews) that would have been anathema to his predecessor; but he was too much involved with the general thrust of the régime and too powerful a man within it to make a credible claim for working against the system in racial matters or anywhere else. And, yes, Vichy can be feelingly and empathetically construed as Barthélemy's Calvary, but the New Testament imagery finally implicates Barthélemy in a very different kind of narrative, in which one man's private and spiritualized agony translates into thousands of other people's quite public and thoroughly physical destruction. We must not forget that many deeply believing Catholics managed both to cooperate with Vichy on its legislative programs and to feel that the nation's great suffering somehow opened up promise of spiritual revival

---

[38] Barthélemy, *Ministre,* 569.

[39] Jean Barthélemy, personal interview with author, Paris, November 1988.

[40] Ibid., apparently in a remark to his daughter.

[41] Cointet-Labrousse, "Le Conseil national," 840.

linked to the new régime (see chapter 10).[42] Who was doing most of the suffering?

This leads us back to *"ressentiment,"* the spiritual malaise connected to Alibert but so far not to Barthélemy. My claim here situates Barthélemy within a respectable tradition of French Catholic thought, which still exists in polite circles,[43] and which would never find itself uttering the obscene forms of Catholic Jew-baiting most recently described by Pierre Birnbaum in his comprehensive study.[44] Yet, as Birnbaum observes, in the prewar writings of François Mauriac, or Emmanuel Mounier, or Stanislas Fumet—all "Catholic personalities [who] were opposed to anti-Semitism, [one finds] terms that were more than equivocal in respect of the experiment Léon Blum was conducting."[45] We have already noted in chapter 1 that Barthélemy's scribblings about the same perennial whipping boy, Blum, were unfortunately marked by explicit antisemitic slurs, not once but several times.[46] I believe that Barthélemy offers an example—of primary importance for lawyers and thus for this study—of the tragic near-inevitability of Catholic resentment when it comes to the Jewish people. On a purely personal level, the *ressentiment* of a distinguished man like Barthélemy may have been triggered by his actual prewar dealings with Blum;[47] but in his own formulation, the liberal Catholic jurist puts it far better: "I have said, I have written, while I was Minister, that it was necessary to study 'humanely, fraternally, the Jewish problem.' "[48]

---

[42] Michèle Cointet-Labrousse, in her chapter on "The Catholics," cites *Conseil national* member Hervé Budes de Guébriant, a fervent Catholic: "If God has not granted us the victory that we were imploring, it's because he reserved for us a greater gift still: the return to him of our dear and beautiful country. Let us bless and praise the Love that will find us at the cost of salutary sufferings," *Vichy et le fascisme,* 146.

[43] I recall the gracious Parisian countess, an elderly woman of impeccable manners, once saying of the Jews: "But why don't they just accept Jesus? It would be so *easy* for them after that. So much suffering they have to endure because they just won't do that simple thing."

[44] Birnbaum, *Anti-Semitism,* chapter 8, "The Antichrist."

[45] Ibid., 182.

[46] See chapter 1, text at footnote 68.

[47] Barthélemy, *Ministre,* 226–29.

[48] Ibid., chapter 9, "Les juifs." The internal reference is to Barthélemy's August 1941 article of the same title in *Patrie.*

As early as 1937, the liberal academician was noting in his *Précis de droit public:*

> The fact of the persistence of the Jewish race as a race within national communities that have forgotten the notion of race merits attention and meditation.[49]

The man who would, as Justice Minister, eventually attempt to introduce race as a *formal notion* into the proposed constitution of Vichy, added however in 1937:

> Here's a fact about public law in France: the French nation contains an element of the Jewish race. But as opposed to Hitler's Germany, this feature carries with it no legal inferiority or superiority of any kind.[50]

The struggle within him between paternal political liberalism[51] and maternal religious conservatism, a struggle benignly evoked in the 1937 Barthélemy, came to typify the stance of a learned profession when Vichy provided an opening for the *legal* stigmatization of that "race" that had offended and insulted by remaining "apart" within French boundaries. Although Barthélemy and people like him would continue to dissociate themselves from "Hitler's Germany," the irony emerged that they would do so *by an appeal to the very Christianity* that, at its origins, conjured the Jews as a constant irritant and implied enemy.

First elaborated by Nietzsche—to describe, by the way, both German antisemites and the origins of Christianity as a Hellenic variation on the Jewish priestly class[52]—*ressentiment* is described most fully by Max Scheler as a reactive condition that comes to see everything as an insult to it, organically reverses the good and makes it into the bad, and lashes out at innocent victims of its rage instead of at those really responsible

---

[49] Noted at ibid., 320.

[50] Ibid.

[51] To some readers, the term "liberal" to describe a paternal influence for which the word "radical" is technically appropriate (see Jean Barthélemy's description of his paternal great-grandfather earlier in this chapter) may be confusing. But the "radical" party in France lined up somewhat as a "liberal" movement would today. See, e,g. Cointet-Labrousse, *Vichy et le fascisme,* 63.

[52] See Friedrich Nietzsche, *The Genealogy of Morals,* tr. Kaufman (New York: Vintage, 1969), Essay I, aphorisms 10–17; see also *Beyond Good and Evil,* tr. Cowan (Chicago: Regnery, 1966), aphorism 52, for a typically strong philosemitic outburst.

for offending it.[53] Nietzsche, unlike his student Scheler, of course felt that Christianity's single most spiritual "accomplishment" was the institutionalized spreading of *ressentiment* across the continent of Europe; uneasy at the healthy values of those belief systems it replaced, Christianity instilled a reactive hatred of life into its followers. Thriving on a consistent sense of having been insulted at birth (original sin), Christianity in this view inspires the organic mendacity that causes good to be seen as "evil"—indeed, Christianity *requires* the positing of another's basic healthiness (now perverted into sin) in order to define itself at all. The basic sign of the resentful individual is its total lack of integrity, of self-naming, of valuation. Instead, it must conjure an enemy against which its reactive energies and those alone can thrive and make its own existence "worthwhile."

The history of French antisemitism combines, as Pierre Birnbaum has recently shown,[54] a religious hatred of the unassimilable Jew (raised occasionally to the level of racial distinctions between the ensconced, agrarian European with organic attachments to French soil and the Asiatic, nomadic Jew, who sets himself up in cities and pillages the native population) with an antipathy to republican principles and an omnipresent urge to authoritarian régimes. Vichy, seen this way, is less an aberration than a cyclical French phenomenon. And it is wholly consistent with this view that a "liberal" Frenchman like Barthélemy could both conceive of Pétain as a savior whose sad but ecstatic mission involved a restoration after dismal defeat of France's historic values, and propose a new constitution bringing everyone under the banner of the restored values; his "Calvary" at the same time included the sad duty of dissociating the country from its racial nemeses.

I cannot doubt—having studied his record in office at great length—that Joseph Barthélemy deserves significant credit for ameliorating the fates of many individual Jews. His sense of legality and a certain kind of

---

[53] The central essay is "Das Ressentiment im Aufbau der Moralen," in Max Scheler, *Gesammelte Werke* (Bern: Francke Verlag, 1955), vol. 3, 33–147. See the excellent translation by W. W. Holdheim, *Ressentiment* (New York: Free Press, 1961). For a complete discussion of literary *ressentiment*, with a general connection to Vichy, see Richard Weisberg, *The Failure of the Word* (New Haven: Yale University Press, 1984), 1–41 and Appendix.

[54] Birnbaum, *Anti-Semitism in France*, passim.

due process[55] extended even to a man he apparently detested as "that Jew," Léon Blum. Had Alibert remained at the *Sceaux,* Riom might have yielded to the unilateral declaration of guilt pronounced by Pétain. Blum and Daladier (like the unhappy Mandel) might have been shot, instead of suffering as they did a five-year-long imprisonment, worse perhaps at home then it was in Germany. Unhappy with his leader's *Diktat,* Barthélemy, although incapable of validating the defendants' incontrovertible claim that a judicial panel specially created by the new government could hardly be impartial once the head of that government declared their guilt,[56] nonetheless successfully maintained the jurisdiction of the court. But beyond this no fair-minded analyst can really go. To explain the racism, the special section courts and their wholesale murder of Jewish hostages and others, the legalistic nitpicking that brought increased terror to innocent Jews, the rigorous exclusion of all Jews from the magistracy even when Vichy litigiousness made the use of their talents virtually mandatory—against these terrible irrationalities the observer may be justified in conjuring the *respectable rancor* that still blemishes French culture at its highest levels and that surely had a central place in Vichy's notion of law.

## B. A Racist Constitution?

From the beginnings of the régime, there was a vague sense of illegitimacy about its legislation and even its constitutional mandate.[57] It would be wrong to say that this sense blossomed into a vigorous contemporary debate about the legal basis for the régime; although there was some concern with the issue.[58] As we have noted and discussed—for it is a central thesis of the present study—lawyers during Vichy almost always

---

[55] See chapter 1, note 70. This should not, however, be overly exaggerated. Despite Barthélemy's own assessment, the Riom defendants and their lawyers did not have much faith in the court deciding their fates (nor even in its jurisdiction).

[56] See AN 72 AJ 411, dossier no. 7.

[57] See chapter 1, note 32.

[58] Moulin de Labarthète describes the uneasiness with Vichy legitimacy felt even by Pétain at times in his *Le Temps des Illusions,* 110–20.

failed to face the most central legal issues of the time, instead opting for lower level discussions that had the effect of legitimating the whole.

But *was* the whole indeed legitimate? Perhaps only the Riom trials brought forth sufficient rhetoric to challenge the régime's very basis. Because he was both a constitutional scholar and the man charged with organizing Riom, Barthélemy was consistently sensitive to those arguments, which I like to call "jugular" in nature since they attacked the very lifeline of Vichy's legislative approach.[59] Some of these arguments were constitutional in nature, and Barthélemy was prone—to his credit—to reflect on their assertions, as when he writes to himself:

> The National Assembly didn't really abdicate—they really gave their mandate to the Marshal to draft a constitution, for it, with it and under its control and then to resign.[60]

For everything that a man of law spent a lifetime supporting, this line of argument must have been disturbing to say the least. If there was no right to create constitutional law, then there was surely no "Cour suprême de justice." Established by Pétain's fifth constitutional act of 30 July 1940,[61] organized in detail under the law of the same date,[62] and further implemented by the Marshal's decree of 1 August,[63] this body must have struck most lawyers as not just new but—in its first setting—also unusual. After all, the *senate* was traditionally the body that tried alleged crimes by high office holders. If the supreme court was not lawfully created, then it had no jurisdiction over these men.

The Riom dispute pitted the still-existing constitution of 1875 against Vichy's theory of legitimacy, and its implications go significantly beyond even that portentous political trial. If Riom was a sham, so arguably was the entirety of Vichy's legislative scheme, because it emerged from a series of laws and decrees passed by the government, with no action by any parliamentary body, supposedly on the basis of Vichy's sole constitutional authority.

---

[59] For Jacques Charpentier's attack on Riom, see chapter 1, text at note 43.

[60] AN 72 AJ 411, dossier no. 8, in Barthélemy's handwriting.

[61] Dominique Rémy, *Les lois de Vichy* (Paris: Romillat, 1992), 60–61.

[62] Ibid., 61–65.

[63] Ibid., 64–66.

Of course, such a question might quickly be dismissed as purely academic, since by the time Barthélemy took office the régime had already issued 950 laws and 750 decrees! If a régime gives every appearance of legality, and if an entire professional community is acting as though its laws are operative, can it be said that nonetheless the régime and its edicts lack some other quality that might be called "legitimacy"? Barthélemy himself, in an ironic post-Liberation response to the writer François Mauriac, questions the distinction.[64] Yet, as Justice Minister, he was sufficiently troubled about it to credit the assertion that the National Assembly, on 10 July 1940, was not so much putting itself totally out of business than establishing a holding pattern until the régime proposed to the whole French people a new constitution.[65] To some, then, Vichy could not delegate to itself any legislative function *except* that of preparing a new constitution, which then had to be ratified by the people. Others would eventually go even further: the National Assembly, they argued, was itself *ultra vires* and had no right to delegate constitutional reform powers that *it alone possessed* under the constitution of 1875.

For post-Liberation legal purposes, legitimacy ended even earlier: the date chosen was 16 June 1940, the very date on which Pétain formed a government bent on ending the war and bowing to Hitler's demands.[66] More recently, the question plaguing Barthélemy and the Liberation lawyers continues to intrigue legal academicians,[67] and to obsess the French more generally. Barthélemy's refusal to resolve the legitimacy issue is the first cause of a form of Vichy mythmaking, epitomized perhaps in the declaration by former President Mitterrand as recently as the end of 1992 that:

> there is no juridical responsibility in the French Republic [for Vichy's religious laws and actions against Jews].... The French nation was not involved in that, nor was the Republic. It was a new régime, and a different

---

[64] Barthélemy, *Ministre,* 432f.

[65] Thus part of the 10 July language is that the new constitution "will be ratified by the Nation...," Rémy, *Les lois,* 31. This, of course, never happened.

[66] See the ordinance of 9 August 1944, *Journal officiel,* 10 August 1944.

[67] See chapter 1, note 32.

kind, occasional in nature. The French state that takes that terrible responsibility,... that is the régime of Vichy.[68]

What became, for everyone from de Gaulle to Mitterrand, an opportunity to dismiss all of Vichy's complex legality as somehow aberrational began, for Barthélemy, in a struggle to wield power while also seeking *eventual* constitutional legitimacy. The primary conduit both for technical legitimation and for a more liberalizing politics was to be the constitutional reform project. This venture originated in the Conseil national, the stopgap and potentially liberalizing body created virtually at the moment of Barthélemy's entry into the government, on 22 January 1941.[69] Flandin, who was the Conseil's visionary vice-president, helped to appoint its first 188 members (increased to 213 members by mid-1941) drawn from various "élites," and the body might have exerted greater influence had Flandin himself not soon been forced from the government, to be replaced by Darlan, with whom the Germans felt they could work.[70] Barthélemy is "the loyal figure to whom Flandin confides the mission of watching over the Conseil national."[71] Barthélemy becomes its president.

Although it never was to meet in plenary session,[72] the Conseil national nonetheless exerted influence throughout the Barthélemy years. It was a pure Vichy project, applicable to both zones, and almost entirely free of any German constraint or censure.[73] It was indigenous, it had every "liberal" tendency that Vichy could muster; what did it say and what did it do? Since Barthélemy was the primary author of the first draft

---

[68] *Le Monde,* 15–16 November 1992, 6.

[69] Rémy, *Les lois,* 105. As Rémy observes, the *Conseil* was established under two threatening clouds: first, its origins were in a *law* and not a constitutional act, perhaps signalling a lack of permanence or real power; second, its founding vice-president, Flandin, was to have little time left in the government to oversee his vision of a parliamentary, neo-liberal body.

[70] See, e.g., Marrus and Paxton, *Vichy France,* 75. Barthélemy himself specifically attributes the firing of Flandin, whom he admired, to Abetz. Barthélemy, "Mémoires," (unpubl. ms.), 24. (I will occasionally cite to Barthélemy's unpublished "Mémoires"—which Jean Barthélemy was kind enough to show me—as opposed to the recently published *Ministre,* particularly if there is some divergence in the two texts worth noting.)

[71] Cointet-Labrousse, "Le Conseil national," 155.

[72] Rémy, *Les lois,* 107.

[73] Cointet-Labrousse, "Le Conseil national," 389.

constitution, his own notes serve as best evidence for the values he felt were at the heart of Vichy.[74]

Barthélemy ruminates at some length about the charge of the constitutional committee:

> Let's be frank straight off—*there is at present no constitution* [*sic*! except for several explicitly repealed provisions, the constitution of 1875 was still operative until the new Vichy constitution, in part based upon it anyway, was signed by Pétain on 30 January 1944] There are just preparatory projects. But the Marshal is only reflecting for the moment; he will pass to the time of decision when he believes that the hour of national interest has rung out, the definitive hour of a France restored to herself in a peaceful Europe.... *There are no constituents*. We are no longer in an age by which the truth is decreed by a vote of seven to six. It is urgent *to prepare a constitution*.... But it is not urgent to publish or promulgate a constitution.[75]

Substantively, Barthélemy notes that the constitution must include:

> The grouping of rights that constitute the notion of the human personality. The family—source of conservation and development of the race. The present constitution is not simply political. It concerns itself with family life, professional activity, the manifestations of the spirit. The state presents itself as *the juridico-political expression of the Nation.*[76]

This informal text is rich in nuance. Drawing from the régime's motto of work/family/homeland, Barthélemy begins to paint a picture that focuses on small groupings or communities rather than on the individual. Duties and responsibilities will be rewarded by communal rights; in Pétain's own words, "before the idea of law, the rule of duty."[77] But this is not

---

[74] There is also a short chapter in Barthélemy, *Ministre*, chapter 6, to which I shall refer here and in chapter 9 at notes 63–71, but most of the quotations are from the Barthélemy archival material, Paris AN 72 AJ 413.

[75] AN 72 AJ 413, dossier no. 2. Dean Roger Bonnard, *Revue du Droit public et de la Science politique*, vol. 58, 72 (1942) gave the assessment that Vichy France still had a link to all prior governments: "Thus were promulgated under the name of 'constitutional acts' a series of constitutional laws that were to modify the constitutional laws of 1875 without abrogating them altogether but in stripping them of their fundamental character [en les amputant de leurs dispositions fondamentales],". Dean Bonnard edited this journal that was unabashedly *Pétainiste;* see idem., "La Reconstruction de la France," *Revue du droit public,* 57 (1940–41), 143–150. See chapter 10, notes 15, 27, and 28.

[76] AN 72 AJ 413, dossier no. 2, emphasis in original.

[77] Ibid.

to be confused with the fascist model of presumed values, incarnated in "the state" (and its leader) at the expense of the juridical "nation." Instead—and here Barthélemy undertakes to distinguish his constitution from the Nazi model—the state and the nation will retain an identity familiar to republican thought.[78] He continues:

> The state considers itself constrained by the higher rules of morality and law, superior creations that impose themselves upon it. *By this, the State differentiates itself from totalitarian states.*[79]

Barthélemy, influenced here by Duguit,[80] insists that the state—however authoritarian in conception—is always subordinated to higher ideals. Refusing to his credit to avoid the question of what these latter *are*, Barthélemy instead consistently associates the higher force with Christianity. Beginning with the words of Pétain himself, for the constitutional committee explicitly sought guidance first from the Marshal and only then from Barthélemy,[81] the drafters of the new constitution were reminded of Pétain's vision, as follows:

> The institutions that have brought upon us moral dissolution, economic ruin and military defeat can only be irremediably condemned. France, with a sure instinct, attributes to them the unhappiness of the nation. It wishes never to see them again. It will never see them again.... The cornerstone of the future Constitution will be the primacy of the State.... It is in sacrifice to the State, in discipline to the community, whether consented to, accepted or imposed, that each will find the guaranty of his own interests.... The State, nonetheless, proclaims loudly its respect for the human personality, first conquest of Christian civilization. It remains, absolutely, separate from the Churches.[82] But it retains to itself the power, if necessary, to take—in

---

[78] See also Cointet-Labrousse, *Vichy et le fascisme,* 178.

[79] AN 72 AJ 413, dossier no. 2.

[80] See Barthélemy, *Ministre,* 615; Cointet-Labrousse, "Le Conseil national," 397.

[81] Barthélemy, *Ministre,* 288.

[82] We will foreground church-state issues in chapter 10. It is surely true that neither Pétain nor Barthélemy, although both believing Catholics, surrendered much to the Church in terms of the latter's direct property interests. Despite fervent advocacy by distinguished figures such as law school dean Auguste Rivet, the Church could not elicit from Barthélemy major statutory concessions that would have benefitted it economically; see, e.g., AN $BB^{30}$ 1708.

conjunction with them—such acts and such measures as seem to it in conformity with the deep and permanent interests of the Nation.[83]

Eventually, the committee issued, through its reporter Henry Puget, this central observation:

> Between the constitutional project and the political system that predominated in France for many years, the rupture is complete. Still, if it rejects the official ideologies of the III Republic, the project stands completely distanced from fascist or hitlerian theories; just as it gathers the recent tendencies of our people, it restores and prolongs ancient national traditions, it sets itself in the line of civilization issued from Christian ideas.[84]

Christianity was to save Vichy constitutionalism from any taint of Nazi theory. But it was also to move the nation from the dissipated values that had cost it defeat and degradation.

Barthélemy's constitutionalism relied not solely on a kind of Christian narrative overlay that would be to Vichy law what the person of Hitler was to the Nazis. Barthélemy was *both* a liberal and a Catholic. In the draft constitution created during his months as Justice Minister and president of the Conseil national, there are specific allusions to the great revolutionary texts of the late eighteenth century. Let us cite a few:

> Titre I. No. 5: Property is the right to enjoy and dispose of one's possessions and one's revenues, the fruit of one's work and one's industriousness. (Decl. of 1795)
>
> No. 6: No one can be deprived of any part of his property without his consent unless the public benefit as legally set forth so requires and on condition of a fair and established compensation. (Decl. of 1793)
>
> No. 11: No one can be accused, arrested, or detained unless the law so dictates according to prescribed forms...but any citizen sought or seized under law must obey instantly and becomes guilty if he resists. (Decl. of 1789)
>
> No. 12: No one can be judged unless he has stated his case in a lawful hearing. The law may impose only those sanctions that are strictly necessary and that fit the crime. Anything imposed in excess of the sentence declared by law is a crime. (Decl. of 1795)

---

[83] AN 72 AJ 413, dossier no. 2.

[84] AN 72 AJ 413, dossier no. 2, p. 6 of the report.

No. 13: No law, civil or criminal, may have retroactive effect. (Decl. of 1795)

Titre II. No. 2: The right to assemble peaceably; the right to freedom of religion cannot ordinarily be abridged, except to respond to abuses of those rights as determined by law.(Decl. of 1789)[85]

The paradox of intertextual social liberalism in the Vichy constitutional context emerged from Barthélemy's own bipolar beliefs. He did not wish to let go of the ideals of his own past career. The challenge was to preserve those while also "cleansing the nation." Vichy's ability to adapt flexibly to this paradoxical situation, that makes its whole legal approach unique among the vanquished states of Europe, is disclosed by the very conditions of membership in the constitutional committee. Article IV of the draft constitution originally stated, explicitly, that "No Jew, as so defined by the law of 2 June 1941, can be named as a member of the Conseil national." As Barthélemy explains in his notes:

> The problem about Article IV was that we had to exclude Jews [il y a lieu d'exclure les Juifs]. The committee tried to do so without so stating, by adopting the following formula: "No one can be named to the Conseil national if he does not possess the general ability to accede to public functions; and if he is deprived of (or does not enjoy) his civil and political rights."[86]

When faced with logical and moral dilemmas, Barthélemy, no less than other lawyers, hid behind his professional language.[87]

The draft constitution marries racial exclusion to liberal humanism. Barthélemy, always capable of the most subtle and elegant writing, could still call a Jew a Jew if that was his inclination. So it was the liberal Catholic, and no one else, who introduced into the constitutional scheme an explicit notion of race. Article IV:

> The French community requires of its members an exclusive allegiance. It does not take into its bosom [elle n'admet pas dans son sein] and as a

---

[85] AN 72 AJ 413, dossier no. 2. These ideas of Barthélemy were by and large carried through in subsequent drafts with no recognition at any time of the contradictory nature of the Jewish laws passed and signed often by the same figures debating the constitution.

[86] Ibid. For a further discussion of the draft constitution and the Jews, and for the eventual fate of the Vichy constitution, see chapter 9, notes 63–71.

[87] Richard Weisberg, *The Failure of the Word: The Protagonist as Lawyer in Modern Fiction* (New Haven: Yale, 1984), chapter 9.

> constitutive element a race that behaves like a distinct community or resists assimilation.[88]

Barthélemy, who as a prewar law professor surely would not have dreamt of lending his name publicly to such a text,[89] furthered it in a variety of Vichy settings. Thus, on his Justice Ministry letterhead, the "Legislative Work of the Government of Marshal Pétain" is seen to include:

> 3e. Cleansing of the Nation. The government of the National Revolution has recognized the necessity, as quickly as possible, of removing from the French community [de débarrasser au plus vite la communauté française] certain elements that have insinuated themselves into leadership positions in the state, in industry and in finance. There, they elevated their own private interests, often even foreign interests, over those of the French nation; they played an insidious role [un role néfaste] in the years that preceded the war, in fact contributing in large measure to that event.[90]

To be French was to possess a package of qualities available to others only by dint of a long sojourn on French soil, typically in a certain place and attached to certain land generation after generation.[91] Otherwise people who happened to be on French soil were "elements," to be removed from time to time from the healthy organism that had generously abided them for a certain period until recognizing them to be a threat. They were another "race."

How much is left—on the level of law—of the supposed differentiation between hitlerian and Vichy values? What at first stood proudly as a kind of self-evident difference (Vichy's Christianity) now seems solipsistic at best. Vichy racism was every bit as exclusionary and reeked of the same verbal violence. Could *it* be "cleansed" through the mere mention of the Christian religion?

So the constitutional project, while considerately declining to accept the Justice Minister's explicit use of racial distinctions, did finally appropriate the narrative model of good and evil. In its Article VI, it declared what

---

[88] The text, which was not accepted by the rest of the committee, is set forth in Cointet-Labrousse, "Le Conseil national," 389.

[89] See note 50.

[90] AN 72 AJ 412, dossier no. 2.

[91] See Pierre Birnbaum, *Anti-Semitism,* chapter 6.

was good: "The French nation is the solidarity of a community of human beings animated by the desire to live together and in whom the soul is formed by traditions, memories, hopes, mores [*moeurs*], the attachment to the same soil, aspirations."[92]

Government was continuously defined as in the service *solely* of those who already "belonged." Almost every "liberal" intervention in the constitutional scheme was contradicted by a companion provision relating to outsiders. Sometimes the internal sense of a single phrase demonstrated its threatening quality:

> I, 16: Religious beliefs of recognized sects must be respected by those Frenchmen who may not share them. Tolerance is the measure of a civilization.

But what if your belief was no longer "recognized"? Or:

> II, 3: The law may only prohibit actions harmful to society. Everything not prohibited by law may not be barred, and no one can be forced to do what it does not require.... The law must be the same for all, whether it protects or punishes. All citizens are equal before the law, are equally accessible to every public honor, status, and employment according to their ability and with no other difference except that of their character and talent.

When does an action—or a state of being—become "harmful to society"? When does a law stop being the same for all? When does a citizen stop being a citizen? May character and talent be ignored if one belongs to the wrong "race"?

It is clear from reading Barthélemy's full set of constitutional notes that the exclusion of the Jews from legal protection—despite the religious laws' clear violation of most of the eighteenth-century principles drafted by him into the Vichy charter—was necessitated by "Frenchness" and its priorities. Thus, the legislative development from the constitutional source works explicitly as follows:

> 2. Protection of national values.... B. Protection of French nationality and property.... (b) the law relating to the Jews.[93]

---

[92] Cointet-Labrousse, *Vichy et le fascisme,* 177.

[93] AN 72 AJ 413, dossier no. 2.

The Vichy draft constitution thus reflected the degraded idealism of its primary creator.[94] Barthélemy included the great prose of the 1780s and 1790s, but he declined to apply it to everyone. Not a single protection afforded to French criminal suspects, except (as we shall see in the next chapter) some courts' salutary insistence on retaining the state's burden of proof against suspected Jews and not shifting that to the individual, was extended to the beleaguered Jewish individual brought before the law. As we shall see in chapter 7, the rights of property ownership were obliterated. And a Jew could not even contemplate the noble conceptions of peaceful assembly, or of freedom of religion.

The Justice Minister believed firmly that authority legitimately passed to Pétain on 10 July 1940.[95] As Barthélemy put it on the day in mid-1941 when Pétain spoke to the assembled Conseil d'État:

> Like all those who care for the well-being of the State above passions, resentments or individual egos, the *conseil* believes that salvation for France [le salut de la France] lies in an authoritarian régime. But it believes that once the tempest is quieted, an authoritarian régime will only be solid, valid, and healthy under the reign of law.[96]

On that very day, Barthélemy elicited and obtained from the officials of the Conseil d'État a personal oath to Pétain, addressing these words directly to his leader:

> Today the time of the equivocators is over.... It is not just to your office, but also to your person, that this body has just sworn an oath.[97]

As Cointet-Labrousse puts it well, describing Barthélemy's constitutional vision, "Whoever fights against the régime will be legitimately set outside of the national community."[98] Authority controls, and if it determines that individuals—or groups—are inherently threatening to the whole, it may without further justification exempt them from the constitutional framework.

---

[94] See J. Lubetzki, *La Condition des Juifs en France sous l'Occupation allemande* (Paris: CDJC, 1945), 22–24.

[95] Barthélemy, *Ministre,* 615.

[96] Ibid., 630 (annex).

[97] AN $BB^{30}$ 1711. For the text of the oath and its significance, see chapter 5, notes 111–17 and 123.

[98] Cointet-Labrousse, "Le Conseil national," 387.

The American generation that drafted its constitution also set a group apart. This racial exclusion, which required a civil war to correct, was to the minds of many today an inexcusable error, blotting out the magnificence of their original egalitarian vision. But slavery existed at the time they wrote; the choice of the excluded group was not their original contribution to constitutional law. And so we return to the unique intervention of Vichy: the *definition*—and not the retention—of a pariah group, outlawed *from the beginning* from legal protection, an ostracizing step justified by a return to older values.

Why? It would be easy to blame the Germans, yet they took no interest in these developments whatsoever. The French stretched to find their own way and Barthélemy, as much as Alibert, loudly proclaimed France's autonomy from German jurisprudential and constitutional models. And this brings us back to *ressentiment,* the reactive venom that seeps with greatest fecundity into the intellectualized vision of an unhappy and defeated spirit. In Alibert, it was palpable. In Barthélemy, as for the French generally, it was far more subtle.

I think the explanation for Barthélemy's jurisprudence goes beyond the nod to authoritarian law, interesting though that is in suggesting that the French have not yet really learned to live comfortably with their own revolutionary ideas.[99] It lies instead in the linkage of authority with a Christian concept of a savior, and of the suffering legitimately imposed on those who refuse to accept him. As Admiral Auphan put it, writing in 1971:

> [Regarding the Jews] there was a *ressentiment* [his word] that could not remain unexpressed. From the moment constitutional law permitted France to put its house in order...the distinction between two categories of French, Jews and non-Jews [became]...the social transcription of a grand mystery: the inability that stopped the people of the Bible, endowed beyond peradventure with so many gifts of the intellect and the heart, to find a collective equilibrium since the death of Christ, or to assimilate except by a long familial conversion, to the Christian nations.[100]

The constitutional project of Barthélemy, never completed during his term as Justice Minister, envisioned the eventual continuation of republican forms of government. While perhaps far from what Flandin may

[99] See, e.g., Birnbaum, *Anti-Semitism,* 19f.

[100] Paul Auphan, *Histoire élémentaire de Vichy* (Paris: France-Empire, 1971), 149f.

have wanted, Barthélemy would have eventually sought moderations on authoritarianism such as a ten-year term for the leader, who would be elected by a form of popular ballot; the restoration of the Senate and Assembly, although not in the same form as in the Third Republic; joint lawmaking power in the executive and legislature but to be monitored by a Supreme Court of Justice with powers of judicial review.[101]

Yet, despite these republican inclinations, Barthélemy remained virtually fixated on the authority whose will was (almost always) done during his ministry. If Vichy was Barthélemy's "Calvary," the suffering he experienced internally in the service of Philippe Pétain by design produced the actual misery of those his leader ostracized—those whom Barthélemy the liberal was willing to sacrifice to Barthélemy the Catholic.

## C. An Authoritarian France

"It has been said and repeated too often that the major benefit of the National Revolution was to give to France the leader for whom it was waiting and of whom it was deserving. We finally have a government of the one and only, the 'my-nasty' [*la mon-archie*]," says M. Charles Maurras.[102]

> In an authoritarian régime, a régime of one leader, there is no real cabinet that becomes a collegial authority; nor is there a head of the cabinet. The president of the United States works with his cabinet ministers individually, and if he chooses to speak with them collectively, he can conclude with Lincoln, "Seven no, one yes, the yes's have it...!" We had no other quality than that of the Marshal's agents.[103]

Joseph Barthélemy was a man of law, but he was Philippe Pétain's man above all. In his attraction to the person of the Marshal, he may have been highly typical, and so suggested his grandson when he told me "there were 40,000,000 Pétainists until July 1941."[104] But if represen-

---

[101] See Lépagnot, *Histoire de Vichy,* vol. 3, 98.

[102] Barthélemy, *Ministre,* 125. Maurras is cited frequently and without apparent disapproval in Barthélemy's book.

[103] Ibid., 126f.

[104] Jean Barthélemy, personal interview with author, Paris, 1988.

tative, the allegiance becomes all the more interesting. It proves to have nothing in common with the American executive Barthélemy conjures, and everything in common with traditional pre-Revolutionary patterns of French zealotry. Barthélemy describes it this way:

> There has been a cult of Pétain. In the aftermath of the defeat, France, disoriented and in dreadful chaos, saw him as the master who would restore order, the leader who would muster minds and hearts, the savior who would raise the country from its ruination. Pétain was the great lifter of French morale. During the two years after the armistice, all the hopes of the French crystallized around him. He thus gave the nation service so exceptional, so high and so eminent that history must preserve an unflinching gratitude to him.
>
> This cult was crucial to the welfare of France. And that is why I was not only one of its adherents, but also one of its most fervent priests. Fervent, but also sincere. It was not only politics, in the highest sense of the word; it was something other than the highest interest of the country. This cult was spontaneous. France loved Pétain and was happy to love him....
>
> I believed in a miraculous salvation for France, in a renewal of Joan of Arc's mission. I practiced this cult, I had this faith.[105]

The man who eventually would see Vichy as his Calvary first saw himself as the priestly follower of France's new Joan of Arc. These personalizations, drawn from iconographies dear to the French, help us to understand a super-rational (or irrational) component of Vichy behavior. If Barthélemy, the urbane lawyer *par excellence,* felt and retained this Christological conception of Vichy and its leader, how much more likely is it that many other Frenchmen adulated, revered, and followed blindly the words of the decorated old man?

How does a tangible human crisis, involving Vichy law, pass through the metaphoric crucible of Christian iconography? How, for example, does the cult leader respond to pleas for help from a follower? Who counts as a follower? A meritorious Jew? Recall that, under Section 8 of the first religious law, a decree could be published exempting individual Jews from the harassment and the punition of the statute. But by mid-1941, an internal Vichy memo entitled "Note on the Situation of Jews Having Been Made the Object of Individual Decrees by the French Head of State," observes that "the very small number of decrees allowed"

---

[105] Barthélemy, *Ministre,* 61.

saved a mere *seven* individuals,[106] and this despite the observation that "it can easily be agreed to by the occupying authorities that the beneficiaries of individual French decrees will be relieved of all obligations and prohibitions resulting from the [German] ordinances against the Jews already or eventually taken in the occupied zone."[107]

The leader on the white horse had "washed his hands of the great majority of Jews," as Marrus and Paxton put it.[108] Occasionally, France's love for him was returned even to a Jew. So Pétain gave his blessing to Étienne Frois, bestowing upon him the decree "relieving him of the prohibitions declared by the law of 2 June 1941...and authorizing him to be reintegrated into his duties as a secondary school teacher."[109] Frois had been able to prove that his family had been established in Bayonne for several centuries (having "lived on the same land, transmitted from father to son, since 1650"); that his father, although already in his forties and head of a large family, had volunteered for the '14–'18 war and had "brilliantly served at the front" (joining in a long line of war veterans going back to Napoleon I); that Étienne himself had earned three citations of merit in the present war; and that the family entertained only the most "moderate political opinions."[110]

One month later, Dr. Tabet, gendarme Orbeck, and army sub-officer Prigosine, fared more typically and lost their positions for being Jews who "however good and loyal they might be," did not present the requisite combination of long attachment to the French soil and estimable family or personal contributions to the state.[111]

Midway into 1943, Gaston Israel joined many of his co-religionists in writing desperately to the French savior to help his brother. Now the stakes surpassed mere employment. Moïse Israel and his family awaited deportation. Gaston writes:

> I must express to you, M. le Maréchal, my sad astonishment. My brother is French, he did his military service [as a volunteer] and later was mobilized

---

[106] Memorandum, 6 May 1941, CDJC CXIV-13.

[107] Ibid., 2.

[108] Marrus and Paxton, *Vichy France and the Jews,* 86.

[109] CDJC CXIV-54.

[110] Ibid., the last phrase and some of the details coming from supporting papers forwarded to the Marshal.

[111] CDJC CVX-79.

for the war as a sub-officer. Thus, both on the military and civil level (he paid all his taxes), he did his duty and fulfilled his obligations. My brother also never indulged in politics, sticking to the sciences exclusively. He was continuing his medical studies.

> Being unexceptionable, morally, professionally, and civilly, he has the right to the protection of his country and of his government. It is this protection that I now solicit. I do not think of myself, M. le Maréchal, of asking you for a favor or a personal solicitude but merely the fulfillment of your own qualities [vos propres attributions] conforming to the duty that the Nation has bestowed upon you.
>
> We are dealing with a Frenchman who has done his duty, who has not betrayed, who has not fled, and who, respectful of all your laws [toutes vos lois], placed himself with confidence under the protection of the leader of his country. Is the Nation just a word? It is true my brother is named Israel. He was not named Dupont when the Nation called him to arms.
>
> That is why, despite the chaos [incohérence] in which we live, the vanity of beliefs, the reversal of every basic precept of the human conscience, I dare to raise my voice towards one of its children.[112]

Moïse Israel, the Marseilles pharmacist, along with his wife and her 15-year-old brother were deported on 31 July 1943.[113] If the octogenarian Joan of Arc ever saw this eloquent but representative prayer, the sad duties of leadership drove the horseman on, impervious.

Joseph Barthélemy, one of the faithful, was experiencing his own Calvary, as we know. On the Jewish question, he was willing to play the faithful cleric to this high priest. In lines originally written for the journal, *Patrie*[114] and reproduced in part in the footnotes of the chapter "Les juifs" in his book-length memoirs,[115] Barthélemy spoke in his polite way of the irredeemable "other" that could never follow his leader:

> We must speak seriously, serenely, amicably, fraternally, but also frankly and courageously about the Jewish problem. Most of us have had Jews among our friends. I have had friends of that race and I hope to keep them. It's a fact nonetheless that for centuries they have refused to meld into the French community. "Put a glass of oil into a tub [barrique] of water, a chief

---

[112] CDJC CXV-118.

[113] Serge Klarsfeld, *Memorial to the Jews Deported from France, 1942–44* (New York: Beate Klarsfeld Foundation, 1983), 438.

[114] See note 48, above; and the citation in Lubetzki, *La Condition des Juifs,* 15.

[115] Barthélemy, *Ministre,* 319.

> rabbi used to say to me proudly, the oil will remain separate. Double the quantity of water, triple it, increase it a hundred fold, the glass of oil will never mix itself into the vile liquid. So it is with our race."
>
> This is the fact that the French government had to face.... I am obsessed in writing these things by the specter of great Jews who are my colleagues, partners, or friends, like the great Bergson, that undeniable glory of French philosophy and literature, and I add, one who thinks French [et j'ajoute, pensant français]. The Marshal foresaw ostracizing measures [des mesures d'exception] ... I also have a heavy heart when I think of the tragedy of so many individual situations.
>
> I need all my reason to think that it was really necessary to take such measures, even against one's will, to heal surgically this suffering French soul of the sickness that has taken us where we are.
>
> The law is cruel. Those who bear responsibility for the destiny of the country have judged it necessary.[116]

As Lubetzki has put it, "Thus does a lawyer who, in numerous works, has defended the grand principles of law and liberty, justify measures that constitute the most abominable attacks on human dignity, liberty, and property."[117]

Yet it may be that an even greater irony than this lies in Barthélemy's *associating* the laws of his régime with his own prewar observations about the irredeemable other. In one of several locutions from this polite man that approach vulgarity, his anecdote about oil and water—placed in the mouth of a rabbi as though to blame the religious laws on their victims—indicates not so much a falling off as a fulfillment of the whole Joseph Barthélemy.

It is not for nothing that the *Patrie* essay proceeds to invert the Pétain iconography:

> When the war broke out, Jews had an exaggerated place in France. They were so numerous in all leadership positions that they seemed like a governing *race* installed in the midst of an inferior indigenous population. Look at the propaganda in the Foreign Ministry: a Jew was in charge; and at the head of each bureau a Jew sat enthroned, without exception: print, science, film, etc.... In the town of Joan of Arc, Orléans, at a certain moment, the mayor, the top military leader, the district prosecutor, were Jews. Well, Jewry [la Juiverie] is not a religion, as Naquet proclaimed, "My

---

[116] Ibid.

[117] Lubetzki, *La Condition des Juifs,* 15.

> religion or better yet my race." "My race," Léon Blum used to say. It's a question of moderation. The measure had been surpassed. Some of my Jewish friends were themselves upset about this.[118]

Joan of Arc's town, and her country, may be excused for ridding itself of a threatening and basically exogenous population. Barthélemy's racism is of a piece with prewar antisemitism on several planes; it lies in this association of Christian iconography with Jewish subterfuge. Joan of Arc is an archetypal reminder of what it is to be racially pure, to belong to the land, to be (like the Marshal) singlemindedly devoted to an identifiable people, to resist or ignore the outsiders. It is purity of mission, acceptance of internal suffering and infliction of external torment on the irredeemable other. Barthélemy raises the prewar imagery to an official and acceptable level. As Birnbaum says:

> Joan, the peasant maid, the Christian, the virgin, the Celt, has carried all the hopes of the nationalist and anti-Semitic Right from the end of the nineteenth century to the present day. During Vichy, "with Pétain as with Joan, the battle remains the same."[119]

In Barthélemy, however, there is the additional element of a pragmatic, *legalistic* racism. It harkens more to the respectable discourse of Stanislas Fumet, who condemned "racism in the name of Catholicism."[120] Unlike overt antisemitism, this strain utilizes Catholicism to distinguish France from Hitler while at the same time accomplishing similar levels of suffering; so, Fumet:

> But the nations are justified in defending themselves from the excessive percentage of Israelites in the highest positions in the country. National susceptibilities, for example, are rightly alarmed when a Léon Blum calls on disproportionate participation by the Jewish element to form his ministry. It is this lack of discretion, this lack of tact, peculiar to a certain type of Judaism.... It is possible that the *numerus clausus* is not an arrangement to be rejected.[121]

---

[118] Barthélemy, *Ministre,* 311, emphasis in original.

[119] Birnbaum, *Anti-Semitism,* 148, citing Michel Winock, who has also analyzed the Joan iconography in his *Edouard Drumont et Cie.: Antisémistisme et fascisme en France* (Paris: Le Seuil, 1982).

[120] Birnbaum, *Anti-Semitism,* 186, citing Fumet in early 1940.

[121] Ibid., citing Fumet, 186.

Barthélemy the Catholic, as his grandson recently remarks, was fond of the rejoinder made by Cardinal Mathieu to the cliché about the Jews, "They brought the blood of Christ upon them," to which the Cardinal riposted "The blood of Christ can only fall as a benediction."[122] Like Fumet and other elite Catholics, he sincerely believed that his "profound and unshakable Christian faith"[123] automatically set him apart from any hitlerian strain of antisemitism. But, like Cardinal Mathieu, he was less interested in *correcting the libels against the Jews* than in lodging them within an ongoing myth of blood that could only bring real suffering upon them by legitimating their otherness.

Pétain led French law less into new territory than back to the old virtues that foreign elements alone had temporarily undermined; Barthélemy, his constitutional apologist, made the return to pre-Revolutionary values seem somehow essentially French. Catholicism and its iconography could be conjured whenever anyone dared suggest that Vichy's Joan of Arc looked too much like a *deutsches Mädchen*. For that irksome drop of oil had also been a bother to the Holy Water.[124] Christ's beneficence would descend on those who betrayed him, despite themselves; but that "benediction" would occur selectively and metaphysically, long after legalistic suffering indistinguishable from the German model had been inflicted upon them.

Not all Catholicisms dovetailed with overt persecution of the Jews during World War II, and I shall reiterate this important caveat in my concluding chapter. But Barthélemy's strikes me as indicative of a rationalistic Catholicism in France, eager to season its purely logical urges with an appropriate dose of archetype, image, and symbolism. Where there is a Joan of Arc, there must be an enemy; where there is Catholic suffering and the need to blame it on someone else, Jews will often suffer physical torment while Christians privately (and with far less actual discomfort) undergo spiritual Calvary.

Between the single-minded horseman and his devout follower, there is always a gulf, of course. As Dostoevsky shows us in his character, the "Grand Inquisitor" in *The Brothers Karamazov,* the priest has a legalistic side that can seem to distort the pure message of the cult leader, which

---

[122] Barthélemy, *Ministre,* 320.

[123] Ibid.

[124] See Birnbaum, *Anti-Semitism,* chapter 8, "The Antichrist."

if left unadulterated might be unassimilable to the masses. Yet Riom produced the lone incident of tension between the two. In our final section, we delve closely into Barthélemy as legislator and implementor of his leader's vision.

## D. Barthélemy and the Régime's Special Legislation

Towards the Christmas of his first year as minister, Barthélemy granted an interview to journalist Maurice Vallet. Reflecting on his accomplishments, he declared that he was "first and foremost a minister of legislation...a provider of good legislative texts."[125] This modest self-assessment serves to remind us that Barthélemy's social, constitutional, and religious beliefs converged around his principal task, which was *technical* in nature. As Claude Singer says of him very recently, in a quotation with which I agree except for its final seven words:

> Barthélemy, as opposed to Alibert, was neither an ideologue nor a militant antisemite. He was above all a man of order, of duty—an administrator. Thus he never made glaring declarations in favor of Franco-German collaboration or the antisemitic legislation, of which he was not the instigator.[126]

For the heroic parliamentarian renegade, Philippe Serre, Barthélemy was one of the faceless technocrats that Pétain occasionally required, a man with "absolutely no personality"—far less interesting—and therefore to Serre far less bizarre and threatening than his predecessor, Alibert.[127]

Yet Barthélemy's 1941 interview really underscores his power, as opposed to his passivity, in the elaboration of Vichy law. Prone though most commentators have been to see the legislation as monolithic, or to reside responsibility for the religious laws at any rate in Alibert, Barthélemy's own words about himself contradict that benign view. While called to Vichy as a member of the government, Barthélemy realized that the constitutional "legitimacy" granted Vichy on 10 July 1940, em-

---

[125] Joseph Barthélemy, interview with Maurice Vallet, 13 December 1941, AN BB[30], 1708.

[126] Singer, *Vichy,* 90.

[127] Philippe Serre, personal interview with author, Paris, 21 December 1988.

powered his ministry, in particular, to be "a provider of good legislative texts."

Yet Barthélemy, unselfconsciously proud of his legislative achievements during that busy year of 1941, hedged about the powers of Vichy and its leaders when it came to the religious laws. Just that past summer, he was insisting in his article, "Les juifs," published in *Patrie,*[128] that "this legislation is not initiated by the French; it is entirely of German origin."[129] Few were ignorant at the time, and many fewer now, of the *exclusive* French origin of the 1940 religious and denaturalization laws. But what of the 1941 developments, which included what Singer calls "a boulimia of legislation by Vichy, which prided itself on marginalizing the Jews in order to remove them from the French community"?[130] With an average of one law and one decree on the Jews signed *each week* during the year that Barthélemy was Justice Minister,[131] is it likely that this "provider of good legislative texts" was distanced from their promulgation?

Barthélemy tended to denigrate sharply his influence upon religious law. Although he signed most of the 1941 legislation, including the definitive and expansive law of 2 June 1941, he claimed that "as to the anti-Jewish legislation, it was done apart from me [Quant à la législation antijuive, elle se faisait en dehors de moi]."[132] Yet, as Marrus and Paxton indicate, that statute "was carefully prepared in cabinet meetings during May, with technical improvements added by Justice Minister Barthélemy. It was a properly French initiative without direct German intervention."[133] The documents further indicate that, on the French view itself, the statute of 2 June 1941 "was the fruit of special comparative legislative studies" by the CGQJ and the ministries, designed to benefit from the experience the French had had with the 3 October statutory scheme.[134] Barthélemy and Pétain were the sole signatories to the 16

---

[128] See note 48.

[129] The essay is reprinted in Barthélemy, *Ministre,* 311.

[130] Singer, *Vichy,* 71.

[131] Ibid.

[132] Barthélemy, *Ministre,* 313.

[133] Marrus and Paxton, *Vichy France and the Jews,* 98.

[134] Memo, CGQJ to the Admiralty (Darlan), 28 March 1942, CDJC, CVX-22a.

July 1941 statute on Jewish lawyers, discussed in chapter 3.[135] And Barthélemy signed on (with Pétain, Bouthiller, and Pucheu) to the law of 22 July 1941,[136] compendiously regulating the ownership of Jewish property. Although such "aryanization" laws form a separate chapter in this study, Barthélemy's own comments about his participation in promulgating the July statute require immediate attention.

In his 1941 piece on the Jews, Barthélemy writes in detail solely about the July property-stripping law. Having already disingenuously blamed the Germans for Vichy's 1940 racial innovations, and falsely dissociated himself from the 2 June 1941 statute, Barthélemy here describes a process of internal ministerial protest to parts of the aryanization law. He depicts himself as sickened to read the draft bill, which effectively would have thrown Jews out of their own homes, divested of their family property, and also aryanized their businesses, rental properties, bank accounts, etc.

> In returning from Paris for that meeting, I found in my office a bill prepared at the Majestic by the Germans and transmitted for approbation by the French government. Following the praiseworthy procedure of Darlan, and regrettably abandoned by Laval, this [proposed] law had to be signed by the cabinet, because of its importance. I spoke up with my somewhat brutal sincerity: "I read this text an hour ago, and I am still burning with indignation. I want the cabinet to have my comments about this text. First, Article I speaks of the liquidation of real and personal property. Real property? Thus the house that the Jew lives in? The apartment he occupies? His personal property, so the bed in which he sleeps, the chair on which he sits?" At this moment, I was interrupted by a colleague. "But Vallat will not do that!" "Then why give him the right to do it?," I riposted.[137]

Thanks to Barthélemy's intervention—others also protested, perhaps for the first time when confronted with anti-Jewish legislation[138]—the elaborate new law permitted retention of the Jew's individual homestead.

> They gave me satisfaction on nine of the 12 amendments I suggested. I finally signed in order to preserve my right of oversight and caution

---

[135] See R. Sarraute and P. Tager, *Les Juifs sous l'Occupation: Recueil des textes officiels français et allemands* (Paris: CDJC, 1982), 60.

[136] Ibid., 62.

[137] Barthélemy, *Ministre,* 313f.

[138] Marrus and Paxton, *Vichy France and the Jews,* 101.

> [surveillance et frein]. But from that day on, I was no longer consulted about the Jewish laws or Jewish matters [au sujet des lois ou des affaires juives].[139]

There is something disturbingly slippery about this prose. Putting aside matters susceptible of proof, the rage experienced by Barthélemy as he read the draft legislation seems myopically self-limiting. Here again, as we have seen with Haennig, Maury, and Charpentier as well, solicitude for the Jews emerges on low levels of lawyerlike generalization. Let them be stripped of their hard-earned property *ex post* and without due process of law—sure. But we cannot permit their apartments to be grabbed, too! Barthélemy's riposte parallels that of one of his favorites, Cardinal Mathieu.[140] It protests, but too feebly.

As to the passage's more factual aspects, it creates two major internal self-contradictions. If the Germans alone initiated and controlled the Jewish laws, how could it be that they were debated and even sharply modified by French cabinet action? And why is the aftermath of the promulgation of even this proposed aryanization law described as a purely French concern, contingent upon decisions by Jewish Question Commissar Vallat, as overseen and cautioned by the Vichy Justice Minister even then?

By reference to extrinsic sources, the passage of course becomes still more questionable. We know that the French controlled their own fates legislatively and that Vichy religious laws prior to the aryanization statute were exclusively of French origin. If it was in any way fair to say that the aryanization laws "originated at the Majestic in Paris," it would be true in the limited sense that the Germans were especially interested in Jewish booty and had become more active in that area as 1941 progressed. But, as we have already signalled, Vichy always argued for its autonomy over *all* aspects of religious law—definition, punition, aryanization, everything.

More disturbingly when it comes to Barthélemy's own self-descriptions, how seriously can we take his contention of removal from Jewish matters after mid-1941, particularly as this contention has been repub-

---

[139] Barthélemy, *Ministre,* 314.

[140] See note 122.

lished and reaffirmed in 1989?[141] When Barthélemy granted his interview to the journalist at the very end of 1941, is it possible that the "good legislative texts" he says he furnished excluded all the Jewish material? As he proceeded until resigning, through 1942 and part of 1943, is it credible that he had no part in "des affaires juives"?

As quickly as the August following the contentious cabinet meeting that supposedly led to his isolation from religious legislative developments, Barthélemy was engaged in the kind of correspondence with the CGQJ that permeated his full term as Justice Minister. True, not all of Barthélemy's work literally had to do with legislative reform or innovation, although some of it did; much effort involved interpretation and implementation of existing law. So, on 19 August 1941, we read of an exchange between the CGQJ's service of legislation and disputes and the Justice Ministry. The point raised is the standard legalism of the four-year Vichy period: who has the burden of proof on Jewishness and what means of evidence can be used to carry or rebut that burden?

> You have graciously transmitted to me, by your letter of 8 August, a memorandum relating to the interpretation of the first article of the law of 2 June 1941.... This memo asks, first of all, if proof as to adherence to the Catholic religion can be provided solely by a baptismal record or if, on the contrary, the production of a certificate attesting to the beginning of religious instruction, or even the fact of being the issue of a marriage with disparity of belief where the commitment was made to bring children up as Christians, can suffice.... The second question concerns children born after 25 June 1940 and who have two Jewish grandparents.[142]

Barthélemy never gave up his interest and his active intervention in this ongoing interpretive dispute. As we shall see, his support of the courts (as opposed to the administrative agencies) on this question tended in the main to liberalize *some* contested areas of the religious laws. So here, his ministry was seeking wider forms of proof of Catholicism, and the CGQJ was insisting that a baptismal certificate alone was necessary—but not

---

[141] In the notes to the chapter, "Les juifs," Barthélemy's editors contend that "It is still a sure fact...that as Minister Joseph Barthélemy opposed himself to the extent possible to the projects of Jacques Barnaud and Xavier Vallat, to the extent that after November 1941, he was no longer consulted about them." Barthélemy, *Ministre,* 320.

[142] AN $AJ^{38}$, 118.

sufficient—to prove non-Jewishness. The fact remains that Barthélemy's participation was constant.

On 27 January 1942, Barthélemy personally signed a letter to the head of the CGQJ responding to the latter's request for his comments on a proposed reformation and tightening of the Jewish statute. This document, among others, specifically rebuts the recent repetition of the claim that he had no role after 1941 in reforming religious statutes.[143] It is worth citing at length:

> To the Commissaire générale aux questions juives. You have asked me, by your letter of 9 January 1942, to submit my agreement to a bill [projet de loi], prepared by your departments, to modify Paragraphs 1, 2 and 3 of the law of 2 June 1941. I am pleased to give you the following observations: 1. The definition of Jew itself is profoundly undermined by the *projet;* in the text of 2 June 1941, only race was taken into consideration and belonging to the mosaic religion only counted as a subsidiary matter to determine the status of someone who had only two Jewish grandparents as a way of determining the race of the grandparents. To the contrary, the proposed text considers Jewish one who "belongs to" the mosaic religion. Religion now seems of equal importance with race. From this point, it is hard to conceive that one who has converted, for example to Catholicism, before June 1940 could escape from the Jewish law, nor could the Catholic who adhered to the Jewish faith even though racially non-Jewish [de pleine race non juive], not be considered Jewish. Even if this reciprocity seems worthy of modification, the proposed text will need to be further perfected. From what facts are we to deduce "belonging to" the mosaic religion? Does this mean every religious rite required from birth till death by the mosaic religion, or just a few and if so which few? How will proof be furnished that the individual did or did not adhere to these rites? Such questions must be resolved in the text itself that would modify the law of 2 June so that the modification neither remains a dead letter nor gives rise to arbitrary interpretations.
>
> 2. To the extent the proposed text does follow the criterion of race, it no longer looks at the number of Jewish grandparents, as does the 2 June statute, but instead derives adherence to the mosaic religion from the number of known ascendants of the first and second degree. According to your letter, this change is inspired by the need to include foreigners and out-of-wedlock children [des enfants naturels]. As to the former, it seems that they will continue to escape for the most part from the law because the research of your operatives on their ascendance and their religion will generally be

[143] See note 141.

impossible to pursue beyond French territory. As to out-of-wedlock children, we must ask the question if this research *should* proceed. Should their ascendants be legally determined, or just factually? If the former, proving legally the ascendants of the children of adulterous or incestuous parents would contradict the formal strictures of Article 335 of the Code civil.... [If the inquiry is based just on common knowledge], out-of-wedlock children would be forced to establish their ascendancy in fact, in violation of the provisions of the Civil Code. Either way, it seems that these situations require an explicit solution.

3. As your letter of January 9 indicates, the prior limitation to religions recognized by the State prior to the law of separation [December 1905] is excessive, and the *projet* correctly wants to enlarge this provision by admitting proof of belonging to any religion besides that of the mosaic religion....

I would add that no other portion of the *projet* poses any problem for me.

Signed—Joseph Barthélemy[144]

Remarkable in this response is not only the obvious continued participation by Barthélemy in racial policies but also the substantive concerns he had in early 1942. He declares himself satisfied with a CGQJ reform project that would have made life far more difficult for Jews or suspected Jews. His *caveats* are restricted to maintaining *race* as a key element in legal definition; protecting the privacy rights of out-of-wedlock children; and broadening—*but only modestly,* and in line with the CGQJ—the kinds of evidence available to prove non-Jewishness.[145]

---

[144] AN AJ[38], 118. Barthélemy ratifies the CGQJ on other issues not addressed by his letter. He thus consents to what would have been a significant shift on the question of burden of proof, from the traditional criminal law imposition *upon the state* to a proposed "double (or mixed) burden" in which the state comes forward with minimal "proof" and the individual then must carry the burden of persuasion on non-Jewishness. This was Alibert's approach, but it somehow seems less appropriate for a man like Barthélemy to leave it unquestioned. See below, note 151.

[145] Barthélemy's final paragraph fails to propound the already available suggestions that *all* evidence should be admissible on this point, not simply the adherence to an organized religion besides Judaism. Indeed, Barthélemy notes this lack in a part of the letter not cited, but declines to endorse further liberalization to include, for example, atheists and freethinkers who, although they have only two Jewish grandparents, would not be able to show adherence to a non-Mosaic faith. These would still be considered Jews under the CGQJ's proposed "broadening." See generally chapter 5(A).

The following month, Vallat and Barthélemy correspond directly on the former's idea of innovating a "specialized jurisdiction" on aryanization questions, since so many connected issues are "sensitive" and difficult. Barthélemy, sticking to a position he maintained against the agency throughout his term as minister, ripostes that the ordinary courts are the perfect vehicle for adjudicating such delicate matters, since they are the "traditional guardians of property and of the honor of individuals."[146]

Among the ancillary issues raised in these continuous calls on Barthélemy after late 1941 was the matter of out-of-wedlock children. Barthélemy cites an article of the Civil Code that long antedates the Jewish laws to protest an aspect of the latter that might contradict settled law. The French have had a special solicitude for the privacy rights of such children, and the idea of disturbing those to research racial genealogy bothers the Justice Minister so much that he devotes half of his answer to the CGQJ to that specific conflict in the law.[147]

Also on his mind at the time—and another area in which his influence on race matters was clearly felt—was the issue of name changes. In a statutory innovation largely ascribed to him personally, the law of 10 February 1942 revised such older laws as one dating to 1870 and *prohibited*

---

[146] CDJC CXV-8a. This response concerns only the law of 22 July 1941. It appears that Barthélemy was more scrupulous in safeguarding traditional proof burdens when it came to this law about property than when it came to the 2 June definitional statute, where he seems willing to shift the burden to the individual.

[147] Not long after Barthélemy's memo, CGQJ advised its regional director in Nice that an out-of-wedlock child suspected of being Jewish but whose parents were completely unknown would "without a doubt be considered Jewish, unless baptized," 3 March 1942, CDJC CXV-19. Even in this harsh letter, however, the agency, perhaps increasingly responsive to Barthélemy's notion of conflicting French law protective of such children's privacy, cites possible problems with certain Civil Code articles and also prewar statutes of 1925 and 1939. On 29 May 1942, CGQJ (through its service on legislation and litigation [contentieux]), wrote to an agency dealing with wards of the state: "You have suggested that it would be too much to ask of a child born of unknown parents and carrying a name that sounds Jewish to prove his non-affiliation with the Jewish race. I am pleased to tell you that I agree, as long as the parents are unknown in fact, that is if nothing in terms of documents or proceedings reveals their existence. On the other hand, the mother, for example, whose name is mentioned on the birth certificate of the child, must be considered as a known parent. In this case the child must establish that his ascendant was not Jewish," AN $AJ^{38}$, 118. See also chapter 9, subsection C.

*name changes by Jews.*[148] Again, Barthélemy was in close touch with CGQJ on this issue; Vallat wrote to him to make sure that the new legislation would "offer special measures to facilitate name changes by non-Jews who bear names of israelite or biblical origin."[149] They worked out a system in which the agency monitored requests and permitted name changes after it felt a certificate of non-affiliation with the Jewish race was mandated. A special internal department, run by Colmet-Daage, was set up, and Jews were quickly prosecuted for using "pseudonyms."[150]

By contrast with these specific areas in which Barthélemy exercised power and remained a potent force in racial policy, he rather shockingly submitted explicitly to what the CGQJ itself called "the most significant reform,"[151] that would have altered the burden of proof as a matter of formal law, imposing a heavier load still upon those charged with "being Jewish." About *that* proposal, even the Admiralty office took greater umbrage than did Barthélemy, in a memo to the CGQJ of 15 March 1942, signed by Admiral Auphan, at that time chief of staff of naval forces.[152] On the other hand, Barthélemy did object at that time when CGQJ appeared to shift the burden of proof on *property* matters arising from the 22 July statute.[153]

Barthélemy participated fully in racial policy debates well into 1942. While from time to time using his influence to protect or at least give solace to individual Jews,[154] and while hewing a somewhat more liberal line on specific lawyers and magistrates than the agencies did, as well as on identifiable single issues such as the effect of the *numerus clausus* on

---

[148] *Journal officiel,* 27 March 1942, 1190.

[149] AN AJ[38], 116.

[150] Ibid. Nonetheless, Barthélemy was criticized by some for moving too slowly on name changes; in the context of a memorandum written anonymously—after he left office—the former minister was accused of not implementing the new law against name changes until 9 January 1943, hence permitting some Jews to camouflage their racial heritage, CDJC, XXVII-9; see chapter 5, note 76.

[151] CDJC CXV-22a, 2. Barthélemy surely realized that he was consenting to an explicit change in the 2 June statutory formula that would have flown in the face of foundational French notions of justice. Indeed, his ministry was vigorously opposing any burden shift in law proposals that had nothing to do with Jews. See chapter 5, text at note 9.

[152] CDJC CXIV-24.

[153] CDJC CXV-3a and 8a.

[154] See especially, Barthélemy, *Ministre,* 312–14 and accompanying notes.

a student who had been promoted and was seeking rematriculation,[155] Barthélemy's unmistakable presence on racial matters legitimated Vichy's antisemitism by moving it to the center of legal acceptability.

Barthélemy rigorously insisted on the exclusion of Jews from almost all posts in government law—especially including the magistracy—despite his knowledge that Vichy needed experienced judges as attrition hit this profession badly.[156] This paradox was joined by an even more sinister one, as the Justice Minister often found himself pleading that his Jewish-free magistracy gain increased power over the racial matters themselves! Barthélemy's whole training and intuition geared him well to fight the battle (which our next chapter explores fully) on behalf of *magistrate jurisdiction above that of the administrative courts*. When it came to Jewish-related litigation, he repeatedly insisted on the primacy of the ordinary courts; thus on 12 February 1942, he responds to the CGQJ's request for his opinion on statutory reform of the aryanization laws as follows:

> I am pleased to inform you that "the conscience of the judge" [la conviction du juge] as to knowing whether a given sale—prior to the appointment of an Aryan trustee [administrateur provisoire]—effectively eliminates all Jewish influence, derives from several factual and legal aspects (the race of the vendee, relationship to vendor, actual payment of purchase price, origin of payment funds, scope of certain contractual provisions) for the examination of which the qualifications of magistrates and tribunals seem especially well suited, because of their experience in civil and commercial cases.

---

155 See CDJC CXV-49, 5, where Barthélemy (as of 30 June 1942) is cited as wanting such students to retain their right to study, even if the total number of Jewish students had by then surpassed the allowable quota.

156 See, e.g., AN BB[30], 1716, where Barthélemy and his ministry are described in late 1941 as opining that Jewish lawyers could not serve as magistrates or in other such capacities: "the provisions of the law of 2 June 1941 seem to keep Jews and Freemasons from any participation, even quite temporary, in the makeup of courts and tribunals." Six months later, Barthélemy's ministry denied the request of Jewish former magistrates to exercise their rights—under a law dating back to 6 July *1810*—to continue to sit in deliberative conferences of their former courts. "To do so," opined the Justice Ministry's division of civil policy, "would constitute their participating in the judicial function." Even *inviting* them to attend in silence would "raise a delicate problem" that could only be resolved through legislation!

> The common law judge, called on a daily basis to rule on criminal matters that implicate questions of intention, offers, because of his training, particular safeguards of psychology and perception....[157]

Yet, as late as 19 March 1943, Barthélemy was routinely signing into law such decrees as the following:

> Examinations for the post of Justice of the Peace.... Article 2. To be admitted for the examination are only those candidates fulfilling the conditions of article 2 of the decree of 4 July 1936 and of the law of 3 April 1941, and who are not excluded by the laws of 2 June 1941, and 11 August 1941.[158]

Jews and members of secret societies were not to apply for positions in Barthélemy's courts although the logic of his own support of the magistrates, during one of France's historically most litigious periods (1941–1944), required all legal talent available.

Barthélemy personally signed many interministerial letters and memoranda as 1942 progressed, and the aryanization of property was often, as we have seen, much on his mind. Thus on 18 May 1942, he replied to a request by the CGQJ for his opinion relating to what was becoming a crucial question of property ownership as the French and German administrations fought for control over Jewish booty in occupied France. What should happen, asked the agency, if a German—rather than a French—administrator handles the transfer, "with the view to eliminating Jewish influence over property in the Occupied Zone"? Always contentious (see chapter 7), this issue would have brought Barthélemy in direct conflict with the Germans, as the property in question was owned by Jews of either German origin or of a nationality now at war with the Germans. Barthélemy, consulted fully as he usually was on racial questions, decided to refer the matter to the Minister of Foreign Affairs.

Little that took place in the area of law during his months in office escaped Barthélemy's attention (even when he decided to take no action on the matter in question), and there is nothing at all to his claim that after 1941 he was no longer a participant when it came to the religious

---

[157] Memorandum, Barthélemy to CGQJ, 12 February 1942, CDJC CXV-8a.

[158] Law of 19 March 1943 (repeating those of 9 September and 3 March 1942), AN $BB^{30}$, 1713. This would have been one of Barthélemy's last official acts before resigning several days later. For discussion of manpower shortages and other demoralizing tendencies among magistrates, see chapter 3, text at notes 63–67; chapter 5, notes 59–60.

laws. There, as is in one sense also true of the dreaded special jurisdictions—such as the special section courts that Barthélemy signed into existence in summer 1941[159]—the liberal law professor had ceded the uppermost levels of his conscience to Pétain, whose authority he followed almost to the letter. As Arnaud Teyssier observes in a recent thesis on Barthélemy, it seemed to some that his greatest doubt about the special arenas of administrative detention lay in their being confused with his beloved ordinary courts.[160] To the extent that the excesses of the special jurisdictions looked like Vichy law to the common observer, Barthélemy feared that "the magistracy would be discredited."[161]

## E. The Final Days

Barthélemy's final days merit sympathy, but there is a part of someone looking at the end of this witty and highly literate man that cannot help but note a kind of poetic justice even he might have appreciated. Leaving the government, Barthélemy turned in spring 1943 to the writing of his memoirs and to the resumption of his academic duties. Barthélemy saw himself as one who "fought, often with success, for the hierarchical place of the Justice Minister [la place protocolaire du Garde des Sceaux], because I saw that as the symbol of the primacy of law."[162]

Flushed with the Liberation, and during the relatively short period of widescale French reprisals (or "épurations"), the restored republican prosecutors had Barthélemy arrested on 6 October 1944.[163] There was a series of interrogations,[164] and Barthélemy continued writing his "Mémoires." But he was also fatally ill, having been diagnosed the previous June with cancer of the tongue.[165]

---

[159] Rémy, *Les lois de Vichy,* 140.

[160] Teyssier, "Joseph Barthélemy," 98, n. 2.

[161] Ibid.

[162] Barthélemy, "Mémoires," 225, from spring 1944.

[163] Barthélemy, *Ministre,* 553.

[164] See text at footnote 38.

[165] Barthélemy, *Ministre,* 553.

Until his release from incarceration—through the mediation of many friends, and particularly of Cardinal Gerlier, archbishop of Lyon[166]—Barthélemy suffered physical and mental torment, losing weight and experiencing all the horrors of a final illness unmediated by full and sympathetic care. He died on 14 May 1945. It strikes me as fully relevant to this chapter and to the larger study to publish here a portion of his "Mémoires" written in his prison hospital:

> 2 December, 1944. The hardest is the physical pain, which does not exist for most of the prison population. I am only a number, an object worthy of no attention... [recalling the words of Electra] more than 2000 years ago: "Show them that we are of a royal race."[167]
>
> ...
>
> I do not project myself as a hero, nor as a saint; I do not demand sainthood or martyrdom. I am—or if it is better to speak of myself only in the past—I have been a just man [un juste]. I ask for justice.[168]

Perhaps the garde des sceaux received more "justice" than he knew. Earlier in his ordeal, Barthélemy penned the following anecdotal lines:

> While describing the cell in which he was shut at the prefecture for several hours the day after the July Revolution, Chateaubriand notes: "in a corner, an infamous furnishing." That infamous furnishing is painlessly taken care of during the lives of free men, following mores [moeurs], custom and habit. But in prison life, it is constantly in question and always talked about. In the basement of the hospital of Grave, there is a morning and a nighttime schedule. At night, from 7 in the evening until 7 in the morning, they set down a pail [seau] they call, alas!, a sanitary pail, at either end of the dining table. Two pails [sceaux, *sic*] of customary size, like those one sees for a family, for about 30 men. No use dwelling on this. From 7 in the morning until 7 in the evening, the pails were set before certain beds and a dark hole was used, installed at the right of the threshold, on the landing that led to the stairway that descended, *ad inferno*. Opposite this hole, on benches, officials are chatting. In front of the door, a spigot for washing up. A hole and a spigot for 50 to 60 men.[169]

---

[166] Ibid., 554.

[167] Barthélemy, "Mémoires," 689–91.

[168] Ibid., 720.

[169] Ibid., 668.

# Chapter 5

# The Fight to Control the Legal Fate of Jews: Administrators versus Magistrates

Although innovating to some extent, with its Cour suprême de justice and its special section courts, Vichy by and large retained France's centuries-old bifurcated system of adjudication.[1] In that system, unknown to most other countries including England and America, cases originate either in the ordinary (or civil) courts or in the administrative system of tribunals. Disputes involving most crimes, and civil litigation not touching on government activity, arise, generally speaking, in the ordinary courts, adjudicated by magistrates; but cases in which the actions of a government administrative body are being challenged fall under a separate jurisdiction and may not be heard by magistrates. Ordinary courts are checked by courts of appeal and ultimately the Cour de Cassation, France's ultimate jurisdiction in this half of the system. The decisions of administrators, and administrative tribunals can be appealed to the other half of the hierarchical summit, the Conseil d'État.

We have already seen in various contexts that the Vichy religious laws quickly became highly contentious and remained so until Liberation vir-

[1] See, e.g., Charles Szladits, *European Legal Systems* (Columbia: Parker School Publication, 1972), 214–32, for a description of the two-tiered system. Although retaining the traditional courts throughout the period, the Vichy government did consider reforms of both of the highest courts.

tually rescinded them.[2] However, this chapter's focus on the jurisdictional battle regarding Jews between ordinary and administrative courts will help us to situate more precisely both the issues involved and the systemic thinking brought to them by hundreds of French lawyers, litigants, officials, and legal analysts.[3]

We will recall that the first Vichy religious statute of 3 October 1940 quickly became subject to judicial interpretation, particularly as to the ambiguous status of people with two Jewish and two non-Jewish grandparents. But by the time the definitive statute was passed, on 2 June 1941, the new agency for Jewish questions was fully in place, having been created on the previous 29 March, with broad statutory powers to propose and implement "all legislative and regulatory acts...relating to the condition of Jews." From that time forth, this special administrative jurisdiction (the CGQJ) deemed itself to be *solely competent* to interpret the religious statutes and to make all decisions about "Who is a Jew?" After the aryanization statute of 22 July was passed, CGQJ further insisted that the removal of Jewish influence from French business and property was *uniquely* its affair. No ordinary court, in the agency's view, was competent to hear any question about Jewishness, unless the relevant statute explicitly granted the magistrates such authority.

CGQJ decision-making occurred not, of course, as a court, but rather in the everyday workings of religious policy under Vichy law. Three main kinds of decision were made almost daily, affecting thousands of individuals and billions of francs of property:

1. whether to aryanize a piece of property or to take over a business because of Jewish influence;
2. whether to grant an individual a "certificate of non-adherence to the Jewish race" [*certificat*];
3. whether to arrest, through the special police arm created by CGQJ itself, or through the regular police, individuals for failure to register themselves or those for whom they were responsible, as Jews.

Although each of these three crucial decisions involved questions of religious definition, CGQJ insisted they were *administrative*. If anyone

---

[2] See especially chapter 2.

[3] Information about substantive (as opposed to jurisdictional) caselaw dealing with Jewish lives and liberty can be found in chapters 2, 3, and 6; with careers in chapters 3 and 8; and property in chapter 7.

had any trouble with them, their sole recourse would thus be to the Conseil d'État.

But meanwhile, the magistrates understood the question differently. Particularly as regards the 2 June statute, they saw racial matters (and Barthélemy, their ministerial ally, tended to agree) as supremely within their own competence, since they involved questions of *personal status;* even on aryanization, they felt the statute gave them some jurisdiction, although here they tended to be more deferential to the administrative side.

The struggle that arose indicates, once again, how autonomous Vichy law was and how much leeway existed for limiting (or even sidestepping) racial persecution. Magistrates, as they would in any country and in any period, sought in Vichy to expand their jurisdiction. They wanted to be the arbiters on such crucial issue as "Who has the burden of proof," our first subtopic in this chapter. But the CGQJ and the administrators fought just as hard to retain a monopoly over this new and rich statutory area, a struggle described in sub-section B.

Although somewhat technical in nature, this part of our study is worth the close attention of even the non-lawyer, for it lays bare the fascinating relationship between legal developments and Vichy racial politics. We watch as the CGQJ gradually softens its *political* stance on legal issues that it sees "going the wrong way" in the ordinary courts. At first baffled by, and then increasingly frustrated by, the decisions of many magistrates, CGQJ vents its spleen in letters of protest to the ordinary courts and their prosecutorial agents, in internal memoranda questioning the judicial trend toward "liberalism," and in detailed program papers sent to government ministries at the highest levels. Eventually, CGQJ officials engage in compromise, and even in an early version of what we today call "plea bargaining," as they find their rigorous original position continuously threatened by judicial decisions.

Not all ordinary courts disappointed CGQJ. For, until the highest court spoke directly, all of France's original courts and courts of appeal were free to interpret the religious statutes as they saw fit. As courts of appeal and even an arm of the Cour de Cassation began to find against the agency's interests, reactions at CGQJ varied from Darquier de Pellepoix's intransigence to other leaders' pragmatism. Finally, CGQJ resentment simmered in the face of what it found to be an increasingly liberal Conseil d'État, the administrative high court that, earlier in the régime, it could usually count upon.

There is simply no doubt that these developments, which often left the Germans bemused and almost always on the sidelines, further indicate the vitality and the importance of Vichy law and its direct connection to the fates of thousands of Jews.[4] Ordinary courts and administrative jurisdictions employed traditional strategies as they sought to elucidate Vichy racism.

## A. Who Has the Burden of Proof? Conflicting Views

Already familiar to the reader is the acrimony attending the crucial question of *burden of proof*. Since the proof submitted in many cases of religious definition was balanced evenly between "Jewishness" (surname or first name, circumcision, some history of Jewish religious practice, general reputation as being a Jew) and "non-Jewishness" (baptism, some evidence of Catholic religious practice, laxness of Jewish ancestors' keeping of rites, non-participation in any synagogue, etc.), the question "who has the burden?" took on capital significance. Where proof is equally balanced, the party bearing the burden on that issue will lose: if the individual, he was doomed; if the state, it could no longer impose the awful strictures of racial persecution. Like other analysts, I have indicated thus far that the CGQJ theoretically wanted the burden in all cases to be on the individual.[5] Yet the basic religious statutes—those of 2 June and of 22 July 1941—left ambiguous whether the state or the individual must carry the burden of establishing Jewish identity. Where someone had only two Jewish grandparents, or could not ascertain the status of their grand-

---

[4] Michael Marrus and Robert Paxton, *Vichy France and the Jews* (New York: Basic Books, 1981), were somewhat premature in suggesting that, even after 1942, only "a tiny handful of Jews" and others applied to the courts for race-related reasons. Specific cases (whether actually initiated by individuals or by the state in one form or another) number in the hundreds, and their effect on many non-litigious individuals extends the number affected into the thousands.

[5] See, e.g., chapter 2, text at notes 110 and 111; and chapter 4 at note 151; see also Joseph Billig, *Le Commissariat général aux questions juives* (Paris: CDJC, 1955), vol. 2, 248–62. Although my conclusions differ from Billig's on occasion (e.g., he sweeps too broadly in saying that the ordinary courts always placed the burden on the state, ibid., 250), and although his purposes did not extend to analysis of caselaw, I benefitted greatly from his treatment.

parents, the burden placement became especially important. Contentious enough if left to one jurisdiction, this grey area muddied further when trampled over by competing systems.

In early 1942, when the CGQJ tried to push through formal legislation eliminating the loopholes in the religious statutes, the agency retained its firm belief that the individual should shoulder the full burden. In theory, at least, they believed that the fictitious "legislator" always cited during Vichy, even though there was no longer a legislature, intended the individual to shoulder the burden both as to personal definition and property transfers. However, their reform projects modified that view, calling on the state and its agencies to have a preliminary burden to "show that the suspect is probably Jewish" and then on the individual to disprove the assertion.[6] The latter solution, which it called the "mixed burden" approach,[7] was apparently acceptable (at least as to the reform of the 2 June statute) to Joseph Barthélemy.[8] Although a compromise of sorts, it would have constituted a significant closing of the statutory loophole, because for the first time the textual language itself would conform to the agency's firm view that the individual must bring most of the proof relating to Jewish definition.

To shift the burden as a matter of explicit statutory law from the prosecuting authority (state or agency) to the individual would also have been to violate another basic "given" of French law. Particularly since in criminal matters—and we must recall that Vichy often sought to punish criminally those who failed to register as Jews or who otherwise violated the increasingly complex system of racial prohibitions—the burden was always on the state. Except for the antisemitic legislation, Vichy held to this fundamental principle. Thus Barthélemy's colleague at the Justice Ministry, Camboulives, had successfully fended off a proposed law that would have required all French citizens to "justify the nature of their income and the origins of their property since 1 September 1939." The Ministry objected that the burden under the proposed legislation would

---

[6] CGQJ memorandum, 16 February 1942, distributed to Barthélemy and to other ministries; see, e.g., CDJC, CXIV-24, and chapter 4 at notes 144, 145.

[7] The mixed burden approach goes back at least as far as to Alibert, who opined that a Jewish last name, or physiognomy, or known religious practice, would satisfy the administrator's burden, after which the individual would have to disprove Jewishness; see chapter 4 at note 30.

[8] See chapter 4, text at notes 151–53.

shift to the individual in matters that might incriminate him; it also felt that the law wrongly vested judicial authority in administrative agencies and that it violated the *ex post facto* principle.[9] The bill never became law. But the same issues, as related to the class of Jews or suspected Jews, were left to the courts and the agencies to decide. There was no equivalent protest.

It is nonetheless true that CGQJ's "mixed burden" statutory approach never saw the light of day. The radical idea of locking into law a shift in the burden of proof that would shock the conscience of most French lawyers did not take hold. But this was probably less because of anyone's firmly objecting than because the matter was already being handled vigorously—as a matter of interpretation of the existing statutes—both by the ordinary and the administrative jurisdictions. Yet the CGQJ's proposal for reform does signify a political reality always closely interconnected in Vichy to the theoretical world of statutory hermeneutics: CGQJ was ready in early 1942 to compromise somewhat on its original, severe "full burden" stance.

CGQJ's mild flexibility on such a crucial question can best be explained by the cases and commentaries that were abounding on the burden of proof question. *Realpolitik* forced the agency, despite its theoretical position, to take note of a significant doctrinal trend in the ordinary courts that violated its own deeply held convictions. Most tribunals were assuming that the traditions of French law imposed the burden of proof of religious status upon the agency or prosecutor; where criminal sanctions were involved, they tended all the more to expect the state and not the purported Jews to carry the burden.[10] Only an explicit legislative text, they felt, could have shifted the burden to the individual, and neither the basic religious statute nor the aryanization statute contained such language. However furious CGQJ was to see the civil court system stepping on its toes in matters of Jewish status, the agency had to

---

[9] AN 72 AJ 412, dossier no. 6.

[10] See, e.g., the *Sorkine* case, in which a Montpellier court exonerated a man for not registering his children as Jews, imposing the burden on the state because of the "repressive" nature of the law, that therefore had to be interpreted strictly against the prosecutor, decision of 14 January 1943, AN $AJ^{38}$, 99. Accord, e.g., Montpellier decision of 17 December 1942, *Gazette du Palais,* 3–4 February 1943; and a Paris Court of Appeals decision of 26 October 1942, AN $AJ^{38}$, 99.

reckon with the legal realities that affect political behavior even in a régime such as Vichy.

Thus, in the *Dorfmann* case, which involved an allegedly Jewish movie theater owner from Toulouse, the ordinary court system wanted to force the agency to prove that Dorfmann was in fact Jewish before it would let the CGQJ aryanize his well-known cinema house, the "Mazamet." Dorfmann had only two Jewish grandparents and was married to an Aryan, placing him in the by then well-established grey area. In November 1941, CGQJ bemoaned the Toulouse prosecutor's position, claiming that "the burden of proof, in every case relating to the Jewishness of an individual, falls on the individual and not on CGQJ."[11]

Dorfmann, who claimed throughout that he was a baptized Catholic, fought for several more years to retain his theater, and we shall revisit his case in due course. His was surely among the first under the 2 June statute to demonstrate that the ordinary courts were ready to challenge the administrative approach to a basic question of religious law; but Toulouse's view was shared by civil courts in such jurisdictions as Bergerac, Aix, and Nice, who also were placing the burden on the State.[12]

Yet, further to complicate matters, the *ordinary courts were hardly of a single mind on the burden of proof question!* If most courts tended to be liberal, Rabat and Brive had shifted the burden to the individual.[13] So had Marseilles.[14] Rabat, in Morocco—which had been made subject to the 2 June religious law by action of the *dahir* on 5 August 1941—had a particularly active jurisprudence that, at least throughout 1941, delighted the agency. Its illiberal *Benaim* decision was described in chapter 2.[15] In the late 1941 case of *Raymond "L,"* the tribunal de première instance of Rabat decided that the burden was on the individual and that it had not been carried.[16] "L" had only two Jewish grandparents; he was not circumcised; he was married to a Catholic; and there was no real proof linking him to Judaism. The problem for "L" was that *he* could

---

[11] *Dorfmann* file, CDJC, XVIIa-45 (250).

[12] See CDJC, CXV-61, CXV-119.

[13] See chapter 2 at notes 113 and 114.

[14] The Marseilles case involved criminal sanctions against Valentin and Soffer, who had resisted the aryanization of their business; see CDJC XVIIa-45 (246).

[15] See chapter 2, text at note 113.

[16] CDJC, LIV-23.

also prove nothing about being a Catholic, for indeed he admitted that he belonged to no organized religion whatsoever. The court placed the burden on "L" and found him to be Jewish.[17]

These contrasting lines of decision within the ordinary courts might have left CGQJ in no mood to compromise when it floated its statutory reform provisions in early 1942, were it not for the harsh reception the illiberal decisions had received in the commentaries. Thus *"L"* had been proclaimed an absurdity by Decroux, the very reporter who wrote up the decision, who declared, in what then became an oft-cited phrase, that the decision would make any Muslim a Jew if he had two Jewish grandparents. Decroux opined that the statutory mention of belonging to an established religion was not a *requirement* to disprove Jewishness but an administrative guideline to establish that fact.[18] Others were observing that, if the "legislator" had intended to create a new classification of Jews, namely those people with two Jewish grandparents who were atheists, Muslims, or Greek Orthodox (not established categories before the 1905 law mentioned in the statute), it would have explicitly said so.[19]

Constrained by the caselaw and prevailing commentary to seek some political consensus in favor of a *textual change* in both the 2 June and the 22 July statutes, CGQJ argued extensively with various cabinet ministers, including as we have seen, Joseph Barthélemy. But the result of the exchange of memoranda during the first few months of 1942 was no statutory reform on burden of proof whatsoever. That key issue was left to play itself out in the bifurcated and already internally divided court system.

There was no dearth of cases in 1942, as the CGQJ itself was passing from Xavier Vallat's leadership to that of the yet more dogmatic Darquier de Pellepoix. In at least one jurisdiction, the agency was finding an ally.

---

[17] See chapter 4 at notes 144–45, for Barthélemy's willingness to yield to the CGQJ in such situations by *not permitting* people like "L" to disprove Jewishness through a show of atheism or freethinking. However, in this particular case, Lubetzki reports that the tribunal's decision was eventually overturned and "L" deemed to be non-Jewish: J. Lubetzki, *La Condition des Juifs en France sous l'Occupation allemande* (Paris: CDJC, 1945), 35.

[18] Report of the "L" case, *Gazette des Tribunaux* (Morocco), 7 February 1942, 49, CDJC LIV-23.

[19] *Pierre Bloch* case, Bergerac tribunal de première instance, 12 June 1941, CDJC CXV-61, 2.

Its hierarchical superior, the Conseil d'État, established a position regarded as clearly placing the burden on the individual. In two cases, *Bloch-Favier,* and *Guy Lévy,* the Conseil d'État, acting through its judicial department (contentieux) showed that the highest administrative court was likely to ask more, on the question of Jewish identity, from the individual than from the state agency.

Both cases involved appeals by state workers who had been fired because they were allegedly Jewish. Bloch-Favier, a teacher at the École pratique in Bourgouin, was fired in December 1940; he had two Jewish grandparents and simply had no evidence to bring to show that he was not Jewish. The Conseil d'État affirmed his dismissal.[20] Just as importantly, the Conseil d'État for the first time formally declared itself competent to rule on "non-adherence to the Jewish race."[21] Meanwhile, in *Guy Lévy,* the high administrative court sustained the appeal brought by a draftsman in the government communications office who had been fired and barred from further government service or even from taking competitive examinations for related positions. Guy Lévy also had two Jewish grandparents, and he also was required to submit proof of non-Jewishness; unlike Bloch-Favier, however, he was able to demonstrate that he had been baptized in the Boucicaut Hospital in Paris on 17 September 1914. The Communications Secretary was thus deemed to have made "an imprecise application of the relevant text" (Article 1 of the law of 2 June 1941), and Guy Lévy was permitted to reclaim his job.[22]

---

[20] The decision of 24 April 1942, was reported in the *Gazette du Palais,* 11–13 November 1942; see CDJC XVIIa-45 (245). The Conseil d'État, while retaining jurisdiction over the appeal from the firing itself—a clear matter for the administrative courts, since it related to government behavior—expressly declined to rule on Bloch-Favier's demand for an Article 8 exemption under the religious statute itself. That matter was for the ordinary courts, not for its contentieux.

[21] Ibid; see the next section of this chapter, particularly the similar language used in the Conseil d'État's 1943 *Maxudian* case.

[22] Both *Bloch-Favier* and *Guy Lévy* are mentioned in AN AJ[38,] 118, the files of the "Service de législation et du contentieux" of the CGQJ. *Guy-Lévy* is noted in the "Bulletin quotidien d'études et d'informations économiques," a handwritten daily information sheet dealing with economic matters, for 19 August 1942. Noting that the religious law of 2 June 1941 "does not shine for its simplicity of expression nor for its clarity of draftsmanship," the writer accurately sums up the confusing condition of the caselaw in the ordinary courts, and cites *Guy-Lévy* for the proposition that, in any battle for jurisdiction won by the Conseil d'État, the individual at this point would be disadvantaged, ibid., 2.

Of greater importance to the CGQJ than the substantive outcome in either case was the support it felt it had gained on the crucial burden of proof issue. Indeed, the agency quickly used the Bloch-Favier decision to claim that any *ordinary court* placing the burden on the state was now clearly in error. Thus Darnieu, chief of staff of the agency, immediately wrote to his regional director in Toulouse ordering him to tell the district prosecutor there that the civil court had badly erred in the recent *Pinto* case, decided 17 February 1942.[23] In that quite unusual matter, Pinto—although not himself a practicing Jew—had *two Jewish parents,* yet his racial status became contentious. (The Germans always considered it absurd that Vichy law could theoretically find someone whose parents were both Jewish nonetheless to be an Aryan if he had three non-Jewish *grandparents*).[24] No one could prove anything about his grandparents' race. If Pinto had the burden of proof, as CGQJ now claimed was inscribed in the law by the *Bloch-Favier* decision, he would clearly be Jewish unless he could show that three or more of his grandparents were Aryans. But if the state had the burden, and knew nothing else, it could not prove by mere virtue of Pinto's Jewish parents that he indeed had more than two Jewish grandparents and hence the state would have to show more about Pinto himself than they were prepared to do.

During the same first six months of 1942, however, the civil courts vigorously adjudicated this doctrinal problem, and the predominant trend was liberal. Thus a civil court in Aix-en-Provence filed a decision in May indicating that a mixed-heritage individual need only show his non-Jewishness—as opposed to his affirmatively belonging to another accepted faith.[25] Although that decision, per se, spoke more to the kinds of evidence admissible than to the burden of proof itself, the decision was cited favorably one month later, in *Pierre Bloch,* a case specifically engaging the burden of proof issue. In *Pierre Bloch,* a criminal court in Toulouse released Bloch, who had been arraigned for failure to register

---

[23] CDJC XVIIa-45 (245).

[24] Memorandum, 12 July 1943, Dr. Hans-Gustav Tweer, Berlin, forwarded to the SS in Paris, CDJC XXVII-25. The Germans chart the French approach, adding "Any German who has mastered even a bit of racial knowledge and Mendelian rules will laugh over the naiveté, indeed the stupidity of these tables," ibid., 3.

[25] This unnamed decision of 12 May 1942, is cited about a year later in the *Langellier-Bellevue* decision, Nice, CDJC CXV-119.

his two minor children as Jews, under the law of 2 June 1941. The children were found to have an Aryan mother and not to have had imposed "at the time of their birth the rituals of the hebraic religion"; hence, despite their having two Jewish grandparents, their status was interpreted by the court as non-Jewish, and their father absolved of criminal charges.[26] The court reporter, admitting that the definitional part of the 2 June statute "is not unproblematic," cited the Aix decision for the proposition that it did not unalterably shift the burden to the individual to prove adherence to an accepted religion but rather "it is for the prosecutor who claims Jewishness to prove adherence to the Jewish religion."[27] "If [the legislator had had a different intention] paragraph 2 would have been rewritten" to say "he or she not belonging to one of the other religions recognized by the state...and who has two Jewish grandparents of the Jewish race."[28]

In a similar case from the same period, a Limoges court released Robert Meyer, who had failed to register his two children. These latter, born respectively in 1927 and 1929, were not circumcised and seemed to have received a Protestant religious upbringing. On the other hand, Meyer apparently only had his children baptized when he feared reprisals against Jews. Bemoaning this decision, the CGQJ's director of its legal department, Armilhon, strongly requested in August 1942 that the agency urge the Limoges prosecutor to appeal.[29]

Toulouse and Montpellier also continued in their liberal tradition during these six months.[30] In fact, Montpellier's courts, firm in placing the burden on the state, were building a reputation for liberality that gained dubious but special mention in late 1943. It was then that the CGQJ's regional director for aryanization of Toulouse declared that "the prefects and above all the courts in the Montpellier [that word emphasized by

---

[26] CDJC CXV-61.

[27] Ibid., 2.

[28] Ibid.

[29] AN $AJ^{38}$, 118.

[30] See Lubetzki, *La Condition,* 36.

being handwritten in the text] region have a marked tendency to protect Jews and their property."[31]

Analysts reflecting in mid-1942 on the civil courts' behavior might have agreed with Lubetzki's postwar assessment that

> the civil court jurisprudence, criminal and administrative, with the exception of some isolated instances (judgments of Rabat and Brive) and doctrine, interpreted the statute, not in a broad sense, but judiciously, in the spirit of just proportions, with respect for principles. Judges and professors avoided falling into the errors and exaggerations of the Administration, notably that of the CGQJ.[32]

The CGQJ and its operatives were quite worried. Their reform project earlier in 1942 had not gotten off the ground, despite minimal objections to it by such important figures as Barthélemy. The Conseil d'État, which it felt it could rely on as an administrative partner,[33] had made only a few decisions touching on the burden of proof question and had not vigorously enough asserted its unique jurisdiction over Jewish matters. The civil courts were now edging strongly towards placing the burden on the state—meaning in many cases on the agency itself—to prove Jewishness, never an easy matter, particularly in view of the difficulty of attaining documents when so many of the targets of prosecution were

---

[31] Monthly report, November 1943, Service of Economic Aryanization of Toulouse, CDJC XVII-36 (153) (154). The agency, faced with such civil court behavior, explicitly pondered a way to remove the courts from all jurisdiction except in criminal matters, CDJC XVII-36 (152).

[32] Lubetzki, *La Condition,* 38. Accord, far more recently (at least as to the behavior of the ordinary courts), Danièle Lochak, "La Doctrine sous Vichy ou les mésaventures du positivisme," in Serge Klarsfeld, ed., *Le statut des juifs de Vichy* (Paris: F.F.D.J.F., 1990), 131. However, Lochak disagrees with the contention that the professors and other analysts during Vichy took a liberal view of this and other contentious questions. Her thesis is rather that the analysts' seeming *objectivity* in and of itself obscured [occultait] the larger issues of legalistic racism.

[33] Indeed, there was often a reciprocal give and take between the two bodies on developing questions of religious law. For an example from this period, the Conseil d'État's head of legislation and litigation, wrote to the CGQJ's director of aryanization on 3 March 1942, to ascertain whether, under the 2 June statute, all Jewish property must be registered or only that above a certain economic value. One month later, the Jewish tailor Lazare Gorodetzki was indeed arraigned for not registering his sewing machine and tables, AN AJ[38], 118. See chapter 7, text at note 77.

foreign Jews. And even French records were notoriously unavailable or untrustworthy on these matters.[34]

No wonder that an operative in the Vars region was predicting complete disaster. Referring to that area's *Claude Lévy* case, a certain Estève writes to the central CGQJ office on 24 June 1942, indicating that a high appeals court is about to impose the burden of proof formally on the state.[35] Furthermore, Estève conjures a worst possible scenario for the agency in its ongoing dispute with the ordinary courts:

> If the Cour de Cassation [the highest civil court] holds that the burden of proof falls on the public minister, it will become impossible to pursue a foreign Jew.[36]

Meanwhile, intrigued as they often were by all this frantic French concern, the Germans in mid-1941 decided to intervene formally. Why all the fuss, they queried? In Germany, they dared to suggest, this question of Jewish definition was handled more politely. So Buhrig, an official in the German High Command in Paris whose job brought him into contact with the CGQJ on aryanization questions,[37] penned a memorandum for all interested parties on 4 July 1942 strongly urging the French to downplay their legalistic zeal in requiring individuals to proffer so much evidence to disprove Jewishness. In Germany, he revealed, a person's mere declaration of "Aryan" status (in a situation not obviously negating it) would suffice.[38]

Autonomous to a fault, as Vichy often was in deciding their own racial matters, CGQJ in mid-1942 pressed again for some statutory reform. By now, too, they had in place a leader who was disinclined to give an inch. Darquier de Pellepoix wanted statutory reform. His legalistic concerns were varied and have been well described in such pioneering books as that of Jean Laloum[39]; although overshadowed in 1943 by the denaturalization reform struggle (see chapter 9), the burden of proof question also

---

[34] See, e.g., Xavier Vallat's postwar account of the difficulties felt by CGQJ if burdened this way, chapter 2, text at note 109.

[35] AN $AJ^{38}$, 118.

[36] Ibid.

[37] See, e.g., Billig, *Le Commissariat général* (Paris: CDJC, 1960), vol. 3, 57.

[38] CDJC CXV-51; identical document, AN $AJ^{38}$, 80.

[39] Jean Laloum, *La France antisémite de Darquier de Pellepoix* (Paris: Syros, 1979), particularly 25-57.

plagued him and his office throughout his reign as head of CGQJ. In what was styled an "Exposé" on "Reforms envisaged for the Legislation on the Jews," CGQJ decidedly resisted all pleas to show restraint and declared the following:

> *As regards proof:* In practice the CGQJ esteems that the currently operative texts reverse the burden of proof and permit the Authority to pursue any individual as a Jew by recourse to simple indices and without having to furnish a formal proof, [since] the alleged Jew, by the mere fact of this pursuit, is bound to bring contradictory proof or otherwise to conform to the obligations incumbent upon Jews. This thesis is mandated by the most obvious practical necessities: to give up would be the same as giving up on pursuing all foreign Jews or Jews of foreign origin, theoretically the most dangerous, and therefore to act for their profit and actual privilege. In fact it is almost always materially impossible to establish the ascendancy of an individual born (or whose parents were born) in Odessa or Budapest. It has been necessary therefore to invoke this legal presumption. But this legal presumption, which violates by definition certain fundamental principles of our law, can only result juridically from a precise and formal legislative pronouncement. Thus on this point discussion is appropriate. The legislator [*sic*] seems to have had the intention of reversing the burden of proof, but it is surely true that he did not say so clearly, and there is now serious disorder in the cases, some jurisdictions accepting the view of the CGQJ, others more numerous remaining loyal to the liberal solution that conforms to tradition. It is this conflict in the cases that we are seeking to remedy with a new text in which the question of proof is firmly resolved.[40]

Even Darquier's agency had to admit that the courts' concern about French traditional law was not unreasonable. Of course, neither CGQJ nor anyone else bothered to question the breach of French legal tradition embodied *in the statute as a whole!* But, the absurdity of racial distinction once successfully posited, the agency wanted to go further and also reverse formally the longstanding placement of the burden of proof squarely on the state.

In only one document does Darquier's agency seem to lose its fervor. This glitch occurred as 1942 wound down and not only the majority of Vichy courts—but also Darquier's Nazi overlords—persevered in their liberal tendencies on the burden of proof question. The result of the

[40] Memorandum, 30 June 1942, CDJC CXV-49.

interaction of Nazi ordinance and Vichy law was an anomaly that Darquier could not help but notice, and that we shall explore fully in chapter 6: the Nazis on their own would have persecuted many fewer Jews in the Occupied Zone than the number who suffered under Vichy definitions:

> The question can be summed up in this way: must we continue to apply all the measures concerning Jews to all Jews registered in the census, without distinguishing those who are Jews only under French law from those who are [Jews] under the German ordinances? In other words, must the measures drawn up against Jews by the latest German ordinances affect people who are not Jewish under the terms of the German ordinances and who are only considered Jewish through a particular interpretation of the French law of 2 June 1941, which has been so far the official interpretation of the CGQJ, but which the jurisprudence of several French appeals courts and tribunals have just recently refused to follow?
>
> [The fact that French law made more people Jewish than did the German ordinances applicable in France had created] two categories of Jews: those who are Jews under the German ordinances and those who—not being Jews under the latter—and against whom therefore those ordinances would not be applied—only become Jews through a particular interpretation of the law of 2 June 1941 that [most of] the cases these days refuse to accept.
>
> It is perfectly illogical and even perfectly unfair to be obliged to apply the most rigorous of the German ordinances concerning Jews uniquely to people who are not Jewish under the terms of those same ordinances....[41]

The science of hermeneutics had permitted an excess of definitional zeal to ensnare an excessive number of presumed Jews. The Germans, perhaps less concerned about textual theories when it came to law, were willing to snatch fewer "Jews."

The overbreadth of the Vichy statute, coupled with the interpretation of the burden of proof question, caused CGQJ to sit for a moment and ponder what they had wrought. Should the police arrest all "Vichy-variety Jews" under laws passed only by the Germans, which therefore should only be applicable to "German-variety Jews"? Thinking only of recent ordinances passed, like the "Ninth Ordinance" of 8 July 1942, should "French-variety Jews" caught off limits, or found marketing outside the hours of 3 and 4 p.m., be incarcerated in "Jewish camps" at

---

[41] Memorandum, CGQJ to prefecture of police, 17 August 1942, CDJC CXV-63.

the will of the police—even if the Germans did not think of them as Jews?[42]

Had the agency decided that it was (in Darquier's term) "unfair" to have treated a certain Robert Lévy the way it had just a few weeks before the memorandum was written? As Lévy's employer, M. Behin, had informed the agency, "M. Lévy seems to be Jewish under the terms of French law of 2 June 1941 but not under the terms of German law." Lévy indeed had two non-Jewish grandparents, and was married to an Aryan; thus he was free and clear, and felt himself to be so. Fatally, Lévy decided on 17 June 1942, to go to the CGQJ office to be relieved of the obligation to wear the Jewish star, an obligation imposed solely by German ordinance as of ten days before. He was promptly arrested, because the agency placed the burden on him to show non-Jewishness; it had less interest in his marital status than did the Germans,[43] and CGQJ thought of him as Jewish until he proved otherwise. By the time he did—by the December following—Robert Lévy had been deported. The agency informed M. Behin that "the German authorities do not accept intervention in favor of Jews incarcerated in concentration camps."[44]

Whatever temporary pang of conscience or warped sense of fairness may have motivated the CGQJ's August memorandum, it died by its own absurd lack of rationality. Was this the only "perfectly unfair" aspect of all of French religious legislation? What about the two-tiered structure *as a whole,* that Professor Maury courageously noted had created at its origin "two categories of French people"—the Jews and the Aryans?[45] With this far larger inquiry neglected, quite naturally by the agency charged with regulating Jewish matters (not so naturally by every other arm of French law, public or private), CGQJ returned to pondering decision after decision that went against it on the burden of proof debate.

Early in 1943, perhaps the year in which the battle between ordinary courts and administrative adjudicators became fiercest, CGQJ found its position on burden of proof rejected by courts of increasingly greater authority in the civil system. The Court of Appeals in Agen squarely placed the burden on the state in the *Scali-Cohen* case, which reversed

[42] R. Sarraute and P. Tager, *Recueil des textes,* 161f.

[43] See, e.g., chapter 2, notes 95–101, and chapter 6.

[44] AN AJ$^{38}$, 118.

[45] See chapter 2, text at notes 60–62.

a lower court finding of criminal liability (a fine of 3000 francs) for failure to register as a Jew.[46] At around the same time, as predicted by the agitated Estève,[47] even weightier civil side authorities were getting involved. An authoritative commentator for the highest non-administrative court, the Cour de Cassation, opined in the *Hazan* case that—at least as to all criminal matters—"it is certain that, unless legally excepted, the pursuing party—to wit the prosecutor—bears the burden of proof."[48]

Losing on the burden of proof question in ever higher courts of ordinary jurisdiction, the CGQJ had to decide whether to continue to press for reform legislation. It did have an alternative, short of conceding the point altogether, and this was raised explicitly as a response to *Hazan* by the head of the agency's individual Jewish status department, Boutmy. Writing to Boué, CGQJ's head of aryanization, Boutmy counsels less statutory reform than increased care as to the individuals against whom the agency begins to proceed:

> We must now be extremely careful about the appellation "Jew" and only attribute it to an individual when his *dossier* will include all the necessary data to conform with the law of 2 June 1941. [He notes the Conseil d'État's declaration of 11 December 1942 about admitting all kinds of proof. As to the burden of proof, he cites *Hazan*.] A criminal law is a law of exception and thus must be interpreted narrowly.[49]

---

[46] Decision of 6 July 1943, CDJC XVIIa-45 (251).

[47] See note 35.

[48] However, Hazan's conviction for failure to register as a Jew as required by the 2 June statute was affirmed by the high court nonetheless, since he had two Jewish grandparents and had confessed he was a Jew, thus leaving it up to his judges to determine whether Hazan's later retraction was to be believed (they did not, apparently), and whether they would credit Hazan's doubts as to his grandmother's religious status in Syria (they also did not, apparently). *Hazan,* Cour d'assise criminelle of the Cour de Cassation, 14 January 1943, CDJC XVIIa-45 (249). This case is listed by Lochak, "La Doctrine sous Vichy," 145, who says that it is "unsigned" in its *Journal officiel* report. But in fact, the decision is signed and commented upon extensively by Marcel Nast for the proposition noted in this text, with which Lochak is in full agreement, ibid., 131.

[49] Internal memorandum, 29 September 1943. Boutmy replaced Loffet in this crucial position at around this time; see Billig, *Le Commissariat général,* vol. 1, 136. It would be wrong (considering Billig's careful research) to think of Boutmy as anything more than an enemy of the Jews and a real collaborator with the Germans, particularly on aryanization. But in the overheated atmosphere of the CGQJ, he did seem to stake out a position more sensitive to the ordinary courts than that of his colleagues. His scrupulousness

Although Darquier, pressured from the outside and from within, might have opted for a defensive strategy of using more care and hence avoiding embarrassing and damaging legal decisions, he instead decided to keep to what must have seemed a reckless course. Shortly after the *Hazan* case—although surely not exclusively responsive to it— Darquier gathered his forces, rejected the uncharacteristic moral questioning of the August memorandum, and issued a new reform project in which the law would place the burden of proof expressly on the individual and on all people

> about whom has been raised a presumption of belonging to that race, notably because of racial characteristics, of the sense of the patronymic name, or of the choice of first name, of the religious practice, or of the practice of a Jewish religious rite, of the burial in a Jewish cemetery, or of the membership in a Jewish community or in a Jewish group.[50]

CGQJ's staunch allegiance to the burden of proof position was buttressed by Conseil d'État decisions well into 1943. Although, as we have seen,[51] that same high administrative court contemporaneously undermined the agency by vastly increasing the *kinds* of evidence the individual could offer to disprove Jewishness,[52] the alliance of the Conseil d'État and CGQJ on the burden of proof issue was a stable ingredient in the legalistic picture, one which could only have disheartened individuals and their lawyers as they contemplated doing battle with the French government. Indeed, the very declaration by the Conseil d'État that broadened the *kinds* of proof allowable to the individual restates in so

---

extended to keeping careful copies of all the certificats de non appartenance granted by his office, the last for which we have records is Caen, née Saurois, Augustine, born 14/8/74, living at 72 rue Monge in the 5$^{e}$, certificate number 10,766. For the 11 December 1942 ruling, see notes 52, 104.

[50] See AN AJ$^{38}$, 118.

[51] See chapter 2 at notes 132–135, where Joseph Haennig's analysis is cited and discussed.

[52] In its declaration of 11 December 1942, the Conseil d'État, by its committee on the Statut des Juifs, issued perhaps its most cited statement on the Jewish laws. Signed by no less than Conseil Vice-President Alfred Porché, the opinion declares that "no text of [the law of 2 June 1941] nor legal policy of the statute requires that only one method of proof be allowed and no other; in these circumstances, any competent jurisdiction must decide in each case whether the individual has brought forth sufficient proof to show that he has never belonged or has stopped belonging to the Jewish community," CDJC CXIV- 2a; CDJC XVIIa-45 (241).

many words the high court's view that it was that individual (and not the state) who bore the burden.[53] A representative decision from 1943 indicates the Conseil d'État's firm resolve, while in its substantive outcome also reveals that the high court would not act as a mere rubber stamp for the agency on Jewish questions.

Brigitte Sée, like thousands of other business owners in France at the time, found her shoe store taken over by an "administrateur provisoire," the Aryan "trustee" whose job it was to oversee and manage the business while any Jewish influence over it was removed. So dictated the law of 22 July 1941, the very statute that Barthélemy anguished over but eventually signed.

But Brigitte Sée showed that she had two non-Jewish grandparents and another of uncertain religion (the fourth being Jewish) and that she had been baptized at birth. She decided to fight the aryanization of her store on that basis. Her first recourse was to the ordinary court that seemingly had jurisdiction over the matter. But the civil courts in Montpellier, which first assigned the case to a referee, wound up affirming the latter's decision that they had no jurisdiction over the CGQJ's aryanization decision! Although the decision indicated that ordinary courts might be able to intervene if the "trustee" breached his responsibilities while administering the store, they could not tamper with the administrative decision that required aryanization in the first place.[54]

Brigitte Sée did not give up. She changed her venue and went to the administrative courts, to whom jurisdiction in her case had been yielded by the ordinary courts. Her case had become even more pressing, because the shoe store was up for sale on 4 May 1943. Less than a week before, on 30 April 1943, her case was finally decided by the Conseil d'État, through its "section du contentieux."[55] The high administrative court first imposed the burden of proof on Sée to show that she was not Jewish, a threshold necessity if her store was to be de-aryanized and the "trustee" removed.

Brigitte Sée claimed that even the CGQJ had first issued her a "certificate of non-adherence to the Jewish race," but the latter contended that

---

[53] Ibid.

[54] Decision of the Court of Appeals of Montpellier, 22 October 1942, CDJC XVIIa-45 (244).

[55] CDJC XVIIa-45 (252).

they had done that on an incomplete record and prior to the promulgation of the now operative 2 June religious statute that was harder to satisfy than the earlier 3 October statute had been; that the agency indeed had retracted her certificate on 18 August 1942, admittedly after the commencement of aryanization but nonetheless within the allowable procedural period to reverse such decisions. Furthermore, claimed CGQJ, the shoe store was also under the control of Ms. Sée's nephew, Pierre, who was clearly a Jew since he had three Jewish grandparents.

Yes, said the Conseil d'État, the reversal of Ms. Sée's status was lawful. Now *she* must prove her non-Jewishness, and this she had done, by producing a baptismal certificate, from the date of her birth, an event attested to "by witnesses worthy of belief"; she had never renounced Catholicism. She had been wrongly divested of her non-Jewish status and may continue ownership of her store. As to her nephew, he is less a manager of the store than a mere employee, and thus his Jewishness is irrelevant to the aryanization proceedings.

As was occurring more and more frequently, CGQJ won only a Pyrrhic victory in *Sée*. Its stance on burden of proof was ratified again by its hierarchical superior. But its substantive decision was called into question, and it lost its control over what it deemed to be a Jewish business. Suffering such outcomes from the administrative tribunal, how could CGQJ hope to battle the ordinary courts effectively?

## B. Who Has Jurisdiction?

*Brigitte Sée* indicates that ordinary courts could be highly respectful of the administrative courts and even yield jurisdiction to the latter on key questions of religious status. But this did not always occur, and the encroachments of civil courts into matters of religious definition and treatment of Jews irked both the CGQJ and the Conseil d'État for years, until the latter changed its position in early 1944, perhaps as it foresaw the Allied victory that lay ahead. But let us not anticipate quite so much the end of the story.

Instead, let us cast our minds for a moment on the *beginnings* of the Vichy legal nightmare. When the new religious laws were first passed, a brand new slate was created, upon which nothing had been written. Who was going to control the slate? Whose judicial words would supply its content? It was by no means clear that the ordinary courts had any jurisdiction whatsoever over these new laws. Were they not public laws, designed to eliminate Jewish influence in France and hence purely matters of administrative jurisdiction? Or were they—because of the highly personal subject matter, dealing as they did with family charts, marriages, and individual practices—supremely within the competence of the ordinary civil courts that dealt with these problems every day?[56]

At his most vociferous, Joseph Barthélemy consistently fought for the jurisdiction of the magistrates, directly answering on more than one occasion the opposite perspective voiced by Xavier Vallat and Darquier de Pellepoix.[57] Faced in early 1942 with CGQJ's potential reforms, Barthélemy insisted—particularly as regards the aryanization law—that the ordinary judge should not be stripped of jurisdiction. Battling Vallat's call for an entirely new, "specialized jurisdiction" that would expedite the transfer of Jewish property into Aryan hands, Barthélemy as much as says: "Slow down! My magistrates know all about property, and they also know human psychology and the way lawyers operate. They're the best! Keep your hands off!"[58]

Deeply disturbed by the diminishing morale of his magistrates, whose salaries declined in real terms,[59] and who enjoyed very low levels of

---

[56] See the excellent review of this debate and those writing about the question contemporaneously in Lochak, "La Doctrine sous Vichy," 129–31.

[57] See, e.g., chapter 4, text at note 146. As for the agency, as Billig points out, *Le Commissariat général,* vol. 2, 249, CGQJ made at least one substantial jurisdictional argument: if the ordinary courts reached these racial cases through personal jurisdiction of a traditional kind, how could that extend to *foreign nationals* on French soil?

[58] Ibid., exchange between Barthélemy and Vallat on potential reform of statute of 22 July 1941; see also chapter 7 for an extensive look at the 22 July law, its "reform" and the general unwillingness of magistrates to take on the administrative agencies and courts in the aryanization domains.

[59] There is considerable documentation on magistrates' salaries in the archives; see AN BB[30], 1716. To take just a few cases: one Jean Joulia, an examining magistrate in Annecy, wrote to the justice ministry on 7 July 1941 to note that even if their salary were to be doubled, magistrates would return only to 1930 levels, since the cost of living had gone up 190% since that time. Joulia opines that a dignified salary is linked to the public perception of Vichy justice: "A suitable rise in judicial salaries will indicate that an era of new justice has opened for Frenchmen...and that the National Revolution has been worked within a judicial organism." A procureur de la République, 3e classe, M. Mabelly of Orange, writes that, for his family of wife, three teenage daughters, and two elderly parents, his salary of 40,330 francs must cover 4,500 for rent; 850 for taxes; 18,000 for food;

respect as well,[60] Barthélemy may have had more than theoretical reasons for insisting on their jurisdiction over such a complex and even prestigious new area. By early 1942, everyone was looking for a piece of the action, since the "blank slate" of Vichy racism had grown, by March 1942, to an impressive pile of *80,000* separate documents![61] But, to his credit, it is also the case that Barthélemy felt the magistrates provided the only potential buffer to a repressive state that was too much in the hands of the administrators and of the police. "The magistrature never let itself be swept up in this [repressive] fury. We are not enjoying a 'season of the judges'; instead, I regret to say, we are in the age of repression, of the triumph of punishment, the summit of tortures. This is not the time [for a decent person] to be opposed to the judges."[62]

As indicated by *Brigitte Sée,* however, Barthélemy's courts sometimes yielded to the administrative jurisdictions, particularly when it came to the aryanization of property. Even though pillaging required first a legalistic show of the owner's Jewishness, an issue arguably to be resolved by ordinary courts, and even though Article 7 of the 22 July aryanization statute explicitly called on the ordinary courts to take part,[63] the latter had no experience with such matters and demonstrated far less assertive-

---

2,800 for gas and electricity; 3,000 for a maid; 10,000 for clothing; 1,500 for schooling (his oldest daughter was a second year law student); 900 for medical; 1,500 for house repairs; 200 for journals; 500 for unavoidable travel; the total places him in the red every year by over 7,000 francs.

Despite concerted efforts by Barthélemy and others to procure wage increases in the vicinity of 10–20% for magistrates, each year brought raises of about 3% at best.

[60] An interministerial memorandum of 17 February 1943 notes that, despite vastly increased workloads and dockets, there was no equivalent interest among the French in becoming judges. "During this period [of litigiousness] there has been a great reduction in the workforce of the magistracy.... [There is] difficulty recruiting because of the deep disaffection felt for the judicial career." The number of candidates for judicial posts had gone down, despite liberalized rules for examinations. In 1941, there were 395 candidates for the magistracy, and in 1942 only 215. Only 38 positions out of an available 132 had been filled by the time of the memorandum, which goes on to call for an immediate repatriation of magistrates still held by the Germans (no call was made, however, to use Jewish talent permanently barred if readily available in France), AN $BB^{30}$, 1715.

[61] The figure was cited by Admiral Auphan, writing to the CGQJ in response to their first reform *projet de loi,* CDJC CXIV-24.

[62] Barthélemy, *Ministre,* 252f.

[63] Dominique Rémy, *Les lois de Vichy* (Paris: Romillat, 1992), 42.

ness than they had shown under the 2 June statute. Exemplified in *Sée,* this reticence was replicated in the case of *Fourcade,* whose leather goods shop in Pau had been aryanized. He claimed he was not Jewish, but the tribunal civil of Pau, on 8 March 1943, ruled itself incompetent to hear his plea. The court found that the 22 July 1941 statute vested exclusive jurisdiction over such issues in the administrative agencies and courts.[64]

The complicated *Dorfmann* case, involving the Toulouse movie theater owner,[65] went through a phase in which the ordinary courts also declined jurisdiction. Dorfmann had managed to build up a convincing case that he was a Catholic. Since he was married to an Aryan and had only two Jewish grandparents, the aryanization of his "Mazamet" theater seemed questionable. Yet, when he took his case to court to have the trustee divested of the theaters, Dorfmann saw his case thrown out on jurisdictional grounds dating to the first French Revolution; the tribunal correctionelle of Toulouse decided on 18 March 1943 that "[Both the appointment of the trustee and his acts] escape the competence of judicial authority, the law of 16 and 24 August 1790 prohibiting the civil judge from evaluating administrative acts, or disturbing administrative operations, or sanctioning administrators within the scope of their function."[66]

Dorfmann was a fighter, however, and, like Brigitte Sée, was willing to shift venue and try the administrative courts. He also benefitted from the fact that the case had attracted a lot of attention. Indeed, Boutmy of the CGQJ, although he had received a gossipy letter from a minor Toulouse official accusing Dorfmann of being a well-known Jew who was

---

[64] Decision of 8 March 1943, CDJC XVIIa-45 (248).

[65] See text at note 11. *Dorfmann* was the more important of two cases involving religious law status of the owners of movie houses in Vichy. The other, *Loubradou,* involved the "Cinéma-Rex" in Antibes which had been purchased from Samsovici, a purported Jew, and subsequently aryanized because the latter continued to manage the Rex. Loubradou argued that, since Samsovici only had two Jewish grandparents, there was in fact no "Jewish influence" and hence the CGQJ had erred. The Conseil d'État quashed his appeal from the aryanization order, AN AJ[38], 99.

[66] CDJC XVIIa-45 (250). The court's view here seems at an extreme of judicial reticence. Other ordinary courts were willing to yield jurisdiction as to the appointing of the trustee but not as to his subsequent behavior in dealing with the aryanized property. See, e.g., the tribunal civil of Marseilles in *Regneault,* AN AJ[38], 99. Regnault was admittedly appointed as trustee in the proper manner by the CGQJ; however, the court saw Article 7 of the 22 July statute as specifically empowering it to monitor the aryanization process.

just saving his skin by lying about Catholicism,[67] adopted the view ascribed to him earlier in this chapter: don't force dubious cases upon the courts because you will wind up with precedents detrimental to the agency.[68] Dorfmann's baptism, although "suspicious because procured during the exodus [from Paris on 18–19 June 1940]" had been accepted as valid, his Jewish ascendancy was quite hard to prove, and there was too much of a record favorable to his legal position. In 1944, Boutmy argued for, and apparently received, permission to enter into a settlement with Dorfmann in which Dorfmann would drop his administrative case in exchange for a certificat de non appartenance à la race juive.[69]

Boutmy's point of view had become fairly consistent as he pragmatically analyzed both the changing tides of the war[70] and (more to the point) a body of caselaw during 1943 and the first half of 1944. Unwilling to change the agency's *public face of defiance* before the encroachments on its jurisdiction, Boutmy and others were prepared to plea bargain quietly, or even to refrain from commencing matters that, earlier in Vichy, they would never have compromised.

Although most ordinary courts still tended to yield jurisdiction on the kinds of aryanization issues that had affected *Dorfmann,*[71] and others tended to be skeptical when litigants proposed new theories of non-

---

[67] CDJC XVII-36 (150).

[68] See text at note 49.

[69] Boutmy to regional director, Toulouse CGQJ, 28 July 1944, CDJC XVIIa-45.

[70] Boutmy's position late in Vichy may have been of a piece with others at CGQJ, who "wanted to attenuate at the last moment [their] disastrous reputation," Billig, *Le Commissariat général,* vol. 1, 308. But even earlier, his pragmatic sense of compromise contradicts the view, expressed by Marrus and Paxton, for example, that adverse judicial decisions and interdepartmental defeats had no effect whatsoever on CGQJ operatives "simply going their own way," in *Vichy France,* 292.

[71] Thus in two separate cases in 1943, *Lévy vs Bethouart* and *Weill,* civil courts declined jurisdiction over aryanization questions, yielding them to the administrative side. In the first, a court in Chateauroux declared itself incompetent, under both Vichy statutes, to tamper with the sale of Lévy's lingerie business, despite the latter's claim that the "trustee" had violated several criminal statutes while administering the property, AN $AJ^{38}$ 99; and in *Weill,* the court managed first to declare a businessman not Jewish (overturning a CGQJ claim that he was) but then to declare itself incompetent to prevent the aryanization of the man's business pending Conseil d'État deliberations as to the appropriateness of naming a "trustee" to a business that an ordinary court declared owned by a non-Jew! See CDJC XVIIa-45 (203).

Jewishness,[72] the civil courts in some respects were starting to prevail. Courts otherwise deferential to the CGQJ on the *need to appoint* a trustee under the 22 July statute, for example, occasionally took jurisdiction to monitor the aryanization process once it had started and to make sure there were no egregious breaches of standards. Although even to this degree in the minority when it came to aryanization, such courts are exemplified in a 1943 Marseilles decision,[73] which had less to do with the freewheeling buying and selling of Jewish property as it did with the failure of the trustee to file an accounting or inventory of sale within the appropriate period. The Marseilles court perceived an important policy behind what it viewed as the 22 July statute's granting to ordinary courts this kind of jurisdiction:

> It would be to misconstrue the text and the spirit of this law to decline to apply its Article 7 during the period of the trustee's management; if that were decided, the simple refusal of the CGQJ to intervene in the face of prejudicial behavior by the trustee, because the CGQJ decided it was of insufficient importance to the state, but only important to the Jew [Israélite], would leave the latter without recourse.[74]

Attitudes such as articulated by the Marseilles court and others could not be dismissed out of hand as CGQJ pondered the jurisdictional dilemma. In this sense, a prudent internal awareness of the need to compromise was occurring; yet, in its stance to the outside world, the increasing urgency of satisfying Nazi demands for Jewish bodies, coupled with the fury CGQJ felt in watching the ordinary courts take control, led to periodic stiffening of the agency's backbone. The battle for control of Vichy law was going to last as long as the war itself.

As 1943 progressed, deferential attitudes seen in cases like *Fourcade* and *Dorfmann* were found less frequently and instead the ordinary courts became somewhat aggressive on the issue of jurisdiction. In an unusual variation involving name changes,[75] where CGQJ was pressing the ordinary courts and the district prosecutors to bring charges against Jews using pseudonyms—for in this area the agency had no independent arrest

---

[72] See chapter 7, text at note 175 for discussion of the *Razon* matter.

[73] The *Regneault* case, AN AJ$^{38}$, 99.

[74] See also chapter 7, note 158.

[75] See chapter 4 at notes 148–50.

mechanism—ordinary courts *declined* to take jurisdiction and the name changes were permitted to occur *de facto.*[76] In *Langellier-Bellevue,* a Nice tribunal sitting in mid-1943 resisted calls to desist adjudicating the alleged Jewishness of Ms. Blum (whose hyphenated married name appears as the title of the case); here, oddly, the jurisdiction's own public prosecutor as well as the CGQJ insisted that the court had no authority to do so. Citing both the 2 June and the 22 July statutes, the Nice court forged ahead and declared the lady to be non-Jewish.[77] About a month later, the court of Montpellier, in what CGQJ describes as a "lamentable" decision, intervened against a trustee to find that a Jewish father had the right to transfer property to his children (declared non-Jewish as part of its decision), who could thus hold it free of aryanization.[78] CGQJ lodged an immediate request for an appeal to the Conseil d'État, both on the jurisdictional and the substantive issues.[79]

Just a few months afterwards, in September 1943, two more situations revealed the civil courts' ever-increasing audaciousness in seizing jurisdiction over combined aryanization/Jewish definition cases. In *René Lévy,* a natural child wanted the court in Perpignan to annul a paternity declaration by his putative father, who was clearly Jewish. This the court declined to do, and by a decision of early 1942, it appointed a court-ordered specialist to examine Lévy "to see if he is circumcised."[80] However, the Court of Appeals of Montpellier reversed this decision, clearly

---

[76] See *Seile known as Raymond Seiler,* in which the Montpellier court declined to prosecute. CGQJ bemoans this in a letter to the justice ministry, 4 April 1943, AN $AJ^{38}$, 118.

[77] Decision of 12 April 1943, CDJC CXV-119.

[78] Internal memo, CGQJ, 5 July 1943, CDJC XVII-38 (161).

[79] Ibid. The agency believed that the court had erred in crediting the children's baptism, which was of uncertain date and hence not necessarily accomplished within the statutory period. But, as CGQJ put it, "the decision has no relevance, since it was rendered incompetently [i.e., from the point of view of lack of jurisdiction]. Under these conditions, nothing should bar the sale of the property."

[80] Decision of 9 February 1942, CDJC XVIIa-45 (243). Although not all ordinary courts placed this much emphasis on circumcision, it was almost always one of the key evidentiary factors. For the CGQJ, as the *Yousouf Behar Kouly* case in August 1943 reiterated, a circumcised individual was strongly presumed to be Jewish, CDJC XVIIa-38 (165); and (same case) AN $AJ^{38}$, 118: "If circumcision is not proof of adherence to the Jewish race, it certainly creates a strong assumption." But since "it is just about impossible to distinguish medical from ritual circumcisions," an "ethno-medical examination is required." See chapter 10, note 54.

articulating its view that sticky definitional issues like this one[81] were best handled by the ordinary courts. The CGQJ continued its official objection to such reasoning, adding perhaps a new twist:

> The law of 2 June 1941 is a public order law of an exceptional kind and should be thought of as a policing statute.... [It] can only be handled by administrative authorities. Under these conditions, common law tribunals are not competent, and only the CGQJ has the power to declare who is or is not Jewish, controlled, of course, by the Conseil d'État.[82]

Whatever internal softening of approach was occurring, the agency obviously would not publicly step down on jurisdiction, even regarding the 2 June statute (much less the aryanization law of 22 July). It instructed its regional officials "never in future to take positions contrary to CGQJ's, as occurred from time to time in this *dossier*."[83] It even innovated by proffering the theory that the religious statutes, which had generally been perceived as laws of personal status, were in fact policing rules—like parking regulations or highway laws—and hence clearly outside the limits of ordinary court adjudication.

Yet only a week or so later, in the *Leboucher* matter, the agency found itself admitting to the prefect of Montpellier that "in the most extreme cases [à l'extrême rigueur]" ordinary courts might have jurisdiction over "persons not yet assigned a trustee" who otherwise contested their Jewish status.[84] The Lebouchers, husband and wife (and first cousins), had been so assigned, and their Beziers novelty shop "Au petit Paris" was about to be aryanized. They wanted to prove in the ordinary court that they were not Jewish. CGQJ, on the other hand, insisted that the Beziers district prosecutor notify the court there of its lack of competence to handle the case:

> The trustee [administrateur provisoire] imposed by the CGQJ on the business called "Au petit Paris" is an act of public power against which a decision by the Beziers court would bring prejudice. It is a corollary of the

---

[81] Recall Barthélemy's solicitude for the natural child in his responsive memoranda of early 1942 to reform legislation proposed by CGQJ. See chapter 4, note 147; chapter 9, sub-section C; chapter 10 (B) (2) (b).

[82] Memo, 3 September 1943, circulated by the CGQJ regional director of Toulouse.

[83] Ibid.

[84] Memorandum, CGQJ to prefecture of Montpellier, 9 September 1943, CDJC XVIIa-38 (163). For another aspect of *Leboucher*, see chapter 6, notes 129.

> decision that I made regarding the Lebouchers as Jewish, a decision that inheres uniquely in the administrative service, and not the judicial. If the Lebouchers protest that they are not Jewish under the 2 June statute, and that therefore my assignment of the trustee is erroneous, they should not take the erroneous step of going to the judicial side but instead must go to the administrative side, to wit here the Conseil d'État.[85]

Despite the agency's aggressive tone, *René Lévy* and *Leboucher* demarcate for the jurisdictional debate—as *Hazan* had for the burden of proof struggle—the end of any real hope that CGQJ had for dominance, and the effective beginning of the Boutmy period of cutting losses through compromise and plea bargain. As 1943 wound down, CGQJ still wished for a new and stronger Conseil d'État opinion that would match its own public stance;[86] but the fact is that the highest administrative court was decreasingly likely to do so.

There was already reason to sense some softening in the Conseil d'État's substantive positions. The Conseil d'État had already broadened the *kinds* of evidence of non-Jewishness it might permit the individual to submit, and it was capable of reversing the agency's judgment about specific matters of definition and aryanization (the *Sée* case, for example).[87] What would it do in late 1943?

In fact, the Conseil d'État chose to rest upon its decision in a case called *Maxudian,* decided in April 1943. Mme. Maxudian had apparently petitioned her local police precinct to remove her name from the list of Jews kept there. When the police failed to respond, and the CGQJ also failed to grant her request, she appealed to the Conseil d'État. She claimed to have only two Jewish grandparents; furthermore, there was testimony to the effect that she had been baptized in 1938 and was married to a Protestant. The Conseil d'État held as follows, again declaring its jurisdiction as an explicit part of its decision:

> Whereas it is stipulated that the petitioner is an issue of 2 Jewish grandparents in the maternal line; that, if she produces a document originating from the consistory church of Verdun of the reformed faith from which it appears that her paternal grandparents, Moses and Sarah Lang, received the nuptial benediction in said church, on March 14, 1843, this evidence is not

---

[85] Ibid., 2. For other cases involving first cousins, see chapter 2, note 103.

[86] Memo, 3 September 1943, CDJC XVIIa-38 (162).

[87] See notes 54-55 above.

> of the sort to establish that neither one nor the other of those people belonged to the Jewish religion; [therefore a presumption] arises from the entirety of the evidence in the dossier which, apart from such proof, disallows Mme. Maxudian from justifying the claim that she cannot be considered a Jewess under the law of 2 June 1941.... By this decision, the Conseil d'État declares itself competent to rule on the adherence or non-adherence to the Jewish race.[88]

The *Maxudian* case, seemingly rigorous on both substantive and jurisdictional points, is in fact a kind of oddity. The last line, included as an authoritative "note" to the case, really concedes as much as it takes. All it proclaims for the Conseil d'État is the right to make judgments—*along with the ordinary courts*—on questions of personal status that had been arising under the 2 June statute for years. It makes no claim for exclusivity there. It merely reiterates what it had already declared in 1942 in the *Bloch-Favier* case.[89] More surprisingly still, the high administrative court makes no mention whatsoever of the most contentious issue then raging, the control over *aryanization* proceedings commenced under the 22 July 1941 statute by its hierarchical inferior, the CGQJ and appealed to ordinary courts by people like the Lebouchers, René Lévy, and Mme. Langellier-Bellevue.

On 23 February 1944, in the *Françoise Raphael* case, the Conseil d'État seemed in its final major decision to betray the CGQJ altogether. With a litigation history rivalling *Dorfmann,* this case commenced when CGQJ appointed a "trustee" to subdivide real estate that Françoise had received as a gift along with her three (clearly Aryan) brothers. The agency considered her to be Jewish because, while of mixed ascendancy, she failed to bring affirmative evidence of non-Jewishness and apparently had "spontaneously declared herself to be Jewish" by registering in the census. In early 1943, insisting that the state had not proven her to be a Jewess, Françoise brought an action in the ordinary courts of Agen. In a compendious and learned decision, the tribunal de première instance of that town held itself to have jurisdiction; it made note of the divided Vichy courts on this point, but then made use of prewar statutes—particularly Article 325 of the Code civil—to find its "status civitatis"

[88] CDJC, XVIIa-45 (242).

[89] See text at note 20.

contained in the matter.[90] Recognizing that the burden of proof issue was legitimately in dispute in the courts, because the 2 June statute was ambiguously worded, the Agen court placed it upon the state, citing the absurdity first mentioned about the Moroccan case of "L" [91]: "a person with a Muslim father and a Jewish mother, being a Muslim" would otherwise be forced to prove he was not Jewish.[92] Permitting all kinds of evidence on the issue—and citing the Conseil d'État's own 1942 statement to that effect[93]—the court declared Françoise non-Jewish, largely on the basis of her having begun instruction in the Christian religion! (This was by no means the only time that an individual who apparently practiced Judaism nonetheless argued for Aryan status due to a combination of factors including her grandparents' status.)[94] The Agen ordinary court then had the temerity to block the aryanization of her part of the property, giving her time to appeal the CGQJ's finding of Jewishness to the Conseil d'État.

All of this infuriated the agency. Aside from trampling on its authority and also permitting the question of burden of proof to dictate what it saw as a ridiculous outcome, CGQJ must have wondered what happened to the doctrine that hitherto prevented ordinary courts from issuing injunctions on aryanization while the administrative courts worked out definitional conflicts.[95] But the worst was yet to come.

In a decision that, effectively speaking, conceded the administrative court's submission to the magistrates regarding Jewish affairs in Vichy, the Conseil d'État reversed its agency's finding on Françoise's Jewish status and affirmed the view of the ordinary court in Agen that her

---

[90] Decision of 12 February 1943, 8, CDJC XVIIa-45 (247).

[91] See text at notes 16 and 17.

[92] *Françoise Raphael,* CDJC XVIIa-45 (247), 11.

[93] See note 52.

[94] On 25 April 1942, the CGQJ regional director for Nice wrote to the aryanization service of CGQJ in Vichy wondering whether a certain *Raoul Valéri,* who had three *Aryan* grandparents could be considered Jewish because he admittedly practiced that religion! Under the approach of the 2 June statute, there was no readily available affirmative response. Instead, the agency marked the question "to be classed under the rubric of the need to reform Article I," AN AJ[38], 118. Darquier, who endorsed the religious approach, did not move to remedy this anomaly.

[95] See, e.g., *Weill* at note 71 for a 1943 Pau case still somewhat deferential to the administrative agencies and courts.

property should not be subject to aryanization.[96] Although explicitly no more conceding jurisdiction to the civil courts than it had monopolized it from them, the Conseil d'État thereby set in motion a series of events that had the effect of declaring the ordinary courts to have substantial jurisdiction in the questions of Jewish status.

On 5 April 1944, the CGQJ informed its regional offices that an individual's unknown ancestors were henceforth to be presumed non-Jewish.[97] Following quickly on a Conseil d'État decision that it knew was disastrous, this reversal of the agency's dearly held view on burden of proof indicates both its defeatism at this stage and its allegiance, however reluctant or resentful, to traditional French legal hierarchies.

On 20 April 1944, the CGQJ also gave up on the jurisdiction issue. Françoise's trustee was informed that he no longer had any right to deal with her property. The agency advised him to discontinue his appeal of the Agen court's finding that Françoise was not Jewish. As though to pour salt on its wounds, the Court of Appeals of Agen a month later threw out the appeal as a formal matter and imposed all costs on the trustee.[98]

There is a certain pathos in reading the words of the agency's regional operative, who was left to wonder out loud "how such a finding of the Conseil d'État will be applied...? Should we continue to treat as Jewish any person who has two Jewish grandparents but belongs to no religion? If so, won't that person appeal to the Conseil d'État if proof of his belonging to the Jewish religion has not been established?"[99]

Forty-eight hours after D-Day, the *Weiller* case, which involved a painter facing criminal penalties for failure to register as a Jew,[100] provided some answers to the operative's baleful queries. When the tribunal de première instance of St. Ceret decided that, even though Weiller had two Jewish grandparents, was circumcised, and seemed to practice

---

[96] Conseil d'État decision, 23 February 1944, CDJC XVII-36 (154a); see also, Conseil d'État decision, *Bickert dit Picard,* 16 July 1943, AN $AJ^{38}$, 99 where the high administrative body overturned the aryanization of a non-Jew's property and found the CGQJ to have erred in thinking that Bickert's *renting* of the property to Jews for long periods of time constituted "an exceptional circumstance" justifying the aryanization.

[97] CDJC XVIIa-38 (164).

[98] Ibid., internal CGQJ memorandum.

[99] Ibid.

[100] See discussion of this case in chapter 2, note 119.

some of the rites of Judaism, he was not legally Jewish, the CGQJ no longer expressed anger or amazement. Instead, it simply noted in its report of the case:

> This judgment conforms with the jurisprudence of the Conseil d'État, which regards as Aryan any person descended from a mixed marriage who does not clearly belong to the Jewish religion. [Citing *Françoise Raphael*][101]

## C. The Conseil d'État's Reorganization for Exclusion

Aware of its special mission on Jewish matters, France's highest administrative jurisdiction tried throughout the Vichy period to keep ahead of the ordinary magistrates when it came to religious law. We have seen that morale was low in the magistrature and that the number of ordinary judges was in decline; but the Conseil d'État had a kind of resurgence of spirit, partly encouraged by its new religious jurisdiction.

The vice-president of the Conseil d'État, Alfred Porché, enjoyed considerable power over individual requests for exemptions under article 8 of the law of 2 June 1941. The high council [haute assemblée] of the full Conseil d'État voted ultimately on Porché's affirmative recommendations. Meanwhile, Porché moved to expand his bureaucratic base on Jewish matters by establishing within an already expanded Conseil d'État a special "Committee on the study of the Jewish Laws" [Commission du statut des juifs]. The task of this group was to study and clarify for the government and others thorny issues, all of which by now have been covered in this and earlier chapters, raised by the new statutes.[102] Its key pronouncement, cited by Joseph Haennig[103] and by numerous Vichy courts, involved an expansion of the *kinds* of proof admissible to include not merely affiliation with a religion recognized prior to 1905 (typically Catholicism, as well as some Protestant sects and—in North Africa—Islam) but also all other indices of "Jewishness" or its opposite.[104] The Conseil d'État seemed to feel that this pronouncement

---

[101] Memorandum, 8 June 1944, CDJC XVIIa-45 (254).

[102] Statement of purpose, Alfred Porché, 1 February 1942, AN BB$^{30}$, Conseil d'État file.

[103] "What Means of Proof Can the Jew of Mixed Blood Offer to Establish his Non-Affiliation with the Jewish Race?," *Gazette du Palais,* 1$^{er}$ trimestre 1943, 31.

[104] Declaration of Conseil d'État, through its special committee, 11 December 1942.

would "put an end to all controversy on the matter,"[105] and (except for the churlish bureaucrats of the CGQJ) it largely did.

However, the performance of the special committee and, indeed, that of the Conseil d'État overall (as we have seen in many decisions of its regular judicial sections) were hardly as liberal as the committee's most famous pronouncement might indicate.[106] The majority of its decisions, until the very end of the war, either overtly prejudiced individual litigants fighting with the state or its agencies about their Jewish status, or more quietly affirmed CGQJ decisions on status and property rights. Was the Conseil d'État a rubber stamp for Vichy or an independent force? Without doubt, the Conseil d'État enjoyed considerable prestige, unlike the magistrature. Their numbers increased during Vichy, while the magistrature was in decline.[107] The Conseil d'État, apart from its adjudicatory capacity, had limited advisory powers as to proposed legislation, although the latter was controlled by the government ministries in theoretical dialogue with the new Conseil national.[108] Barthélemy, ever the defender in bad times of the magistrates, nonetheless respected the Conseil d'État, too, visiting it as its nominal "president" and even arranging for Pétain to appear before the haute assemblée personally.[109] For awhile, the Conseil d'État established its seat of operations right in Vichy, although apparently the lack of material comforts there quickly

---

105 Memorandum, 7 February 1943, AN AJ[38], 118.

106 Accord Marrus and Paxton, *Vichy France,* 141f. For a fine analysis of the Conseil d'État's jurisprudence, see Jean Marcou, "Le Conseil d'État sous Vichy," (Ph.D. diss., Law Faculty, Grenoble II, 30 June 1984). I thank Serge Klarsfeld for bringing this thesis to my attention.

107 Laws of 1 October 1941 and 18 May 1942 increased the number of conseillers above prewar levels; see AN BB[30], "Conseil d'État" file.

108 It is probably fair to say that, by constitutional act number 2 of 11 July 1940, Article 1, paragraph 2, Pétain committed himself solely to the advice of his cabinet. Rémy, *Les lois de Vichy,* 41. See also, Barthélemy's formulation of his own considerable legislative power, both in chapter 4 and in *Ministre,* 282. At one point the cabinet seems to have considered a *formal* decree suspending the Conseil d'État's legislative function, AN BB[30], 1716, but it did continue on a sharply limited and discretionary basis, whereas its adjudicatory functions were considerable. Accord René Rémond, ed., *Le gouvernement de Vichy* (Paris: A. Colin, Fond. nationale des sciences politiques, 1972), 34: "The Conseil d'État...saw sharply reduced activity on the legislative front.... It was not actively consulted."

109 As recalled in Barthélemy, *Ministre,* 576; see also chapter 4, note 96.

led most of its bureaus to return to Paris.[110] Their temporary physical proximity to the core of Vichy power was symbolic of a far more significant actual collaboration.

To their sworn allegiance to the person of Marshal Pétain[111], an oath that the magistrates[112] but not private lawyers[113] also had to take, there was also for all "high functionaries" a special statutory obligation to be "personally liable before the Marshall...including in their person and their property," subjecting many in the Conseil d'État to punition for violating their oath.[114]

In fact, all adjudicators—magistrates and administrators alike—took the oath, and when Pétain personally visited the Conseil d'État on 19 August 1941, he heard the following words uttered by the assemblage:[115] Je jure fidelité à la personne du chef de l'État. [I swear allegiance to the person of the Head of State]

How could the Conseil d'État function as ultimate arbiter of disputes between the state and the individual when it had staked all on the supreme head of Vichy? Yet only one member abstained the day of Pétain's visit, and after receiving some assurances about the meaning of the oath, he agreed to take it the following November.[116]

While the oath as a breach of separation of powers might have bothered some, for Porché—discussing the situation with Barthélemy—there was no conflict. On the contrary, Porché wanted Barthélemy to know that his Conseil d'État had always been at its best historically when

---

[110] AN BB[30], "Conseil d'État" file.

[111] See constitutional act number 9 of 14 August 1941, Rémy, *Les Lois de Vichy,* 140. As high functionaries, the Conseil d'État seems to have been bound also in their person and their property by the terms of Articles 2 and 3 of constitutional act number 7 of 27 January 1941, applicable to "high functionaries," ibid., 108.

[112] Under constitutional act no. 9, ibid.

[113] The absence of an oath to Pétain was cited to me by Philippe Serre as one of the areas in which private lawyers distinguished themselves by their autonomy from the régime, especially as contrasted to the magistrates, whom he felt had substantially merged their power with that of the régime by taking the oath, Philippe Serre, personal interview with author, Paris, 21 December 1988.

[114] See note 111.

[115] Barthélemy, *Ministre,* 576.

[116] The member was Eugène Blondeau, as reported by Barthélemy, *Ministre,* 577; see also note 123 below as to the similar minority of one among the magistrates.

asked to work with authoritarian leaders demanding full allegiance. As Porché put it:

> The past teaches us...that our role has been greatest under authoritarian régimes; the last few months have already brought preliminary verification of this law of history; we are confident that we will be called upon at last to take on the legitimate role which is restored to us in the great work undertaken by the head of state to "gently rehabilitate," in Catherine de Medici's expressive turn of phrase, to "gently rehabilitate what the evils of time may have spoiled in this realm."[117]

The Conseil d'État's rehabilitative role has been in part illuminated as seen in its major decisions about race. So pervasive was the interplay of religious legislation and the Conseil d'État's perception of its own role in the national revolution that Porché argued for—and received— permission to reinforce the litigation arm of his agency. In early 1942, he wrote to the Justice Department asking for a suspension of the usual rotation of his junior staff among the Conseil d'État's various departments, instead requesting saturation of the litigation [contentieux] unit.[118]

The litigation unit was split into eight sub-sections during the Vichy years. Each case was assigned to one of these, and appeal could lie from any single decision to the full unit or even to the plenary assembly of the Conseil d'État.[119] Despite its diminished role as a legislative advisor, these were busy times for one of France's most honored adjudicatory institutions.

## D. The Post-Liberation Fate of the Magistrates

We have seen that, although producing a sometimes contradictory and always complex body of caselaw, on balance Vichy's magistrates more than their administrative adjudicators offered some means of escape to individuals caught in Vichy's racial net. Indeed, their very battle to retain and extend jurisdiction over religious laws speaks well for the magistrates who (as we have seen here and in chapters 3 and 4) were themselves beleaguered, demoralized, underpaid, and little respected.

---

[117] Barthélemy, *Ministre,* 47; see chapter 10, note 10.

[118] Memorandum, 13 January 1942, AN $BB^{30}$, 1714.

[119] Ibid.

Perhaps for these reasons, an element of public opinion just after the Liberation tended to think highly of the ordinary courts' performance during Vichy. At its most extreme, this admiration emerged in the speeches of judicial functionaries themselves; thus the assembled Cour de Cassation, on 16 October 1944, heard one of its own opine that "a considerable majority [of magistrates] courageously resisted" the régime.[120]

More realistically, the official report on the performance of the magistrates opined that resistance among them was "very limited" [très minoritaire].[121] Its author, Maurice Rolland, a member of the Paris magistracy who had escaped to London and worked in the Resistance, cited the awful conditions of wartime Vichy courts, and the unpredictability of careers during the régime, but nonetheless noted that—analogously to the Conseil d'État[122]—only *one* magistrate had refused to take the oath of allegiance to the very person of Pétain.[123]

Rolland observed that magistrates making judgments about magistrates—as they had to do in the immediate post-Liberation atmosphere of reprisal that we have seen affecting Barthélemy[124]—would not lead to the most objective findings. "Reprisals [L'épuration] placed all judges into a crisis of conscience," as one historian put it. "How can a high functionary friendly to Laval be tried by judges who themselves obeyed the orders of their hierarchical superiors?"[125]

In the end, 363 magistrates, of whom about 100 sat in the special repressive jurisdictions of Vichy, were stripped of their function, of whom six were from the Cour de Cassation, and nine from the Parisian Court of Appeals and tribunal de la Seine.[126] One can ask, at the close of a chapter such as this, whether distinctions apart perhaps from the special section terrors, could be made between, say, the magistrate in Marseilles

---

[120] Félix Mazeaud, presiding judge of the Cour de Cassation, cited in Christian Lépagnot, *Histoire de Vichy* (Geneva: Editions Idégraf, 1978), vol. 5, 72. Mazeaud was himself appointed by Barthélemy to an important division of the Cour, the chambre des requêtes, Barthélemy, *Ministre,* 195.

[121] Lépagnot, *Histoire de Vichy,* vol. 5, 73.

[122] See note 116.

[123] Lépagnot, *Histoire de Vichy,* vol. 5, 73.

[124] See closing section of chapter four.

[125] Lépagnot, *Histoire de Vichy,* vol. 5, 73.

[126] Ibid., 157.

who placed the burden of proof on the Jew Soffer[127] and the one in Toulouse that released the ostensibly Jewish Pierre Bloch, having placed the burden on the state.[128] Should the ordinary court that declined jurisdiction and hence yielded its potentially balming judgment to the rigors of the CGQJ and the Conseil d'État be more blameworthy after the fact than the one that vigorously seized the subject matter of Jewishness and went on to contradict the administration's actions?[129]

As soon as one moves to a slightly higher level of generalization, the meaningfulness of such distinctions disappears. The Vichy problem in all its human, moral, and legalistic significance concerns the inability of all magistrates to address directly the corruption, the unconstitutionality, and the fundamental illegality of racial persecution, arbitrary incarceration, and mass pillage of property. Before that universal failing, the spectrum that may be found in the cases cited in this chapter closes in upon itself, a tiny and pathetic dot along the broad span of possibility that no magistrate or administrator attempted.

For that reason, I leave the final judgment in this study to a lawyer and contemporary observer of Vichy. For Philippe Serre, a man who voted with the minority to deny full powers to Pétain: "the magistrates did not distinguish themselves under Vichy."[130]

---

[127] See note 14.

[128] See note 27.

[129] Contrast *Langellier-Bellevue,* note 77 (taking jurisdiction) with *Weill,* notes 71 and 95 (refusing jurisdiction).

[130] Phillipe Serre, personal interview with author, Paris, December 1988.

# Chapter 6

## Out-Naziing the Masters

The Vichy approach to religious definition encouraged the Nazis to use it even in the Occupied Zone. While their own first ordinance of 27 September 1940 adopted the Reich's preliminary statutory requirement of at least three Jewish grandparents,[1] Vichy's law of 3 October 1940 had added a well-stocked category of mixed-heritage individuals,[2] and the Nazis followed suit with their next definitional ordinance on 26 April 1941.[3] Not to be outdone, as we have seen, Vichy on its own initiated the even more expansive 2 June 1941 categories of mixed-heritage Jews married to other *mixed-heritage* Jews and also restricted the date and arguably the proofs by which individuals might demonstrate their non-Jewishness.[4]

The German conquerors seem almost to have been prescient about Vichy zealousness on race, although of course that is only implicit in their earliest declarations about comparative law in the Occupied Zone. Their original position, articulated for all conquered countries in an

---

[1] R. Sarraute and P. Tager, *Les Juifs sous l'Occupation: Recueil des textes officiels français et allemands* (Paris: CDJC, 1982), 18; the 1935 Reich statute had a similar formulation, see, e.g., J. R. Desbaines, ed., *Le statut des juifs en France en Allemagne et en Italie* (Lyon: Express-Documents, 1943]), 4, citing Law of 15 September 1935 defining Jewishness for the Reich.

[2] Ibid., 19; see chapter 2.

[3] Sarraute and Tager, *Recueil des textes,* 41.

[4] Ibid., 51.

ordinance of 10 May 1940 insisted that "the ordinances and decrees of the German High Command take primacy over [priment] those of the country itself," but left the opening that "the laws of the country remain in force so long as they do not contradict the aims of the Occupation."[5] And Vichy agreed wholeheartedly, taking an early position that they pridefully maintained throughout the régime's four years; it was articulated by Darlan, contemporaneously viewed by resistance and communist partisans to be basically a German martinet,[6] yet on 7 June 1941, he informed all Vichy ministries:

> the occupation does not destroy the prerogatives of the sovereign French state.... It may happen that functionaries of the French state in the occupied zone find themselves charged by the local occupying authorities with abusive tasks that are not compatible with French legislation nor with texts and treaties that are currently operative. On the other hand, any abandonment on our part furnishes to the occupying authority a juridical base that is not in accord with the armistice convention.[7]

By late 1941, with most of Vichy's comprehensive religious legislation fully propounded, both sides agreed that neither German "primacy" nor French "abandonment" of tradition had been troubled by the Vichy approach to the Jewish question. On 9 December, Vichy formulated to the German High Command what was then a *fait accompli:* "the German authorities and [Vichy] have been in agreement on the principle of the substitution of French regulation against Jews for the German regulation thereof."[8] And the Germans, through Dannecker, concurred formally in mid-1942: "the French definition being broader, it will now serve as a basis in all doubtful cases."[9]

French law about race had originated in the autonomous actions of a newly-formed government and moved along in an astonishingly rapid sequence of further laws and decrees, detailed interpretations, and frenzied internecine conflict. We have seen packed into a four-year period marked by political and even geographical upheaval a single-minded focus by

[5] Cited as applicable to France in AN BB$^{30}$, Gabolde papers.

[6] See, e.g., Daniel Cordier, *Jean Moulin: L'Inconnu du Panthéon,* (Paris: Lattès, 1993), vol. 3, 387, citing a 1941 piece in *L'Humanité.*

[7] AN BB$^{30}$, Gabolde papers.

[8] CDJC CVIII-5; see chapter 5, notes 41–44.

[9] Memorandum, 1 July 1942, CDJC XXVI, 36.

courts, agencies, lawyers and writers upon the theme of race. There was little German interference in, yet much German appreciation of, this phenomenon. The French somehow found their own way to reach conclusions that matched—sometimes more than matched—whatever demands the Germans might conceivably make.

Yet it is vital to remember that the *cause* of Vichy's legalistic single-mindedness was decidedly *not* appeasement of their Nazi vanquishers. On the contrary, from Alibert to Xavier Vallat, and from Barthélemy to Darlan, the policy makers of religious law in Vichy insisted on publicly dissociating themselves from German precedents. If their approach on any given law found favor in German eyes, so be it, but that was a matter of relative indifference. Magistrates and ministers, bureaucrats and barristers—all were playing by French rules. Whatever apprehensions they had at the beginning (and these seemed few in import and in number) tended to diminish as time taught them that everyday French legal reasoning, under everyday French legal procedures implemented by everyday French institutions, by and large controlled the newly created world of French religious law. If the Germans' direct intervention increased as the war's imminent end found their thirst for Jewish blood unappeased, it was more a matter of administrative efficiency than of dissatisfaction with French behavior. By then, however, Vichy had contributed to the Holocaust more than three years of laws, regulation, and manpower that made possible the horrific climax of the occupation of their country.

I do not mean to say, of course, that the German presence in much of France had no influence on these legalistic developments at all. One of the functions of this chapter's first three sub-parts, in fact, is to indicate that that presence occasionally *checked* what might have become even more extensive Vichy excesses in religious law! Of course, the Nazis did pursue at first their native racial approach in the Occupied Zone. However, their ordinances were overtaken and in some key respects replaced by Vichy methodologies and statutes. More and more people were changed by Vichy definition into grist for the Nazis' holocaustic mill, and at very small cost in German manpower or treasure. In the third sub-section, the way in which the legalities of Jewish definition directly affected arrest and deportation decisions is emphasized.

As the chapter closes, I will move towards the specific subject matter of chapter 7 with some observations about Vichy's pillaging of Jewish property in both zones. Although, of course, the aryanization of Jewish holdings—and the "elimination of Jewish influence" in commerce—were common aims of both the Germans and the French, the focus for the purposes of this chapter will be upon *legalistic* zeal by the latter in a number of specific realms.

German willingness to adopt a case-by-case approach dependent (until 1944) on French laws, rules, and interpretations—even for arrest and deportation decisions—goes beyond cynicism or the desire to confuse both the French and the victimized Jews. Instead, I believe that in the legal areas emphasized here (as well as in their response to French denaturalization laws, discussed later in this book), the Nazis genuinely depended on Vichy authority, for it had the twin merit of keeping the local population relatively assuaged and of bringing *more* people into the scope of persecution than would have occurred under their own system.

In this chapter we track four major developments in Vichy law that attracted Nazi attention and that tended to go beyond German precedents. Each area involves an interweaving of law and regulation, policy and application, but each is based on statutory formulations that permitted the French to contravene and contradict more liberal Nazi outcomes. (Beyond the scope of this chapter are other, less legalistic, areas in which French behavior arguably exceeded German models and definitely provoked German irritation, such as racial propaganda.)[10] In each domain, I will present documentation tending to show that Vichy *willfully* surpassed Nazi precedents, and that, anticipating contentiousness, the régime expected its policies to be implemented in both zones. Finally, Vichy hewed to its positions quite rigorously, even as the war wound down and part of France was already liberated. Something about the French mind—perhaps especially the legalistic and bureaucratic mind—wanted to bring systemic closure to any given task, no matter how absurd the subject matter in light of extrinsic events; but, in these areas, unlike the purely Franco-French debates we saw in the previous chapters, Vichy discovered a kind of logic in outdoing the Germans on racism at the same time as the Allied troops were outdoing them on the battlefields.

---

[10] See Jean Laloum, *La France antisémite de Darquier de Pellepoix* (Paris: Syros, 1979), 87–143 for an excellent analysis of competitive racial propaganda during Vichy; Laurent Gervereau and Denis Peschanski, *La Propagande sous Vichy* (Paris: BDIC, 1990).

## A. How Seriously Should the Baptismal Act Be Taken?

German and French views may not have differed much about the need to punish France's Jews through legalistic means, but on the basic question of "*who* is a Jew," there was quite a difference indeed. Perhaps the most pervasive of these contrasts, although as we shall see later in this chapter by no means the most extreme, involved the value of proof of Christianity through baptismal and other clerical records. For Vichy law, the need to examine such proof arose fairly often, particularly for mixed-heritage individuals.[11] There was a score of litigated cases in which baptismal records were offered into evidence, but the need to scrutinize church documents occurred far more often at the agency level, when the CGQJ decided whether or not to issue a certificate of non-adherence to the Jewish religion. German attitudes about the reliability of sacramental data emerged in reaction to French legal and administrative developments.

Paragraph 2 of Article 1 of the law of 2 June 1941 explicitly states that, since individuals with only two Jewish grandparents will be deemed Jewish only if they "belong to the Jewish religion," their *non-affiliation* "is established by proof of belonging to another religion recognized by the state" prior to 1905, the year in which such distinctions were removed from French law.[12] Quite apart from the portentous legal issue of who bears the burden of proof on this question—examined in chapter 5—the *nature* of the proof offered by individuals might well include a baptismal certificate. How seriously was this proof to be taken? Was it dispositive? Did it at least create a rebuttable presumption of non-Jewishness? Or was it just one piece of evidence among many, to be taken perhaps less seriously, say, than circumcision, and to be given no more weight, say, than attendance at synagogue or marriage in a church or the possession of Hebrew religious relics?

---

[11] See, e.g., the following cases discussed in chapter 5: *Brigitte Sée* at note 55, and *Dorfmann* at note 66. For the CGQJ position that baptism was relevant *only* in cases involving people with two Jewish grandparents able to show two non-Jewish grandparents, see CGQJ to a Paris police official, 27 February 1942, CDJC XXI-42, chastising him for being influenced by such records when the status of the individual was otherwise clear.

[12] Sarraute and Tager, *Recueil des textes,* 49.

In terms of statutory interpretation, the first serious question was whether proof of belonging to an accepted Christian faith (normally Catholicism) was the *only* evidentiary route to non-Jewish status; the CGQJ quickly took the view that it was, but the Conseil d'État (as we have seen) finally quieted the debate in late 1942, when its special committee on Jewish questions declared that *all* forms of proof were admissible.[13] However, that decision did not deal with the still tricky matter of baptismal and other church records as the *best* means to the end of proving non-Jewishness through a clear showing of what the statute explicitly mandated: adherence to a recognized Christian religion.

Earlier, the CGQJ had taken a position that superficially, at least, implied strong reliance upon baptismal records to demonstrate one's Catholicism:

> [M]ust adherence to Catholicism be demonstrated exclusively by the production of a *baptismal record* or may, on the contrary, the production of evidence showing the beginning of religious instruction, or even being the child of a marriage where there is official dispensation or where there has been an agreement to bring the children up as Christians, suffice?
> We [CGQJ service of litigation and legislation] believe that the production of a baptismal certificate is indispensable. It is the only irrefutable way to prove one's adherence to the Catholic religion. [Other kinds of proof] would too easily permit fraud and would impede the implementation of the law. [Underlining in red pencil in the original.][14]

Perhaps the key word in this document, written only two months after promulgation of the 2 June 1941 statute, is "fraud," a word that conjures for the very first time the CGQJ's pervasive skepticism about proof of Christianity. Although the agency's position here surely indicates acceptance of baptismal records themselves, CGQJ took the view that a certificate was necessary *but not sufficient* to prove Catholicism. If the individual failed to produce his baptismal record, he would not satisfy what CGQJ took to be his burden of proof. At best, the baptismal record provided a rebuttable presumption of Christianity.

Whether understood this way, or as granting a greater presumption to the production of a baptismal record, the 1941 statement of policy

---

[13] See chapter 5 at notes 102–105.

[14] Memorandum, CGQJ to Barthélemy, 19 August 1941, AN AJ[38],148; see also chapter 4, note 142.

marked the apex of CGQJ's faith in clerical documents. Early in the following year, the agency demoted baptismal records from providing a rebuttable presumption of Christianity to being totally irrelevant on the issue. And by the end of 1942, it was explicitly declaring church records to be a suspect evidentiary category in the determination of non-Jewishness.

In articulating for its regional director in Nice the agency's policy about out-of-wedlock children,[15] where the grandparental heritage was indicated as mixed, CGQJ opined in early spring 1942 that "if the child is not baptized, there is no doubt at all: he is Jewish. If he was baptized before 25 June 1940 [the statutory cut-off date], there remains against him a presumption of belonging to the Jewish race that he must rebut [qu'il lui appartient de combattre]."[16]

Part of CGQJ's minimizing of baptismal records in the latter situation reflected the "substance over form" position often evident in the agency's approach to children; it was being taken contemporaneously by rigorous courts such as the criminal court in Brive, which held in the *Charles-Robert Lang* case that neither the baptism of Claude and Jack Lang, aged 2 and 3—nor the fact that they were uncircumcised—legally absolved their father from his responsibility to register them as Jews.[17]

The agency also wondered about the relevance of baptism where, as was true in the *Lang* case, the rite took place *after* the statutory cut-off date of 25 June 1940. On the other hand, CGQJ finally decided that such baptisms would be relevant if the child was indeed *born after the statutory date* (as was true of one of the two infants in the Brive decision) since, as it put it, using all the rigor of Vichy legalistic thinking at its most "logical":

> Obviously the child could not have been baptized before June 25, 1940, because it was not yet born.[18]

---

[15] See chapter 2 at note 116, and chapter 4 at note 147.

[16] Memorandum, 26 March 1942, CDJC CXV (19).

[17] *Charles-Robert Lang* case, 30 April 1942, reported in *Semaine juridique*, 12 July 1942. Lubetzki, *La Condition des Juifs en France sous l'Occupation allemande* (Paris: CDJC, 1947), 34, reports that the case was reversed on appeal; see chapter 2, note 114.

[18] Letter, CGQJ to its regional director, Toulouse, 18 August 1942, CDJC XVIIa-38 (158).

Yet, as we saw in its response to the Limoges tribunal's decision in the *Robert Meyer* case,[19] where a father had his adolescent children baptized into Protestantism just after learning of the Jewish law, CGQJ pursued its "substance over form" sense that baptism was irrelevant unless sincerely undertaken.[20] CGQJ's reluctance to accept the baptismal form as probative became more generalized as 1942 progressed, and as the cases in 1943 increasingly worked against its racial viewpoints.[21]

Yet, both within and without CGQJ, the gradual denigration of baptismal evidence by ignoring it was developing, paradoxically, a two-sided nature that might assist people incapable of producing church records almost as often as it persecuted them by finding that their records were suspect. For example, even some ordinary courts were tacitly agreeing in effect with CGQJ that baptism was irrelevant while at the same time using that logic to declare the Aryan status of non-baptized people.[22]

In the same vein, a CGQJ lawyer, Jacques Ditte, garnered (until March 1943, when he was fired by Darquier) something of a reputation for "softness" on the Jewish status matters he administered; those who felt that way criticized (or credited)[23] him for dispensing with the need for

---

[19] See chapter 5, note 29.

[20] The substance over form approach surfaced in CGQJ's reaction to at least one *adult* baptism, that of movie theater owner Dorfmann (see chapter 5, notes 11 and 65). Dorfmann was baptized on either 17 or 19 June 1940 (the evidence on the date was conflicting), both of which fall just within the statutory period. Boutmy of the agency continued to call Dorfmann's baptism "suspect," but the agency did not press the point.

[21] See chapter 5, passim.

[22] Thus in a divorce proceeding before the tribunal civil de la Seine, both parents asked for a judicial finding of non-Jewishness for their minor children. These latter each had two Jewish grandparents; they were circumcised, although it seemed not in the Jewish ritual manner, at ages 22 months and 2 years respectively. They were *not baptized in a timely manner,* but a priest testified that they had received a Christian upbringing and education from their earliest childhood. The court, on 14 May 1943, while agreeing that they were legally not baptized for purposes of the statute, placed the burden on the state and found the religious education to suffice. The children were declared non-Jewish. *Clerc vs. Lévy,* CDJC (unnumbered).

[23] See Joseph Barthélemy, *Ministre de la Justice: Vichy, 1941–1943* (Paris: Pygmalion, 1989), 321, where Ditte is depicted assisting Barthélemy's daughter to help Jews by "delivering questionable certificates of Aryan status." The picture of Ditte, "an antisemite for many years," is quite different in Joseph Billig, *Le Commissariat général aux questions juives* (Paris: CDJC, 1955), vol. 1, 109, although Billig allows that Ditte did

baptismal records in determining whether to grant the precious certificate of non-adherence to the Jewish race. One cranky CGQJ operative in Toulouse wrote of his concerns just a month before Ditte left the agency:

> Subject: Bizarre approvals of the *certificat.* I must signal you that Jacques Ditte—who is still around although the Minister [of the Interior, under whose aegis CGQJ operated] in person told me he would be fired—at the *statut des personnes* in Paris, delivers certificates of non-adherence on a showing, for the grandparents, of religious burial certificates.
>
> *He does not require baptismal records.... Conclusion*
>
> I ask, once more, for the rescission of all *certificats* approved—too easily and even illegally—by Paris. (Emphasis in original.)[24]

Jacques Ditte's attitude on baptism during his direction of the CGQJ's bureau of persons is, however, exaggerated in this letter. It is true that, as Ditte opines to a police official in mid-1942, proof of schooling at a Catholic institution that does not admit non-baptized students, created for his agency a rebuttable presumption of non-Jewishness, even in the absence of a baptismal certificate.[25] But this "liberality" on the kinds of evidence allowable simply reflects what by then was the dominant attitude throughout Vichy, if not within the CGQJ itself. His actions in granting non-Jewish status to some individuals unable to proffer a baptismal certificate was less a sign of "softness" than of political pragmatism in the face of changing currents in Vichy's ordinary and administrative courts (see chapter 5) and of a creeping hostility towards clerical records that became overt only somewhat later and that eventually disturbed the Germans almost as much as it did certain Vichy constituencies.

More likely yet, Ditte's flexibility probably reflected a kind of seat of the pants approach to these life-and-death decisions typical of some bureaucrats suddenly vested with great power. To a few unlucky lawyers, like those of the *Union général des Israëlites français* (UGIF), it seemed as though Ditte might just as well find against someone as for him, with baptism or non-baptism an inevitable sideshow of an arbitrary decision-making process. So in the case of Alexander Saul Bernholc, Ditte ignored the fact that Bernholc had produced convincing baptismal records from

---

give certificates to a few Jews.

[24] Memorandum, 2 February 1943, CDJC CXV-101.

[25] Memorandum, 4 July 1942, CDJC CVX-50.

his native Russia and, in the words of a lawyer who had spoken to Ditte's secretary about the case, "Ditte feels that M. Bernholc is Jewish. I don't know on what basis he reached his conclusion [je ne sais pas sur quelle base il fonde sa conviction]...."[26]

To the contrary effect, in a case with virtually immediate life and death consequences, Ditte decided in favor of an individual with a questionable baptismal record, but his confirmation of her non-Jewish status came too late. Since it involved the interrelationship of crucial CGQJ decisions with caselaw on Jewish status when baptismal records were questionable, and since the German authorities were ultimately involved, the matter deserves detailed attention at this point. This case was several months beyond the *Bernholc* set of facts; the jurisprudence increasingly placing the burden of proof on the agency was in full blossom, and even Darquier had taken notice of the fact that CGQJ's hardline positions conflicted not only with those of the ordinary courts but, on some issues, with the German approach, too.[27] Lucienne Morel (née Weissmann) claimed to be a Catholic, but she failed to produce a baptismal certificate. A mixed-heritage individual married to a Catholic, her life was now a chaotic ride with twists and turns supplied by Vichy law, which first offered the golden ring of non-Jewish status and then took it away. In a case precisely exemplifying Darquier's momentary contrition at seeing individuals arrested for violating German ordinances whom German law would not have defined as Jewish,[28] Lucienne was arrested and sent to Drancy for failure to wear the Jewish Star. Her rollercoaster ride began when her father apparently elicited from CGQJ assurances of Lucienne's non-Jewishness. She herself appeared at the agency without incident, asking for an identity card in the name of her husband. But fifteen days later she was summoned back and required to show a baptismal certificate.

Unable to proffer the baptismal records, Lucienne and her husband had to re-register her as a Jew, and dutifully reported to CGQJ, where M. Morel was summarily fined 1200 francs for not having registered her to

---

[26] Correspondence, Lucienne Scheid Haas, 10 August 1942, YV C-3.

[27] See chapter 5 at notes 41–44.

[28] Ibid.

begin with.[29] A few days later, she was ready to report to CGQJ to pick up her Star, but in the meanwhile she received a summons to appear at the police station, where she expected to get her new identity card; instead, she was directed back to the CGQJ, where she was arrested for her delay in obtaining and wearing the Star.

On 28 October Ditte opined that Lucienne Weissmann

> was not baptized within the statutory period, her baptism occurring only in 1942. She has not belonged to the Jewish religion, nor is she inscribed with the *consistoire* of Paris, as attested to by the Chief Rabbi. Her paternal line is Jewish. Her maternal line is Aryan.... Under these conditions, and in conformity with new caselaw [la nouvelle jurisprudence], there is reason to view the individual as non-Jewish....[30]

Ditte's order was immediately communicated to officials at Drancy, with an urgent demand that Lucienne be released. When the French authorities failed to do so by 6 November, and with transports now routine, an appeal was made "to the German authorities to obtain a discharge order."[31]

Lucienne Morel, née Weissmann, may have escaped deportation. But if so, it was only after French law changed to accommodate the kinds of evidence her husband desperately managed to produce on her behalf; as for the Nazis, as we shall see, French citizens like Mme. Morel should not have been arrested to begin with once they showed that they were married to an Aryan.[32]

At around the time of the Weissmann matter, Ditte made explicit his relative indifference to the mere showing of baptismal records as a factor in determining Jewishness. His memorandum indicates how far CGQJ's substance over form policy had taken it from its original position of the prior year, which declared baptism to be a *sine qua non* for a finding of non-Jewishness; but it also conjures what had become for the French

---

[29] Under Vichy law, based on its reading of the 2 June statute, most registration requirements for a family suspected of having Jewish members fell on the husband and father, including that of declaring his wife's or children's Jewishness, and—in the Occupied Zone—of having them obtain and wear the Star. See, e.g., Franco-German agreement on these principles in correspondence ranging from late 1942 to early 1943 as regards the Mazaud matter, CDJC XXVa-161a.

[30] Lucienne Weissmann file, YV C-3.

[31] Ibid.; for a similar case, see discussion of Robert Lévy, chapter 5, note 44.

[32] See sub-section C below.

(although not for the Germans) the most basic component of their skepticism:

> [R]egarding what value to attribute to baptismal certificates delivered by M. Henri, vicar general of the liberal Catholic Church, or more generally to all records coming from dissident sects of recognized religions:
>
> ...
>
> 1. *We are solely concerned with* knowing if *someone does or does not belong to the Jewish religion* or still belonged to it on June 25, 1940.
>
> 2. We have no reason to care about the religious value of the cult or dissident sect to which the individual claims affiliation, *to prove his non-affiliation* to the Jewish religion, this being the sole point of interest, indeed the entire question, for us.
>
> 3. We need be bothered only by *the probative value of the alleged affiliation claimed,* that is did it really exist and did it exist prior to 25 June 1940.
>
> It is by sticking to these three principles that we can determine, in each specific case, whether we should consider as probative the alleged affiliation claimed, in other words whether the proffered baptismal act can be verified on regularly kept records or whether it has on the contrary a purely irregular and strange character that renders it suspect.... [Emphasis in original][33]

Jacques Ditte cared about baptism only if it evidenced true non-belonging to the Jewish religion. If no timely baptismal proof was available (as in Weissmann's case), this would not be fatal to a showing of non-Jewishness, otherwise convincingly indicated; in this, although deciding too little and too late, he joined a predominant trend in the caselaw thinking. But, on the other hand, if there was *insufficient* demonstration of non-Jewishness, as in the Bernholc matter, Ditte would not be moved by the mere showing of a baptismal certificate. The aversion to the fact itself of clerical evidence had been building throughout 1942.

---

[33] Memorandum to the police, 2 November 1942, CDJC CXV-80. Ditte was deluged with questions from the police about Jewish matters, in part because the police often had to make preliminary determinations of religious status that would permit some regularization of ordinary commerce and human interaction pending the longer-term process of receiving a certificat, which of course only Ditte's agency could deliver. On one occasion, the Paris prefecture asked Ditte if the agency had, "given the difficulties presented by the determination of the Jewish or non-Jewish quality of names, established a list of names that evoke Jewishness or are presumed to be Jewish [des noms à consonance juive ou présumés juifs]." Ditte drew two exclamation points in the margin of the inquiry note and instructed his subordinates "Not to bother answering the letter of the police prefecture," AN AJ[38], 148.

Baptismal records lost credibility in Vichy eyes from early in that year, when a series of forgeries emerged from the parish of Chateauneuf-sur-Loire. One of the first Chateauneuf cases provides an analogy to, but also a highly dramatic reversal of, Lucienne Weissmann's tragic baptismal story. It was one of those "only in Vichy" cases, for the person in question would almost definitely never have been troubled had she lived in Nazi Germany. Irene de Leusse (née Manheimer) was married to a Catholic count and incontrovertibly was herself baptized. She seemed to have only one Jewish grandparent, but even with two would have probably been safe under German law. Irene's maternal grandparents were clearly non-Jewish.

Then, a scrupulous inquiry into the religion of her paternal grandmother, Jeanne Halphen, cast doubt on whether the latter had been baptized on 28 October 1854, as Irene had asserted. In dialogue with the police over a three-month period, CGQJ determined that

> verifications we have made regarding the baptismal register at the parish of Chateauneuf-sur-Loire, where the said Jeanne HALPHEN was supposedly baptized, indicates that there has been an interlineation [intercalage] of the baptismal act for her between other baptismal acts recorded in the same time period."[34]

CGQJ demanded a full inquiry, threatening judicial action against both Irene and "all those who might have permitted this falsification of the baptismal certificate." It was discovered that

> The act is registered at the bottom of a page numbered 91 in handwriting different from the page that preceded it and the one that follows. It was hard to fit the act in at the bottom of the page, its first line encroaching a bit on the signature of the preceding act. The ink is unequally aged.... There is definite fraud here.[35]

Irene was reclassified as of 13 July as a Jew, and the matter of fraud further investigated.

Meanwhile, the parish at Chateauneuf-sur-Loire was implicated in another allegation of fraud. André Boas had requested from CGQJ a reversal of his Jewish status, claiming that his paternal grandparents, his father and himself had all been baptized there. His sister, Claire, made a similar

[34] Letter, CGQJ to Paris prefecture, 23 March 1942, CDJC CXV-6.

[35] CDJC CXV-7.

request. This time, the special police for Jewish questions, through its investigator, Jean Bouquin, discovered multiple acts of seeming fraud in the record keeping, including erasures, different handwritings, interpolations, and multiple inkage. He interrogated the vicar of Chateauneuf, M. Mansion, its curator, M. de la Bigne, and M. Yanka of the archdiocese of Orléans. The first two confessed to altering the records, while Yanka confirmed that the records had been temporarily removed from their usual place and authorized the police to inquire further and to seize the records.[36] M. de la Bigne observed that "No more than did my vicar did I proceed for lucre, because we received no remuneration. We only proceeded from a goodness of soul."[37]

Reaction inside Vichy intensified and ranged from polite indignation to pugnaciousness. In April 1942, the Ministry of the Interior complained to an official in Lourdes that the curator of Nistos, Abbé Bourdette, had falsified a baptismal certificate to assist a Marseilles woman named Amadja-Bourdilla around the religious laws. The courteously firm letter took pains to stress the government's surprise to see Catholic officials violating the religious laws.[38] The government's hope that the church would "reform" from within was reflected in a 1943 letter to Bishop Roserot of Troyes, apparently permitting him to handle the chastisement of an Abbé Simonnet and hence "to avoid bringing publicity to this regrettable incident." CGQJ asked to be kept informed of the nature of the punition, and also "of the steps you intend to take to inform your clergy of the dangers of any repetition of such initiatives."[39] For, as the agency proceeds:

> It seems to me ignominious that members of the clergy would lend themselves to such deviousness, designed to undermine the execution of the laws, notably that of 2 June 1941, promulgated by the French State under the signature of the Marshal.[40]

As Jean Laloum indicates, by the end of 1943, there were enough such cases as to place Vichy ministries generally on their guard, particularly

---

[36] CDJC CXV-7.

[37] Ibid.

[38] CDJC CXI-32.

[39] Letter, 4 February 1943, CDJC CXV-7.

[40] Ibid.

about certain parishes; but the reputation of some of the high officials in some of the more active archdioceses, like the one in Marseilles, made overt prosecution of churchmen difficult.[41] However, in others, the SEC (Section d'Enquête et de Contrôle) would use force to impound church records, and would hand churchmen who tried to assist Jews directly over to the Nazis.[42]

Vichy's relationship with religious institutions will be more fully examined in chapter 10 and is of course both complex and entirely relevant to many legalistic developments. But the episode involving baptismal forgeries surely raises the question not only of Vichy law's scrupulousness in questioning non-Jewish status but also the effect of the anti-clerical campaign on the Germans, who saw neither the legal nor the political issues the same way. For Vichy's campaign against those who would try to interpose baptismal form over real non-Jewish substance was self-generated, and there is some indication that German punition was limited to the falsifying clerics, and did not extend to the presumed Jews they helped. These latter were handled by French justice.[43] If Vichy's racial decision-makers believed that Jewishness, which status the Nazis had left to their understanding and control, required for its undoing at least an unsullied and superficially valid baptismal record, they would proceed to investigate until every possibility of forgery and fraud was removed.

The reasons for such hostility, which German law did not share, may have something to do with the historically uncomfortable relationship of secular French governments to the clergy. Yet, if specific legal developments provoked Vichy anti-clericalism, it was sharply mitigated by the Catholic faith of many of the régime's leaders,[44] the Christian imagery in the new mythology of the state,[45] and the need to work with the Church to develop the ideals of the "revolution" of family, work and nation.[46] Also, as we shall see in the next sub-section, Vichy antipathy

---

[41] Laloum, *La France antisémite,* 169ff.

[42] Ibid., 115.

[43] Ibid., 114.

[44] See Michèle Cointet-Labrousse, *Vichy et le fascisme* (Paris: Editions complexe, 1987), 142–56 ("Les Catholiques"); see analysis of Joseph Barthélemy, chapter 4.

[45] See chapters 1 and 10.

[46] See chapter 4 at note 83.

to baptismal records extended to the numerous requests for Aryan status by members of *non-French* churches against which there was no historical lay animosity whatsoever. The French just liked to go as far as they felt the law positively required on any given legalistic issue. And, having expanded "Jewishness" to include many hundreds of mixed-heritage people, Vichy wanted to be sure of their alleged Christian religious status.

Why would this basically Franco-French phenomenon interest the Germans? No doubt they cared if the aryanization of Jewish property in their zone might be adversely affected by fraudulent clerics bent on increasing the number of people Vichy law would see as Catholic or Protestant, whose property would then not be ripe for pillage. On the other hand, the constant French tendency to pile legalistic requirement upon legalistic requirement—to replace for the *feel* of an Aryan a rationalistic and picayune inquiry—this was both inefficient and foreign to Nazi jurisprudential notions.[47] Perhaps they saw overzealous bureaucrats muddying the waters unnecessarily, alienating significant constituencies not usually inclined to protest vigorously against religious laws with which they had learned to live.

So, in the midst of the scandal of clerical forgeries, Buhrig of the German High Command cautioned Vichy that its legalistic insistence on having the individual compendiously prove his non-Jewishness was the real threat to the pace of aryanization in the Occupied Zone. On 4 July 1942, he wrote:

> Generally speaking, to require that Aryan origins be proved, not by a simple declaration but instead by formal evidence, presents in my opinion serious problems. Based on our experience in the Reich, we know it can take a while, during wartime, to prove one's origins by documentation relating to one's ascendants. Since, over the past two months, aryanization has completely stopped, any new delay would be inexcusable, if only for the impression that would make on the public.... When there is no particular reason to suspect the *bona fides* of the parties, it will be enough to go by a declaration of Aryan status and, only if necessary, to probe for retroactive presentation of documents. Approval would be considered to have been fraudulently received and would be retracted once it were proven that the declaration was false. I ask you therefore to stick to the present procedure.[48]

---

[47] See note 51 and sub-section D.

[48] CDJC CXV-51, and (same document) AN $AJ^{38}$, file 80.

This statement signifies a fundamental difference between French and German approaches to law.[49] For the French, Aryan and Jewish status needed to be proven by painstaking, nitpicking, and skeptical inquiries into racial and religious origins. For the Germans, it was a question of "feel." You can *see,* Buhrig seems to be counselling Vichy; use your racial sensors and improve the efficiency of a process that has to roll along. Buhrig proposes not only a political or economic argument for less contentiousness and litigiousness; in a way, although not without paradox in this specific context,[50] he is reflecting the jurisprudential views of a system that had forsworn legalisms in favor of arbitrary outcomes predicated on an intuitive sense of National Socialism's goals and those of its supreme leader.[51]

While Buhrig's memorandum does not explicitly mention clerical records, several months later Heinz Röthke, usually involved in deporting Jews,[52] does bring it up. Himself a lawyer, like his predecessor Theodor Dannecker (SS head of the Paris Jewish Affairs bureau),[53] Röthke was capable of explaining the Germans' position on baptism to the CGQJ, and he did so on various levels of generalization. Röthke writes from the perspective of a legal system that had less need for baptismal records (because it defined mixed-heritage individuals as clearly non-Jewish unless they actually practiced Judaism)[54] and fewer problems with accepting baptism as competent evidence of Christian status when the

---

[49] See below, sub-section D, and chapter 10, notes 28–32.

[50] The French after all, when it came to baptismal records, replicated the Nazi tendency to elevate spirit above text, and substance above form. But, as we shall see, most other Franco-Nazi legal conflicts exposed to German criticism the *excessive literalism* of the French.

[51] Perhaps they even perceived in this campaign against baptismal records an example of a *basic jurisprudential difference between Nazi conceptions of law and those of the Vichy lawyers.* For the Germans feared in Vichy too strict and too rigorous a conception of law; the gallic mentality was inclined to overstep the bounds required by the "spirit" of the law, which was far less prone to blow into every logical corner of a situation. See chapter 10, notes 29–31.

[52] See, e.g., Lucien Steinberg, *Les Allemands en France* (Paris: Albin Michel, 1980), 219, for Röthke's central place in the final solution for France, contemporaneous with the letter cited.

[53] Ibid.

[54] See next sub-section of this chapter.

need arose.[55] His plea to the French is less that they should ignore the problem of clerical forgeries than that they might cure it by *elevating the evidentiary status of church records to replicate the law of the Reich:*

> Paris, 7 November, 1942. A specific case that came to my attention[56] has led me to examine the legal validity of clerical records, notably baptismal acts and marriage certificates, so that one might better understand if these documents are to be considered as official (public) records or simply private agreements [actes sous seing privé]. Prevailing [French] law clearly holds that these, in the absence of some express declaration that they are official, can only be considered private.
>
> If this opinion is indeed dominant in France, I find myself obliged to emphasize that, according to the German approach, it is indispensable that clerical records be deemed official in the legal sense. This is all the more important precisely because the Jewish laws in France hinge racial classification almost exclusively on the production of clerical records. Thus, these records form the basis of decisions in such cases.
>
> This necessitates, in law as in principle, the granting to these records of a value that corresponds to their importance. The relatively high number of forgeries of clerical records would no doubt be reduced thereby, because the penalties are greater for falsifying official records.[57]

Unlike straightforward statements we have already seen contrasting to Vichy legal developments some "liberal" Nazi precedent and imploring the French to adopt it,[58] Röthke's advice is indirect: elevate in law the value of clerical evidence and hence provide disincentives to forging clerical documents. But the sense of his memorandum is similar to that of his

---

[55] This was also the understanding of French analysts such as Jacques Maury. See, e.g., chapter 2, text at notes 83, 124, and 125, where Maury cites to German laws of 15 September 1935 and afterwards protecting baptized individuals and opines that this should be the position of French courts.

[56] Röthke certainly knew of the Chateauneuf clerical forgery cases, ibid., 114. Billig reports another case, later in November, of a purported Jew arrested by SEC and turned over to Röthke's jurisdiction, for using a false baptismal certificate. Billig, *Le Commissariat général,* vol. 2, 86.

[57] Memorandum to CGQJ of 7 November 1942, CDJC CXV-83.

[58] See, e.g., Buhrig's statement in the text above at note 48, Jacques Maury's opinion that, in cases involving the baptism of children, German law was more lenient than some Vichy variations, chapter 2, notes 125 and 129; Joseph Haennig's call to his colleagues in 1943 to adopt "the liberal spirit" of German law on the question of the kinds of evidence admissible to disprove Jewishness, chapter 2, text at note 132.

colleague Buhrig: define Jews without undue legalistic procrastination. If baptismal records must provide the linchpin of religious definition, any losses incurred to the state by lending greater credence to clerical documents will be more than offset by the increase in efficiency that a less legalistic inquiry will produce.

The nitpicking about baptismal records was of a piece with Vichy's rigorous approach to religious definition, but unlike the majority of French legal developments, it produced consequences deleterious to German self-interest. For the zealous interdiction of baptismal records could have been no more pleasing to the Germans as a political matter than it was as an inefficiently legalistic tendency foreign to their thinking. Perhaps they felt that the French insufficiently realized that racial politics had its own dynamics quite apart from individual cases in which prelates might have tried to help mixed-heritage individuals to improve their chances before Vichy law. So they chose to face up to what was inefficient in Vichy law, and—in any event—quite different from the approach *bei uns in Deutschland.*

## B. Are Mosaic Georgians Jewish? Are Sepharadim Christian? Franco-Nazi Disputes about Ethnic Groupings and the Religious Laws

The tension in approaches to "Jewishness" between a racial and a religious conception of "belonging" occupied the French mind as Vichy law was propounded[59] and then implemented. While Nazi jurisprudence faced the same duality—for, after all, how *does* one discern a Jew for legal purposes when the definition must trace "race" back to people long dead whose only ascertainable association with "Jewishness" was a religious one—Third Reich theorists always emphasized race.[60] In their first ordinance, the requirement of at least three Jewish grandparents signalled their predominantly racial assessment; yet the word "race" was missing from that ordinance and centrally present in the first and all subsequent

---

[59] See chapter 2, notes 16–20; see also Barthélemy's allegiance to a racial approach in the face of CGQJ reform ideas, chapter 4.

[60] See Ingo Müller, *Hitler's Justice: The Courts of the Third Reich,* trans. Deborah Lucas Schneider (Boston: Harvard, 1991).

Vichy statutes. Ironically, though, the French expanded the category of Jews to include mixed-heritage individuals with less than three Jewish grandparents, and this expansion coerced detailed and complex inquiries into those same religious questions that the Germans seemed inclined to forego.[61]

As we examine in chapter 10, religious groups—whatever their ultimate stance on Vichy legislation—tended to try to eschew the racial approach. For some Christian sects in France, an emphasis on religious affiliation became vital, as they found themselves racially implicated as Jews; on the other hand, a Jewish group—the Sepharadim—enjoyed for awhile a privileged status under Vichy law because it was felt they might be racially different from the bulk of their central and eastern European brethren.

In the majority of these cases, the Germans took positions that conflicted with the French view. For example, the *Greek and Russian Orthodox* churches in France were not recognized prior to the law of 1905 to which the Vichy statute refers. Like Muslims and atheists, they found some of their members subject to the religious laws without recourse to their established beliefs, which were Christian. Yet, from quite early in the occupation, the Germans relied on high leaders in these churches—particularly Metropolitan Séraphin in Paris—as their only authority on ecclesiastical matters in France.[62]

Séraphin took personal umbrage at the fact that his church had to fight for a status in Vichy that it already enjoyed with the Nazis. To the amazement of Jacques Ditte's CGQJ, who dotted his correspondence with two marginal exclamation points and the phrase "Erroneous! Not at all! Strict, but not erroneous," the religious leader wrote to the agency accusing them of taking an "erroneous" perspective on the law of 2 June 1941.[63] Séraphin, for his part, disliked being accused of insufficiently

---

[61] This was not an uncommon perspective on Franco-Nazi differences. Thus in a late 1942 or 1943 note to the CGQJ, a former lawyer in Russia, Kossecki, offered a learned treatment of the conflicts-of-law question, raising the irony that, under French law, "people who have nothing to do with the Jewish race cannot get any respect, while others wrongly are given validation by proffering false evidence.... The best solution would be to modify the French law on Jews, using the model of the German ordinances that respect much less the religious than the racial aspect," CDJC CXIV-26.

[62] Séraphin to CGQJ, 15 October 1941, AN $AJ^{38}$, 148.

[63] Ibid.

inquiring into the religious status of people asking to be converted into his sect. His letter traces the history of White Russian, anti-Soviet membership in the Russian Orthodox church and proudly asserts that it had accepted merely ninety-nine applications of one thousand for adherence.

Ditte held quite firm, and even announced to Dannecker that Séraphin would have to rely upon German policies in protecting his co-religionists from the dreaded status of Jew.[64] The case of Archimandrite Serge Fefferman of Meudon, a leader in the Russian Orthodox Church there is instructive. In late 1942, he found himself required to wear the Jewish star. Yes, he admits, in complaining of this to CGQJ, he does have four Jewish grandparents; but

> urged on by a precocious faith, I left the hebraic religion and at the age of 16 converted to the catholic-orthodox religion.... During my long career, I have progressed through all the levels of the monastic life, always advancing until reaching the high echelon that is that of the Archimandrite.
>
> A half-century of service to the catholic-orthodox church made me confident that no one would remind me ever again of my distant israelite origins.
>
> Now, because of the regulation, perhaps overly rigorously interpreted, I am made to wear the Star of Zion that I have rejected forever [and which] brings about the saddest sacrifice imposed on a priest—that of not being able to participate in the celebration of a religious service.[65]

Two months later, René Laithier of the CGQJ turned down his request, admonishing the Archimandrite to go to the Germans, "who are alone qualified to judge this matter."[66] Laithier's disingenuousness may have been apparent to Fefferman, who, however, was left without recourse: although the Nazis originated the law on wearing the Star of David, *who* had to wear it was a matter of Vichy law.

Religious leaders of these minority sects were quite vocal about the German reliance on Vichy definitions of religious status, and they did not hesitate to flag greater Nazi liberality on the latter. Thus the Diocese of Russian Orthodox churches in Western Europe, through its member A. Filonoff, complained of the insult to his church in not making it an

---

[64] Billig, *Le Commissariat général,* vol. 2, 230.

[65] Archimandrite Serge Fefferman, 17 December 1942, AN $AJ^{38}$, 148.

[66] René Laithier, note, 27 February 1943; ibid.

officially recognized sect, as the Germans had done. Filonoff stoked up the coals of Franco-Nazi contention for the purpose of redeeming his "persecuted" religion:

> As to the ordinances passed by the occupation forces, one should naturally look to the certificates of churches that they recognize. If, at present, the French administration rejects the latter, the issue now reaches a level of disagreement between France and Germany that will only confuse the question.
>
> Such are the consequences of the law of 2 June. In order to avoid unfavorable as well as unjust commentaries, this text demands an interpretation more in conformity with present necessities; it is not advisable to leave the matter to the operations of the prefecture or the CGQJ.[67]

Members of lesser known and statutorily unrecognized groups who had some Jewish grandparental heritage but felt they were religiously nonsuspect may have had their problems under Vichy law. But surpassing these and in greater jeopardy were members of the *Mosaic Georgian* sect, who honored and revered the Torah and hence were suspect even as a religious matter. By German approximation early in 1941, there were some fifty Mosaic Georgians in France whose fate would have to be decided under the religious laws.

The occupiers quickly made clear their own sense that these individuals were not Jewish, both by the Nazis' race-oriented lights and by their view of the sect's religious practices, too. "These Georgians are not Semites but rather Chaldeans converted to Judaism and having emigrated, in antiquity, to the Caucasus." As to their religious practice, what was most important to the Germans was that the group *never revered the Talmud.* They were relieved, under German interpretations, of all Jewish obligations, even including the need to have their property handed over for aryanization, always a particular area of Nazi interest.[68]

The French rigorously refused to adopt German standards on the Georgians. Ditte's colleague at CGQJ, Armilhon, who increasingly had authority over such questions,[69] reflected the increasing harshness of the Dar-

---

67 A. Filonoff to Vichy, 28 July 1941, AN AJ$^{38}$, 148.

68 AN AJ$^{38}$, 148. See Billig's excellent account of this Franco-German dispute, *Le Commissariat général,* vol. 1, 337ff.

69 Ibid., vol. 2, 226.

quier period at the agency in opining strongly in mid-1943 (after some equivocation beforehand):

> [F]rench law incontestably views these Georgians of Mosaic belief as covered by the racial statute. This derives from the fact that the statute is essentially based in determining the race of an individual upon the religion practiced by his grandparents.[70]

CGQJ eventually allowed that the German opinion on the sect might relieve its followers from having to wear the Star. But, remarkably:

> This exemption from wearing the Star does not lead, *ipso facto,* to the removal of trustees [administrateurs provisoires] that it was thought should be placed on the property of Georgians of Mosaic belief. In fact, I am deciding now that, in all cases, Georgians of Mosaic belief should be subject to aryanization measures.[71]

At least fifteen Georgian business people are cited in 1944 as being targets of persecution under the final Vichy definition of their religious sect.[72]

That German emphasis on race occasionally and ironically assisted groups whom the French were managing to persecute religiously is borne out in the analogous case of the *Karaites*. This Jewish sect numbered in France no more than 270 people.[73] The Karaites believe in the Pentateuch and their name itself derives from the Hebrew for "scriptures,"[74] but they reject the Talmud. The Karaites came into existence some time around the eighth century.[75]

Debate about the status of this tiny group began in 1941 and engages the attention of the Roman Catholic Church, from whose Parisian archdiocese the cleric Bénusart writes as follows in December:

---

[70] Ibid., vol. 1, 339.

[71] Ibid., vol. 1, 340.

[72] AN AJ$^{38}$, 148.

[73] Memorandum, probably internally prepared by the CGQJ on 8 February 1943, describing the Karaites, whose status was still being contested, YV 0-9/20-5; see Michael Marrus and Robert Paxton, *Vichy France and the Jews* (New York: Basic Books, 1981), 93, who put the figure at 250. A later analyst puts it at 240, see below at note 84.

[74] YV 0-9/20-5.

[75] Vichy expert Peter Bogdanovitch eventually opined that the Karaites were not Jewish; see AN AJ$^{38}$, 148.

> The Karaite religion is practiced by a small number of Russians established in France after the Revolution, for the most part. It is considered by the Catholic Church as completely autonomous, and leaning more towards Islam than the Jewish religion. The Imperial Russian government recognized this independence, by the way, and exempted Karaites from measures taken by the Empire against Jews.[76]

Metropolitain Séraphin also moved to dissociate Karaites from Judaism.[77] And the Nazis quickly took the same position they had taken on the Mosaic Georgians. So did self-styled "ethnographical experts" such as Professor Montandon, whose distinctions between hereditary racial qualities and those he favored ("based on all qualities of the man: physical, mental, moral") had been well noted and utilized on just such issues.[78]

After some internal discussion at CGQJ, Cabanis of that agency informed the Justice Minister in March 1942, that the agency considered Karaites to be Jewish.[79] The Interior Ministry wrote to a Catholic Church official (Père Robert Léon) that Vichy believed the sect broke off from Jews only because of a theological quibble and decreed Karaites as falling under the statutory definition.[80] Many months later, as Vichy seemed to be changing its mind, a compendious analysis called for adoption of the German approach. It sympathized with the Karaites, opining that "For these people, then, the French legislation has proven more severe than the German measures, even on their terrain of race and the fight against Jews.... [But] the Karaites seem not to be of the (biologically) Jewish race."[81]

Ultimately, the Karaites fared better than the Georgians. By early 1943, possibly because of such studious research, and surely because of the diligent efforts of Paul Bogdanovitch, an increasingly influential authority at the Office of Russian Emigrés in France, Vichy policy shifted. Bogdanovitch, who as we shall see was by no means a reliable force for good in these kinds of disputes, finally opined that the Karaites were not

---

[76] CDJC XXXII, 108.

[77] YV 0-9/20-5, 5.

[78] Ibid., 6; on Montandon, see below, text at note 103.

[79] YV 0-9/20-5, 3.

[80] AN $AJ^{38}$, 148.

[81] Ibid., 8.

Jewish for the purposes of the religious law. Bogdanovitch apparently convinced Darquier,[82] and Vichy informed its regional directors that "the Karaites are no longer to be considered as Jews."[83]

One of the ironies, again, of these debates, is the elevation of race over religion in the attempts *to protect* minorities from the stain of Judaism. As one observer put it, to persecute Georgians, Karaites and other such sects would be to puzzle "the great mass" of French public opinion, which is

> indifferent to religious ideas and has even a hostile and skeptical tendency [toward religion]. Public opinion does admit well the notion that there is a Jewish race; it accepts that but has never concerned itself with the Jewish religion. If you tell people that to be Jewish you must be in the Jewish religion, they're ready to believe that not to be Jewish requires belonging to the Christian religion. The case of half-Jews confirms their view. The Jewish question will seem to them like a form of clericalism and a religious bromide. "You know," said a street vendor in the presence of one of our friends, "I'll need to push my wagon with a baptismal certificate in my pocket." ... In privileging religion above race, one flies in the face (this time, for no reason whatsoever) of the occupying authorities.[84]

Did the average Frenchman better understand the Jew as a racial entity than as a participant in an organized religious group? In a legal area that ambiguously combined the language of race and religion, such popular views might indeed have affected both administrative and judicial policy. CGQJ's first leader, Xavier Vallat, seemed as a *theoretical* matter to have preferred a religious conception of Jewish status, as we saw in his exchanges with Barthélemy from early 1942[85]; yet, as time went on, both he and his successor, Darquier, inevitably became involved in what seemed to many an official racism,[86] backed by native French conceptions. Ironically, their zealous (nay, compulsive) overinclusiveness coerced the language of race from the lips of legal players trying hard to protect these smaller groups; doubly ironic, such language evoked Nazi decisions that had long since left these groups alone. The resultant dis-

---

[82] AN AJ[38], 148.

[83] Ibid., memorandum, 22 January 1943.

[84] Analysis, uncertain date and origin, CDJC CXIV-25.

[85] See chapter 4, text at note 144.

[86] Marrus and Paxton, *Vichy France and the Jews,* 93.

course again demonstrates the ability of analysts and participants alike to use low levels of generalization to engage in seemingly complex discussion, in this case situating through their drily logical rhetoric tiny groups while only *exacerbating* the effect of religious legislation upon Jews.

So, in representing another sect that eventually gained exempted status—the *Jugutis*—the lawyer Julien Kraehling found himself using tactical language for his client that surely might have surprised him a year or so earlier from the pen of any colleague in France, much less his own:

> To Doctor Atchildi, Leader of the Jugutis community [Président de la Communauté DJOUGOUTE], Paris, 22 August, 1941. Sir: In accordance with your instructions, I spoke this morning to the delegate of the German High Command attached to the CGQJ [Dr. Amon].[87] I elaborated for him the special condition of your group's members and asked him as a minimum, before he made a definitive decision, to order provisionally that any iniquity or sale of property be avoided. After examining the various relevant questions, the representative of the High Command told me that he was going to refer the matter to the Racial Bureau in Berlin and would expect an opinion with which he could comply.[88]

Four days later, Kraehling confidently informed his client that Amon would instruct CGQJ to stop bothering the Jugutis, expressing his "certainty that CGQJ will immediately inform its relevant departments."[89]

Kraehling's association with the occupying authorities in order to assist a client was hardly unique, as we shall see in a later chapter of this study. Nor is it necessarily blameworthy, even though the tactics more or less required recourse specifically to Nazi racial theories. But, as it turns out, Kraehling's counsel was retained for life-and-death issues as well as property matters, and it was here that he learned how chancy racial advocacy was, and how independent Vichy was from the German "opinion" on the Jugutis.

Collaterally with his representation of the full community, Kraehling had as a client a certain Abramoff, a man whose liberty and life, as well as his grocery store, were being threatened because Vichy believed that

---

[87] Amon dealt at the time with the aryanization issues that preoccupy this letter; see Billig, *Le Commissariat général*, vol. 1, 145.

[88] YV 0-9/20-4.

[89] Ibid., letter to Atchildi, 26 August 1941.

Jugutis were Jews for their statutory purposes.[90] In August 1941, Kraehling may have had reason for optimism, although he was mistaken at the time in urging similar treatment for his clients as he thought was going to be given to the Georgians—and we know how they eventually fared. But 1942 and 1943 brought no resolution to the question of his clients' status; the Nazis were *not,* in fact, uniformly favorable to the Jugutis (as they had been to the Georgians and the Karaites),[91] although CGQJ by early in 1942 expressly restated the Nazi position as exempting them.[92]

While the Nazi position was crystallizing around the earlier view Kraehling confidently expected, Vichy held firm against his clients. As late as May 1943, the Swiss had to intervene on behalf of what they called "Iranian emigrés of the Jugutis faith" who found themselves under Vichy authority, pleading for "treatment similar to that applied to their co-religionists in the Occupied Zone."[93] At least four of their sect, including Kraehling's client Abramoff, were arrested, and Abramoff's grocery store was also aryanized.[94] It was not until mid-1943 that Vichy declared Jugutis to be racially uncompromised. Abramoff seems to have been released and his store de-aryanized.[95]

Private legal advocacy also was needed to keep the *Subbotniks* distinct from all Jewish tincture. A lawyer listed as LaPaulle had been representing four members of the sect since 1941 in dialogue with Ditte of CGQJ; the agency was at first as unremittingly against the Subbotniks as it had been against the Russian Orthodox. Ditte maintained that these little "Mosaic" groups could not be distinguished one from the other, at least not in a manner convincing to his agency.[96]

Lawyer LaPaulle argued into mid-1942 that Russian law exempted Subbotniks from antisemitic measures (although allowing that the group

---

[90] AN $AJ^{38}$, 148.

[91] Ibid. Röthke, for one, is cited as saying that "Jugutis must not be thought of *a priori* as non-Jews. Each case must be examined on its own."

[92] CGQJ aryanization department, 19 January 1942, YV 0-9/20-4.

[93] AN $AJ^{38}$, 148.

[94] Ibid.

[95] On 3 March 1943, an "Aron Abramow" is referred to in a letter from the police to CGQJ, in which "the annulment of his declaration as a Jew" is reported, ibid.

[96] AN $AJ^{38}$, 148. We shall meet Lapaulle, most probably this same lawyer, at chapter 8, note 150.

had "Judaizing tendencies"), perhaps assimilating analogous arguments made for the Karaites. Like the latter, however, his clients were made to suffer longer than they had under either Russian or Nazi definitions. Surely, too, his argument stressing *religious* distinctions between Subbotniks and Jews were unlikely to find favor in Vichy eyes, since the régime proved itself less amenable to these than even the Germans, who were interested to learn that Mosaic Georgians rejected the Talmud. Still, LaPaulle tried:

> The best proof that Subbotniks are in no way a Mosaic sect is that they accept the New Testament, which is totally rejected by the Jewish religion.[97]

Only in the case of the Ismaelites, a Shiite Muslim sect with 500,000 members worldwide—all of whom would surely have been shocked to hear someone call them Jews!—did Vichy finally show itself less persecutory than the Germans. It took until 21 January 1944, however. While the Germans continued to examine this sect's members case by case, Vichy decided that these Muslims were indeed not Jews.[98]

Stranger and stranger, and increasingly reliant on "expert" assistance, Vichy's ruggedly individualistic stance on race extended to *Armenians*. Throughout 1943 and into 1944 this ethnically distinct group found some of its members fighting racial battles it thought had been won a full ten years and more ago, at the very origins of the Third Reich. On 3 July 1933, the Interior Minister of the Reich had issued an "Expert Racial Letter" classifying Armenians as Aryans.[99] Vichy for awhile tended to agree, but then some creeping aryanization of Armenian-held property began to occur. The problem seems to have been a typically Vichy-based legalistic distinction—applicable to the Armenians but not to the earlier groups discussed—between nationality and religion.

In early 1943, CGQJ asked its regional directors dealing with the aryanization of Jewish property not to bother Armenians, since "there are no Armenian Jews [*sic*]." The Toulouse regional director responded as follows, with an eery wit appropriate to the dispute:

---

[97] Ibid.

[98] Ibid.

[99] Ibid.

> I would like to believe that, but aren't we confusing nationality with religion? I find it hard to believe that a Jewess married to a Jew would not permit herself to give birth to a Jew in Armenia. To my knowledge, this is not a materially impossible situation. If the "jus soli" had this purifying quality in and of itself, people would know about it, I believe.[100]

The central office in Paris gave in to this argument, responding straightforwardly that only the expert, Dr. Berberian, could definitively rule on the non-Jewishness of stateless Armenians. Pending such an opinion in disputed cases, Armenians had to rely on a certificate from the "Bureau of Stateless Persons."

Matters got worse when the dreaded Professor Montandon joined the issue of the Armenians' religious status. As late as 13 January 1944, CGQJ informed the SD's Röthke that arrested Armenians might have "to undergo the ethnoracial examination of Professor Montandon, who will verify that they are not circumcised."[101] Circumcision inspection, a big business for Montandon,[102] was only one of the sub-specialties of his "field."

Montandon's very name would strike fear in the hearts of the most fiercely proud and racially self-satisfied individual. Indeed, the professor had been a favorite at the CGQJ from "before the beginning" and was even—along with the likes of Darquier, Céline, and Serpeille de Gobineau (the latter "with reservations") on the short list submitted by the Germans to be the first head of the agency![103] A professor of ethnology at the School of Anthropology, Montandon had assisted for over two years in the legal determination of Jewish status, and his weird approach to ethnology had commended itself so highly to Vichy and the Nazis that he had become connected to the Final Solution itself in France.[104]

---

[100] Ibid.

[101] Ibid.

[102] Note the case of Yousouf Behar Kouly, August 1943. Kouly was a circumcised Muslim. The agency stated that "If circumcision is not proof of belonging to the Jewish race, it constitutes a serious presumption of Jewishness, as it is almost impossible to differentiate ritual from medical circumcision." CGQJ advised him, if dissatisfied with its findings, "to undergo the ethno-racial" examination of Prof. Montandon, CDJC XVIIa 38 (165); AN $AJ^{38}$, 148.

[103] Billig, *Le Commissariat général,* vol. 1, 55.

[104] Ibid., vol. 2, 141.

The conjuration of experts such as Berberian and Montandon indicates that determining the racial characteristics of central and eastern Europeans had become a kind of cottage industry in France. It was intimately connected with legalistic decisions, and it is perhaps best exemplified by the work of Paul Bogdanovitch, whose name we saw earlier in connection with the Karaites' dilemma.[105]

Apparently, almost all questionable cases of racial and religious affiliation from eastern Europe would be mandatorily referred to Bogdanovitch's "Office of Russian Emigrés in France." So authoritative was his counsel that eastern Europeans seeking Aryan status at the CGQJ were first *required* to go to his offices with all their documents in hand to solicit his opinion. Then, armed with a card of introduction signed by him, and only with such a card, would they gain entrance to the Paris CGQJ at number 1, place des Petits Pères.[106] Even regarding established sects such as Roman Catholicism, Bogdanovitch's opinion could be definitive and fatal. In one such case, a Michel Niewiazski presented CGQJ with a baptismal certificate allegedly from the Roman Catholic church in Lodz. No!, opined Bogdanovitch, "All these documents must be considered false."[107] Niewiazski was arrested.

Bogdanovitch enjoyed sufficient prestige at CGQJ to complain to the agency if they violated the confidentiality of any of his reports on the Jewishness of individuals, as he did in late 1942 when he learned that two people he had found to be Jewish had gained access to his expert opinions on their cases.[108] His counsel extended to matters that were entirely legalistic in nature, such as whether Russians could understand the French procedural device of answering "without prejudice" [sous réserve]. Bogdanovitch wanted the agency to know that such equivocation "does not correspond to the Russian mentality nor to juridical ideas in Russia. One would say "yes" or "no," one would confess or no, but one never got the idea of affirming something "without prejudice."[109]

Whether or not Bogdanovitch was right that "Russian law was much more simple, more elementary, than French law," his expertise only

---

[105] See note 83.

[106] Ibid.

[107] AN $AJ^{38}$, 148.

[108] *Abramovitch* and *Poczer* cases, ibid.

[109] Ibid.

helped to complicate Vichy's already detailed approach to religious law. More to our point here, the result of such "expertise" as his own was an expansive and agonizingly detailed treatment of ethnic categories long before dismissed as Aryan by the laws of the Third Reich. By comparison to other European legal systems, Vichy's thoroughgoing curiosity dovetailed with France's traditional sophistication to produce horrified individuals whose only recourse was to ratify the laws against Jews by forcefully distinguishing themselves from everything that was Jewish.

The epitome of this phenomenon, and a further mark of the blinders Vichy wrapped around its zealous investigations of race, was the régime's policy towards the *Sepharadim.* In almost any other situation, the idea of making clear distinctions between these Jews of peninsular origin and their Ashkenazi brethren would have been laughable. But as Vichy moved from religion towards race as the defining element under its statutes, the Sepharadim found themselves with a "benefit"—to quote a prescient government minister who helped propound the 3 October statute[110]—albeit of shaky substance and limited duration.

In September 1941, a Parisian organization of Sepharadim was writing directly to Marshal Pétain, asking him not to require Jews to wear the special insignia of the Star, and reminding him how all Jews (but particularly these "Latins of Mosaic belief") had traditionally loved "this dear France, which you are saving from dissipation."[111] No one in Vichy, however, credited the implication that such a big group of believing Jews, who prayed to the same Deity as the Ashkenazim, revered the same sacred and interpretive texts, and formed basically the same community of cultural interests, however nuanced, could be set apart and specially privileged. Xavier Vallat, then in the business of balancing a "religious definition" of the Jew against the statute's explicit invocation of "race," laughed off the notion that the Sepharadim were a "Latin" people, closely aligned to the French themselves.[112]

---

[110] Marrus and Paxton, *Vichy France and the Jews,* 99.

[111] AN AJ$^{38}$, 148.

[112] Ibid. Vallat's *official* position when it came to religious arguments for non-Jewishness remained, of course, consistent. As his subordinate writes, on 13 August 1941, to a Roman Catholic priest in Aubenas, who seeks relief from Jewish status for three of his colleagues with Jewish grandparents: "It is race, contrary to what you seem to believe, which determines for French law the legal Jew," CDJC CXIV-46.

The Germans, however—in what amounted to an extreme example of an otherwise consistent position about religious sub-groups with "acceptable" racial qualities—were intrigued by the suggestion. By late fall, a Nazi official in Bordeaux wrote to the prefect of la Gironde to find out more about this curious sect. The Vichy official dampens German enthusiasm and responds that there is no difference between one kind of Jew and another.[113] But, already engaged in controversies with the Germans and with their own "experts" about Mosaic Georgians, Karaites, Jugutis, Subbotniks, Ismaelites, and Armenians, Vichy began to intervene in mid-1942 on the matter of the Sepharadim. CGQJ wrote to the Spanish Consul General in Paris for his opinion of the group. The Consul, Bernardo Rolland, penned the following artful reply:

> I am happy to inform you that Spanish law makes no distinction among immigrants as to their religious belief; thus it considers Spanish Sepharadim, although Jews, to be Spanish. I would advise the French authorities, as well as the occupation authorities, not to apply the Jewish statute to them.[114]

We move into 1943, the year in which Vichy was holding firm on Mosaic Georgians but conceding at least the possibility of the non-Jewishness of other controversial groups. Early in the year, a CGQJ operative in Lyon tells the Paris office that, as he hears it from the capital, "the occupiers think of the Sepharadim as being like the Karaites; they are thought of as Aryans. Please advise." The response admits the operative's basic premise, and informs the regional bureau for aryanization that "we now must know upon what proof one bases his affiliation with that sect."[115]

Until Paris fixed its position—some six months later—Sepharadim gained some respite from the burdens of the religious laws. That this potential loophole was chancy and likely to close quickly in any individual case was signalled by an unsigned, handwritten letter, again directed to the Marshal, during this period; a self-described "Israelite Sepharadi of the Latin race" begged for special relief.[116] Vichy squeezed the ropes

---

[113] *Feldkommandant* Shrader, 18 December 1941; reply to him, 8 January 1942, AN AJ[38], 148.

[114] Ibid., Rolland to CGQJ, 23 July 1942.

[115] Ibid., correspondence 19 January and 1 February 1943.

[116] Ibid., anonymous letter to Pétain, 22 September 1942.

tight on 2 September 1943, however: "The Sepharadim are a Spanish Jewish sect. Thus, the Jewish statute is applicable to them."[117]

Notable in these cases of religious allegiance, neo-ethnic expertise, and racist "theory" is Vichy's unending aptitude for injecting legalistic terror into the corpus of groups left untouched by the Nazis. As we have seen time and again, within and without the government, both by judicial and extra-judicial mechanisms, thoroughness vied with common sense and decency in Vichy's single-minded quest for doctrinal coherence in matters of race.

## C. Mixed Heritage and Mixed Marriage as an Element in Ultimate Religious Persecution

Faithful to a kind of traditional gallic rationalism, Vichy also tried to bring order to the troublesome categories of mixed heritage and mixed marriage individuals whose religious status might be in question.[118] As Ingo Müller has indicated recently, these sorts of people remained puzzling to the Nazis, whose law and practice sometimes seemed to privilege them even when there were strong indices of "Jewishness" in a specific case.[119] While subject to some uncertainty, a comparative inquiry might well conclude that, once again, Vichy surpassed German precedents and demands in their persecution of such people. As we have shown elsewhere,[120] Vichy statutory law and interpretations of the law's grey areas affected Nazi thinking, for they relied almost exclusively on the French legal system to establish broad categories and then to make case-by-case decisions, where necessary, about who was ripe for every form of persecution that came into practice.[121]

---

[117] Ibid.

[118] See chapter 2 at notes 23-29.

[119] Müller, *Hitler's Justice*, 98ff.

[120] See chapter 2, text at notes 34 and 71 for crucial examples.

[121] Serge Klarsfeld, while thorough in tracking the documentation dealing with mixed-status individuals, see, e.g., *Vichy/Auschwitz* (Paris: Fayard, 1983), 42, 111, 113, 199, 238, 358, opined in his earlier work that the differences between the Vichy 2 June 1941 statute generally and the eventual (seventh) German ordinance of 24 March 1942 were "minimal." But regarding these two categories, it is Vichy doctrinal leadership that led to eventual German agreement.

First, as to mixed-heritage individuals: the Nazis had to play leapfrog with the French in order to keep their ordinances for the Occupied Zone as comprehensive as the Vichy statutory definitions. The French were familiar with the laws of the Reich, and they would not have been surprised that the first German ordinance for France limited the application of racial prejudice to those with at least three Jewish grandparents.[122] In German law, too, the earliest attempts fell short of including those with only two Jewish grandparents, such people being considered "crossbreeds" and not Jewish unless practicing the religion or married to a Jew.[123]

Alibert's 3 October statute disavowed any special category for what the Nazis called "crossbreeds" (our "mixed-heritage individuals") and simply included those whom the German ordinance had disregarded altogether: Jews with only two grandparents but married to another Jew. Omitted from the Alibert definition were those mixed-heritage individuals who also practiced Judaism. But the definitive 2 June statute, the product of extensive agency and ministerial study in Vichy, closed the loophole for those practicing the religion[124] and also developed the following fatal extension of all precedents, German or French:

> Art I. A Jew is...[one] with only two Jewish grandparents if his or her spouse is also the descendant of Jewish grandparents of the Jewish race.[125]

Absurd in the literal language of the statute is its apparent limitation of Jewish status to those who marry *other mixed-heritage individuals,* thereby excluding from Jewishness half-Jews marrying someone with *more*

---

[122] See note 1.

[123] Müller, *Hitler's Justice,* 98.

[124] Marrus and Paxton, *Vichy France and the Jews,* 291, erred in stating that "Vallat's statute"—meaning that of 2 June 1941—exempted mixed-heritage individuals "who were not married to a Jew." On the contrary, much of the contentious caselaw and doctrinal theory discussed earlier in this study was of course generated by the need for such people to prove their non-Jewishness, whatever their marital status and—if they practiced Judaism as of 25 June 1940—they were Jewish under the explicit terms of the definitive statute.

[125] Sarraute and Tager, *Recueil des textes,* 49.

than two Jewish grandparents.[126] While no private lawyer, to my knowledge, dared that argument in favor of a mixed-heritage client, the lawyers in the CGQJ did notice it, and offered the following internal advice in December 1941:

> We are faced with a defect in the drafting of the law that will soon be corrected. [It never was; it never needed to be.] But good sense requires that it be interpreted as though it said: "if his/her spouse is Jewish," and not "if his/her spouse is an issue of two grandparents of the Jewish race."[127]

No laughing matter, however, the *effect* of the statute was to supersede German models[128] and to implicate many mixed-heritage people whose mates carried the same description, even though they married long before the costs of such a decision could have been predicted in their worst nightmares.[129] One extreme example of this is the case of *first cousins* with largely non-Jewish grandparental heritage who marry each other. Vichy debated the question, which the Germans probably would not have reached at all, whether one set of common Jewish grandparents between them might turn each of the spouse-cousins into Jews! Although extensive charts were drawn by Vichy lawyers, and at first CGQJ seemed to answer the question in the negative, the extensive history of one of these cases *(Leboucher)* indicates that the matter was not resolved either way.[130] As we have noted, too, some internal Vichy criticism was

---

[126] See on this point Klarsfeld, *Vichy/Auschwitz,* 86. Klarsfeld seems to stress the literal limitation of the statute to cases in which *both* spouses are of mixed heritage, but it is clear that Vichy from the beginning implicated a mixed heritage person who had married a full Jew or Jewess. Klarsfeld also in this brief section on comparative statutory law makes no mention of the attribution of Jewishness even to unmarried mixed-heritage individuals—or to those *married to Aryans!*—who could not disprove their Jewishness; see chapter 5.

[127] CDJC XVIIa-38 (156). In this letter to the regional director of CGQJ in Toulouse the reference is to the *Leboucher* case, see chapter 5 at note 84.

[128] The 1935 German law did not include "crossbreeds" marrying other "crossbreeds," Müller, *Hitler's Justice,* 98, note 34; see also Desbaines, *Le statut des juifs en Allemagne,* cited at note 1.

[129] This retroactive effect argument (see chapter 2, note 27) was unsuccessfully raised in Vichy against the 3 October 1940 statute.

[130] See discussion of *Leboucher* at its later stage, with Jewishness still contentious, chapter 5, notes 84–85. For another mention of an early first cousin case producing CGQJ stubbornness, see the *Jacques* case, chapter 2, note 103; see chapter 8, text at note 208.

levelled at the idea that religious status would be affected by marriage at all, but this early objection also carried no eventual weight.[131]

Comparison of the German to the Vichy scheme reveals two other elements that might have induced such French analysts as Joseph Haennig to describe Nazi religious law as possessing, in some senses, "a largeness and objectivity of spirit"[132] First, the German statute took a substantially different approach to nationality, implicating as full Jews only those "crossbreeds" who were or became citizens of the Reich, and *not* those of other nationalities.[133] Vichy included everybody under its mixed-heritage umbrella and was particularly hard on foreign and stateless people.

Second, German religious definition tended to be more *prospective* than did the French statutes. For example, the German statute labelled as Jewish only those "issue of mixed marriages contracted after 15 September 1935," or (after revision to include the category) of "free unions born after 31 July 1936."[134] These nuances permitted at least some planning for the fate of children, unlike Vichy's retroactive inclusion of people who could in no way predict what a statute passed after their actions might prohibit or define. The French statute, over preliminary internal objections, defined Jewish status retroactively, either through marriage (3 October 1940)[135] or through actions indicating "affiliation" with one religion or another (2 June 1941).

Thus, as to attempts to prove "non-adherence to the Jewish race," the latter Vichy statute penalizes all those who could be considered Jewish as of 25 June *1940*. Now many good-faith conversions to Christianity may have occurred in the more than eleven months between the Nazi occupation of France and the promulgation of the 2 June 1941 statute; indeed, it is this statute alone that for the first time *penalized* mixed-heritage Jews who could not prove their "adherence" to another religion,[136] so it would be difficult to impute any false motives to such

---

[131] See chapter 2 at note 26.

[132] See chapter 2, text at note 132.

[133] Müller, *Hitler's Justice,* 99.

[134] See note 1 statutory reference.

[135] See chapter 2, note 23.

[136] The 3 October statute, of course, had included only mixed-heritage individuals married to Jews.

conversions. Thus there is a retroactivity element not only in the *ex post facto* legal definition of Jew itself, but also on the smaller scale of disallowing specific actions that a mixed-heritage individual might have taken (like baptism) during the intervening eleven months. Remarkably, the Germans' "fairer" approach extended late into the occupation, in a Nazi directive *about arrest and deportation* from France. In April 1944 the Dijon SD informed its operatives that "all Jews...except those married to Aryans before 10 July 1940" were to be arrested.[137] The date establishing the cut-off for mixed marriages reflected the notion that people acting prior to a set of events—legal or military—that they could not have anticipated (here the Nazi occupation of France) should be credited with good faith decision-making; Vichy took the opposite attitude in many of its laws and regulations.

None of this is to suggest that life under the Nazi legal system was easy for people with even the slightest trace of Jewish blood. But it became at least as hard for someone on French soil, and in some ways harder. As legalistic Vichy translated itself into the enormity of genocidal Vichy, the fine-tuned interpretations of an already expansive statutory law placed at risk of ultimate destruction individuals whom Nazi law, together with Nazi policy, might have left free. The explanation for this, as we have suggested elsewhere, too, lies less in any form of antisemitism than in a relentless gallic rationalism, desiccated and free of the constraint on occasion, even of the occupier. Serge Klarsfeld has put it best, perhaps, in describing the comparative responsibility of the French and the Germans for the roundups of 1942 and 1943; his example is Jean Leguay, a lawyer whom René Bousquet brought to the service of the National Police:

> We can debate extensively whose responsibility involved the most personal commitment: that of the SS, involved in eliminating Jews after nine years of Hitler, or that of the high French bureaucrat who perhaps has nothing against the Jews but who acts as Leguay did.[138]

Mixed marriage cases, quite apart from the jeopardy that one of mixed heritage might find himself or herself in, also deserve some elaboration

---

[137] See chapter 2, note 101.

[138] Serge Klarsfeld, *Vichy/Auschwitz,* 141.

here upon our earlier mention.[139] The French were aware that the Germans started by favoring the exemption from arrest and deportation, "as in the Reich," of Jews married to Aryans.[140] Both as a legalistic matter, and in terms of the Final Solution, the Nazis tended to be more open than the French to arguments based on intermarriage. Indeed, marriage to an Aryan was, for the French, either a matter of indifference or—in cases of mixed-heritage individuals seeking to establish their non-Jewishness—just one piece of evidence among others of the non-Aryan spouse's religious status. Reminiscent of, but undoubtedly not as morally charged as Vichy's insistence on sending Jewish children with their parents "to the East"—despite the Nazis disinterest in having them sent there[141]—Vichy's attitude about Jews married to Aryans was simply that they were, after all, Jews.

By at least March 1942, Vichy was familiar with Eichmann's directive that no Jew (whatever his or nationality) married to an Aryan was to be arrested or deported from the Occupied Zone.[142] As we saw in the unfortunate Taub matter mentioned earlier,[143] the French police nonetheless arrested and sent to Drancy individuals who should have benefitted from the exemption, but for whom intervention even by the Germans sometimes proved too late. (Taub seems to have been deported in one of the first convoys to Auschwitz from French soil.)

By the time of the roundups of summer 1942 and 1943, the Nazis' mixed marriage exemption had been removed from entire national categories, including, by 1943, Austrians, Bulgarians, Greeks, Dutch, Belgians, Norwegians "former Poles," "former Luxembourgers," "former Czechs," a half-dozen Germanic regional categories and all "stateless

---

[139] See, e.g., chapter 2 at notes 26–30, 95–101.

[140] CDJC IV-183.

[141] Parisian SS to Eichmann, 6 July 1942, indicating Laval's suggestion about children—Bousquet extended this to children from *both* zones; Eichmann response, 21 July, that "Kindertransporte rollen können (children's trains can roll)," CDJC XLIX-3, YV 09/23-2.

[142] Chapter 2 at note 96; Klarsfeld, *Vichy/Auschwitz,* 199, citing Eichmann to SS in France, memorandum, 12 March 1942.

[143] See chapter 2, note 97.

Jews."[144] However, other "Jews in mixed marriages with children" were still "exempted from arrest."[145]

By 1944, the perception of Nazi policy had changed. More importantly, camps like Drancy were now almost entirely under German administration.[146] People no longer could hope that a combination of national status plus marriage to an Aryan would bring them either immunity from arrest or—if persecuted by the French, anyway—at least a trump card against deportation.[147] To the extent that arguments against deportation could be mounted at all during these late stages, they nonetheless took the form of a variation on the older German theme of intermarriage exemptions for certain national groups.

An increasingly rare but probably not unique case exemplifies the synergistic (and controversial) interchanges between the Nazis and UGIF that sometimes led to the release of people whose destinies French law might earlier have subverted.[148] Renée Kyburz, née Meyer, was a French native married to a Swiss national and hence considered Swiss under the laws of that nation. Arrested in Paris in late 1943, she had survived in Drancy—or more specifically in the satellite "hospices" that by then imprisoned various categories of Jews[149]—for four full months,

---

[144] SS memorandum to all Paris prefects, 16 July 1943, CDJC XXVI-76.

[145] Ibid. Meanwhile, in the Unoccupied Zone, the French did not identify for exemption the category of mixed marriages, but their formal arrest techniques had been limited to the same national groupings whose exemption from Eichmann's March 1942 policy had since been lifted by Nazi directive for the Occupied Zone, Klarsfeld, *Vichy/Auschwitz*, 318.

[146] Cynthia J. Haft, *The Bargain and the Bridle* (Chicago: Dialog, 1983).

[147] See, e.g., chapter 2, note 97.

[148] Mrs. Morel's case, discussed above at notes 30–31, is another example of this interrelation. And in the *Bernholc* matter (note 26), there was explicit SD intervention in the case, even after Bernholc was in Drancy, to seek additional data about Bernholc's maternal heritage in Russia, SD note, 27 August 1942, to Israelowitch, UGIF, YV (not numbered) Bernholc file. Although beyond the scope of the present study, the Germans apparently did work directly with UGIF (and Israelowitch in particular) to release some individuals in these questionable categories. See Georges Wellers, *L'Activité des Organisations juives en France* (Paris: CDJC, 1983), introduction, 215.

[149] Haft, *Bargain and the Bridle*, 95. Mrs. Kyburz in fact had been moved from the relative safety of the Rothschild Old Age Home (where foreign nationals were kept who had some claim of immunity from deportation) to the Rothschild Hospice, where mixed-marriage individuals (no longer immune from deportation) were imprisoned, YV, Kurt

despite the accelerating and increasingly indiscriminate deportation schedules. But by the end of the following February, Mr. Kyburz began to fear her imminent "transfer." "They have changed her category," he writes to UGIF, from protected national to "spouse of an Aryan," a status increasingly at risk if the nationality no longer counted.

UGIF responded to the pleas and to the detailed letter handwritten by Mr. Kyburz and reminded the Germans that the Swiss were a protected national group and that Renée Kyburz was to be considered Swiss and not French, under the terms of Swiss law. (French law would have labelled her French, ironically sealing her fate in this case where in so many thousands of others it had doomed people by refusing to call them French.) Interestingly, Mr. Kyburz apparently by this time felt that any ambiguous racial question should be addressed directly to the Germans—"Should we contact Avenue Foch?"[150]—he asks UGIF, referring to the French branch office of the genocidal Nazi police service IV-B.[151]

Not too long after UGIF reported Renée's situation to the Nazis, she received free passage to Switzerland, signed personally by SS Obersturmführer Hans Röthke. That a Jew in 1944 would occasionally be liberated by a man like Röthke, who was dedicated to having all of France's Jews annihilated,[152] indicates again that the Germans always considered other nation's legal perceptions as a real potential check on the Final Solution. By this time, the French administration was gone from French prisons, but the Jews could utilize Swiss law, for example, to make viable arguments to the Nazis. Renée Kyburz, like dozens of others before her, gained her freedom because, amidst the grimmest example of organized cruelty humankind had ever seen, the executioners tended to listen to voices of law that were authoritative.

So UGIF still referred to the "Avenue Foch," and their appeals were not simply rendered from naiveté or foolhardiness. To whom else could they go? For one thing, in 1944, Jews found that French law, although still an essential barometer to Nazi action in some arenas (denaturalization law, for example), was no longer a major component of prison camp

---

Schendel file.

[150] Kyburz to UGIF, YV file.

[151] See, e.g., Klarsfeld, *Vichy/Auschwitz,* 147; Steinberg, *Les Allemands en France,* 217.

[152] See, e.g., Marrus and Paxton, *Vichy France and the Jews,* 344; Steinberg, *Les Allemands en France,* 222.

decision making. Sadly, too, they knew that even when the French *had* most of the legal power, it was not often used for humane ends. Like a starving plant that reaches up for nourishment when deluged, or down when pulled violently by its very roots, France's Jews found what nourishment they could from two rotten sources.

## D. Law and Pillage: Keeping Pace (at a Minimum) with the Occupiers

While the laws of property under Vichy, as they relate to the Jewish population, await fuller exposition in the next chapter, a fitting introduction to their breadth and imagination takes place here, where French legalistic greed is shown to have exceeded, on occasion, the highly comparable German lusts. As dispassionate as the historian tries to be in dealing with this subject, he has some difficulty avoiding the image of the hunt: the lion may stray from his own territory to produce victimized flesh, but the indigenous jackals—if they remain alert—sometimes reap the richest rewards from the kill.

When it came to property law, the French were at least as concerned as they were regarding religious definition to insist that even the Occupied Zone continue to be their own province. In January 1941, Vichy invoked the Armistice Convention once again,[153] along with Articles 43 and 46 of the Hague Convention, to proclaim Vichy control over the majority of seized property—and the entirety of Jewish property—despite existing German ordinances.[154] This memorandum displays Vichy's comparative zeal to aryanize Jewish property holdings. The inter-relation of French and German laws and regulations on property seizures awaits fuller analysis in the next chapter, but, as Joseph Billig well contends,

> It is the Vichy law of 10 September [1940] that prepares the terrain for a much more extensive seizure by the [French] *administrateur provisoire* than was brought about by the [German] ordinance of 20 May [1940].[155]

---

[153] See note 7.

[154] See chapter 2, text at notes 51–53, for this important document.

[155] Billig, *Le Commissariat général,* vol. 3, 69.

Two aspects of Vichy intervention in the aryanization of property replicate similar patterns we have seen regarding religious definition. First, to the Germans' delight, the French initiated involvement of their own ministries and courts in the seizure of property;[156] second, they considerably broadened (vis-à-vis the first German ordinance) the *scope of coverage* to include seizing businesses "where, for whatever reason, the qualified directors cannot possibly exercise their functions."[157] The German ordinance had mentioned only absence and *force majeure* as justifications for property takeovers.[158]

The memorandum proudly setting forth French legal resistance to German initiatives on property law suggests that French "concession"[159] was perhaps less a factor in their increasing role than was a determined policy overtly to limit German jurisdiction over Jewish wealth. The Germans, as we shall see, needed French law to rationalize their seizures of Jewish property, but the French often refused to display a converse willingness to have German ordinances co-exist with theirs, unless the German outcome worked greater hardship on Jews than would their own law.[160] (Indeed, the height of Vichy collaboration with the Germans on matters of pillage involved a Vichy law promulgated to implement the Nazi "fine" of 1 billion francs on the Jewish community.)[161] From the earliest seizures of property in the Occupied Zone, during which the French nominated countless thousands more Aryan "trustees" than did the

---

[156] Law of 10 September 1940 (J.O., 26 October 1940), Article 2; see Sarraute and Tager, *Recueil des textes,* 20.

[157] Ibid., 17: Article I.

[158] Ibid., 15: German ordinance, 20 May 1940, Article 2.

[159] Billig's term, *Le Commissariat général,* vol. 3, 73.

[160] On these occasions, French administrators might cite favorably to German ordinances. In an interesting example from mid-1941, SCAP declined to grant the Jewish wife of a French prisoner of war an exemption from the aryanization rules, although the exemption seems warranted under the *French* law of 2 June 1941 (see chapters 2 and 3). Mrs. Kuperberg wanted to maintain her husband's radio store in the rue Magenta of Paris' 11^e^ arrondissement. But an administrateur provisoire, M. Guth of Houilles, insisted that she leave the store permanently. CGQJ replied to her that the German ordinances pre-dating the French law were solely applicable and did not permit her any exemption, CDJC CXIV-34.

[161] See chapter 7.

Germans,[162] the French exhibited a zeal to clamp down economically even in the victors' private arena.

By April 1941, SCAP leader Fournier had decided to take the lead in *liquidating* many Jewish businesses, a step not called for as yet by any German ordinance.[163] As that year progressed, the Germans and French competed to control Jewish property. SCAP's leadership passed to those under the control of the newly created CGQJ, men like de Faramond, an anti-German[164] who realized that "the way aryanization is carried out in the Occupied Zone is bound to have an influence on whether we can substitute French regulations for German regulations in the aryanization business."[165] De Faramond's mix of hostilities (like Alibert, he was as anti-German as he was antisemitic) was not untypical of SCAP administrators during the early CGQJ years.[166]

In large ways and small, Vichy endeavored to make aryanization and the "de-Judaification" of the French economy its own projects. In mid-1941, Vichy took the largely uncoerced step of extending by statute the process of aryanization to the Unoccupied Zone.[167] At around the same time, the Germans interpreted French law to have extended to North Africa such aryanization measures as the blocking of Jewish bank accounts.[168] Vichy introduced and then implemented other, specific laws to maximize the economic hardships of Jews in both zones. Thus, by its law of 10 February 1942, Vichy reversed a 150-year old legal approach to name changes; whereas all could previously change their names largely at will, now Jews were not permitted to do so.[169] Moving

---

[162] Billig reports that the Germans named about 30 administrateurs provisoire between November 1940 and March 1941; during the same period, the French nominated over 4,500 of them in *one week alone,* Billig, *Le Commissariat général,* vol. 3, 80; see also chapter 7.

[163] Ibid., vol. 3, 82.

[164] Ibid, vol. 1, 97.

[165] Marrus and Paxton, *Vichy France and the Jews,* 83.

[166] Billig, *Le Commissariat général,* vol. 3, 95–96.

[167] Law of 22 July 1941; Sarraute and Tager, *Recueil des textes,* 62.

[168] Secret German memorandum, 10 April 1941, citing the Vichy statute of 3 October 1940, Article III, YV V-87.

[169] Ibid., 140. The struggle by Vichy to determine "who is a Jew?" included a pervasive attempt to link Jewishness to certain names, and the régime did not want variations on those "noms de consonance juive" with which it thought it was familiar; see, e.g., chapter

with typical logic, the régime then barred the payment of royalties to any Jewish author who had ever used a pseudonym.[170]

By 1942 and 1943, Vichy had moved to seize even businesses that only Jews patronized, a domain largely untouched by the Germans. Thus a young man named Jacques Stutwoyner, both of whose parents had been deported in July, sought permission to keep their family bakery running in the Marais, in order to support himself (aged 19) and his two younger brothers. Although the clientele was "purely Jewish," and although the business grossed no more than 500 francs a day, it had been aryanized, a practice that had become general.[171] The bakery was already in the hands of its administrateur provisoire, M. Gresley of the 15[e] arrondissement; but now the CGQJ was threatening to close it up and sell it. In early 1943, UGIF reported that the CGQJ had exclusive jurisdiction over such enterprises, and that "the Occupation Authorities are not competent to deliver the requested authorization [to stay in business]."[172]

But the CGQJ, which under Darquier had fully taken over SCAP,[173] had shown itself indomitable on aryanization questions. It was unlikely that the poor youthful baker would gain relief from such a source. It had been the CGQJ, after all, that had already exceeded the German view on more general questions of Jewish property law. For example, in the face of Jews fleeing to the south, something had to be done with the furniture they had left behind; the Germans insisted that such property not be sold out from under the Jewish tenants, a policy that went so far as to see

---

2, note 16; AN AJ[38], 100.

[170] AN AJ[38], 100; CGQJ memorandum, 4 April 1942.

[171] See UGIF memorandum, 8 January 1943, in which they report that the CGQJ now ordinarily aryanizes even business not really touched by any formal statute or ordinance; the only difference between such aryanizations and others seemed to be that there would not be a total forced sale, CDJC CDXXIX-1. The case of the baker discussed here, however, indicates that even forced sales of such businesses became common.

[172] Stutwoyner matter, UGIF documents, 31 December 1942, 6 January 1943.

[173] A decree of 19 June 1941 placed SCAP under CGQJ control, but under Darquier—as of 18 May 1942, SCAP was formally annexed to the agency's Direction générale de l'aryanisation économique; see AN "Inventaire," AJ[38], "CGQJ."

them refusing to have implemented French judicial orders to the contrary.[174]

Occasionally, Vichy excess had to be checked by the Germans, who—from the top down—scrupulously followed every development in Vichy property law.[175] As we remarked, Buhrig of the German High Command had to caution the French at around this time; he felt that their basic approach to economic cleansing had gotten out of hand.[176] After the war, Dr. Knochen of the Paris SS would put it this way: "[A]fter its arrival on the scene, the CGQJ showed too much zeal, going beyond our wishes and sometimes engaging in outbidding us."[177]

The next chapter proceeds with an inquiry about property law generally during the Vichy years. In many areas discussed there, race became intertwined with legal doctrine in a purely "franco-French" manner, with little German intervention or interest. But in slicing the pie of Jewish wealth, the zeal of Vichy policy-makers to retain a maximum of legalistic autonomy over an increasing amount of booty often came into direct conflict with strong German self-interest. Nonetheless, as in the areas we have discussed throughout the present chapter, Vichy property law tended to proceed according to a self-referential logic, heavily influenced by its own developing analyses of older precedents and the new laws[178]

---

[174] AN AJ[38], 118. The German motivations for such beneficence might, of course, have included a desire to see Jewish property remain under seal instead of shifting to French Aryan hands; see chapter 7, e.g., at note 74. Still, the effect was to save certain Jewish property.

[175] As Billig remarks about one of the top German bureaucrats for economic aryanization in France: "Dr. Blanke placed under a microscope the legislative work of Vichy!," *Le Commissariat général,* vol. 3, 161.

[176] See full text at note 48.

[177] CDJC LXXIV-7 (13), cited in Laloum, *La France antisémite,* 78.

[178] Accord on the question of Vichy aryanization legislation often exceeding German requirements, André Kaspi, *Les Juifs pendant l'Occupation* (Paris: Seuil, 1991), 116, and (citing Henri Rousso on spoliation generally), ibid., 121.

# Chapter 7

# Property Law

## A. Landlord-Tenant Relations Under the Exclusionary Roof

We begin an inquiry into Vichy property law with the study of a body of caselaw affecting hundreds of Jewish lives. In its interweaving of various strands of French legislation, it further indicates how agonizing and unstable Vichy law became once it—Haennig-like—substituted the freedom of the discursive moment for the constraint of constitutional ideals. By a decree of 26 September 1939—pre-dating by a year all antisemitic legislation—any tenant who had been mobilized for the war could benefit from a 75% reduction in rent during the period of his military service.[1] Furthermore, the decree permitted tenants the right to reductions, even after mobilization, if debilitated, economically or otherwise, by "a circumstance of war" (un fait de guerre).[2]

The question to which dozens of lawyers and judges had to turn was whether Jews disadvantaged by the Vichy statutes could benefit from the rent reduction prescribed by the 26 September 1939 decree. The latter was silent as to Jews, of course, since its promulgation pre-dated any concept of race-specific legislation. Yet Jews were now losing jobs, being

---

[1] *Gazette des Tribuneaux* 47 (20 October 1939); see also the modification to this decree, (although not relevant to this discussion) of 1 June 1940.

[2] See, e.g., opinion of Justice of the Peace, 20e arrondissement, Paris, 2 April 1942, in *Gazette des Tribuneaux* 50 (6–12 December 1942), CDJC CDXXIX-2.

arrested, facing deportation. Could they or their families benefit from the 1939 decree? Lawyers for landlords who might never have seen the religious statutes, and lawyers for Jews who had been living with them on a daily basis, now had to endeavor to harmonize two unrelated statutes and to use them for their clients.

We have no documents indicating any interest by the German occupiers in this jurisprudence, even though most of the cases arose in occupied Paris (the situation is somewhat different when the cases also encroach on property aryanizations). Here was a purely internal matter of law, subject—perhaps even more than was the rhetoric we have examined in earlier chapters—only to the usual discourse among lawyers and judges. In this situation, too, there were none of the jurisdictional conflicts that raged between the civil and administrative courts. Magisterial discourse floated freely into the air of Vichy religious legislation.

Many landlords, faced with Jewish tenants unable to pay their rent, went to court to evict. From mid-1941 until the end of the war, before justices of the peace in many of Paris's twenty arrondissements, before other civil courts of original jurisdiction, and before various courts of appeal, lawyers argued the legal niceties of the 26 September 1939 decree on rent reductions.

As developed regarding the 2 June statute, so here, so everywhere that the interpretive community of French lawyers focussed its attention, the debate was confined narrowly to several issues. The main question was whether unemployment, detention, or deportation constituted a "circumstance of war," so that victims might claim the rent reduction; or whether it was a "fait du prince"—an act of the French state, quite apart from the war. In the latter case, the tenants or their survivors would have no recourse. The vicissitudes of legal argument further created mini-debates on whether the results of the anti-Jewish climate might not have been a circumstance of war *prior* to 2 June 1941, and an act of state afterwards; or whether "mere" job loss might be an act of state, whereas arrest or deportation would be an act of war. Because it *was* a Vichy statute, now applicable to the Occupied Zone as well, the 2 June 1941 law marked a reasonable date to infer purely French activity of a racially restrictive nature, arguably unconnected with the war, but not all courts were willing forthrightly to say so in all cases; just as many were unwilling to look reality in the face and take note of the much earlier French legislation calling for the firings, arrests, and detention of thousands of Jews.

Further squabbles arose as to the resolution stage of these trials. If a rent reduction was called for, courts still had to decide whether the adjudged reduction (set by the decree at 75% for any period of actual mobilization) should be the same or less when the circumstance of war was forced unemployment, detention, or deportation.

What developed is—in one respect anyway—unique in the jurisprudence of the Vichy years. Courts of first jurisdiction showed themselves to be philosemitic. They overwhelmingly allowed some rent reduction to the Jewish tenants; they indicated thereby that Vichy magistrates—so sadly conformist in accepting the basic outrage of religious definition itself—were capable of extending a kind of legalistic logic towards a benign doctrinal result. There is not a jot of antisemitism to be located in these decisions; they flow freely from the internal dynamics of a system striving to interpret what was, indeed, a pre-"religious" statute. Furthermore, the judges in some cases openly admitted that the religious statutes affecting their decision were of Vichy origin and *could not be blamed on the Germans.*[3] Yet the manner in which even favorable decisions were rendered served to promote uncertainty and confusion among similarly situated tenants who could not, chose not to, or would only later, litigate the question of their monthly rent. The caselaw here, like Joseph Haennig's or Jacques Maury's approach to the 2 June 1941 statute, forces on the analyst an inquiry as to the effect of legal discourse that chooses to work with—rather than centrally challenge—a grotesque superstructure of law.

Although I have analyzed elsewhere a considerable cross-section of these landlord/tenant cases,[4] a brief perspective here on cases from two Parisian arrondissements indicates how conflicting rhetoric confused Jews in trouble with the law.

In a typical case in the 20[e] arrondissement, the justice of the peace there found for M. *Bankhelter,* who received the full 75% reduction for his army period (4 months) and 35% for his period in detention, which

---

[3] See, e.g., the *Tenenbaum vs. Berger* case, 11[e] arrondissement, granting a rent reduction to the family of a Jewish man who had been arrested and sent to Drancy: "The laws that have established a special status for Jews are incontestably measures that do not bear a cause and effect relationship to the war...; they could have been promulgated in other circumstances than those of the war," CDJC CDXXIX-2; see note 8.

[4] See Richard Weisberg, *Poethics, and Other Strategies of Law and Literature* (New York: Columbia University), 158–69.

the court formulaically asserted to be "by order of the Occupying authorities." Forced detention was viewed by the court as a circumstance of war, relieving Bankhelter of that much of his rent from the date of his internment until the date of the decision, 12 December 1942, a period of nineteen months.[5]

The 20e arrondissement had by then developed a small body of caselaw on this issue. On 19 June 1941, in the *Lerman* case, the court allowed a non-veteran a 70% reduction for having been fired the year before, leaving him without resources.[6] While there is no discussion of the cause of Lerman's unemployment, it seems probable that he demonstrated its link to the religious laws. And in *Baraban,* decided 30 July 1942, a detainee at the camp at Beaunes la Rolande was relieved of 75% of his rent obligation during his mobilization and 50% since his internment some fourteen months prior to the decision.[7]

The 11e arrondissement, faced squarely the long history of Jewish incarceration by Vichy law. In *Tenenbaum,*[8] this court explicitly stated that the religious laws were of French origin, not directly connected causally to the war, of unlimited duration, and "could have been promulgated in other circumstances than those of the war."[9] Only the court's decision to emphasize the *internment* of the tenant, which it managed to connect (unlike the religious statutes themselves) to the war, justified the outcome of a rent reduction, permitted here to the extent of between 30% and 50%. Even as to internment, the court took a realistic view of French

---

[5] CDJC CDXXIX-2.

[6] See also *Reiner* decision, 22 October 1941, CDJC CDXXIX-1; and *Miodowski* decision, 7 January 1943, CDJC CDXXIX-2.

[7] CDJC CDXXIX-2.

[8] See note 3. *Tenenbaum* expanded on briefer decisions in the same arrondissement stating that internments were always to be deemed acts of war. See, e.g., *Talvy vs. Roserans,* decision of 26 October 1942, Justice of the Peace, 11e arr., CDJC CDXXIX-2. This decision was apparently not the first by Judge Marbeck that helped Jewish tenants, as one of his earlier decisions to the same effect (i.e., that arrest and internment place the tenant in the same situation as mobilization, regardless of the origins of the laws that detained him) was cited by the UGIF regarding a dispute in July 1942 between Klein and Kappelmeister as to the rents due on an apartment in the rue d'Angoulême, CDJC CDXXIX-2. See also this arrondissement's decision of 16 November 1942, granting (on the advice of a court-ordered expert) a rent reduction for M. Gutmann, CDJC CDXXIX-2.

[9] Ibid., decision of 1 February 1943.

participation: "It is not greatly important that the camps are under French administration; it is the exceptional [and temporary] nature of these measures that form the sole criterion on this subject."[10]

Thus, while the 11ᵉ and 20ᵉ arrondissements found ways to grant relief to most Jewish tenants seeking such relief, their differing rhetoric created confusion among the families of many other Jews potentially seeking such relief later. The 11ᵉ, by freely admitting French authorship and activity in anti-Jewish legislation of all kinds, produced a more realistic rhetoric but nonetheless used statutory interpretation to grant rent reductions; the 20ᵉ, on the other hand, used a formula to create less forthright distinctions that kept similarly situated Jews in the dark about their rights. Furthermore, once beyond the dominant jurisdictions of the 11ᵉ and 20ᵉ arrondissements, cases at the level of original jurisdiction become still more difficult to rationalize according to any predictable principal. Relatively early, for example, the Tribunal de la Seine denied a rent reduction to a Jew who had "merely" fled the Occupied Zone and whose inability to pay rent was ascribed by the court purely to his own behavior.[11]

More disturbingly, perhaps, an appeals court for the jurisdiction of the Seine (including Paris) had, also at an early stage, issued a negative decision that cast into question the logic and the liberality of such arrondissements as the 11ᵉ and the 20ᵉ. In the case, decided 29 September 1941,[12] the Chambre des référés of the Cour de Paris unfortunately decided to construe each of the two doctrines I ascribed to the 11ᵉ and 20ᵉ arrondissement in a manner detrimental to the Jewish tenant, with a resulting authoritative declaration that "mere" job loss had to be connected to French legislation and hence was not an act of war permitting a rent reduction. First, the court held (unlike that of the 20ᵉ arrondissement) that even very early legislation was of Vichy origin: the August and September 1940 decrees restricting the practice of medicine by Jews were deemed pure acts of Vichy administrative law; second (unlike the 11ᵉ arrondissement), this court specifically declined to associate that legislation with the necessities of war:

---

[10] CDJC CDXXXIX-2.

[11] See decision of 18 March 1941, CDJC CDXXIX-2.

[12] CDJC CDXXIX-2.

> As to that last order of administrative law" [the decree of 16 August 1940 prohibiting such practice],[13] it cannot be said that it bears a cause-and-effect relationship to the war; rather it derives from measures adopted by the legislator [*sic*] that might have been taken in circumstances having nothing to do with the war....[14]

Thus, the doctor was allowed his 75% reduction dating from his mobilization until 10 September 1940, the exact date when he was informed by the French police that he could no longer practice medicine because of the religious laws. But he was not permitted any other reduction in rent under the 29 September 1939 decree.

The appeals court's frank admission that the racial policy of France was unconnected with the war not only confirms my basic thesis, but essentially also ran counter to the earlier cases discussed.[15] It stood as an authoritative roadblock to any sense of security, even under this uniquely benign set of cases, that impoverished and terrified Jewish tenants might retain for their chances in court.

Other decisions might have continued to afford to Jewish tenants or their survivors some consolation, as the horrors of the experience in both zones increased. But they provided no doctrinal anchoring, no sense of predictability. While some courts showed explicit sympathy to the horrible fates of those left behind by arrested and deported Jews, the basic jurisprudence remained too chancy.[16]

No wonder that the Jewish legal service of the Union générale des Israélites français (UGIF), in advising hundreds of tenants and even their landlords' lawyers, could not rely on this jurisprudence to make legalistic

---

[13] For the basic Vichy text creating a *numerus clausus* and other restrictions on the practice of medicine by Jews, see the Decree of 11 August 1941, *Journal Officiel,* no. 3474; and chapter 3.

[14] CDJC CDXXIX-2.

[15] Accord, however, Tribunal de la Seine, 10 February 1941, that permitted a doctor to have a slight rent reduction not because of the religious laws barring him from practice but because of an earlier falling off in clientele, CDJC CDXXIX-2.

[16] Some jurisdictions afforded rent reductions for arrested Jews and chose simply not to engage in the logical game of connecting or disconnecting the fact of arrest with the war itself. See, in the fashionable 8ᵉ arrondissement, the granting of a 65% rent reduction to the *Sliwka* family, whose breadwinner and supplier of income towards the substantial rent of 2800 francs had been "interned and can no longer pay his rent," CDJC CDXXIX-2, decision of 23 March 1943.

distinctions with any confidence.[17] In many such situations, disequilibrated by the jurisprudence, Jews were first advised to ask their landlords to decide the matter "à l'amiable"—without recourse to litigation. Thus for example, in October 1942 UGIF offered its help to the *Topolanski* family, whose breadwinner had been arrested and deported after the enactment of the 2 June 1941 statute. UGIF, despite the tenant-favorable cases already on the books, had to write to the landlord's lawyer, a certain M. Poisson, as follows:

> 30 October, 1942....
> May we not try to arrive at a friendly agreement here...? Mr. Topolanski, employed before the war in the Commercial Pharmaceutical Office, volunteered at the beginning of hostilities. He always paid his rent fully and on time.
>
> On 20 August 1941, he was interned at the camp in Drancy, on the order of the Occupation authorities. He was freed on 5 November for reasons of health; but on 16 July 1942, he was again arrested and on the 22d of the

[17] For detailed descriptions of the work of UGIF, see André Kaspi, *Les Juifs pendant l'Occupation* (Paris, Seuil, 1991), ch. 9; Cynthia J. Haft, *The Bargain and the Bridle* (Chicago: Dialog, 1983) and G. Wellers, and I. Schneerson, eds., *L'Activité des Organisations juives en France* (Paris: CDJC, 1947; repr. 1983).

The legal service itself was apparently established by UGIF internal decision during summer 1942. It was immediately controversial, as the CGQJ (with note taken by the Germans) at first politely protested that aggrieved Jews might better use the ordinary courts, and that UGIF's budget was not designed to provide legal assistance, CGQJ to UGIF, 28 July 1942, with German translation, YV 09-28. UGIF's response, apparently successful to a limited extent, was that Article 1 of the originating law of 29 November 1941, explicitly authorized it to "represent Jews before the public authorities," e.g., André Baur (UGIF director in the Occupied Zone) to Darquier de Pellepoix, 22 December 1942, ibid.

The legal service, and indeed André Baur, did not fare well. In the late December 1942 dispute, for example, UGIF had directly intervened to assist the *Trevgoda* family in their futile dealings with their a.p., M. Miard. Darquier sternly warned Baur that this was not the function of the legal service arm of UGIF, which was to report only to the CGQJ's UGIF department and never to deal as a Jewish agent with an a.p. By March 1943, Baur's dealings with Darquier, and with Antignac (who finally would not tolerate Baur's strong support of foreign Jews employed by UGIF), deteriorated to the point that CGQJ brought about his arrest by the Germans; see Jean Laloum, *La France antisémite de Darquier de Pellepoix* (Paris: Syros, 1979), 83–84. By June 1944, the legal service had been reduced to two staff members, Minutes of UGIF administrative committee 13 June 1944, 2, YV 09-27a.

> same month deported to an unknown place. His wife has had no news of him since then.
>
> Mrs. Topolanski has remained behind with three young children of 7, 5½ and 20 months, and without any source of funds. She has been described to us as particularly worthy of note.
>
> Could you not, under these conditions, ask your client...if he could grant these pitiful tenants a reduction of 50%....
>
> We ourselves will guarantie that M. Poisson receives the balance of the rents due from these tenants.[18]

UGIF's strategy of seeking "friendly" resolutions, instead of relying on the doctrinally confusing philosemitic judicial precedents, reveals a sophisticated appreciation of the trickiness of even "favorable" rhetoric regarding their persecuted clients. The case of Mme. Palestar, who lived at 28 rue Besfroi in the 11ᵉ, is instructive. Unable to pay her annual rent of 800 francs, she is described by UGIF as "a poor woman who can scarcely walk and who is likable (elle peut à peine marcher et qui a l'air sympathique),"[19] who has no resources and who is having problems with her concierge. UGIF decided to treat directly with her landlord and to offer its own subvention towards her rent; but five months later, her case had worsened: "she finds herself threatened by her neighbors, her concierge, etc."[20] UGIF does not inscribe her fate.[21]

On the other hand, some matters—most with negative outcomes—had become sufficiently well settled to afford UGIF a degree of confidence in advising either Jews or their lawyers.[22] In early 1943, UGIF replied to a request for information from Charles Charrier, a Parisian lawyer whose client, Marc Rosen, had fled Paris to the "free" zone. A dental surgeon, Rosen was looking for a rent reduction on his now useless lease

---

[18] CDJC CDXXIX-1.

[19] Memo, UGIF service juridique, 15 April 1942, CDJC CDXXIX-1.

[20] Ibid.

[21] Often landlords wrote to UGIF in hopes of having the organization pay back rents due to them. Thus, for example, on 10 November 1943, M. Philippow's landlord complained that his commercial tenant, a photographer who "was arrested by the Authorities on 17 July 1942," owed him 11,693.30 francs, CDJC CDXXIX-1. In another such case, UGIF responded to landlord Gilliard that it could not help in cases where no Jewish tenant remained on the premises, correspondence, 5 and 12 June 1944, ibid.

[22] For an analysis of the way private lawyers and notaries engaged in race-related practice during the Vichy years, see chapter 8.

in Paris. But UGIF had to report to Maître Charrier that court decisions refused to grant reductions to those fleeing the Occupied Zone, even though laws prohibited them to engage in their chosen career. A "voluntary" departure from the Occupied Zone could not be attributable to any law, "since no authority has ordered the evacuation of Paris."[23] UGIF could report that "we have obtained, fairly often, both from the tribunal de la Seine and from diverse justices of the peace," some rent reductions due to loss of jobs;[24] more "optimistically," UGIF proceeds:

> Finally, we should add that the *tribunal* along with the justices of the peace, very frequently accord rent reductions to Jewish tenants who are interned in concentration camps, such measure considered to be a result of an act of war unless the internment is due to an *individual* infraction committed by the Jew under the terms of legislation passed against the Jews.[25]

Like UGIF in its contemporaneous exposition, present day historians are left with a body of legal rhetoric, facially favorable to a class of Jewish litigants but still somehow dissatisfying. True—and in some ways most significantly—landlord-tenant law does show that the rigors of "autopoeitic," self-referential, Vichy legal logic could just as easily lead to philo- as to antisemitic results. Once again, no particular religious animus explains the volumes of ink spilled on the Jewish question in Vichy. Finally, however, even these cases contributed to the terror, as they placed a further blotch of ambiguity on the face of French doctrine regarding the Jews.

The caselaw's ambiguities certainly afforded relief to those Jewish tenants—or their families—who might eventually fall within the developing doctrine. But to the many Jews in the 20$^{e}$ arrondissement who were arrested after 2 June 1941 and who could never be sure thereafter that such arrests would not be ascribed solely to the French state and not to an act of war; to those advised by lawyers of the many courts that saw job loss as an act of state; and to those in the 11$^{e}$ who saw confirmed by the courts that their countrymen—and not the Germans—were responsible

---

[23] Accord, decision of the Tribunal de la Seine, 18 March 1941, described at note 11.

[24] But see notes 13–15.

[25] Correspondence, 1 February 1943 and 4 February 1943, emphasis in original, CDJC CDXXIX-1.

for the incarceration of men, women, and children—these cases created only further confusion and terror.

## B. Aryanizing Jewish Property by Operation of Law

Pillage in wartime France was a legalistic preoccupation. The Germans had moved quickly, and far more attentively than they had as to actual religious definition, to seize property in the Occupied Zone. As early as 20 May 1940, the High Command was empowered to appoint a trustee—German: *kommissarische Verwalter*—for any property (with no specific mention of Jews) left empty by fleeing owners.[26] On 18 October and on 26 April 1941—in ordinances influenced by the Vichy law of 3 October 1940[27]—the Germans explicitly targeted Jews. The 18 October ordinance—against Vichy protestations that their own jurisdiction was thereby illegally invaded[28]—aryanized "Jewish enterprises," and the 1941 ordinance both denied to Jews even the fruits of the sales of their lost property and forbade them to exercise numerous careers. This latter

---

[26] Sarraute and Tager, *Les Juifs sous l'Occupation: Recueil des textes officiels français et allemands,* (Paris: CDJC, 1982), 15; see also Marrus and Paxton, *Vichy France and the Jews,* (New York: Basic Books, 1981), 7.

[27] See especially, chapters 2 and 6.

[28] See chapter 6, section D. Between May 1940 and July 1942, the Germans retained their formal right to mark with the status "nullité" any transaction involving Jewish property, even if it had met with French approbation, and even involving the Unoccupied Zone. There were many such nullifications; see AJ[38], 80. Although, as we shall see, the bulk of the booty wound up in a special account in the Occupied Zone—the caisse des dépots et consignations—and although that account was largely controlled over time by the CGQJ, the Germans also insisted that the fruits of sales of property held by Jews of certain nationalities (those countries in the Reich or annexed to it) be kept in a separate German account, that of the *Deutscher Generalkommisar für das jüdische Vermögen* at several banks in Paris, including the Barclay's Bank. On 22 July 1942, Dr. Elmar Michel of the German High Command signed an order turning over to the CGQJ most of the final aryanization decisions not relating to Jews of these nationalities, ibid. This hardly marked an end for keen German interest in the aryanization of Jewish property, however.

brought on increased aryanizations and the associated penury that we have seen exemplified in landlord ejectment cases.[29]

Meanwhile, as early as 10 September 1940, Vichy statutes contrived to seize legally the property of newly denaturalized individuals.[30] On the same day, Vichy introduced the "administrateur provisoire" (a.p.) whose function was to manage the property and businesses of all individuals who might become legally incompetent to own or run such enterprises.[31] This innovation brought with it the creation of the "commissaire aux comptes,"[32] a figure attached to the Court of Appeals of the district in which the aryanized property was located. This functionary would gather the a.p.'s data and other information on the property and report to the Minister of Finance or other relevant cabinet ministers. The a.p. would often—as we shall discuss below in sub-section E—sell the enterprise to Aryans or liquidate it altogether, with the proceeds of the sale often going to a specially-created account.

Explicit Vichy mention of Jewish enterprises awaited the detailed law of 22 July 1941, contentious in some Vichy circles because it extended breaches of due process on property ownership to the "free" zone.[33] Meanwhile, with the creation of the CGQJ in March 1941, much of the direct control over the aryanization process was passing to that agency.

Aware of Vichy's enthusiastic initiation of many kinds of religious legislation, the Germans quickly decided to utilize French administrative departments to aryanize Jewish property, under their own as well as under Vichy's laws.[34] This collaboration's early phase was epitomized by

---

[29] See above, notes 6, 13, etc. In a decree of 13 June 1941, a Neuilly-sur-Seine court specifically cited the German ordinance of the prior April as the causal impetus for the rent reduction it then permitted the Jewish tenant, CDJC CDXXIX-2.

[30] Dominique Rémy, *Les Lois de Vichy* (Paris: Romillat, 1992), 79: Law of 10 September 1940, Article 2.

[31] Sarraute and Tager, *Recueil des textes,* 17.

[32] Originated in a decree of 16 January 1941, reported in Sarraute and Tager, *Recueil des textes,* 35; see also "Inventory" to AN AJ[38], collection.

[33] See chapter 4, at notes 136–39.

[34] See Joseph Billig, *Le Commissariat général aux questions juives* (Paris: CDJC, 1955), vol. 3, 75 for the key memorandum to this effect of 1 November 1940 from Dr. Elmar Michel of the Economic Bureau of the Military High Command. Michel notes that "First, we must do what is necessary to eliminate Jews [from the economy] even after the Occupation. More important, we cannot from our side provide sufficient manpower to

the creation of a special agency, the Service de Contrôle des Administrateurs provisoires (SCAP) in December 1940. Created under the direction of the Vichy Ministry of Industrial Production, as extended to Occupied France through the offices of the "General Delegation of the French Government to the Occupied Territories," SCAP applied the German ordinances while appointing French a.p.'s. The Germans were largely delighted with this collaborative effort—particularly at first. It saved them manpower while costing them little, since they had ultimate veto power over the nominations of the a.p.'s.[35] Indeed, the Germans largely relied on French prefects to identify "Jewish" enterprises in the Occupied Zone. They aryanized on their own initiative only thirty-one businesses between November 1940 and March 1941; and they left to the French the seizure of thousands of other Jewish enterprises during this period.[36]

Both to protect their self-interest in the Occupied Zone, and to define the administrative, ministerial, and judicial responsibilities for the seizure of property, Vichy sought better to regulate the process of property transfer. The 16 January 1941 decree, itself perfected by changes made in August of that year, set forth the manner of choosing the a.p.,[37] a task that was pervasive and vital to French economic activity during the war. One prominent documentary center has amassed a file of some 45,000 indivi-

deal with the great number of Jewish enterprises. These two factors have led us to have the French authorities participate in the elimination of Jews. We thereby gain shared responsibility by the French and we have at our disposal the French administrative apparatus," ibid.; see also Billig, vol. 1, 35–37 on the establishment of a "French Governmental Delegation to the Occupied Territories," established under General la Laurencie in fall 1940.

[35] Billig, *Le Commissariat général,* vol. 3, 77; Marrus and Paxton, *Vichy France and the Jews,* 8.

[36] Ibid., 80. Billig, *Le Commissariat général,* vol. 3, supplies an excellent "Annex of Aryanized Businesses." Documentation at AN, especially $AJ^{38}$, 592–96 also gives a flavor for the vast numbers of Jewish enterprises assigned (or awaiting) an a.p. As late as September 1941, CGQJ's judicial bureau notes over two thousand such enterprises then awaiting appointment of an a.p., memorandum, 25 September 1941, AN $AJ^{38}$, 592. For the global figures, see sub-section E.

[37] The Vichy Secretary of State, advised by other ministers and by local committees familiar with the business being seized, made the appointment by decree; Article I, decree of 16 January 1941, Sarraute and Tager, *Receuil des textes,* 35.

dual Jewish enterprises and properties that were aryanized;[38] well into 1944, this process of locating and appointing a.p.'s was to continue undaunted.[39]

This seminal decree also described the scope of the a.p.'s discretion:

> Article 2. The powers of the a.p. can extend to the totality of the enterprise or only to a part thereof, depending on the instructions accompanying the nomination;
>
> Article 3. According to the limits fixed by the nomination decree, the a.p. exercises the broadest powers for the account of the owners [des ayants droits]. [These may include:]
>
> 1. All operations tending to modify the principal purposes of the enterprise;
> 2. All operations tending to raise or lower considerably the production or sales capacity of the enterprise;
> 3. All operations that might lead to the liquidation of the enterprise.[40]

Article 5, creating the Commissaire aux comptes was amended that August to place the latter official under the management of SCAP, which by then had been subsumed into the CGQJ. But Article 9 gave ultimate supervisory responsibility over the a.p.'s to the Minister of Justice, the Finance Minister, the Secretary of State for industry and labor, and several other ministerial authorities if the enterprises in question were associated with their portfolios.

The CGQJ officially took over direction of the a.p.'s in the Occupied Zone under the law of 22 July 1941.[41] The law also extended to the "free zone" for the first time—and in the face of modest objections by

---

[38] CDJC, "Un Fichier des spoliés et des administrateurs." AN AJ[38], 528, offers numerous examples of 5–8-inch slips of paper, each one representing a Jewish enterprise either aryanized or awaiting aryanization. For May–June 1941 alone, there are collected some 550 of these, most involving businesses still needing an a.p. This collection represented only a tiny fraction of the real number of nominations, deriving from the towns of Pithiviers, Beaune-la-Rolande, and Romanville; for the full dimension of French activity in this regard, see chapter 6, note 162, and below, note 79.

[39] From January to June, 1944, in Montpellier, Toulouse, and Pau, for example, eleven private and corporate a.p.'s were newly decreed to manage twenty-six separate Jewish properties, CDJC XVII-10 (41).

[40] Sarraute and Tager, *Recueil des Textes,* 35.

[41] Ibid., 62.

Barthélemy that it violated most principles of French property law[42]—the legalized concept of aryanization. It made explicit (as did the voluminous regulations that were promulgated under it)[43] that aryanization aimed "to eliminate all Jewish influence in the national economy." In the face of increasing allegations of corruption among the a.p.'s (see sub-section E), it established (by its Article 7) that:

> The a.p. must administrate as would a head-of-family [en bon père de famille]. He is accountable before judicial tribunals, as a salaried agent, conforming to the rules of the common law.[44]

We will shortly describe the operation of this head of family "standard" in day-to-day transactions and in the courts.

By a decree of 20 October 1941, CGQJ was centralized bureaucratically to reflect its increasingly dominant role in aryanization.[45] Although we have seen how active the agency was in matters relating to Jewish definition, caselaw, and punition, it is hard to argue with Billig's evaluation that CGQJ's aryanization division eventually became its "most developed service."[46] The constraints placed on a.p. behavior by the early leaders of SCAP gave way to the condoning of more obvious forms of pillage under such Darquier cronies as Lucien Boué, head of the aryanization office. But these developments, too, occurred under color of Vichy laws, decrees, and regulations. On property as on religious definition, on Aryan "trustees" as on the creation of concentration camps, Vichy legalisms either preceded Nazi intervention or directly assisted the Germans to reduce their own manpower needs on racial policy in France.[47]

If there is a difference between property transfer law and the legalized violence we have described in earlier chapters, it relates to the *kind* of collaboration and the *intensity* of the competition that persisted between

---

42 See chapter 4, text at note 137, for Barthélemy's "hesitation" before signing on to this law; see also Marrus and Paxton, *Vichy France and the Jews,* 104.

43 See Sarraute and Tager, *Recueil des textes,* 115–27.

44 Ibid., 63.

45 SCAP and its other aryanization arms were joined to CGQJ's two principal administrative sections. See Billig, *Le Commissariat général,* vol. 1, 77; see also Sarraute and Tager, *Recueil des textes,* 55. Eventually the CGQJ would have eight sections and its own police arm, the "Police aux questions juives."

46 Billig, *Le Commissariat général,* vol. 1, 79.

47 Accord Marrus and Paxton, *Vichy France and the Jews,* 296–97.

the French and the Germans[48] as lucrative Jewish property was made available to Aryan greed. Billig describes the collaborative pillage well in his mandatory volume on the process of aryanization.[49] The Germans realized early that *French legislation* was a necessity if their own pillaging of Jewish property was to be legitimized under international law; in their memorandum of 26 August 1940, they state explicitly that "in order to avoid the appearance of international law violations, the transfer of Jewish enterprises into German hands must seem, to the outside world, as following the norms of private law."[50] The French, who (as we saw) utilized international law to proclaim their own unique jurisdiction over Jewish property in both zones, proved willing to provide laws that gave choice tidbits of Jewish wealth to the Germans as long as big chunks of the carcass were indeed left over for their delectation.

This mutual effort in the elaboration of property transfer laws for the Occupied Zone reached its apex when the French promulgated—exactly a year to the day after their first major aryanization statute—the law of 16 January 1942.[51] The law, designed to facilitate the German imposition on the Jewish community of a "fine" of 1,000,000,000 francs, called upon UGIF to "borrow" 250,000,000 francs, largely to be paid out of aryanized property and blocked Jewish bank accounts. As Billig puts it, "This law is unique in the history of Vichy in that it is explicitly limited to the Occupied Zone and it serves specifically an act of Nazi repression."[52]

Just as the kind of collaborative legislation on property differs in its mutuality from the leapfrogging in the legislative domains of religious definition, so the extent of continuing German interference—even after Vichy had given the occupiers more than what they might have demanded—surpasses what we have seen in earlier chapters. Where the

---

[48] See, e.g., the German ordinance of 9 December 1942, claiming for the Reich property once held in France by "Jews holding or once having held German nationality," a category that they defined very broadly, memorandum, German High Command, 16 January 1943, YV IV-209.

[49] Billig, *Le Commissariat général,* vol. 3, passim.

[50] Ibid.

[51] Sarraute and Tager, *Recueil des textes,* 134.

[52] Billig, *Le Commissariat général,* vol. 3, 112. For complications arising from UGIF's status as a borrower against blocked Jewish accounts, see also chapter 6, section D, and below, notes 94–97.

Germans' bloodlust largely could be satisfied by "letting Vichy do the work" on defining live Jewish prey, when it came to lucre, the rival fortune hunters were often at each others' necks. The Germans might have been more amused than annoyed when Vichy law managed to exceed its own precedents as to the question "Who is a Jew?"; but they could not be quite as dispassionate about wealth.

We proceed to elaborate specific areas of French property law that came into play as aryanization produced legalistic opportunities and dilemmas. As with landlord-tenant law, to which we return to find it overlapping with aryanization, so with other legal sub-categories, the Germans rarely interfered in these internal matters of French doctrine. But we shall see that their greed made them more vocal in responding to property developments than they had been about religious definition.

## C. Landlord-Tenant Law: Commercial Properties

The set of cases we have already treated largely concerned rent payments by *private* Jewish tenants.[53] But what recourse would a Jewish property owner (or tenant) have if French law stripped him of his interest altogether and placed it in the hands of a non-Jewish "trustee"? The Paris Court of Appeals in the *Lapinski* case made clear that property interests—from ownership to leaseholds—could be protected in court *only by Jews who still could claim the interest in their own names.*[54] Yet, increasingly, the whole range of Jewish property interests was being expunged by aryanization laws.

Although Article I, paragraph 3 of the 22 July 1941 law exempted the personal residence and furniture of the Jew from aryanization,[55] a few situations arose in which Jewish tenants—whether or not able to pay

---

[53] See Section A.

[54] *Laporte and Luc vs. Lapinski,* decision of 24 May 1943, reported in the *Gazette du Palais,* 11–13 August 1943. CGQJ characteristically (see chapter 5) complained that the non-administrative courts had no jurisdiction at all over aryanization questions.

[55] Sarraute and Tager, *Recueil des textes,* 62; and p. 97 for the law of 17 November 1941, making clear that only the "personal residence" of the Jew was protected from aryanization. In another law of 17 November 1941, Jews were forbidden to hold property out for lease. See Billig, *Le Commissariat général,* vol. 3, 154. And the question of second homes, etc., was subject to fluctuating perspectives throughout the war; ibid., 154–57.

rent—faced one form or another of aryanization and potential loss of leasehold, furniture, or other possessory interests. One fairly typical case involved a Jewish landlady, Mme. Maxine Kahn, who found her entire building—including the floor on which she had her personal residence!—being sold out from under her by an a.p. She appealed the decision of the CGQJ all the way to the Conseil d'État but (as we often saw in chapter 5) suffered defeat in that court, for:

> It is no longer in question that the laws of 22 July 1941 [etc.]...seek so meticulously the social aryanization of the country that this policy cannot be abandoned under the pretext that the Jewish owner only occupies a part of the building.[56]

Another typical case involved Mrs. Mendelson, who both lived and worked in the rue du Petit-Thouars of the 3e arrondissement. Her case tested whether exceptions under the basic 2 June 1941 definitional statute could be extended to the laws of aryanization. By March 1942, she had fallen behind on her rent payments. Her husband was a prisoner of war in Germany, a status arguably inducing more solicitous treatment of relatives left behind who would otherwise be subject to the religious laws.[57] She managed to continue their small men's clothing business at the address of their domicile, but the business had been aryanized as early as the previous May, under the terms of the 16 January decree. Her a.p. was M. Desplanques of the 18e arrondissement.

Desplanques, although informed of the status of Mr. Mendelson, sold the business's stock and most of Mrs. Mendelson's equipment as well. But when Desplanques and the buyer sought to remove the property, the building's concierge intervened. Her outrage related to the rent arrears, for which she felt the landlord should be entitled to a claim against the business's property. She did not want anything taken out of the building.

---

[56] Conseil d'État, litigation bureau, decision 831-LG, no. 73-768, AN $AJ^{38}$, 593. Accord, CGQJ memorandum, 24 June 1942, distinguishing Jewish buildings mostly used for rental purposes (but in which the landlord continued to maintain his residence)—that would be sold in their entirety—from such dwellings virtually entirely occupied only by the Jew, which would not usually be sold, CDJC CXI-37.

[57] The law of 2 June 1941 set up by its Article 7 a temporary exception for the family of prisoners of war, an exception that was to terminate two months after the release of the prisoner.

Desplanques desisted, and sought the aid of the courts, who appointed a referee, Georges Hereil of the rue de Savoie.

Meanwhile, Mrs. Mendelson asked that some of the business equipment be safeguarded for her. Could she not at least keep her sewing machine, a few tables, and some irons? UGIF took up her case and wrote to the CGQJ "to intervene with the a.p.,"[58] wishing to have it stressed that the law of 2 June 1941 excepted from its rigors the families of prisoners of war. UGIF at this stage seemed to feel that that Article 7 exception to the general religious statute might also be applicable to the *aryanization* statute of 22 July 1941.

CGQJ's regional director in Nice had already asked the agency, on 26 March 1942, whether Article 8 of the 2 June statute—excepting those families of vieille souche—worked to exempt such Jews from the aryanization laws. The Nice office elaborated:

> [A] fabric manufacturer from the free zone has a sword of Damocles hanging over his head because of [the law of 22 July]. He has experienced current prejudice and a status that, although only potential, is nonetheless real. What can he do?[59]

In its legalistic and niggardly way, CGQJ quickly burst this bubble. Unarguably, the 2 June statute's dérogations (or exceptions) had not explicitly been extended to the later statute, which literally excepted only the Jew's personal domicile and no category of Jew per se. On 22 April 1942, CGQJ pointed this out in the *Leman Schwab* matter. Schwab contended that, since his son was a prisoner of war in Germany, he should not have lost his real estate brokerage business until the boy was released. No! The a.p. was properly assigned to Schwab's business because the exception to the 2 June statute did not become an "exemption" to the 22 July law.

UGIF, which used the prisoner of war argument to try to help in arrest as well as aryanization cases,[60] persisted in trying to link the statutes, at least for awhile. On 4 May 1942, they wrote on behalf of a certain Rapoport, whose imprisoned son "is to get his hardware business upon

---

[58] Correspondence, 28 March and 6 April 1942, CDJC CDXXIX-1.

[59] CDJC CXV-19.

[60] On 31 July 1942, for example, UGIF represented a child, Bernard Pejsachowicz, in an attempt to have his mother freed from Drancy. She had just been arrested, although the child "pointed out that his father was a prisoner of war," CDJC CDXXIX-18.

his return."[61] Was the a.p. properly assigned in such a situation? It took some time for UGIF to realize that the statutory linkage argument was futile, and that immunization to the 22 July 1941 law—arbitrarily assigned in the absence of statutory direction—was to be even scarcer than under the 2 June statute.[62]

Occasionally, Aryan landlords or their employees would petition UGIF for help with Jewish tenants.[63] So M. Moreau—an architect by training and also the landlord's agent for an apartment building in the rue Neuve des Boulets—wrote to UGIF urging their aid for his employer. Two Jewish tenants "are gone," he reports, and their rents remain due. M. Sybulski had been a tailor on the building's main floor; Mrs. Peczenik was a non business-related tenant. Her tenancy, of course, was purely a private affair; M. Sybulski's, though, had been aryanized.

Moreau received no satisfaction from Sybulski's a.p., M. Quercy. The latter felt that there was nothing left of the tailor shop to sell. Could UGIF pay the arrears, he asks, "to preserve for your co-religionists the enjoyment of the premises upon their return?" UGIF responds politely that they have no capacity to help directly, but that perhaps Quercy should proceed to dissolve the lease.[64]

Dissolutions of commercial Jewish leaseholds were by then common practice. Only the modalities and consequences of dissolution remained. How might the landlord's interests be "guarantied," for example, against the risks of the commercial market place in wartime Paris? So, in late 1942, a lawyer in the Parisian Public Assistance Office asked CGQJ if the former Jewish business, now in the hands of an a.p., could in fact act as guarantor of the rents until a subsequent tenant was found and proven viable? After all, this would be common practice in commercial leasehold situations were it not for the racial element. No!, contests the CGQJ legal

---

[61] CDJC CDXXIX-1.

[62] Billig, *Le Commissariat géneral,* vol. 3, 234.

[63] See, e.g., the *Opatowski* matter, memo, 11 September 1942, CDJC CDXXIX-1; the *Rodier* matter, memo, 14 September 1942, ibid.; the *Ocherowitz* matter, memo, 17 January 1944, ibid.; the *Farouche* matter, memo, 17 March 1944, ibid.

[64] Correspondence, 30 June and 2 July 1943, CDJC CDXXIX-1. Compare a request to UGIF, very late in the war, by a Parisian architect representing a landlord's demand for back rent in the *Pitkowski* matter, Lambla de Sarria to UGIF, 30 June 1944, CDJC CDXXIX-1.

office, with impeccable aryanization logic; even if the lease has a clause to that effect, it is unenforceable in a.p. cases:

> Although the sale [of a lease by an a.p.] has the appearance of a voluntary transaction, it is closer to an expropriation; it is not a case of voluntary termination but rather of forced sale, in which the Jew is not intervening, because he is stripped of his rights and of all correlative responsibilities. Since the Jew cannot stand as surety, it appears that the boilerplate clause of guaranty is without force both for the original and subsequent lessee, the latter now solely responsible to the landlord for the payment of rents.[65]

CGQJ suggests that the a.p. seek a common law remedy here—court approval to substitute another guarantor.

Despite the detrimental effect of aryanization upon its clientèle, UGIF occasionally would be in the unusual position of *requesting* appointment of an a.p. for Jewish property! During the winter of 1942, Mrs. Rosenstein of Nancy requested assistance in receiving a considerable monthly rental on her former house there. Apparently, she had sold the property but retained a life estate that was to pay her in excess of 16,000 francs every month—income largely derived from those rents. UGIF wrote CGQJ, which promised "an inquiry" to be conducted by the prefect of the Meurthe and Moselle district.[66]

Such a route, although fraught with risk, was by then the only one to follow. The CGQJ had already enunciated a quasi-official policy that Aryan tenants of Jewish landlords should simply cease paying their rents, unless there was an Aryan agent of the landlord in place. Otherwise, no rents were to be paid until an a.p. was installed as manager of the Jewish property.[67]

Many aryanized tenancies left open the question of furniture or other personal belongings. Parisian police decrees of June and July 1941 forbade all relocation of such property from Jewish apartments in the Occupied Zone to new residences taken by tenants who might have fled to the south, although as time went on it became clear that the southern

---

[65] CGQJ memorandum, 11 November 1942, AN $AJ^{38}$, 118.

[66] Correspondence, 18 February, 12 March and 16 March 1942, CDJC CDXXIX-1. For another case involving an a.p. for a Jewish landlord, here asked to give a rent reduction to a Jewish tenant, see *Fostel v Cérèze* (3^e^ arrondissement, Justice of the Peace), 2 July 1942, CDJC CDXXIX-2.

[67] Memorandum, 8 July 1941, AN $AJ^{38}$, 118.

zone was no safe harbor for such possessions anyway.[68] The press ran notices that such furniture could be sold, on the other hand, but only upon friendly or judicial termination of the Jew's leasehold and then only for payment of back rent to Aryan landlords or of arrears in utility payments or taxes.[69] Later, seizure of Jewish furniture was also permitted when, as in the matter of *Blum and Weill*—shop merchants—Aryan landlords were happy to repossess, and Aryan a.p.'s feared that the Germans would seize the furniture first if it was not relocated.[70] In such cases, the absent Jewish tenants' furniture might be removed and stored, a list of its contents registered with the local police.[71]

However, the fate of Jewish furniture kept in storage during the war was by no means secure. Thus Mme. Feldstein, domiciled in 1942 in an Aryan friend's 16[e] arrondissement apartment, reported to UGIF that she would like to take there her own property, which had been in storage. Unfortunately, she found that the storage company had "lost half of it." Furthermore, the storage people would "denounce" her if she filed a claim for the missing half.[72]

Dealings with the Germans about Jewish furniture sometimes led to happier results. In an interesting case, reflecting German solicitude for some nations' protection of their own Jewish nationals, the Swiss were again involved.[73] Mrs. Marckus lived in Paris with her three children, all German nationals. Her mother and sister, Swiss nationals, resided with them. In the summer and fall 1942, she and her children were arrested and deported; the remaining two women, both named Brunschweig, lived under Swiss protection in the same domicile. The Swiss also gave their permission to UGIF to lodge two French Jewish women in the same apartment.

---

[68] By November 1943, so many Jews had disappeared that the furniture in their empty domiciles all over France became ripe for pillage. Thus the CGQJ regional director wrote in his monthly report for that period: "Given the increasing frequency of arrests of Jews, it would be worthwhile to find out if it is necessary to name a.p.'s for the possessions in their apartments that have been left vacant and placed under seal," CDJC XVII-10 (37).

[69] Notice, 22 July 1941, AN $AJ^{38}$, 118.

[70] UGIF correspondence, 23 and 27 April 1943, CDJC CDXXIX-1.

[71] Ibid.

[72] UGIF memorandum, 24 June 1942, CDJC CDXXIX-1.

[73] See also chapter 6, text at notes 93 and 149.

In February 1943, the Brunschweigs were repatriated safely to Switzerland. The authorities now moved to take away the furniture that remained, claiming it belonged to the Marckus's. UGIF intervention with the German authorities led to an agreement that the furniture could be picked up from storage in Montbéliard—where it had been held pending resolution of the matter—and returned to the Paris apartment.[74]

Where a powerful neutral state was not involved, of course, Jewish belongings of the most personal kind would often remain in Aryan hands. Thus, André Thielen of Reims wrote the CGQJ as follows:

> Sirs. I would be much obliged if you could let me know to whom must be made a declaration about property belonging to persons of the Jewish race but held by a third person. In fact, my parents now have in their attic a baby carriage that had been left with them by a person of the Jewish race, Mme. Simon Lévy, of whom there is absolutely no news since the exodus of June 1940. Since my wife is now about to have a baby, I would like to know if I can use this carriage, because these are now rare and particularly expensive. I would not like to do this, of course, without assurance that no proceeding of any kind will later be initiated against me.[75]

Perhaps, as to furniture, the best plan would be to remove the belongings from the Occupied Zone altogether. Although inter-zonal transfers not involving changes of ownership were not permitted, the legal situation might be different if the furniture was being sold or given away. Thus a Jewish engineer named Lehman asked UGIF if he could send some of the furniture from his own 17$^{e}$ arrondissement apartment to his son, now living in Nice. Lehman considered his son (perhaps inaccurately) to be "Non-Jewish, because he had two Aryan grandparents." UGIF replied that, in any case, no German ordinance precluded the sale of non-aryanized Jewish property, if the sale would not bring proceeds of more than 15,000 francs monthly.[76] So UGIF concluded that a transfer, tantamount to a gift, of such furniture would not be prohibited.

---

[74] UGIF memorandum, 24 September 1943, CDJC CDXXIX-1.

[75] AN AJ$^{38}$, 118.

[76] UGIF cites here the German fourth ordinance, erroneously dated 28 February 1941, but in fact dated 28 *May,* for which see Sarraute and Tager, *Recueil des textes,* 48; *Lehmann* matter, memorandum, 20 February 1943, CDJC CDXXIX-1.

Yet a Jew making this kind of transfer had to be very careful to abide closely to the statutory valuation above which sales would become unlawful. The sad case of tailor Lazare Gorodetzki indicates that *criminal* penalties descended on businessmen failing to abide by the letter of the law on aryanization. Gorodetzki had failed to list his sewing machine and tables when he registered as a Jew under the law of 2 June 1941.[77] In April 1942, he was indicted for this infraction, despite the relatively small value of his meagre business equipment. This incident encouraged an official in the Conseil d'État to ask CGQJ if property of negligible value, left undeclared, might lead to its owner's arrest.[78]

In fact, commercial leaseholds and businesses were being aryanized at every level of identifiable net worth and gross income,[79] and in numbers that must have taxed the emerging Vichy aryanization bureaucracy.[80] In their race against the Germans for Jewish lucre, the French further benefitted from the concomitant pace of roundups and arrests in 1941 and 1942. Indeed, the harsh fact of increased deportation only strengthened the flow of aryanizations of Jewish homes, tenancies, and businesses during the Vichy years. With a dead or imprisoned Jew incapable of asserting rights against the pillage, or with surviving family either legally incompetent to stand in their loved one's stead or too impoverished or demoralized to try to do so, aryanization proceeded apace.

Many of the individualized 5x8-inch sheets of paper devoted by SCAP to each aryanized business took casual note of the extreme penalty for being Jewish; so, on 19 May 1941, Salomon Lerner's business was turned over to an a.p. with the notation, "absent since 14 May 1941 after having been taken to police headquarters. Must be in a concentration camp."[81] Sometimes detailed descriptions of the fate of such businesses during aryanization are noted by the agency:

---

[77] The census law of that date required, in its Article I, a declaration including "the condition of the belongings" of the registering Jew, Sarraute and Tager, *Recueil des textes,* 53. See also chapter 5, note 33.

[78] Correspondence, March and April 1942, AN $AJ^{38}$ 118.

[79] AN $AJ^{38}$, 528; a.p. 5x8-inch slips indicate interest in such enterprises as Henri Polak's watch and jewelry business in the Faubourg Montmartre (with stock in hand valued at 200,000 francs), to the more representative 20,000-franc annual income brought in by straw wholesaler J. Guggenheim on the rue Lafayette.

[80] See above, note 37.

[81] AN $AJ^{38}$, 528, "A.P."

*WAYNTRAUB,* Israel, 56 rue du Temple. small craftsman. 3 Aryan and 3 Jewish employees. Gross income: 435,000 francs. Merchandise in stock: 15,000. A.P. or no: No. Seals[82] affixed or no: No. Observations: Interned in a concentration camp—business continued by his wife.

Signed: Paris, May 20, 1941. Provisional administrator, Jacques Dupuis.[83]

Nearing the end of the war, aryanization policy involving real property seemed to have softened not one whit. Even the exception to the 22 July 1941 law that Joseph Barthélemy claims to have authored—that involving Jewish private domiciles[84]—did not hold firm. Thus the brother and sister Marx family, from the town of St.-Dié (Vosges), wrote to UGIF on 3 June 1944 that their family home had been aryanized by M. René Metz, who in turn sold it from underneath them to M. Wackenhalter. Amazed at the process, and strongly unwilling to ratify it by any action, the Marx's nonetheless found themselves forced to accept a leaseback from Wackenhalter or else to be evicted. When Wackenhalter's lawyer refused to enter a provision in the lease asserting the Marx's protest to the sale of the house in the first place, the brother and sister asked UGIF for advice. So late in the war, and with the tide turning, UGIF answered that formally they must write to the CGQJ but that "it might be better if you do nothing."[85]

---

[82] The affixing of seals on apartments, homes, and businesses was a common practice affording both the French and German authorities some security and some time in dealing with the enclosed contents. Dozens of individual questions arose as to the legalities connected with the sealing of Jewish properties. For example, if a Jewish tenant continued to pay rent even though her apartment had been sealed, could she be assured that it would not be leased to a new, Aryan tenant before she could re-possess?, UGIF memorandum, 21 March 1943, CDJC CDXXIX-1. If an Aryan had leased a piano to a Jew before the war and now wished to repossess—but the apartment is under seal—may he unseal and take back the piano?; on this latter question, CGQJ answered affirmatively in a memo, 10 November 1942, despite prewar laws relating to the Code of Civil Procedure, Section 909 that seemed to disallow such a practice, AN $AJ^{38}$, 127. If an Aryan had just purchased a fabrics business from a Jew and herself possessed a certificat de non-appartenance à la race juive, did the French authorities nonetheless have the right to seal the business pending further investigation of Jewish influence?, Mlle. le Bars, Dinard, to UGIF, 12 March 1942, CDJC CDXXIX-1, complaining that her newly-acquired business was under seal and that repeated inquiries to CGQJ had not yielded any answer as to why.

[83] AN $AJ^{38}$, 528.

[84] See above, note 40.

[85] Correspondence, 3 and 9 June 1944, CDJC CDXXIX-1.

To be Jewish in wartime France was to be unsure of the ground underneath one's feet. Aryanization was a legalized process that affected all forms of real property ownership; it affected any personality attached to real property that might be deemed "Jewish." It shut you out of your apartment or your business or your home. It introduced you to "trustees" who were suddenly in charge of your domicile, your enterprise, your sewing machine, your stock-in-trade. And, when you went outside the domain that you once thought was yours, you were in for further shocks.

## D. Regulating the Economy, Subject by Subject

Real property and its contents, business leaseholds and their accompanying equipment and stock—these were not the only kinds of Jewish property rights to be compromised by Vichy law. As aryanization continued, and as the economic burdens placed on the Jewish community in France increased, almost every area of French law became infected with racial bias. The purpose of this section is by no means to bring exhaustive treatment to any given legal subject;[86] rather, I intend to flag the many marketplace arenas affected by such laws and to exemplify each by at least one real case.

### 1. Banking

The first non-governmental or non-media related career path banned by Vichy statute writers to the Jews was that of banking.[87] Conversely, one of Vichy's top functionaries for economic aryanization—Regelsperger—was chosen from the ranks of the Bank of France.[88] The banking industry participated in aryanization more generally, distinguishing itself as one of the few professions that *anticipated* the promulgation of laws by instituting anti-Jewish policies *avant la lettre*. Hence, on 23 May

---

[86] As in the area of real property law, Joseph Billig, *Le Commissariat général*, particularly vol. 3, remains mandatory reading for the issues discussed in this section.

[87] 2 June 1941, Article 5. Sarraute and Tager, *Recueil des textes*, 50. There was preliminary confusion among bankers as to whether this law meant that even Jewish bank tellers had to be dismissed, AN $AJ^{38}$, 58.

[88] Billig, *Le Commissariat général*, vol. 3, 103.

1941, the following "Circular of the Association of Bankers" was published:

> By letter dated 21 May, I am informed by the head of the Banking Oversight Office that, according to information he received from the German Military Command, that administration is about to issue an ordinance under which Jews and Jewish companies will retain only limited withdrawal rights at their banks. It is envisioned that only amounts absolutely necessary for subsistence will be withdrawable.
>
> The Oversight Office asks me to let you know this immediately and to inform you that you must act accordingly as of this notice, even if the projected ordinance has not yet been promulgated. In this regard, the Office calls our attention to the second ordinance against the Jews of 18 October 1940, where the 4th paragraph states that any legal stipulation dealing with Jewish property (individual or corporate) can be annulled.[89]

This remarkable document, although in fact followed quickly by a German ordinance that deals indirectly with banks,[90] was cited by French courts for the next few months as authoritatively regulating the blockage of Jewish deposits. The sources of its authority to do so are both articulated and sanctioned in two decisions of a Parisian court, one *permitting* and the other *blocking* the withdrawal by Jews of money to which they were otherwise entitled. In the first decision, the Tribunal civil de la Seine expressly legitimated the internal memorandum blocking Jewish accounts but at the same time sustained the prayer of a small Jewish depositor:

> the ordinance of 22 July 1940 of the occupying authorities has created a Banking Oversight Office in the Occupied Zone, specifying that banks will be required to follow the instructions of that Office.
>
> [The May instructions] constitute an act by the occupying authorities that is binding on banks placed under its control.

---

[89] Sarraute and Tager, *Recueil des textes,* 47. The bankers' citation to Article 4 of the German ordinance of 18 October 1940, is correct, ibid., 25. On the curious *ex ante* imposition of this French view of forthcoming German regulations, accord, Jacques Adler, *The Jews of Paris and the Final Solution* (New York: Oxford U. Press, 1987), 22.

[90] See the fourth ordinance of 28 May 1941, which on its terms prohibits transfers of debt, letters of credit, etc., but does not directly block bank accounts. Sarraute and Tager, *Recueil des textes,* 47. For a superb treatment of the limited rights enjoyed by Jews on occasion to maintain some activity in their bank accounts, both in the Occupied and Unoccupied Zones, see Billig, *Le Commissariat général,* vol. 3, 109–10.

> Since, in this case, Mr. C. asks to withdraw the sum of 8,000 francs; he is the father of four; he receives nothing from his trade; so the requested withdrawal falls within the letter's instructions and is necessary to the existence of his family.[91]

In the same tribunal's later decision, however, the bankers' understanding that the industry need no longer recognize any legal or contractual barrier to the blockage of Jewish accounts was recognized. Thus on 23 October 1941, the tribunal, citing Article 4 of the German ordinance of 18 October 1940,[92] permits the bankers to disregard any prior legal or contractual constraint upon them in its dealings with Jewish clients. So the Revels, a Jewish couple who had received a loan *in 1934* from the Crédit foncier for 2.8 million francs, were denied their right to draw down 600,000 francs of the loan. Their only recourse, according to the court, would be by letter to the German authorities.[93]

By the end of 1941, the focusing event of the Germans' 1,000,000,000-franc fine against the Jewish community brought greater statutory "regularity" to the problem of blocked Jewish bank accounts.[94] Hence, German ordinances of 17 and 22 December 1941[95] and the French law of 16 January 1942,[96] sharply restricted Jewish withdrawals from banks and furthermore permitted blockage towards the payment of the communal fine of at least 50% of existing accounts. This amount would

---

[91] Decision of 31 May 1941, Tribunal civil de la Seine, published 18 September 1941, YV IV-210. The fatal combination of aryanization of a business, blockage of a bank account, and inability to pay rent was quite common and—in the comparable *Bercovici* matter—combined with the breadwinner's arrest and detention in "Dortoir 7" at Drancy, CDJC CDXXIX-1. The Red Cross, on Bercovici's behalf, wrote on 18 May 1942 to UGIF, asking if his bank account could be unblocked to pay his rental arrears of 4636 francs. His business had been sold by the a.p., and his sickly wife and two teenage children were "without resources." Even after such decisions as the one in the principal case noted here, UGIF could only recommend that Bercovici write to CGQJ [!] for permission to have part of his bank account unblocked to pay the landlord.

[92] See note 89.

[93] AN $AJ^{38}$, 596.

[94] See text at notes 51. For an account of the cause-and-effect relation between this fine and blocked bank accounts, see also Adler, *The Jews of Paris,* 25–26. Adler observes that the fine "was finally paid by 15 April 1942."

[95] Sarraute and Tager, *Recueil des textes,* 107–109.

[96] Ibid., 134.

be automatically blocked, quite apart from the individual or corporate need of the depositor. As Article 7 of the latter French law put it:

> Every bank can participate in the procedures dictated by the present law, any legal or contractual barriers to the contrary notwithstanding.[97]

Catastrophic results multiplied rapidly. Thus Georges Paraf, an elderly Parisian bachelor of limited means who had hitherto in part cared for his two siblings and himself, wrote to the CGQJ a mere ten days after promulgation of the French law:

> On 2 January 1942, my savings account had 20,000 francs. Due to the regulations in effect, 10,000 francs have been removed. I thus have 10,000 francs at my disposal. Besides a modest pension of 480 francs, I have nothing except those 10,000 francs. Can my case, in view of the extreme modesty of my means, be reconsidered?[98]

Apparently unanswered, Paraf sought solace from UGIF (whose office, as we should recall, the 16 January law made responsible for borrowing one-fourth of the billion francs and depositing that sum in a special account, the "caisse des dépots et consignes"); the agency held out little hope, however, that even such small accounts could be unblocked.[99]

Blockage was a fact of life, affecting all Jews and Jewish companies, great and small. By October 1941, the CGQJ had established the official policy that accounts would not be unblocked merely because the Jewish owner had himself (or, in the case of a company, itself) relocated to the Unoccupied Zone.[100] Debtors were to pay their Jewish creditors not personally but only into the latters' blocked bank accounts.[101] Jewish

---

[97] Ibid.

[98] Letter of 27 January 1942, CDJC CDXXIX-1.

[99] Ibid., letter to Paraf, 5 March 1942. By September 1942, UGIF estimated to CGQJ that in excess of *60%* of the average bank account had already been turned over to the Caisse des dépots et consignes, André Baur to Darquier de Pellepoix, 18 September 1942, YV 09-40c-3.

[100] Financial Bureau memo, 11 October 1941, AN $AJ^{38}$, 596.

[101] De Faramond, memorandum, 27 September 1941, AN $AJ^{38}$, 594. Accord, a few months later, the CGQJ's response to an inquiry about a Jewish doctor: if still practicing, he can be paid directly, but if prevented from doing so and owed more than 1000 francs, the doctor can only be paid into a blocked account and the payment must be reported to the agency's financial bureau, AN $AJ^{38}$, 596.

employees, now fired but still owed back wages or commissions, were to be compensated by indirect payments to such blocked accounts.[102]

Meanwhile, by Darquier de Pellepoix's hand, Vichy at its highest level announced an additional "fine" on the beleaguered Jewish community throughout France. Using the law of 29 November 1941 that had created UGIF, Vichy declared by a decree of 28 August 1942 that it was incumbent on the Jewish community to pay—mostly from already blocked bank accounts—or to give voluntarily [!] a monthly sum totalling 6,000,000 francs to support the organization and its increasing responsibilities.[103] UGIF's considered response to the new decree mixed amazement with concern, wondering how such a sum could be raised rapidly and then in each successive month and finally suggesting that every Jew above the age of eighteen be "taxed" 120 francs annually and that 5% of every withdrawal from a blocked account go towards the payment of the newly announced obligation.[104]

## 2. Corporate Law

As we shall see in greater detail in chapter 8, Vichy's religious laws became part of many a legal practice as lawyers performed the various tasks associated with representation of corporate clients. Jews were dispossessed, by Article 3 of the basic Vichy law of 22 July 1941, of

---

[102] Ibid., memo, 20 March 1942.

[103] UGIF memorandum, 10 September 1942, attaching the decree which was published in the *Journal officiel* of 5 September, YV 09-28. For the decree itself, see Sarraute and Tager, *Recueil des textes,* 166. The monthly figure is considerably in excess of UGIF's monthly expenses, deemed by the agency to have risen in March to 771,662 francs, minutes, 15 April 1942 meeting of UGIF Finance Committee, YV 09-28. It is possible that the authorities envisioned—as specifically flagged during UGIF's 15 April committee meeting—that UGIF "repay" the eighteen wealthy owners of blocked accounts and vaults who had "loaned" them 250,000,000 francs under the terms of the law of 16 January 1942. Furthermore, as suggested by Marrus and Paxton, UGIF may have borrowed considerably more towards repayment of the 1,000,000,000-franc fine; their creditors may well have included Aryan bankers themselves, encouraged to loan the agency money by which to pay the huge fine. These bankers received back amounts from the largest Jewish blocked accounts. But they, and the creditors of Jewish depositors, now might demand from UGIF both interest and principal still due. See generally Marrus and Paxton, *Vichy France,* 111.

[104] Baur to Darquier, memorandum, 18 September 1942, YV 09-40c-3.

their corporate ownership of Jewish "enterprises" defined in Article 1 of the same law:

> The a.p. enjoys the fullest administrative and dispositive rights, and from the moment of his nomination, he exercises them instead and in place of the named owners of any rights or shares, or of their agents; and, in a company, in place of any proxy or partner, with or without their agreement.[105]

Except for certain businesses, "serving only a Jewish clientèle,"[106] the a.p.'s powers extended to complete sale of the Jewish-owned corporations or partnerships, as long as the statutory requirement (under Article 14) of approval by the CGQJ had been met; in many cases in the Occupied Zone, German ratification was also required. Jointly-held property as between Jewish and non-Jewish co-tenants could be divided and redistributed separately, whether or not an a.p. had been appointed over the Jewish co-tenancy.[107]

Questions occasionally arose as to whether a given corporation was, in fact, "Jewish." In the Occupied Zone, a note from the Barclay's Bank in France to one of its clients indicates both one way of determining such ownership and the consequences of such a decision not only upon an a.p. but upon the business' suppliers of goods and services:

> 29 October, 1941, to the
> Atlantic Express Co., 7 Boulevard
> des Capucines, Paris
>
> Sirs, Given recent instructions from the CGQJ, we must ask you to have signed by M. Ch. F. Lacomme, agent, the attached declaration, which we ask you to send back to us by return mail. This formality must be completed rapidly, so that any obstacle to the smooth running of your account can be avoided.[108]

Bankers and others were instructed on the role of Jewish shareholders or partners in businesses that were predominantly Aryan-owned. The same October that saw the Barclays Bank and their competitors

---

[105] Sarraute and Tager, *Recueil des textes,* 63.

[106] See chapter 6, note 171.

[107] 22 July 1941, Article 20.

[108] Correspondence, Barclays Bank letterhead, YV 09/28. Barclays was one of the main banks at which the *Germans* maintained an account carrying the proceeds of sales of property of certain Jewish foreign nationals with holdings in the Occupied Zone.

frenetically moving to block Jewish corporate accounts found the CGQJ informing the President of the Professional Banking Association that:

> Jews in no manner may exercise their right to vote relating to ownership of shares in corporations or to partnership interests they may already own.[109]

Whether Jewish or Aryan, corporations needed to find out how voting on basic corporate matters could proceed in the face of Jewish ownership of shares. A variety of situations arose, including that of majority Jewish shareholders who had fled the Occupied Zone with their corporate shares in hand. By mid-1943, this eventuality had been resolved by the CGQJ; in the case of a large company about to be sold to or swallowed up by an even larger French corporation but stymied by the continued existence of Jewish shares that had been taken south, the agency simply instructed the company's a.p. to annul the Jewish shares and reissue to Aryans the same shares of stock, exhibiting the identical share numbers.[110] In another common scenario, banks dutifully blocking the use of safety deposit boxes to their Jewish clients effectively immobilized many Aryan corporations whose occasional company business required presentation of documents preserved in such bank vaults. For beleaguered Jews in particular, against whom nothing explicit in the new laws worked to prevent the mere collection of stock dividends, the inability to clip coupons that were blocked in these boxes was especially grievous.[111]

There were some odd rules, too. Although Jewish corporate shareholders usually had to sell off their shares, often through the mediation of an a.p., it was not clear that individual Jews lost all capacity to serve on corporate boards of governors. CGQJ's litigation department in fact noted that companies capitalized by less than 33% of Jewish money could retain the services of Jewish board members unless otherwise prohibited by law.[112] Furthermore, until shares were officially sold, Jews had the right (if they could gain access to corporate coupons) to receive dividends from them and even to take such income—but not the shares—

---

[109] Letter from Financial Office of the CGQJ, 9 October 1941, AN AJ[38], 594.

[110] See Billig, *Le Commissariat général,* vol. 3, 135.

[111] UGIF memo to German High Command, 20 April 1942, CDJC CDXXXIX-1. For similar corporate matters, as assisted by private lawyers during Vichy, see chapter 8.

[112] AN AJ[38], 592.

to the Unoccupied Zone.[113] This constituted one of the few areas where Vichy authorities did not scrupulously track down—often with the help of a.p.'s appointed in the Unoccupied Zone for the specific task—transferred Jewish wealth.[114]

As we turn, however, from corporate law to the law of gratuitous transfers, we shall find that oddities in the law of property under Vichy generally worked against Jews. Any conceivable exercise of Jewish influence over wealth was to be monitored and scrupulously barred in advance. For gifts and legacies, even if the destined owner were clearly Aryan, the authorities often refused such traditional means of wealth transfers.

## 3. Gratuitous Transfers

### a. Gifts *Inter Vivos*

Suppose a Jewish property owner wanted to give the property away to his Aryan spouse or children? Whether as an obvious device to avoid the a.p., or as a natural part of the life cycles of a family, such proposed transactions fell under Vichy scrutiny. A poignant case raising once again the name of Pierre Masse, one of France's most distinguished lawyers,[115] involved an attempt by his Aryan wife to unblock his account at the Banque Comptoir d'Escompte. The occasion, in early 1942, was the marriage of their son. Masse wished to give the boy a wedding present of 500,000 francs, and his wife formally petitioned Vichy to that end. No! responded CGQJ's litigation department: the German ordinances of 28 May and 12 December 1941 prohibit such a transfer.[116]

The department's refusal demonstrates that gray areas worked for the most part against either a Jewish interest or that of an Aryan (like Mrs. Masse or her son) seeking a benefit from Jewish property. Neither of the cited German ordinances *specifically* related to gifts; both permitted

---

[113] De Faramond of SCAP, memorandum, 5 May 1941, AN $AJ^{38}$, 594.

[114] See correspondence, litigation section, CGQJ, 31 July 1942; correspondence with the Interior Minister, 18 June 1942, citing the problem of Jews fleeing the Unoccupied Zone with wealth, sometimes derived from the proceeds of sale of corporate or real property, CDJC CXI-36.

[115] See chapter 3, notes 41–44.

[116] Memo, 16 March 1942, reply to Mrs. Masse's request of 6 February 1942, AN $AJ^{38}$ 593.

exceptions to be made from prohibitions upon "transfer to another place."[117] Yet Mrs. Masse, acting for her arrested husband, found no relief.

On the other hand, such a gift might have been allowed if it were for the basic necessities of "starting out in life" for the married couple.[118] In the Unoccupied Zone, gifts were usually allowed from Jewish parents to Aryan children, as long as no reversionary rights were preserved by the donor.[119] Such inter-familial gifts became one of the few areas where property transfers might be made relatively free of administrative control or a.p.; even in the Occupied Zone, as we have just noted, special permission could be given and often was, even for gifts of real property, but never for corporate property.[120]

Race-related property law, now sorting itself in various sub-divisions, became an active part of many private legal practices. The complexities of gift law appealed to the bar, because they might do some small good for a Jewish client otherwise everywhere persecuted and because—hard though it might be to succeed— gray areas did exist. So, in the matter of "my Jewish client, French for many generations," lawyer Paul Scapel of Marseilles asked the CGQJ if the Parisian client's gift to various national museums of valuable artwork might be completed. Stored in crates, the gift had not been delivered, and the client feared aryanization of the artwork. Scapel advocated his client's interests well by adding the following facts:

---

[117] The earlier ordinance, as we have seen, aside from excepting 15,000 francs a month from the rule of non-transfer, also permitted SCAP to take a case-by-case approach to such requests, Sarraute and Tager, *Recueil des textes,* 48. The later one, that seems more applicable to gifts, permitted exceptions to be made by the Service du contrôle, ibid., 107.

[118] Ibid.

[119] CGQJ to notary M. Henri Fargeat of Thizy, 11 March 1942, AN AJ[38], 127. The operative consideration was always whether there was "complete elimination of Jewish influence" over the property; hence gifts to fully emancipated adult children were often permitted after application for approval to the CGQJ, CGQJ memo, 20 May 1943, AN AJ[38], 592.

[120] Ibid.; see also YV 09/94 ("Spoiliation" file), stating analogously that "the law of 2 November 1941 intends to perfect legislation by prohibiting all acquisition of corporate or business property by Jews, unless so authorized [by the prefecture]. This prohibition is imposed not only on sales of corporate property but also as to gifts."

> I call upon your services so that I may give my client an answer. I have found no answer to his question in any legal publication that I have received. I add that the case of this client is unique, because as the war was starting, he lost his wife—herself 100% Aryan—and hence became the legal guardian of these collections that were part of the community property that had not yet been liquidated.[121]

Lawyer Scapel's additional information would hardly have clarified the legal issues involved, however, as we are about to see in our next two sub-sections.

### b. Legacies or Intestate Property

What happened when a Jew died, either intestate or specifically attempting to leave property either to other Jews or to Aryans? The CGQJ interpreted the 22 July 1941 Vichy law to set forth the following rules, which we have seen reflected already in the decision of bankers as to whether to release funds held on account of deceased Jewish clients for the satisfaction of death transfers[122]:

1. Aryans can take such property;
2. Jewish legatees cannot,[123] but instead the gift ordinarily must be handed over to an a.p.;
3. these rules are exclusively derived from French law, and no German laws contravene them;
4. they apply in both zones.[124]

What if a non-Jew attempted to leave property by will to a Jew? Although sophisticated estate planning techniques would of course in most

---

[121] Letter, 30 August 1941, CDJC CXIV-50.

[122] For more on legacies, see chapter 8 (C)(3)(b).

[123] An exception we have dealt with, for the personal residence of the Jew, extended to permitting him to leave that property to "his ancestors or heirs," Law of 22 July 1941, Article I, paragraph 3 as amended by the law of 17 November 1941, Sarraute and Tager, *Recueil des textes,* 62. A seemingly liberal interpretation of this exception was given by none other than Xavier Vallat in a letter to a woman from Montpellier, dated 2 March 1942, who had asked the CGQJ whether she could leave her family house to her *niece,* a mixed-heritage Jew who had herself married a Jew. "There is nothing in the present state of the law," responds Vallat, "to keep a Jewess from receiving a house by will," AN $AJ^{38}$, 127.

[124] Letter from agency in reference to the Leopold Weill estate to a Valency notary, Adrien Plat, AN $AJ^{38}$ 127.

cases have limited such situations to a handful, some cases did arise. Thus, Robert Castille, a Parisian lawyer, inquired of the CGQJ on behalf of a corporate client that found 30,000 of its shares descending to a Jewish legatee of its former CEO, M. Maldant. Apparently, the recently deceased CEO left his shares to M. Weyler, causing the Gnome and Rhone Motor Company some distress, because they wished to be acquired by prominent industrialists who needed clarification of the company's ownership. Writes lawyer Castille:

> The buyers wish to know the status of Paul Louis Weyler, both as to his person and his property, and also want to know by what method they can acquire [the business].[125]

CGQJ responds:

> Cher Maître. In response to your request for information concerning the shares of Gnome and Rhone Motor Company..., I am pleased to tell you that the surrender of these shares has caused no difficulty. In fact, M. Weyler has been stripped of his property by the French Government, and the company through this fact has become aryanized.[126]

In a few parallel situations, Americans became involved. Vichy chose to exempt from the usual aryanization rules a bequest to an American Jew; CGQJ answered on behalf of the foreign minister an inquiry from the United States:

> If the decedent is not Jewish, the Jewish beneficiary finding himself abroad can profit from reciprocal agreements just as if he were not Jewish.[127]

The agency hastened to observe that if the testator were Jewish, the decision would have to be left to an a.p. as to whether to distribute the bequest or leave it in France for some other purpose.[128]

An a.p. would be given broad discretion once testamentary or intestate property fell into his hands. Suppose in a situation such as that of the American legatee, above, a Jewish testator had left a residuary clause leaving everything to a French (Aryan) charity. Not surprising would be

---

[125] Undated "Castille" file, AN $AJ^{38}$ 331; for more on Castille, see chapter 8, notes 154–158.

[126] Ibid.

[127] Internal memorandum, 10 March 1943, AN $AJ^{38}$, 127.

[128] Ibid.

an a.p. decision to allow a specific bequest (even to a foreign Jewish legatee) lapse in favor of the Aryan residuary taker; in these situations, the a.p. had virtual control over Jewish testamentary wealth.[129]

Furthermore, the French authorities would not hesitate—even where foreign (and specifically, American) interests were involved—to aryanize testamentary property where it saw fit. Thus Billig reports the case of a wealthy American with significant property in France; her will, probated in the United States in 1940, sought to have her French real estate in the Alpes-Maritimes transformed after her death into a charitable residence for French artists. Instead, suspecting the testatrix of being Jewish, the CGQJ aryanized the property, named an a.p., and eventually authorized the sale of the estate for 9,000,000 francs. Her lawyer, picking up the matter again in July 1944, writes to CGQJ to complain, and notes "scandalous local pressure" upon the a.p. to sell the estate.[130]

Estate taxes were very much on the minds of Vichy officials such as Paty de Clam—the third and last head of the CGQJ—when he complained of the German's pillaging.[131] Thus, quite late in the game, Paty writes to a Vichy functionary that "In all these cases, the *Einsatzstab* grabs the property without any honoring of the formalities designed to guarantie the rights of creditors or of the fisc." (No mention is made of Jewish rights.)[132]

Estate distributions, with their emphasis on race-based distinctions both as to the decedent and to the presumed objects of his bounty, often raised again the perennial question of "Who is a Jew?" under French law. Gifts to children under a will, or intestate distributions to issue, combined with mixed-marriage and mixed-heritage complexities discussed earlier in this study to block many death transfers to needy or deserving individuals. The following sub-topic develops an analogous area of legalisms.

---

[129] See discussion by CGQJ of Eugène Dreyfuss' estate, where the Pasteur Institute in Paris was named in a bequest that might have come into conflict with the same will's treatment of bequests to individual Jews, AN AJ[38], 127.

[130] Billig, *Le Commissariat général,* vol. 3, 205–206.

[131] See also chapter 6(D).

[132] Correspondence, 4 April 1944, AN AJ[38], 127.

## c. Community Property

By law, the French system mandated that property acquired during a marriage ordinarily be treated under a régime of community property, giving both spouses equal possession of the property and also giving the survivor (absent some pre-nuptial agreement) full ownership upon the death of the other spouse.[133] Jointly held property also existed, of course, by operation of partnerships, joint ownerships, and other legal arrangements.

What was to happen to such property in the case of a mixed marriage (or partnership between Jew and non-Jew) during Vichy? Under Article 20 of the law of 22 July 1941, the non-Jewish co-owner was given the right to divide the communal assets, that is to restore separate ownership of the property, as long as this was done within four months of the promulgation of the law.[134] Furthermore, even the Jewish wife of a Jew was given a right to nullify communal ownership of marital property.[135] Many such divisions were made, but then again many partnerships remained unified, either for pragmatic or sentimental reasons. Various rules developed over time.

In cases where joint marital ownership of property was retained, the ancient system of patriarchy held sway. By Article 1421 of the Code civil, "The husband alone administers the communal property.... He can manage the property, unless there is fraud...."[136] Hence a mixed marriage involving an Aryan husband and a Jewess was usually unproblematic: the entirety of the jointly held marital property was deemed free of any need for aryanization. Upon the death of the Jewish wife, if the Aryan husband survived, he was free to do whatever he wanted with the

---

[133] See the applicable statutes during Vichy in, e.g., Dalloz *Code civil* (Paris: Dalloz, 1978–79), "Marriage Contract," Chapter 2, "Communal Property," Articles 1443–1467.

[134] Sarraute and Tager, *Recueil des textes,* 65.

[135] Article 20, paragraph 4, ibid.

[136] Dalloz, 687. Former Article 1421 stated simply: "The husband administers the communal property. He can sell, assign, or mortgage it without the consent of his wife," ibid., 721.

community property now entirely in his hands.[137] Lifetime transfers were unnecessary in this situation. As a CGQJ official put it:

> The Aryan husband is the master and lord of the communal property. He manages it and there is no obstacle to his administration of it. The Jewish wife is burdened by a legal incapacity. She can do nothing. Jewish influence is non-existent.[138]

Almost all other cases relating to community property created complexities, however. As we have seen, a Jewish surviving spouse would *not* receive legacies or intestate property free and clear, and if theoretically entitled to full ownership of the prior community assets, these latter would have to be aryanized. Furthermore, during the lifetimes of the spouses in a mixed marriage, many complexities arose if the *wife* was the Aryan marriage partner. Whereas the Aryan husband was usually granted unencumbered privileges over the communal property, the same ancient civil law paternalism worked doubly against a *Jewish* husband. Barred personally from dealing with most of his own assets, as well as those of the marriage, he also could not—short of divorce[139]—rely on his Aryan wife to "take over." She, after all, was not the "lady and mistress" of the estate. Indeed, the law imposed on such a marriage the contrary assumption: a Jewish husband was deemed a continuing—Jewish—influence upon his wife and hence upon marital property even in her Aryan hands.

---

[137] See, e.g. litigation department of CGQJ responding to a private lawyer, Jean Gay, on 29 April 1944, AN $AJ^{38}$, 596. Less clear was the mixed couple's right to *purchase* real property anew, even if the husband was not Jewish. Thus M. Moulin, married to a Jewish spouse under the community property rules, sought approval from CGQJ to buy a small garden. The agency took pains to observe that such a purchase might be problematic, but it approved in this case because the 22 July 1941 law as amended on 17 November 1941, *excepted* such personal use properties connected to the primary residence of a Jewish owner, correspondence, 17 December 1942, $AJ^{38}$, 593.

[138] See, e.g., CGQJ memo, 1 August 1941, AN $AJ^{38}$, 118.

[139] Divorce itself was a delicate issue in Vichy, as the government's "values" generally tended to discourage dissolutions of marriages. See, e.g., chapter 4, where Barthélemy's distaste for divorce is evident. When it came to Aryan divorces from Jewish spouses, however, that same Barthélemy's justice ministry issued a directive on 25 September 1942, advising all chief district attorneys to "make sure that such divorces do not undergo unjustified delays," AN $AJ^{38}$, 592.

Perhaps nowhere else is Vichy racism so closely interconnected with a form of Vichy sexism. None other than Marshal Pétain himself, after all, had promulgated a new Civil Code section 213 as follows:

> The husband is the head of the family. He exercises this function in the common interest of the couple and of their children.[140]

Even where an Aryan wife sought to gain back her own assets free of community status, this perspective dominated, despite Article 20 of the 22 July law. Hence the CGQJ's legal department, referring to provisions of the Code civil (rather than to Article 20), determined that real property restored by separation of marital assets to an Aryan wife still had to be controlled by an a.p. and the proceeds thereof paid into a special account, "because the Jewish husband is the administrator of property owned by his wife and cannot enjoy the proceeds thereof."[141]

Case-by-case determinations of joint or community property rights under Vichy would prove just as confusing and ultimately persecutory as they had been in other areas we have examined. In some ways, the CGQJ's attitude was specially acrimonious in this unique situation, because their antipathy extended not only to lenient judicial decisions (as in chapter 5) but even to the statute itself![142] Indeed, for the most part, they had greater success in this doctrinal realm than elsewhere in gaining judicial support for some of their legal positions, and this certainly did not help those who were trying to use Article 20 to protect Jewish property. A 1942 memorandum, for example, displayed the agency's ire that

---

[140] Ibid. This section, by revision of 4 June 1970, reads "Spouses produce together the moral and material direction of the family. They provide for the education of their children and shape their future," Dalloz, 140.

[141] See, e.g., memorandum, 13 March 1942, litigation department of CGQJ, AN AJ$^{38}$, 592. For a variation on the paradigm case, see the *Tchenic* matter, involving the attempt of an Aryan wife to regain the community property *after* her Jewish husband's death. She managed to have the seals removed from the Parisian apartment in the rue du Temple, hoping to remove and sell all the marriage's possessions and then return with the proceeds to the unoccupied zone. UGIF's legal department, to whom she had gone for advice, opined that she should be able to retain "her" half of the property, UGIF memo, 8 May 1942, CDJC CDXXIX-1.

[142] For example, the CGQJ resented the 22 July 1941 statute's granting to the husband of the right of separation of assets and made the claim that this contradicted the Civil Code, which had only given that right to the wife, largely to protect her dowry, CGQJ memo to regional director, Toulouse, 24 August 1942, CDJC CXIV-82.

some courts had permitted immediate (common law) dissolution of the community and separation of marital property under Civil Code Article 1483 for the sole reason that an a.p. had been named for the communal property. CGQJ's view was that the 22 July law insisted on a judicial proceeding that would permit division of assets only after full investigation of the status of both partners and of all their property.[143] Within a few months, an appeals court in Toulouse reversed the lower court's liberality. In the *Lindenfeld* case, applauded by the agency, the appeals court held that only if aryanization itself had created a real threat to the woman's own property would dissolution of the community be permitted instantly; in most cases, the mere appointment of an a.p. did not constitute such a threat, according to the court.[144] This permitted, in case after case, the legal pillaging of the *entirety* of a mixed couple's property, all of it—especially if the husband was Jewish—deemed to be "Jewish" until legal division of assets was declared.[145]

Similarly to the agency's liking were judicial developments involving the statutory time limit of four months subsequent to the promulgation of the 22 July statute. The time constraint was often difficult to honor, and many partners and spouses tried to divide the communal ownership well after 22 November 1941. While, as we might by now expect, the magistrates began by taking the more liberal position that the common law protections of a woman's dowry worked an extension of the statutory

---

[143] Ibid. Similarly, the CGQJ advised the Aryan mother-in-law of Mme. Renée Ronanet (née Kahn) that Renée's grandparental status made her almost certainly a legal Jewess, and that a "competent authority" would therefore have to approve a sale to her of Renée's premarital and hence individually owned assets, letter signed by Boué, 8 January 1943, $AJ^{38}$, 593.

[144] Memo, Toulouse regional director to CGQJ, 20 January 1943, reporting the decision of exactly a week before, AN $AJ^{38}$, 80. The director exults that the case "is very interesting jurisprudentially, because it consecrates the CGQJ position, whereas the earlier doctrine was unanimously opposed to us."

[145] The case of an UGIF employee, Maurice *Ryba,* is poignant and typical. Although married to an Aryan, Ryba in early 1943 had been threatened with the removal of the *entirety* of the furniture in the couple's Bordeaux house. Despite the wife's ownership of the latter, and despite the community property laws that made half the furniture hers as well, the operative policies—shared by the Germans and the French in such cases—placed all the personal wealth in the marriage at risk, UGIF letter, 7 January 1943, YV (Baur file, unnumbered).

period, eventually the CGQJ's rigorous retention of the limit prevailed in court, and many attempts to divide assets were barred as untimely.[146]

## E. The Administrateur Provisoire under a Microscope

Thousands of ordinary Frenchmen took up the task of a.p., as defined by the law of 22 July 1941 as well as by earlier and subsequent regulations. By early 1942, Vallat reported that 1500 of 3000 Jewish enterprises had been aryanized in the Unoccupied Zone, and SCAP counted at the same time 4540 of 26,570 such enterprises in the Occupied Zone.[147] By July 1943, 39,000 enterprises in the Occupied Zone alone had been placed under the control of an a.p., including 28,000 businesses and 11,000 buildings; of the latter, 12,000 businesses had been either fully aryanized or sold off and 700 of the buildings had been sold.[148] The wealth therefrom that had been deposited in the special account established for the purpose had risen to 1,289,139,095 francs, most of which had been used to pay the German "fine" on the Jewish community, although 2 million francs had gone directly to the CGQJ.[149] By April 1944, CGQJ was putting the global number of Jewish enterprises for which an a.p. had been appointed at 42,227, of which over 17,000 had been aryanized or sold off.[150] A representative list of over 300 a.p.'s from the Lyon region alone indicates the saturation of ordinary Frenchmen in the task of aryanization; many of them had more than one or two Jewish enterprises under their control.[151]

But the figure of the a.p. was virtually brand new to French law. To the extent that the a.p. looked like a "trustee," someone legally authorized

---

[146] Billig, *Le Commissariat général,* vol. 3, 258.

[147] Laloum, *La France antisémite,* 113–14.

[148] Ibid., 119.

[149] Ibid.

[150] Ibid., 118.

[151] Several lists of administrateurs provisoires, some of them consisting of more than two hundred names of ordinary Frenchmen, can be found in CDJC general files (unnumbered). A five-page undated document offers some 225 names of Lyon-area a.p.'s, including in some cases, their names, addresses, and telephone numbers. On the *effect* of aryanization upon individual Jewish property owners, see, e.g., AN AJ[38], 528 for actual artifacts of index cards listing businesses victimized by the a.p. régime.

to deal with property for the benefit of another, Anglo-American law might have provided some useful precedents; but French property law contained no such institution as the trust. Useful analogies to English law fell flat, considering not only the political aspects of the wartime situation but also the fact that a.p.'s had been granted limited powers to encourage *criminal* sanctions against people dealing fraudulently with Jewish-owned property under their oversight.[152] The novelty of the a.p. brought with it a degree of complexity requiring a whole new course of study in the nation's law schools.

Perhaps the most significant pragmatic question involved the *standard* to which the a.p. was to be held in his dealings regarding property at once with the former Jewish owner, potential Aryan vendees, actual Aryan vendees if the transfer was suspect, government bureaucrats, and occasionally the Germans themselves. Despite salient differences, here some comparison with the British model may have been contemplated; in Article 7 of the law of 22 July 1941, the standard is defined:

> The a.p. must administer with due diligence [en bon père de famille]. He is liable before judicial tribunals as a salaried agent, under the rules of the common law.[153]

As matters developed, the a.p.'s collective adherence to the statutory standard came into question. In the words of Joseph Billig:

> Except in rare cases, the a.p. was a plague [*fléau]* upon the administered enterprise. The hybrid nature of his task prevented impartial management [*une gestion saine*]. Among the a.p.'s, there were some whose administrees[154] described after the Liberation as having had a fair and solicitous attitude.... But the Minister of Justice [just after the Liberation] stated with good reason in August 1944 that "placing it under an a.p. usually led the enterprise to its ruin."[155]

---

[152] Law of 2 November 1941, prescribing fine and imprisonment for anyone falsifying records about or making fraudulent transfers of Jewish property, Sarraute and Tager, *Recueil des textes,* 94; see also Billig, *Le Commissariat général,* vol. 3, 151–52.

[153] Sarraute and Tager, *Recueil des textes,* 63.

[154] We must use this awkward term since, again, the Anglo-American word "beneficiary" is inappropriate here.

[155] Billig, *Le Commissariat général,* vol. 3, 282; see also ibid., vol. 1, 314. Billig observes that the "bon père" standard itself derived from indigenous Nazi law, ibid., vol. 3, 129.

Cases of bad faith abounded in a statutory context calling for a "bon père." Billig continues:

> The management of enterprises was often conferred upon a.p.'s chosen more for their antisemitic zeal than their knowledge of the business.[156]

A harried Jewish entrepreneur might on his own transfer his business to an Aryan. By the time the CGQJ became involved, its a.p. would often displace the latter—theoretically from skepticism of "continuing Jewish influence"—and proceed through ignorance or worse to drive the assets down.

Against these breaches of duty by the a.p., parties managing to gain standing could go to court under Article 7; so, for example, the Aryan partner using the same statute's device of separating joint assets (see above, section D[3][c]) might complain if those assets had been wasted during the period of administration.[157] Jews, too, as we saw first in chapter 5, occasionally were granted standing to contest the behavior of an a.p.; hence a civil court in Marseilles declared itself competent to appoint an expert to render an inventory account for a Jewish business whose a.p. had failed to submit such an account for over a year. The suit for "failure to perform" basic duties was granted, and an accounting ordered.[158]

Delicate jurisdictional questions suffused such cases, even where the a.p. was ultimately chastised. For one thing, the breach of "bon père" behavior by an individual a.p. almost always implicated the CGQJ itself, for under Article 14 of the 22 July statute:

> No sale by an a.p. of a business, a house, or any personalty, except for shares sold on the stock market, is valid until approved by the CGQJ, which verifies whether all Jewish influence has been effectively removed and whether the price of the sale is fair.[159]

---

[156] Ibid., vol. 3, 282.

[157] Ibid.; Billig reports that an Aryan spouse went to court, upon division of the marital assets, to complain that the a.p. had allowed the estate to fall to 10% of its original value.

[158] *Regneault* decision, 6 April 1943, AN AJ[38], 99; see also chapter 5 at notes 73 and 74.

[159] Sarraute and Tager, *Recueil des textes,* 64. For the German's self-preserved right to stamp "nullité" on any such sale, see below at note 179. The Germans also kept track of certain a.p.'s performance under the "bon père" standard, including the duty to account, and the Germans occasionally slapped CGQJ wrists for replacing a.p.s without informing them, AN AJ[38] 80.

From the earliest period, Vichy realized that the statute might impugn its *own* good faith if a.p.'s misbehaved, especially given the statute's grant to the agency of patronage powers under Article 15[160]; given the eventual finding that CGQJ had received some 2,000,000 francs into its own coffers from sale of Jewish interests, this fear was well-founded.[161] Hence the Justice Minister hosted an inter-ministerial meeting as early as 22 August 1941 to consider revisions of the statute. In the words of Darlan himself, writing to Xavier Vallat:

> The meeting undertook in my name the essential task...of eliminating at all costs from the process of sale of Jewish property the risk of scandalous embezzlements and failures, whose political ramifications will not be answered even if finally laid at your doorstep.[162]

Darlan specifically recommended four further constraints on a.p. behavior: first, that sales be made at public auction wherever possible; second, that prices be established with the concurrence of a court-appointed expert; third, that the agency's own Article 14 consultancy committee always include objective and even judicial members; and fourth, that supervision of the a.p. be "permanent, scrupulous, and severe."[163]

When the revisions of the 22 July statute appeared in the *Journal officiel* of 2 December, however, they contained none of these liberalizing suggestions. Dated 17 November 1941, the revised statute retains the basic form of the mammoth 22 July law, and adds in pertinent part only a provision giving the CGQJ its Article 15 patronage leverage over the consultancy committee, hence flying in the face of Darlan's recommendations.

Perversely, the revisions *deleted* the Article 14 responsibility of CGQJ to verify the fairness of prices. Instead, a new Article 25 gave the agency broad investigatory powers for *all* aspects of the aryanization process, including *criminal* investigatory powers, to be imposed on any Jew or non-Jew behaving "fraudulently" to impede the removal of Jewish eco-

---

[160] Sarraute and Tager, *Recueil des textes,* 64.

[161] Laloum, *La France antisémite,* 119.

[162] Darlan to Xavier Vallat, 10 November 1941, with copies to the ministers of Justice, Interior, Finance, and Industry, CDJC CXIII-76.

[163] Ibid.

nomic interests.[164] The latter, plus the principal revision, permitting a.p. assignment retroactive to sales made by Jews since 23 May 1940, indicate the true direction of Vichy thinking, Darlan to the contrary notwithstanding.[165]

That Vichy would ignore Darlan's fears that "fraud" (or worse) would be imputed to the CGQJ—that the revised statute would instead shift the notion of "fraud" to its Jewish victims—raises moral as well as legal questions, and we shall re-approach those in chapter 10. Suffice it to see in Vichy, especially here, the vice associated in the antisemitic mind with Shylock, a reversal evident throughout this chapter anticipated by Shakespeare himself when his Lorenzo speaks for the assembled Christians of Shylock's stripped Jewish property as "manna in the way/Of starvèd people."[166] Vichy magistrates, ever mindful of the play of jurisdictional tensions in Vichy law, proceeded by and large to protect the CGQJ from many causes of action challenging a.p. standards of behavior.[167]

Hence, in *Lévy vs. Bethouart,* a Chateauroux civil court declared itself incompetent to hear a Jew's complaint against the alleged mismanagement by the a.p. assigned to his lingerie business. The tribunal civil would not tamper with what it felt was a purely administrative matter under the 2 June and 22 July statutes, not subject to magistrate jurisdiction.[168] Similarly, a Nice diamond dealer was not permitted to pursue his action against the a.p. who had sold his stock at scandalously low prices; the court held, and it was affirmed on appeal, that the 22 July law went beyond any personal interest in property over which a civil court might have jurisdiction; only administrative agencies, not subject to magisterial control, can rid the nation of Jewish influence.[169] And a

---

[164] Sarraute and Tager, *Recueil des textes,* 66.

[165] See also Billig, *Le Commissariat général,* vol. 3, 152–53.

[166] Shakespeare, *The Merchant of Venice,* 5.1.16 (New York: Folger Paperback edition, 1957).

[167] See, in addition to the cases cited here, those mentioned by Billig, *Le Commissariat général,* vol. 3, 258–59, reach the same conclusion about generally deferential judicial behavior on aryanization.

[168] AN $AJ^{38}$, 99. The court declined to recognize Lévy's citation of a criminal statute, Penal Code section 405; see also chapter 5, note 71.

[169] Tribunal civil of Aix, decision of 6 October 1942, *Helft* case, affirmed by the court of appeals of Aix, 10 November 1942. AN $AJ^{38}$, 99.

Toulouse court declined to review, on similar grounds, the complaint of an optician against the price established for his business by the a.p.[170]

As noted in chapter 5,[171] although civil courts had *explicit* jurisdiction under the 22 July statute to review a.p. behavior, they showed far less inclination to intervene against the CGQJ in property matters than they had demonstrated under the personal definition aspects of the 2 June statute. It is as though the broad national policy of stripping Jewish influence from the French economy might be wholeheartedly endorsed by courts as an administrative matter analogous to the improvement of various specific industries by national committees appointed by ministers to advise or regulate them.[172] Yet, as aryanization became a massive project, a.p.'s eventually raised questions of criminal law wholly similar to the fines and arrests that grew out of failure to report as a Jew under the 2 June statute.[173] Surely the ordinary courts could have played a greater role in monitoring this phenomenon. They chose not to do so.

Despite the deference generally granted to them by the courts, the CGQJ's hypersensitivity about jurisdiction led them to emphasize the few adverse magisterial decisions and to plead (unsuccessfully) for statutory reform explicitly creating a brand new administrative court to handle aryanization issues.[174] But in fact they had little to fear. Theory after theory that might protect Jewish property was rejected by the magistrates.

---

[170] *Lion* case, Tribunal civil of Toulouse, decision of 12 December 1942, AN AJ[38] 99.

[171] See, e.g., chapter 5 at notes 54–64, the *Sée* and *Fourcade* cases.

[172] For this analogy, see an article by law professor Edmond Bertrand, cited by Danièle Lochak, "La Doctrine sous Vichy," in Serge Klarsfeld, ed., *Le statut des juifs de Vichy* (Paris: F.F.D.J.F., 1990), 129–30. But Bertrand's 1943 article went on to protest that, since the distribution of Jewish wealth went into the hands of *private* Aryan vendees, it was more comparable to a bankruptcy or other enforced wealth distribution typically handled by magistrates! ibid., 130.

[173] Article 24 of the law of 22 July 1941, as amended by the law of 11 November 1941, gave the CGQJ, through its various agents, the power to punish Jew or non-Jew who attempted to defraud the law's insistence on the removal of Jewish influence from the economy. The criminal sanctions included imprisonment from one to five years, and statutory fines ranging from 10,000 to 250,000 francs. For an example of the form document that almost any vendor of property would have had to sign under the 22 July law to show his *bona fides* on economic aryanization, see CDJC XVIIa-44.

[174] See chapter 4 at note 146 for the battle between Darquier and Barthélemy on this unsuccessful agency law reform proposal.

A fascinating example of frustrated innovation involved the 1943 claim of a Turkish Jew, *Razon,* before a civil tribunal in Lyon, that the 1923 Treaty of Lausanne protected him from the aryanization laws and from the control over his property by an ordinary French court. Razon was moving to protect a business in Lyon that he co-owned with a naturalized French Jew. The tribunal civil rejected both parts of his claim, labelling as "Platonic" Razon's reference to a treaty and hence finding it not legally controlling and—as to the jurisdictional aspect—finding the treaty irrelevant since, under the French law of 16–24 August 1730 and 16 Fructidor, an. III, courts "cannot impede in any way whatsoever the operations of the administration." The court advised Razon to try instead to prove that he was not Jewish and then to use the division of assets provisions (Article 20 of the 22 July law) to regain ownership from his Jewish partner.[175]

*Razon* indicates the degree of deference—and of sarcasm against theories prejudicial to administrators of Jewish wealth—exhibited by many ordinary courts dealing with aryanization questions. However, once a matter was firmly in the control of the administrative agencies—as we recall from chapter 5—one might still appeal to the Conseil d'État. Although most often, the high administrative court affirmed CGQJ decisions on aryanization, even where a non-Jewish vendee from a mixed-heritage prior owner had become subject to an a.p. over his business,[176]

---

[175] *Razon* decision, 4 March 1943, AN AJ[38], 99. This was not the only case in which Jews tried to use international treaties to find some modicum of protection. The principals of *Lazar and Co.* in Montpellier tried to use the 1934 Sarrois treaty, but their argument was rejected on the highest Vichy levels, by Laval's chief of cabinet, Pierre Chamel de Jarnieu, CDJC XVIIa-43 (225–26). See Raoul Hilberg, *La Destruction des Juifs d'Europe* (Paris: Fayard, 1988), 535.

On the sensitivity of Vichy to a variety of international problems arising under their racial policies, see chapter 6. An early example of this is CGQJ's note to all prefectures that many individuals had sought certificates of non-adherence from them before travelling to foreign countries; that these requests of course fell within their exclusive jurisdiction, but that they would not affect the ordinary courts' right to decide whether the individual was entitled to a passport to begin with as a matter of French law, memorandum, 9 October 1941, CDJC CXIV-67.

[176] Typical is the *Loubradou* case, also mentioned in chapter 5 at note 65, in which the latter appealed the appointment of an a.p. to run his business, the Cinéma-Rex in Antibes. Loubradou wanted to show that his vendor, Samsovici, was not Jewish because he had only two Jewish grandparents. Despite this claim, and despite Loubradou's production of

occasionally the Conseil d'État did reverse. As we saw in chapter 5, such intra-administration tension increased as the war progressed. So in July, 1943, the first and third sections of the high administrative court quashed the agency's decision to appoint an a.p. to a small business operated from a family house in Isle-d'Abeau (Isère); since the owner and his family lived there for part of the year, "absent special circumstances," an a.p. was not to be appointed.[177]

But if ordinary courts by and large were proving impermeable to Jewish arguments on aryanization matters, surely reliance was inappropriate on administrative courts to overturn the property-related decisions of the a.p. and the CGQJ that appointed him. The conclusion seems fair that the "bon père" statutory standard was simply not enforced. The legalized looting of Jewish property surely stands as one of the blackest and still least-understood chapters of the Vichy years.

A few final examples are necessary, for they tend to show that pillage occurred in many ways, not all of them obvious even when one looks at the figure exceeding 1.2 francs deposited into the central Caisse des dépots et consignes.[178] In a classic breach-of-trust situation reported by Billig, an a.p. of a large real estate concern was culpable of self-dealing. The Jewish owner had found buyers offering six million francs for the business, but "Jewish influence" was suspected and a bid of 3 million accepted from an anonymous competing group. When another group bid 4.5 million, the a.p. chose the former nonetheless. It then came out that the a.p. was a director of one of the companies associated with the anonymous group of low bidders, and that he had fraudulently declared that the sale to the latter had been completed when the higher bid came in, although in fact it had only been registered nine days after receipt of the more favorable offer. The German High Command, consulted on the matter—as in all cases theoretically[179]—approved the a.p.'s group, despite acknowledgment of the fraud.[180]

---

an authorizing letter from the Ministry of Information, the Conseil d'État rejected his appeal, granting to the agency "measures designed to eliminate from the business all Jewish influence," AN AJ[38], 99.

[177] *Bickert (dit Picard)*, AN AJ[38], 99.

[178] See Laloum, *La France antisémite,* 119.

[179] The Germans had to approve all sales in the Occupied Zone, AN AJ[38], 596.

[180] Billig, *Le Commissariat général,* vol. 3, 105.

In a similar vein, an a.p. appointed to administer no fewer than twelve businesses between May 1941 and April 1944 was officially found to have self-dealt by stealing for his own personal use thousands of francs worth of products; in addition, he took in annual fees of around 89,000 francs for "managing" this sole concern, although officially permitted less than half that amount. Finally, he stalled off a perfectly good buyer for the business, apparently both to safeguard his little dominion and to avoid having to account for his excesses.[181]

Nor was the corrupt practice associated with aryanization limited to breaches of a.p. standards. The documentation further reveals a kind of feeding frenzy for vacated Jewish office space, with the French and the Germans equally voracious. When, for example, some large Parisian buildings previously owned by Jews became available in the rue Monceau during fall 1941, the Germans saw what they called an *Arisierungsangelegenheit:* an aryanization situation. Rudolf Schleier, a diplomat and consul general to Otto Abetz,[182] was looking for more space and more illustrious quarters for himself, his embassy, and his staff; number 71 on that block would fill the bill beautifully. The building itself

> [w]as formally owned by the Jew, Meunier. We will thus have to come to an agreement about lease or sale of the property with the French government.[183]

Schleier, like most Germans, knew full well that the French were zealous and even xenophobic when it came to *all* Jewish matters—that (as he reported to Berlin) it was the French, after all, who had thought up the idea of concentration camps in which to place Jews on their soil![184] So careful negotiations for the prime space in the rue Monceau, that included smaller but no less attractive properties formerly owned by the Rothschilds, would have to ensue. Such bargaining could be just as important

---

[181] Ibid., vol. 3, 274.

[182] See, e.g. Lucien Steinberg, *Les Allemands en France* (Paris: Albin Michel, 1980), 49, 208.

[183] Memorandum, 8 August 1941, YV 5-112.

[184] Marrus and Paxton, *Vichy France,* 223–24.

whether it dealt with persons, property, or even the right to the best boxes at the Paris Opéra or the Opéra comique.[185]

The French variation on the theme in fact seems taken from light opera, until we recall the context. If the German interests ranged from the Rothschilds' lucrative properties[186] to the largest corporate conglomerates in the Occupied Zone, to relatively large sums left behind by recently victimized Jews who had arrived in the German camps from France,[187] Vichy (often bidding for the same lucre) sometimes found itself wallowing in the underflow of petty cash, the portable property of Jews still surviving, and the pittance of those not so lucky, who had left behind them in Drancy or other French camps small sums for the use (they thought) of their families. So there is a tragic flavor to these anecdotes that surpasses the show of greater greed.

In a memo of June 1942, Monsieur G. Lien of the CGQJ asks the director of SCAP to remind all a.p.'s that "Rule 4375 of 4 June 1942" must be interpreted to give any French bureaucracy that has set up shop in "vacated Jewish storefronts" at least fifteen days notice before being asked to leave in view of a permanent sale of the space to a private Aryan vendee.[188] Franco-French tensions over aryanized Jewish real estate were entering a new phase.

Meanwhile, personal property had to be dealt with, as Jews "disappeared," leaving money, cars, and debts behind them. An UGIF social worker wonders, in September 1942, if 2,765 francs can be restored to the family of a M. Hugo Becker: "M. Becker has been de-

---

[185] Memorandum, 16 August 1941, YV V-7 (Schleier file). Here Schleier complains of being locked out of the best box at the Opéra one evening when he arrived "for half an hour to observe the scene," because French and German military riffraff had taken the seats. To cure this "evil" [übelstand], Schleier proposes a special plaque for the door of these boxes and even the firing of any usher who thereafter unlocks the box for such unworthy competitors.

[186] See the Schleier file, ibid., where the Rothschild's buildings in rue de Monceau are divided up by the German ministries, YV V-112. The Germans also bought up shares of the aryanized Rothschild corporations on the open market. See von Bose file, YV V-115, memorandum, 9 June 1941; see also Marrus and Paxton, *Vichy France,* 7, 29, 109.

[187] See, e.g., a memorandum, Auschwitz officials to the High Command in Paris, 18 April 1942 wondering what to do with 183,903.50 francs left behind by the deportees. The writers opine that, whatever else is done with the money, it should first be used to pay costs of Jewish "damages" and upkeep totalling 21,222 francs.

[188] G. Lien to SCAP, June 1942, CDJC CXI-38.

ported, but this money remained at the camp [Drancy], so his wife asks if she can now retain possession of that sum."[189]

Some prisoners learned to take the precaution of giving their wives or others powers of attorney to deal with such property. Some months later, UGIF wrote to one of its board members in the southern zone this perennial and perhaps paradigmatic Jewish property question. What, the central office asks, can be done with "property belonging to Jews who have been deported from the camp at Casseneuil, and whose close relatives would like to retrieve it?" The pitiful remnants of Jewish deportees from French soil could not expeditiously be handed over to their surviving families.[190]

The Lenczicki family had left behind only a debt on their car, which they had purchased in 1939 from the Ropelux Company in Levallois, agreeing to make six payments on it of 1300 francs each. Their debt had been underwritten by a M. Vainrib, but by January 1943 there remained a balance of 3,800 francs on the payments due. Ropelux itself was being sold off, and it had an "administrateur" who sought the payment from UGIF, because:

> Before seeking criminal sanctions under Articles 400 and 401 of the Criminal Code, I preferred to bring the matter to your attention. M. Lenczicki has apparently been imprisoned at Drancy, and his wife has left their former domicile, 42 rue de Trévise in Paris, without leaving a forwarding address, which is also true of the guarantor.[191]

As for those lucky enough to have survived and remained in France, everyday sights of French pillage could not have been inspiring. Eight Paris policemen, as 1944 begins, appear at the apartment of the Odesser family in the rue de la Roquette. Two remain in the street, two stay with the concierge, and four break into the apartment, taking with them as they leave not the Odessers themselves but instead:

2 food tickets;
packages to send to internees;
all the clothing;
6000 francs in cash.

---

[189] Letter, 15 September 1942, CDJC CDXXIX-1.

[190] For an example of the power of attorney form used, see Drancy internee *Lang's* power, granted to his wife in April 1943, CDJC CDXXIX-1.

[191] UGIF correspondence, 12 and 15 January 1943, CDJC CDXXIX-1.

The cries of the family for help are ignored by workers in the street below. The Odessers report the theft to UGIF but "ask for no special assistance, realizing that others are far worse off."[192]

[192] UGIF social service memo, 3 January 1944.

# Chapter 8

# The Professional Lives of Private Lawyers

What was it like for the ordinary attorney during the Vichy years? How much did he know—or care—about the plight of his Jewish colleagues or about the numerous religious laws that occupied so much space in the courts and in the lawbooks? Beginning with the collective voice of France's professional legal associations, we will "see from within" how Vichy's approach to the Jews became a detailed and sometimes preoccupying matter. This view from the inside out will be greatly assisted by the very first official declarations issued by the Bar Association of the City of Paris about its work under Vichy.[1] We then examine the relationship to the German authorities of private legal service providers, including the difficulties that arose with interzonal transfers of various kinds. Communications from lawyers to Vichy agencies and government offi-

---

[1] On 6 January 1992, M. Azanam, archivist of the Association at the Palais de Justice, transmitted to Serge Klarsfeld and to myself (who were then present) and to Marc Knoebel (a researcher who was not present on that date but was to receive the communication in the mail) a four-page memorandum bearing that date, together with 12 annexes relating to this topic. M. Azanam informed us that, ordinarily, only the bâtonnier (head) of the Association, or members needing a file for a pending case (not alone for reasons of historical interest), had the right to see the archives. He said that, given my own interest—first expressed to him three years before—and given increased general research interest in the Vichy period, the Association had authorized him to let us have the memorandum and annexes. They collectively bear the title, "Note sur l'attitude des avocats à la Cour d'Appel de Paris à l'égard des autorités de l'État français de 1940 à 1944," hereinafter "Bar Memorandum."

cials are analyzed. Throughout, we try to sustain the perspective of the active individual practitioner of law, as conveyed by a score of examples, and as epitomized perhaps by the wartime professional practice of a highly distinguished French lawyer, Maurice Garçon, again with the help of hitherto underexamined archival materials.[2]

## A. Collective Associations of Legal Professionals

We have pertinent information now about the wartime activity of traditional associations of French legal professionals, and particularly about the largest of these, the Bar Association of the City of Paris. These groups, whose collective voice spoke for avocats, avoués, and notaires practicing their craft in various localities, fulfilled a familiar function: to assess and articulate the interests of their members. Consistent with this aim, legal associations during Vichy differed only somewhat from other groups of legally trained individuals previously examined, such as magistrates and government officials. In their pronouncements and—although here we can be less certain of our conclusions—in their activities, they displayed that characteristic gallic mix of fierce autonomy and restrained acceptance: autonomy before the autocratic French régime and even before the German occupiers, but acceptance of what was newest and weirdest in the laws they all served, the racial exclusion of some of their own oldest and dearest colleagues on the basis of race and religion alone.

Some bar associations, and analogous representatives of solicitors and notaries, felt empowered during those years to pursue what the Paris Bar calls their "independence before the Vichy régime,"[3] a veritable "souci d'indépendance" [striving for autonomy][4] that could lead to overt criticism of Vichy's highest authorities. Many lawyers shared the view of Philippe Serre, the renegade whose vote against Pétain in July 1940 sent him into exile, that the bar managed to retain its honor far better than had

---

[2] I refer to the collection of papers contributed by Garçon to the French government and now held at the Archives nationales in Fontainebleau (hereafter AN 304 AP).

[3] Bar Memorandum, 1. This chapter occasionally contrasts to the Paris Bar and other local associations the *generally* more "corporatist" and pro-Vichy approach of some national associations; see below, note 115.

[4] Bar Memorandum, 1.

the magistrates[5]; the Paris Bar, for example, explicitly opposed itself to the courts and to the Ministry of Justice—at least whenever these competing legal establishments sought in any way to regulate the internal governance of their own group.[6] Jacques Charpentier, head [bâtonnier] of the Paris Bar expressed in no uncertain terms to Marshal Pétain himself the unwillingness of his association to be controlled on its membership decisions by Vichy[7]; as counsel for Riom defendant Paul Reynaud, Charpentier proffered a written protest directly to Pétain eloquently contesting in majestic terms that leader's violation of the separation of powers by declaring the Riom defendants guilty prior to trial[8]; he emphasized in the name of the Bar generally the enduring rights of people prosecuted in France to have the zealous advocacy of independent lawyers who would be permitted to play the game on an equal footing with the government.[9]

When several members suggested that Pétain's political speeches and inspirational locutions be affixed prominently on the wall of every association local, the full membership of the Paris Bar declined to do so.[10] When the latter grudgingly agreed to mount the Marshal's portrait in its library at the Palais de Justice, it took pains contemporaneously to emphasize that it would never—as the magistrates had done—swear to

---

[5] Philippe Serre, personal interview with author, Paris, 21 December 1988. As we shall see, the Bar often explicitly set its independence up against what it saw as the servility of the magistrates during Vichy.

[6] Bar Memorandum, 1.

[7] Jacques Charpentier, *Au Service de la Liberté* (Paris: Fayard, 1949), 199 et seq.; Bar Memorandum, 1; see also chapter 3 at notes 8–11.

[8] Jacques Charpentier to Marshall Pétain, 28 August 1941, in Barthélemy papers, AN 72 AJ 411.

[9] Ibid. Vichy was not impervious to what they felt was the "party spirit and the immunity of the Bar" that sometimes led defense lawyers, in particular, to contradict its legislative policy. Ministry of Justice memorandum, 11 November 1940, AN BB[30], 1708, complains at an early stage of the zealous advocacy mounted by private counsel on behalf of youngsters who had been delinquent in reporting for mandatory national service under the Vichy law of 30 July 1940. Instead of pitching in, the Bar was seen here as deliberately turning the tables and attacking the Vichy implementation of the national service policy, particularly conjuring in their pleadings "before judges and public opinion dark portraits of the life in these youth programs; individual cases, isolated facts, are generalized. The most praiseworthy efforts, even those that have met with success, are left in the shadows."

[10] Bar Memorandum, 1.

that leader a political oath of allegiance.[11] It was a proudly autonomous association, not untypical of others like it around the country. It brooked no interventions by governments, no matter how autocratic. But it picked and chose the issues for which it would fight.

In Belgium, as we might recall, one of the first acts of the organized bar had been to protest vigorously the persecution of its own Jewish members. Citing the constitutional law of Belgium, these leaders protested the exclusion of Jews from the magistracy and,

> as for lawyers, they can be removed from the lists of their Bar Associations only by disciplinary action. It is the irreconcilability of these principles with the [German] ordinance that makes it a duty for the undersigned, sir, to contact you, hoping that you will keep these in mind before proceeding to apply the measures that have been announced.[12]

In France, the Bar did not apparently consider the segregation and ostracism of its Jewish members to be a priority in its fight to maintain the autonomy of private lawyers from government edict and control.

With the exception of its attitude on the affixing of the Star of David to the outside of the robes worn by Jewish advocates at the Palais de Justice, to which we shall return in due course, the Paris Bar (like most other associations) displayed little or no organized opposition to the treatment of their racially persecuted colleagues. Let us examine this behavior, issue by issue.

## 1. Removal of Jews from Practice

### *a. Xenophobia: The Law of 10 September 1940*

Vichy moved quickly to eliminate foreign influence in the legal professions. By Article I of the law of 10 September 1940, no one could remain inscribed at the Bar who did not possess "French nationality...being born of a French father."[13] The obligation of bar associations to participate actively in the firing of their members under this law—and also in originating whatever formal exceptions could be brought under it—

---

[11] Ibid.

[12] YV IV-203. See chapter 2, note 49.

[13] Signed by Pétain and Alibert, published in the *Journal officiel,* 11 September 1940. See earlier discussion, chapter 3, note 9.

caught the attention of Jacques Maury in one of the articles he wrote for the Constitutional Law commentaries in 1940.[14] Maury, whose courageous attack upon the denaturalization laws as violating basic French legal principles was noted earlier in this study, emphasizes that the law "is retroactive and hits lawyers already inscribed for whom, therefore, the Bar Association must now pronounce removal [or exception therefrom] by formal decision."[15]

Speaking of this law after the war, Paris *bâtonnier* Charpentier takes a different position. He allowed that "for several years, this measure was dearly anticipated by the Paris Bar."[16] The strange customs, dialects, and appearance of those who "invaded" the Bar during the late 1930s had "covered us with ridicule"; foreign lawyers settling in France "brought to the conduct of litigation the procedures of their bazaars."[17] Charpentier speaks of a kind of "honeymoon" with Vichy during the early months that produced this law.[18]

It is not surprising that Paris (among other bar associations) went about the work of firing non-French colleagues with considerable efficiency. As their memorandum puts it, "The Bar Association assured the application of the law by calling, on its own motion, for appropriate documentation; by excluding lawyers not fulfilling the requirements; and by proposing in exceptional cases that some lawyers stay on."[19] Charpentier was himself a part of this process, sometimes asked to communicate with former colleagues as to why they had been fired.[20] The Paris Bar innovated in several respects, going beyond the letter of the law in deciding that it could define one of the statutory categories of exception from the law ("service in a combat unit of the French army during the wars of 1914

---

[14] Maury, *Semaine juridique,* (1940), 169; see chapter 2, text at note 60 and at notes 122–24.

[15] Ibid.

[16] Charpentier, *Au Service,* 127.

[17] Ibid.

[18] Ibid.

[19] Bar Memorandum, 2.

[20] See Charpentier to Machetto, 3 July 1941, assuring his "dear colleague" that the decree of the previous December that disbarred Machetto was "solely" due to "the Italian nationality of your father," and that "such a decision in no way blemishes your honor and carries with it no critique of your professional life," CDJC XXXIII-7.

or 1939") and in surrounding with impressive legalisms the process of firing even its most illustrious members.

Pierre Cot, whom we met as a defendant *in absentia* at Riom, was fully French under the statutory definitions. But his name had appeared on a special decree signed by Pétain on 6 September 1940, stripping him of French nationality, an honor bestowed simultaneously upon all the brothers Rothschild, among others.[21] Pétain surely was "rewarding" Cot as one of many prominent Frenchmen who had left the country around the time of the armistice, which Cot had "adamantly opposed."[22] His colleagues at the Bar, who had seen Cot rise to be Air Minister under the Third Republic, moved by dint of the 6 September decree to remove him from their rolls. Their methods, cited by Yvon Martinet in a moving eulogy to his colleague in 1991, were perhaps more troubling than their substantive act:

> Pierre Cot could read, with sadness and rebellion, the reasons for his removal from the Bar. The committee's decree gave three reasons; first, that the 22nd article of the decree of 20 June, 1920, required all those seeking admission to the apprenticeship [*stage*] of a Bar to provide documentation of their status as French.
>
> This text, concerning apprenticeship, hardly applied to Pierre Cot, who had been a member of the Bar since June 22, 1921.
>
> Second, reference was made to the law of 10 September 1940...which did not apply to Pierre Cot, who possessed French nationality as being born of a French father.
>
> Finally, there was reference to the personal decree of Marshal Pétain of 6 September 1940, the only reference justifying the Bar's action.[23]

Martinet continues:

> Why then this barrage of juridical sophistry? [Alors, pourquoi ce luxe de pécautions juridiques?] Why try to justify by other texts than the Vichy-ist decree the unfair [inique] measure taken against Pierre Cot? Why cloak the diabolical and undignified measure in a legalistic fabric woven with compromise [dans un habit juridique couleur de compromission]?

---

[21] Bar Memorandum, annex 12: eulogy for Pierre Cot by Yvon Martinet of the Paris Bar Association, 22 November 1991.

[22] Robert O. Paxton, *Vichy France: Old Guard and New Order* (New York: Knopf, 1972), 6.

[23] Bar Memorandum, annex 12; see also chapter 3, note 9.

No one can understand this.[24]

Avoiding disbarment for lack of French nationality could only take place with the help of the same bar associations that did the work of removal itself, and we saw in chapter 3 how rarely lawyers benefitted from such largesse. But a personal interview with a lawyer in Paris indicated to me recently that the Bar could move in mysterious ways to safeguard some legal careers. His story is worth recounting in some detail.

Emmanuel Blanc, fully Jewish and of Romanian parentage, recalls that Vichy moved with alacrity to adopt religious laws[25]; but it was the xenophobic September law and not antisemitism that placed his legal career at risk. Born in Kishinev, Romania, he came to France in 1928 and was naturalized in 1931. He received his law degree the following year and was a stagiaire in Paris from 1935–39. Called up for the drôle de guerre, he was demobilized in Toulouse in 1940 and soon returned to Paris, where he formally was inscribed at the Bar that year.

Emmanuel Blanc never declared himself to be Jewish. With his non-Jewish wife—herself an avocate—they "house-sat" in Paris for a philosopher who was away. M. Blanc recalls that one day the Germans entered the apartment and asked the couple why they were there. "Because it doesn't cost us anything," was the reply, and the interrogators left peaceably.

Removed from the lists at the Paris Bar, because he was not the son of a French father, Blanc moved to convince the Paris Court of Appeals that he should be reinstated. His argument centered on his active service in Lebanon during the hostilities. But to perfect his file for the proceeding, Blanc had to go both to his law school records and to the Ministry of Justice on the Place Vendôme. In both instances, evidence of his Jewishness was to be found in the files; almost miraculously, no official bothered him about his racial and religious background.

Armed with "pièces justificatives," M. Blanc eventually prevailed before the Court of Appeals. He was reinstated for his active service in the war and resumed a daily practice at the Palais de Justice. There, he sadly observed the fate of the arrested Jewish lawyers, most or all of

---

[24] Ibid.

[25] Blanc contrasts Vichy in this respect to Italy. He ascribes Vichy policy directly to the antisemitism (as he sees it) of the régime's leaders. Emmanuel Blanc, personal interview with author, Paris, 20 December 1991 (hereafter, Blanc interview).

whom were his acquaintances. He saw the star on the robes of some Jewish colleagues, and he recalls little or no protest of that necessity. After the roundups of mid-1942, he recalls seeing fewer and fewer of these persecuted men and women.

The Bar, in Blanc's recollection, lodged various objections to incursions on its own autonomy. He remembers working with Charpentier to protest against a German measure—"par intermédiare du Parquet"—requiring the Bar to identify to the occupiers any lawyer who defended communists or gaullists.[26] The tactic used was to rotate such defense work among the entire membership and hence keep it fairly anonymous. This device, like many clever strategies devised by lawyers, seemed to have worked.

But there was almost no talk of the Jewish laws themselves. At our interview, M. Blanc confessed that I probably knew much more about the latter than he did.[27] What he did want to convey was his strong belief that his bâtonnier, Jacques Charpentier, was a basically good man. Side by side, they helped late in the occupation to defend the Palais itself against German tanks.[28] After the liberation, it was Blanc personally who received Charpentier back into the Palais.[29]

### *b. Ostracism: The* Numerus Clausus *for Jewish Lawyers*

Chapter 3 fully reviewed the totalistic approach of Vichy regarding its judicial functionaries. The story private lawyers had to live with was more subtle, and we have largely preserved it for this section of our study. Its central theme is the *numerus clausus*. The origin of this concept—at least as regards student access to higher education—has been ascribed recently by Claude Singer to education minister Jérome Carcopino, in collaboration with Admiral Darlan.[30]

---

[26] Blanc interview; see also sub-section (C)(3)(c), on Maurice Garçon, below.

[27] Blanc interview.

[28] Ibid. (Maître Blanc showed me a printed pamphlet, "Six jours au Palais," detailing this event.)

[29] Ibid.

[30] Claude Singer, *Vichy, l'Université et les Juifs* (Paris: Les Belles Lettres, 1992), 78.

It is worth noting, however, that the concept that was finally inscribed in the law of 16 July 1941 for practitioners[31] seems to have been developed by Justice Minister Joseph Barthélemy considerably earlier in 1941, before much was being proposed by Carcopino. Indeed, Barthélemy took the stuff of the 3 October 1940 Vichy statute, which *did not* set up any proscriptions for the liberal professions, and—at least as early as 11 February 1941, solicited approval of the eventual law. Thus, in a memorandum of that date to the War Veterans League, signed individually by Barthélemy, he seeks comments:

> Article 4 of the law of 3 October 1940 states that access to and exercise of the liberal professions are permitted to Jews, unless public administrative regulations have set up for them a fixed quota.
>
> I would like you to know that, applying that article, my ministry has developed a public administrative regulatory scheme that, in the jurisdiction of each court of appeal, fixes the proportion of Jewish lawyers at 2% of the total of non-Jewish lawyers at the bar in that jurisdiction. This scheme envisions that Jewish war veterans of the 1914 and 1939 wars can, over and above and up to half of this quota, remain in practice. Beneficiaries of this measure would be designated by a special Commission, made up of one judge and four war veterans....
>
> This scheme was proposed to the Conseil d'État. Using Article 3 of the law of 3 October 1940 that deals with the access of Jews to certain public offices, the High Assembly was inclined to permit—without limitation—access to the legal profession for Jewish war veterans who can satisfy one of these qualifications: a) hold the carte de combattant 1914–18 or have been cited during that war; b) have been cited in the ordre du jour of the campaign of 1939–40; c) decorated with the Légion d'honneur in military or military medal status.[32]

On 18 February 1941, the War Veterans League responded to Barthélemy in the affirmative.[33] The original scheme, liberalized in part over Bar-

---

[31] R. Sarraute and P. Tager, *Les Juifs sous l'Occupation: Recueil des textes officiels français et allemands* (Paris: CDJC, 1982), 58.

[32] CDJC CCCLXXIX-9.

[33] Ibid. The requirement of holding a carte de combattant or of otherwise proving service in actual hostilities was to become a stumbling block to some veterans asserting exceptional status just by that fact alone.

thélemy's draft by the Conseil d'État,[34] was then reduced to statute on 16 July.

The statute stipulated that each juridical district in France (or under Vichy control elsewhere) was counted upon to list its Jewish lawyers and to calculate, using a *numerus clausus,* those who must be expelled from the Bar or those who could remain in practice. The total number of Jewish lawyers could not, except in one prescribed way, exceed 2% of the total number of non-Jewish lawyers inscribed in any Bar jurisdiction, and in no case could the absolute number of Jewish lawyers in any district exceed their numbers as of 25 June 1940 (the same cut-off date that the 2 June statute used to define proof of "non-Jewishness").

The statute required each Jew—as defined by the 2 June statute—to inform the administrative committee of his local Bar Association of that fact. The latter was then to determine the number of Jewish lawyers "in excess" [*en surnombre*] of the quota and to remove such from the lists. With those numbers established, the district prosecutor was to inform the Court of Appeals of each district of three statistics: first, the number of non-Jewish lawyers inscribed at the Bar; second, the number of Jewish lawyers and stagiaires inscribed as of 25 June 1940; and third, the number now reportedly still inscribed—after the necessitated de-listings—with a special list of those satisfying the June 2 Article 3 exceptions.

Indeed, various routes were available to Jewish lawyers—as they were not to legal functionaries such as magistrates—to remain listed, and all of these demanded at least some intervention by the bar associations. First, there was the "exception" with which we are already familiar under Article 8 of the 2 June statute, permitting individuals to escape the strictures of the religious laws *altogether*; here, the Bar played a role, because in many cases (including the Paris area, with its thousands of practitioners) the Bar was specifically asked by the CGQJ to opine as to the meritoriousness of the Article 8 petitions.[35] Those able to show Article 8 exceptions for old-line families (vieille souche) and for service

[34] As we noted in chapter 5, the Conseil d'Etat retained substantial review powers over Vichy legislation. As to the *numerus clausus,* a CGQJ memorandum of 29 May 1941 to Vichy's Foreign Secretary explicitly notes that the bill is "now in the hands of the Conseil d'Etat," CDJC CX-47. See also the formal decree of the 16 July 1941 law by the Conseil, CDJC CXCIII-23.

[35] Bar Memorandum, 2.

to France remained in practice without regard to the *numerus clausus*. There then arose the statutory possibilities under the law of 16 July—which we call "exemptions" to distinguish them from Article 8 "exceptions" permitted under the earlier statute. These included prisoners of war or their relatives, who were given temporary solace, although this exemption was to terminate two months after either the liberated lawyer's return to French territory or confirmed proof of his death in battle or in prison.[36] The bar associations had to monitor requests, primarily by practitioners whose sons or husbands were imprisoned or missing in action, and many such bereaved practitioners in fact were thus enabled to remain at the Bar for several years.[37] Next, those fulfilling the exemptions of paragraph 5 of Article 1 of the 16 July statute—mostly war veterans (as further defined) and those holding the légion d'honneur—were given priority in determining who would fall within the 2%, and if their number resulted in more Jewish lawyers remaining than was technically allowed, that would be permitted, and no new lawyer could be added to the list until the number reached back down to 2% through deaths or other attritions.[38] Determinations of what constituted appropriate military service were usually left to the individual bar associations. Finally, on the recommendation of the Bar, the statute permitted special recognition of "the eminent quality of the professional merit" of individual lawyers; as with the Article 8 exceptions, this group, too, could serve over and above the *numerus clausus,* but like the latter, this path to continued practice needed the subsequent confirmation of each name by the Court of Appeals. As we shall see, even with the court's approbation in hand, a lawyer exempted for special professional merit was still at risk of being

---

[36] Article 3, paragraph 2. The difficulty of establishing the fact of the death of one thought to be a war prisoner is exemplified in the case of Mme. Kraemer Bach, herself a Parisian lawyer, whose son was presumed killed during the 1939–40 war. The Paris Court of Appeals, by decree of 2 January 1942, specifically permitted her to remain in practice "until the death of her son is officially established," CDJC CXCV-18.

[37] By April 1943, twelve women were permitted to practice in the Paris region because they were considered a "war widow," "mother of a son killed in action," or "prisoner's wife."

[38] See, e.g., J. Lubetzki, *La condition des Juifs en France sous l'Occupation allemande* (Paris: CDJC, 1947), 51.

rejected by either the Justice Minister or the CGQJ, under the terms of paragraph 5 of Article 1.[39]

Once formally in place, the *numerus clausus* became a matter of mathematics, bar association politics, and inter-agency contentiousness for the duration of the war. The CGQJ indeed displayed its almost Germanic sense of precision throughout the war when it came to the *numerus clausus*. On 9 October 1941, it hastened to impose its mathematics upon all those who had to calculate the quota. Thus, this analysis was sent to the Ministry of Justice:

> Please let all your *procureurs généraux* [district prosecutors] know that, to calculate the *numerus clausus* established by the decree of 16 July 1941, they must keep track of fractions that cannot be less than 25 [*read:* 2.5]. For example, where in a Court of Appeals there are fewer than 124 non-Jewish lawyers, the *numerus clausus* of 2% will leave room for two Jewish lawyers. If there are 126 non-Jewish lawyers, there will be room for three Jews, if there are 176 there will be room for four....[40]

The CGQJ's magic fraction of 2.5—meaning that any multiplication leaving less than that fraction would work against permitting an additional Jewish lawyer to practice—seems to have derived from a suggestion that it had received from the district prosecutor in Lyon. There, the number of non-Jewish lawyers was less than 325, so the *numerus clausus* was set at six. "If the number of non-Jewish lawyers at the moment of the decree had been above 330, the number fixed by the *numerus clausus* could have been set at seven."[41]

The 16 July statute required the CGQJ to confer with bar associations in their determination of exceptions and exemptions under the *numerus clausus*. Most Jewish legal practitioners now had to register with their professional associations all relevant information on religious status. The associations then had to amass the relevant lists and convey them to the

---

[39] The Paris Bar recommended fourteen of its colleagues for special recognition. None was affirmed by Darquier's CGQJ; see Bar Memorandum, 3.

[40] CDJC CXCV-158.

[41] CDJC CXCV-156.

district prosecutor. The CGQJ took a detailed interest in every phase of this process.[42]

The necessity of having the private bar associate with any government agency as to its most precious internal decisions must have been irksome. Yet no collective group managed to protest formally against the *numerus clausus*. In Paris, "the majority of the Bar," Charpentier would later observe, "disliked the 'racial' laws."[43] Yet he did not think it feasible to muster effective sentiment against a strong minority of his antisemitic, avaricious, or merely neutral colleagues.

Furthermore, the active statutory period affecting Jewish lawyers still fell into the self-described "lune-de-miel" (honeymoon) between the Bar and Vichy.[44] As Charpentier observed of the possibility of formal objection to the quotas, speaking also of the North African Bar, which had another considerable body of Jewish lawyers in its midst:

> It [protest] would only have interested the Bars of Paris and North Africa, which—since it was in major part antisemitic—would not have joined our efforts.[45]

Eventually, a policy of *attenuation,* a kind of "working from within" was agreed to, Charpentier says, adding that such esteemed Jewish colleagues as Masse and Crémieux concurred that this offered the best hope of "mitigating the suffering of their co-religionists."[46] The Bar would move to "conserve among us the majority of those colleagues who had won our esteem or who absolutely depended on their profession to support their existence."[47]

---

[42] See, e.g., CGQJ to district prosecutor in Cusset, 25 September 1941, on the racial declarations of lawyers Maître Dreyfus-May and Abramovitch, CDJC CXCV-155; for other examples of CGQJ micromanagement, see chapter 3, e.g., at notes 73 and 89.

[43] Charpentier, *Au Service,* 151. Charpentier mentions that one of his association's strongest protests related to the 2 June statute as it persecuted Freemasons. Joseph Barthélemy insisted that the *bâtonnier* of the Bar Association in Amiens be removed for belonging to that secret organization. Again, however, the argument with Vichy related not so much to the substance of the removal as to the private lawyers' objection to incursions on their own autonomy in admitting or firing their own, ibid., 143–44.

[44] Ibid., chapter 9 (entitled "The Honeymoon"), although by the end of summer 1941, relations with Barthélemy were indeed wearing thin.

[45] Ibid., 151.

[46] Ibid., 153.

[47] Ibid.

So the Bar Association of the City of Paris, the country's most powerful, began the process of racial computation, compromise, and choice. The first task, which culminated on 2 January 1942, resulted in a list of seventy lawyers from the greater Paris region who would be allowed to continue in the practice of law.[48] Thirty-three of the Parisian lawyers were listed as holding the carte de combattant from one of the two World Wars.[49] One woman lawyer (there were five in all), Mme. Kraemer Bach, earned additional notation as "retained provisionally on the list of the Bar of the Court of Appeals of Paris until the official declaration of the death of her son who, as it appears from documents submitted to the court, fell in battle in a light armored division on May 10, 1940."[50] In addition, twenty lawyers from these jurisdictions who were still prisoners of war gained "provisional continuation, their cases to be re-evaluated after their liberation."[51]

The decree and its appended list are interesting in several respects. First, no total number of Aryan lawyers at the Paris Bar is cited, so it is difficult to assess the liberality or stinginess of the number (forty-eight) permitted to remain in practice. In spring 1943, Charpentier would estimate that there were 2,035 lawyers (including stagiaires) at the Paris bar.[52] This, if roughly the figure in 1941 over to 1942, would permit forty Jewish lawyers to remain in practice. The decree exceeds that number, but it explicitly cites Article 1, paragraph 4 of the 16 July law, permitting an excess for lawyers gaining exemption due to accepted war veteran status, Legion d'honneur, etc. Second, the list includes such

---

[48] CDJC CVIII-6.

[49] Ibid.

[50] Ibid.

[51] Ibid.

[52] See Antignac, CGQJ to Paris Bar, 17 March 1943, CDJC CXCIII-176, demanding the number of lawyers and stagiaires at the Paris bar; and response, Charpentier, CDJC CVIII-15. At roughly the same time, the Germans—always prone to exaggeration when it came to the influence of lawyers—estimated more than 2300 Aryans and more than five hundred (instead of the accurate 305) Jews at the Paris Bar, CDJC LXXV-172. Further to demonstrate their obsession, see Röthke to SD, 8 March 1943: "As far as I can tell, from reading the *Journal officiel,* the philo-Semites in certain ministries still admit, or re-admit, Jews to the exercise of leading professions." He then lists nine such categories, including "Jewish lawyers," "Jewish notaries" and—even more fantastically (see chapter 3)—"Jewish judges (are some still there by chance?)," CDJC XXIII-21.

already familiar names as Samuel Spanien (Blum's defense counsel at Riom), still obviously active in their practice; but it also includes names such as Pierre Masse, Marcel Uhry, and several others who had been arrested on 21 August 1941 with thirty-eight other prominent Parisian lawyers.[53] Many of these were still in Drancy, and in fact never to return to their homes, much less their practice. Did the Bar and the court, by listing these names, hope both to honor and to encourage such victims? Arrested by French police and in a camp run largely by French administrators, would the action of a French court at least serve to give them solace that they had not been forgotten?

Contemporaneous with the judicial decree, the CGQJ set the number of Jewish practitioners in the capital region at 305 and the number effectively disbarred under the *numerus clausus* at 250.[54] With forty-eight, plus Mme. Kraemer Bach, now permitted to practice, it was clear that a sizable number were out of work. The Paris Bar attempted to increase accessibility to practice by means of the two other available routes. Under the Article 8 exceptions stipulated by the definitional statute of 2 June, the Bar, in its own recent words:

> rendered an opinion on each petition submitted by Jewish lawyers to the CGQJ. The opinions varied with each lawyer according to the following

---

[53] See chapter 3, notes 12–45.

[54] The global number 305 comes from the covering memorandum, CGQJ to Dr. Schneider, German High Command, 16 January 1942, CDJC CXCV-18. Jacques Adler, *The Jews of Paris and the Final Solution* (New York: Oxford University Press 1987), 27, seems to have misreported this number as 250, and perhaps misinterpreted the figure as referring to lawyers still remaining in practice (as opposed to the global number of Jewish lawyers in the Paris region). In fact, the number 250 in our text—the number actually *disbarred* in early 1942—comes from an interesting exchange between CGQJ and a former bâtonnier, Charles de l'Estoille. The latter had written to the agency on 26 January 1942, complaining apparently that the Paris Bar Association was trying to protect its Jewish members. The CGQJ responded politely but firmly three days later that these charges "are unjustified. The administrative committee of the Bar has engaged in no tactic whatsoever to protect Jews." CGQJ tells its correspondent that the Bar will, under the statute, advise the CGQJ who it thinks deserves an exemption; that there will "apparently be very few names" on the Bar's list, and that "you can be sure that the CGQJ will present to the Court of Appeals of Paris only those names of Jewish lawyers that fall well within the requirements stated in the law of 17 July." The letter further indicates that, like de l'Estoille, a number of "lawyers from the Northern region" had expressed some dismay, but that the explanation was "the result of insufficient information," CDJC XXIII-2.

hierarchy: unfavorable; no objection; honorable [exercice honorable]; favorable [avis favorable]; most favorable [avis très favorable]. The Court of Appeals then rendered its opinion, denying almost all the petitions in its session of 13 February, 1942.[55]

The 2 June exceptions yielding little benefit to petitioning Jewish lawyers, the Paris Bar (and others) sought to take advantage of the *exemptions* specially provided by paragraph 5 of Article I of the 16 July law establishing the *numerus clausus*. Here, lawyers cited for "professional merit" might, if their status were confirmed by the Minister of Justice and then the CGQJ, specially continue in practice. The Paris-area bar associations recommended fifteen such lawyers.[56] The Court of Appeals affirmed in its plenary session of 13 February 1942.[57]

Joseph Barthélemy—in his statutory function under the 16 July statute of "designating" to the CGQJ such eminent individuals—quickly advised Vallat of the names proposed,[58] appending the Court of Appeals decision to that effect of early January 1942 that listed all the names.[59] On 4 April, Xavier Vallat permitted five to gain an exemption on the basis of extraordinary professional merit.[60] But the CGQJ chief denied the recommendations for the others, "seeing no reason at all to maintain them on the lists" and inquired further as to one of the candidacies. Then came the changeover to Darquier de Pellepoix.[61] On 24 August the new head of CGQJ wrote to Barthélemy:

> My predecessor has issued you a favorable opinion on maintaining, over and above the *numerus clausus* [five of the lawyers] proposed by their bar associations and by the Court of Appeals of Paris....

---

[55] Bar Memorandum, 2, with annex 8, dated, however, *12* February 1942.

[56] Fourteen were recommended by the Paris Bar, ibid., 3; one was recommended by the Bar of Reims; memorandum, Ministry of Justice to CGQJ, 28 March 1942, asking for the latter's opinion on each of the fifteen, CDJC CXI-25.

[57] CDJC CVIII-8.

[58] Ibid.

[59] Named were Crémieux, Hollander, Ignace, Javal, Lemant, Loeb, Loewel, Lyon-Caen, Montel, Netter, Rein, Mme. Scheid, Simon (of Reims), Vidal-Naquet, and Widal, CDJC XI-25.

[60] These were Mme. Scheid, and Maîtres Lemant, Netter, Raphael Eugène Crémieux, and Charles Lyon-Caen.

[61] See, e.g., Jean Laloum, *La France anti-sémite de Darquier de Pellepoix* (Paris: Syros, 1979), 13.

I now inform you that I am issuing an unfavorable opinion on the maintaining of these lawyers.[62]

Their sad fates (at least one, Vidal-Naquet, was probably already deported by the time Darquier acted against him on French soil) may well have been appreciated by the Bar groups that recommended them in the first place, but the eventual treatment of the originally designated fourteen Parisians is described recently as follows:

> The Bar asked for the maintaining of 14 Jewish lawyers by reason of their professional merit. It could only deplore the rejection of these proposals by the CGQJ in October 1942. The lawyers so excluded from the Bar were made the subject of a special petition, asking that the clients of these lawyers be safeguarded for them. The administrative committee of the Bar rejected this petition in November 1941. It adopted, on the other hand, in February 1942 the principle of a pension for Jewish lawyers excluded from the Bar who had practiced for at least 35 years.[63]

Although on rare occasions, associations of lawyers or avoués were to achieve success—even with the redoubtable Darquier, in seeking exemptions for their exceptional members[64]—some of those already included under the *numerus clausus* and declared by the Court of Appeals to have their veterans status proved by a *carte de combattant* could not feel completely at ease in their status as lawyers. The CGQJ and others were always on guard, making sure that the bar associations, the courts and even the government agencies were being rigorous.[65]

Charpentier generally tried to resist the agency in its frequent demands for precise statistics about Jewish lawyers continuing to practice. In fall 1942, he notes to CGQJ of his remaining Jewish colleagues that:

---

[62] CDJC CXI-25. See Lubetzki, *La Condition des Juifs,* 51.

[63] Paris Bar memorandum, 3, with attached minutes of the meeting of the administrative committee, 17 February 1942. The idea of providing a pension to discharged lawyers was not new; even legal functionaries, summarily discharged *en masse* from the courts (see the early Vichy law 3194 of 1940, *Journal officiel,* 23 July 1940, permitting without justification the firing of magistrates and functionaries; and see chapter 3) were permitted their pension by law 3364, *Journal Officiel,* 19 September 1940.

[64] Success was rare but is exemplified by the case of Lucien Cohen Solal of an old Algerian family. The approval by the CGQJ on 25 March 1942, of this avoué's exception combines all three of the elements available to private lawyers (vieille souche, special service to the state, and personal professional merit), CDJC CCXXXVII-27.

[65] CDJC CXCV-18.

> I have no way of telling you with certainty who are those who continue to plead. In Paris, there are many jurisdictions, often at great distances from each other, and many lawyers practice only intermittently. To satisfy your inquiry, it would be necessary to impose individual scrutiny on each person, and this is neither possible for me nor part of my duties.[66]

Yet Charpentier did report, for the first quarter of 1943, that there were ninety-two lawyers by then theoretically permitted to practice, many of them the already cited combination of forty-eight from the January 1942 Court of Appeals decree, twenty or so wives and mothers of prisoners of war or as yet missing in action and others who had during the prior year received either Article 8 exceptional status or exemptions for war veteran status.[67] At around the same time, it was reported that only one Jewish notary retained clients in the Paris region (Robert Revel), but that this person "never comes to the Palais,"[68] and that there were only two Jewish avoués still practicing, "Frank and Dreyfuss. These never come to the Palais, and they appear only by an Aryan clerk."[69]

The double dose to Jewish legal talent found in the laws of 2 June and 16 July, 1941, combined with the tacit acceptance of the situation by the Bar Association, dissolved Jewish legal talent, once such a solid element in the practice. Six months after Charpentier's estimate of ninety-two remaining Jews at the Bar, the group consisted of twenty-seven prisoners of war, twelve war widows, and sixty others including such as the already deported Pierre Masse, and at least a handful of Parisian lawyers who had relocated to the southern zone[70]; no wonder that Emmanuel Blanc, whose Jewishness was concealed throughout the war, noticed the decreasing numbers of Jewish lawyers in his day to day practice at the

---

[66] Charpentier to district prosecutor, Paris, 16 October 1942, CDJC CVIII-13.

[67] Charpentier to CGQJ, 7 April 1943, CDJC CVIII-15.

[68] Report of Ziegler de Loes, 2.

[69] Ibid. The references are to Lucien Frank (see chapter 3, note 98, and below, note 232), and Jean-François Dreyfuss.

[70] The October 1942 list of Jewish lawyers allowed to practice in addition to those from the original January decree, which later list Charpentier managed to procure, under pressure from the CGQJ, already contained six out of the fifteen named who were either in the Unoccupied Zone, in foreign countries, or in other cities besides Paris, CDJC CVIII-13.

Palais.[71] By late 1942, the CGQJ endorsed Dardot's estimate that "14 or 16 Jewish lawyers now practice at the Palais."[72]

In the other area of Vichy control that had sizable numbers of Jewish lawyers, the situation was equally depressing. North Africa, whose countries each had a *numerus clausus*[73] also had cases of attempted exemption for exemplary professional service. These, too, did not often end successfully for the applicant. In Morocco, thirty-three lawyers were removed by the quota, out of thirty-seven at the bars of Casablanca, Marrakech, Fes, and Oujda.[74] On 30 January 1942, the Court of Appeals of Rabat issued its decree on who could continue and who could not, generally affirming the decisions of several months before by the local bar association. Three lawyers were maintained under 2 June, Article 3 exceptions.

Algeria had a sufficient number of Jewish lawyers to attract the attention of one of its bâtonniers somewhat *avant la lettre*. On 16 May 1941, Henri de Bourges, head of the Bar for Setif, wrote to Vallat ("Monsieur le commissaire général et cher Confrère") begging the CGQJ to establish a *numerus clausus*.

> The number of Jews inscribed at the bar associations of Algeria (17 Bars, with the largest Court of Appeals next to that in Paris) is much too high. At our Bar, for example, four out of 12 lawyers are Jews.... Under the rubric moral and social influence, the result is bad. Thus in certain jurisdictions, a unique "morality" exists, so that there is a tendency among many colleagues to consider their profession as a kind of "noisy business" [contentieux commercial] absolutely opposed to the noble traditions of the Bar.[75]

The agency replied later that same month that relief was on the way.[76] By early 1942, Algeria had its *numerus clausus*.[77]

The *numerus clausus* seems to have been generally accepted without major protest by almost all French professional organizations, on the mainland as well as in North Africa. So, in a series of "Bulletins of the

---

[71] See above, notes 25–29.

[72] Report, 16 October 1942, CDJC VIII-13.

[73] See above, chapter 3, note 78.

[74] See judicial decision of the Court of Appeals of Rabat, CDJC LIV-24.

[75] CDJC LXXX-2.

[76] CGQJ to Henri de Bourges, 23 May 1941, ibid.

[77] See chapter 3, note 78.

National Association of Registered Lawyers," for fall 1941, a group that occasionally disagreed on important issues with the Paris Bar, one finds a piece entitled "New Legislation: Dangerous Innovations."[78] The article complains of Vichy's violations of separation of powers and incursions on the right to defense counsel.[79] However, their protest makes no mention of the *numerus clausus* or other persecutory legislation affecting Jewish colleagues.

Somewhat more overtly, the "22nd Trimestrial Bulletin of the Conference of Bâtonniers" in April 1942[80] specifically notes the "Special Laws for the Jews."[81] It makes no comment on the laws, while noting that avoués (solicitors) had sought to extend their rights to plead before courts and while expressing "delight" that the Vichy "legislator," by law of 26 June 1941, had enhanced the powers of lawyers generally.[82]

## 2. The Bar's Relationship to the Germans

There is no indication, at least at this stage of the uncovering of documents, that collectivities of legal service providers collaborated significantly with the Germans. While we have seen very occasional anecdotal evidence of individual deal-making involving Germans and French private lawyers,[83] the bar, on the contrary, seems in the main to have kept its distance from the occupier, neither rebelling nor conforming but instead saving its protests for incursions by Vichy itself on its own autonomy.

Nonetheless, from time to time, it was in the interest of legal professional groups to communicate with the Germans and even to participate with them in working out problems inevitably connected to a dual system of justice such as existed in France during the war. One question that confronted individual lawyers and the bar associations was whether

---

[78] The bulletins were published in the widely-read *Gazette du Palais,* September/October 1941.

[79] See below, note 106.

[80] Available in the Library of the Bar Association, Palais de Justice.

[81] Ibid., 14.

[82] Ibid.

[83] See chapter 3, notes 31–40, for a description of the process that led to the release of a few of the Jewish lawyers who were arrested in August 1941.

or not to offer French legal defense counsel for people hauled before the Gestapo and its "courts."

There was little zeal to perform such work and there was also, of course, the related question of French counsel's ability to speak German, an issue flagged by the occupiers themselves in a mid-1941 memorandum that in the main accepted the concept itself of French lawyers defending people before German tribunals.[84] Once in place, French counsel sometimes found that their clients had been executed before they could gather any evidence, much less plead or appeal. Yet German justice—although "ferocious"—often respected the forms of a defense and, in Jacques Charpentier's accurate memory, sometimes acquitted.[85] As to his own constituency's attitude, "Our relations with German justice were proper [Nos rapports avec la justice allemande étaient correctes]."[86]

The behavior of French associations for legal service providers, in the face of pragmatic (not necessarily legal) obstacles posed by the German presence in France, by and large displays a gritty gallic perspicacity. Whatever one may think of the substance of some of the tasks performed by the legal profession under Vichy, the willingness to carry on with a sense of solidarity and professionalism merits a degree of respect.

## 3. Charpentier, the Paris Bar, and Non-Quota Issues Relating to Jewish Lawyers

### a. *The Wearing of the Star of David*

Like other Jews in the Occupied Zone, lawyers had to wear the Star of David. While largely outside the scope of this study, it is probably fair to say—with most earlier historians—that Vichy finally did distinguish itself on Jewish questions by refusing to extend the special insignia to Jews in the Unoccupied Zone and by tending to raise a voice of protest against this odious usage even to the German overlords in the north.[87]

---

[84] High Command memorandum, 9 May 1941, YV IV/14.

[85] Ibid., 167; accord AN $BB^{30}$, 1713. The French legal system did not always accept either the acquittal or the conviction as binding on its courts.

[86] Charpentier, *Au Service,* 167.

[87] Even notably antisemitic lawyers such as Alibert, the first Justice Minister, thought of the Star as "ignominious," Moulin de Labarthète, *Le Temps des Illusions* (Geneva: Bourguin, 1946), 280. See generally, Léon Poliakov, *L'Étoile jaune* (Paris: Éd. du Centre, 1949); also, Michael Marrus and Robert Paxton, *Vichy France and the Jews* (New York: Basic Books, 1981), 235–40. Yet, French police often arrested Jews in the Occupied Zone

Zeitschel realized, in early June 1942, that lawyers and notaries were planning to demand that their groups be exempt from the wearing of the Star; he told Dannecker to have such protesters arrested.[88] Then, by specific order of Röthke, indicating again the Germans' peculiar attention to French lawyers:[89] "all Jewish notaries, avocats, and avoués, whether in the Palais de Justice or in other jurisdictions, must wear the Jewish star."[90] The Nazi obsession with this issue provoked a kind of cat-and-mouse played out, in descending order of approval for the policy, among the Germans, the CGQJ, the Paris district prosecutor, and Charpentier's bar association.

The Germans heard from their sources at the Palais, as that summer of 1942 turned into fall, that very few Stars of David were to be seen on legal professionals around town. Röthke wrote to the CGQJ asking for an explanation, but that agency, which particularly in Darquier's hands usually did the Germans' bidding, replied with uncharacteristic slipperiness:

> I must tell you that the Palais is on vacation from July to October. The inquiry we plan cannot, under these conditions, produce any results.[91]

But a few weeks later, the French agency persevered. They sent their man, R. Ziegler de Loes, into the Palais to meet with his self-described longterm acquaintance, the advocate-general, Dardot. Ziegler asked Dardot about the paucity of Stars at the Palais. But that official of the district

---

for infractions relating to the Star, for example, failure to wear it (*Cahen,* August 1942, UGIF correspondence, CDJC CDXXIX-1), or even to have it properly sewn on (*Largilliere,* January 1943, UGIF correspondence, CDJC, ibid.). Marrus and Paxton, *Vichy France,* 240, end their extensive treatment of the subject by noting that Vichy took an "even more threatening" step when it imposed on all Jews the affixation of the word "Jew" or "Jewess" on "all Jews' vital personal documents."

[88] Poliakov, *L'Étoile jaune,* 86; in the margin of Zeitschel's memorandum someone (probably Dannecker) wrote "To Drancy!"

[89] See chapter 3, notes 15–19.

[90] Order of 15 July 1942, CDJC XXXIII-6.

[91] CGQJ to Röthke, 2 October 1942, CDJC CXV-80. Darquier had already told the Germans six months earlier to expect no French enthusiasm anywhere for the Star, much less initiatives to enforce its appearance on Jewish outerwear. Poliakov, *L'Étoile jaune,* 31. Later he told the Germans that "the wearing of the Jewish Star...is becoming ever more inconsistent," YV, Klarsfeld Notebook 1.083.

prosecutor's office passed the buck, noting "the hierarchy at the Palais"[92]; he advised seeing Charpentier. The bâtonnier, in his turn, responded that there were twelve to fourteen Jewish lawyers at the Palais by that date, and that they "on their own motion were not wearing the Star, despite it being called to their attention."[93]

Ziegler seems to have realized that he was being forestalled by the lawyers to whom he directed his agency's inquiry, and especially perhaps by the bâtonnier. Ziegler describes Charpentier's attitude as follows:

> This latter...showed his obvious bad faith in proclaiming that it was impossible for him to monitor the frequency of the attendance of certain Jewish lawyers at the Palais. To put it succinctly, he demurred to our petition.[94]

In this situation, at least, the leader of the major bar association in France took direct action to forestall an additional humiliation against Jewish lawyers. Although the Bar generally has been portrayed to me by Jewish survivors of the period in terms of "antisemitism,"[95] and although Charpentier's actions about colleagues wearing the Star amounted perhaps to less than the self-described complete refusal mentioned in his postwar memoirs,[96] the bar's overall contempt for the practice merits praise and reflects the resistance of most Frenchmen to the sight of ostracizing insignia.[97]

### *b. Lawyers in Drancy*

Whatever the final verdict on Jacques Charpentier in his dealings with Jewish colleagues, it is clear that the man was deeply moved by the fate of some of his oldest and most revered confrères at the Bar. A true "resistant" as the war progressed, and a man who himself would be im-

---

[92] Ziegler to CGQJ, 22 October 1942, CDJC CXV-80.

[93] Report, R. Ziegler de Loes, 22 October 1942, CDJC CVIII-13.

[94] Ibid.

[95] Roger Berg, interview with author, 16 December 1991, Paris. Berg's own story has been published in *Le Monde juif,* 51 (July-September 1968).

[96] Charpentier, *Au Service,* 154.

[97] Marrus and Paxton, *Vichy France and the Jews,* 236, put the following conundrum forward on this issue: "It is worth pondering why the Vichy government was so much more recalcitrant about the star than about the deportation of foreign Jews." Something of this puzzle is also present in reflecting on the Bar's behavior.

prisoned by the Germans in 1943,[98] Charpentier's self-described "honeymoon" with Vichy undoubtedly disintegrated into a "rupture" because in part of his own personal observations of the camp at Drancy. His words are inspired by visits to the camp to see his revered and beloved colleague, Pierre Masse (and others):

> Drancy. The first of those Hells...during a time in which we still did not know of Dachau or Ravensbrück; it was already a strong piece of evidence about the return of humanity to savagery.... Like the opening to a zoo, with its grotesque cement statuary...2000 poor souls—dirty, scared, of whom half did not know French. [Charpentier asked to see Pierre Masse.] As I was waiting, I heard a scream. I saw a policeman grasp a person by the neck and shake him....
>
> Masse said it is like that all the time. You don't even notice it after awhile.... He took me to his room. A cement room. Wooden blocks, with straw mattresses. The 40 [lawyer] prisoners...could not believe they had been imprisoned by the French police. Masse was their one ray of hope. They gathered around me with messages for their family. One of them was reading the *Journal* of Gide in the Pleiade edition.... Everyone recognized Masse as a leader, who walked with the same tranquil assurance he showed at the Bar.[99]

Charpentier returned to Drancy several days later:

> To demoralize them...the lawyers were dispersed...recognized as leaders wherever they were sent.... Whoever has seen Drancy understands Babylonia.[100]

As to the final hours of Masse himself on French soil:

> I never saw Pierre Masse again. His friends had vainly tried to lodge against him a false accusation that would bring him under French jurisdiction. They took him in one of their trains from Compiègne...their cargo condemned to death.[101]

---

[98] Ibid., 202.

[99] Charpentier, *Au Service,* 154–55. Of course, these relatively prominent forty lawyers were only the first of their colleagues to pass through Drancy on the way to the death camps. Consider Maître Claude Rosenthal, himself a war veteran, whose mother pleaded in vain for his release from Drancy and his reinvestiture at the bar during the first three months of 1942, CDJC CDXXIX-6.

[100] Charpentier, *Au Service,* 155–56.

[101] Ibid., 154. On Masse, see below note 192 and chapter 3, notes 41–45.

On 14 December 1941, Masse wrote the following to Charpentier from Drancy, in a manner evoked by other colleagues who would fall for their faith or for their political beliefs:[102]

> I am called. I will probably die. I will die, I hope, for my country, my faith, my profession [mon ordre]. Please watch after my son. Pierre Masse.[103]

## B. Fighting Barthélemy, Laval, and Gabolde

Charpentier had abided "the strange M. Alibert," that well-known antisemite.[104] Yet his relations to Barthélemy, the liberal, were ironically far less cordial. Some of the change, of course, derived from Charpentier's response to Riom, where men like Blum, Daladier, and others were already guilty by proclamation of Vichy's leader.[105] Charpentier called this violation of the separation of powers "an enormity."[106] The Bar leader's letter to Pétain indicated again how formidable Charpentier was when his instincts as a lawyer provoked him to see under attack something basic in his legal training.

So, too, the Paris Bar would not tolerate the idea of a political oath to Pétain. That was for the judges, perhaps, but not for proudly autonomous private lawyers. Charpentier conveyed a proclamation to Barthélemy, taken by the Bar, that

> the most vital of our principles is independence.... A lawyer must never be deprived of that liberty of judgment and of freedom to criticize, not for any man, not for any institution. The bâtonnier is therefore asked [to tell the Justice Minister] that there shall be no change in the oath.[107]

---

[102] Compare the letter to Charpentier from a communist lawyer about to be shot by the Germans as a hostage, Antoine Hajje, cited in Charpentier, *Au Service,* 158; and chapter 3, text at note 25.

[103] Charpentier, *Au Service,* 157. Protests for Masse's release continued into spring 1942, but on 30 March 1942, Knochen declared that all such petitions for Masse would be firmly denied. Poliakov, *L'Étoile jaune,* 24–5. As for subsequent legalities regarding Masse's son, see chapter 7, note 117.

[104] Charpentier, *Au Service,* 127.

[105] See chapter 1, note 43.

[106] Charpentier, *Au Service,* 147.

[107] Ibid. 141.

After receiving this proclamation, Barthélemy—whose reverence for Marshal Pétain was overt and non-negotiable[108]—never spoke to Charpentier again.[109]

Eventually, Charpentier's spirit of resistance sought even grander battles. Pierre Laval, a member of the Paris Bar, tried on several occasions to intermeddle with the association's decisions on who belonged and who should be disbarred. Again, lawyers would not permit this kind of incursion, but their ire centered on several specific situations and not on the mass disbarment of their Jewish or "non-French" colleagues. One of these cases involved an unnamed extreme right-wing lawyer, (actually Jean-Charles Legrand),[110] who had been disbarred prior to the war. The Germans and Laval pressured Charpentier to reinstate Legrand, who had been used by these régimes to head the propaganda radio network out of Paris.[111] Barthélemy may have slowed the process down,[112] although Charpentier does not so credit him.[113] But in the late spring and early summer 1943, under the leadership of Vichy's third Justice Minister, Gabolde, the authority of all relevant players was brought down upon Charpentier and his association. When they continued to refuse reinstatement, and when Gabolde issued an edict, signed by Laval, accomplishing by a *fait du prince* what the Bar refused to do, not only Paris (which vowed a collective resignation), but most of France's organized Bar,[114] rebelled.[115] It is a measure of the courage and the principle of a man

---

[108] See chapter 4, section C and, e.g., Barthélemy, *Ministre,* chapter 3.

[109] Charpentier, *Au Service,* 142. Barthélemy, *Ministre,* 553, however, credits Charpentier with offering and probably implementing assistance to the imprisoned Barthélemy in early 1945. In general, and perhaps understandably, the postwar Charpentier, *Au Service,* 140, is far less generous in his memories of the Justice Minister, ascribing the decision of this distinguished and fully established figure to join such a government to a "psychosis of vanity," to "pathology."

[110] See Barthélemy, *Ministre,* 58, for his account of the following incident, which differs in some respects from Charpentier's but affirms the latter's eloquence and courage.

[111] Ibid.

[112] Ibid.

[113] Charpentier, *Au Service,* 199.

[114] Barthélemy, *Ministre,* 58.

[115] Charpentier, *Au Service,* 205, however, excepts the rival National Association of Registered Lawyers; but see Barthélemy, *Ministre,* 58, where he indicates that that group did in fact support their colleagues at the Paris Bar. The difference between these two groups

like Charpentier—but also of the tendency of his instincts to protest here but not elsewhere—that this conversation could then take place:

> JC: The Bar has spoken, following its conscience.... I have the duty of defending the integrity of the Bar.
> Laval: Your association, always your association. You are about to lose it. The [German] Embassy has its eye on you. You'll find out.
> JC: Is that a threat?
> Laval: Yes. I've had enough. I'm going to send you my resignation from the Bar.
> JC: M. le President, that will certainly anguish us.
> [Laval hangs up the phone.][116]

The government retreated.[117] Legrand was eventually indicted for collaborating with the enemy.[118]

The Bar uniformly resisted incursions on its membership decisions. So, when Gabolde actually passed a law on 2 June 1943,[119] precisely two years to the day after Barthélemy's anti-Jewish statute, giving his ministry the right to regulate vacancies arising in the administrative committees of any Bar, the Paris association instructed Charpentier through a formal decree to protest, which he promptly did.[120] The Bar's ferociously intelligent defense of the historical autonomy of French lawyers situates, by contrast, its failure to see racial and religious ostracism as similarly unacceptable:

---

is also alluded to in a Vichy memorandum that tries to remind the Bar that, although it is "in principle, a free profession...yet it is not possible to agree that a corporation, of whatever kind, retain sovereignty over its membership, without control and without assuring that all candidates meet the requirements of law and regulation. Indeed, the Bar is not a private organism...a decree of the Cour de Cassation of 8 January 1868 [declares] that the administration of the Bar is a *public authority*.... [T]he new régime's tendency to include corporations as part of the state thus implies, as opposed to what the bâtonnier of Paris maintains, that the Bar must be under the supervision of the Courts of Appeal," AN $BB^{30}$, 1711.

116 Charpentier, *Au Service,* 119.

117 Barthélemy, *Ministre,* 58.

118 Ibid.

119 *Journal officiel,* 18 June 1941; see also AN 72 AJ 413, Dossier no. 1 for text of law and the protest that followed it.

120 Ibid.

> The provisions [of the law of 2 June, 1943], on which the Paris Bar was not consulted, are without precedent in the history of our Order.... [T]he independence of the Bar, without which there could only be the appearance of justice, rests on the double privilege of recruiting for itself and of electing its own leaders. These rights have been respected by all earlier French régimes....
>
> [H]aving been charged with defending the institutions confided to its care, it must raise its voice with strength against the gravest attack that has ever been mounted against the freedom of the Bar....[!][121]

With all that we are now learning about the Bar's relationship to its persecuted Jewish membership, there is finally no small irony in the words of this proclamation. Indeed, the many cases of personal and association-wide courage showed by the leaders and by the lawyers in their groups lead to a paradoxical conclusion: there can be little real doubt that if the same energies had been mustered against the *numerus clausus,* there would have been no realistic way of implementing the quotas. But exclusion, imprisonment, deportation—these were not enough to provoke the "dignity" of the Bar towards full-fledged protest.

## C. Individual Legal Lives

The average practitioner's life went on pretty much as it had before the defeat, except that the newly promulgated religious laws made the stuff of law-related practice more complex, more rich—or in the untranslatable French phrase, *plus délicat.*

### 1. Advocacy in the Face of Deportation

In the Paris phone books of December 1941, as the *Pariser Zeitung* observed gleefully, there appeared 477 Levys compared to 747 in 1939; 114 Dreyfuses compared to 203; 87 Kahns compared to 142, etc. Although it was distressful to that journal that there were two more Bernstein's (15 compared to 13 in 1939), the paper took solace in reporting that "the name Léon Blum can no longer be found among his 80 homonyms" in the phone book. Many of the missing or deleted, like Blum, were in

---

[121] Ibid.

prison. Many were in Drancy, where there were no telephones for the private use of its inhabitants.

Lawyers were assisting some of these dispossessed Jews in the most desperate moments of their lives, in some cases indeed the final moments prior to deportation. Life on—and death from—French soil remained for victim and oppressor alike matters of law, negotiated by ordinary people using the tools of their seemingly prosaic craft. It is thus too simplistic to say, as a recent commentator put it in an otherwise sound sketch of the Vichy judiciary, that "rapidly, and especially after the occupation of the free zone in 1942, police action replaced judicial criteria. The Vichy police, or the Gestapo, did not bother with more or less subtle legal distinctions as they seized those Jews who had not yet hidden themselves away."[122] Right up until the Liberation, lawyers worked to find loopholes for the Jews of Drancy and other way-stations to the East.

In Drancy, prisoners desperately sought the certificat de non appartenance that would be their exit ticket. If impossible in their own cases, they would urge their Aryan spouses to present their certificats, or at least their baptismal records, to the CGQJ. If the French would not listen, perhaps the Germans—with their differing approach to *Mischehe* (see chapter 6)—would at least bestow upon the Jewish partner some additional degree of protection against whatever lay ahead. Not surprisingly, prisoners who had lawyers, and both time and means to contact them, solicited legal counsel on deportation itself.

The case of *Samy Rothschild* exemplifies the perspicacity of various French lawyers in assisting clients to escape Drancy through legal means.

If only thirteen of thirty-one Rothschilds remained in the Paris phone book in late 1941, according to the *Pariser Zeitung,* at least some of these were already in Drancy. Others would follow, and more than one Parisian Rothschild would be deported over the next three years.[123] Although Samy Rothschild (whose surname was occasionally rendered "Rotschild" in the documents) had lived in Brest—a fact that became significant in proving his religious status—his brother Albert retained Parisian counsel to assist them. By November 1942, Albert had won a

---

[122] Bernard de Bigault du Granrut, "Les Tribuneaux et le statut des Juifs d'Octobre 1940 et Juin 1941," *Tenou'a/Le Mouvement* 62 (Spring 1992).

[123] See Serge Klarsfeld, *Memorial to the Jews Deported From France* (New York: Beate Klarsfeld Foundation, 1983), 446, 566.

decree of non-Jewishness from the Tribunal civil de la Seine. But would this help the imprisoned Samy? Word was conveyed to the legal department of UGIF, which helped to amass all probative documentation. The aim was to convince the authorities that Samy, under the Vichy law of 2 June 1941, was also not Jewish.

Counselor Claudien Pelletier, who worked from an office in the rue des Mathurins, had already transferred documents about the family to Samy's private lawyer, Maître Stoeber in the Place Vendôme. Pelletier, having helped Albert, wrote to the lawyers at UGIF that "Having the same parents as his brother Albert, M. Samy Rothschild can benefit from the judgment" of non-Jewishness rendered by the Paris court.[124] The UGIF lawyers, noting that Samy's present residence was "Drancy, V-20-3e," proceeded to ask Stoeber for the documentary file. There was considerable urgency, as the forty-fifth convoy from Drancy to the East had just departed two days before, and deportations were progressing at a fevered pace.

Stoeber had already forwarded Samy's file to the Germans[125] in an attempt to gain his client's freedom. He reported to UGIF that, at least on the current state of the file, the Germans were unwilling to release Samy.[126] More work would have to be done. Stoeber provided UGIF with Rothschild's racial profile, which was unfortunately full of *lacunae*. Samy did not know the date of his grandmother's death, nor whether her burial in Paris was done religiously; nor whether his parents had a religious ceremony at their marriage. Samy was not baptized but neither had he ever belonged to any organized religion. Samy points out that leading citizens both of Brest and Caractec could confirm this and that "the proof that he did not frequent Jewish religious circles is that Brest does not have a religious Jewish community."[127]

The end of the story appears to have been satisfactory to the client, at least as far as we can surmise. Two beneficial factors arose, one thanks

---

[124] Pelletier to UGIF, 13 November 1942, CDJC CDXXIX-1. Given Vichy law's attitude that siblings might well have conflicting legal status (chapters 2 and 6), Pelletier's optimism was unwarranted.

[125] "Avenue Foch" designated the Gestapo's anti-Jewish bureau at that address.

[126] UGIF to Maître Stoeber, 18 November 1942 with accompanying handwritten notes about the matter, CDJC CDXXIX-1.

[127] UGIF to Stoeber, 27 November 1942, ibid.

to Stoeber, one thanks to German policy on deportations. Stoeber apparently managed to obtain by the first week in December, a certificat de non appartenance for Samy and to send it along to UGIF at their urging, "within several hours" of receipt. UGIF would then copy the document and send it to Drancy (Stoeber would get back the original for his files).[128] Meanwhile, convoys from Drancy had grounded to a halt. There would be no deportations again until 9 February of the following year.[129] On 21 December UGIF and Stoeber seem to have closed their file on the case, but although there is no mention of Samy Rothschild's name on any subsequent list of deportees known to researchers at this time, we also have no definitive sign of his ultimate fate. Clearly, lawyers gave Samy Rothschild a fighting chance.

Not so satisfying—and perhaps more typical—was the result of an intervention by Maître Pierre Mallard for his client Andreas Nissim Bitton. Writing in mid-1942 to UGIF from his offices in the rue de Rivoli, Mallard asks to find out "as soon as possible at which concentration camp my client now is held.... I must tell you that he left Compiègne on 27 March 1942.[130] Mallard needed to locate his client for a pending judicial process. UGIF realized, of course, that the departure from Compiègne was for "a concentration camp in the East," as their followup memorandum puts it.[131] No forwarding address was supplied in such cases. When Bitton's wife tried, several months later, to verify her husband's presence on French soil, UGIF reported to her that the request had been denied.[132] Her husband's lawyer knew only that Bitton had left Compiègne on 27 March. He had no way of knowing at the time that Convoy #1 from French soil, bound for Auschwitz, had left at 5 p.m. that day, with some 1150 Jews aboard.[133] Not yet 37 years old, an "Andreas Bitton" was on the list of deportees.[134] Only about 20 of the human cargo were to return.[135]

---

[128] UGIF to Stoeber, 7 December 1942, ibid.

[129] Klarsfeld, *Memorial to the Jews Deported From France,* 360.

[130] Pierre Mallard to UGIF, 19 June 1942.

[131] Memorandum, 20 June 1942, ibid.

[132] Ibid.

[133] Klarsfeld, *Memorial to the Jews Deported from France,* 1.

[134] Ibid., 10.

[135] Ibid., 1.

A year after the tragic Bitton case, and some six months after the seemingly happier resolution of the Samy Rothschild matter, a complicated situation arose, one that involved both zones and a number of legal issues now familiar to us. The saga of the *Nizard* family seems to have involved two branches. Simon and Marthe Nizard had been arrested and were in Drancy as of early March 1943, when Simon's brother, Armand, arrived in Paris from Marseilles to try to help them out. The brothers had owned a business in Marseilles, the "Ancienne Maison Nizard Frères"; that business was now in the hands of an a.p., a certain Vitton-Laval, a fact that soon became crucial to Armand's own fate.

Armand wrote to UGIF, seeking at best the release of his brother and sister-in-law and at least the right to bring them the *colis* (parcels) that might ease their burdens while imprisoned. UGIF alludes, however, to "the nature of the indictment against M. Simon Nizard" and counsels Armand to "get a lawyer."[136] By 18 March, UGIF's lawyers explicitly removed themselves from the case,[137] and on Convoy 53 from Drancy—thirteen days later—Simon and Marthe Nizard joined about a thousand other Jews in a voyage of death.[138]

Armand returned to his domicile at Fay-sur-Lignon and to his wife and son who also lived there. On 8 June, whatever peace they had achieved was brutally interrupted. Two men had arrived in the town and were directed to the Nizard residence. They blocked the exits of the house and demanded from Simon and the son (who was in the family business himself) the sum of 150,000 francs that they claimed was owed their agents, a Parisian firm, as an outgrowth of litigation with the Nizard's now aryanized company. When Simon pointed out that the family no longer had any income, since their Marseilles business was in the hands of the a.p., and that he would not compromise the case (which had already cost the family 8000 francs to defend), the two men drew revolvers. Claiming to be authorized to do so by the Germans (who had by then overrun the southern zone), they "arrested" the father and son.

Horrified, Mrs. Armand Nizard quickly called in the local police. The latter demanded identification from the intruders but, when told that the German local office in Puy would validate their status, left the house.

---

[136] UGIF memorandum, 5 March 1943, CDJC CDXXIX-1.

[137] Ibid.

[138] Klarsfeld, *Memorial to the Jews Departed from France,* 423.

Mrs. Nizard then offered the two men all that she had—110,000 francs—if they would leave her family alone. They took the money, and even signed a receipt for it. Nonetheless, they forced the Nizard men at gunpoint into their car and left.

Armand and his son followed a path that then took them to Valence, Tarascon, and Marseilles, where they wound up in a German prison called St-Pierre. From there, after almost two weeks, they were sent to Drancy. Meanwhile, the two interlopers had been arrested in Marseilles for false arrest and false identity and were being inculpated by the district prosecutor for Puy. Needing the Nizards' evidence, the French authorities in Puy solicited their release from the Parisian camp.[139]

Mrs. Nizard sent a trusted lawyer, Albert Exbrayat, to Paris to further attempts to release her husband and son. Lauding Exbrayat as the "the only person who, in my despair, thought it his duty to help me," she also asked him to bring precious care packages to her imprisoned family. But she wondered if UGIF could recommend a specialist in the field of internment law, conjuring the name of lawyer Baudoin-Bugnet.[140]

Any legal assistance proved to be in vain. By 12 July, UGIF lawyers still maintained an active file for the Nizards. But on 31 July, father and son, aged 61 and 29 respectively, were deported.[141] Of the approximately one thousand Jews sent to Auschwitz from France that day, 727 were gassed immediately. Of the 273 spared, only 44 returned.[142]

## 2. Lawyers as Informants

A certain percentage of the French population revelled in the opportunities created by the Vichy religious laws. From out of the woodwork came people of all types and trades, eager to inform French or German authorities about suspected Jews. The documents provide examples—outside the scope of this study—of sordid notes delivered to the Gestapo

---

[139] Mme. Nizard to UGIF, 30 June 1943 (with her account to the Puy prosecutor attached), CDJC CDXXIX-1.

[140] Ibid.

[141] Klarsfeld, *Memorial to the Jews Deported from France,* 445.

[142] Ibid., 435.

by eager informants.[143] And Vichy had its own governmental network of informants, eventually associated with the Section d'enquête et de contrôle (SEC) and with the Police aux questions juives. The prefectures were a constant source of information, reporting all the time about any questionable individual.[144]

Inevitably, legal service providers comprised a fraction of the private individuals who delighted in informing on suspected Jews, or in otherwise capitalizing on their suffering not just in the material sense but almost as a mark of their prestige in the "Vichy revolution." There numbers were small, but they were noticed. One of these, a member of the Paris Bar, was seen swaggering around Drancy:

> thought little of before the war, he is now the leader of the Aryan Lodge. This guy was accompanied by German officers and seemed odious during his visit, surpassing in his cynicism even that of his masters. He gave out information to the camp commander, permitting new arrests.[145]

Other such groups had formed, sometimes led by lawyers. In the corporatist manner that typified Vichy ideals, one of these—Henri Labroue of the Monte-Cristo Bar—originated the "Bordeaux Institute of Jewish Studies." He proudly sent a description of his organization to the Bordeaux German field-commander's office, in formal German, closing with a *vorzueglicher Hochachtung*. The board, which consisted largely of lawyers and avoués, passed the following corporate by-laws:

> Article I. An institute of Jewish studies is created in Bordeaux.

---

[143] In one of these, cryptic language of a ludicrously cinematic nature revealed that "Mr. and Mme. DELAPCHIER escapees to Nice: 7 Place Cassini. arrive tomorrow. Camouflaged Jews—British agents—agitators—possessing numerous anti-Nazi books." The Nazis used such data, of course; see SD memorandum, 20 June 1941, YV V-31.

[144] For example, on 27 September 1941, the prefect of Lot s/Garone wrote to the Toulouse regional director of the SEC about "ALASRAKE, of Turkish origin, the son of a Jewish father and grandfather. Does not know the religion of his great-grandfather. His mother was Protestant, his grandmother orthodox, but he does not know the religion of his great-grandmother. This foreigner is married to a Catholic. He is a commercial agent. Although he denies it, it seems nonetheless that he must be considered a Jew," AN $AJ^{38}$, 1090.

[145] "Physionomie de la Quinzaine," undated document (probably mid-1944), a resistance pamphlet, YV 0-9/9(2)-26.

> Article II. This institute has as its function the study and the popularizing of Jewish questions in the interests of France and of international peace.... Article VII. No Jew may be admitted to take part in the institute.[146]

A percentage of the bar, a collectivity that usually reflects dominant rather than radical contemporary *mores,* replicated what they saw Vichy doing to the Jewish population. Charpentier reports, of a minority of his own colleagues, that they quickly capitalized on Vichy policy by assuming a dominion over Jewish property. Nonetheless, Charpentier noticed that

> when I returned to Paris, in the latter half of July 1940...there were some 100 lawyers who had remained behind there. Among these...some were actively 'aryanizing' Jewish property.... During that period, the Bar was really in danger.... The ground was being prepared. There were among us many antisemites.... The Catholics had not pardoned the Republic for its secular policies.[147]

Later his colleagues could observe Joseph Barthélemy (discussed in chapters 1 and 4) proposing to a gathering of *constitutional* draftsmen that Jews were a race apart. How surprising is it, given these models, that otherwise respectable lawyers became outright racists during Vichy? And then, why not go the extra yard, as Vichy had done with such exhibits as that on Jews presented in Paris in 1941, and expend one's energies on the direct "study" of the ostracized group? The corporatist model, attractive to many lawyers, brought even the occasional "autonomous" private lawyer to imitate his Vichy leaders. In that context, information disadvantageous to Jews flowed freely from the private to the public sectors.

## 3. Day-to-Day Practice

In the main, neither the Henri Labroue model nor that of extreme protest (think of Hajje, the communist lawyer, of Léon Blum, or of Philippe Serre), nor even that of gradualism (Jacques Charpentier) predominated among private lawyers. For most lawyers, Vichy simply provided an opportunity to continue one's practice. Many Parisian practitioners, like thousands of their lay compatriots, had of course suffered the twin humiliation of their country's defeat and the exodus towards the south. But, as

---

[146] Letter, 28 April 1941, signed by Labroue and the institute's secretary, Barkhausen.

[147] Charpentier, *Au Service,* 97.

summer 1940 progressed, the majority of lawyers were back at their offices or in the Palais, and this was true of the bulk of other law-related professionals. In the Unoccupied Zone, there was even less disruption. Like Maurice Chevalier, whose "Paris sera toujours Paris" could be heard in the nightclubs of the capital, many ordinary practitioners could say "the law will always be the law." Only with a difference, as we shall see.

This chapter's final sub-section extrapolates, from the experience of about a dozen lawyers, the picture of a pragmatic professional, by no means necessarily antisemitic or racist but nonetheless opportunistic in his use of the new Vichy environment. There is little evidence here—as with the "squealers"—of outright collaboration with the Germans. But unlike some of his colleagues whose practice never touched on racial issues, our subject here did voluntarily undertake matters that grew out of legalistic racism. In general, this lawyer would even-handedly accept a Jewish client along with an Aryan; he might be capable of courageous representation while at the same time serving as an a.p. over Jewish property or at least representing one against Jewish interests. He was, in the main, a "hired gun." He was a lawyer.

### a. Practitioners in Frequent Contact with CGQJ

At least a handful of private practitioners dealt frequently with CGQJ. In correspondence with Boué, the agency's chief of economic aryanization, they dealt as advocates for individual clients on a wide range of issues. They mastered the Vichy laws of religious definition; the aryanization statutes; the caselaw on landlord-tenant[148]; the corporate law of shareholders rights and rights of acquisition where Jewish participation applied; the complexities of what it was to be an a.p., a role actually played by at least one of them. They scheduled conferences with CGQJ officials to plead their cases or to give the agency needed information; more rarely they corresponded with Germans when Nazi approval was necessary to sign off on a deal.

---

[148] Private lawyers would write to the CGQJ to ask about the rent-reduction laws (see chapter 7), even though as we saw this was one area where even the CGQJ was willing to leave the doctrine almost entirely to the ordinary courts. They advised private lawyer René Paillière of this fact in a letter to him, 30 September 1942, citing prominent decisions relevant to the issue, AN AJ[38], contentieux file.

In the first case, that of lawyer Pierre Lepaulle, there seems to be good evidence that his skills were placed in the service of at least one Jewish client on the most basic question of religious definition, while they also served to further the process of aryanization, however marginally in this case. Lepaulle, with law offices in the avenue d'Iéna, wrote in mid-1941 to Boué regarding the troubled administration over Jewish property of a colleague, P. Charles Gervais. (It is not clear whether Lepaulle officially represented Gervais or was inquiring on his behalf less formally.) The Tribunal civil had appointed Gervais the a.p. over the property of David Weill, a collector of choice paintings. Gervais understood the standard for his "trusteeship"[149] to be the following:

> [T]o amass and list all the assets [of whatever kind], to manage them and to administer them both actively and passively, to safeguard them, with the aim of recuperating and taking possession of his property in the occupied zone and to fulfill the duties and responsibilities attached to them.[150]

The problem here was that the Germans had apparently already grabbed Weill's artwork, and a good deal of it had been sent for storage at the *Jeu de Paumes,* the famous museum requisitioned by the Germans to "safeguard" such French collections. It might have been just a matter of time before some of Weill's canvasses passed beyond French borders and even into the hands of that connaisseur, Field Marshal Göring.[151]

The ambiguous nature of so much of this data emerges once again here. The specific legal issue flagged by Lepaulle and Gervais was limited to the duty owed by an a.p. to the property in question. The actual owner of the property, because he was Jewish, hardly affected their thinking. Yet, the lawyers exhibited their professional pride in challenging the bigger fish who had grabbed the prey, even as they seemed to ignore the victimized organism whose efforts had first gathered it up.

About eighteen months later, Lepaulle more squarely advocated the interests of a Jewish client who was in the deepest kind of *personal* trouble. Moreau, an avoué in the rue des Mathurins, had written to UGIF in desperation, as follows:

---

[149] See chapter 7, Section E, for a discussion of the French aryanizing "trust" concept.

[150] Lepaulle to Boué, 6 May 1941, AN $AJ^{38}$, 331; see chapter 6, note 96.

[151] For an acerbic account of Franz Wolf Metternich's "protection bureau" for French art, see Gilles Ragache and Jean-Robert Ragache, *La Vie quotidienne des écrivains et des artistes sous l'Occupation* (Paris: Hachette, 1988), 146.

> As Raymond *Blum*'s solicitor...I wish to inform you that he has asked the court to find that he is not Jewish under the law of 2 June, 1941. This petition is now before the first section of the court and may be taken up any day now; Maître Lepaulle, an advocate at the court...has the file. I must also point out that a certificat of Aryan status is pending at the CGQJ. I inform you of this so that you can take all necessary steps to prevent M. Raymond BLUM from becoming the object of a deportation order [toutes demarches afin d'éviter que RB...soit l'objet d'une mésure de deportation].[152]

Lawyers like Lepaulle may have saved the lives of people like Raymond Blum, and avoué Moreau also played a part.[153]

Lawyer Robert Castille seems to have been involved in a number of aryanization matters, dealing directly with the CGQJ's Boué.[154] A number of Castille's matters commenced with a piece of paper containing a typewritten file number on the upper left and the name of the CGQJ's legal contact on the upper right.[155] In other situations, Castille was named personally as the a.p. In one such situation, a Parisian pharmacy in the rue de Grenelle called Georges Meyer was sold to Aryan interests, but the new owners had a problem: the Minister of Public Health has closed down the store. The purchasers begged for Castille's intervention. What will happen to their income? And what about their landlord, who is insisting on back rent?[156]

In certain other situations, Castille was a "fact-finder" for CGQJ, either following their lead or initiating the inquiry himself. Central to many such situations was the quest to make sure that sales of property to Aryans were indeed "sincere" as opposed merely to creating straw men still

---

[152] Moreau to UGIF, 14 February 1943, CDJC CDXXIX-1.

[153] Although there are scores of victims named "Blum" listed in Klarsfeld's volume as deportees after the date of this letter, there are only two "Raymond Blum"—one from Strasbourg, the other, listed as being from Paris VIII, was deported on 30 June 1944. (The blvd. Richard Lenoir, however, is in the 11$^{e}$, not the 8$^{e}$.) Klarsfeld, *Memorial to the Jews Deported from France,* 575.

[154] See also chapter 7, note 125.

[155] See, e.g., the discussion of a realty company in Vouzeron, where the inquiry involves "whether the company is Jewish. In the affirmative, name an a.p. immediately, preferably one who lives in Paris." CGQJ learns that "M. *Etlin,* a Jew, is the chief executive" and owns forty of the fifty shares outstanding. "An a.p. is urgently required," 5 December 1942, AN $AJ^{38}$, 331.

[156] Early 1944 file, AN $AJ^{38}$, 331.

in the service of Jewish agendas. Solicitors and sheriffs [huissiers] had already complained to a Parisian court of "Jewish manoeuvering" in corporate transactions.[157] One of Castille's 1943 matters involved a "T.S.F. Ariane VII," in which the business might have been "fraudulently" sold to "insincere Aryans," meaning of course that the Jewish influence allegedly survived the sale. The a.p. was replaced, and a new one named. "The new a.p. must ratify the authenticity of the sale; otherwise we will demand a rescission. March 5, 1943."[158]

Some of Castille's type of work with CGQJ originated in legal correspondence with the Germans, who in most cases were content to transmit such inquiries to Vichy. For example, a Parisian lawyer wrote to the French Center for German Economic Groups, asking whether a client who had been baptized (like his father) but also had Jewish grandparents "might remain as a director of a French corporation doing business with German companies. I also need to tell you that this person has a 1941 certificat from the CGQJ declaring that he is not Jewish." This letter was transmitted to Blanke, the aryanization director of the German High Command, who passed it along to the CGQJ.[159]

Lawyer Pierre Gide, with offices in the avenue Georges V, also maintained lively relations with the CGQJ, but his practice seemed to conjure more contentiousness than cooperation with the agency. In one of the few conciliatory exchanges available in the documentation, Gide and Boué put through a plan selling the French Jewish shares of the Polak and Schwartz Company to its Dutch subsidiary, which had been aryanized by the authorities in The Netherlands.[160] But Gide could push home a very different kind of "deal," too.

Camille Bloch, Gide's client, convinced a Paris tribunal in early 1943 that he was not Jewish under the 2 June statute. He now wished to regain control of his business in the rue St. Honoré, which had been aryanized for the prior two years. Gide complained to CGQJ that the a.p., M. de Villers,

> holds on to it desperately, which is inexplicable to me given the assurances that you made to me at our meeting.... I would be much obliged if you

[157] CGQJ legal service memorandum, 10 March 1942, AN $AJ^{38}$, 596.

[158] AN $AJ^{38}$, 331.

[159] Blanke memorandum, 15 July 1942, AN $AJ^{38}$, 80.

[160] Correspondence, December 1942, AN $AJ^{38}$, 331.

> could give instructions so that M. Bloch, indisputably a non-Jew, can take back control of his business, from which he has been kept for almost two years. Additional stalling procedures, which seem to me to be superfluous at this time, would thus be avoided.[161]

But the a.p. remained obdurate. Even direct phone calls from Boué would not move him. Eight days after the first note, Gide tried again:

> Under these circumstances, I certainly thought that the instructions you led me to believe would be given had as their aim purely and simply to relieve M. Villers of his function. *Despite the intervening orders* [he] *insists on staying in place and naming a director.* This is obviously unacceptable. Let me further observe that M. Villers was apparently named by the Prefecture of Police to deal with a [mere] storefront.[162]

About a year later, Gide's adversarial posture re-emerged. CGQJ had appointed an a.p. to a banking company he represented. Yet, Gide insists that since its founding in 1912, the company had never had Jewish managers or even shareholders. He contested, in strong and sometimes sarcastic tones, the justification given by the a.p., whom he names:

> One need only cast a glimpse at the reports of M. Gallay to be convinced of the fragility of his reasoning.[163]

Gide uses even stronger language in a landlord-tenant dispute involving a Jew, Joseph *Levy,* who rents an apartment from an Aryan corporation. Apparently, the agency has considered this one fact sufficient to investigate the corporation for having a Jewish "tincture." Gide writes:

> We applaud the infinitely meritorious efforts of the Commissariat général as it uncovers Jewish enterprises masked as Aryan, but it must, it seems to us, make distinctions among the files submitted to it and to examine with

---

[161] Pierre Gide to SCAP, 8 April 1943, AN AJ[38], 331.

[162] Ibid., emphasis in original.

[163] Ibid., correspondence, 25 February 1944. Gide's evident animus against a.p. stupidity or inefficiency exploded earlier in the Helios Archerau and Georges Lang case, where the latter's debt to his printing company had been amicably resolved by having his Aryan children cede to the company their interest in lands owned by their father on which the company had an option. Gide is incredulous, as he sets up a meeting with the CGQJ's Regelberger, placing an exclamation point after the phrase "deux commissaires (!)"—*two* a.p.'s over the enterprise, "which has as a result that no decision can ever be made," Pierre Gide correspondence, 14 January 1942, AN AJ[38], 331.

> generosity those that only contain doubtful elements, dubious witnesses, and fantastical deductions.[164]

Pierre Leroy, a Parisian lawyer with offices in the rue de la Paix, seems—somewhat like Gide—to have developed a bit of a specialty in business matters relating to race. Like Gide, his cases include at least one in which he argues that an a.p. has been erroneously assigned to property owned by a non-Jew:

> Samuel *KAHN*...has been assigned an a.p. in the person of M. Moizey [address omitted]. But M. Kahn possesses a certificat de non appartenance, no. 7,927, which was granted to him on 15 October 1943. Under these circumstances, it seems incontestable that the a.p. should purely and simply be relieved of his duties.[165]

The post of administrateur provisoire was much sought-after and well-remunerated.[166] There were dozens if not hundreds of applications by 1943 and 1944, and Boué told many applicants that "most Jewish enterprises are by now aryanized or about to be aryanized."[167] Leroy's good word surely must have helped those aspiring a.p.'s he was supporting.

Leroy assisted clients in their corporate acquisition attempts, and here again he occasionally argued for their non-Jewishness, not only to the CGQJ but even to the German authorities if they might take an interest. Thus Blanke writes to Leroy about a contentious plan mounted by his client, Propper de Callejou, to buy 12,000 shares of the Springer Corporation in Maisons-Alfort:

> It seems from the marriage contract that has been submitted to me that at least one of the grandmothers, specifically Mme. Jean Kohn, was Jewish. The name Alois Propper, is also neither French, nor Spanish, but instead German, and as Jews in France frequently have German names, I am inclined to believe that Alois Propper was also Jewish. You will kindly supply

---

164 Ibid.

165 Pierre Leroy, correspondence, 15 February 1944, AN $AJ^{38}$, 331.

166 Ibid.; Leroy's file indicates that 4,000 francs per month was not untypical for the position. See correspondence, 9 November 1943 requesting reduction of fee paid by one of Leroy's clients to an a.p.; and correspondence, 17 November 1943, decision to reduce by 50%.

167 Ibid.

me with the place and date of birth of Maximilian Propper and also of Alois Propper, along with the professions they exercised.[168]

Another client, Burckle, experienced difficulties gaining approval of his company's acquisition of the Jewish cotton company, Rozendaal, Inc. The Belfort company, Somatex, frustrated by the delays, mounted this argument through Leroy:

> It is curious that this matter, having once been approved, now reappears. Might this not be the result of the more or less capable means used to stretch this out, permitting Jews to keep the upper hand?[169]

A solicitor, with law offices in the blvd. de Courcelles, queried Boué with a complex variation on *landlord-tenant* law such as we saw it so often in chapter 7. His clients, the Durands, purchased a building in the rue Maspero from an a.p. of the property, which was formerly owned by a Jew, Mme. *Behrendt*. But the latter leased the building to her son, Dr. Landowski, whose widow still resided there. The Durands sought to eject her. A Paris court supported the tenant, citing the exception in the 22 July 1941 statute, with which we are already familiar, for the personal residences of Jews. The court's decision emphasized the statutory language "personal residence of the parties or of their ascendants or descendants."

The stakes on appeal were high for the solicitor's Aryan clients, for not only might the Durands fail to eject Mrs. Landowski, they also risked having their purchase rescinded as improperly performed by an a.p. who should not have been there to begin with. In fighting for his client's position, the solicitor urged the agency to find an exception to the exception:

> The statutory exception...may have been construed by the Commissariat in such a way that if the building was rented, in other words if it brought in revenues, the Commissariat had always considered appointment of an a.p. to be justified.

Boué adopted the solicitor's argument and agreed to argue an appeal that the Jewish tenant should be ejected: no exception was to apply where rent had entered the picture.[170] Although the agency knew that magistrates

---

[168] Ibid.

[169] Ibid., correspondence, 29 December 1943.

[170] Ibid., correspondence, Loncle file, 21 March 1944.

exhibited no obligation to adopt CGQJ's interpretations, the solicitor's argument had given the Durands a leg to stand on in their appeal of the lower court's tenant-favorable decision.

As in many other law-related situations already examined, the choices these lawyers had to make involved complex combinations of legal, ethical, and moral factors. Whatever internal struggles they may have had—or failed to have—the result in the handful of cases contained in the Boué file indicates that professionalism could be defined quite narrowly; that zealous advocacy could continue in a racial environment quite foreign to the beliefs and practices of these lawyers prior to 1940; and that no overriding ethical or moral principle kept them from dealing with bureaucracies that they increasingly had reason to know were culpable of not only pillage but far worse.

### *b. Related Work of Notaries*

Individual notaries seemed to have been less directly in contact with the CGQJ, but their work collectively was vital to aryanization, and the agency took pains to inform them of changes in the law regarding transfers of property. Notaries traditionally play a significant role in France in these matters; after the law of 22 July 1941, all transfers of covered Jewish property held by a.p.'s (small lots of corporate shares seem to have been excepted) had to be approved by the CGQJ, and—in the Occupied Zone—by the Germans, too. "Notaries must be so informed," writes CGQJ in early September, as many legal practitioners were returning from vacations.[171]

As time went on, a huge number of individual situations arose, many resulting in questions from notaries directly to one service or another of the CGQJ, with followup inquiries on occasion to the UGIF, the latter usually upon the advice of the CGQJ itself. Two comparable examples involve probate, another area of notary specialization in France. Both cases interweave Jewish wealth with religious law and administrative policy. In the first, the estate of a wealthy Jew from the Gironde, Abraham Louis Garcias, awaited distribution. Garcias, who died on 23 July 1942, left behind his Jewish daughter and his Aryan granddaughter, represented by notary G. Brisson. His last will and testament, and a codicil thereto, left real property to two towns (Bayonne and Arcachon) for char-

---

[171] AN AJ[38], 593.

itable uses, with a remainder to his daughter. But Brisson's client, a divorcee currently married to orchestra director Angelo Mihaiti of Bordeaux, also had an indefeasible right to part of her grandfather's estate.[172]

We are familiar with many cases like this, in which the same family produced Jew and non-Jew. So, Brisson confidently argued for the Aryan granddaughter against the interests of her Jewish aunt, citing "the laws and ordinances in effect" to support the opposing racial description of the two.[173] But Mrs. Mihaiti, his client, had not been able to collect everything due her under the relevant laws of decedents' estates.

On her behalf, Brisson reported to the CGQJ that, as part of the massive plunder of Jewish accounts to pay the German-imposed fine, 165,398 francs were taken from Garcias' deposits in the Occupied Zone as of 14 February 1942. The other half of his funds on deposit, or "183,775 francs and 52 centimes," was blocked in an account established the previous month.[174] As we saw in chapter 7, millions upon millions of francs so withdrawn were then placed in an account—the Caisse des dépots et consignations—nominally to be used by UGIF for varying lawful purposes, but in fact not really "touchable" by that organization in its own right.[175]

CGQJ and the managers of the Jewish account advised Brisson to write to UGIF, both perceiving Garcias' estate as a kind of "creditor" of the Jewish agency. Brisson thus writes to UGIF to find out

> the exact sum which UGIF owes the estate of M. Garcias. An agreement having been worked out between [the executor] and Mme. Mihaiti, if the sums can be unblocked, I would appreciate [finding out] what I need to send you to facilitate the payments of these sums.[176]

---

[172] In France, unlike the United States, issue of decedent take a share irrespective of a will disinheriting them. Thus, in *Garcias,* the daughter and granddaughter (who represented a predeceased parent) stood to take their forced share–or légitime–and the daughter also was the residuary taker of the "quotite disponible," i.e., the remaining amount after satisfaction of the légitime and the specific bequests to charity.

[173] G. Brisson to UGIF, 21 January 1943, CDJC CDXXIX-1.

[174] Ibid.

[175] See chapter 7, notes 99–100.

[176] G. Brisson to UGIF, 21 January 1943, CDJC CDXXIX-1, 2.

Of course, UGIF never attained actual power over the blocked sums, much of which had already been distributed to pay one fine or another. There, in Estate of Offenstadt (a wealthy publisher until barred from that activity by Vichy law),[177] similar issues arose involving similar players and a blocked account of some nine and a quarter million francs. Offenstadt died on New Year's Day 1943, at his chateau in Suresnes. He was survived, like Garcias, by two generations of issue: a son and a grandson, the latter taking by representation of Offenstadt's predeceased son. The notary asked UGIF how and when it would pay its "debt" of the blocked funds to the estate?[178]

The beleaguered and impoverished Jewish agency was in no position to help the estate. On 4 May they replied to the notary that UGIF "cannot consider itself a debtor of the Offenstadt estate and can make no commitment involving the return of principal and whatever interest may accrue." They further declined to play the part of guarantor for the blocked accounts, explaining:

> In fact, although the sums deposited in the Caisse des dépots and consignations were made in the name of UGIF, they are controlled by the CGQJ and seem to have been used to pay the fine of one billion francs imposed on Jews by order of the German High Command on December 14, 1941.[179]

Meanwhile, the everyday work of notaries continued, although it was complicated rather than facilitated by problems such as the blocked accounts of Jewish people. Just as troubling could be their blocked *apartments,* as we explored in chapter 7. Thus, in May 1944, a Parisian notary represented a landlady, Mrs. Guenne. Her tenant, the Jew Patalajean, "left his apartment in September 1942 and owes rent since accruing to 14,659 francs and 5 centimes."[180] The Germans have sealed up the place. If UGIF cannot help, the notary says he will be constrained to "ask the occupying authorities to remove the seals, and to free the apartment for

---

[177] His enforced retirement is explicitly averred in the first line of his estate's notary's letter to UGIF, 3 March 1943, CDJC CDXXIX-1.

[178] Ibid.

[179] Ibid.

[180] Correspondence, to UGIF, 26 May 1944, CDJC CDXXIX-1.

a new rental."[181] As with the blocked accounts, however, UGIF could only indicate its powerlessness to assist such a proceeding.[182]

As the war drew to a close, most activities engaged in by notaries—if Jews were involved at all—suffered similar fates of frustration and complexity. The CGQJ's aryanization service thus notes in February 1944 that sales of Jewish enterprises had dwindled. Their specific example is the Mediterranean region, where in the towns of Pau, Toulouse, and Montpellier, only five sales were effected since the beginning of the year, with four remaining unsold. The service largely ascribes this deficiency to the "demands and needs of the notaries."[183]

### *c. The Files of Maurice Garçon*

The files donated to the French national archives by the distinguished lawyer, Maurice Garçon, comprise some 11,000 separate dossiers spanning a career of five decades. There are almost 1000 from the war years alone. It is largely, but by no means exclusively, to the Vichy law idiosyncracies in such a practice that we now turn our attention. For Maurice Garçon, perhaps best known during the Vichy years for two cases that do not concern us centrally here,[184] was to take on approximately the percentage of race-related matters that the reader might by now expect of an ongoing French wartime practice. Not all of such cases were new, of course; prewar files involving Jews or Jewish property had to be carried over and their analysis sometimes altered to suit Vichy's *ex post facto* legislation. But a fair number of fresh files relating to race were opened, too. Garçon's competence spanned many fields of law, and his papers offer enforcement and enrichment of some of our earlier chapters and sections. But perhaps the most accurate way to grasp the man

---

[181] Ibid.

[182] Ibid., note, 31 May 1944.

[183] CGQJ, February 1944, CDJC XVII-10 (39).

[184] His son points to the "piqures-d'Orsay" and the *Guillaume* matters. Pierre Maurice Garçon, personal interview with author, 27 December 1991. It is clear that not every file begun by Garçon during the Vichy years is present in the archives, nor that all the available dossiers are themselves complete. As would be natural for a busy practitioner over five decades of practice, there were occasional periods of re-organization and even disposal of the files. One of these "classification" periods occurred in February 1944. See Garçon to Amathieu, 7 February 1944, AN 304 AP 8872.

and the lawyer is by starting with several widely separated libel cases that he took on between 1935 and 1943.

### *(1) The Defamation Cases*

The files—before, during, and after Vichy—reveal a man of goodwill and courage, an advocate who surely could pick and choose his clients but who rarely flinched before controversial, unpopular, or even quite risky causes. In 1935, for example, Garçon aggressively prosecuted a defamation action for a member of the Parliament, Louis Louis-Dreyfus. The defendant was the virulently antisemitic weekly, *Le Porc Epic*. In the same sheet that pilloried Georges Mandel, Léon Blum, and the Rothschilds, and in the tone to which we referred in chapter one's brief look at prewar propaganda against Blum in particular, the weekly had vilified Garçon's client. The problem for Garçon was to distinguish the weekly's debasing comments about Louis Louis-Dreyfus the parliamentarian from its sickening attacks on Louis Louis-Dreyfus the private man of commerce and the marketplace. Libels of the former category would be much harder to prosecute, according both to statute and to Cour de Cassation decisions. Garçon's analysis on behalf of this client aptly presages the consistent acuity of his legal thinking during Vichy, when sometimes the stakes would prove even greater than that of mere reputation.[185]

The next libel case places us squarely in the war years. Sacha Guitry, the playwright, actor, and filmmaker, retained Garçon for a variety of purposes during Vichy. The first situation offers a little-known preface to the story of Sacha Guitry as alleged collaborationist arrested after the Liberation[186]; it arose from a scurrilous column published on the last day of 1940 in *La France au Travail,* under the pseudonym "Diogène." The columnist, apparently Henri Coston according to Garçon's notes,[187] satirized a "M. *Moa,*" obviously Guitry, whose caricature appeared next to the opening paragraphs, and whose film, *En Remontant les Champs-Élysées,* was mentioned later. We then read of "Moa's" return to Paris and an errand he performed for a friend named "Bernheim." "He was told by his Hebrew friends," Coston writes, "to recoup certain canvasses [that had been safeguarded before the occupation] and to bring them

[185] Memorandum, 31 January 1935, AN 304 AP 9690.

[186] See, e.g., Ragache and Ragache, *La Vie quotidienne,* 133, 144, 264–67.

[187] AN 304 AP 8426.

down to the unoccupied zone. For a trifling one million francs as commission."[188] But the authorities block the transfer.

> Our great man must stay in Paris. A bit uneasy at first, he quickly gained assurance. "They don't know about my ancestry [*mes origines*]," he confided in his pal Levy, with a conspiratorial wink of the eye. Of course! He scarcely brags about it.[189]

Guitry writes an impassioned response to the paper, but it is not printed. He denies all the facts, and especially takes umbrage at the prolonged racial slur, only part of which has been cited here. "But it is not to you that I will furnish proof of my complete and total 'aryan-ness,' and since the law punishes defamation, know that I will have recourse to it."[190]

Garçon moves quickly, with the help of a colleague, Fernand Paresys. Their action is set for trial as quickly as 31 January 1941; their target is the head of *La France au Travail,* M. Saint Serge, who faces a 50,000-franc criminal fine, with a possible 500,000 francs in additional liability under the libel law of 29 July 1881.

The legal cause of action is fascinatingly framed:

> To claim that someone is Jewish during the German Occupation and at a time when French laws and German ordinances are promulgated to regulate the situation of Jews, and to keep them from attaining certain jobs or exercising certain professions, is without any doubt to lower that person's reputation.... The [statement] intended nothing less than to prevent M. Sacha Guitry from exercising his profession and his art, the German authorities in the occupied zone prohibiting for the most part the publication of the works of Jewish writers and absolutely barring Jewish artists from appearing on the stage or producing films....[191]

The case may well have been settled, because there is no further record of it, at least not in the Garçon files. However, Garçon goes on to represent Guitry a few more times during the Vichy years. In one case that he

---

[188] Ibid., the attached article itself, "La Lanterne."

[189] Ibid.

[190] Ibid.

[191] Ibid.

took over from his colleague Pierre Masse,[192] Garçon defends Guitry against a claim that he had fraudulently failed to honor a 1937 promise of an acting role in one of his films, the role to be given the holder of the winning lottery ticket in a charitable function held that year. Guitry supposedly promised some 20,000 francs in remuneration to the winner, who turned out to be a M. Bontemps. The latter had sued him, but his chances were again to be questioned, in part because

> With that rigorous exactitude for which he is known at the Palais, M. Maurice Garçon, his file under his arm, appeared at the Bar, ready to take the last swipe at M. Bontemps' hopes.[193]

Garçon's relationship to Guitry was sometimes rocky. In 1943, having handled part of yet another defamation action—relating to Guitry's marital problems—Garçon learned that his client was seeking a new lawyer, Maître Delzons. Garçon writes to his colleague on the Guitry case, M. Houssard, that "I would be much obliged if you will communicate to M. Sacha Guitry that he must transfer to me the sum of 5000 francs."[194] But he seems to have genuinely felt the outrage of his famous client for what he calls the "inadmissable" behavior by the press "in invading the private life of people."[195]

### *(2) Early Cases Involving the New Legislation*

It is hard for a late twentieth-century professional to feel the seismic change that shook the French legal community during that first summer of occupation of 1940. When Garçon joined the mass exodus from Paris on 11 June, he could not even foresee resuming his practice at all. Yet, as with so many other lawyers, he was back behind his desk by July. And now he had to master so many new laws. For some of his prewar clients, the catastrophe seems to have ameliorated their legal difficulties; so one of Garçon's first notes in resuming his practice:

---

[192] Ibid., appearing for Guitry in May 1942, Garçon asks the court for a continuance, "since I am replacing my colleague, Pierre Masse." There is an eloquent reference to Masse in Guitry's letter to Garçon of 28 November 1942, ibid. See discussions of Masse in chapter 3, notes 41–45, and above at A(1)(b).

[193] AN 304 AP 8716, including newspaper article, 26 January 1942.

[194] Ibid.

[195] Garçon to Guitry, 24 February 1943, AN 304 AP 8715.

> I have been away from Paris until yesterday and found your letter upon returning. Don't worry at all about the case involving your son. All criminal cases antedating 10 June 1940 have been continued indefinitely. The absence of the defendants makes any judgment impossible. We will take up this matter much later, unless a general amnesty intervenes to end it definitively.[196]

Maurice Garçon had no way of knowing—any more than did his bâtonnier Jacques Charpentier, who expressed the same uncertainties upon his own return to the Paris Bar in July[197]—that cases would overwhelmingly resume their prewar character and follow forms virtually unchanged from before the debacle. In fact, Garçon still seemed in late July to have been contemplating a kind of semi-retirement at his country home. So, on the day he was writing to the father of the boy burdened with criminal charges, he told a client who himself had relocated in Lyon that a matter they had last discussed on the fateful 10 June might not resume at all:

> If in fact the courts and tribunals have theoretically started up again, it is almost impossible for them to judge prior criminal cases. There is little communication between the occupied and the free zones.... As to myself, as I've told you, even if my colleague Menesclou can't take your case [a third party civil complaint] nor Maître Carouche, I doubt that I personally can handle it. I'm again leaving Paris, to return to my lands, where I intend to stay for quite awhile.[198]

What Maurice Garçon did know, and was already professionally touched by, was the part of the seismic disruption affecting Jews and others. In that brief Parisian stopover, he learned of the fate of M. Maligne, imprisoned at Gurs. Garçon responds cordially to Mme. Maligne, who asked him for help in their desperate and unprecedented situation:

> I am distressed.... Your husband, who of course is now in the same condition as a certain number of others for whom the situation seems insoluble. Arrested in Paris by the military authority, he was evacuated, to a concentration camp.[199]

---

[196] Garçon to M. Auerbach of Sanary-sur-Mer, 11 June 1940, AN 304 AP 8295.

[197] See, e.g., text at chapter 1, notes 41–42.

[198] Garçon to M. de la Perrelle, 27 July 1940, AN 304 AP 8350.

[199] AN 304 AP 8179.

With petty crimes and related civil actions in legal disarray, and the chances great that some prewar wrongdoers would be amnestied, others who had no reason to believe that they had ever done anything wrong now found themselves in French concentration camps. Perhaps such thoughts occupied Garçon's mind as he withdrew for what amounted to a rather short late summer hiatus in the provinces. By October, he had returned to the office, attending to the interests of the *Comedie française*. And by the November after the defeat, his practice resumed according to his diaries and his files, on a fully active basis.[200]

Among the early cases are landlord-tenant matters familiar to us, dealing usually with rent reductions demanded under the law of 26 September 1939.[201] In mid-November, Garçon can write to his client, Korab, that in view of his lack of income and resources he has been granted a 50% rent reduction and that the court is also giving him extra time to repay back rent.[202] Garçon also represented landlords.[203] In one significant case, finally decided by the Cour de Cassation in 1942, the tenant—named Miraschi or Misrachi—had given notice to landlord Paunin that he was vacating as of 1 November 1940. But the notice was given in early May, just before the occupation, and the tenant eventually decided not to leave. Furthermore, he now asks for a rent reduction, despite the uncertain condition of his leasehold. The high court holds:

> Due to the privation of a good part of his resources because of the state of war, the tenant has the right to obtain a rent reduction, whatever the term of his lease....[204]

In a landlord-tenant representation that carried over from pre-Occupation days, Garçon takes note of the religious status of his client.

---

[200] November calendar entries average four listed clients a day, peaking toward the end of the month with nine matters or meetings on the 29th, AN 304 AP, 1940 diaries.

[201] See chapter 7, A.

[202] Correspondence, 11 November 1940, AN 304 AP 8243.

[203] See, e.g. the Desforges matter, in which a farm owner was able to reclaim his estate from a war veteran tenant named Barre, AN 304 AP 8862.

[204] Cour de Cassation, session of its chambre sociale, 24 December 1942, AN 304 AP 8069.

Dr. *Kahan,* no longer practicing his profession,[205] but still able to edit the journal, *Hippocrate: Revue d'Humanisme medical,* who sought the reduction after his mobilization for the war itself. But in picking up the file some time later, Garçon writes, "Jewish client. Where is he?"[206]

*(3) Researching Questions of Religious Definition*

As 1940 yielded to 1941 and its ever stronger foundation of Vichy laws, colleagues, friends, and individuals seem to have felt quite comfortable approaching Maurice Garçon on the most "delicate" questions of religious status itself. The first case in the files is apparently that of a *Haguenauer,* a mixed-heritage Jew married to his first cousin.[207] The case was referred to Garçon by a mutual friend, Dussaud. The time is just after promulgation of the 2 June Vichy statute. Haguenauer, a teacher of Japanese, visits Garçon's offices in the rue de l'Eperon and outlines the facts of the case. Is there some hope?

Garçon focusses on this new area of law. Neither law school nor decades of active practice had prepared him for the substance of the religious laws—quite the contrary—but like the majority of his colleagues, Garçon managed to repress his egalitarian instincts and to make technical arguments on the hitherto bizarre question of racial status.

On 23 June, Garçon wrote for Haguenauer what might have been the first memorandum of law by a seasoned practitioner about the 2 June statute:

> M. Haguenauer, who practices no religion and who is part of no Jewish circle, is from an Alsatian Jewish paternal line and a Norman Catholic maternal line. He therefore has two Jewish grandparents on the paternal side. In addition, he is married to a first cousin who is also the issue of Jewish grandparents.

---

[205] Claude Singer, lecture, 13 December 1991, series directed by André Kaspi, the Sorbonne, spoke recently on the behavior of the medical profession during Vichy. Similar to lawyers, physicians cooperated in the *numerus clausus,* responding in their formal associations to Vichy's corporatist approach. At least one lawyer, Roger Berg, interview with author, Paris, 16 December 1991, opined that doctors as a group were in fact more difficult to Jews than were the lawyers, particularly to Jewish surgeons.

[206] AN 304 AP 8518.

[207] See chapter 2, note 103; chapter 5, note 85; chapter 6, note 130, for other examples of first cousins.

> He must therefore, under Article 1, paragraph 1 of the law, be considered Jewish, because anyone descended of two or more Jewish grandparents and married to one who is descended from two Jewish grandparents—whatever his religion—is statutorily Jewish.[208]

Garçon does not try to argue that the first cousin marriage is an anomaly, nor does his memorandum in any way challenge the broader questions raised by such a statute. In this he is again typical of his colleagues; surely no adherent of such a law, but also incapable of seeing (for he does not articulate them, even for purely internal office analysis) larger *legal* arguments that might undermine the statute altogether or at least minimize its effects.

Instead, Garçon rationalizes the most absurd aspect of his client's dilemma: it is based on marriage only, and then, too, on a first cousin marriage. Garçon opines:

> The justification for such a marriage-related classification may be because, if it were otherwise, the children and grandchildren who would be Jews would be burdened with legal incapacities while these parents would not.[209]

Garçon, by this reference, must be assuming that Mme. Haguenauer, unlike her husband-cousin, is fully Jewish, and this of course *would* make their children Jewish as having had three or more Jewish grandparents. (If Haguenauer himself, however, remained an Aryan in this situation—or if, as in the *Leboucher* case discussed in chapter 2, the Haguenauers *shared* grandparents in common—it is unclear that Garçon's other assumptions here would follow.) Garçon does not articulate the absurdity of such a view in light of his conclusion about the children of Mme. Haguenauer's first marriage to a Catholic; these, he concludes, are clearly not Jewish. Nor, at the moment, could he conceive that children such as those, although baptized, would by no means be considered automatically non-Jewish under Vichy interpretations.[210]

The lawyer ends this section of his analysis by stating that, "under these circumstances, there is no doubt that M. Haguenauer is burdened

---

[208] Garçon to M. Dussaud about *Haguenauer*, memorandum, 23 June 1941, AN 304 AP 8523.

[209] Ibid.

[210] See chapter 2, note 114 and chapter 6, sections A and B.

by the incapacities that now cover Jews." Although in so doing, he surrenders on the key issue, where so many legal arguments still seem untapped, he does not concede everything. He now turns to the *exceptions* under the 2 June statute. Since Haguenauer is a teacher, he can benefit from the Article 3 exception for holders of the Croix de guerre. Furthermore, Garçon finds in the dossier Article 8 exceptional status in Haguenauer's career, and a strong argument for this because "he is the only person in France now capable of teaching Japanese." And Haguenauer's family is vieille souche.[211]

So there is some hope for the client, at least in the preservation of his function as a teacher. And then again, even this is to reckon without Garçon's contacts; these shall be conjured in Haguenauer's poignant letter of thanks to his counsel:

> Maître. I will let no time go by to express my appreciation for your cordial welcome; such signs of sympathy are especially comforting for a provisional "pariah," separated from his family. I also thank you for what you have told M. Dussaud in enlisting him to find the person on whom the decision depends. Thank you too for all you can do personally to draw the attention of that latter personage to what can only be thought of as an atrocious injustice.[212]

Haguenauer promises to come by and pick up the documents that have formed much of the file.

The career-related part of this episode, whose racial dimensions extend as a formal legal matter through early 1944, does not end happily, despite Garçon's best efforts. Dussaud writes his learned friend, thanking him warmly of course, but expressing the view that Garçon's opinion on Haguenauer's Jewishness closes the books on his remaining at his job, at least in France. "The occupying authorities," he suggests, "are not recognizing the exceptions delineated by Vichy." Dussaud's judgment about Vichy's subservience to German authority on racial questions is of course not borne out over the course of the four-year period, during which Vichy very much seemed the master of its own fate on questions of exceptional status under the religious laws; Dussaud will now approach his own contacts and endeavor to:

---

[211] AN 304 AP 8523.

[212] Ibid.

use H., for example, in Indochina or Japan. What a silly impulse, this marriage! [Quelle mauvaise inspiration, que ce mariage!][213]

A year and a half later, but now armed with a significant amount of Vichy jurisprudence and German and French bureaucratic behavior, Garçon takes on the case of Paul Bernard. In mid-May 1942, Bernard has been called into the police prefecture in the quai des Orfévres and challenged as a Jew for non-declaration of certain property under the law of 2 June 1941. Although not a real estate holder, Bernard does own shares in several publicly-owned French companies. He is indicted and a criminal hearing set for November.

Paul Bernard, who pays Garçon 2000 francs as a retainer, gives the usual genealogy to his lawyer at their interview: his grandparents, spouse, children, etc. His war veteran status and legion d'honneur. His holdings. The fact that Vichy fears not so much the "Jewish nature" of the companies in question as Bernard's personal failure to declare his share of them. The fact that Bernard *did* register as a Jew under the first German ordinance but then "discovered" that his paternal grandparents were Catholic and so is now applying for a certificat de non appartenance for himself and his children. He is married to an Aryan. And—noting a physiological detail often discussed among Vichy practitioners of racial law—Garçon observes that his client is not circumcised.[214]

The next two months are full of activity for this client. The period since *Haguenauer,* we can infer, has armed Garçon with increased knowledge and expertise about religious definition and also lent him *finesse* with the bureaucratic structures. He attacks on several fronts. By 4 December, the CGQJ has informed the prefecture of police that Bernard should be considered a non-Jew.[215] This finding, however, does not dispose of the pending proceeding against Bernard for non-declaration of

[213] Ibid., Dussaud to Garçon, 24 June 1941. Well into 1944, we learn from other files, Haguenauer's racial fate is still being reckoned by Vichy legal bureaucrats. The question is no longer Jewish definition and career, but property. And Haguenauer's lawyer is now a Roger Sarret, arguing with Boué of CGQJ, whom we saw active with lawyers in our prior section, that Haguenauer's life and lineage should lead Vichy to remove the a.p. over his property. In the first quarter of 1944, Boué indicates to the lawyer that the a.p. had indeed been removed on 3 May 1943. Haguenauer, with perhaps too little, too late, had finally won a legal victory; see Boué file, AN AJ[38], 331.

[214] AN 304 AP 8692.

[215] Ibid., Bernard to Garçon, 9 December 1942.

property during his "Jewish period." Garçon takes collateral action against that charge: in early January, he argues before the 12th Criminal Section of the Tribunal de la Seine that Bernard was exempted from the duty to declare!

Garçon's intervention in court is masterful. True, as he stipulates, Bernard did not declare his stock ownership. But when he first declared himself to be Jewish, on 6 October 1940, his "good faith" was obvious, and *no German ordinance* required any statement of holdings at the time. Only under Vichy law, as of 2 June 1941, was there a technical violation. However, at that time, and until the present date, Bernard's son Henri "has been a prisoner at Stalag V B No. 33." Under Article 7, paragraph 14 of the 2 June law, Bernard "as ascendant of a prisoner of war, need not make the declaration until two months after the liberation of his son."[216]

On 11 January, Bernard writes to thank his lawyer. Unfortunately, there is one remaining problem. His daughter, Jacqueline Lise Annette, has been omitted from the document granting non-Jewish status to the other Bernards. Can Garçon handle this by calling the CGQJ, specifically the office of Jacques Ditte, head of the agency's personal status bureau?[217]

A final example takes us briefly out of the realm of criminal sanctions for religious law violations and into the world of estate planning. A true generalist, Garçon was able to provide clients with a wide range of services and to apply his increasing awareness of the intricacies of Vichy racial policy to civil and criminal matters. Thus, in mid-1942, when approached by a client whose Jewish father-in-law's fortune was at risk, Garçon immediately comes up with a plan. Mme. Charet of Chartres, referred to him by a mutual friend, is married to a M. Ochse, who has adopted the two children of her first marriage. Ochse's father is Jewish, and his accounts have been blocked; he is authorized to receive only 3500 francs a month. There is an a.p. assigned to his assets; this situation is hardly tolerable as it is but, in Garçon's words, "they are expecting more severe measures."[218]

Garçon devises a plan whereby Mme. Charet's children, who are clearly Aryan, can be best situated to receive old M. Ochse's estate. "I pro-

---

[216] Ibid., argument to the tribunal.

[217] Ibid., Bernard to Garçon, 11 January 1943.

[218] Garcon's notes, 22 June 1942, AN 304 AP 8507.

pose that we consult a notary," he writes. "A gift or advancement [to the children] seems scarcely possible.[219] But maybe we can arrange a division [to the grandchildren] which will establish as of the present moment that the donees are Aryan so that from the time of the opening of the probate, the property will become Aryan."[220] Although the notary may not be able to fulfill Garçon's estate planning concept to the letter, the case demonstrates the flexibility of the lawyer in dealing with religious definition and pragmatic problems hitherto unthinkable under French law.

### *(4) 1941–42: Riom and Less*

It was probably as much statistical inevitability as an actual craving for, or specialization in, Jewish matters that accounts for approximately 10–12% of Garçon's wartime files touching on various Jewish questions. Yet even his more general practice occasionally demonstrated Garçon's approach to the oppressed religious minority. Perhaps the most visible example during the first half of the Vichy experience was his representation of Georges Mandel, a Riom defendant *in absentia*. Here, Garçon replicates the autonomy of the Bar generally, including that of his bâtonnier, Jacques Charpentier, with whom he met fairly often on many matters.[221] Eventually, the Germans would go so far as to *arrest* Garçon, together with a colleague, Maître Besselere, and to hold them for the better part of a day while their apartments were being ransacked and files removed concerning Mandel and the infamous *Grynszpan* matter.[222]

To this grievous insult, Jacques Charpentier was quick to respond. He writes to Laval, via Pierre Cathala:

> You cannot but be struck by the gravity of these measures, which deprived of their liberty two lawyers against whom no wrong had been charged and which also violated professional privilege. I must ask you to intercede with

---

[219] See discussion of inter-generational gifts in chapter 7, notes 116–21.

[220] AN 304 AP 8507.

[221] AN 304 AP; see, e.g., diary entry, 8 June 1942.

[222] Herschel Grynszpan shot a German diplomat in the rue de Lille in 1938. The case became an antisemitic *cause célèbre,* both in Germany and among right-wing circles in France. See Marrus and Paxton, *Vichy France and the Jews,* 43; the Grynszpan affair was connected in the German mind with Riom, see Barthélemy, *Ministre,* 222.

> the occupation authorities and to give voice to an indisputably justified protest to make sure that such incidents will never be repeated.[223]

Garçon regretted that he could not do much for Mandel at Riom; he writes his client in 1943 telling him of some good he managed to accomplish by safeguarding some of the files amassed by the court at Riom. He closes eloquently:

> I have been kept informed by my friend Besselere of your travels, and I have felt your tribulations. Let us hope that better times will come soon and that we will arrive at the end of the overturning of everything [à la fin du bouleversement des mondes].[224]

Garçon was never, in fact, to rejoin his client. Georges Mandel was brutally assassinated by the milice in July 1944. But Garçon, along with Léon Blum, had the opportunity to speak at the opening of the Mandel Memorial in the forest of Fontainebleau two years to the day after that despicable event. The Society of the Friends of Georges Mandel spoke of its being "honored" by his presence.[225]

His practice during the Riom span of events brought him far less notable criminal clients whose Jewishness is also a factor. *Katzensztein* was arrested on 10 April 1941 for stashing metals unlawfully. Garçon took the case on that same day. Shortly thereafter, his client's brother-in-law, David Lewin, was arrested on similar charges. Lewin, a naturalized French Jew, was sentenced to six months in prison. Katzensztein, who was not naturalized, suffered a more severe fate. Arrested "as a Jew," in Garçon's words, he was sent to the concentration camp at Pithiviers, where Garçon was not permitted to visit him.[226] Lewin survived the war, where his record was preserved for the criminal conviction during Vichy. Katzensztein was not heard from again.

1941 also brought at least one case to Garçon in which Vichy's policies about Freemasons needed to be analyzed for a client. While away from Paris during that summer, the lawyer received a letter from Dr. Paul Chevallier, whose membership in the "secret society" had just cost him his

---

[223] Charpentier correspondence, 25 November 1942, with amiable covering note to Garçon, AN 304 AP 9703.

[224] Garçon to Mandel, 28 October 1943, AN 304 AP 9703.

[225] Letter to Garçon, with photograph attached, 28 June 1947, AN 304 AP 9703.

[226] AN 304 AP 8517.

jobs on the Faculty of Medicine and as resident physician in a hospital. Chevallier describes the law of 11 August 1941 dealing with Freemasons as though it "conflates me with a Jew" [Cette loi m'assimile à un juif].[227]

With his typical thoroughness and flair, Garçon challenges that comparison upon his return to the capital. A memorandum indicates that Chevallier is both prejudiced and benefitted by the *difference*—not the conflation!—of the two statutes. First, the exceptions permitted under the 2 June 1941 statute for certain categories of Jews do not seem to apply to Freemasons, since there is no cross-reference to them in the 11 August law. So the doctor will not be able to argue, for example, exceptional professional merit under Article 8 of the Jewish law. He will therefore lose his job on the medical faculty, considered (like a law professor's) to be a government function.

But Garçon does not give up his client's whole position. If the Freemason law excludes exceptional status, it also stops short of covering all the activities banned by the Jewish law. The cross-reference is only to *Article 2,* and not Article 3, of the 2 June statute. Since Article 3 bars "General residencies" to Jews, there is no indication that these were off limits to Freemasons. So Garçon can conclude, "Dr. C. apparently cannot be relieved of his post as a hospital doctor."[228] Half a loaf but something to chew on. So it went in Vichy law offices.

Jews, Freemasons, those stigmatized by denaturalization laws,[229] communists,[230] alleged pornographers,[231] and many other specially victimized people came to see Maurice Garçon during those first two years of Vichy power, and beyond. As the 1943 letter to absent client Mandel indicates, Garçon must have been quite distressed by these legal developments. It may have saddened him in particular to see colleagues like Mandel forced to retain his services. It may have demoralized him

---

[227] Chevallier to Garçon, 25 August 1941, AN 304 AP 8907.

[228] Garçon memorandum, ibid.

[229] See, e.g., Adamoff case, AN 304 AP 8398.

[230] See, e.g., Maurice Dine matter, AN 304 AP 8926; or Ginette Decker matter, AN 304 AP 9204.

[231] See the *Hirsch* case, from 1943–44, where Hirsch and his daughter, proprietors of a Paris bookstore, "La Librairie du Palais royal," are investigated for selling such books as *Mystère de Vénus* and *Nouvelle Sapho,* AN 304 AP 9973; see also the Cornil file, AN 304 AP 9914.

on a purely personal basis to take cases left behind by Pierre Masse. Or to deal collegially with a Jewish avoué like Lucien Frank, one of only two (as we saw) left in Paris, neither of whom—in Charpentier's words to the CGQJ—was appearing any more at the Palais.[232] Other lawyers, too felt these things; others had the mixed emotions involved in maintaining the interests of clients by providing continuity in their representation when a Jewish lawyer had been removed from the Bar, arrested, or worse.[233] They may have wondered how it could have happened so quickly that bizarre issues of heritage, race, secret society membership, circumcision, etc., had become part of their workday. They may have done their best to do some small good for clients.

But throughout 1941 and 1942, they were like Garçon in another way. They did not lift their voice in protest, certainly not collectively and apparently not singly either. They may have done other work for charities or the downtrodden—usually good people unable by dint of training or inclination to challenge centrally the laws against the Jews.[234]

### *(5) Towards the Liberation and Beyond*

Maurice Garçon pursued his active career until the very end of the German occupation. Cases involving Jews, or the mention of Jews, were as plentiful during the final years of Vichy as they were before. They had at least the same poignancy, as more and more Jews were departing French soil for "the East." Some of these were clients or family of clients known to Garçon for some years. Thus the *Caen* family appealed to him in their moment of urgent need, late summer 1943. The family, like their

---

[232] For Garçon's collegial dealings with Frank, see, e.g., AN 304 AP 8428, the *Intransigeant* matter of early January 1942. For the Charpentier reference to Frank, see above, note 69.

[233] One lawyer I interviewed had his own practice taken over in this way. An avoué, Maître Jeramec was advised not to return to his practice in Ghiens. (Good advice: his father, "the only one in Ghiens to wear the Star," was sent to Drancy, where he spent time with the poet, Max Jacob, and then went to his death in the East.) That practice was taken over by another avoué. After the war, Jeramec's practice was largely restored to him, good fortune that he attributes to the fact that the lawyer last involved in his practice "was more a man of the left" and acted honorably to him. Jeramec, interview with author, Paris, 13 December 1988. See also chapter 9, note 18.

[234] Among other wartime charitable activities connected to his expertise, Garçon devoted time to the rebuilding of the *bouquinistes* familiar to strollers along the Seine but at that time in dire straits as a commercial group; see, e.g. AN 304 AP 10284.

lawyer, had departed Paris ahead of the German troops several years before, leaving their Parisian apartment in the rue Beaubourg. Unlike their lawyer, they could not safely return to the capital. But M. Georges Caen met commercial success in the Unoccupied Zone, setting up a retail business. Although aryanized, his a.p. considered Caen so important to the business that he had been kept on and so had earned his living.

Suddenly, Caen was arrested. Apparently denounced anonymously for having kept a gun in his Paris apartment, his fate quickly followed that of many Jews in the last period of the German presence in France. Imprisoned in the south, he was then sent to Drancy. His wife asks Garçon for any help he can give, "remembering your fine family and hoping for a favorable response."[235] Whatever he could do was not enough. The file closes with a single sentence that speaks volumes:

> Jew deported to Silesia.

At around the same time, another individual hoping to make a comeback from his Parisian days wrote to Garçon. M. Amathieu, now setting up a business in Bordeaux, sought "a lawyer from Paris and even a great one [même un grand maître]" to attack calumnies by his former employer, the Auto-Thermos Company. The latter allegedly fired him, failed to pay his back wages and accused him, among other insults, of being Jewish.[236] His problems have followed him, and he was finding it difficult to get bank loans and to function effectively. He wanted Garçon's representation in directly attacking the company for "false accusations and accusation of Jewishness."[237]

Still in 1943, Garçon takes on a torts case, representing the plaintiff against a formerly Jewish company, now in the hands of an a.p. The facts predated the war. On 3 January 1940, at the intersection of the Blvd. Malesherbes and the Blvd. de Courcelles, the Dreyfus Company's driver failed to reduce his speed and ran over and killed a man in a pedestrian crossing zone. Once the Germans entered Paris, they apparently changed the rules that formerly required drivers to slow down in these zones [passages cloutés]. But Garçon argues that the prewar standard is applicable and gains a judgment of 40,000 francs for the victim's widow and

[235] Mme. Caen to Garçon, 13 August 1943, AN 304 AP 8901.

[236] Amathieu to Garçon, 8 June 1943, AN 304 AP 8872.

[237] Ibid., Amathieu to Garçon, 5 July 1943.

6,000 for his son. Although in other circumstances, he might have appealed for more, Garçon here insists that the complexities of aryanization (among other factors) militate against seeking greater compensation.[238]

By 1944, there is detectible in Garçon's available files a growing prudence about the cases he will take on. Although by then, even a lawyer of his breadth and sensitivity had begun using the word "juif" pretty much as a term of art,[239] he surely grasped that the tide had turned and that soon the normalcy he craved in his touching letter to Mandel would, at long last, return to France. By February 1944, he was putting his files in order.[240] He took few or no cases outside of Paris, whereas his practice earlier was to take selected trips fairly often on behalf of clients.[241] To a client's request to defend her husband in Périgueux, Garçon offers his regrets; communications have now become almost impossible, he says, and he has "just about given up all cases outside of Paris."[242] He is still quite capable of raising the Germans' hackles,[243] but the tone of his practice seems generally to relax just a bit and to await the inevitable restoration of sanity.

After the war, Garçon consulted with Jews hoping to regain property,[244] and with non-Jews whose title to property was blurred because before Vichy it belonged to a Jew.[245] He defended collaborators and even those accused of trafficking in Jews by fraudulently eliciting sums of money from the desperate families of Drancy inmates.[246] He was honored for his work for Georges Mandel. He died a pillar of the Bar.

---

[238] *Coutin vs. Dreyfus,* decided 9 March 1943, Tribunal civil of Paris, AN 304 AP 8747.

[239] See, e.g., the Jacquet matter, a real estate file from mid-May 1944, AN 304 AP 9622 *bis*. One vendor is called "juif," even though from what we can see of this case, his religion is irrelevant to the issues Garçon deals with. Interestingly, Garçon adopts this usage as late as 1958, in describing *Josilovici,* who wished to take advantage of a new French law permitting name changes by anyone with a "biblical or oriental-sounding name." This man, referred to somewhat atypically by Garçon as "un juif," wanted to assume the name Molière, AN 304 AP 14206.

[240] Garçon to Amathieu, 7 February 1944, AN 304 AP 8872.

[241] See, e.g., ibid.

[242] The *Abride* matter, AN 304 AP 8854; accord, *Dupommier* file, AN 304 AP 8938.

[243] *Eckerling* matter, April 1944, AN 304 AP 9307.

[244] See, e.g., the *Rueff* matter, 1945, AN 304 AP 10612.

[245] See, e.g., the *Lamadon* matter, November 1948.

[246] See the *Ickowicz* matter, 1945, AN 304 AP 9783.

# Chapter 9

# Reforming the Courts, Reforming the Law: Denationalization, Special Sections, et al.

Thoroughgoing as Vichy law may have been on issues of race and nationality, there were always those who felt it had not gone far enough. Law "reform" in these areas was a recurrent theme from the beginning, and the impulse persevered into 1944. As we have noted, besides race and nationality, questions ranging from the constitution down to divorce law (both of which had antisemitic "reform" tinctures) occupied Vichy lawyers and strategists, too. This chapter indicates that, at the same late period assumed by most historians to signify Vichy's political decline, legal activity mounted, peaking in late 1943, when many lawyers still believed that Vichy needed to do still more to perfect its "revolution." Reform of technical aspects of the religious laws, mostly at the urging of the always frustrated CGQJ, has been covered in earlier chapters[1]; the focus here is on *denaturalization* and its strong linkage to Nazi deportation policy on French soil.

We will see that the Nazis hung on every rumor and fact of Vichy legal planning on the rollback of citizenship status, because as the year of valid naturalization to French status wound back to 1933, 1931, 1927,

[1] See, e.g., Darquier's jousts with Barthélemy and the courts on explicitly shifting the burden of proof to the suspected Jew (a reform that Barthélemy seems to have endorsed), and on making religion, rather than race the criterion for Jewishness (which Barthélemy opposed), chapter 4, notes 140–145; chapter 5, note 40.

more Jews on French soil became legally ripe for arrest. We will also cover the perennial phenomenon of reformist impulses in the areas of constitutional law and court procedure in general, as well as fascinating ancillary issues such as Vichy protectionism towards out-of-wedlock children [*enfants naturels*] even if the latter were putatively Jewish. Perhaps the most basic reform of all to the notions of French justice were the "special sections" for the summary prosecution of crimes "committed with a communist or anarchist intent," and since many Jews lost their lives under this "reform," it finds a place in this chapter as well.

## A. Denaturalization for Death

We begin with the most intense period since Alibert's justice ministry for proposals regarding race and nationality—the latter three-fourths of 1943. The Germans of this period, unlike their counterparts in 1940, were fully focussed on arrest and deportation; but because of Vichy's earlier enthusiasms, they were also substantially dependent on French law. New arrests and deportations of Jews on French soil were to be driven by new laws rescinding the citizenship of thousands of people and hence subjecting them to already existing laws and policies that had had the effect—if probably not the intent—of protecting most of France's "own Jews." As to denaturalization and other aspects of the attack upon the Jewish population, the year 1943 stands most of all for the remarkable reliance by the Nazis upon French law, both as it had developed in the past and as they hoped it would in the future. Indeed, the temporal dimension of Franco-German relations cannot be overemphasized: had Vichy law moved in different directions on race prior to 1943, it is unlikely that the Germans would have expected as much from the French legal community in the late stages of the war. A less enthusiastic Vichy in 1940 and 1941—when there was still a kind of legislative *tabula rasa*—might well have produced a less expectant Berlin in 1943. Nor is it at all clear that Vichy resistance to racial persecution could have been overcome, either at the beginning or in 1943, by a German war machine sorely tested and suffering everywhere from the Russian front to North Africa.

But the die was cast: Vichy laws, interpretations, and infusive legal practice had made race an integral part of the French system. The Germans felt they had a virtual right to expect the French to reform their own laws to meet new exigencies; yet, if Vichy found the strength to reverse its own legalistic path, there were few options open to the Nazis to enforce solutions unacceptable to French law.

As we focus on the denaturalization reform projects, the reader is thus asked to entertain a somewhat paradoxical but arguably precise set of conclusions: 1) French zealousness in outdoing the Nazis on many points of religious law between 1940 and 1942, coupled with undeniable German manpower insufficiencies, had rendered Berlin almost fully dependent on further *Vichy* legal developments that would satisfy their insatiable demand for Jewish bodies, irrespective of nationality; 2) although Vichy finally hesitated in its otherwise headlong rush to expand the number of people defined as Jewish and thus subject to arrest and deportation, the régime's prior policies alone had made possible the eventual grotesque combination of unprecedented German *Diktat* and typically cooperative French police power that finally swept thousands of new Jewish victims towards the East.

To put it this way is to suggest that the usual apology for Vichy holds no water. Even those who have come to see the pervasiveness and the autonomy of Vichy racism still tend to argue that the régime protected its "native" population by admittedly sacrificing "foreign" Jews to the Nazi blood lust. A prime focus of their argument is on Laval's "resistance" to German pressures about denaturalization reform in 1943.[2] Our entire set of data and analysis to this point requires consideration of the upsetting possibility that Vichy first wilfully and lawfully disposed of a large segment of its foreign Jewish population in both zones, and that the early forms of that "sacrifice" *made possible* the ultimate (and largely subsequent) loss of tens of thousands of "its own Jews." Autonomous

---

[2] For two recent examples from somewhat surprising sources, see John P. Fox, "How Far Did Vichy France 'Sabotage' the Imperatives of Wannsee?," (unpubl., symposium on the 50th anniversary of the Wannsee Conference, London, 1992), 16. Fox goes so far as to say that the Germans were "thoroughly hoodwinked" by Laval in their quest for French Jews in 1943. He claims that, although Vichy is guilty of a "*degree of complicity* in the Nazi extermination process" (his emphasis) after 1943, that both prior to then and until acting "with much vigour" in 1944 to arrest its own Jews, "it undoubtedly prevented the extermination of at least over 200,000 [Jews]," ibid., 16–18. Fox is cited favorably in Abraham Brumberg, "Nuances of Evil," *Tikkun* 7, no. 3 (1992): 23; see my response, Richard Weisberg, "Cartesian Lawyers and the Unspeakable: The Case of Vichy France," *Tikkun* 7, no. 5 (1992), 46.

developments in Vichy law brought about the arrests of Jews in 1940–42 and not a clearly bifurcated scheme designed to protect French Jews at the expense of foreigners—consider only Laval's volunteering in 1942 of thousands of children born on French soil! And, as we shall now show, those developments created a momentum that *permitted—not* impeded—fresh arrests and deportations.

From at least March 1942, German diplomacy on its highest levels in France foresaw the bulk of future deportation events as linked to the progress of Vichy law. For the *Unoccupied* Zone, hopes were high of sweeping new legislation the impact of which would well affect the Occupied Zone, too. So Carl-Theo Zeitschel, the Jewish specialist in the German Embassy in Paris, writes to Krug von Nidda, his colleague delegated since the prior October to Vichy:

> Dear Herr von Nidda!... There is now talk that from the French side there will be the proclamation of a law project by which all non-French Jews in the Unoccupied Zone will be interned. Since I am particularly interested in this opportunity at this time, when a new Jewish Commissioner [of CGQJ] is anticipated, I would appreciate your keeping me informed of developments on the subject. Should this opportunity not ripen soon, I intend to ask the new Jewish Commissioner to seize the issue immediately. With best wishes, and *Heil Hitler*![3]

That new commissioner was, of course, to be Darquier de Pellepoix, who took up his post at CGQJ a few months later. And he did, in fact, become a central player in the story of developments relative to French "reform" of denaturalization (or, as Marrus and Paxton helpfully call them, "denationalization" laws).[4] The story has been told before. I contribute here only a few documents that, to my knowledge, have not hitherto been emphasized and an interpretation of events that only mildly departs from that of the two sources perhaps most consulted on this subject, Marrus and Paxton[5] and Serge Klarsfeld:[6] Vichy, in summer 1943, can be credited with taking one stand—finally—that interrupted a

---

[3] Zeitschel to von Nidda, 14 March 1942, YV 98d/13-57.

[4] Michael Marrus and Robert Paxton, *Vichy France and the Jews* (New York: Basic Books, 1981), 324.

[5] Ibid., 321–29.

[6] Serge Klarsfeld, *Le Calendrier de la Persecution des Juifs en France* (Paris: FFDJF, 1993), 739–930, passim.

legislative flow otherwise disastrous for the Jews; but, in Marrus and Paxton's phrase, "its import should not be exaggerated."[7]

Until 1943, by an agreement with Pierre Laval, people naturalized as French citizens since 1933 were stripped of their status as nationals.[8] By mid-1943, 6,307 Jews had been thus denationalized. These joined the pool of stateless Jews, and of French citizens (such as the group of distinguished lawyers discussed in chapter 3 and 8), and French native-born children of immigrants already grist for the mill under Vichy laws.[9] But there was still grumbling in Berlin. Habitually tending to inflate the Jewish population numbers greatly, and sometimes assisted by Vichy in this respect, the Germans knew that pools of Jewish cargo had not yet been touched by Vichy law. The target was *not* every single Jew on French soil, even this late in the game. (Or perhaps we should say especially this late in the game, because the manpower needed as a simple concomitant of mass roundups was not available to Berlin, as we have indicated in chapter 2, and as Klarsfeld confirms.)[10] But surely the denaturalization of additional Jews would help fill the trains. In the early spring of 1943, Paris SS Jewish Question leader Knochen writes to no less than Eichmann of his hopes that the French will sign such reform ideas into law and of his eventual need for *Sonderzüge* to take care of a potential additional 100,000 Jews.[11]

The German attitude is remarkable precisely for its faith that eventually French law would do whatever was necessary to widen the net. During the reform period central to the present chapter, even the slightest rumor of Vichy amendments to such laws was carefully noted by the Nazis and sent along to Berlin:

---

[7] Marrus and Paxton, *Vichy France and the Jews,* 328.

[8] See Serge Klarsfeld, *Vichy/Auschwitz* (Paris: Fayard, 1983), 429 and 451–53; Marrus and Paxton, *Vichy France and the Jews,* 324. In summer 1942, both before and after the big roundup in Paris, German memoranda mention the rollback to 1933 explicitly. See, e.g., memorandum, 30 July 1942, 3, CDJC XXVI-50. Two days earlier, Röthke conjures the eventual move by the French to 1927 as the earliest date naturalizations are to be recognized, CDJC XXVI-48. Both ideas are attributed to occupation police chief Jean Leguay (himself a lawyer), to the CGQJ, or to the Vichy government generally.

[9] Klarsfeld, *Calendrier,* 876.

[10] "As we have consistently suggested, the Germans depended on the complicity of French police power to conduct mass arrests of Jews," Klarsfeld, *Calendrier,* 922.

[11] Knochen to Eichmann, telegram, 29 March 1943, CDJC XXVI-235.

> Paris, February 2, 1942. To the Reich Security Office, Berlin.... Press notices from Vichy of February 24, 1942, speak of a development in the French Jewish laws whereby in the future Jewish definition will no longer be decided on the religious, but instead on the racial characteristics of the individual. A draft law is to be prepared by the Ministry.[12]

Well into 1943, much faith was placed in Darquier de Pellepoix, the aggressive and radically antisemitic leader of the CGQJ. Indeed, Darquier initiated in December 1942, as part of an aggressive legislative reform program, a plan to roll back valid naturalizations to 1927.[13] The number of potential additional deportees was significant, although not nearly as exaggerated as the numbers the Justice Ministry first gave to Heinz Röthke of the Paris SS Office on Jewish questions.[14] But even the interim figure of almost 25,000 Jews waiting in the wings, so to speak, many of whom were naturalized between 1927 and 1933, must have been tantalizing.[15]

During that summer, Smarda of the Reich Security Office tells the Paris SS, in a long memorandum coupling legalistic detail with an almost comic tone of sarcasm and befuddlement, of the need for reform so that the 2 June Vichy statute will no longer be able to protect so many Jews. While Smarda grants that Vichy law is perhaps "well meaning," it nonetheless contains too many loopholes. Primary among these are the Article 3 exceptions for people with certain kinds of military service and the statute's inadequate definition of half-Jews. His Berlin office queries:

> How can it be that, despite all the seeming trouble, the Jewish problem in France has still not been brought to a satisfactory conclusion? The German assumes that that land, with its ancient antisemitic traditions, which soon will have undergone three years of occupation by the most anti-Jewish nation [*der judenfeindlichsten Nation*], would not have made it so difficult to find strong and radical measures.[16]

---

[12] CDJC XXVI-17.

[13] Darquier broadcast the idea on Vichy radio the following February; see Marrus and Paxton, *Vichy France and the Jews,* 324.

[14] Klarsfeld, *Calendrier,* 876, 883; Gabolde first estimated some 200,000 Jews naturalized since 1927, but his eventual realistic figure was upwards of 24,000.

[15] An internal Vichy Naturalization and Reintegration chart shows the number of immigrants to France from other European countries peaking in 1927–28, AN BB$^{30}$, 1711.

[16] Memorandum, 12 July 1943, CDJC XXVII-25.

Smarda had been hopeful that Darquier, with his "long experience as fighting journalist and anti-Jewish politician," might speed up the process, but his hopes had been dashed. "Darquier de Pellepoix proposed to the régime a group of laws and also won from Vichy a series of compromises that would allow a small number of his reforms to go through. The rest of his overall program remains unfulfilled. He cannot for the moment push the rest through. Why not?"[17]

Smarda runs through the "loopholes" in the Vichy law, while also recognizing that some Vichy definitions of Jewishness go beyond Nazi models but are nonetheless ridiculous from a purely racist perspective. He allows the good faith of the French in promulgating the 2 June law but wonders at the exceptions for meritorious service or vieille souche. Then, too

> There is more. Article 3 of that same law gives special rights [*besondere Rechte*] to all Jewish war veterans who in the last War were decorated or who have won the Légion d'honneur.[18]

Smarda notes that, in Vichy alone, there are still some sixty Jews in "leading ministerial positions," but here his figures are inflated and his blaming the law for such few cases is incorrect.

---

[17] Ibid.

[18] Ibid., Smarda memorandum, 2. We have noted that the ministry most pertinent to this study—Justice—rigorously excluded Jews from service and of course as well from the courts; see chapters 3 and 4. However, I personally know of at least one Jewish lawyer who *did* serve in the government of Vichy. M. Jeramec (see chapter 8, note 233) was originally retained by the Youth Ministry, where his cousin helped to get him a job. He lasted only three months in this position and was asked to leave for "an attitude tending to denigrate the policy of the government," but his service to Vichy was not over. He had become friendly with Aline Béringuer, herself a friend of Xavier Vallat's, and he also had made the acquaintance of a Quaker named Gilbert Lesage. The latter worked for René Belin, the Labor Minister who had (against his better judgment, according to Lesage) signed the first Vichy religious law of 3 October 1940. Lesage helped Jeramec get a job in that ministry, and they worked to try to develop as many cases of exceptions to the Jewish laws as they could find, and particularly to keep Jewish children from deportation. Jeramec actually used his legal skills and served on some interministerial missions with the likes of Gazagne of the CGQJ, who always referred to him as "the Czech" in order to avoid acknowledging that he was Jewish. He later served as a juge d'instruction in the maquis, survived the war, and resumed his practice of law in Ghiens. Gilbert Lesage and Jeramec, interview with author, Paris, 13 December 1988.

Fascinating in this memorandum is its tone of sarcasm and almost teasing irony. If the French are to do "better" by German lights—this late in the occupation!—it will be by French law reform and not by German power, and Berlin will wait and see if they can wake up to their own legalistic foibles. Reflective observers such as Smarda realized that frustration should be tempered with tolerance. Much less had been accomplished than he would have liked, but much more than other countries might have done who had been left equally on their own to do the legislative job. And, after all, Vichy had sometimes exceeded the scope of German precedents, too. So there was a kind of balance.

Subtexts, by definition, are open to controversy. On the level of Smarda's literal language, at the very least, it is clear however that Germans were content to pin their hopes on internal French legal reform. Smarda is explicit on this point as he concludes his analysis with a detailed summary of the Vichy denaturalization laws upon which the Nazi greed for Jewish bodies so much depended:

> Weitere Probleme warten dringend auf ihre Lösung. [Broader issues await their urgent solution.][19]

The verb "await," like the memorandum as a whole, links German success in France to *Vichy law*.

Well into 1943, as Klarsfeld observes, "we can see a relative absence of brutal German pressure on the Jewish question."[20] Only by November of that year, and arguably only because by then the French had equivocated about the denaturalization rollback, Herbert Hagen's SS would define "French Jews as those naturalized before 1927" and attempt to coerce the French police to arrest people who were still arguably citizens of France.[21]

This German *Diktat*—the first real imposition upon France of German policy going beyond Vichy's on questions of status—emerged with great ambiguity after four separate "reform projects" on denationalization had been floated by the French themselves, and two signed by high

---

[19] Smarda memorandum, CDJC XXVII-25, 4.

[20] Klarsfeld, *Calendrier*, 861.

[21] Ibid., 915–16.

government leaders. Both Laval and Darquier (not often allied)[22] had suggested major denaturalizations, including back to the year 1927, as early as July 1942.[23] Chronologically, the first draft legal proposal was Darquier's, in a bill dated 31 December, 1942:

> Article I. Upon the promulgation of the present law, French nationality is fully retracted from any Jew who has become French by virtue of one of the following texts: 1. Law of 10 August 1927 [others omitted] ...
> Article II. Also losing their nationality are even non-Jewish wives who attained it as a result of their marriage with a naturalized Frenchman whose French nationality has been retracted by this law.
> Article III. Also losing their nationality are the issue of Jews [denaturalized by this law].
> [Article IV omitted.][24]

Darquier's draconian approach received little approbation at first,[25] although his innovation of stripping even entire families of citizenship would eventually create a stir when the rest of his idea had become more palatable to Vichy.[26] The Germans knew of it, and in detailed correspondence during March with Eichmann, pegged their hopes on its eventual promulgation.[27]

---

[22] One of the "reforms" of this period of Vichy history was Laval's attempt to have Darquier's CGQJ replaced by interministerial departments centered in the Justice Ministry; Conseil d'État lawyer Georges Monier even drafted such legislation; see Christian Lépagnot, *Histoire de Vichy* (Geneva: Editions Idégraf, 1978), vol. 1, 93.

[23] See, e.g., Lépagnot, *Histoire de Vichy,* vol. 4, 97. Laval's idea of deporting virtually all the stateless Jews in France was articulated at about the same time as he asked the Germans to include children in the deportations of July 1942, ibid., 95.

[24] CDJC XVII, draft legislation of 31 December 1942.

[25] Even nine months after its drafting, when the Germans had already to some extent relied upon its language, Darquier's "reform" had made little progress; Marcel Déat, a friend of Otto Abetz and about to join the government, observed "About this project [as about Darquier's other reforms bills], the same reticence from the provisional capital of France. M. Röthke went to Vichy recently on the instructions of the German government to insist that this reform be rapidly promulgated, threatening otherwise to take the same steps against Jews in the southern as in the northern zone. The Marshal replied that he would never accept mass retractions and that he would have to view each case separately," CDJC XXVII-51.

[26] Röthke memorandum, 15 August 1943, 1, CDJC XXVII-36; see also Klarsfeld, *Calendrier,* 865.

[27] Klarsfeld, *Calendrier,* 784.

The second reform project, little mentioned in earlier analyses,[28] is emphasized in the recent compilations of Serge Klarsfeld: it relates to the initiative of none other than the head of French police in the Interior Ministry, René Bousquet.[29] This collaborator, who as early as February told the Germans that a law would be necessary if French police were to arrest people thought of as French, although also indicating that those then in Drancy could be deported anyway,[30] was anxious to find a way to please his own government as well as the Germans. His deputy for the Occupied Zone, lawyer Jean Leguay, told the Germans in March that there might be some resistance from Vichy because "there are still so many other Jews in France," but that the government itself would take care of the problem.[31] Bousquet proposed a rollback, but only to 1932. Additionally, his draft law granted exceptions identical to those in Article 3 of the 2 June 1941 statute and excepted those connected to prisoners of war.[32]

Above all, this collaborator, who gave over his men to the filthy work of rounding up Jews the summer before, hoped by his "reform" to remain in a controlling position over the Jewish question. Bousquet's idea received favorable readings both among the French and the German bureaucracies. But, upon close study comparing the two proposed years, German lawyers insist on 1927, claiming erroneously that some 50,000 Jews had been naturalized between 1927 and 1932.[33] Multiple German memoranda further opine that "90% of the currently naturalized French Jews received their citizenship between 1927 and 1932."[34]

Bousquet had little choice before his warlords but to amend his proposal back to the year 1927; rejecting, however, Darquier's draconian inclusion of Aryan spouses and children of such naturalized Jews, and

---

[28] See, e.g., Marrus and Paxton, *Vichy France and the Jews,* 325.

[29] See Klarsfeld, *Calendrier,* 788. Bousquet was assassinated just prior to his projected and belated trial in 1992.

[30] Paris SS memorandum, 10 February 1943, CDJC XXVC-204. This same memo observes that "Already in 1942, we have shot French Jews who violated the Jewish ordinances."

[31] Röthke memorandum, 23 March 1943, CDJC XXVC-228.

[32] CDJC XXVII; see Klarsfeld, *Calendrier,* 788–89.

[33] Klarsfeld, *Calendrier,* 807.

[34] SS memorandum, 11 June 1943, CDJC XXVII-12; see an earlier memorandum to the same effect, 12 April 1943 under Röthke's signature, CDJC XXVII-5.

preserving the exceptions of Bousquet's earlier draft; there was reason to believe it might be acceptable to Vichy on the highest levels. As for the Germans:

> The moment seemed at hand for Röthke to get hold of a mass of deportable Jews. The naturalization law, whether that of Bousquet or that of Bousquet as amended by Darquier with more bite, would be quickly promulgated, or so it seemed. Röthke now had to tell Eichmann of the problems that followed upon this great opportunity for the Gestapo. The undertaking of a roundup of denaturalized Jews over the whole territory would be quite complex, since one would have to determine who, among Jews in the census, have been naturalized and find the means to get ahold of them thanks to the French police; and then one would have to consider Drancy, with an influx of thousands of French Jews, men, women, and children. Röthke counted on tens of thousands of French Jews.[35]

Bousquet's revision was circulated interministerially in June, and signed by Justice Minister Gabolde and Pierre Laval on the tenth.[36]

Meanwhile, Darquier waded in and added a version of his earlier bill; now, not the Aryan but still the *Jewish* wife and all minor children would lose their nationality along with the husband and father personally stripped of it by the new law.[37] Laval signed this fourth and last version of denationalization "reform" on 20 June, and Gabolde on 22 June. Meanwhile, the French police, willing and able to send thousands of French born Jewish children to the East during the big roundup of 1942, scrupulously inquired as to whether the new "law" applied to French children as well as naturalized ones, and whether Jewesses born on French soil were to be included with the other women covered by the bill's second paragraph.[38]

The Germans reported that "the law retracting naturalizations granted to Jews prior to August 10, 1927 is to appear in the *Journal officiel* on June 24 [1943]." They linked the promulgation of the law explicitly to the "actions"—the roundups—that would follow hard upon Vichy legislation. At 5 a.m. on that day and the next, French police and gendarmes,

---

[35] Klarsfeld, *Calendrier,* 818.

[36] Ibid., 823.

[37] CDJC XXVII.

[38] Klarsfeld, *Calendrier,* 853–54.

with a few SD supervising, will make the arrests. Everything would be done with lists in hand, according to the dictates of the new law.[39]

The German analysis of the situation was inaccurate. The French "legislative" mechanism, truncated if compared to Third Republic models, still had a ways to go before the fourth version would become Vichy law. The council of ministers still needed to inspect the proposals closely;[40] the Marshal himself might be needed (although it had been a while since his signature was required for new laws) for such a significant change in policy.[41] Moreover, central Vichy players were having second thoughts. Police czar Bousquet told SS Jewish affairs specialist Hagen—who was under direct orders from Himmler to proceed rapidly to the "action"[42]—that he did not realize Darquier's controversial additions had been superimposed on his own draft. He wondered if even Laval realized what he was signing. (Later, when confronted with Pétain's objections, Laval would in fact claim that he did not read the bill when he signed it, with all the other papers he was always being asked to sign.[43]) Knochen agreed to a delay in the promulgation of the law until early July.

Meanwhile Knochen sought reenforcements of at least 250 SS from Germany—he told Berlin that the scope of the operation, coupled with the over-extension of occupation forces already combatting "Communists, terrorists, saboteurs, etc.," make this imperative.[44] In the event, Röthke would be granted only four new men.[45] The French have always done it themselves; with everything else on Berlin's mind in summer 1943, they could be depended upon to do it now.

Typically, there is no thought to arrest Jews in France until such "actions" are fully lawful. (The previous March, Hagen, amazed at the slowness of French arrests of their "own" Jews when "the Führer [repetitively]...has called for a radical solution of the Jewish problem,"

---

[39] CDJC XXVI-77; YV 09/32.

[40] Klarsfeld, *Calendrier*, 865.

[41] See Constitutional Act No. 12, 17 November 1942, essentially giving Laval the right to sign into law all non-constitutional texts, Rémy, *Les Lois de Vichy* (Paris: Romillat, 1992), 198.

[42] Klarsfeld, *Calendrier*, 816–17.

[43] Ibid., 865.

[44] See Röthke to Group Leader Muller, memorandum, 28 June 28 , CDJC XXVII-20.

[45] Müller, Berlin to Knochen, Paris, 2 July 1943, CDJC XXVII-23.

nonetheless decided to await Vichy denationalization laws.)[46] Given the absolutely minimal time required to investigate and denationalize the potential group (now understood to be around 22,000 people) of deportable Jews, the Germans finally settled on 23 and 24 July as the proposed roundup date.[47] In a memorandum of 16 July that repetitively uses the phrase "Auf Grund des französischen Gesetzes" [according to the French law][48]—the still unsigned *bill* is being referred to by Darquier and other proponents as "law number 361"[49]—the numbers are stated, and the usual German exceptions for certain nationalities *and for Jews living in mixed marriages* are again enunciated.[50]

It was at this stage that Vichy, having initiated the idea of denationalizations a full year before,[51] and having sent a bill that was signed by Laval and Gabolde over to the Germans, finally balked. They had not realized that full families were implicated, nor that arrests would follow so quickly; they also reacted, perhaps, to the news of Mussolini's downfall, which occurred the very same day that Laval decided to shift gears.[52] The next few weeks saw manoeuvering, as on the one hand the French police devised a method to determine clearly the naturalization status of remaining Jews, while Laval insisted that Bousquet's less draconian rollback—still to 1927, however—replace Darquier's version.[53] On 14 August, a crucial meeting between Röthke and Laval occurred (preceded by a briefing from Bousquet). Röthke's minutes[54] depicted a Laval, described marginally as "der alte Parlamentarier" [that old

---

[46] Hagen memorandum, 25 March 1943, CDJC XXVC-232.

[47] Klarsfeld, *Calendrier,* 847.

[48] Röthke memorandum, CDJC XXVII-26.

[49] Darquier to Röthke, 17 July, CDJC XXVII-28.

[50] CDJC XXVII-27. See chapter 2, section C, and chapter 6, section C.

[51] See above, note 8.

[52] Klarsfeld, *Calendrier,* 854–55.

[53] Ibid., 863–64. See SS memorandum, 11 August 1943, CDJC XXVII-35, characterizing this position of Laval's. Christian Lépagnot may exaggerate somewhat in suggesting that "Laval and Bousquet try to fend off the zeal of Darquier de Pellepoix, who wants to denationalize the bulk of French Jews," *Histoire de Vichy* (Geneva: Idégraf, 1979), vol. 2, 169. All were united in principle, and the difference between them amounts to what we have noted: the minimum rollback feasible given French elasticity on, and indeed initiation of, the issue.

[54] Röthke memorandum, 15 August 1943, CDJC XXVII-36.

parliamentarian], who was clearly begging for time by claiming that the full cabinet council must now approve the bill. The Italian situation was raised, too: Vichy asked why the Germans had not moved the Italians, their allies, to a position on the Jews approximating that of Vichy's even prior to this proposed "reform"? And now Laval threatened to bring Pétain back into the review process.[55]

Although Röthke concludes that the French can no longer be counted on to "go with" the Germans on the Jewish question,[56] he has no intention of dislodging from its base in French law Nazi behavior towards their Jews. As Serge Klarsfeld sums up German thinking at the time:

> Röthke suggests to Knochen the use of German police force against the Jews, although he knows that Knochen already thinks them to be insufficient to combat resistance, and he will not trade off order in France, for which he is responsible, against some total fulfillment of the *idée fixe* of Hitler's top leaders. After all, when Himmler and Kaltenbrunner were in Paris, they did not importune Knochen with the Jewish question, and they did not even meet with Röthke. When Knochen communicates with Müller, the head of the Reich Gestapo, Berlin never in the slightest criticizes Paris in this area. Of course, Knochen will do his best to seize as many Jews as possible, but never by compromising the political edifice of Vichy nor the team of Laval-Pétain, who have satisfied the notions of Hitler fully, as well as the interests of the Reich....[57]

Yet the Germans play rhetorical hard ball, threatening to make arrests of all Jews, without regard to nationality, and to do this themselves if necessary. Marshal Pétain, meanwhile, has a rare bout of conscience. His office writes to Laval on August 24:

> The Marshal will not sign the bill. By its collective nature, it does not allow him to make any distinctions among individuals, some of whom have rendered service to France....
>
> But the Marshal wishes to indicate that he has given too many proofs of his collaboration [*volonté d'accord*] with Germany to have his motives suspected in wishing to regulate, under the best conditions, the demand that the Occupation Authorities now make to him. Not only has he actively accepted the principle of retracting naturalizations, but for a long time he

[55] See above, note 40; see also Lépagnot, *Histoire de Vichy,* vol. 2, 146.

[56] CDJC XXVII-36, 3.

[57] Klarsfeld, *Calendrier,* 866–67.

has insisted on speed from the committee within the Justice Ministry. At frequent intervals, the Marshal signs denaturalization decrees taken on the advice of that committee.[58]

The Marshal is giving orders immediately to the Justice Minister to cease as quickly as possible the project of retracting naturalizations of Jews since 1927....[59]

Knochen reports of Pétain's position that it is in part based on the Marshal's personal emotion when advised by Monsignor Chapoulie that such a measure would shock the Pope himself. He would not bring himself to sign a bill so that French people would be immediately turned over for transport [*um von den Deutschen dann abtransportiert werden]*. But he will continue to handle denaturalizations on a case-by-case basis.[60]

By the following month, the figure representing the number of Jews actually seizable by virtue of a rollback to 1927 was cut by more than half from the interim figure to a mere 10,000 still-unexamined cases.[61] The entire process of "reform" would have implicated less than 10% of the total number of Jews left on French soil. Perhaps its primary lesson is to re-enforce the control maintained by Vichy over *all* questions of Jewish definition, up to and including deportation decisions, at least until quite late in 1943. Its speculative quality would be surpassed only by its tragic undertone if the thought again were uttered—the thought that originated in the mouth of Philippe Serre, one of the eighty on Pétain's legislative enemies list:

There would not have been a racial policy in France had the French refused.[62]

---

[58] Such decrees were published in the *Journal officiel* under the Marshal's signature. The Justice Minister, according to Barthélemy himself, was primarily responsible for most denaturalization decisions. Joseph Barthélemy, *Ministre de la Justice: Vichy, 1941–1943* (Paris: Pygmalion, 1989), 307.

[59] CDJC XXVII-38.

[60] Knochen to Kaltenbrunner, 25 August 1943, CDJC XXVII-40.

[61] Marrus and Paxton, *Vichy France and the Jews,* 329; see generally CDJC XXVII-50.

[62] See chapter 2 at note 9.

## B. Franco-French Legal Reform Projects

Fulsome and complex as promulgated Vichy law surely was, there existed strong sentiment in many French quarters that the new legislation did not suffice to carry out Vichy's "revolution." Although Vichy policy makers scrutinized many French institutions, and many aspects of French life, the urge to reform the law persevered with great intensity in the specific areas central to the present study. This subsection proceeds to review the projects of Darquier de Pellepoix and others to "perfect" Vichy's internal persecution of the Jews.

Between the virulent Darquier and the realization of his many legalistic schemes, there stood only other Vichy constraints, constituted by public opinion or institutional hierarchies. We shall see how almost all of the CGQJ's projects failed, while also noting that disparate ministries in Vichy became involved in discussing them, or indeed offering other kinds of reform laws that might have equally affected racial policy.

Doubtless, the urge to overturn every facet of French life that had led to the debacle and defeat lessened somewhat over time in the face of shifting public opinion, likely German defeat, and the innate strength of some challenged French institutions. On the other hand, and this is a crucial tenet of the wider study, the ability of French intellectuals, bureaucrats and lawyers to "follow through" with Cartesian logic on any process once begun, gave sustained impetus to "reforms" that really stood no realistic chance of being implemented once the Germans left French soil.

An excellent example of the self-contained, almost myopic enthusiasm generated across four full years of the Vichy experience was the urge to draft a new constitution. Originated in the legalistic necessity thrust on Vichy by the departing French parliament on 10 July 1940,[63] the redaction of the new text finally received Pétain's signature in early 1944, when German defeat was a foreordained conclusion.[64] As Barthé-

---

[63] The second paragraph of the basic transfer of powers to Pétain agreed upon that day by the Parliament required the new government to promulgate a constitution, and the third paragraph required that the new constitution "be ratified by the Nation," Rémy, *Les Lois de Vichy,* 31. For a complete discussion of the early constitutional project, see chapter 4, text at notes 72–101.

[64] See Lépagnot, *Histoire de Vichy,* vol. 2, 199.

lemy envisioned it, the new constitution was to be "based entirely on the principle of Christianity and of the French Revolution."[65] The paradoxical combination, with a further emphasis on legality, an empowered magistracy and especially an authoritative Conseil d'État,[66] survived Barthélemy's departure from government.

After Barthélemy left the Justice Ministry in 1943, the committees that had been set in motion by himself and by Pétain continued their work under the leadership of such men as Lucien Romier and Henry Moysset, who, together with distinguished parliamentarians like Jacques Bardoux (until 1943, when differences caused him to quit the committee), had been leaders on the reform project virtually since it began.[67]

Constitutional reform work had already emitted an undertone of responsiveness to the "Jewish question" as somehow fundamentally needful of sweeping solution.[68] Nothing in the aims or discussions of the reform committee's work negated even the most radical sense of what the new constitution would look like. At an extreme, certainly, was the continuous thunder from the hysterical press, sometimes couched in legalistic terms. Thus, the Paris weekly, *Au Pilori,* mounted a campaign to "abrogate the decree of 27 September 1791," under which the National Assembly majestically universalized the constitutional rights of all French citizens by granting them under condition of a civic oath to be faithful to its principles. *Au Pilori*'s reform rhetoric surely exceeded what any polite constitutional draftsman would declare publicly—it seems, in the phrase of Henri Amoureux, to be "the least readable of all collaborationist weeklies"[69]—but its sentiments were not foreign to mainstream Vichy thinking at a certain level of generalization, and the exaggerated legal

---

[65] Barthélemy, *Ministre,* 290.

[66] Ibid., 295. The new Cour suprême constitutionnelle, partly based on the American model, also took its place in the reform. See also AN 72 AJ 412, Dossier no. 2 for a description in the archives of this reform project along the lines of an American High Court that could strike down unconstitutional laws.

[67] See AN 72 AJ 413, for Barthélemy's notes about Bardoux, as well as Barthélemy, *Ministre,* e.g., 289. On Romier's completion of the project for Pétain's signature in 1944, see ibid., 295. See also Lépagnot, *Histoire de Vichy,* vol. 2, 199 and vol. 3., 96; and Jean-Paul Cointet, *Pierre Laval* (Paris: Fayard, 1993), 444.

[68] See chapter 4, notes 86–94.

[69] See Amoureux, *Les Beaux jours des Collabos* (Paris: Laffont, 1978), 474.

reforms of Vichy's waning months probably all stood some chance of passing into law because of such thinking:

> Naturally, everyone hastened to take this [citizenship] oath, which cost them little, most with the intent to break it. And, from one day to the next, these strangers from all corners of the globe, these who were immigrants yesterday now became citizens of the country with the same rights as the descendants of the oldest families of our ancient Gaul. And soon there was a flood, a tide of the circumcised, of every color and shade, spilling onto our shores, here sometimes without knowing a single word of our language, to participate in our national business.
>
> The worm was in the fruit.... We must now remove it before the fruit, our France, drops putrid from the European tree. And here are the terms on which we propose to guaranty our future by abrogating the decree:
>
> *Article One.* The decree of the National Assembly of 27 September 1791, is abrogated as regards the Jews....[70]

The reformist impulse, sustained by thousands of people who perhaps had nothing else in common with *Au Pilori,* contributed to the denaturalization laws and religious statutes passed as among Vichy's very first acts and proposed as an ongoing series of increasingly burdensome restrictions. Without explicit constitutional sanction, *Au Pilori*'s program of extirpating the Jewish worm gained *partial* currency. On the level of governmental discourse, as we examined in chapter 1, the radical antisemitic constitutional reform program found more threatening form in the more polite language of Pétain's pronouncements about the causes of the recent defeat.[71] Was it the extent of those first laws, and of that early exclusionary discourse, or was it the evident logical zeal shown by Vichy institutions in debating and extending them that made reform of many established institutions through exclusionary measures a viable possibility throughout the period?

### *1. Reforming the Courts*

*Au Pilori* did not rest content with frontal attacks on the idea of Jewish participation in French civic life. By the end of the Vichy period, *any* institution was grist for its mill if deemed soft or deleterious on the

---

[70] The *Au Pilori* text is from an article by Lucien Pemjean, May 1942, cited extensively in YV 0-9/9-3, 14–15.

[71] See chapter 1, text at notes 10–20.

Jewish question. The magistrates, the appeals courts, and the venerated Cour de Cassation itself were chastised; consider the timing of the following pronouncement, published two weeks and one day after the Allied landings in Normandy:

> We all know that just about every judge in France has linked hands with the Jews and the Freemasons. We could cite you 50 decisions in which the most prestigious judges have tripped up the laws concerning either the Jews or Freemasonry.[72]

The weekly zooms in on its latest target, Donat-Gigue, whose latest decision exemplifies the magistracy's softness. But then, he is "one of the most notorious Gaullists in the Palais de Justice.... If the police had handled things well, [he] would have been in a concentration camp a long time ago."[73]

The hysterical press was merely parroting sentiments harbored in far more serious places. In chapters 4 and 5, we analyzed the behavior of the courts and saw that, politically, Justice Minister Barthélemy walked a fine line between support for his magistrates and endorsement of policies that the judges sometimes seemed to dislike. He had to be especially scrupulous—as the Garde des Sceaux—to protect his underpaid and demoralized magistrates from the attacks of the increasingly powerful police, the always strident CGQJ, and nationalist groups like the *Légion d'Honneur*.[74] Some police informed periodically on judges viewed as "weak."[75]

Reform of the courts, and particularly of the magistrates, simmered as a Vichy project. Despite their personal oath to Marshal Pétain, and despite their participation in the special jurisdictions discussed a bit further on, magistrates seemed to Vichy's unrepentant supporters to be irksomely independent at times. Perhaps something could be done.

So Jean Labre, head of the lawyer's liaison committee from the Conseil d'État to the Cour de Cassation, suggested directly to the latter, in a series of memoranda, that reform of the ordinary court was in order.

---

[72] *Au Pilori,* 28 June 1944, AN $BB^{30}$, 1716.

[73] Ibid., the article cites Donat-Gigue's decision in the case of "M.B." from the *Gazette du Palais,* 3 June 1944.

[74] See Barthélemy, *Ministre,* 186–95.

[75] Ibid., 189.

Labre freely criticized the Cour de Cassation, a venerable institution dating in France (like the Constitution) to 1790. He criticized its concern "about basic principles in dealing with the new legislation."[76] He noted "contradictions" among the court's four distinct sections in interpreting these laws. Labre's reform—reminiscent of FDR's court-packing scheme of the 1930s—might involve replacing "aging" members of the Cour de Cassation and establishing at the same time "a leading group of magistrates...that would consist of [sitting members left on the court], lawyers assigned to it, selected district prosecutors assigned to the sections, etc., and advisors [*collaborateurs*] helping them with the administrative duty imposed on them by this reform."[77] A second memo followed from the same pen, suggesting to the Ministry of Justice that the sole reason for reforming such a bulwark of French justice would indeed be because "it might not be ready to expedite the appeals that are made to it." Reform would be modeled somewhat on the (more authoritarian)[78] structure of the Conseil d'État or the Cour des comptes, and might involve decentralization so that the newly staffed sections could make rapid decisions without referring to a plenary session of the court.[79]

Although such notions never gained legislative ratification, they indicate that radical reform was always in the Vichy atmosphere. *Because* they never attained to the level of new law, these proposals once again indicate the firmness and the relative autonomy under which Vichy maintained most of its traditions while also accommodating laws on race and religion that would have been anathema to the traditions of the judges now interpreting them.

Although the ensconced courts not only survived but thrived in the reformist atmosphere of Vichy, new jurisdictions were created. We have seen how the Cour suprême de justice, created by constitutional act number five,[80] handled what turned out to be its unique adjudication, the

---

[76] Correspondence file of Georges Dayras of the Justice Ministry, AN BB[30], 1708.

[77] Ibid.

[78] See chapter 5, note 111. The Conseil not only took a direct oath to Pétain (as did all the magistrates); it publicly exulted in working with an authoritarian leader. Nonetheless, even the Conseil came in for some threats of reform; see chapter 5, note 108.

[79] Dayras correspondence, AN BB[30], 1708.

[80] Rémy, *Les Lois de Vichy,* 60; see also Lépagnot, *Histoire de Vichy,* vol. 1, 54.

Riom prosecutions.[81] Also reaching its zenith of power at Riom was Pétain's hand-picked "counsel of political justice," which so raised the hackles of the French Bar.[82] Far more active, and more pernicious, too, was the essentially extralegal Tribunal d'état, a special court noteworthy for issuing Vichy's only death sentence for abortion (and in the process France's first execution of a woman since the Revolution).[83] Perhaps most distanced of all from French tradition, the sections spéciales arose under the law of 14 August 1941, signed among others by Joseph Barthélemy.[84] Georges Dayras, a perennial in the Justice Ministry, would barely escape with his life after the Liberation for his participation in the running of these courts.[85] Interior Minister Pierre Pucheu, another signatory to the special sections law, would not successfully answer those and other charges against him when he appeared before a military court in liberated Algeria. He would be executed there in 1944.[86] The postwar

---

[81] See chapter 1.

[82] See chapter 1, note 43 and chapter 8, note 106, on Jacques Charpentier's vigorous reaction to this obvious breach of separation of powers.

[83] See Barthélemy, *Ministre,* 249–50. Described as "l'avorteuse de Cherbourg," she appealed to Pétain, but "the defender of the family and guardian of childbirth refused to pardon her." See Maurice Gabolde, "Justice," in Chambron, ed., *La Vie de France sous l'Occupation,* (Stanford: Hoover Institute, 1957), vol. 2 , 625.

[84] See Rémy, *Les Lois de Vichy,* 140; chapter 4, note 159; and Barthélemy, *Ministre,* 244–49, 582. See also Lépagnot, *Histoire de Vichy,* vol. 1, 161, for a description of the pressure placed on Vichy by the Germans to create such a repressive jurisdiction.

[85] See Lépagnot, *Histoire de Vichy,* vol. 5, 144. Dayras was pardoned of his capital sentence.

[86] See an excellent book about Pucheu's trial by his lawyer, Paul Buttin, *Le procès Pucheu* (Paris: Amiot-Dumont, 1948). On 11 March 1944, Pucheu was sentenced to death by a military tribunal in Algeria; although the sentence was specifically limited to his behavior regarding the special sections, he was found guilty of several capital crimes, including the following: "7. ...[while] secretary of State for Production and then Minister of the Interior...promulgating or contributing to the promulgation of laws claiming to be those of the French state, favorable to the policies of Germany, in time of war...." and "8. ...placing at the service of the German occupying forces all or part of the organs of public power in time of war...." ibid., 210–11. He was executed less than two weeks later. Among other law-related figures, only Pierre Laval would see a formal capital sentence executed against him. See Jean-Paul Cointet, *Pierre Laval,* chapter 15. Barthélemy, arrested after the liberation, would die in a prison hospital. See above, chapter 4.

For Pucheu's central place in establishing the special courts, see also Barthélemy, *Ministre,* 244–49, and Marrus and Paxton, *Vichy France,* 224.

filmmaker Claude Chabrol later told of the abortionist's joust with Vichy justice in *Une Histoire des Femmes*.[87] The filmmaker Costa-Gavras named a motion picture after the infamy of the special sections.[88]

*2. The Sections Spéciales*

The Vichy law of 14 August 1941, reads as follows:

> Article I. There is now instituted, as part of each military tribunal or each maritime tribunal, one or several special sections to which are referred the perpetrators of all penal infractions, whatever they may be, committed with the intent of communist or anarchist activity.
>
> In the parts of the territory where military or maritime tribunals would not sit, the jurisdiction of the special sections provided for in the paragraph above will be transmitted to a section of the Court of Appeals which rules without announcing its reasons [*sans énonciation des motifs*] by deciding only on guilt and penalty....
>
> Article VII. Judgments rendered by the special section are not amenable to appeal; they are executed immediately.
>
> Article IX. Penalties available to the special section are life imprisonment with or without a fine, hard labor for a term or for life, or death, and no sentence can be less than that prescribed for the crime alleged....
>
> Article X.... All existing bodies of inquiry or of judgment are stripped of jurisdiction in favor of the special section, which will in addition hear any complaint against judgments made for failure to appear or *in absentia*.[89]

The law was both procedurally and substantively startling, as it was designed, *ex post facto,* to punish people unconnected with the actual "crime." Although antedated to August 14 in order to legitimate the special trials of individuals already arrested in connection with "anarchist activity" and the killing of a Wehrmacht officer in a Paris subway,[90] it was published in the *Journal officiel* for 25 August 1941. By the time of the law's subsequent modifications on 5 June 1943, the special sections had been integrated into French legal discourse, subject to polite debate as to their jurisdiction, their procedures, and the substance of their work.

---

[87] *The Story of Women* (Chabrol, 1988) recounts fictionally the true-life prosecution of Marie Latour, who was guillotined under Vichy law.

[88] *Section spéciale* (Costa-Gavras, 1975).

[89] Rémy, *Les Lois de Vichy,* 142 et seq.

[90] See Barthélemy, *Ministre,* 572–83; also Marrus and Paxton, *Vichy France,* 138, 224.

As with the religious laws already analyzed, which were equally in violation of French traditions still available to legal discourse if people wanted to invoke them, the special section legislation provided fecund analytical soil for lawyers tilling and talking, harvesting and writing, doing what they do best.

The new jurisdiction had its source in Nazi reprisals against trouble-makers in the Occupied Zone, most of whom were Communists, whether Jew or non-Jew.[91] German violence on French soil had become accustomed to, and hence craved in the particular case, Vichy legitimation.

Apologists for Justice Minister Barthélemy blame German "blackmail" for the law, and the Nazis did appreciate gaining his distinguished signature under the promulgation of such an extreme measure.[92] But there was no cause to believe that Vichy would *not* give the Germans what it usually gave them without any such pressure. For without Vichy law's already situated violations of French legal traditions, epitomized the prior September and October and carried through with fervor on 2 June 1941, would the Germans in August 1941 confidently elicit the legitimation of their casual violence against victim populations?

Members of the first special sections were to be chosen by the Justice Minister himself[93]; they were to be attached to existing French jurisdictions, usually culled from the magistrates of the Court of Appeals where the trials were to occur. Although they ultimately adjudicated cases largely involving Communists, they were intended to try and execute "those hostages...who fall into the same category or the same 'race' as that of the guilty (or presumed to be guilty) assassin."[94] In the first incident that provoked the Germans, Pierre Masse was conjured as a possible hostage, further forcing those French lawyers who so admired Masse to move with their own law.[95]

Barthélemy, called to Paris to sign the law—and fresh from the shock of hearing Pétain announce over the radio that other "special

---

[91] Marrus and Paxton, *Vichy France,* 225, observe that "proportion...of Jews among the hostages was high from the beginning."

[92] Barthélemy, *Ministre,* 578.

[93] See ibid., 582–3.

[94] Ibid.

[95] Ibid.

jurisdictions" would pronounce the guilt of the Riom defendants[96]—apparently wondered aloud if Vichy magistrates might cooperate in prosecuting and trying such cases, which smacked more of summary military justice. "The creation of such an exceptional jurisdiction would conflict with the reticence of magistrates, who defend the principles of liberal law"; yet Barthélemy not only signed the law but agreed to study another related reform: the amendment of the Code of Criminal Law to include sanctions against non-informers![97]

Vichy manoeuvering by Pucheu (according to Barthélemy) quickly brought about the designation of the first special section. Manned by Paris-area magistrates, with only one refusing to serve on such a court,[98] it decided the fate of four men, among whom was Abraham Tryzbrucki, a Jew. With apparent unanimity, the court condemned three to death. One was given a lesser sentence: forced labor for a term of life. The three were guillotined at dawn, without right of appeal, the day following the "trial." Some 500–550 other Frenchmen would eventually be shot as hostages.[99]

Barthélemy, self-described as "in a state of torture," consoled himself with having avoided greater slaughter.[100] In legalistic character, he speaks of:

> assuring essential guaranties. First, there was the make-up of the courts: they consisted of magistrates from the judiciary, who had a professional conscience. Then, too, in principle criminal procedure had to be observed. The accused were to be represented by counsel. There were indisputably some extreme sentences at first.... Shortly, things quieted down. The special sections could be more lenient than regular criminal courts. They issued a sentence of eight months where a court would have sentenced to five years.[101]

Indeed, the special courts turned into an almost everyday phenomenon. Such eminences as Maurice Garçon took on notorious defendants before

---

[96] See chapter 1, text at note 43; Jean-Paul Cointet, *Pierre Laval* (Paris: Fayard, 1993), 354.

[97] Barthélemy, *Ministre,* 584.

[98] Ibid., 583.

[99] Marrus and Paxton, *Vichy France,* 225.

[100] Barthélemy, *Ministre,* 245.

[101] Ibid., 245–6.

these courts.[102] Lawyers might "forum shop," deciding for their clients whether an ordinary court, or the new variety, might best serve their interests. But this was risky: ordinary courts might be held no longer to have jurisdiction over suspects whose behavior now seemed covered by the special sections. And this might apply even for infractions brought before the ordinary court *prior* to the promulgation of the special section law. In a situation that arose literally days after the new sections were legally created, the special section attached to the Court of Appeal of Caen stripped the ordinary court of its jurisdiction over the prosecution of a distributor of Communist tracts. The alleged criminal act occurred prior to 14 August 1941, the date of inception of the special jurisdiction. Here, the non-retroactivity principle, never raised formally to protect Jews against the basic religious legislation, was at least conjured (unsuccessfully in the situation) to safeguard the defendant from the rigors of the brand new courts:

> If the rule against non-retroactivity of the laws, whether civil or criminal, is well recognized in Article 2 of the *Code civil* and Article 4 of the *Code pénale,* this rule only applies to the substantive aspect of the law [and not necessarily to which court has jurisdiction over it]. But it is a recognized principle that especially as regards criminal procedures and jurisdictions, these are applicable from the date of their promulgation to infractions committed during the pendency of the former laws. The law of 14 August 1941 turns over to a special section of the Court of Appeals...those who have committed any criminal act with the intention of communist or anarchist activity.... Thus the Court of Appeals must declare itself incompetent to hear a case against a distributor of communist tracts even if the summons to appear before it was served on the defendant prior to the promulgation of the law of 14 August 1941.[103]

Another procedural anomaly involved the skipping of a vital hierarchical step in the prosecution of such suspects. Debate ensued on whether the figure who usually investigated serious crimes, the juge d'instruction (examining magistrate), could be replaced by the hierarchically superior and politically more correct district prosecutor, who could then

---

[102] See ibid., 248, for a description of what the Justice Minister calls Garçon's "tightrope act" defense of a communist former deputy, Gabriel Péri, who was shot as a hostage on 15 December 1941.

[103] Decision of 2 September 1941, *Gazette du Palais,* 1–2 October 1941.

unilaterally invoke the court's jurisdiction.[104] The judicial rhetoric on this procedural nicety is altogether typical of Vichy lawyers, once they accommodated to a seemingly appalling *substantive* innovation. Lower-level issues quickly dominated the discourse, and the enormity of the legal change itself—here the execution of "hostages" under cover of law—was obfuscated by the precision of the procedural debate:

> In fact, Article 22 of the Code of Criminal Procedure seems to be interpretable as permitting district prosecutors to pursue all crimes and offenses as opposed to simple breaches of the peace. [Yet the revisions of 5 June 1943 leave vague whether their competence extends to many infractions handled by the special sections.] It seems that sound policy would dictate an interest in finding parity on these matters between the juge d'instruction and the district prosecutor.[105]

A draft bill was circulated, but no further changes to the new jurisdiction were formally made after June 1943.

By most accounts,[106] the special sections were ultimately responsible for summary executions, and countless long sentences rendered without the usual protections of French—and Vichy—procedures. Many Jews lost their lives before successor special courts to the one in Paris in August 1941.

## C. The Case of Out-of-Wedlock Children

Vichy demonstrated a strange solicitude for children born out of wedlock, even if they might be Jewish.[107] Although the case of such children never gave rise to explicit reform legislation, Barthélemy and others had to fend off reforms by the CGQJ that would have *implicitly* subjected them to investigations foreign to established French law. As we saw in the landlord/tenant section of chapter 7, Franco-French autopoeitic legal reasoning—on rare occasions—would draw a line that might protect certain Jews. But here, for the first time, a Vichy minister opposed measures by CGQJ that otherwise would disturb settled principles deemed "fundamental."

---

104 See internal Vichy memorandum, 22 October 1943, AN $BB^{30}$, 1709.

105 Ibid.

106 See above, notes 99–101.

107 See chapter 4, notes 144 and 147; chapter 5, note 81.

When the Justice Minister heard from the CGQJ in late 1941 and early 1942 that plans were afoot to modify the first three articles of the basic religious law of 2 June 1941, his response largely focussed on out-of-wedlock children.[108] Barthélemy responded that a quest to find parents and grandparents of out-of-wedlock children would violate rights to privacy that these people had been given by already existing legislation. He cross-referred to Article 335 of the Code civil,[109] and to other "provisions.[110] These strictly prohibit *legal* inquiries, except at the behest of the child. (If factual inquiries are to occur, they will of course pose the usual difficulties in cases of unknown ancestry.)

French law had protected these children from precisely the inquiry now proposed against them to determine potential Jewish ancestry. The CGQJ's reform implicated this older doctrine in an attempt by the agency to fight some Vichy courts that had been tending to assume non-Jewishness in cases of unknown parentage.[111] The result, in Barthélemy's word, would be "unfair" to these children.

This formalistic debate, which has been previously discussed to excellent effect by Joseph Billig (but apparently without benefit of the

---

[108] For the text of Barthélemy's response, see chapter 4, note 144.

[109] For the postwar rights of out-of-wedlock children—considerably greater than they have been even in the more liberal American states—see Lucien Isselé, *Les Successions* (Paris: Éditions sociales mercures, 1957), sections 67–76.

[110] "Article 335. Recognition of an out-of-wedlock child will be done by notarized formality if it has not been done on the birth certificate.... 340–2. The [paternity] action belongs only to the child," Dalloz, *Code civil* (1978), 206–8. For a Vichy-era exemplification of the former section, see the case of a woman whose lover was imprisoned in Drancy. She wanted his declaration of paternity so that their child could gain the benefits of a legal father. To do this, the lover needed permission to leave Drancy and to go to the town hall of the 12ᵉ arrondissement and make the proper declaration. UGIF wrote to the SS as the child neared the age of two months; a few days later, SS *Untersturmführer* Ahnert afforded Thomas *Fogel* and his newborn son provisional relief: the father could go to the town hall of Drancy to make the appropriate declarations and to sign the paternity forms, Anna Neishtat/Thomas Fogel file, beginning 19 May 1943, YV/Leo Israelowicz file.

[111] See, e.g., Trib corr. of Toulouse, 22 December 1941; and the *Touati* case, discussed at chapter 2, note 116, where the son of two out-of-wedlock children was deemed non-Jewish by a Paris tribunal in 1943 because his grandparents were unknown.

Barthélemy papers),[112] begs the question of why equally applicable collateral statutes were *never* flagged about the Jewish statutes more generally. The stripping away of property, the imposition of *ex post facto* criminal sanctions, the shifting of the burden of proof (by judicial, if not statutory, mandate), the evisceration of still-recognized basic rights—all of this occurred with no such legalistic protest. What strange compulsion led intelligent and seemingly logical lawyers to find their personal "degree zero" at such low levels of generalization as the case of the out-of-wedlock child?

In this legal area, at least, the Nazi models were harsher; the Germans had long before changed their own laws to permit detailed legal inquiries into the ancestry of such children.[113] But Vichy, on the ministerial level, fiercely insisted on protection against CGQJ reforms for this tiny sub-group of Jewish unfortunates.

In the event, there were more than a few cases. As quickly after this correspondence as the following month, a court in Perpignan issued a mixed decision in the case of an out-of-wedlock child named Levy. The court disallowed his plea that a declaration of paternity by his putative father (a Jew) in 1910 should be annulled. Levy claimed that this man was not even in Paris when he was conceived. The court nonetheless assumed that Levy had two Jewish grandparents on his paternal side, yet it permitted him to show that he personally had never practiced Judaism. The burden remained on Levy, and the protections (of non-inquiry into parentage) usually afforded to such children were not honored by the court, but at least Levy was not required to prove adherence to another religion besides Judaism. Nonetheless, the court ordered him to have a circumcision inspection within fifteen days.[114]

Not long after this decision, CGQJ advised its regional director in Nice that an out-of-wedlock child suspected of being Jewish but whose parents were completely unknown would "without a doubt be considered Jewish,

---

[112] See Joseph Billig, *Le Commissariat général aux questions juives* (Paris: CDJC, 1955), vol. 2, 173–77.

[113] For the usual German rule, see Billig, ibid.

[114] Decision of 9 February 1942, CDJC XVIIa-45 (243); see also Danièle Lochak, "La Doctrine sous Vichy, ou les Mésaventures du positivisme," in Serge Klarsfeld, ed., *Le Statut des Juifs de Vichy* (Paris: 1990), 131.

unless baptized."[115] Even in this harsh letter, however, the agency, perhaps increasingly responsive to Barthélemy's notion of conflicting French law that protected such children's privacy, cited possible problems with certain Civil Code articles and also prewar statutes of 1939 and 1925. Several weeks later, CGQJ (through its service on legislation and litigation [contentieux]), wrote to an agency dealing with wards of the state:

> You have suggested that it would be too much to ask of a child born of unknown parents and carrying a name that sounds Jewish to prove his non-affiliation with the Jewish race. I am pleased to tell you that I agree, as long as the parents are unknown in fact, that is if nothing in terms of documents or proceedings reveals their existence. On the other hand, the mother, for example, whose name is mentioned on the birth certificate of the child, must be considered as a known parent. In this case the child must establish that his ascendant was not Jewish.[116]

CGQJ's increasingly softened position indicates—as so much else in this study already affirms—the elasticity of racial policy under Vichy law. Its concession on paternity is even more striking when we recall that the 2 June statute itself literally prohibited all attempts by Jewish parents or grandparents to *disavow* ties to children trying to avoid Jewish status. This provision could have been used by the agency, or the courts, to infer a "legislative" intention to burden all children with the *factual* Jewishness of their ancestors, whatever the latter's subsequent status or declaration might provide as an argument for non-Jewishness. Yet, virtually all known cases and policy statements on this issue from 1942 on affirmed the special rights of the out-of-wedlock child to certain assumptions of unknown grandparental heritage and also of presumptive non-Jewishness.

In the *Bouchard-Levy* matter, brought on at around this time in mid-1942, the individual had been baptized at age 25. Prior to this, however, his father (M. Levy, unconnected to the Levy just discussed above) had confessed paternity and in fact married his mother (Bouchard, an Aryan). Levy was himself an out-of-wedlock child and hence *his* parents were also legally unknown. Bouchard-Levy won an annulment of the declaration of paternity, the right to take his mother's name as his own, and

[115] Note, 3 March 1942, CDJC CXV-19.

[116] CGQJ correspondence, 29 May 1942, AN AJ$^{38}$, 118.

CGQJ recognition that he would be considered non-Jewish.[117] In early 1943, the Tribunal de la Seine held that, where an individual's grandparents were legally unknown, that individual would be considered non-Jewish.[118] In 1944, an Algerian was permitted to argue (in the spirit of Barthélemy's 1942 letter) that the "legislator" of the 2 June statute intended a legal and not a factual inquiry as to the parentage of out-of-wedlock children.[119] And, as we have noted earlier, by April 1944, the CGQJ advanced to the position that all unknown ancestors would be presumed non-Jewish.[120]

The reasoning process that disallowed reform of the 2 June statute to burden out-of-wedlock children with legal presumptions about ancestry otherwise not permitted by French law deserves one last underscoring in terms of our thesis as a whole. The French legalistic machine forged ahead during Vichy, with all engines at the ready. Every argument familiar to French lawyers was *always* there to be taken out of storage. The existence of the statutes of 3 October 1940, of 2 June 1941, and of 22 July 1941—the dominant texts of racial persecution authored by Vichy—did *not in and of themselves dictate any particular outcome in individual cases*. If hundreds of persons with two Jewish and two non-Jewish grandparents could muster arguments to avoid Jewish status, if Jewish out-of-wedlock children and if Jewish tenants were favorites of the law, why could not an individual with three or even four Jewish grandparents mount arguments *under French law* that could save them from some or all of the mandated persecutions?

The only respectable answer is that the French *chose* not to make those arguments. The "simplicity" of the text on any given point was not an unalterable "given"; its "simplicity" (or unavoidability) was the *result* of a process of reasoning that decided to draw lines in one place and not in another. In Italy, a fascist neighbor, the Jewish laws were simply ignored until the Nazis invaded the country in 1943. In Belgium, powerful lawyers made clear that persecution of Jewish colleagues was unthinkable under Belgian law. In Denmark, despite burdensome German ordinances against the Jews, 7500 of 7800 were saved under the nose of the very

---

[117] YV unnumbered, date of CGQJ memorandum on the case being 22 July 1942.

[118] Decision of 12 February 1943, CDJC unnumbered.

[119] Reported in Billig, *Le Commissariat général,* vol. 2, 176.

[120] See internal CGQJ memorandum, 5 April 1944, CDJC XVIIa-38 (164).

Nazi overlord[121] who had formerly watched the French fall into (or beyond the) line with German racism.[122]

Vichy's acceptance of some reforms, and its resistance to others—particularly to Darquier's package of draconian policies formed in late 1942 and throughout 1943—may serve as a source of limited pride to Vichy apologists. Unfortunately, "liberal" choices within illiberal frameworks indict rather than justify the behavior of authorities. In Vichy, they not only went to bed with the bad guys—they built the bed, called it a bed, and then managed only to nitpick about what outfits to wear to bed. The latter, mere adornments, were sometimes called "reforms."

---

[121] Werner Best, Head of Military Operations in Paris, went on to watch the massive rescue of Jews by the Danes. See Marrus and Paxton, *Vichy France and the Jews,* 218.

[122] See, e.g., Henry Kamm, "Danes Commemorate Rescue of Jews from Nazis," *New York Times,* 28 September 1993, A3; Leo Goldberger, "Nazi Understaffing Helped Danish Jews," *New York Times,* 11 October 1993, A16, citing Tamara Bernstein's findings on the Danish rescue in *Rambam,* 2 (1993).

# Chapter 10

## Why Lawyers Underperformed: Xenophobia, Catholicism, and the Talmudic Outsider

This final chapter attempts to explain what our study has shown: the pervasive and largely voluntary acceptance among French wartime lawyers of a non-egalitarian theme totally foreign to their earlier custom and practice. Some of the sources emphasized here will be more academic in nature—the book-length contemporary studies of the religious statutes, and jurisprudential works, as well as the manuals and law review articles also analyzed in the recent work of others.[1] I will reopen only a bit the discussions of the writings of perhaps the most infamous of Vichy legal academics, Maurice Duverger, whose 1941 article on the Jewish laws has become a barometer of Vichy academic discourse and has been much de-

[1] See, e.g., the articles in the symposium entitled "Que Faire de Vichy," *Esprit,* May 1992; see also Dominique Gros, "Le statut des Juifs dans les manuels en usage dans les Facultés de Droit," in Philippe Braud, ed., *La violence politique dans les démocraties occidentales* (Paris: L'Harmattan, 1993); see especially, the articles in Serge Klarsfeld, ed., *Le Statut des Juifs de Vichy* (Paris: FFDJF, 1990), including Danièle Lochak, "La Doctrine sous Vichy ou les mésaventures du positivisme," 121–50. Prof. Lochak's article first appeared in CURAPP, *Les Usages sociaux du droit,* (Paris: P.U.F., 1989), 252–85. with a brief response from Prof. Michel Troper. (Citations in this chapter to Lochak will be to the Klarsfeld edition; citations to Prof. Troper's response will be to *Les Usages,* as the response was not included in the later Klarsfeld edition.)

bated and even litigated.[2] Although connected to this study's earlier examples of seemingly "neutral" discourse (Broc, Baudry and Ambre, Haennig, and Maury),[3] the use of the sources in this chapter is somewhat different.

I draw here an overall conception of legal discourse during Vichy. I will differ in this conception from the very few French analysts who have so far looked into Vichy reasoning, for I make the claim that the treatment of Jews by the Vichy legal establishment cannot be fully explained by the existence alone of specific laws addressing the Jews; countries such as Italy had similar laws and (to a large extent) did not apply them, and the participation of so many thousands of French legal actors already ensconced in a libertarian legal tradition might have led to the same result under Vichy. Instead, the majority of legal actors affirmatively produced a position that ruled Jews out of the entire structure of law—including constitutional law—a structure that still protected "real" Frenchmen. This strategy, which I call "Vichy hermeneutics," fairly quickly came to inform virtually the whole of legal practice and dictated more than any written set of laws the dismal outcome we have elaborated. It was a way of seeing the law that colored the legal act before it even began, and existed irrespective of the facts or the statutes in question. It "trumped" (that is to say, it automatically overcame) all competing perspectives on the given situation and posited in advance of

---

[2] Maurice Duverger, "La Situation des fonctionnaires depuis la Révolution de 1940," *Revue du Droit public et des Sciences politiques*, vol. 57 (1940–1941), 277–332, 417–450. For an extensive *apologia* and review of the debate and the litigation arising from his piece, see idem, "La Perversion du droit," in n.a., *Réligion, Société et Politique: Mélanges en Hommmage à Jacques Ellul* (Paris: P.U.F., 1983). See also Michael Marrus and Robert Paxton, *Vichy France and the Jews* (New York: Basic Books, 1981), 145, for a description of the 1941 article; and Jean-Marc Théolleyre, "Les Années 40 de M. Maurice Duverger," *Le Monde*, 22 October 1988, 22, for a more recent discussion of various libel suits brought by Duverger against people who cite his 1941 work. In one of these suits, the moving papers for which I have seen, Duverger challenges the review *Actuel* for asserting, e.g., that his wartime articles on the religious laws were written "in a judicious and cold tone, without the slightest reproach, the slightest irony." Complaint in the case of *Duverger vs. Bizot* (and *Actuel*), Trib. de grande Instance (Paris), session of 17 November 1988.

[3] See, on Broc, chapter 1, note 56; on Baudry and Ambre, chapter 1, note 55 and chapter 2, notes 14–17, 77–78, and 83–84; on Joseph Haennig's discourse, chapter 2, text at notes 130–35; on Jacques Maury's discourse, chapter 2, text at notes 60–61 and after note 122.

any legal act an overriding interpretive principle. It greatly helps explain the community's utter failure to heed Prof. Jacques Maury's prompt constitutional attack in late 1940 on these grotesque laws.

Once and forever missing that salutary opportunity—the rejection as "non-French" of the whole of the religious legislation—Vichy legal actors turned to the statutes on a detailed basis. But even with this tragic move made, there were many interpretive options, at least through fall 1942 (not, perhaps, well into 1943, when we have seen Joseph Haennig still disingenuously calling for them). All of the data tends to support the conclusion that legal actors could have rendered the religious statutes a virtual nullity: French lawyers held all the cards, and they often did manage to trump other governmental initiatives viewed by them as unacceptable. As we have seen over and over again, however, they read the religious statutes in a niggardly and myopic manner, each stingy interpretation leading to yet another, until more Jews were persecuted than even the literal language demanded.

The phenomenon of an overriding interpretive strategy riding herd over both basic principles and specific written texts, while not before applied to Vichy law, has historical precedent. It has been discussed by scholars in the context of America's antebellum constitutional law, where constitutional due process and Christian humaneness managed with considerable ease to coexist with the persecution of a specific group.[4] Contemporaneous with Vichy, Nazi Germany itself was producing an analogous yet ironically conflicting legal hermeneutic that insisted (like Vichy) on flexible manipulation of principles to suit greater needs but that (unlike Vichy) resisted all forms of legalistic narrowness.

The French phenomenon developed, however, its own peculiar legal and cultural jurisprudential lines. The historical link to antebellum America, and the wartime link to Nazi jurisprudence take us only so far. As I have discussed elsewhere, flagging an issue that cannot be fully elaborated here, the closest twentieth-century analogy to Vichy methods of reading might be found in a surprising and non-legalistic place: the French-influenced school of deconstructionism![5]

---

[4] See, e.g., Robert Cover, *Justice Accused* (New Haven: Yale U. Press, 1975).

[5] See Richard Weisberg, "On the Use and Abuse of Nietzsche for Modern Constitutional Theory," in Sanford Levinson and Steven Mailloux, eds., *Interpreting Law and Literature*, (Evanston, IL: Northwestern University, 1988), 181–85.

The Vichy hermeneutic ran as follows: *French lawyers managed to interpret the still extant constitutional principles of their training flexibly, i.e., in a manner permitting relatively open-ended understandings of once-ensconced concepts such as "equality"; at the same time, they brought to the new statutory texts a rigorous, low-level technical precision that inhibited them from making liberal legal arguments extending protection to thousands of additional people.* This double hermeneutic first creatively reinterpreted the great foundational stories of French constitutional law, displaying an ability to deconstruct long-accepted texts and to use them for the given perceived purpose whatever prior understandings of their meaning seemed to require. Extended forward, this first prong is not dissimilar to post-modern strategies of reading; it is also historically and ironically close to a form of French Catholic reading of dominant texts, dating to at least the manner in which early Christians such as St. Paul managed to read the Tanakh (Old Testament). Such readings produce striking and disharmonious understandings of stories (such as those of the Bible), readings designed to further a cause (such as a new religion). The second prong of the hermeneutic brought the skills and eloquence of Cartesian logic to the task of interpreting the actual racial and religious legislation. Here, exactly contrary to their flexible readings of foundational texts, lawyers insisted on narrow, almost myopic readings that lost in potential power of protesting argument anything they may have gained in technical acuity and rhetorical coherence.

Vichy legal hermeneutics inevitably encroaches upon religion, a domain that, as we have already shown, touched legal analysts of the new racial laws. This book's proclivity to use the adjective "religious" in front of the noun "laws" indeed (as I mentioned in the Preface) was largely inspired by the willingness among Vichy lawyers not trained in theology to rationalize statutory ostracism far more on the basis of beliefs than of race. Readers will note in what follows an emphasis on the religious sources of Vichy legal hermeneutics.

The proposal of these pages, in its ultimate articulation, is that a form of French Catholic reasoning greatly influenced the ability of Vichy racial laws to infiltrate a culture otherwise antipathetic to them, and that this influence—far from being understood or even reckoned with by postwar thought—has itself contributed to the baleful evasiveness of "post-modern" discourse on the issue of the Holocaust. As the November 1995 assassination of Israel's Prime Minister Yitzchak Rabin has indicated, the link between religious interpretive practices, legal reasoning, and violent victimization of others is hardly limited to the French Catholic hermeneutics studied in this book as it applies to Vichy law. But neither would it be sensible to universalize religious systems or to suggest that the work of a few in the destruction of a peaceful leader can be equated in significance with the work of thousands in the destruction of the millions.

## A. Clearing the Ground: Neither Positivism nor Carl Schmitt

### 1. Neither the Statutes On Their Own Nor "Positivistic" Responses to Them Dictated Legal Outcomes

One of this book's major theses has been sustained and, in a sense, is no longer in controversy among historians of Vichy: Nazi Germany neither was at the origin nor dictated the flow of Vichy religious law. Its source was France, its development was French. I believe I have also proven that the religious laws were *pervasive,* that is, they rapidly gained a major place in the legal community, private as well as governmental. They were implemented by agencies and courts, interpreted by hundreds of magistrates, utilized by practicing lawyers on behalf of clients, discussed for potential reform on the highest levels of government, as well as by scores of academicians and manual writers.

Less clear are the reasons for this pervasiveness. The direct tie to German *Diktat* having been removed, the analyst is temporarily unanchored both from his own intuitions about Nazi power and from whatever naive faith he may still have harbored in the five-decade-old myths created by the French themselves, myths of "universal resistance," "puppets in Vichy," or "at least we saved our own Jews." Two other grounding devices seem ready to take over, both of which have been offered recently as part of excellent legal analyses of the period. They create in common a strict dichotomy, the first political, and the second jurisprudential, between the promulgation of the laws and the *reception* of them by the Vichy legal community. First, there is the claim of Franco-French *coercion:* official Vichy racism forced antisemitism upon an otherwise unreceptive constituency of French legal actors. The second is the claim of *positivism:* regardless of how lawyers felt about Jews, the antisemitic laws flourished because of a literalistic and value-neutral allegiance to whatever the "sovereign" (here Pétain and his ministers) might dictate. Both claims are helpful but, in my view, go only part way at best to resolving our questions.

An adequate and indeed quite interesting formulation of the claim of coercion has been rendered in a decade-old doctoral dissertation on the Vichy Conseil d'État by Jean Marcou. He begins by saying that traditional French antisemitism coupled with sharply contextualized anti-Jewish political strategies lay behind the creation of the Vichy statutes (an unexceptionable claim endorsed earlier in our discussions of Raphaël Alibert, the first Minister of Justice), *and* that the statutes once in place inspired and produced such antisemitism in others (a more dubious claim). The two-step process is described as follows:

> The legal definition of Jewishness is a fundamental element of the antisemitic policies of Vichy because it appeals to the traditional French antisemitism that inspired those policies. The originality of that definition, its insistence upon legal precision, indicate that such policies were not at first imported. Maurras and Vallat were shocked, after the Liberation, to be labelled "collaborators" because (among other things) of their antisemitism.[6] ... The elaboration of a specific law—far better than imported or imposed norms—had permitted antisemitism to become implanted, in fact, in the administrative and judicial structures and, after a time, to penetrate society as a whole. And this is indeed an illustration of what the Nazis were expecting as they tolerated the existence of the Vichy government.[7]

Marcou is right to suggest that the statutes derived from a uniquely French conception of antisemitism, unneedful and indeed resentful of Nazi influence (see chapters 2 and 6). But he then makes the questionable move of asserting that the statutes *worked their will* first upon an otherwise unreceptive legal establishment and then upon the population as a whole. Their existence, primarily, made antisemitism legally pervasive. He elaborates, in a manner both harmonious with and antithetical to some of our earlier conclusions:

> The antisemitic bureaucracy [i.e., the CGQJ or its predecessor] was, of course, the first charged with the realization of these measures, but the question also concerned most [other] administrators and certain courts. In the end, Vichy antisemitism leads to recognition of an administrative and

[6] See, on the "defense" mounted by Vallat at his trial of being a true anti-German patriot by being a true French antisemite during Vichy, Éric Conan and Daniel Lindenberg, "Que faire de Vichy?," *Esprit,* May 1992, 5–15.

[7] Jean Marcou, "Le Conseil d'État sous Vichy (1940–44)," (Ph.D. diss., (Law), Grenoble II, 1984), 223.

> judicial apparatus that was still basically republican, confronted with an anti-republican legislation of Maurassian inspiration that also played the Occupier's game. The Conseil d'État, in its consultative and especially its litigious functions, was going to experience this kind of challenge [*ce type d'épreuve*].[8]

Here Marcou asserts that the Vichy statutes stood on one side, and the community that had to implement them stood on another, until the first overwhelmed the second. It is this move that my study as a whole, and this chapter in particular, tends to challenge. While I agree that antisemitism of a peculiarly Vichyist strain influenced a still-enduring "republican" structure, I have weighted the *latter* as the key part of the legal phenomenon. Thus, in the case of the Conseil d'État, the tradition was already highly authoritarian. So when Marcou assumes that the Vichy legal community as a whole was not always already prepared to be so infected—that instead it was challenged to become antisemitic by the laws themselves—he is neglecting the peculiar *openness* to those laws of the legal community as it was already constituted.[9]

Far from seeing the imposition of Vichy law as a "challenge," in other words, the Conseil d'État perceived authoritarian laws as almost wholly *harmonious* with their preconceived sense of themselves and their function. (For private lawyers, as we have seen, the "already-there" strain was a tendency to see low-level legalistic nitpicking as a creative good,

---

[8] Ibid., 224.

[9] This is an argument in line with the suggestion of Stanley Fish, whom I have mentioned in earlier writings about Vichy, and also elsewhere in this study; see chapter 2, note 122. Fish, although not yet ready to discuss the Holocaust directly, has posited in numerous other contexts that it is the community that creates, at every moment, the meanings that it brings to its practice and to that practice's central texts. It is emphatically not the reverse. So any explanation of institutional behavior that would hold people defined or constrained by a text (here, the Vichy statutes) would be suspect, Stanley Fish, *Is There A Text in this Class?* (Cambridge: Harvard U. Press, 1980), particularly chapters 15 and 16. I welcome Fish's view and have applied it to Vichy, recognizing that on one level it seems to condone *any* behavior acceptable to the community. But Fish's approach can be read to *empower* the community—always and at any moment—to rise above the ostensible constraints of a text (or external political program) that it might choose to reject, in this case the Vichy statutes alleged to have been controlling. See Dominique-Gros' citation to my Vichy work in this sense, "Le 'Statut des juifs' et les manuels en usage dans les facultés de droit (1940–1944)," *La Violence politique dans les Démocraties européennes occidentales,* 140–41; see chapter 2, note 43.

whatever the context.) Yet this welcoming of the religious laws does not, without further discussion, prove that the Conseil d'État was "antisemitic" as that term is traditionally understood. The laws instead played into other features of the Conseil d'État's self-perception, precisely their long-standing appreciation of strong leaders. Hence, a wartime academic commentator on the institution put it this way:

> The role of the Conseil d'État is more that of a collaborator and a counsellor. In the entire history of the Conseil d'État, we hear of no cases of overt conflict with the government. [The author cites the "suppleness" with which the Conseil d'État affirmed prefectural arrests and detentions under the laws passed in fall 1940, without inquiry into the motives of the arresting officers.] If we assume that the authoritarian tendencies of the régime continue to display themselves and are even set down in a definitive constitution, the discretionary power of the government and the administrators will be broadened.... Finally, the Conseil d'État, in its jurisprudence, gains inspiration from the entirety of the legislation and places itself above word-by-word textual literalism.[10]

The calculus shifts and becomes more subtle than Marcou might want: the laws did not require major adjustments by the constituent legal groups in France; their willingness to work with the new statutes was a function of intrinsic factors native to each specific body. Nothing delighted the Conseil d'État more than an authoritarian leader with a broad vision. The hermeneutics of Vichy law played out fully in the work of that administrative body, and it did so with little or no forced adjustment to the new realities of religious persecution.

The second recent academic explanation draws a sharp line between the politics and prejudices behind the promulgation of the statutes and the ensuing growth and saturation of the laws through case-by-case analysis and expansion. This "positivist" argument holds that the French legal community, which was committed to obey the promulgated laws, had little choice but to follow the statutes once they were in place. To this

[10] Wei Teng-lin, "Le Pouvoir discretionnaire de l'administration et le contrôle juridictionnel en droit français," (prizewinning Ph.D. diss., law Faculty, University of Lyon, 31 May 1944), 199–200. See also, for the Conseil's overt preference for periods of authoritarian leadership, chapter 5, at note 117; for its oath to Pétain, chapter 4, note 97 and chapter 5, notes 111–15.

extent, the argument here goes beyond that of Marcou: he allows (as I do not) that the statutes coerced antisemitism where it might not otherwise have existed; the appeal to positivism asserts that the statutes *compelled* a certain kind of anti-Jewish behavior from the legal community, "neutrally," as it were, and without regard to religious attitudes.

The strongest proponent of the latter view, Danièle Lochak, goes on in an influential article[11] to attack positivism itself and in the process joins a reputable jurisprudential debate about the Holocaust that previously had most often focussed on the behavior of *Nazi* courts.[12] Lochak's position is bottomed on the premise that the statutes, once promulgated, dictated the reaction of the legal community, which took as its rule of interpretation the time-honored approach that the job of the courts and the commentators is, respectively, to *interpret* and to *analyze* the existing law according to "objective" or indeed "scientific" norms of understanding. Rigorously to be avoided would be the interjection of any personal assessment or critique of those laws. Her article tests this approach against Vichy results.

Prof. Lochak emphasizes the oft-cited 1941 article of Toulouse Law Professor, E. H. Perreau, entitled "The New Jewish Law in France."[13] Perreau there established what Lochak sees as the paradigmatic attitude of "neutrality" before the law; typical of his language is the following:

> One must avoid oneself [*se défier de soi-même*], noting above all what is concrete, objective, and generally abstaining from *judgment*.[14]

---

[11] See note 1 above.

[12] See, most recently, Ingo Müller, *Hitler's Justice* (Cambridge: Harvard U. Press, 1991), 220 for his discussions of such positivists as Hans Kelsen; for a superb account of the postwar debate between Kelsen and H. L. A. Hart about positivism in the Nazi context, see David Richards, "Terror and the Law," *Human Rights Quarterly* 5 (1983), 171–85; and "Positivism and Natural Law," 172–77.

[13] Perreau's "neutral" work on the racial laws was widely cited by other positivist analysts during Vichy; see, e.g., Baudry and Ambre, *La Condition publique et privée du Juif en France* (Lyon: Desvigne, 1942), 37.

[14] Lochak, citing Perreau, in Klarsfeld, ed., "Les mésaventures du positivisme," 135. For another "neutral" assessment of the religious laws, this time by a private practitioner, see René Floriot, *Le Droit Nouveau: Lois, Décrets, Circulaires et Ordonnances parus entre l'Armistice et le 20 Novembre* (Paris: Librairie française de documentation, 1940), "Les textes relatifs aux Juifs," 29–43.

Prof. Lochak is doubtless correct that this stance of normative purity, in which the scholar or writer removes himself from the analysis, indeed characterizes the *ostensible* tactic of most Vichy lawyers who considered the religious laws[15]; we have seen this to be true not only in the academy but also among practitioners, in doctrinal articles (Haennig),[16] or legal memoranda (Garçon.)[17] And, of course, judicial opinions on the various religious laws maintained the French form of objective deduction from statute to the facts of the case at hand, up to and including the fiction of a "legislator" whose intent the court would glean from the statutory language itself. But it is in the articles and books that Prof. Lochak's observation most holds sway. Thus Duverger, after the war, explained his task in writing about the new laws as follows:

> This [formalistic] style is designed not only to reveal the lawyer's duty, but still more to underscore that he is erasing himself totally from the laws and regulations in order to derive from them an objective significance.[18]

Baudry and Ambre, two lawyers whose book-length volume on the religious laws we have noted earlier, put it this way in their preface:

> The reader, before going any further, will want to note that we are writing here as lawyers and not as polemicists. The Law has no place for partisan shouts, and it has seemed less useful to us to give in to the hurrahs or to the boos than to analyze with serenity and probity the numerous texts promulgated since the new régime has come into being. Complex and unprecedented legal problems have arisen from the legislative structure that is the Jewish statute, a structure moving constantly towards improvement [*ce monument législatif qu'est le statut des Juifs en voie de perfection constante*].[19]

---

[15] An exception among academic polemicists for the Vichy laws is Dean Roger Bonnard, the influential editor of the *Revue du droit public et des Sciences politiques*. Bonnard distinguishes "science," which he endorses, from "neutrality," which he claims is no longer appropriate. On his journal's enthusiasm for the Marshal's "political and social" program, see below at notes 27 and 28.

[16] See chapter 2 at notes 130–35.

[17] See chapter 8 at notes 208–34

[18] Duverger, "La perversion du droit," 707.

[19] Baudry and Ambre, *La Condition publique et privée du Juif en France*, 16.

André Broc, whose doctoral dissertation on "La Qualification juive" was published as a book in 1943 by the Presses universitaires de France, notes prefatorily that two questions must be analyzed "with care":

> that of the definition of the Jew, in a country where nothing distinguishes him legally from others, and, subsequently, the attribution of Jewishness to economic entities or corporate structures in which Jews participate. It is to this dual study, of a legally technical nature [*de pure technique juridique*], that the present monograph is devoted, to the exclusion of all other considerations.[20]

But does this oft-used rhetorical gambit in fact constitute "positivism," or is it not a mask for value-imbued, unscientific discourse that derives from the writer's preconceived view as tempered (or, indeed, as furthered) by the then-prevailing view of his colleagues? Do we have a recognizable, and indeed in most situations a highly respectable, appeal to positivism, or do we have a debased discourse that—like the "science" of ethnography that contemporaneously measured people's noses to see if they were racially Jewish—wraps apology around the flag of neutrality?

Prof. Troper answers Prof. Lochak by positing a drifting away from objectivity by that same Vichy legal discourse; he defends positivism, properly understood, and finds in Vichy analysis a departure from the purely descriptive function claimed by these writers, whose

> approach to law agrees to reckon with values, as opposed to a purely positivist legal science, and furthermore...departs from positivism not only in observing the values of the legislator, but even those coming from the political, religious, social, or psychological environment that might influence the legal system.[21]

Troper's model, as opposed to Lochak's, looks beyond the offer of objectivity alone to the rest of the speech act performed by the analyst. As I have indicated elsewhere in appraising their debate, Troper adopts a model more fully in tune with Vichy legal discourse.[22] The debate is

---

[20] André Broc, *La Qualification juive* (Paris: PUF, 1943), 6.

[21] Troper, "La Doctrine et le Positivisme," in *Les Usages du droit,* 286.

[22] See Richard Weisberg, "Autopoeisis and Positivism," *Cardozo Law Review,* 13 (1992), 1721–27. Autopoeisis, a concept applied to legal sociology by the German theorist, Niklas Luhmann, holds that systems operate within their own self-contained framework, adapting

quite important, for if we are convinced that Vichy lawyers were positivists, we would excuse their behavior (while condemning positivism), which we would admit was "constrained" by the statutory texts as promulgated.

But instead, one needs only to move a paragraph or two from most of the "positivistic" declarations cited thus far to get closer to the systemic heart of the matter. So Duverger, in explaining after the fact how the "neutral" observer [comme un spectateur non concerné] was brought to bear on Vichy legislation, allows that:

> Charged with looking over the new government's texts that affected public service, I had to peruse them each day in the *Journal officiel,* interpret them according to the established method [*la technique précédente*], and expose them to students in a few sessions of directed work. *The subject matter did not permit the same detachment as [say] the* conveyance of real property. It brought out *fundamental questions,* among which the gravest affected me personally, through ties of friendship.[23]

Baudry and Ambre, in their turn, while paying lip service to their "scientific" function as analysts of a preordained statutory system about

---

to changes (or resisting them) according to a network of self-reproducing operations. The mechanisms of response are not always fully articulated, in fact they rarely are. The autopoeitic system is alert to the "irritants" of systems outside itself, but its choices as to which extrinsic factors to adapt are its own; it may act independently of (and often obliviously to) extrinsic factors such as the will of the sovereign (including positivistic allegiance to the sovereign's statutory dictates). Their tendency is to work always in the direction of their "operations," an undefined term importing the system's unarticulated sense of what is appropriate to its function. See Gunther Teubner, ed., *Autopoeitic Law: A New Approach to Law and Society* (Berlin: de Gruyter, 1987). Autopoeisis is helpful in understanding how seemingly stable "norms," such as equality before the law, can be internally transformed through acts of communication—which Luhmann has recently called the "basal operation" of law that, however, "never becomes thought"—that subtly shift notions of right and wrong to accommodate new realities acceptable to the system although previously foreign to it. See Niklas Luhmann, "Operational Closure and Structural Coupling: The Differentiation of the Legal System," *Cardozo Law Review,* 13 (1992), 1419–41, 1424 and 1433. Although the system in Vichy, as we have demonstrated often, allowed for protest, generally the organism accommodated racism into its sense of its "operations"; see chapter 2, note 42 above. The appeal to positivism, understood this way, was a justifying strategy that permitted the system to bring out *other*, unspoken aspects of itself that were hitherto unthinkable.

[23] Duverger, "La perversion du droit," 706, emphases in original.

the Jews, just as quickly into their treatise make the following observations about "the law":

> The Jewish statutes are, without any doubt, one of the characteristic monuments of the legislative system of the new France.... The number of texts so far published is rising towards several hundred.... But already, the thought that presided over their promulgation is unfolding: the desire to define the Jew precisely, the desire to individualize Jews as so defined, the restoration of public service to its eminently national characteristics, the freeing from the Jewish grip of the French economy, all measures that will bring back to France its true face.[24]

Where do they get their sense of France's "true face"? Not from any statute; not from all, collectively. As we shall observe in our next section, they reach into history and even theology to rationalize their acceptance of the new texts.

André Broc, using his "purely technical legal method," launches into pages of analysis associating Jews with a foreign way of thinking, specifically with a foreign conception of law itself. We shall explore the devices by which science becomes polemic, much as we saw "the Talmud" integrated subtly into the prosecution of Léon Blum at Riom.[25]

Both Marcou and Lochak, otherwise dealing with different legal subgroups and arriving at differing conclusions, share the view that the statutes in and of themselves explain Vichy legal behavior. Marcou allows that antisemitism—so central to the promulgation of the written texts—eventually prevailed in a community that might otherwise still have been thinking like republicans. Lochak believes that Vichy lawyers (especially courts and professors) declined to factor in any fixed beliefs and instead opted for the "objective" assimilation and analysis of the written texts. Neither reckons with the conclusion that my data most brings forth: *there was always available to each and all of the Vichy legal communities the option of rejecting the statutes or interpreting them on high levels of generalization that would have minimized their effect on most people.* The Italians did it, the Belgians did it, and France—unique among its neighbors in the autonomy of its institutions from Nazi control—could also have done it (chapters 2, 3 and 6). Even later in the

---

[24] Baudry and Ambre, *La Condition publique et privée du Juif en France,* "Préface."

[25] See discussion of legal scholarship contemporaneous with the Riom trials at chapter 1, notes 56–57.

war, with Germans occupying the full country, French legal institutions remained intact and were open to revisions and retractions of the antisemitic laws with little viable threat of Nazi retaliation (chapter 9).

The inanimate ink of statutory law does not explain legal outcomes: people and institutions bring about these outcomes. French legal institutions reacted as they did because of a peculiar combination of factors. Marcou and Lochak have surely helped in locating two of these: traditional antisemitism and traditional legal positivism. Their joint efforts assist particularly to illuminate *half* of the legal hermeneutic: Vichy literalism. We are going to see what lawyers said to explain the laws and then add another category of explanation. First, however, it will be necessary to understand Vichy strategies of reading in comparison with those of their Nazi conquerors.

## 2. Nazi "Authoritarian Racism" With a Difference

In France, as in Germany, the authoritarian bent of the population as a whole quickly became dominant in the thinking of leading academic lawyers. Less so than in Germany, but still quite overtly, they turned to the overall program of the leader of the State—as much as to the statutes themselves—as a source of law.[26] Thus Dean Roger Bonnard sets forth in a preface to his well-known journal, *La Revue du Droit Public et des Sciences politiques* for 1941 the following program:

> By its long tradition, and by the authority it has acquired, our *Revue* must take part in this effort of national restoration. It will doubtless, as in the past, refrain from partisan political conduct. It will remain on the scientific grounding it has never left. But its science cannot be neutral, indifferent to truth and falsehood and refusing all value judgments. For now one must take sides and "embark." The resurrection, the grace of our country comes at this price.
>
> And, with our "leader," M. the Maréchal Pétain, France now has a guide whose wisdom and mastery of thought are incomparable and almost superhuman, who will keep it from wandering and lead it on the path of truth. In his admirable messages, the Marshal has indicated the goals and the directions of the work ahead. The policies he proposes are of no party. For they rid us of those partisan struggles that have led us to misfortune. It is

---

[26] Recall Joseph Barthélemy's devotion to Pétain's ideas as virtually foundational, at Riom and elsewhere; see chapter 4.

> instead a national policy, the policy capable of installing a living program in the French community and which will be concerned uniquely with "the real France." To such a policy, all Frenchmen can and must adhere to form that one national party that will eventually be organized.[27]

Bonnard now calls upon "public lawyers" specifically—those engaged in administrative, constitutional, and academic law—to take leadership roles in the Marshal's program:

> To this work of restoration, we who specialize in public law, because we are among the most qualified and the most skilled, we especially must bring a passionate and ardent collaboration. Rebuking that false critical mentality that instilled in many a veritable mania for contradiction and divergence, and thereby caused so much decomposition and deconstruction, let us strive on the contrary to contribute together and with a unified soul to the political and social structure that the Maréchal asks of us within the limits and the tasks he gives to us.[28]

Lawyers are to be part of the political and social—not just the legal—restructuring of France. The Marshal's addresses, as much so or more than his statutes (not even mentioned here), lead public lawyers both to the truth of the leader and to the "false critical mentality" of *others*.

It had quickly become apparent that certain categories and groups were no longer in the polity, no part of the program of French reconstruction. So Vichy made an exclusionary principle foundational, by merging hermeneutically French past principles of egalitarianism with their new policies of religious exclusion. And, in France, too (although surely not in the writings of Dean Bonnard) the exclusionary hermeneutic brought with it racial elements, generally connected to French soil and specifically embodied in the notion of grandparental heritage as a defining feature of the excluded group.

Yet the language of racial hierarchies gained little currency in France. The codeword of unity and "one France" never really caught on; indeed, there was never any simplistic vocabulary of national vision or exclusion. Rhetoric, as we have seem throughout this study, was far more subtle in the hands of French legal actors. Vichy authoritarianism depended at least as much on an explicit appeal to Christianity, for example, because it was

---

[27] Bonnard, "A Nos lecteurs," *Revue du droit public,* 1940–41, 141–42.

[28] Ibid.

a repetitive vision of the Jew as Talmudist—and hence outsider to the Christian spirit—that rationalized on the level of law the Marshal's call for a new and repentant France. It illuminates the half of the legal hermeneutic untouched by Marcou and Lochak.

Vichy legal actors responded, as had Nazi theorists, to the notion of a legal interpretive principle embodied in the authoritarian leader. Yet we cannot forget, in pondering the special strain that was Vichy law, the Nazis' chagrin towards what they saw as French literalism. The occupiers sometimes attempted to slow Vichy's rush to persecute as many Jews as possible by challenging French definitional and evidentiary nitpicking, which was often far in excess of Nazi precedents.[29] They responded skeptically to the kind of French formalism that discovered *low* levels of literal problems in the statutes; the Nazis, under their jurisprudential source, Carl Schmitt, wished to find law in the person of the *Führer,* as merged with the people through their racial identity—they did not believe in legal sophistries or excess literalism.[30] The Germans feared in Vichy too strict and too rigorous a conception of law; the gallic mentality was inclined to overstep the bounds required by the "spirit" of the law, which was less prone to blow into every logical corner of a situation.

The French learned quickly about the legal theories of their new colleagues in racial persecution. They had read Schmitt and cited him as the "highest juridical authority in the new Germany," the academic lawyer who had

> devised this original notion of law conceived as the expression of the "racial and sanguinary unity of the nation." Formal law, for the Nazis, dissolves into vital law.... [T]he dynamism unique to the 3rd Reich has given to law a new feature: that of the preeminence of the social interest above the rigidity of that conventional view that serves merely egotistical and private interests.[31]

The Germans, with some legitimacy, suspected the French of failing to adopt this new, "vital" notion of law. In many respects, Vichy lawyers felt more comfortable plodding along on a case-by-case basis, using their

---

[29] See chapters 2 and 6, particularly chapter 6, note 51.

[30] See, e.g., Carl Schmitt, *Staat, Bewegung, Volk, Die Dreigliederung der politischen Einheit* (Hamburg: Hanseatisch, 1934), 12.

[31] AN BB[30], Gabolde papers, Justice Ministry memorandum titled *Droit formel et Droit vital.*

desiccated Cartesianism even on questions of racial and religious exclusion otherwise foreign to their training and best professional instincts. But the *other side of the Vichy hermeneutic coin,* the *non-statutory* flexibility of the Vichy community, expressed in Dean Bonnard's preface, was just as figurative or even "spiritual" as Nazi jurisprudential thinkers like Schmitt might have wanted. Vichy legal actors were asked to recognize an authoritarian principle that crossed doctrinal areas of law and merged all questions into the program of the Marshal. Distinguished French academicians invoked Pétain and the National Revolution much in the way Schmitt invoked "Führertum."[32]

Furthermore, the Nazi lawyers' linked conception of Führertum and *Artgleichheit* (substantial equality in racial purity)[33] had its Vichy analogue, although strongly tempered by an absence of virulent race theory among mainstream French legal thinkers and a peculiar religious perspective that at once negated racism and encouraged a kind of exclusion that produced virtually similar results. To adopt the exclusionary principle, Vichy lawyers also did not apparently need to buy into that part of the Franco-German propaganda program that stressed the "lazy, parasitical, decadent" features of republican government viciously associated with "the Jew." Legal analysts tended instead to stress the Jew's *religious* otherness (sometimes the opposite of laxity or moral looseness).

Arguably, it was the uniquely French dualistic approach of a spiritually exclusionary constitutionalism and a literalistic statutory logicality that worked fatally to do more injury to the Jewish population than was required by the Nazi overlords or mandated by the letter of Vichy positive law itself.

## B. The Choice of Vichy Academicians: Stressing Religious, not Racial, Otherness

### 1. Modifying, Without Eliminating, the 150-Year-Old Story

In chapter 1, we flagged the legalistic attempt to tar defendant Léon Blum with the brush of "Talmudism." We saw there that constitutional

---

32 See, e.g., Schmitt, *Staat, Bewegung, Volk,* 42.

33 Ibid.; see also, e.g., Koellreutter, *Grundriss der Allgemeinen Staatslehre* (Tubingen: Mohr, 1933), 54.

principles managed to cohabit with racial and religious persecution. Several insights from the Riom experience help us here to fathom how a discourse of "otherness" placed the burden on Jews to demonstrate why—given their bizarre[34] beliefs—there should *not* be a special set of laws applicable to them.

We have asked how it could be that the egalitarian and due-process traditions of the 1790s, still in force through the never-repealed constitution of 1875,[35] coexisted with exclusionary rules of exceptional harshness launched, *ex post facto,* against a group defined by immutable or private characteristics. The declarations of "neutral" discourse reveal a hermeneutics capable of carving from the story of equality an elegant slice, without doing away with the story itself.

The existence, along with statutory literalism, of a more spiritualized component of Vichy legal hermeneutics permitted religious persecution to be assimilated into the ancient story of constitutional egalitarianism without doing away with the main narrative theme. Unlike the case in Nazi Germany, adoption of this interpretive strategy involved offsetting a century and a half of French legal tradition. The Nazis in 1933 had no qualms about transferring absolute power through enabling acts to Hitler, and there was very little talk throughout the Third Reich (as there always was in Vichy) of writing a new constitution while preserving much of the old. It was going to take more in France so to discombobulate the egalitarian traditions as to assimilate exclusion into equality. Any talk of race as a *central* component of the Vichy revolution would be anathema to a wide spectrum of legal, social, and political forces necessary to buy into the new narrative of egalitarian exclusion.

---

[34] The word is used with particular care not only to bring precision to the analytical perspective of the academicians and doctrine writers cited here, but also to recall the homonym "bazaar," used by bâtonnier Jacques Charpentier to describe the behavior of foreign Jews who had joined the Bar; see chapter 3, note 10. The outer display of weird professional behavior, annoying enough to many French lawyers, disclosed more subtly the "bizarre" approach to life and law that these outsiders practiced.

[35] Recall Dean Roger Bonnard's statement to this effect in the same *Revue du droit public,* 58 (1942), 72: "Thus [under Pétain's early leadership] were promulgated under the name of 'constitutional acts' a series of constitutional laws intended to modify the constitutional laws of 1875 without completely abrogating them...." See also Riom counsel Ribet's argument to the court for Daladier, citing Article 9 of the law of 24 February 1875 and Article 12 of the law of 16 July 1875, both relating to the non-retroactivity principle, AN 72 AJ 411, Dossier no. 15.

Rather than emphasize race, therefore, French academicians tended to stress *religion,* and their peculiar definition of the Jew as literal Talmudist provided the basis of the hermeneutic exclusionary principle: if a person uses the literal law to dictate his every act, they would say, his conception of law is so foreign to ours that he no longer fits into our community. (Thus, in a real sense, the Nazi misconception of French legal theory replicated the Vichy attitude about Jewish law! Each system produced a theory that elevated it above those over whom it had power. Like the Aristotelian view that man was superior to woman in his greater spirituality and indifference to the material and the corporeal, so the German jurisprudential thinkers debunked literalism in favor of a metaphysical "archimedean point" of true law; and the French, deemed too legalistic by their Nazi overlords, turned around and chastised the Jews for being literal, textual, in a word "Talmudic"!)[36]

Vichy's strategy of reading the constitution, as much as its approach to reading the statutory texts about the Jews, eventually permitted acceptance of the persecution of an entire group because of that group's own unacceptably *legalistic* tendencies. For, in the perception of the Jew as Talmudic "other," a creature so removed from the French conception of law that he needs a rigorous legal system to regulate his every act, Vichy found its normative sense of any Jew. Such a creature, constructed not in the rantings of vicious antisemites but rather in the rationalized discourse of Vichy law, extended to the community as a whole the hermeneutics of exclusion that, unless restored by a literal statutory text, read any Jew out of the word "French."

The spiritualized hermeneutic co-existed with (was the same as) the maintenance of egalitarian and due process foundational beliefs, embodied in the still-extant constitution of 1875. As we saw in chapter 4's discussion of Barthélemy's draft constitution, Vichy intended to distinguish itself from the Third Reich by pressing those beliefs; but the Jew was simply *read out* of them. An organic constitutional text, like the actual polite antisemitism of Charles Maurras, could display an "antisémitisme de peau."[37] Its protections were designed for the non-Talmudic, uncircumcised many. The exogenous few were shaken off. Lawyers could

[36] See chapter 1, notes 54–56 for Riom's reinvocation of the old Talmudic slur, as Vichy prosecuted Léon Blum.

[37] Cited in Baudry and Ambre, *La Condition,* 13.

move on to playing with the specific enactments about Jews that gave them as much opportunity to save as to persecute some in the already disembodied group.

Any protection afforded the discarded minority would have to come from an interpretation of the special statutes concerning that group, *not* from a foundational source of human equality and judicial process. How lawyers collectively decided to interpret and implement those statutes now became vital. This protective opportunity, afforded a French lawyer only when such positive texts existed, compared (ironically) to an inelastic prejudicial practice when no text was present to mitigate it, is emphasized in one of the stronger parts of Maurice Duverger's postwar apology for his "neutral" writings on the statutes; the context is a passage relating to the elimination of certain categories of government workers:

> [Liberal treatment] was accorded only one category of concerned individuals, by playing on the legal definition of the victims of unequal treatment. This could not apply to denaturalized people nor to women, for whom no contest was possible, nor to agents threatened with firing, because of the purely discretionary aspect of the procedure. On the other hand, the texts about Jews *permitted an interpretation capable of paralyzing their application in most cases, by making it extremely difficult to prove that a person fell under the legal definition of "Jew."*[38]

Duverger proceeds to suggest an always available view of the main religious statutes that, he says (after the fact), would have negated the statutes' application; in the process—and this is less significant to this phase of our study—he attempts to show that *his own wartime* articles clearly evoked or even suggested such an interpretive strategy:

> [T]he law of 2 June 1941 considered "as being of the Jewish race any grandparent who belonged to the Jewish religion." My article showed that this was "one of the most important innovations" of the text, one that led to the following consequence, "Belonging to the race is established by belonging to the religion, and this belonging must be established, ordinarily, by the usual means of proof." The essential is in the last clause. For a lawyer, "the usual means of proof" must be carried by the complainant [*sont à la charge du demandeur*].... This meant that the Vichy administration could only fire from their posts as "Jews" those workers whom *it on its own* could establish were the issue of three (or, exceptionally, of two) Jewish

[38] See Duverger, "La Perversion du droit," 708, emphasis added.

> grandparents who belonged to the Jewish religion. Such a burden [on the government] would have been very difficult if not impossible to carry in most cases. Although this conclusion was not stated clearly, any head of department, any magistrate, would be directly led there by the preceding formulation.[39]

Although we might wonder why Vichy law turned out not to be so clear (perhaps no one read Duverger! perhaps no one understood his unstated conclusion!), the theoretical point is valid and underscores the well-known phenomenon that positive texts give rise to arguments, where, as in the case of discretionary acts not based on written codes, such arguments may not be available. Vichy positive law, on this account, could have worked to minimize Jewish persecution even if it failed to reject the laws outright. Instead, the sources of France's unwritten hermeneutic strategies worked the desultory contrary result that the earlier part of this book has elaborated.

One of those sources was a French Catholic brand of theological reasoning that, as we shall shortly see, became overtly connected to Vichy social law. For the link between law and religion, both historical and metaphysical, was present often in the work of Vichy's "experts" on the new statutes. In this linkage, we may hope to find potential answers to the "ultimate" questions raised by the Vichy legal experience.

## 2. The Dominant Strategy: Depicting the Jew as Legalistic Other

### *a. Why the Jew can be "Read Out" of Basic Law*

Fundamental to the exclusionary strategy are passages such as the following, from Baudry and Ambre's legal treatise:

> Good minds, in no way sectarian, eventually came to believe that safeguard measures would sooner or later be imposed to protect at one and the same time the French nation against the seemingly pernicious action of heterogeneous elements and the French Jews against the vigorous reaction which popular irritation pushed to the limit would not fail to provoke.
>
> Thus, Pierre Gastineaud wrote in the piece he edited in the work "The Jews" [Paris: Plon, 1937]: "There is a Jewish problem. Given the character of the Jew such as it is, it is not at all certain that nations have not legitimately been led to take certain measures against the Jews, the *numerus*

---

[39] Ibid., 709, emphasis in the original.

> *clausus* for example. But this problem cannot be solved by violence or massacres, nor even, I believe, by deportations to Palestine or elsewhere. The ultimate point of my thought is that the Jewish problem is put to the World in such a way that it cannot have a human solution. It must be, I imagine, one of those *scandals* about which it has been said that they were needed for the order of God's designs. But this religious, metaphysical problem, if I intuit it correctly, I find myself unable to solve it. It seems to me to mean nothing less than an interrogation into the final end of humanity."
>
> Beyond this spiritual and moral claim, which it is not ours to judge, let us remember that as of 1937 a man whose good faith could not be questioned, utters in relation to the Jews the dreaded words *numerus clausus*.
>
> Similarly, René Schwob, the famous author of "Moi, Juif," having found *his* solution (if not *the* solution) of the Jewish question in conversion to Catholicism ("Conversion is the only way to resolve their survival into the modern world") has noted: "Giving non-Christian Jews a particular status strikes me as strict justice. But let us not forget that the only solution to the Jewish problem is not a political solution; it is nowhere else but in conversion, but it lies entirely therein precisely because the Jewish people remains the chosen people, whose mission is spiritual, the priestly people, the protected people. And a people who owes the frenzy of its impure curiosities, of its dangerous fevers, the disturbance it generates only to the infidelity which it put in the way of the mission with which God entrusted it. And this is not a humanitarian or philosophical, or financial or artistic mission. It is to praise Christ who is of its flesh...."
>
> Bonsirven, in more than one work, Denis de Rougemont, Jacques Maritain, and others have brought up and analyzed this notion of the betrayal of Israel's mission better than we could. Such a study would not belong in this volume with its purposely narrow focus.
>
> But is it not, there again, symptomatic to indicate the position taken by René Schwob, a cultured man who could not be suspected of antisemitic phobia?[40]

Baudry and Ambre then make a still traditional but quite essential move, highly typical of collegial discourse on the subject during Vichy, from a mere notation of Jewish numbers in the population to a normative claim about Jewish values:

---

[40] Baudry and Ambre, *La Condition,* 13–15.

> We will not take up again [*sic*] the well-known grievances imputed rightly or wrongly to the Jews. These have often been reduced, *grosso modo*, to two essential points: 1. too many Jews in high positions of leadership; 2. absence of a *truly* national sentiment, or, to cite the famous *bon mot* evoked above, "absence of French soil in their sandals."[41]

As Pierre Birnbaum has shown, French xenophobia worked with French antisemitism to bring great pain to Jews on French soil historically and particularly during the 1930s.[42] But Baudry and Ambre, inverting their syntax to make the point more strongly, feel duty-bound to emphasize the newest element in the equation:

> This group that has poorly assimilated (and we are not forgetting the exceptions that prove the rule) the Nation will obviously have a tendency, especially during periods of crisis, to neutralize if not to expel. The disastrous war from which we are emerging will have precipitated the course of events. Under the pressure of new factors, the Jewish statutes have just been born.[43]

Expulsion means, at least as a first manoeuver, removal from the polity. Laws are passed that expunge, without formal amendment of egalitarianism, a group that (after all) does not really live, walk, or respond the way those do who are meant to be covered by the foundational guaranties against discrimination.

Yet another move, more subtle, and to my mind more revelatory of Vichy legal hermeneutics, now follows hard upon. Employing a graceful sequence of negative clauses that hide the real importance of the gambit, Baudry and Ambre begin their first principal chapter as follows:

> It is not our intention to offer at the beginning of this work a detailed picture of the Jews from antiquity to our time. But it does not seem to be without interest to provide a summary historical sketch.[44]

Having laid a politically viable groundwork of attack—too many Jews in Republican governments, too little French nationalism among them—Baudry and Ambre turn subtly to a different set of data: religious

---

[41] Ibid., 15.

[42] Birnbaum, *Anti-Semitism in France*, trans. Miriam Kochan (Oxford: Basil Blackwell, 1992), chapter 4 and passim.

[43] Baudry and Ambre, *La Condition*, 16.

[44] Ibid., 19.

persecution of the Jews *in the past*. While the relationship between the Jewish population and various monarchs had its ups and downs, the ecclesiastical authorities rarely softened in their hatred:

> The Carolingians having been assisted to power somewhat with their help, they proved quite hospitable to the Jews, against whom, however, the ecclesiastics unleashed hostility. Irritated by the favor shown the Jews in the court of Louis the Pious, Agobard, cardinal of Lyon, railed against them in a vigorous treatise suggestively called, "De Insolentia judeorum."[45]

At the time of the Crusades, the first antisemitic measures were promulgated in France. These statutes saw nuances of strictness from the twelfth century until the Revolution, with property occasionally stripped away, or the entire Jewish population expelled in some cases, whereas occasional monarchs treated them more benignly. What was universal is highlighted by these legal analysts in a one-sentence paragraph:

> Let us again note that civil disputes between Jews were adjudicated by Rabbinic courts, relying on a special law.[46]

The authors then take their brief survey from the Revolution through the recent hostilities, emphasizing this as a golden period for Jews under the law, while noting that the Dreyfus affair "split France in two, renewing hatreds, planting in the whole country the murderous seeds of anger and doubt."[47] Yet the Great War helped to heal the wounds, and France became a haven for many foreign Jews escaping the increased tyranny from points east. There follows a description of the legal steps taken in some of these countries (notably Germany and Italy) to promulgate anti-Jewish statutes.

For Vichy, however—and here Baudry and Ambre provide a helpful formulation—"it seems that what is desired, as Christian Renaudin has put it, is to define the limits of the French community before legislating for it."[48] Allowing that "quite naturally, the extent of the French laws is greater than that of the German ordinances,"[49] the authors end their overview and turn to a "technical" appreciation of the actual statutes.

---

[45] Ibid., 20; see also Birnbaum, *Anti-Semitism in France,* 19.

[46] Baudry and Ambre, *La Condition,* 21.

[47] Ibid., 22.

[48] Ibid., 25.

[49] Ibid.

André Broc, too, dwells upon the historical Jewish tendency to rely on a different set of laws. He explicitly equates the Talmud with a universal inability suffered by its devoted followers to understand French nationalism.[50] For Judaism is a "national" religion; lacking any spiritual base, it exists largely to propagate itself and "to defend itself during any crisis against foreign tendencies that might compromise its national soul."[51] Continuing in this vein, which can only be described as a virtually pure projection onto Judaism of Vichy's own ambitions, Broc calls the Jews racists by dint of their legalistic approach:

> Judaism has no real mystical aspect, which might somehow correspond directly to religious needs.... On the contrary, Judaism consists since the Exile essentially of a system, supported by the Talmud, designed to maintain the patriotic goal of the social cohesiveness of the Jews, dispersed in the midst of the Gentiles. This system, although intellectualized, has so marked the Jewish people that it seems objectively today to be their moral law, at least as regards the essential rules, the details having been nitpicked to death by them. One might ask if this system, by its corporeal restraints, particularly as regards sexual matters, has not itself contributed to the enforcement of racial categories.... One can even inquire if that belief, in its physical proscriptions, has not contributed to the preservation and reenforcement of distinct racial types.[52]

Broc argues that the religious criterion, with an emphasis on a set of material practices (rather than metaphysical beliefs) required by the Talmud, best justifies and explains the Vichy religious laws. Neither this law school doctoral candidate, nor his faculty jury, nor the distinguished editors of the *Presses universitaires de France* apparently found it odd to see juxtaposed to "neutral" legal analysis the following call to the weird complexities (as Broc understands them) of circumcision:

> It is difficult for a western frame of mind to account for this mutilation, practiced today, without counting the Jews, by many peoples in Africa, America, and Polynesia. The origin of circumcision, like that of the removal of other dispensable organs of the two sexes, is certainly an ancient one, since it uses sharpened flint for these operations. One can assume that it is a product of a mentality of magic, which, in former ages, religions adapted

---

[50] See also chapter 1 at note 56.

[51] Broc, *La Qualification juive,* 15.

[52] Ibid., 16.

> to their needs by transforming it into a theologically exploitable rite. The initiates will teach that man, for example, in his state of original purity, did not have a foreskin and that it is necessary for the elect to rid itself of this hereditary disfigurement.[53]

(Vichy lawyers will pick up on such nonsensical points in the deadly serious context of figuring out who is a Jew. Thus an anonymous lawyer asks a colleague to push along litigation involving the latter's client by sending the writer a medical document attesting that the suspected Jew "enjoys his entire preputial integrity" [*jouit de toute son intégrité préputialle*].)[54]

Perhaps the dominant theme of these treatises, which count among the lengthiest published during the Vichy period, is the "otherness" of the Jew as translated into the Jew's reliance historically on *other rituals, other authorities, other methods of resolving disputes*. While much else in their fate on French soil has varied, and while the authors show no ambivalence about the suffering brought upon Jews historically by the clergy and by certain kings or influential people (e.g., the anti-Dreyfusards), this legalistic otherness is a constant, worthy of emphasis and repetition.

If Vichy desires to figure out who *is* French before legislating on behalf of insiders, what could be more appropriate than rejecting from that circle a group that has always anyway created its competing circle of insular legislation? As a basic strategy of reading French law, Jews thus will exist only when specially defined by a statutory text, not in any other way. "Equality" survives, but as a concept hermeneutically protected by the assumptions defining the term. The strategy permits what is "great and good" in French tradition to endure, distinguishing French justice (as Vallat and Maurras, and Barthélemy and Darlan always thought) from the hierarchically racist models of the Nazi state.

Finally, Vichy hermeneutics permits its insider legal community to avoid self-scrutiny. For the average French lawyer remains indifferent to the nonexistent category of Jew, and is culpable neither of virulent racial hatred nor even of polite "political antisemitism."[55] We have seen that much of legal discourse is not only apparently, but in fact, fundamentally

---

[53] Ibid., 19.

[54] CDJC XXIII-19.

[55] See, for this distinction, Birnbaum, *Anti-Semitism in France,* 5 and *passim.*

free of either of these aspects. Indeed, we have seen two doctrinal areas that produced a kind of philosemitic outcome unthinkable in other countries applying laws rigorously to the Jews. Shortly we will see how bereft Jewish tenants and out-of-wedlock children who are suspected of being Jewish fall into the dominant strategy.

The hermeneutics of exclusion, or the strategy of reading that permitted the brain of the lawyer to read all French statutes in terms of an absence (i.e., the Jews), differs from the positivistic phenomenon conjured by others discussed earlier in this chapter: it is not that the religious statutes' mere existence compelled performance even by some reluctant legal actors. In a way, it is the reverse: The dominant method of reading the law compelled the existence of the religious statutes![56] Jews had their own laws, and they were fundamentally incapable of understanding French national values. They were "out" already. They constituted an absence from the beginning, as a matter of French fundamental law, because that law existed and was to develop only for the French, only for those entitled to be covered by its protections. It remained only for them to be formally defined so that the already existing strategy of removing them from the texts could be implemented. Seen this way, the exceptions and exemptions provided by the Vichy religious laws were not so much affirmatively designed to protect classes of Jews on French soil as they were meant to re-endow some Jewish individuals (for limited purposes) with the protection of equality under the law.

Two interesting perspectives on this inversion both involve constitutional law. The first emerges from the readings for a 1942 course offered at the University of Dijon. The professor reverses the usual optic through which the religious laws are discussed; he sees them rather as a separate non-enjoining circle than as a punitive sub-category, of Vichy law:

> I. Safeguarding the French Spirit....
>
> 1. The Rights of the French community....
>
> *The Status of the French.* [Le statut des Français]—The benefits provided by French nationality are subordinated to a positive attitude that results in an attachment to the community. If that attachment is proven, the French have reserved to them the exclusiveness of certain prerogatives....

---

[56] The source in Marshal Pétain of all Vichy law demonstrates the inevitability of Jewish expungement, with or without a statute; see chapter 1, notes 12 et seq.

> [Recent immigrants, those recently naturalized, and those French who left the country at its time of need, are to be excluded.]
> II. *The Jewish Laws*. It follows from this observation that, given his ethnic characteristics, and his reactions, the Jew is unassimilable. The régime believes that he must be kept apart from the French community.[57]

The second example, already familiar to us, involves the programmatic *deletion* of the word "Jew" from the texts of constitutional reform. As Barthélemy put it, "There was a need to exclude Jews. The Committee sought to accomplish this, without saying it, in adopting the following formula: 'No one can be named to the National Council if he does not possess the general capacity to accede to high public office.' "[58] Jews existed on the foundational level only through their absence, both rhetorical (they could not speak) and nominal (they could not be spoken of). In a sense, only if the explicitly anti-Jewish legislation (already, of course, in effect) is understood as we have done so here to create possibilities of reappearance—and hence of re-attachment of some "Jews" to the constitutional concept "French"—can such reticence be fathomed.

Given Alibert and the imminent prosecution of such archetypal villains as Léon Blum, the quick promulgation of a positive law against Jews was an inevitable step, but were it not for the definitional problem one might almost say it was of secondary significance. Far less speculative is the conclusion everywhere to be derived from the data of this book (and ironically endorsed by the postwar Prof. Duverger): the existence of a written text provided *opportunities for liberal implementation* that a non-textual strategy alone would not have offered. In the main, as we have seen pervasively, this opportunity was not seized by Vichy legal actors who argued the statutes' meaning on an absurdly low level. But there are several exceptions to this rule to which we now turn as part of an inquiry into religious discourse more generally as it interwove with the hermeneutics of legalized persecution.

### *b. Explaining the Pro-Jewish Outcomes*

Did bereft Jewish tenants or putative Jewish out-of-wedlock children have any more "French soil in their sandals" than other Jews who became non-

---

[57] Prof. G. Burdeau, "Cours de droit constitutionnel" (Paris: Librairie générale de Droit et de Jurisprudence, 1942), 189–91.

[58] AN 72 AJ 413, Dossier no. 5.

persons in Vichy law's method of reading? Arguably not, since these categories included many foreign Jews living in cramped Parisian apartments, or many individuals who, by definition, could not even begin to prove a heritage tracing to the good earth of ancient Gaul. The doctrinal favoritism shown to these two groupings of Jews has drawn our attention in earlier chapters,[59] and indicates that traditional antisemitism cannot be an adequate or even a viable explanation of the work of Vichy lawyers and judges. Unlike individuals *read back in* to French law by the exemptions of, say, the 2 June 1941 statute, these people remained non-French because they were Jewish. Yet they gained the law's protection in highly important aspects of their lives and possessions.

We have analyzed each of these exceptions carefully in terms of legalistic factors unique to landlord/tenant on the one hand (the court's ability to interpret freely a pre-Occupation statute granting rent reductions) and out-of-wedlock children on the other (formalistic respect for longstanding provisions of the *Code civil* granting privacy and procedural advantages to all such children). But these explanations beg the question why similar methodologies available to French jurists and legal actors were not used to protect Jews across the board. Indeed, they render more piquant the dominant choices of Vichy law, choices that ignored equally forceful and equally *legalistic* arguments that could quite easily have been mustered and rendered dominant in the discourse.

Little distinguishes the two exceptional categories from everything else except the creative and even humane discourse generated by legal actors to protect only these Jews. But if Vichy legal hermeneutics organically, as it were, read "Jew" out of protective French precedents, how could these categories gain favor in the eyes of Vichy law?

As we have noted frequently, antisemitism alone cannot adequately explain Vichy legal outcomes; these two protected categories again more than prove Vichy's capacity to bring a peculiar legal logic, rather than a pervasive prejudice, to the French wartime legal system. It turns out that this peculiar logic has, in its rare, *protective* guise, a strongly "Christian"—almost allegorical—component. Consider the following two statements from Barthélemy's office, concerning Vichy's fundamental approach to constitutional law:

---

[59] See, e.g., chapter 7, landlord/tenant law; chapter 9, out-of-wedlock children.

> [Legislative planks...] No. 3. Cleansing of the Country. The Government of the National Revolution considers it indispensable to rid the French community as quickly as possible of certain elements that have insinuated themselves into leadership positions in the State, in industry, and in the banks....[60]

> [The Constitution] will be welcoming for all, even for those who have strayed [*même pour les égarés*], on the condition that they will have repented.[61]

The latter phrase, used by Barthélemy in an important speech on 8 July 1941 to introduce the work of the Constitutional drafting committee, exudes a Christian spiritualism that is integral to the Vichy morality play. "You may have been legally obliterated even from mention in the new ordering of things," the Justice Minister seems to say, "but if you repent, we will include you again in our circle."

But what can it mean to "repent" in the context of a hermeneutic that leaves you out? How does one make amends for being absent? One way might be through suffering, up to and including death. Another might be to return, like the prodigal son, to true Frenchness. Both moves were made by the protected categories of Jewish tenant and (purported) Jewish natural child. The Jewish families whose breadwinners suffered by lost careers or lost lives reemerge in the rhetoric of Parisian magistrates as a group favored by the law of September 1939. They can get a rent reduction, like any Frenchman affected by the war. They may not yet have the true national soil in their sandals, but they have "repented" through suffering, up to and including seeing their loved ones ejected not only from the apartment but also from the physical borders of the Nation. And who is more of an "égaré" (Barthélemy's prodigal term) than the child born out of the legitimate structure of marriage? Who is more defined by original sin? And hence, who is more worthy of reappearance and re-humanization through the longstanding protections of the *Code civil*?

Those who assert that Vichy law can be explained by blanket antisemitism (whether or not predating the positive texts of 1940 and 1941) have been given rightful pause by the pro-Jewish outcomes in these categories. It cannot be said that Vichy legal actors threw themselves headlong into

---

[60] AN 72 AJ 412, Dossier no. 2.

[61] AN 72 AJ 413, Dossier no. 5.

an attack on Jews; furthermore, if legal actors uniformly protected such entire sub-groupings, we have seen that (less often) they might also help some of the targeted population as a whole by making life harder for the state on such issues as burden of proof.[62] Yet, a closer scan of these philosemitic pieces of the Vichy legal puzzle indicates that they are nonetheless a fitting part of the whole, and that the whole—if not comprehensible in traditional terms of antisemitism—evokes a more subtle and equally as damning final amalgam.

The French version of antisemitism, as expressed at least through Vichy law, is now susceptible to generalization. Exclusion of Jews became a strategy of reading almost as soon as the régime came to power, and certainly when Pétain's policies about eliminating those responsible for the defeat became manifest through his speeches and, for our purposes especially, his prosecutions at Riom. Alibert's vicious statutes were a logical although not fully necessitated outgrowth of this already embedded hermeneutic of guilt and expungement; they did not primarily produce (*pace* Marcou) or coerce (*pace* Lochak) antisemitism among legal actors. Legal actors would know *how to read* the law when it came to Jews, with or without a statute. The existence of positive statutory texts instead permitted legal actors to bring all their training and skills to bear on the Jewish question. (They were not able to do so in other cases not embodied in elaborate special status laws, e.g., freemasons, denaturalized individuals, women.) In this sense, paradoxically, the written text could have liberated Vichy legal actors (particularly as the Nazis showed their virtual complete reliance on French law) to protect thousands of Jews who might have been impersonally victimized by the spiritualized hermeneutic standing against them on its own. The written laws against Jews (as Duverger confesses) were the medium always available to clever Vichy lawyers to negate or at least to minimize Jewish suffering. Instead, lawyers, judges, government officials and academicians argued for the protection of only small sub-groupings. Scant gains were made for other Jews through the traditional arguments of lawyers in action, but these were more than offset by the immense suffering caused by the legal community's very willingness to nitpick, hence indicating their basic acceptance of the new laws. Two sub-groups joined with the tiny number of statutory exemptions and were resubmitted

---

[62] See especially, chapters 2 and 5.

into the word "equality," because they were prodigals who had suffered and "returned" to French law.

## C. Contemporary Christian Discourse About Jewish Legal Problems

### 1. Church-State Relations and Religious Persecution

This is not the place, nor am I the specialist, to engage in lengthy ruminations about the role played by the Christian sects in the fate of the Jews under Vichy. Happily, again, the interested community itself is gathering to discuss this question,[63] and the writings are intense.[64] Many Christians were themselves persecuted, and some priests fell prey to the Vichy laws against Jews. There were many acts of Christian charity towards individual Jews.[65] Some Jewish writers have begun to note the complexities of the situation during Vichy, including the varying positions taken on the question of proselytizing Jewish children who were brought under the protection of devout Christians.[66]

The relation of Christianity to Vichy law does, however, pose profound questions that have already proven relevant to this study. We have seen that clerics tried in many cases to assist mixed-heritage individuals by

---

[63] E.g., Colloquium on "Vichy et la Réligion," Sorbonne, Paris, 21 November 1991 (attended by this author). The speakers, Catholic and Protestant witnesses from the period, many of whom had risked their lives and peace of mind to assist Jews during the war, stressed the complexity of Christian response, as well as the sometimes brutal simplicity of the results to the persecuted population of inattention, silence, or worse.

[64] For three examples varied as to publication dates, subject matter, and format, see "Églises et Chrétiens pendant la Seconde Guerre Mondiale dans le Nord-Pas-de-Calais," *Revue du Nord,* 60 (April–June 1978: 451–60; Philip Hallie, *Lest Innocent Blood Be Shed: The Story of the Village of Le Chambon and How Goodness Happened There* (New York: Harper, 1979); and François and Renée Bédarida, "L'Église catholique sous Vichy: Une mémoire troublée," in *Esprit,* May 1992, 52–66.

[65] See especially Philip Hallie's account of the leadership of Pastor André Trocmé in saving Jewish lives in the Protestant town of Le Chambon, note 64. Another Protestant pastor, Marc Boegner, denounced the Jewish laws, as did anti-Pétainist Catholic prelates such as Jules-Gérard Saliège of Lyon. See, e.g., on the latter righteous Christians, Marrus and Paxton, *Vichy France and the Jews,* 203–05. For the Catholic reaction to Boegner, see, e.g., note 85 below, and text at note 88.

[66] See, most recently, Maurice Rajsfus, *N'Oublie Pas le petit Jésus* (Paris: Manya, 1994).

providing baptismal records to carry the evidentiary burden on the issue of Jewishness raised by the law of 2 June 1941.[67] The law's deprecation of the value of these clerical records finally surprised even the Germans and moved the Nazis to recommend less legalistic nitpicking about (and more acceptance of) such evidence.[68]

There were direct confrontations between the clerics and Vichy legal actors. The Church hoped that the new régime would look more favorably on longstanding sources of ecclesiastical resentment. For example, they wanted repeal of some early twentieth-century laws that had affected the rights of congregations to obtain the status of individual associations;[69] this and other changes would have assisted the Church to regain property rights. More expansively, they sought a rescission of the law of 9 December 1905 (which we will recall was a key date of departure in the 2 June 1941 statute requiring people to prove they belonged to a religion recognized as "established" prior to that date); they sought restoration of church-state relations harking to the medieval age of Charles VII and Louis XII. And on this, they received strong lay support from several of the members of the constitutional reform committee, notably Barthélemy's colleague as law professor, Achille Mestre, who believed in a Catholic state.[70] But Barthélemy, in late 1941, apparently decided not to grant substantial legislative concessions to the Church.[71]

Frustrated institutionally by what they saw as an insufficient Vichy attack on laicity, the Christian sects saw many practicing clerics and faithful parishioners fall under the definition of Jew, despite their Christian faith or even priestly professional callings. Thus the head of the Missionary Priests of Notre Dame of Sion in Aubenas had to plead for three colleagues in his religious order in the Ardèche. His case went all

---

[67] See chapters 2, 5, and 6.

[68] See chapter 6, section A generally, and particularly notes 43–51.

[69] The laws in question were those of 1 July and 16 August 1901; see Dayras file, AN $BB^{30}$, 1708.

[70] Mestre called explicitly for repeal of the law of 1905, which he felt "created an obstacle to the concordat"; see 72 AJ 412, Dossier no. 5.

[71] Ibid., Barthélemy two-page memorandum of late summer or early fall 1941. A legal advocate for the Church's cause, who seems to have travelled to Vichy to plead with Dayras for its interests, was Auguste Rivet of Lyon, Dean of the Catholic Faculty of Law in that city, ibid.

the way to the obstinately race-oriented Xavier Vallat, who was willing to protect two of Hungarian origin but not the third, Fr. Jean de Menasce, about whom:

> it is not possible for us not to consider him Jewish according to the law, for it is race, contrary to what you seem to think, which is the decisive factor under French law in determining the legal Jew. Yet the only sanction that might affect Father Menasce would be against teaching in a public facility. It does not seem that he would be actually affected by this prohibition.[72]

As pointed out by André Broc, one of the academicians cited extensively in this chapter, Christians (and even priests) might have reason to fear racial categorizations implicating ancestral heritage.[73] Father Menasce's case exemplifies this concern, and although more mainstream churches under Vichy never formally opted for either racial or religious criteria, we have also indicated that non-established religions like the Greek or Russian Orthodox felt quite threatened by racial analyses that might persecute some of their major figures (see chapter 6). One of these, the Archimandrite Serge Fefferman, actually had four Jewish grandparents; although he converted at age 16 and was now a dignitary of the Russian Orthodox Church, he had to wear the Star because of the laws, "perhaps too rigidly construed."[74]

Individual Christian congregants also felt the tincture of alleged "racial" Jewishness. In a representative situation, the vicar general of the diocese of Marseilles, Audibert, writes in early 1943 to a parishioner in distress, the converted writer Albert Lopez:

> My dear friend: You have shared with me your intense and legitimate hope, having made all the declarations needed on the subject of your Jewish racial origin,[75] to be recognized by all and incontestably as a good Frenchmen and a good Catholic. No one who knows you can raise the slightest doubt about this double claim.... For my part, I want to reassure you and give you my witness in order to satisfy justice and friendship. [Audibert recounts Lopez' conversion at the age of 19, his marriage to a Catholic and the baptism of their many children.] In your literary works, among your poems,

---

[72] Vallat correspondence, 13 August 1941, CDJC CXIV-46.

[73] Broc, *La Qualification juive,* 16–18.

[74] AN $AJ^{38}$, 148; see chapter 6, note 65.

[75] The word "origine" is in the typed text, crossed out and the word "race" handwritten in the margin.

> biographies, critical articles, and novels, you have expressed your Provençal spirit, your feel for the Mistral as we might say. You have always been as regional as you have been French, in the manner that Marshal Pétain likes so much.... Good Frenchman, good Provençal, you have also been a good Catholic at the cost of much sacrifice—this I know. You have suffered, and this is understandable, from the incomprehension, and sometimes the hostility, of some of your race. Yet you have always kept mastery of yourself, in patience and in empathy.[76]

Aware that much was expected of his régime from its devout Christian constituents, some of whom actually suffered from laws directed at Jewish "otherness," Marshal Pétain waffled. He declared, in remarks touching on the proposed new constitution, that Vichy would not go all the way to a Catholic state, but that it did seek greater détente with Christianity than had other recent French governments and especially with the Church to which he belonged and to whose Pope he would soon look for support:

> The State declares loudly its respect for individual humanity, the first triumph of Christian civilization. It remains completely separated from the churches. But it retains the right to take, in accord with them if the need arises, such actions and such measures that seem to it to conform to the profound and permanent interests of the Nation.[77]

For our limited purposes here, it seems correct to state that Vichy air exuded a growing closeness in church-state relations, although little actually changed on the level of legislation. In what we are calling the spiritual hermeneutics of exclusion, however, the Marshal's view of the churches as an integral part of "the Nation" served to bring all Vichy policies—including the persecution of the Jews—under the umbrella of "Christian civilization." Vichy both distinguished its program in this way from the gross barbarities of the Germans and encouraged the internalization by all legal actors of the Jew as religious "other."

If much was only implicit in the Marshal's view of the churches, his reliance on his own Church to legitimize Vichy's religious laws was quite out in the open. For, in 1941, Pétain set in motion an inquiry to the

---

[76] Letter written by Audibert and approved by Monsignor Delay on behalf of the archdiocese of Marseille, 8 January 1943, CDJC CXV-93.

[77] Pétain's written observations about the Vichy constitutional program. AN 72 AJ 412, Dossier no. 2.

highest levels of the Vatican to determine its viewpoint on "the Nation's" religious laws. Perhaps the appeal to Catholic authority was disingenuous, not only because Pétain was far from a devout Catholic,[78] but also because in some ways institutional Catholicism's response to the Jewish question in France was already situated and knowable.[79] From the point of view of the 2 June 1941 statute, however, Pétain's inquiry came early in the game. Let us see what the Vatican said to the Marshal.

## 2. Two Catholic Lawyers: Léon Bérard and Cardinal Gerlier

By August 1941, Vichy legal actors had become extensively engaged in the rhetoric of religious exclusion. Whatever protests might have been lodged on the level of constitutional law no longer emanated from Vichy pens, which had been quieted as the community increasingly accepted the hermeneutics of Jewish absence. Reams of words, on the other hand, had attended the "delicate" new statutory materials, lower level talk that lawyers love, because it engages their narrowest creative impulses and because it keeps them in business.

Curiously, it is Marshal Pétain himself who found the time to seek the moral high ground. Given his Riom-related behavior that summer, given the paucity of individuals he permitted to gain exemptions from the harsh strictures of the religious laws, given the advice and consent of a man like Barthélemy to the program, what besides an inkling of Catholic conscience would motivate him to charge his ambassador to the Vatican with the task of determining Papal attitudes about Vichy legislation? Early that August, Pétain initiated such an inquiry. In a letter that is often cited sparsely, but that is of sufficient importance to our study to cite at some length, Vatican Ambassador Léon Bérard replies to Pétain:

> 2 September 1941. M. le Maréchal: By your letter of 7 August 1941, you honored me by requesting information touching questions and problems that might be raised, from the Roman Catholic perspective, by the measures your

[78] An excellent, and representative, account of Pétain's view of Catholicism is rendered in Lépagnot, *Histoire de Vichy,* vol. 1, 35–41. "The Marshal was not noted for his religious piety," ibid., 40; but he had learned much during his years as French ambassador to Franco about "how a dictator leaning on the Church, the army (that one victorious), and on all conservative forces, could impose himself on a torn people, broken by war," ibid., 37.

[79] See text at note 89, below.

government has taken regarding the Jews. I have had the honor of sending you a preliminary response where I observed that nothing has ever been said to me at the Vatican that would imply, on the part of the Holy See, a critique or disapproval of those legislative and regulatory acts. Now I can affirm that at no time has the pontifical authority been either concerned or preoccupied with that part of French policies, and that no complaint or request coming to it from France has so far given it such an opportunity. [Bérard now notes that it has been difficult to get a copy of the Italian laws, but that he is ready to articulate the "complex" stance of the Church on] the contradictions or divergences that might be found between the teachings of the Church on this question and the fascist legislation, on the one hand, and the French legislation on the other....

A. The Church and Racism. There is a fundamental and basic opposition between Church doctrine and "racist" theories. The Church, by universal definition, professes the unity of all human beings. The same Redeemer died for all men; the Gospel is announced to "every creature".... All these precepts are incompatible with a concept that could derive from the conformity of the skull and the nature of the blood and the aptitudes and the vocation of peoples, their religion itself, to establish finally a hierarchy of the races, at the top of which is found a pure and royal race called "Aryan." [There are then quotations to this effect taken from the words of Pius XI in *Mit brennender Sorge* in 1937, as well as from other authoritative declarations.] The Church thus has condemned racism as it has condemned communism.

From its teachings about racist ideas one should be far from deducing, however, that it necessarily condemns any specific measure taken by any particular state against what it calls the Jewish race. Its thinking on this involves distinctions and nuances that must now be noted. The subject must be treated clearly.

B. The Church, the Jewish Problem, and Antisemitism.

It would be vain to extract from Canon Law, theology, pontifical acts, a group of precepts that resembles legislation on Judaism or the Judaic religion. It would even be difficult to find easily, regarding this subject, a clearly marked doctrinal body.

The first principle that appears, and the surest, is that in the eyes of the Church, a Jew who has been authentically baptized ceases to be a Jew and becomes part of "Christ's flock." But one should not conclude from this that the Church regards religion alone as the thing marking Israel off in the midst of the nations. It does not believe that Jews constitute simply a "spiritual family," as do in our case, for example, Catholics and "reformed" Christians. It recognizes that among the distinctive traits of the Jewish community there appear not so much *racial* as *ethnic* particularities. It discerned this long ago and has always taken this into account. [Bérard then recounts various periods in which such measures as the *numerus clausus* or special signs on apparel were adopted by Catholic authorities such as, respectively, St. Thomas of Aquinas and the Lateran Council.]....

It would be possible now, with the help of these precedents, to determine whether the French laws on Jews contradict or not, and in what ways they contradict, Catholic tenets. But this connection, and this analysis, will be easier to do if we first reckon with the reception three years ago of the Holy See to the Fascist state's laws about the Jews. [There follow two pages on Italian law, opposed in two related ways by the Church, according to Bérard. First, the Church resented any legal incursion on the sacrament of marriage that would prevent a Catholic from marrying either a baptized Jew or even a non-baptized Jew if the couple has received "dispensation." Next, Pius XI had taken special umbrage at the seeming rescission by Mussolini of a 1929 Concordat he himself had signed with the Vatican giving the latter's religious marriage sacraments virtually the force of civil law.]....

D. What Disjunctions Can One Find Between Catholic Doctrine and the French Law of 2 June 1941 on the Jews?

[Bérard reviews the law's exclusionary sections.] In principle, there is nothing in these measures that the Holy See would criticize. It believes that in promulgating such measures a State uses its legitimate power and that a spiritual force should not interfere with the internal politics of States. And, then too, the Church has never professed that the same rights must be given to or recognized in all citizens. It has never ceased teaching dignity and respect for the individual. But it surely does not understand matters in the fashion, strictly speaking, of the spiritual followers of Rousseau and Condorcet.... Yet the law of 2 June 1941 begins with the legislator's giving a juridical definition of the Jew as expressly linked to the notion of "race." Still, if we compare the law of 2 June with that of 3 October (which it replaced), we see that the new text has reduced the reliance on "race." If a Jew proves that he belonged, prior to 25 June 1940, to the Catholic faith, or to the Calvinist or Lutheran faiths, he is no longer "considered as a Jew," as long as he does not have more than two grandparents of the Jewish race. In this case, the law attached legal significance to "conversion." It remains the case that a Jew, if duly converted and baptized, will still be considered a Jew, if he is the issue of at least three grandparents of the Jewish race, that is having belonged to the Judaic religion.

There, one must admit, is a contradiction between French law and Church doctrine.

E. Practical Result of This Contradiction. Conclusion. I just pointed out the sole point at which the law of 2 June 1941 contradicts a principle held by the Roman Church. But it does not follow from this doctrinal divergence that the French state is threatened with...even a censure or disapproval that

> the Holy See might express in one form or another about the Jewish laws.... As an authorized person at the Vatican told me, they mean no quarrel with the Jewish laws. But a double wish has been expressed to me by the representatives of the Holy See, with the clear desire that it be submitted to the Head of State:
>
> 1) that no provision touching on marriage be added to the law on the Jews. There we would have difficulties of a religious nature. They were strongly moved at the Vatican when Romania adopted, on this vital point, legislation modeled on the Fascist laws;
>
> 2) that the precepts of justice and of charity be kept in mind in applying the law. My interlocutors seem to have had in mind particularly the liquidation of enterprises in which Jews have an interest....[80]

Bérard's letter apparently gave considerable solace to Pétain.[81] Although flagging the contradiction on the question of "race," the letter not only denied its significance to the Vatican but, more importantly to our thesis, played into the dominant understanding of the French statutes anyway: that they were religious more than racial and that they responded to special qualities in the Jew (Bérard calls them "ethnic") that take him out of the political and social arena anyway.

Indeed, the only dissonance between Vatican thinking —as summarized by Bérard—and Vichy jurisprudence lay in the distinct distaste the Church explicitly brought to the generation of 1789, embodied in Rousseau and Condorcet. Yet, for the French legal thinker, there was ample room for both Rousseau and Alibert, for the great foundational ideals of egalitarianism, and for an exclusionary interpretive principle that, before the act of reading even began, read Jews out of the majestic vision. Pétain's very resistance to a merger of Church and State undoubtedly reflected this dissonance: Vichy could advance its basic program without leaping to an alliance that denied the overhanging myth of the individual, admittedly chastened but still free. It would be enough for Church and State to agree on a *Christian* sense of human dignity, and there would be no real disagreement from the Holy See.

"Antisemitism" and racism were muted in this exchange of opinions on the Jewish laws. Emerging instead was a vitally significant mutual ability to engage in a flexible statecraft that masks persecution under the felt

---

80 CDJC CIX-102, all emphases in the original.

81 See, e.g., Marrus and Paxton, *Vichy France and the Jews,* 202.

needs of the political moment. Bérard's letter places this under the sign of what the Church calls "hypothesis."[82] This "realistic" hermeneutic strategy is defined for Pétain by his ambassador as "an essential distinction that the Church has never ceased to admit and to practice, for it is full of wisdom and reason: the distinction between *thesis* and *hypothesis,* the thesis in which the principle is invariably affirmed and maintained and the hypothesis, where practical arrangements are organized." It is in the space of this theological distinction that practical arrangements are organized—the Church's alleged theoretical distaste for racism can be made to conform to a given state's actual, racist legal practice. The hermeneutic of easy manipulation is ingrained in both entities, an organic Maurrasian "antisémitisme de peau"[83] and requires no clear articulation on such high levels of authority. Church and State, preserving their historical functions, can reach a détente.

Cardinal Gerlier of Lyon was one of the first clerics to bring closer to the world of real people the flexible hermeneutics of the leadership. On 6 October 1941, this "brilliant lawyer"[84] and cleric sat down and conversed with Xavier Vallat about the religious laws. The conversation—as narrated by the CGQJ chief—reveals both Gerlier's Pétainist leanings and the complex interpretive vision of religious persecution that I claim was more central to the suffering than even the positive statutes of which he spoke:

> His Eminence: I believe that M. Léon Bérard makes many allusions. On who, on what, does he rely?
>
> Me: He relies doctrinally on St. Thomas Aquinas for one. [He briefly reviews how the Vichy law avoids the mistake of the Italian statute in tramping on the Church's feet as to marriage between Jew and non-Jew.] Implicitly this signifies that no provision of the French law is blameworthy to the Vatican. Of course, the Ambassador makes clear that the desire of the Vatican is for us to apply that Law with justice and charity.
>
> His Eminence interrupts me, his face becoming less affable: There's the complex part. [*Voilà le point délicat.*] No one knows better than I the enormous harm the Jews have done to France. It's the damned Union générale the Jews wanted that ruined my family.

---

[82] CDJC CIX-102, section "E."

[83] See note 37.

[84] Marrus and Paxton, *Vichy France and the Jews,* 200.

No one supports more zealously than I the policies of Marshal Pétain. I have compromised myself for him, and I have been bitterly reproached for certain strong words I used about the French people's duty to him. But on this terrain of justice and charity, I cannot follow you.... Your law is not unjust, I know you did not write it, the Germans supposedly imposed it [*les Allemands l'auraient imposée*] and even harsher [*sic*], but it is in its application that justice and charity are lacking. I said this just the other day to the Maréchal in front of Admiral Darlan, and although the latter did not completely agree with me, the Maréchal said: "That's right. That question needs to be looked at."

[Gerlier then brings up the paucity of exemptions under the statute. Vallat replies, "on my honor as a Christian" that only five such cases were clearly exceptional, whereas "in none of the multitude of other cases I have seen would it have been reasonable to characterize as exceptional the services rendered by the claimant." Gerlier wants Vallat to know that he was referring to war veterans, and Vallat tells him that these are Article 3 exemptions and would he care to give Vallat specific names? Gerlier alludes to one case, and Vallat says that if the Conseil d'État and the Vichy government ministry and the Marshal confirm, the exemption will be granted....]

His Eminence: By the way, Pastor Boegner came to see me, also troubled like me, by numerous visits from poor types who see no other choice but suicide.

Me: To my knowledge, there have not yet been any suicides of Jews in the free zone, and if there were, there are certainly fewer than in Germany at the time of the new laws. And, although Your Eminence knows that I feel deference and even zeal about the advice You are giving me, I am absolutely indifferent to the opinion of Pastor Boegner, who has written to us that "all Christians, we have been spiritual Semites."

His Eminence smiled.[85]

## 3. Blurred Vision, Distorted Texts

Part of the legal hermeneutic in Vichy depended on what we have just seen: the acceptance by Catholic authorities, with a few noble exceptions and with some reservations, of the "hypothesis" of legalized Jewish persecution. Surely this consoled many working lawyers and judges, as it did their Marshal, both spiritually and pragmatically. Other Catholic prelates, less apologetic about the statutes, continued to add rhetorical fuel to the

---

[85] CDJC CIX-106.

legalistic fires.[86] Since the war, on the other hand, some Christian theologians have wondered out loud about the enduring validity, in view of the Holocaust, of their religion.[87] For, as Henry Rousso puts it, in a speculative tone that seems appropriate for a topic obviously not amenable to standard academic proofs:

> [I]n Vichy's conception of the struggle, the problem of the persecution of the Jews was less secondary than it was second: it was the tragic and ultimate final point of a policy inaugurated as of June 1940. From this perspective, the reactions of French people, and particularly of the Church, on which you have rightly insisted,[88] seem nonetheless quite tardy. [At the very beginning of the régime] neither the population (and one might be able to understand this, given the shock of the defeat) nor the religious authorities, protested.[89]

Rousso thus reiterates a theme of this study: quick and vigorous protest by authoritative individuals, including lawyers, might have resulted in vastly different outcomes for Jews on Vichy soil. He then continues, distinguishing the responses in Protestant countries from those in France:

> As to the question of the numbers of Jewish victims, proportionately lower in France than in other countries,[90] this is a debate that will last a long time. Paxton and Marrus have proposed an interpretation according to objective criteria that color a bit your idea that the essential factors were the weight of opinion, not favorable to Jews but unfavorable to persecutions. One might say that, by comparison to countries with a Protestant tradition, like the Scandinavian countries and the Netherlands, a whole series of measures was possible in France, because there existed a latent anti-Judaism and antisemitism, and xenophobic tendencies strongly ratified since the Thirties....[91]

---

[86] For other statements by Church officials, see e.g. Marrus and Paxton, *Vichy France and the Jews,* 277–79.

[87] See Franklin Littell, *The Crucifixion of the Jews* (New York: Harper & Row, 1975).

[88] Rousso is here in dialogue with Serge Klarsfeld, who gives partial credit to the Church for slowing down the Nazis in late 1942 in their quest to establish a growing "quota" of Jewish deportees, *Esprit,* 27.

[89] Ibid., 30.

[90] In Denmark, of course, 7500 of 7800 Jews were saved.

[91] Ibid., 31.

I mean here only to probe a bit further, and a bit more generally, the meaning for Vichy legal actors of the Catholic response to Vichy law. To my mind, more was at stake than even spiritual or pragmatic solace; what was meaningful for Vichy legal actors was the Catholic method of reading texts itself! For this method helps explain the hermeneutics of Vichy lawyers (who, after all, were predominantly Catholic and in some notable cases, devoutly so) both as to their capacity to read texts a certain way and as to their quick acceptance of a particular kind of religious victim.

We have seen that the great egalitarian foundations of France did not disappear overnight when the Vichy régime took power. The education of hundreds if not thousands of legal actors—the ingrained professional intuition of all those lawyers—still needed to be engaged for the everyday work of a fully functional system. Antisemitism of various traditional kinds, and virulent racism, would not appeal to mainstream legal actors. Neither were lawyers especially receptive to the occasional wartime evocation of the "lazy, decadent, plutocratic" side of the Jewish story. Stereotypes helped them to abide some changes regarding Jews (Charpentier's distaste for the "bazaars" of his foreign Jewish colleagues at the Palais helped him accept the idea of the *numerus clausus*)[92]; but Barthélemy's flirtation with racist language for the proposed new constitution itself was rejected.[93]

Something far more native to their education and training would have to appeal to them to make the system as pervasively anti-Jewish as it eventually became. Change of this magnitude would occur by appealing to a two-pronged French disposition to read texts a certain way.

Long before—and long after—Vichy, a certain capacity to work with foundational texts and to make them "fit" a certain vision became commonplace. In its signally most memorable and indeed seismically original form, it had rendered possible the complete distortion of the "Old Testament" in order to validate a new spiritual condition. As Nietzsche put it in dissecting the hermeneutic strategies of the Christian exegetes:

> However much the Jewish scholars protested, everywhere in the Old Testament there were supposed to be references to Christ and only to Christ and particularly to His cross. Whenever any piece of wood, a switch, a ladder, a twig, a tree, a willow, or a staff is mentioned, this was supposed to

---

[92] See chapter 8.

[93] See chapter 4.

> indicate a prophecy of the wood of the cross; even the erection of the one-horned beast and the brazen serpent, even Moses spreading his arms in prayer, even the spits on which the Passover lamb was roasted—all are allusions to the cross and as it were preludes to it. Has anyone who asserted this ever *believed* it? Consider that the Church did not even shrink from enriching the text of the Septuagint (e.g., in Psalm 96, verse 10) so as afterwards to employ the smuggled-in passage in the sense of Christian prophecy. For they were conducting a *war* and paid more heed to their opponents than to the need to stay honest.[94]

Vichy knew that obliterating the French constitutional story in one fell swoop would work against its interests in encouraging the kind of pervasive participation in the system that it, indeed, ultimately received. Why expunge the principles which a whole legal community took in with its mother's milk? Instead, a long tradition of distortion in the very optic of the reader was utilized. The constitutional texts of the generation of 1789 could remain in place, much as the Old Testament was left standing by the Gospel writers. It was just a question of recasting it to account for the new program.

Catholic reading strategies assisted Vichy, then, not only morally and pragmatically in affirming its program but even more integrally in providing a way to effectuate the program on every level of legalistic practice. How perfect, too, in isolating the Jew as *Talmudic* other! For the main component of this strange figure's durability was precisely the Jew's ability—at least over the long haul—to interpret the text as the barometer of a legislated and ethical daily routine, the Text as it was originally written and not as it had "accommodated" into the New Policy.

---

[94] Friedrich Nietzsche, *Dawn of Day,* aphorism 84, emphasis in original (my translation). See on Nietzsche's author-centered philological program, Hendrik Birus, "Nietzsche's Concept of Interpretation," *Texte-Revue de critique et de Théorie littéraire,* 3 (1984), 87. Nietzsche's prose often contrasts New to Old Testament values and hermeneutic strategies, the latter of which he sees favorably. See, e.g., Nietzsche, *Beyond Good and Evil,* aphorism 52.

# Selected Bibliography


Adler, Jacques. *The Jews of Paris and the Final Solution.* New York: Oxford U. Press, 1987.

Amoureux, Henri. *Les Beaux jours des Collabos.* Paris: Laffont, 1978.

Aron, Robert. *Histoire de Vichy.* Paris: Fayard, 1954.

Auphan, Paul. *Histoire Élémentaire de Vichy.* Paris: France-Empire, 1971.

Barthélemy, Joseph. *Ministre de la Justice: Vichy, 1941–1943.* Paris: Pygmalion, 1989.

Baudouin, P. *Neuf mois au gouvernement.* Paris: Editions de la Table Ronde, 1948.

Baudry, Henri and Joannès Ambre. *La Condition publique et privée du juif en France.* Lyon: Desvigne, 1942.

Bédarida, François and Renée. "L'Église catholique sous Vichy: Une mémoire troublée." *Esprit.* (May 1992): 52–66.

Billig, Joseph. *Les Juifs Sous l'Occupation.* Paris: CDJC; 1945, 1982.

———. *Le Commissariat général aux Questions juives.* Paris: Editions du centre, 1955.

———. *La Solution finale de la Question juive.* Paris: CDJC, 1977.

Birnbaum, Pierre. *Les fous de la République.* Paris: Fayard, 1992.

———. *Anti-Semitism in France.* trans. M. Kochan, Oxford: Blackwell, 1992.

Birus, Hendrik, "Nietzsche's Concept of Interpretation." *Texte-Revue de Critique et de Théorie littéraire* 3 (1984): 87.

Bonnard, Roger, ed. "A Nos Lecteurs." *Revue du Droit public et des Sciences politiques* (1940–41): 141–42.

Broc, André. *La Qualification juive; une notion juridique nouvelle.* Paris: Presses universitaires de France, 1943.

Brumberg, Abraham. "Nuances of Evil." *Tikkun* 7 (1992): 23.

Burdeau, G. *Cours de droit constitutionnel.* Paris: Librairie générale de Droit et de Jurisprudence, 1942.

Buttin, Paul. *Le Procès Pucheu.* Paris: Amiot-Dumont, 1948.

Chabrol, Claude. *The Story of Women.* Film, 1988.

Charpentier, Jacques. *Au Service de la Liberté.* Paris: Fayard, 1949.

Cointet, Jean-Paul. *Pierre Laval.* Paris: Fayard, 1993.

Cointet-Labrousse, Michèle. *Vichy et le fascisme.* Paris: Editions complexe, 1987.

———. "Le Conseil national de Vichy." Ph.D. diss.: Paris X, 1984.

Colton, Joel. *Leon Blum: Humanist in Politics.* New York: Knopf, 1966.

Conan, E. and D. Lindenberg. "Que Faire de Vichy?" *Esprit.* Symposium Issue. (May 1992).

Cordier, Daniel. *Jean Moulin: L'Inconnu du Panthéon.* Paris: Lattès, 1993.

Costa-Gavras, *Special Section.* Film, 1975.

Cover, Robert. *Justice Accused.* New Haven: Yale U. Press, 1975.

Dalby, Louise Elliott. *Léon Blum: Evolution of a Socialist.* London: Yoseloff, 1963.

Dalloz. *Code civil.* Paris: Dalloz, 1978–79.

Dawidowicz, Lucy. *The War Against the Jews*. New York: Holt, Rinehart; 1975.

Desbaines, J. R., ed. *Le statut des juifs en France en Allemagne et en Italie.* Lyon: Express-Documents, 1943.

Dominique-Gros, François, "Le 'Statut des juifs' et les manuels en usage dans les facultés de droit, 1940–44," in Philippe Breaud, ed. *La Violence politique dans les Démocracies européennes occidentales.* Paris: L'Harmatan, 1993, 139–92.

Duverger, Maurice. "La Situation des fonctionnaires depuis la Révolution de 1940." *Revue du Droit public et des Sciences politiques* 57 (1940–41): 277–332.

———. "La Perversion du droit." in *Réligion, Société et Politique: Mélanges en hommage à Jacques Ellul.* Paris: P.U.F., 1983.

Fish, Stanley. *Is There A Text in this Class? The Authority of Interpretive Communities.* Cambridge: Harvard U. Press, 1980.

Floriot, René. *Le Droit nouveau: Lois, Décrets, Circulaires et Ordonnances parus entre l'Armistice et le 20 Novembre.* Paris: Librairie française de documentation, 1940, 29–43.

Gabolde, Maurice. "Justice." in Chambron, ed. *La Vie de France sous l'Occupation.* Stanford: Hoover Institute, 1957.

Gervereau, Laurent and Denis Peschanski. *La Propogande sous Vichy*. Paris: BDIC, 1990.

Gouin, Felix (introduction) and Christian Howie (trans.). *Leon Blum Before His Judges.* London: Routledge, 1943.

Granrut, Bernard de Bigault du. "Les Tribuneaux et le statut des Juifs d'Octobre, 1940 et Juin 1941." in *Tenou'a/Le Mouvement* (Spring 1992): 62.

Gros, Dominique. "Le Statut des Juifs dans les manuels en usage dans les

Facultés de Droit." in Philippe Breaud, ed., *La Violence politique dans les démocraties occidentales.* Paris: L'Harmattan, 1993.

Haennig, Joseph. "What Means of Proof Can the Jew of Mixed Blood Offer to Establish his Non-Affiliation with the Jewish Race?" *Gazette du Palais.* 1st trimester 1943.

Haft, Cynthia. *The Bargain and the Bridle.* Chicago: Dialog, 1983.

Hallie, Philip. *Lest Innocent Blood Be Shed: The Story of the Village of Le Chambon and How Goodness Happened There.* New York: Harper, 1979.

Hilberg, Raoul. *La Destruction des juifs d'Europe.* Paris: Fayard, 1988.

Kaspi, André. *Les Juifs pendant l'Occupation.* Paris: Seuil, 1991.

Klarsfeld, Serge, ed. *Le statut des juifs de Vichy.* Paris: FFDJF, 1990.

———. *Vichy/Auschwitz.* Paris: Fayard, 1983.

———. *Memorial to the Jews Deported from France, 1942–44.* New York: Beatte Klarsfeld Foundation, 1983.

———. *Le Calendrier de la Persecution des Juifs en France.* Paris: FFDJF, 1993.

Laloum, Jean. *La France antisemite de Darquier de Pellepoix.* Paris: Syros, 1979.

Lépagnot, Christian. *Histoire de Vichy.* 5 vols. Geneva: Idéagraf, 1978.

Littell, Franklin. *The Crucifixion of the Jews.* New York: Harper and Row, 1975).

Lochak, Danièle. "La Doctrine sous Vichy ou les mésaventures du positivisme." in Serge Klarsfeld, ed. *Le statut des juifs de Vichy.* Paris: FFDJF, 1990, 121–50.

Lubetzki, J. *La condition des juifs en France sous l'Occupation allemande.* Paris: CDJC, 1947.

Luhmann, Niklas. "Operational Closure and Structural Coupling: The Differentiation of the Legal System." *Cardozo Law Review* 13 (1992): 1419–41.

Marcou, Jean. "Le Conseil d'État sous Vichy." Ph.D. diss., Law Faculty, Grenoble II, 30 June 1984.

Marrus, Michael and Robert Paxton. *Vichy France and the Jews.* New York: Basic Books, 1981.

Martin du Gard, Maurice. *La Chronique de Vichy, 1940–44* Paris: Flammarion, 1948.

Michel, Henri. *Le Procès de Riom.* Paris: Albin Michel, 1979.

Moulin de Labarthète, Henri. *Le temps des Illusions.* Geneva: Bourquin, 1946.

Müller, Ingo. *Hitler's Justice: The Courts of the Third Reich.* trans. Deborah Lucas Schneider. Boston: Harvard, 1991.

Nietzsche, Friedrich. *On The Genealogy of Morals.* trans. Walter Kaufmann. New York: Vintage, 1969.

———. *Beyond Good and Evil.* trans. Cowan. Chicago: Regnery, 1966.

Paxton, Robert. *Vichy France: Old Guard and New Order, 1940–44.* New York: Columbia U. Press, 1982.

Poliakov, Léon. *L'Étoile jaune.* Paris: Éds. du Centre, 1949.

Ragache, Gilles, and Jean-Robert Ragache. *La Vie quotidienne des écrivains et des artistes sous l'Occupation.* Paris: Hachette, 1988.

Rajsfus, Maurice. *N'Oublie Pas le petit Jésus.* Paris: Manya, 1994.

Rémond, René, ed. *Le gouvernement de Vichy.* Paris: A. Colin, Fond. nationale des sciences politiques, 1972.

Rémy, Dominique. *Les lois de Vichy.* Paris: Romillat, 1992.

Richards, David. "Terror and the Law." *Human Rights Quarterly* 5 (1983): 172–77.

Sarraute, R. and P. Tager. *Les Juifs sous l'Occupation: Recueil des textes officiels français et allemands.* Paris: CDJC, 1982.

Scheler, Max. "Das *Ressentiment* im Aufbau der Moralen." in *Gesammelte Werke.* Bern: Francke Verlag, 1955, vol. 3, 33–147; idem. *Ressentiment.* trans. W. W. Holdheim. New York: Free Press, 1961.

Schmitt, Carl. *Staat, Bewegung, Volk: Die Dreigliederung der politischen Einheit.* Hamburg: Hanseatisch, 1934.

Shakespeare, William. *The Merchant of Venice.* (1596) Maryland: Penguin Books, 1959.

Singer, Claude. *Vichy, l'Université et les Juifs.* Paris: Les Belles Lettres, 1992.

Steinberg, Lucien. *Les Allemands en France.* Paris: Albin Michel, 1980.

Szladits, Charles. "European Legal Systems." Columbia: Parker School Publication, 1972.

Teubner, Gunther, ed. *Autopoeitic Law: A New Approach to Law and Society.* Berlin; de Gruyter, 1987.

Teyssier, Arnaud. "Joseph Barthélemy, Garde des Sceaux." unpubl. M.A. thesis, Paris X, 1980.

Théolleyre, Jean-Marc. "Les Années 40 de M. Maurice Duverger" *Le Monde* (22 October 1988): 22.

Troper, Michel. "La Doctrine et le positivisme." in CURAPP, ed. *Les Usages sociaux du droit.* Paris: P.U.F., 1989, 286–93.

Vallat, Xavier. *La Vie de France Sous l'Occupation.* Hoover Institute, Stanford University, 1947.

Wei Teng-lin. "Le Pouvoir discretionnaire de l'administration et le contrôle jurisdictionnel en droit français." Ph.d. diss., Faculty of Law, Univ. of Lyon, 31 May 1944.

Weisberg, Richard. *Poethics: And Other Strategies of Law and Literature.* New York: Columbia U. Press, 1992, 127–87.

———. *The Failure of the Word: The Protagonist as Lawyer in Modern*

*Fiction*. New Haven: Yale U. Press, 1984.

———. "Autopoiesis and Positivism." *Cardozo Law Review* 13 (1992): 1721–28.

———. "Cartesian Lawyers and the Unspeakable: The Case of Vichy France." *Tikkun* 7 (1992): 46.

———. "On the Use and Abuse of Nietzsche for Modern Constitutional Theory." in Levinson, S. and S. Mailloux, eds. *Interpreting Law and Literature*. Evanston: Northwestern U. Press, 1988, 181–85.

Wellers, G., and I. Schneerson, eds. *L'Activité des Organisations juives en France*. Paris: CDJC, 1983.

Wellers, G., A. Kaspi and S. Klarsfeld. *La France et la Question juive*. Paris: Sylvie Messinger, 1981.

# Appendix

## Constitutional Law

*Declaration of the Rights of Man* (1789–95), 133–34
*Constitution of 1875*, 9, 17, 128, 129, 131, 403, 404

## Constitutional Acts promulgated by Vichy

*Loi constitutionelle* (10 July 1940), 17–19, 40, 129, 137, 146, 232, 370
*Acte constitutionnel # 1* (11 July 1940), 65, 66, 86, 90, 94, 191
*Acte constitutionnel # 4* (12 July 1940), 70, 168, 202, 325, 360
*Acte constitutionnel # 5* (30 July 1940), 17, 128, 244, 295, 359
*Acte constitutionnel # 7* (27 January 1941), 20, 56, 107, 121, 151, 192, 268
*Acte constitutionnel # 9* (14 August 1941), 192, 367, 375, 376, 379
*Acte constitutionnel #10* (4 October 1941), 3, 21, 37, 56–58, 114, 118, 119
*Acte constitutionnel #12* (17 November 1942), 99, 256, 274, 278, 284, 333, 366,387

## Statutes, Ordinances, and Decrees

*26 September 1939*, 241, 242, 343
*1 August 1940*, 128, 278
*3 September 1940*, 16, 185, 186
*10 September 1940*, 107, 236, 237, 246, 251, 269, 296, 298
*27 September 1940*, 39, 42, 44, 50, 57, 196, 268, 326, 371, 372
*3 October 1940*, 4, 21, 37, 39–41, 43, 45–49, 51, 53, 54, 58–61, 63, 64, 66, 74, 77, 82, 85, 101, 104, 120, 147, 160, 178, 196, 226, 229–31, 238, 250, 301, 361, 384, 423
*4 October 1940*, 3, 21, 37, 56–58, 114, 118, 119, 430
*18 October 1940*, 17, 50, 52, 54, 56, 57, 250, 266, 267
*30 October 1940*, 247
*2 June 1941*, 4, 9, 21, 40–42, 41, 43, 45, 54, 58–61, 63, 64, 66–72, 74–76, 78–80, 82, 83, 97, 98, 100–104, 108, 114, 117, 121, 134, 141, 147, 148, 150, 151, 153, 154–56, 160–63, 165–67, 169, 170, 173–76, 178, 181, 184–88, 190, 196, 200, 201, 206, 209, 215, 217, 228, 229, 231, 237, 242, 243, 247, 249, 257–59, 263, 265, 285, 286, 302, 305, 307, 308, 310, 311, 319, 320, 322, 330, 331, 344, 346–48, 351, 360, 361, 364, 377, 381, 383, 384, 405, 414, 418, 421, 423
*16 July 1941*, 49, 65, 83, 101, 103, 107–12, 147, 189, 233, 247, 301–304, 306, 308, 310, 367, 403

## Cases

# Index